Principle and Interest

PRINCIPLE AND INTEREST

Thomas Jefferson and the Problem of Debt

HERBERT E. SLOAN

New York   Oxford
Oxford University Press
1995

Oxford University Press

Oxford   New York   Toronto
Delhi   Bombay   Calcutta   Madras   Karachi
Kuala Lumpur   Singapore   Hong Kong   Tokyo
Nairobi   Dar es Salaam   Cape Town
Melbourne   Auckland   Madrid

and associated companies in
Berlin   Ibadan

Copyright © 1995 by Herbert E. Sloan

Published by Oxford University Press, Inc.,
198 Madison Avenue, New York, New York 10016

Oxford is a registered trademark of Oxford University Press

Library of Congress Cataloging-in-Publication Data
Sloan, Herbert E.
Principle and interest : Thomas Jefferson and the problem
of debt / Herbert E. Sloan.
p. cm.   Includes bibliographical references and index.
ISBN 0-19-505878-X
1. Jefferson, Thomas, 1743–1826–Views on public debt.   2. Debts,
Public–United States–History–18th century.   I. Title.
HJ8032.A2S55   1995
336.3'4'0973–dc20   94-16400

1 3 5 7 9 8 6 4 2

Printed in the United States of America
on acid-free paper

Acknowledgments

Because I am writing about debt, I have become more aware than perhaps I should be of academic authors' efforts to thank their friends, their colleagues, their students, their editors, their families, their favorite late-night radio stations, their word-processing programs, and anyone and anything else somehow figuring in the production of their books. Past and present colleagues on Morningside Heights, if I may be permitted a moment of intertextuality, have given me examples of fine historians at either end of the acknowledgments spectrum—Anne Withington's confessional mode in *Toward a More Perfect Union* (New York, 1991) and Eric Foner's barebones approach in *Reconstruction* (New York, 1988). My sense of what I owe to others, and what I should express here, lies somewhere between these two. If nothing else, I want to avoid overdoing things and at the same time give credit where credit is due. Some of those I thank have helped me more than I can express, and know it; others may be less aware of their role and even be surprised to find themselves listed here. And still others, by simply being there, without reading drafts, doing no more than being themselves, were everything they should have been—and more. To all of them, in advance, my thanks.

But specifics are important, and individuals deserve mention. First are those who did not live to see the publication of this book. My mother, who died in 1989, was loyal to her children despite the harebrained paths they chose to pursue, and of the five of us, I was the most harebrained of the lot. And then there was Bill McNeil, my colleague, friend, and department chair, whose untimely death at the age of forty-seven in the spring of 1993 robbed me of much more than a critic from whom I had hoped to benefit in the final stages of revision. I dedicate this book to both of them—which does nothing to bring them back or fill the gap they have left, but is all I can do.

Many others have had important parts, and I want to begin by acknowledging the Barnard History Department. Successive chairs—we change them rather often at Barnard—Robert McCaughey, Rosalind Rosenberg, and Mark Carnes supported me and assumed that something would come of it in the end. If that was all that they did, it was more than enough, and more than I could have expected—and of course they did more than that. Members of the History Department gave generously of their time and their special knowledge, even though they may not have grasped what I was up to. Jeff Merrick, now at the University of Wisconsin–Milwaukee, was open to an interloper in eighteenth-century French matters, forgave my mispronunciations, and graciously shared his bibliographies and his erudition. Others in the department, then and now, deserve recognition as well. My thanks, in no rank order except alphabetical, to Beth Bailey, David Farber, Joel Kaye, Cathy Kudlich, Richard Lufrano, Alan Potofsky, Ann Ramsey, Deborah Valenze—my partner in eighteenth-century crime at Barnard—and Nancy Woloch, who knows more about the *dix-huitième* in its American and continental contexts than she sometimes lets on. Sully Rios, our long-suffering departmental administrative assistant and general factotum, was always ready with advice on the practicalities that matter; who else could have explained the mysteries of each new Xerox machine we acquired or unravelled the bureaucracies of basement-level Milbank? Eileen Glickstein, our librarian during the years when this book was written, is in a category all her own; she and her staff were magnificent in every respect, and her dedication to acquiring the reference tools historians need, on a budget that defies belief, was positively heroic.

Beyond Barnard, no farther away than the other side of Broadway, there is another world of past and present members of the Morningside Heights community who have had a share in this work. My graduate-school colleagues and their partners—Jeanie Attie, Aaron Berman and Amy Mittelman, Josh and Julie Brown, Elizabeth Capelle, Steve Cohen and Doreen Lomax, Helena Flam, Peggy and Alan Kurtz, Diana Meissinger, Dan and Sharon Richter, and Kristie Ross—all merit kudos because they long ago stopped asking when the book would be finished and accepted procrastination as a given. Bob and Joelle Lionne Scheiber allowed me to indulge in a Jeffersonian walking tour of Paris while I stayed with them on the rue Poulet, making the myth that Americans are naturally at home in Paris come true.

But not everyone was quite so innocent or can be absolved of the result. I owe an enormous debt to Eric McKitrick, who had more faith in this project than it deserved; Stanley Elkins also played a role that, if not quite conspiratorial, nevertheless partook of the hortatory. My thanks are also due to members of the Morningside Heights community who read earlier versions of this book, and first among them Peter Onuf, now Thomas Jefferson

Memorial Foundation Professor of History at the University of Virginia—no longer the Columbia assistant professor I met in a seminar on the Great Awakening, more years ago, I suspect, than either he or I care to remember. Peter will insist that I refused to let him see things, but in fact he saw what mattered or at least heard about it when I tried to explain what I was up to, and I am grateful to him for allowing me to publish some of my unrefined findings in *Jeffersonian Legacies* (Charlottesville, Va., 1993), the volume he edited to mark Jefferson's 250th birthday. Over the years he and Kristin have been good friends, loyal to a fault, and Kristin, no mean Jeffersonian herself, has introduced me to the research department at Monticello, where I enjoyed the hospitality—Darjeeling and Keebler's Sociables—she and Cinder Stanton purvey.

Alden Vaughan supervised my early efforts, which had nothing to do with Jefferson, and stayed the course to sit on my dissertation defense; I broke every rule in his book when it came to the contents of footnotes, but his tolerance for eccentricity served me well. Sigmund Diamond and Eric Foner offered their comments at that crucial stage, and one could not have asked for more discerning readers. If they were formally involved, my colleagues in the Barnard Political Science Department were not; Leslie Calman, Michael Delli Carpini, Ester Fuchs (the resident authority on Microsoft Word), Dick Pious, and Judy Russell were additional members of the support staff without whom little happens in academe.

Others who shared in the process of housing me on research trips and putting up with me also deserve commendation: Anne and Richard Berenberg (sadly, Richard is not here to see the results), Anne Donnellon, Victor Levine, Jonathan Oberman, Katie Sparling, and David and Lisa Sundelson may have forgotten their roles, but they were important, and I want to recognize them. My parents were willing to take in a child they thought they had finally sent out into the world and allowed me to stay with them in Ann Arbor when I was using the University of Michigan libraries; my sister, Ann Devlin, made the poor relation's outings to Mystic and Noank more profitable by opening the Connecticut College Library to me. Librarians at many other institutions have helped; not all of what I looked at has found its way into these pages, but no historian would be able to work without them, and so my thanks to all who put up with my requests, my inquiries, my fumbling use of microform machines.

Thanks are also due to panelists, commentators, and audiences at sessions of the American Historical Association, the Society for Historians of the Early American Republic, the Columbia University Seminar in Early American History, and the Barnard College Willen Social Science Seminar who read and listened to earlier versions of some of the material in the following pages. Dick Ryerson presided on some of these occasions; special thanks to him, and thanks as well for his willingness to listen to my amateur and no doubt unfounded verdicts on the editorial practices at the papers of the Founding Fathers. Another member of the fraternity, John Catanzariti of *The Papers of Thomas Jefferson*, was kind enough to encourage this project, and it says a good deal for his open-mindedness that he would do so despite my less than respectful comments on his predecessor, Julian Boyd, some of them reproduced in the notes.

I have done my best to spare my students the burden of supporting my Jeffersonian obsessions; those who knew what I was working on politely asked when they could read the book and in other ways assumed I was up to something worthwhile; their confidence was its own reward. Finally, and last but hardly least, my thanks to colleagues at the Barnard lunchtime round table for their ability to put everything in proper perspective—the quality of the food we were trying to eat, the latest round of local academic politics, whatever stupidity had appeared on the Op Ed page of the *Times* that morning. Having lunch with scientists is never dull; some of them even think Jefferson is worth studying, and some of them have even been to Monticello and favored me with their impressions (which was a good deal more than I could do when it came to crystallography). To them, to anyone I may have omitted, and to all of those I have named, my thanks; each of you contributed, and my debt is great.

CONTENTS

Principle and Interest

Introduction

Debt is the thread that runs through Thomas Jefferson's private life and public career.[1] From 1774, when he first incurred major obligations in conjunction with the settlement of his father-in-law's estate, to 1826, when he died overwhelmed by a mountain of bills he could not meet, debt was a constant presence in Jefferson's personal affairs. It was also, as we shall see, an issue that preoccupied him politically, whether in the 1780s when as minister to France he found himself struggling with the new nation's foreign debts, or in the 1790s when Hamilton's treatment of the debt looked altogether too much like Walpole's in England seventy years earlier, or during the presidency when he made it his goal to set the debt firmly on the road to extinction, or in the years of retirement when he worried that the sound policies his administration had pursued were no longer being followed. Throughout, Jefferson knew that public debts were dangerous, that they brought corruption and threatened republicanism. And, like most of his contemporaries, Jefferson did not distinguish between public indebtedness and private indebtedness: Both were dangerous; both were threats to independence; both had consequences he could only deplore. Debt, whether public or private, was central to his experience from his thirties to his eighties, and this half-century of concern and worry about debt inevitably left its mark on Jefferson.

Jefferson's lifelong struggle with debt called up responses that go well beyond the standard late-eighteenth-century rhetoric on this subject—which, to be sure, he never abandoned. In the chapters that follow, I offer an account that ties Jefferson's public views to events in his private life. If the culture gave him cues, told him what to say, pointed him in directions that were generally approved, in the end it was the inner Jefferson that made the difference, that made debt resonate so deeply. Who else but Jefferson, those of us who have worked our way through his correspondence are likely to ask, would chide his granddaughter on her failure to write more frequently by drawing up their balance as debtor and creditor in the matter of letters?[2] But, of course, he did exactly that; debt, in one form or another, was never far from the center of his life. Because Jefferson preserved so much of the paper that passed through his hands, we have an unusually large body of data on which to draw, including financial records and the great bulk of his personal correspondence from the 1780s on. His inability to clean out his files periodically is our best guarantee that we are dealing with the whole man. The record as it has come down to us is that debt occupied an extremely important place in Jefferson's life.

Describing the relationship between Jefferson and debt thus threatens to become another way of writing Jefferson's biography. To avoid that danger, and for other reasons that will be apparent in the course of this book, I have centered the story I tell on a key moment in Jefferson's life–the two years or so that stretch from the beginning of 1789 to the early months of 1791. This is the period in which Jefferson writes his famous letter to Madison of 6 September 1789 declaring that natural law forbids one generation to make its successors pay the debts it has incurred; it is also the period when Jefferson finds himself ensnared by Hamilton, consenting against his better judgment to the famous "Dinner Table Bargain" of June 1790 and then discovering by the spring of 1791 that he had been duped; and, just as importantly, it is the period of Jefferson's return to the United States to negotiate with his creditors and reach arrangements with them for the payment of the debts he had "inherited" from his father-in-law. It is, I want to argue, a critical moment in Jefferson's life, and it sets the tone for what comes after; unless we understand it, we cannot follow Jefferson's political career in the 1790s and the opening decades of the new century.

But the events of 1789 to 1791 need to be seen in context. After my initial discussion of Jefferson's debts and his famous letter to Madison, I proceed to explore the eighteenth century's conventional wisdom on the subject of the public debt and assess the fit between the doctrines that Jefferson and his contemporaries are likely to have imbibed from their reading and our own understanding of how wars, debts, and taxes helped to form their world. Next, I look in some detail at the crucial events of 1790, the Dinner Table Bargain and the Arrears of Pay, with particular attention to the way Jefferson's attitudes and reactions mirrored and reinforced those of his fellow Virginia republicans. Two additional chapters take the story down to 1826, though in less detail. The detail is unnecessary, because the attitudes apparent by 1791 undergo little change in later years. Of course, there is always something else to say about Jefferson (the man himself bears a major share of the responsibility for this; his "epistolary corvée," as he would come to call it, has left us an inexhaustible body of evidence from which to work), and no one can hope to have the last word.[3] Equally, it will always be possible to tell the story in other terms or from a different perspective, and I have no doubt that the version I offer is not the only one this subject will support. But throughout, I argue that we are dealing with Jefferson the Virginian, to borrow the title of Dumas Malone's first volume; what finally makes Jefferson's views important in his own day is not so much that he held them, but that they were widely shared and shared in particular by fellow Virginians who were willing to follow his political lead after 1790 and for decades to come.

The picture of Jefferson I offer is, of course, one that takes its place in a preexisting body of scholarship to which I am—inevitably—deeply in debt.[4] "My" Jefferson is one who has much in common with other Jeffersons who historians have given us in the last quarter-century, even with the distinctively Virginia Jefferson whom Henry Adams offered more than a century ago. It is a Jefferson embodying a good deal of the country party persuasion in American politics, and thus a Jefferson implacably opposed to the world of debts and high finance and corruption introduced in Britain after the Glorious Revolution of 1688 and then, to all appearances, recreated by Hamilton in the United States after 1790. In short, this Virginia, country party Jefferson bears a close resemblance to the republican Jefferson familiar to those who have read and profited from—as I have—the accounts of such careful students as Lance Banning and John Murrin; to some extent it may even be the increasingly irrelevant Jefferson more recently identified by Gordon Wood.[5] And yet my Jefferson may also claim some kinship to the liberal figure Joyce Appleby has found so compelling. We are beginning to entertain the possibility that there were multiple Jeffersons, that the republican and country party Jefferson of Banning and Murrin does not automatically exclude the liberal Jefferson of Appleby, that the categories historians have been imposing on Jefferson and his contemporaries for the last quarter-century do not do full justice.[6] The problem is to establish the linkages, to recover what it was that allowed Jefferson to be at once republican in practice and liberal in aspiration. Thus, if only because the dichotomies posited by some earlier forms of the republican synthesis are no longer satisfactory, this will also be a Jefferson who is, to follow J.G.A. Pocock, Janus-faced.[7]

What impresses me about Jefferson is his apparent ability to combine elements of the two modes, to live, as it were, with a foot in two worlds. On the one hand, there is the real world of politics as he knew it, in which the republican mode predominates and in which he plays a crucial part in the American reenactment of an early-eighteenth-century English debate. This is the world in which debt is denounced for the corruption it produces in government, for the dangerous and liberty-threatening military it supports, for the ways it privileges paper wealth over agriculture. At the same time, however, Jefferson envisages a second world, a world still only *in posse*, not yet *in esse*, the liberal world in which the public debt has been extinguished forever. With government effectively limited and resources no longer diverted to pay for the follies and crimes of those who govern, the politics Jefferson knew only too well would be permanently adjourned. Thus, in Jefferson's vision, a harmonious community, no longer condemned to watch its hard-won earnings swallowed up to service the debt, will at last be able to devote its united efforts to moral and material betterment, to the acquisition of knowledge and the improvement of its surroundings.

This second, other Jefferson, then, is not unlike the Jefferson whom Appleby champions. Her case for a Jefferson who looks to the future, who offers new and untried possibilities to his countrymen, is an attractive one, but it gives us only part of Jefferson, and perhaps not the most important part at that, if by important we mean what mattered on a daily basis in the world Jefferson actually inhabited. Appleby is right to insist that we must not ignore Jefferson's visions of the future and the ways he imagined it would be possible to transcend the limits traditional practice imposed. And yet that emphasis leads her to neglect Jefferson's day-to-day experience, privileging his vision over the life he actually lived. It tends, therefore, to slight Jefferson the working politician—and it was as a working politician that Jefferson spent much of his adult life. Jefferson knew, better than any of his contemporaries, that the future he envisioned could be secured only if the present could finally be laid to rest. He differed from some of them in supposing that the enemy *could* be defeated, that the future did not *have* to be one of decay and declension, that a new way of doing things could be inaugurated and, just as importantly, institutionalized. But until that happened, he knew that he was condemned to soldier on in the old cause.[8]

If Appleby's argument that Jefferson was able to move beyond the republicanism of many of his contemporaries and embrace "the principle of hope" suggests change rather than continuity, how are we to explain his lifelong use of country party ideas, his concern that debt inevitably leads to "corruption," and all the other ways in which Jefferson seems genuinely nostalgic? The answer implicit in Appleby's argument is articulated by another scholar working in the field, Isaac Kramnick, who insists that though the vocabulary and the objects of attack are the same, the motives and perspectives are not. Looking with more authority at some of Jefferson's radical English contemporaries than at Jefferson himself, Kramnick posits the emergence of a new petit bourgeois radicalism in England in the last third of the eighteenth century, exemplified by men like James Burgh, Richard Price, and Joseph Priestley, who attacked the debt and corruption not because it threatened to destroy the landed interest, for which they had little use, but because of the ways it blocked the advance of small manufac-turers and others at the cutting edge of Britain's industrial transformation. Radical in their politics, Kramnick says, these men were also radical in their religion and in their pursuit of science. His hypothesis is intriguing, and it makes considerable sense in the English case.[9]

But does it make sense in the American case? Clearly it does not, without real modifications, at least for Jefferson; for some of those identified as "Jeffersonians" in urban centers, it may well be true.[10] The problem, of course, is that Jefferson himself hardly fits the paradigm Kramnick establishes. Granted, he was something of a small manufacturer, keeping his young male slaves busy in the nailery on Mulberry Row and attempting with varying degrees of success to operate a flour mill–though Kramnick does not mention this–but beyond that it is difficult to see how this flower of the Virginia gentry can be turned into a petit bourgeois spokesman for a rising class. Nor does Kramnick's argument that Jefferson's Unitarianism further links him to the English group seem especially convincing. Undoubtedly, Unitarianism was radical and even dangerous in Britain; during Jefferson's lifetime, its main body of adherents in the United States could be found among his bitter opponents, the politically conservative Federalists of New England. Most Jeffersonians were Trinitarians, a good many of them evangelical enthusiasts.[11] Nor was science, the third of Kramnick's trio of markers, especially radical in the new United States; if Jefferson found politically kindred spirits among the members of the American Philosophical Society, if Federalists sometimes ridiculed his scientific aspirations and those of his fellow Jeffersonians, other American scientists flourished in the heartland of Federalism. Yale in the era of Timothy Dwight may have damned Jefferson and all his works, but it was also willing to support Benjamin Silliman's efforts to create an American school of chemistry, and we should not be too quick to conclude that political progressives had a monopoly on science, any more than they had a monopoly on rational religion.[12]

But what needs to be demonstrated, and what no one has shown, is that Americans who read and were influenced by the political ideas of men like Burgh and Price and Priestley understood their works the way Kramnick thinks they must have. It is far more likely that Jefferson and others in Virginia failed to pick up the different use being made of traditional arguments phrased in traditional language; for them, it would only have been familiar words used to support familiar propositions. Yet by showing that opposition to the debt and what it implied was not inevitably connected to the values and interests of the Augustan critics of the first part of the century, Kramnick, too, helps us to see how widely shared were the attitudes Jefferson held and how they could attract support from a variety of quarters.

Again, my argument is that Jefferson was a man of two worlds, that he knew and appreciated the rules of the game in the republican world he lived in but hoped, perhaps too fondly, that the world he knew could be replaced by a new and better system of reformed and purified republicanism. Two Jeffersons, then, and one will ask whether they are Jeffersons in conflict. The answer, on the whole, is no; Faust's "zwei Seelen wohnen, ach, in meiner Brust" does not describe the third president of the United States, at any rate in this regard. What is important to insist on is the coexistence of the two outlooks–and their sequential relationship. For Jefferson was convinced, I think, that his dream of a better future could be realized if and only if–it was the "if" that dominated his career in politics after 1790–the old system, the system he was prepared to expect from everything that history and experience had taught him, could be destroyed. But while he could imagine a world in which that system no longer existed, he never doubted that, as long as it continued, it would produce the results he and his contemporaries observed in Britain, the results whose early stages, they were certain, were already evident in the 1790s in the United States.

Jefferson came as close to destroying that system as anyone could during his presidency and so to establishing the preconditions for the new world he hoped to usher in. But the War of 1812 revived it, both in its old form of massive national debt and in the unanticipated one of banks and paper money. The last decade of Jefferson's life was marked, then, not only by the collapse of his fortunes, but also by the collapse of his hopes, though he could never allow himself to admit this. He fought against that conclusion, founding the University of Virginia to propagate the true doctrine, reviving his states'-rights theories, denouncing the apostasy of the younger generation on every occasion. In the end, he died not knowing whether things would right themselves or whether all was lost; tortured by his inability to ensure an adequate provision for his family, he was at the same time consumed with anxiety for the fate of his country and outcome of the republican experiment.

A large part of Jefferson's determination to expunge every last element of Hamiltonianism in all its forms came, then, from his sense that it was perverting the dream. Jefferson shared the view of many of his contemporaries by the 1780s that the United States had escaped most of "the contagious and ruinous errors" of European life, as he put it to Madison in the 6 September 1789 letter, and it was this strong conviction that the United States was already well on its way to becoming the kind of society he envisaged that was in large part responsible for his alarm once he grasped, in late 1790 or early 1791, what Hamilton was aiming at.[13] Certainly the time he spent in Europe had reinforced his view of America as the great exception to the wretchedness and corruption that prevailed elsewhere, and the realization, within little more than a year of his return home, that all this was threatened—and threatened thanks to mistakes, however innocent, he himself had made—could only have come as a shock. But he was able to recover some of the lost ground and lead the triumphant counterrevolution of 1800, reversing the process that Hamilton had set in motion, or at least containing it. It was the great tragedy of his life that he had to watch these hopes unravel once again, with the War of 1812 and its aftermath, and this time, despite his every effort, he was far less successful in stemming the tide.

Jefferson's commitments to republican values were very deep, deeper than those of almost any of his contemporaries, and more radical than theirs as well; the man who insisted on the right of each generation to write its own constitution—to reenact the moment of founding—and who cherished the ward system that would bring to Virginia's local government the participatory democracy he thought existed in New England's townships, was not a man who had given up on republicanism in its root sense.[14] But it is precisely this kind of republicanism, a republicanism that goes back to the base, to the local community, that distinguishes Jefferson from the other Founders, for whom the issues that mattered were always those of the center, of what sort of constitutional arrangements would produce an acceptable national government. The future that Jefferson envisioned, the liberal future in the current scholarly shorthand, is thus one in which a purified and truer republicanism prevails, a republicanism no longer at the mercy of the forces of debt and corruption, a republicanism with no need to be defensive–and republicanism is always on the defensive for his colleagues among the Founders, whose lack of confidence in their project's staying power is so apparent in the thought and work of Jefferson's friend and ally James Madison.[15]

Jefferson's imagined America is one in which localities and individuals would increasingly take charge, where states rather than the federal center would make the key decisions, precisely because the issues–war, above all, and preexisting debt–that required a federal center capable of acting with energy have been permanently removed from the national agenda. War and debt and the taxes they required led inevitably to a political order that was the antithesis of the one Jefferson hoped to achieve. Remove these, as he attempted to remove them during his presidency, and the possibilities for genuine transformation would no longer be visionary. But Jefferson's dream was compromised, almost from the beginning, by its dependence on the men republicanism had traditionally looked to. Jefferson supposed that local institutions would be run by those who mirrored his own self-image: disinterested, gentlemanly, educated, even erudite, the sort of men his Act for the More General Diffusion of Knowledge was intended to produce.[16] This was not to be; Jefferson's ideal community, the kind he tried all his life to create in Albemarle by enticing his friends to settle there, bore little relation to the emerging pattern of nineteenth-century American life, and though he would never have admitted it–fortunately, he did not live long enough to read *Domestic Manners of the Americans* (1832)–Mrs. Trollope's view of life in the United States far more accurately described his countrymen.[17] As Joyce Appleby reminds us–once again putting her finger on the issues that students of Jefferson must confront–the future that the Jeffersonians and their successors helped to create turned out to be very different from the one Jefferson thought he was establishing; with the passage of time, the liberating effects of capitalism so evident in the late eighteenth and early nineteenth centuries became increasingly difficult to discern.[18]

It is far from clear that even at the height of Jefferson's success, the majority of his followers appreciated the full range of his vision, and, as we shall see, he was always more than a little cautious about giving it full exposure. It was easier, and perhaps more characteristic, for Jefferson to work by indirection, to accomplish, with his trusted aides Madison and Albert Gallatin, the practical goal of retiring the national debt and then letting things take what he hoped would be their natural course. For years, he hesitated to give the public in unvarnished form the principle of his letter to Madison, that the earth belongs in usufruct to the living generation. He knew his followers were with him in abominating the debt; the Virginia view of these matters was all he needed to attract and keep their support. But the larger vision, the inner passion that drove Jefferson to remain in public life and was strong enough to make him suppress his distaste for politics, was rarely articulated in full, if only because Jefferson, experienced politician that he was, knew the dangers of theoretical pronouncements and was determined to avoid the controversy they brought. He sketched some of his notions in his annual messages during the presidency, but these were no more than outlines, barren of detail and without much underpinning; the views that animated them were usually saved for his closest colleagues alone.[19] An intensely private man, Jefferson cannot, I think, have wanted to see an idea that meant so much to him held up to ridicule (the fate it too often met after his death, as we shall see).

But this should not surprise us. In public, Jefferson remained the straightforward man of Virginia, the opponent of debt in simple and uncomplicated ways because the debt was there and nothing could be done until it was gone. Thus it will not be misleading to think of Jefferson's official posture as Virginian in the sense I have specified. It had to be, as long as the debt continued. Only in the last years of his presidency and the beginning of Madison's did he have an opportunity to enlarge on matters, and that opportunity disappeared almost immediately. Jefferson would never cease to deplore the opportunities lost by the return of debt with the War of 1812, but from 1813 until his death he found himself returning to the arguments of the 1790s as the future, once so near, again grew more distant. But Jefferson's lifelong struggle against debt was a failure; when death came in 1826, he had been able neither to clear his own debts nor to convince his countrymen that they must do without debt. Yet the struggle gave his life meaning, and it would be a mistake to suppose it only a minor or an ancillary feature of the legacy Jefferson intended to leave that a republican society was impossible without serious consideration of the ways debt could distort and, ultimately, frustrate the realization of republican dreams.

In 1808, contemplating the burden of personal debt he would carry with him into retirement, Jefferson told his daughter Martha that "not being apt to deject myself with evils before they happen, I nourish the hope of getting along."[20] Like Mr. Micawber—the comparison is unavoidable—Jefferson was forever expecting that something would turn up, and this optimism, if that is what it really was, has been noted by almost everyone who looks at Jefferson's handling of his own financial affairs.[21] Optimism, yes, but a distaste for confronting unpleasant facts as well, and perhaps at bottom an obstinate refusal to let others tell Thomas Jefferson what he had to do. It was a refusal finding its justification in his faith that something would indeed turn up, no matter how bleak the situation, a refusal often leading him to ignore creditors until their duns became too insistent to be put off, a refusal allowing him to see himself as a blameless victim. Hating debt and the thralldom debt imposed on him, he would hate those he held responsible for imposing it as much and more. His sense of martyrdom was acute in the years when he felt himself under the greatest pressures, and, until the end, he never abandoned the hope that the worst could be avoided. He was, in short, all too human.

But Jefferson was unlucky. He lived too long, he invested unwisely, and he endorsed the promissory notes of a friend. One could hardly find a better recipe for disaster, especially in Virginia, and in Jefferson's case it was disaster to the fullest possible extent. At the time of his death, the Piedmont economy, hard hit by the Panic of 1819, was in disarray, and of all his assets only the slaves were readily saleable. Had he not poured some $30,000 into his flour mill and local navigation improvements, he might have withstood some of the pressures that crushed him in his last years, but by 1819 that money was gone, and the mill proved largely worthless. And then there was his standing security for his friend and relative by marriage Wilson Cary Nicholas, whose failure in 1819 added $20,000 of Nicholas's debts to Jefferson's obligations and burdened him with an additional $1,200 a year in interest that he could not afford to pay.[22] If one wants to know why Jefferson died a bankrupt, the elements of the answer are present in these facts—his lands had lost their value, he had thrown good money after bad in an effort to create income-producing property, and he had endorsed the promissory notes of a friend. It takes considerable imagination to suppose that any other outcome was possible after 1819, and given Jefferson's outlook in these matters, it seems equally difficult to imagine that there was a serious likelihood before 1819 that he might have acted differently and in ways that would have prevented the final debacle.

Jefferson's attitude toward his debts, his belief that in time things would right themselves, his certainty that, if allowed to do things his way, everything would turn out for the best, had significant consequences for others. There were, of course, his slaves, most of whom would be sold after his death. Jefferson, it is fair to say, never quite knew where he stood on slavery, either in the abstract or in the very real matter of his slaves at Monticello and in Bedford. Had he devoted his life to clearing his debts, saved as much as he could, and made none of the decisions that came back to haunt him in the years after 1819, no doubt he could have created the conditions under which his slaves could have met a different and kinder fate. But, by his lights, it is important to remember, he did act responsibly, did try to increase the output of his property so that the debts could be retired, did sell assets other than slaves when that was possible (the sale of his library is the great case in point, and there were land sales as well).[23] Yet his efforts failed, and they failed, I think, because he assumed until it was too late that there would always be a way of "getting along." As might have been predicted, that turned out to be a serious mistake, and it had irreparable consequences—for him, for his family, and for his slaves. Perhaps the most depressing thing about the whole sorry business is Jefferson's silence in the last years on the fate his slaves were now condemned to experience. "I am overwhelmed," he said early in 1826, as the end neared, "at the prospect of the situation in which I may leave my family."[24] But there was never a word about the slaves, his other family— except, of course, in the plans to dispose of numbers of them to effect his rescue and save some of his property for the Randolphs.[25] Jefferson knew only too well what debt meant to him and to his country, knew only too well the blight it imposed, the opportunities it foreclosed. But he was remarkably silent on the question of what his debts meant for his slaves.

Jefferson and debt will give us, then, a Jefferson who loses battles as often as he wins them, a Jefferson who struggles and fails. This is not the most common of the many Jeffersons in the repertory, but it is an important one. To be sure, it will not be the whole Jefferson, but what Jefferson ever is? I can only hope that it will not be an unfaithful one.

1

The Thralldom of Debt

I am miserable till I shall owe not a shilling.

Thomas Jefferson, 1787[1]

In the fall of 1788, the American minister to France began making preparations for his return to Virginia. Thomas Jefferson notified his landlord that he did not intend to renew the lease of the Hôtel de Langeac when it expired the following April, and on 19 November he wrote to John Jay, the secretary for foreign affairs, asking Jay to lay before Congress his request for a six-months leave of absence. He had been away from home far longer than he had expected, Jefferson explained, and could no longer put off attending to his affairs in Virginia, "matters of great moment to others as well as myself, and which can be arranged by nobody but myself." There was, in addition, a more delicate consideration: Jefferson wished to accompany his daughters on their voyage home. Congress, he hoped, would see the merit of his application and act on it at once, for "it will be vastly desirable to me to receive the permission immediately, so that I may go out as soon as the Vernal equinox [spring 1789] is over, and be sure of my return in good time and season in the fall."[2] Through the winter of 1788/1789, Jefferson waited anxiously for Jay's reply, but the secretary failed to acknowledge receipt of his letter.[3] Still, Jefferson counted on having the request granted, and he went ahead with his plans. He informed his friends and relations in Virginia that he intended to sail in April 1789, and he worked steadily to dispose of outstanding business.[4] April came and went, however, and there was still no word from Jay. Jefferson fretted, but there was nothing he could do until Congress's permission arrived.[5] At last, on 19 June 1789—seven months to the day from the date of Jefferson's request—Jay wrote with good news. The Senate had confirmed William Short as chargé d'affaires to act in Paris during Jefferson's absence, and the way was now clear for Jefferson's return. Jay's letter took its time reaching the minister, and Jefferson did not receive it until the final week of August.[6] When at last it arrived, he was ready. His baggage, some of it packed since April, was sent off to Le Havre on 6 September; passage was engaged on a ship bound for Norfolk in early October; and on 26 September, Jefferson and his family left Paris.[7] It was the end of his mission to France, though he did not yet know that.

Jefferson's leave was for six months—time enough, he imagined, to permit him a full two months in Virginia, three months for the transatlantic crossings, and a month of leeway.[8] He had every expectation of returning to Paris in the spring of 1790, and good reasons for wanting to do so. The French Revolution, of which he was a more than casual observer, seemed to open new possibilities for American diplomacy, especially in the commercial line, and he took a lively interest in the reforms his liberal friends were promoting in the French National Assembly.[9] He was aware, of course, of the talk in New York that he would be offered a post in the new administration, but he did his best to discourage it. When James Madison wrote him, in the spring of 1789, discreetly inquiring whether he would be willing to serve in Washington's cabinet, Jefferson promptly let his friend know that after the completion of the French mission he intended to retire from public life and devote himself to his family and his plantation.[10] To be sure, he planned to see Madison and Washington during his American stay; there was much to discuss, and he particularly wanted to get a better sense of the new mood of American politics.[11] But beyond that, his trip would be purely personal; he would see his daughters safely across the Atlantic, and in Virginia he would attend to his debts. For it was, in the last instance, his debts that called him home.[12]

Jefferson's financial position in 1788 and 1789 was seriously, though not hopelessly, entangled.[13] No doubt he was solvent in a global sense: On paper, his thousands of acres in the Piedmont and more than 200 slaves made him one of the richest men in Virginia.[14] But this was only the asset side of the ledger. There were also considerable liabilities, and in 1788 and 1789, as in later years, it was the latter that required his attention. The most important, and most pressing, of the claims against him stemmed from his late wife's inheritance. When Jefferson's father-in-law, the wealthy planter, lawyer, and slave trader John Wayles, died in 1773, he left his heirs a sizable estate—at the time, Jefferson estimated that it was worth £30,000 before debts.[15] Wayles's chief English correspondents, the Bristol partnership of Farell and Jones, were the primary creditors, and their demands must have seemed staggering: Wayles died owing them more than £11,000, and this was entirely apart from a further matter of £6,000 arising from a shipment of slaves they had underwritten in 1772. The latter claim was vigorously denied by the Wayles heirs, but it, too, posed a threat to the estate.[16] Still, if Jefferson's estimate of the estate's value was correct, there should have been little difficulty, given sufficient time, in liquidating some of the estate and discharging the obligation to Farell and Jones, with or without the £6,000 supposed due on account of the slave shipment.

John Wayles had been well aware of the magnitude of the balance against him on Farell and Jones's books, and in a codicil to his will, added shortly before his death, he directed his heirs—his daughters Martha Jefferson, Elizabeth Eppes, and Anne Skipwith—to keep the estate "together, and the whole Tobacco made thereon be shipped unto the said Farell and Jones, of Bristol, until his debt and interest shall be lawfully and completely paid and satisfied, unless my children should find it to their interest to pay and satisfie the same in a manner that may be agreeable to the said Farell and Jones."[17] Despite Jefferson's promise to Farell and Jones "to touch no shilling of the estate" before "the paiement of your debt . . . be accomplished," he and his co-executors, Francis Eppes (Elizabeth's husband) and Henry Skipwith (Anne's husband), soon realized that the first of their father-in-law's plans could not be put into effect with any hope of success.[18] The amount due Farell and Jones was simply too great to be discharged out of the annual earnings in a reasonable period of time. As George Mason observed to George Washington in December 1773, even as the Wayles heirs were adopting their new plan, an "Aversion to selling the Lands & Slaves, in Expectation of paying the Debts with the Crops & Profits," had landed James Mercer in serious difficulties; thirty-five years later, so little had things changed in Virginia, Jefferson's daughter would make the same argument, warning her father that "the impossibility of paying serious debts by crops, and living at the same time, has been so often proved that I am afraid you should trust to it."[19]

Clearly, the Wayles heirs were determined to avoid that result. It would be necessary, they concluded, to dispose of the less desirable assets, and after trying to sell some of the land in 1773, in January 1774 they divided up the land and slaves and began selling off the outlying properties.[20] The heirs stood to benefit from this course of action in two important ways. They would gain immediate possession of the land and slaves allotted to them, and the estate would be relieved of years of interest on the outstanding balance of the debts, interest that, as they saw it, would represent a pure loss. It made far more sense to clear the books immediately, or at least as quickly as possible, and that was what the sales would do. Nevertheless, their decision, which seemed appropriate given the circumstances in 1773 and 1774, was to have significant consequences for Jefferson: It was the beginning of his lifelong struggle with debt.

Jefferson, as we shall see, would later claim that the British debts were a kind of perpetual encumbrance on Virginia property, and in a sense he was right. Certainly, matters were not made easier for Virginia debtors by Parliament's Colonial Debts Act of 1732, under whose terms "the *lands, houses, chattels, and slaves* of debtors in the American colonies" were "liable for the satisfaction of debts" due to British merchants such as Farell and Jones "in the like Manner as Real Estates are by the Law of *England* liable to Satisfaction of Debts due by Bond or other Specialty." In short, the debtor's entire property was vulnerable, even though Virginia's laws protected real estate from most creditors.[21] Thus at the time of Wayles's death, all of Wayles's assets were liable for the payment of his debts to Farell and Jones. Yet by distributing the assets before the creditors were satisfied, the executors– Jefferson, Eppes, and Skipwith–extended that liability to their own estates. Had the estate been kept together and used to pay the debts, liability would have extended only as far as its assets. Any deficiency could then have been met by the executors with a plea of *plene administravit*, a statement that all the estate's assets had been exhausted in paying valid claims against the estate.[22] But the decision to divide the estate before the debts were paid radically altered the legal position. A creditor could now sue Jefferson on a *devastavit* for his unsatisfied demand on the Wayles estate.[23] As we shall see, Jefferson was well aware of the elementary principles of law that his conduct brought into play.[24]

In early 1774, however, despite growing imperial tensions, the executors had little reason to fear that they had made a serious error of judgment. True, the 1774 sales brought little in the way of immediate relief to the estate; following the usual Virginia practice, the executors took bonds from the purchasers, who promised to pay in installments. These were offered to Evans, Farell and Jones's Virginia representative, in the hope that he would accept them in payment of so much of the estate's debt as the face amount of the bonds represented. But Evans refused his consent, preferring, no doubt wisely, to let the executors face the risks of collection.[25] Taking advantage of circumstances neither the executors nor Farell and Jones could have foreseen in 1773 and 1774, those who purchased the property availed themselves of Virginia's wartime legal tender act and paid off their bonds in heavily depreciated paper currency. Jefferson, Eppes, and Skipwith did the best they could under the circumstances. In 1779, pursuant to the terms of a statute Jefferson himself had drafted, they deposited the sums received from the purchasers in the state treasury and thereby acquitted themselves, as far as the laws of Virginia were concerned, of the bulk of the estate's obligations to Farell and Jones.[26]

But unfortunately for the Wayles heirs–and for a good many other Virginians indebted to British merchants–the fourth article of the Treaty of Paris of 1783 provided that creditors on either side were to meet no legal impediments as they sought to recover the full sterling value of prewar debts.[27] This left the Wayles estate in a decidedly disadvantageous position. Assets had been sold to pay the Farell and Jones demand, and all that had been gained, it now seemed, was a fistful of paper worth "but a shadow," as Jefferson later informed William Jones, the firm's surviving partner.[28] The heirs could not claim against the purchasers for the "real" value of the property that they had acquired, and the treaty failed to specify relief for those who had paid into the treasury.[29] From Jefferson's perspective, the situation was anything but promising; he and his fellow executors faced the prospect of having to sell still more land and slaves if they were to free themselves and the estate from the burdens encumbering it. And given that they had counted, as husbands of the heirs, on coming into substantial property on the death of their father-in-law, it was a matter of more than academic interest to see what could be salvaged for themselves and their families from the wreck of their once great expectations.[30]

For the moment, there was no need to rush matters. Virginia did not repeal its statutes barring British creditors from the courts, and as long as that continued to be the case, the executors were safe enough.[31] Farell and Jones, like other British firms, sent an agent to Virginia armed with powers to collect outstanding debts, but the agent could only urge debtors to pay; until 1789, he had no way of bringing suit against Jefferson and the other executors.[32] In the meantime, Jefferson, like every other Virginia debtor on the British merchants' books, was convinced that he was in no condition to begin repayment even if the debt were justly due. Virginia's economy was in ruins, and he himself had suffered from Cornwallis's depredations along the James River in 1781.[33] He needed time to reorganize his affairs and put his plantations back on a sound footing; once he had done this, once he had cleared off certain purely local debts—Virginia creditors, after all, could sue Virginia debtors—he would then be able to address himself to the question of his British debts.[34] Congress, however, decided in 1784 to send Jefferson to France, and he accepted the mission. This meant that he would not be able to supervise his Virginia property in person; as he came to realize, without that oversight his plantations were likely to be a good deal less productive than they would have been under proper management. Still, despite the burden of the Wayles debt, Jefferson was willing to serve abroad, and with a substantial salary of £2,100 a year to cover his living expenses, he must have anticipated being free to devote the plantation profits to reducing his debts. Thus in the summer of 1784 he sailed for France, leaving his Virginia problems behind for the moment.[35]

His creditors, however, whether in Bristol, London, or Glasgow, were beginning to grow impatient. Even before Jefferson went to France, their reminders had begun to reach him. Wakelin Welch, surviving partner of the London firm of Cary and Company, was one of the first to present his claims, and these arrived in the summer of 1783, in advance, it may be noted, of the definitive treaty of peace. The amount due—it was on Jefferson's personal account—was seemingly insignificant. The balance in Welch's favor, as of November 1774, stood at £87.4.0, and after crediting Jefferson with the proceeds of a sale of "old pewter," it was £85.1.0. But Welch also claimed interest for the eight years of the war (1775–1783), and this came to a further £30.17.4.[36] Jefferson took his time answering Welch, and it was not until the summer of 1784 that he informed Welch of his hope to pay the debt during the current year. This turned out to be a bit too sanguine—the pattern would be repeated in the years to come—and in January 1785 Jefferson was forced to write again, explaining that his expenses in Paris were greater than he had anticipated and that though unable to pay immediately he would do so as soon as he could.[37] There would then be a conference with Welch when Jefferson was in London in 1786—Welch was a creditor of the Wayles estate, as well as of Jefferson personally, and wished to know where he stood on both accounts–the upshot of which was an agreement on the amount of Jefferson's balance: £128.13.4, £40 of which (representing interest) he promptly paid.[38] And then Welch waited. Years passed; Jefferson returned to the United States; Welch continued to wait. Finally, in 1797, after Welch placed the matter in the hands of a Richmond lawyer, Jefferson executed four bonds to Welch, three totaling £900 to pay the estate's debt and one for £150 to cover his own.[39] But in 1810, Jefferson still had not finished paying them off; one of the £300 bonds for the estate as well as Jefferson's own £150 obligation had yet to be discharged, and so a new bond for £684.6.3 covering both was drawn up at a higher rate of interest (6 percent).[40] Welch showed remarkable patience, all things considered, but the debt remained unpaid at the time of Jefferson's death.[41]

The pattern Jefferson established in his dealings with Welch would repeat itself in his negotiations with other creditors. The estate of Jefferson's father, who died in 1757, was unsettled when the Revolution broke out, and the Glasgow firm of Kippen and Company, known after the war as Henderson, McCaul, and Company, was an important creditor. Jefferson had debts of his own to Kippen and Company, as did his mother–though the latter were minor.[42] Alexander McCaul, whom he had known years before when they were at school together in Virginia, was now a partner in the firm, and it was with McCaul that Jefferson conducted the correspondence relating to the Kippen debts.[43] In the spring of 1786, McCaul wrote to Jefferson, who received the letter while in London, where he was assisting John Adams in an unsuccessful attempt to settle the disputes between the United States and Britain, including, of course, the troublesome matter of the unpaid debts he and other Virginians owed the long-suffering British merchants.[44] Jefferson replied promptly, remembering their old acquaintance with pleasure and explaining to McCaul why Virginians were in no position to pay their debts. As for his own situation, he described his losses to the enemy and those the Wayles estate had suffered as a result of the legal-tender statute. He had sold lands to the value of £4,000, he pointedly remarked, and the money he had received for them was "not worth oak leaves." Indeed, in concluding his review of the state of affairs in Virginia, he thought the plight of the planters far worse than that of the British merchants. But while refusing to concede wartime interest, he promised McCaul that his plantation profits would be devoted entirely to paying the debts to McCaul's firm and to Farell and Jones, proposing to divide them on a pro rata basis.[45]

McCaul must have been pleased to receive the letter, for, as he later remarked to Jefferson, "you will be amazed when I tell you that among the great number of respectable names that owed money to my Partners and myself that not one amongst them have said they would pay their debts except yourself, Mr. John Rose and Mr. John Nicholas." For "when I first knew that Country," McCaul said of his years in Virginia, "I don't believe there was in general an honester sett of people on the face of the Earth, but wonderfully have they changed of late years."[46] Yet even Jefferson, whose honor seemed so bright in McCaul's eyes, took his time making good on his promise. It was not until the beginning of the new year, after receiving encouraging reports from Virginia, that he wrote to McCaul, on 4 January 1787, with a solid proposition. Stating that he did not consider himself bound by Virginia law–which at that point would have protected him from legal action by McCaul's agent in the state, James Lyle–Jefferson set out a carefully drafted plan for paying his debts over a period of several years. He would reserve his plantations' profits for McCaul and Jones, one-third to the former and the balance to the latter. The crop of 1787 would constitute the first installment, and that crop, he reminded McCaul, would not come to market until 1788. But because the state of the tobacco crop–and the price it would bring–was always a matter of uncertainty, he further bound himself to a minimum annual payment of £200, reserving the right to fall behind in a given year on condition that he make up the deficiency in the following one, thus ensuring that his account would be current at least every second year.[47] McCaul was willing to accept Jefferson's proposal for a settlement, though he added a provision–to which Jefferson readily gave his assent– protecting against what Jefferson called "injustice, should the madness of paper money invade our assembly."[48]

But as always there would be a gap between Jefferson's professions and his performance. He made no payments to McCaul in 1788, and it was only after McCaul politely prodded him that he came up with £300 in 1789. There was a reason for this, of course, and it was rather simple: Jefferson was spending all his salary as minister to France (not that he had promised McCaul anything from it), and with his plantations barely producing enough to meet expenses, he had not received a penny in profits during his stay in Europe.[49] Thus the debts to Kippen and Company remained to be dealt with when he returned to Virginia, and in January 1790 Jefferson arranged with Lyle to make five annual payments–to begin the following July–that would discharge the various obligations for which he was respons- ible, amounting, in the gross, to about £1,400 in principal and a further £490 in interest accumulated since 1783.[50]

But McCaul, despite Jefferson's best intentions, despite their ancient friendship, would never be paid in full. During the 1790s, Jefferson fell behind in his installments on these debts, often by several years, and in 1800 he had yet to pay part of the fourth bond (due in 1795), as well as the entire principal and interest of the fifth bond (due in 1796).[51] By 1808, Jefferson would owe £650 (£400 of it interest), and his mother's account–£95 with twenty-eight and a half years of interest at 5 percent–had not been reduced by so much as a shilling.[52] During his retirement, Jefferson attempted to address the Kippen debts; he paid Lyle $1,000 in 1811 (he had already paid him $500 in 1808), but even this was not enough.[53] In 1821, he converted his remaining indebtedness–now $6,580–into five bonds, payable annually from 1823 through 1827.[54] Death and the total collapse of Jefferson's fortunes intervened before these could be discharged, and as late as 1835 his executor still had not finished paying the third bond of this second series,

due originally in 1825.[55] McCaul's misplaced trust thus gained him little in
the way of immediate satisfaction from Jefferson. Although interest partially
compensated McCaul for Jefferson's delays, it was surely false economy on
Jefferson's part to let it mount up, year after year.

If McCaul proved amenable to Jefferson's blandishments and found
himself waiting half a century in consequence, William Jones showed that he
was made of sterner stuff.[56] He would not be put off, and his persistence, or
rather that of his agent in Virginia, Richard Hanson, was duly rewarded:
Jefferson paid in full. Jones, like Wakelin Welch and Alexander McCaul,
began reminding Jefferson of what he owed shortly after the peace of 1783.[57]
As the surviving partner of Farell and Jones, he was, it will be remembered,
the Wayles estate's largest creditor; and because the executors had distributed
the estate's assets (to themselves, in effect) before the debts were paid, they
were, apart from the Virginia statutes barring suits by British creditors,
personally liable for Wayles's debts to Farell and Jones. Jones and Jefferson
met in London during Jefferson's 1786 visit, but they reached no agreement.
Jones was not ready to relinquish his claim for wartime interest, and Jefferson refused to concede the point. There was also the matter of the slave
shipment, for which the estate continued to deny liability, and in any
case Jones was inclined to leave the details of the negotiation to his agent
in Virginia, who, being on the spot, would be able to assess the practical
merits of whatever proposals Jefferson and his fellow executors decided
to make.[58]

What seems mainly to have concerned Jones was the heart of Jefferson's
plan for an arrangement: an alteration of the executors' liability for the
estate's debts. As Jefferson outlined it, each executor would be charged with
one-third of the debt and, once he had paid that, exonerated of any further
liability, despite (and this was obviously a sensitive point) failure on the
part of his co-executors to come up with their full one-third shares. Thus
the executors' joint and several liability for the estate's debts to Farell and
Jones would be replaced by individual liabilities for only one-third of the
amount due, and the security for the debt would be considerably reduced.
The proposition bothered Jones; he feared, though apparently without
reason, that such an alteration might release the executors entirely, and he
wanted to have Hanson work out the details after consultation with Virginia
lawyers.[59]

Jones's refusal to accede to Jefferson's terms—they would, after all, have
been highly favorable to Jefferson, with very little in the way of a solid quid
pro quo other than an unenforceable promise to begin payment—distressed
Jefferson, and his correspondence with relatives and family friends in Virginia began to take on a tone of worry previously absent. References to the
crushing burden of his debts now became frequent, and it was typical when
he wrote to his Virginia agent Nicholas Lewis, whom he had left in charge of
Monticello, that "the torment of mind I endure till the moment shall arrive
when I shall not owe a shilling on earth is such really as to render life of little
value."[60] If this sounded rather melodramatic, it was authentic enough. "I

am miserable till I shall owe not a shilling," he reminded Lewis when urging him to redouble his efforts to make the Albemarle lands productive, and that misery would remain with Jefferson for the rest of his life.[61] Hoping that his Virginia property could be rented out, thereby ensuring a steady stream of income that could be used to pay his debts, he described the plan as "my only salvation" and said that once "this arrangement" was in place he would "feel like a person on shore, escaped from shipwreck."[62]

Yet something had to be done about the Wayles debt to Farell and Jones. Jefferson had already acknowledged that it was due, making no attempt to hide behind the Virginia statutes or claim that it had been discharged by the wartime payment into the treasury.[63] Jones's refusal to conclude an agreement in England left Jefferson with little choice, and the ratification of the Constitution, as we shall see, with none at all. Unwilling to entrust the Virginia end of the business to his co-executors, Jefferson realized that his presence at home was imperative if the estate's affairs were finally to be sorted out.[64] Thus his request, in the fall of 1788, for leave, a request that followed on the heels of two important pieces of news—first the ratification of the Constitution, and then the discouraging reports from his manager Lewis and his co-executor Francis Eppes about the prospects of discharging his debts, to whomever owed, from the sales of his tobacco.[65] When Jefferson finally reached Virginia, Jones's agent, Richard Hanson, proved difficult to appease, and the negotiations for the Wayles settlement consumed several weeks in the winter of 1790. Not until the first week of February did Jefferson complete his arrangements with Hanson—who in the end was willing to accept the change in the executors' liability—turning over to him seven bonds, payable annually from 1791 through 1797, in the principal amount of £2,800, with interest in the further sum of £1,635.[66] The payment of these bonds was Jefferson's great burden throughout the 1790s; lands and slaves had to be sold in significant amounts to accomplish it, and even then it was only by borrowing from other sources that Jefferson was able to rid himself of this incubus.[67]

The question of the slave shipment was an additional worry, and on this point the executors and Hanson were unable to agree. Once the federal courts opened, Hanson brought suit in 1790 to recover the sums claimed by Farell and Jones, and the case dragged on until 1797, when the defendants at last prevailed, despite John Marshall's opinion in 1791 that they had not a leg to stand on.[68] Throughout, the burdens he had to shoulder weighed heavily on Jefferson. His "unfortunate losses of property and particularly by the paper-money for which my lands were sold with a view to pay off Mr. Wayles's debt," he complained in 1791, "cripples all my wishes and endeavors to be useful to others," leaving him without the means to help family and friends. "No circumstances ever made me feel so strongly the thraldom of Mr. Wayles's debt," he told his daughter Martha in 1790, explaining his inability to provide more generously for the newly married Martha and Thomas Mann Randolph, Jr.[69] He would "sell property," he told Eppes, to obtain the money he needed to discharge his bonds to Jones "so as to clear my mind of that oppression"; he was "Haunted nightly," he told the Richmond merchant Daniel L. Hylton, "by the form of our friend Hanson," to which Hylton, another victim of the agent's unwanted attentions, responded by calling Hanson "one of the worst of all the human race."[70] Freedom lay in freedom from debt, but the realities of Virginia agriculture in the 1790s made that an increasingly distant prospect.

Thus the settlement of Jefferson's pre–Revolutionary War debts would drag on for decades. There was nothing unusual about this in Virginia; suits for British debts were still being heard well into the nineteenth century.[71] But for Jefferson, it meant that he could never get clear of the past, never wipe the slate clean. And as new debts joined old ones–try as he might, it proved impossible to escape from the cycle of borrowing and interest and renegotiation–the accumulation all too often seemed to overpower him. His old age would be clouded by it; rather than "retiring unembarrassed and independent," he told Thaddeus Kosciuszko in 1810, he found himself condemned "to pass such a length of time in thralldom of mind never before known to me."[72] But in truth, that thralldom was nothing new in 1810; it had begun in the 1780s, and it would be there until the end in 1826. Jefferson's troubles with debt in later years will be described in the final chapter; for the present, what is important is that the patterns of behavior, the habits of mind evident in his confrontations with debt in the 1780s and 1790s, underwent no real change during the rest of his life. Debt was a horror, a nightmare; his debts stood between him and the realization of his hopes–just as the public debt stood between America and the hopes he cherished for it.

Jefferson's complaints of financial distress were not confined to letters to his family and fellow sufferers from the Wayles imbroglio. Indeed, his best-known description of the position of the debt-ridden Virginia planter stems from the late 1780s, the period when he began to understand the full significance of the Wayles debt. In 1786, shortly before his trip to London to confer with his creditors and to meet with John Adams, Jefferson replied to a series of questions from a French writer who was preparing articles on the United States for the new *Encyclopédie méthodique* by describing the American planters' debts as "hereditary from father to son for many generations, so that the planters were a species of property, annexed to certain mercantile houses in London"–and, he might have added, to firms in Bristol and Glasgow as well.[73] For Jefferson to depict the position of Virginia planters, himself included, in this light was to suggest that their situation was no better than that of their slaves–another "species of property"–who similarly toiled without hope of liberation for harsh and exacting masters.[74] Trained as a lawyer, Jefferson knew that a creditor's claims ordinarily extended no further than the estate's assets and that the heir was not legally responsible for his ancestor's debts, unless that heir chose to bind himself–for example, by taking his ancestor's property before the creditors were satisfied.[75] Virginia realities, however, were different; heirs believed they could not afford to wait until estates were fully settled before taking the property left to them, and whether they kept it together and tried to pay the creditors from the profits or, like Jefferson, Eppes, and Skipwith, sold parts of their share immediately to cover the debts, they did, in fact, act in ways that made debts "hereditary from father to son."

Nevertheless, Jefferson's implied parallel between the Virginia planters and their slaves would be absurd, were it not for the special importance of "slavery" in the rhetoric of eighteenth-century Anglo-American politics. That theme, with its connotations of absolute dependence on the will of another, was central to the self-definition of men like Jefferson; it told them what they must at all costs avoid, and in 1776 they pledged "our Lives, our Fortunes and our sacred Honor" to escape it.[76] However strained it may seem to late-twentieth-century readers, the image of the planter as bonds-man had considerable social and emotional reality for Jefferson and his Virginia contemporaries; capturing their sense of servitude to foreign credi-tors, it was a powerful metaphor that illuminated their society's fears, aspirations, and values. And yet as an image it was badly flawed, or rather it was a little too convenient for planters like Jefferson to seize on. For the planters at least had the option of obtaining their freedom by selling their land and slaves to pay their debts; the real slaves could liberate themselves only by risking death, as many of them recently had during the Revolution and as more would do in the coming decades.[77]

If Jefferson saw himself as a slave to his creditors, he was determined to secure his liberty. Repeatedly, he assured them of his fixed intention to act honorably and see his debts paid to the last penny. "What the laws of Virginia are, or may be, will in no wise influence my conduct. Substantial justice is my object," he insisted to Alexander McCaul, though he qualified this in significant fashion by adding "as decided by reason, and not by authority or compulsion." William Jones was likewise assured of Jefferson's wish to do him "exact justice." As Jefferson stated: "I do not care what the laws or governments may do. I am sure they will never oblige me to do more than I shall do without needing any obligation but that of morality."[78] But Jeffer-son's assurance that the laws of Virginia—which at that point shielded him from British creditors' demands—would not dictate his behavior was a double-edged sword. In fact, he was attempting to do nothing less than move his relations with his creditors out of the sphere of ordinary legality and into one he created and controlled, where the rules would be those of "substantial" and "exact justice," concepts that he, not his creditors, would define and whose application he, not they, would determine.

Writing to his brother-in-law Francis Eppes, Jefferson was more candid about this, explaining for Eppes's benefit what the Wayles estate should, and should not, be liable for. There were debts due from the estate founded in morality, he noted, and others (such as the claim for the slave shipment) that arose from the operation of law only. The former constituted debts "of justice and should be honestly paid, because we have the property bought by him with that money." In the case of the latter, "we have not the property bought by the money for which he was security only." It followed, Jefferson con-cluded, that "we may conscientiously avoid" the claim on the slave ship "by every possible means"; mere securityship did not, for Jefferson, create the kind of moral obligation that made payment obligatory.[79]

Thus Jefferson was especially anxious to obtain his creditors' recognition that he was complying with the most stringent standards of virtue and morality, and he went to great lengths to secure it, marshaling his rhetorical skills to create a persuasive case for his version of the debtor–creditor relationship. Once the creditors accepted his position, it was then as though his debts were as good as paid, and he could rest easy. They had, after all, agreed that Jefferson had no intention of defrauding them, and so in good conscience they could be forced to wait, for years if necessary, until the day when payment was finally possible. Their recognition of his bona fides gave him what he required—acknowledgment that his virtue was intact, his honor still spotless, his credit in good standing. "Reason" and "morality" were the guidelines here, as he had told McCaul and Jones, not "authority or compulsion," and the result was to bend the rules of economic behavior entirely in Jefferson's favor.

This proved a source of comfort when he had to write still another in the endless series of letters postponing yet another installment on a debt already long overdue. Thus when Jefferson found himself compelled in 1792 to tell James Lyle, McCaul's Virginia agent, that short crops and other disappointments, together with the need to meet a pressing bill of £400 or £500 to cover the cost of shipping his goods from Paris, would delay his payments to McCaul, it must have been all he wanted and more when Lyle wrote in reply praising his efforts. "Could you inspire our Debtors in Virginia with sentiments similar to yours, how happy it would make our Companys," Lyle told him. "But alas! I meet with much ingratitude, and dishonesty (as it appears to me). I will wait your time of payment, and am sorry the Honest heart should ever feel distress: I hope yours is nearly at an end."[80]

At the very least, Jefferson's position gave him a sense of moral advantage over his creditors, confirmed his belief that he was acting as a gentleman should, and allowed him to indulge the feeling of martyrdom he cultivated in his thinking about his financial affairs. Particularly in the case of the Wayles debt—for obvious reasons, and ones we may sympathize with—he found satisfaction in casting himself as the victim: It was not he who refused to accept the bonds in 1774; it was not he who incurred the debts in the first place; it was not he who for years lived comfortably off the profits of the Virginia trade; it was not he who failed to stop the ministry's plan to enslave America and so brought on the war that disrupted the trading patterns of the empire and made it impossible for the planters to pay their debts.[81] He was blameless in all this, just as he was blameless when crops were poor or slow in getting to market, or when merchants manipulated the price of tobacco to the planters' detriment.[82]

It was equally part of Jefferson's outlook to suppose that his debts could be retired without too much disruption of his routine and his plans for the development of Monticello. If Jefferson promised to pay—and he did, again and again—he made sure that the promise was framed in terms that reflected his priorities. There were to be no fire sales: When it did not suit him to sell slaves, he resisted; when he wished to hold onto his more valuable lands, he did his best to keep them. And, when necessary, Jefferson sharply reminded his creditors that he had agreed only to allow them a chance to stand in line for the proceeds of his tobacco. Rebuking John Dobson, the assignee of one of his bonds to Farell and Jones and a man with the temerity first to remind him that an installment was overdue and then to do so "in a tone of complaint to which no action of my life has ever justly exposed me," Jefferson insisted in 1792 that "you have not duly attended, Sir, to those letters. If you will have the goodness to look at them, you will find they contain no other promise than that the nett proceeds of the tobacco which should come here [to Philadelphia, where Jefferson was then serving as secretary of state] should be duly divided between that & the demand of another creditor." Over and over he repeated to Dobson that it was not his fault: that he had made less tobacco than he had anticipated, that the costs of transporting it to Philadelphia had been higher than expected—none of this could be laid at his feet. "I carefully avoided saying I would do anything which did not depend on myself," he said. "None of these things depended on me, and therefore in my letters I made myself responsible for none of them."[83] But if these things did not depend on Jefferson, what did? The creditors, apparently, were to run all the risks; Jefferson took no responsibility.

His creditors were thus required to wait their turn for the uncertain results of the year's crop. Alexander McCaul was willing to accept this—just as he was willing to grant Jefferson the recognition he required of his resolve to pay. William Jones was not, and Jefferson bitterly resented his attitude and that of his agent, Richard Hanson. But Jefferson had enormous difficulty making the sacrifices necessary to clear off his debts once and for all; only with the greatest effort could he contemplate reducing his standard of living by selling land and slaves to satisfy Jones in full. He had his own imperatives—the building, or rather the rebuilding, of Monticello, furnishing it to the appropriate standard, assembling a library on a scale few Americans could match.[84] And beyond that there were his responsibilities as patriarch: the preservation and improvement of his property for the benefit of the next generation, his daughters and their growing families—in short, the perpetuation of a traditional way of life neither he nor they could imagine doing without. These duties took precedence over his creditors' demands; as Jefferson saw it, the merchants would have to accept that as a given. Experience ought to have chastened Jefferson, but a sober perspective on his condition was something he was incapable of attaining. To the end, like Mr. Micawber he was convinced that something would turn up; a genuinely radical solution was the last idea he would have entertained, and even in 1826, when he could no longer avoid acting, there was still something of wish fulfillment about the course he chose, the lottery, as though even at this late date he could create a world to his liking, a situation in which he would make the rules and determine the outcome. But always, when things failed once again to turn out as he had so confidently expected, there were others to whom the blame could be shifted.[85]

If he was reluctant to make sacrifices, once they were made Jefferson's frantic efforts to close the books on his debts betray a man in agony. Thus he repeatedly attempted to have creditors accept as payment in full the bonds he received from those who purchased his land–this was true whether the sales were those of 1774 or 1790. After selling his Elkhill lands late in 1790, he tried with one creditor and then another, pointing out that the bonds were secured by a mortgage on the property and thus offered the creditors greater protection than his own unsecured notes they now held. "It would be an infinite relief to my mind, and the greatest favour in the world, if you would take these two bonds and mortgages *in discharge of my* bonds," he begged James Lyle in 1791. Lyle refused, and so did Richard Hanson, telling Jefferson: "I can assure you that your Bonds without security is preferable. . . . Besides," Hanson added, Jefferson's debtor "might pay you sooner than me." But even though his creditors had no compunction about turning over to others the bonds Jefferson gave them, they would not do the same for him. Always preferring to leave the risks of collection to Jefferson, letting him off the hook by substituting others in his place was not an idea they were prepared to entertain.[86]

During the 1780s, Jefferson came to have a strong sense of being oppressed by his debts, and he reacted to his condition in a decidedly ambivalent manner. Professing himself willing to do what had to be done, in reality he was prepared to do only what could not be avoided, and even then it took the pressure of a man like Richard Hanson to force him to act.[87] He used the means at his disposal–considerable charm, official position, skills as a lawyer–to disarm his creditors and win concessions from them, and when those tactics failed, he grew angry and resentful. Debt carried a high charge for Jefferson; it involved him in relations of dependence and even humiliation he would have given almost anything to avoid. The difficulty was that he could not escape without paying a price that, in the end, was always greater than he was willing to accept.

Jefferson's plight was hardly unique. There is a sort of pathos about his Virginia, as its gentry failed to meet the post-Revolutionary challenge. Few of the generation supplying the leaders of independence and the early Republic escaped unscathed. Washington was the exception, but for the rest it was all too often a story of debt and bankruptcy, and worse. National history seems to reinforce the impression individual cases create: After the Virginia dynasty and the Adamses, control passed to Andrew Jackson and Martin Van Buren. Jefferson's plight, the debts that finally overwhelmed him, appears on this reading more than the tragedy of an individual: It is the fall of a class, and Jefferson is never more Virginian than when he plays his part in it. After all, it was not only Jefferson, but also Madison and Monroe. Montpelier was ruined by Madison's efforts to pay his stepson's gambling debts; Oak Hill's precarious survival depended on sales of Monroe's slaves and land and the reluctance of the Bank of the United States to bring suit against a former president.[88] Close behind the Virginia presidents were the figures of the second rank: Edmund Randolph, politically discredited and never able to clear his debts to the United States; Light-Horse Harry Lee, ruined by speculation and ill-health, forced to abandon family and country; Jefferson's son-in-law Thomas Mann Randolph, Jr., sometime congressman and governor of Virginia, lapsing into insanity, his financial collapse mirroring his father-in-law's.[89] And then there were the scandals that could not be kept quiet: the tragedy of Nancy Randolph and the family at Bizarre; the poisoning of saintly George Wythe by a young relative too eager to come into his inheritance; the strange deaths of Jefferson's nephews; Meriwether Lewis's suicide on the frontier.[90] Crippled by debt, troubled in spirit, the Virginia gentry of the early nineteenth century presents a picture of moral and financial exhaustion.

And if we wonder whether we read the evidence correctly, there is always John Randolph of Roanoke to convince us we have. To be sure, Randolph was atypical in one respect: He managed to pay off the debts encumbering his estate and died a relatively wealthy man—wealthy enough to leave his slaves their freedom in his will, an act of conscience few of his contemporaries could afford. But it is Randolph, with his elegies on the vanished glories of Virginia, with his invective, with his brilliant but empty rhetoric, who seems in his person and his politics to provide the final proof of the Old Dominion's decline and fall.[91] Add to him his Tucker connections, George and Nathaniel Beverley, echoing Randolph's nostalgic pessimism in their novels and tracts; add John Taylor of Caroline, convinced that the blood-sucking paper interests held Virginia in thrall; add even so genial a figure as William Wirt, recording the decadence of Tidewater society in his *Letters of the British Spy*—the picture seems complete.[92]

For contemporary confirmation of these impressions, we can turn to George Tucker's novel *The Valley of the Shenandoah* (1824). Pedestrian as literature, this first of the "Virginia novels" finds its subject in the decay and exhaustion of the gentry. Tucker traces the fortunes of the Graysons, proud Tidewater planter stock now—the story is set in 1796, and the tone of the period is faithfully reproduced—fallen on evil days. Colonel Grayson expires shortly before the action begins, leaving debts that promise to consume the estate. His fault, however, was not extravagance; gentleman that he was, he had gallantly, and as it turned out fatally, volunteered to endorse a friend's promissory note. When the friend cannot pay, the creditors look to Grayson, and their suit is pending as the colonel dies. His widow and her two children, the predictably handsome Edward and just as predictably beautiful Louisa, are threatened with disaster. It is, as Tucker remarks, a "tale of the ruin of a once prosperous and respected family." The Graysons' downfall leaves nothing to the imagination. Only the kindness of their old family lawyer enables them to retain a small cottage and a few acres of land in the Shenandoah Valley; all the rest is swept away to pay for the colonel's improvidence. Tragedy on a personal level parallels the financial debacle: Edward, a promising young attorney and the sole support of his mother and sister, dies in a duel fought to vindicate Louisa's honor. He is killed, appropriately enough, by a merchant from New York, a one-time college friend who has abandoned Louisa to pursue an heiress.[93]

Tucker's moral is all too clear. Edward cannot survive in a world where his values—the old gentry values—no longer reflect the dominant ethos. Economically, the Graysons and the class they represent have given way to the shrewd and calculating German farmers of the valley, to conniving usurers and grasping overseers whose greed and narrowness of vision have supplanted the more generous outlook of the gentry. Even the Republican enthusiasms of Edward and his friends are called into question. Their dreams of liberty and equality, Tucker strongly hints, have prepared the way for the breakdown of the old order and its high-minded, aristocratic code.[94]

Tucker's vision of decay and ruin reminds us that contemporaries in the 1820s and 1830s were well aware of the Old Dominion's plight. No longer first in population, Virginia was fast losing its national preeminence, and not even Martin Van Buren's revival of the New York–Virginia axis could restore the political power that was apparently lost forever when Monroe left the White House in 1825.[95] On the economic side, conditions were grim, with few prospects of improvement. People replaced tobacco as the state's staple export; the Virginian in exile was fast becoming a recognizable type.[96] Profits from the sale of slaves to the booming plantations of the cotton region kept many of the remaining estates afloat and paid at least part of the debts of others—Jefferson's among them.[97] As debt and depression enveloped the state, particularly after the collapse of prices with the Panic of 1819, the gentry could only acknowledge that its day had passed.[98]

Granted, this picture of Virginia in decline requires modification. The fall of the gentry—or at any rate the hardships encountered by some conspicuous members of the caste—may not warrant our speaking of the impoverishment of the state as a whole. Scholars have noted continuing, if uneven, agricultural prosperity and stressed the rise of new industries and—for the first time in Virginia history—the growth of a significant urban sector.[99] Surely, many families avoided the stigma of scandal or escaped the end that overwhelmed Tucker's fictional Graysons. In Albemarle, hard hit by the depression though it was, the Coleses were building their distinguished houses at the very time Monticello was going under; even before her father's death, Martha Jefferson Randolph was remarking, with more than a tinge of envy, that "the Coles family are still rising in the world, nor do they appear to have reached the top of the wheel yet." And, she added, no doubt thinking of her own situation, "whether they will be exceptions to the general course of nature in private families as in Empires remains to be seen." Yet the Randolphs eventually managed to restore something of their shattered fortunes; by the eve of the Civil War, Jefferson's favorite grandson, Thomas Jefferson Randolph, was Albemarle's wealthiest inhabitant, with thousands of acres and scores of slaves; his brother, George Wythe Randolph, was sufficiently prominent to become the Confederate secretary of war in 1862.[100] Still, the state's recovery after 1840 should not be allowed to erase the impressions of contemporaries, Virginians and non-Virginians alike, in the 1820s and

1830s, for whom the decay and decline were painfully apparent.[101] At the very least, there is no getting away from the pervading sense of debt as a condition dominating the lives of the gentry.

Debt as a fundamental problem of the gentry long antedated the 1820s. The tableau of gentry in decay and creditors threatening to foreclose— whether we see it in the persons of former presidents or in Tucker's char- acters—had roots deep in the past. If the agricultural depression of the years that followed the War of 1812 contributed substantially to the gentry's financial collapse, the crisis was by no means solely the product of the hard times that came in with the Embargo or after the Treaty of Ghent and the Panic of 1819.[102] Jefferson's troubles, as we have seen, had begun a half- century before. The obstacles he confronted in his struggles to satisfy John Wayles's creditors were typical of those facing Virginians of all classes in the aftermath of the Revolution. By 1790, the state's inhabitants were some £2.3 million in arrears to the traders of London, Glasgow, and the outports, and a substantial proportion of Virginia's 70,825 white families were among the more than 30,000 delinquent prewar debtors whose names figured in the ledgers of the British merchants.[103] This massive indebtedness, widely dis- tributed across the population, had important political, economic, and even psychological effects, and it shaped the Virginia consciousness for decades, from the outbreak of trouble with the mother country in 1765 until well into the nineteenth century, when the last of the suits brought by British creditors were put to rest.[104]

But the British debts were only part of it. Virginians were indebted to other Virginians, as well as to London factors and crossroads Scottish storekeepers, and while it is impossible even to begin to quantify these domestic debts, they were substantial, as Madison would argue in the House of Representatives in 1790.[105] Few important transactions in Virginia were accomplished in cash; credits, short-term or long-term, were the norm, and when Virginians like Jefferson sold land or slaves to other Virginians, they took bonds in payment, realizing that they might have to wait months or even years before the final returns were in.[106]

Moreover, wealthy Virginians commonly acted as lenders for their poorer neighbors. A planter like George Washington or George Mason might have hundreds or even thousands of pounds out on loan at any given moment; it was a way both of earning interest on surplus funds and, at the same time, of satisfying one's responsibilities as a member of the gentry, of filling the patriarchal role which that status entailed.[107] The result of tens of thousands of such transactions was a network of debt and credit that knit Virginia society together. Thus for gentry Virginians, it was more likely than not that one would be a creditor as well as a debtor, and that dual experience, it has been argued, gave gentry Virginians special sensitivity to what it meant to be in debt. On the one hand, as debtors to British merchants, they were well aware of the potential for overbearing and abuse the credit relationship created; on the other, as creditors of their neighbors, it did not escape them that debtors had to be watched or that indulgence might sometimes go too far.[108] What was clear, above all, was that debt was an inescapable part of Virginia life.

There were reasons for this, of course. The Virginia economy in the second half of the eighteenth century depended heavily, if not entirely, on the export of staples, tobacco first and always, and then wheat, the newcomer.[109] In an agricultural economy of this kind, relying on the sale of staples– underdeveloped and lacking in specialized financial institutions–credit and its concomitant, debt, were necessary parts of life. As a contemporary observer put it, "The Virginians are poor to a proverb in money. They anticipate their crops; they spend faster than they earn; they are ever in debt. Their rich exports return in eatables, in drinkables, in wearables."[110] Planters were paid for their crops once a year; in the interim, they made do with credit. They expected their correspondents in Britain or the local storekeeper to extend them every reasonable facility in this, first because all parties recognized the need for it and second because the ability to command credit was an important measure of a man's standing in the community.[111] To deny him credit was to suggest that he was a poor planter–an affront deeply resented by members of the gentry, who took considerable pride in the quality of their tobacco. The testy Landon Carter, forever comparing the prices he received with those given to his neighbors, hardly differed in this regard from Jefferson, who insisted that his tobacco had always commanded a premium price.[112] But denying a planter credit did more than raise questions about his abilities as a tobacco grower, for it also cast doubt on his financial standing, and the insinuation that one was not worthy of credit was a significant insult to men who did not take insults lightly.[113]

Like members of agricultural communities generally, Virginians both needed and feared credit. Real debt–as opposed to advances intended to bridge the gap between purchases and the receipt of payment for a crop–was clearly to be avoided. "Pay as you go," Joseph Jones reminded James Madison in the 1790s, was always the best policy, and within the limits imposed by the nature of their agricultural system, many Virginians strove to do just that. Jefferson himself would tell his daughter Mary Jefferson Eppes in 1798 that "nothing can save us and your children from beggary but a determination to get a year beforehand, and restrain ourselves rigorously this year to the clear profits of the last. If a debt is once contracted by a farmer it is never paid but by a sale." And he would later comment that he knew of no more important lesson to teach the young than "the wisdom, the honor, and the blessed comfort of living within their income," for the alternative, "a few years of splendor above their income," would be followed by seeing "their property taken away for debt when they have a family growing up to maintain and provide for."[114]

Real debts of the sort Jefferson had in mind undercut one's independence, and there were few things the gentry valued more. This attachment to independence, with all its political and economic implications, was not confined to the eighteenth-century Virginia gentry; indeed, it was one of the values that linked them to their English counterparts and to Anglo-

American elites generally.[115] But it was a quality especially prized in Virginia and one that debt easily destroyed. Virginians of the gentry had no desire to depend on the favors of others—and that was the position they would find themselves in if genuinely pressed for money. To ask indulgence from a creditor was difficult for men not accustomed to standing hat in hand before anyone; for men like Jefferson and Washington, it was accomplished only with the greatest reluctance.[116] Nor was it unimportant that the same men, in their other role as creditors, did not hesitate to accommodate their own debtors; such conduct was de rigueur, but it was also de haut en bas, and the point of being a member of the gentry was to be no man's inferior.[117] For it was not only status that might vanish under the pressure of debt: Land and slaves, the two forms of capital the gentry possessed, would also have to go, sooner or later—the Virginia laws were so arranged that it was usually later rather than sooner—and once that happened there was no escaping ruin.[118]

Thus the fear of debt was constant. Matters were not helped by an upsurge in luxury consumption in the two decades or so before the Revolution. This phenomenon, the Virginia part of what we have come to call the eighteenth century's "consumer revolution," placed its own strains on gentry purses and gentry psyches.[119] For while the gentry had inherited a cultural tradition in which luxury—with its implications of self-indulgence and, worse, effeminacy—was roundly condemned, a certain degree of display was nevertheless an integral part of the gentry style, and hence a sometimes feverish effort to keep up with the Carters, the Lees, the Byrds, and the Randolphs.[120] Once some of the great families began raising the stakes by building bigger houses, importing fancier chariots, and spending more on attire, the others could hardly afford to fall behind, though many of them must have been hard-pressed to match the standards set by the grandees. Add to this culturally sanctioned gambling at cards and on horse races, and it is easy enough to see why some Virginians might have begun to outspend their incomes, running deeper and ever more dangerously into debt.[121]

But perhaps the real problem the Virginia gentry had to face was that its chosen mode of life allowed it no escape from the specter of debt. As long as Virginians of the gentry—white Virginians generally—remained committed to producing tobacco or wheat, there was no way out. They had no means of controlling the prices they received, except marginally through the inspection system; they could not control the weather, which might destroy an entire crop in a single summer afternoon's storm; they had never been able to control output; and they lacked the leverage to control their customers, the British merchants and, behind them, the French tobacco monopoly.[122] Wheat, which some historians have seen as the answer to the problems confronting Virginians in the late colonial period, in fact offered no permanent solution to the problems of staple agriculture. Although wheat growers would catch the crest of exceptional prices in the European markets of the late 1760s and early 1770s, in the long run they discovered—as Jefferson did when he turned to wheat as a cash crop in the 1790s—that they were still at the mercy of forces they could not control. The weather, infestation—at least tobacco did not have to contend with the Hessian fly—and international politics plagued them, as similar forces had plagued tobacco growers for generations.[123] Given staple agriculture under eighteenth-century conditions, debt was bound to be a fixture of Virginia life.

The distressed situation of the gentry in the 1820s, therefore, was implicit in the character of Virginia's agricultural economy from the start. Boom and bust, cycles of prosperity and depression had been there since the seventeenth century.[124] And problems of debt had also been there, unavoidably so. Yet the decline that set in by the early nineteenth century—due in part to competition from new growing areas—was perhaps more severe than earlier declines; it unquestionably struck those who experienced it as marking the end of an era.[125] If we are to understand this, we need to take account of the political determinants of Virginia's economic condition, not merely those structural givens inherent in any form of staple agriculture. This will serve to underscore the importance of certain critical experiences that helped to shape the outlook of Jefferson and his contemporaries.

I am arguing, then, that the Revolution made a difference, and in many ways a disastrous one, to Virginia's economic situation. Much of the political context of debt in Jefferson's Virginia was the product of the Revolution and its immediate aftermath; without the break with Britain and the accompanying disruption of the imperial economy, Virginians would not have experienced the full extent of the problems with debt that beset them after 1775. In a sense, Jefferson spent the rest of his life trying to cope with the utterly unforeseen consequences of that break; had there been no rebellion, no war, in all probability he would have been able to collect on the bonds he received when the Wayles lands were sold, pay off his British creditors, and remain relatively free of debt thereafter. But the war changed this. The decision for independence, the outcome of a decade of intensifying crisis, drew a sharp blade through the web of credit that linked Virginia with the Atlantic economy. Virginians may have been uneasy about their British debts before the war; from the perspective of 1790, the conditions of 1775 must have looked attractive indeed.[126] For the war severed the ties to British merchants, disrupting the traditional marketing systems for Virginia staples, systems that would not be satisfactorily replaced for decades to come.[127] Efforts to export tobacco directly to France, whether during the war or after it, never really worked—as Jefferson discovered to his chagrin after 1784—and without a reliable market for tobacco the Virginia economy was in trouble.[128] True, some of the British merchants would return following the end of hostilities in 1783, but hardly in their prewar strength, either in numbers or in the amount of capital they were prepared to pump into the local economy.[129] The result was a Virginia ill-equipped to cope with its debts, whether internal or external.

Indeed, the fact that Virginians—Jefferson among them—would have to pay their British debts was one of the war's outcomes that a good many Virginians found hard to accept.[130] Although it would be wrong to imply

that Virginians sought independence to escape the burden of that indebtedness—almost all the evidence is to the contrary; at most one might
speak of the temporary breathing space some gentry debtors hoped to gain
through court closure and nonexportation—it would be equally mistaken to
disregard the evidence that the war changed opinions on this subject.[131] By
the time news of the peace treaty reached Virginia, more than eight years had
passed since the courts were closed to suits by British creditors, and in the
interval much had happened. Virginians suffered heavy losses during the
war: Slaves were carried away by the invaders (Jefferson lost a good many that
way) or fled to enemy lines in search of freedom; inflation took a heavy toll of
gentry fortunes; and the psychological separation from the mother country
had become final.[132] No one in Virginia was prepared to do the British any
favors in 1783; on the contrary, the mood was one of blaming the British for
the war, which should never have happened in the first place—or so the
Virginians were inclined to think, in the process rationalizing their attitudes
by placing special responsibility on the merchants. They, above all, ought to
have been grateful to Virginia—the source of their wealth—and prevented
this "unjust" conflict.[133] When it became clear that the peacemakers had
decided to reinstate the prewar debts in full (John Adams had said he had no
intention of "cheating" anyone, but that was not quite the phrase some
Virginians would have used to describe their posture), the planters found
themselves condemned to pay both the original debts and, according to
their creditors, a full eight years of interest at 5 percent per annum.[134]

Yet there were some gentry Virginians—Jefferson was one—who argued
that it was time to swallow hard and pay up, provided that the British
performed their part of the treaty.[135] What makes this position particularly
revealing is the way it demonstrates that debt was never a one-sided matter in
Virginia, even for debtors. A man like Jefferson could argue in favor of
payment, though it went against his immediate interests. This suggests that
deeper attitudes were at work, attitudes embodying gentry recognition that
Virginia required a certain measure of discipline if gentry hegemony was to
be maintained. The constant emphasis throughout the 1780s on "justice" in
the letters of gentry politicians like George Mason and James Madison
speaks volumes in this regard, for "justice" as they defined it had everything
to do with relations between debtor and creditor. These gentry politicians
and their followers were shaken by what had taken place in Virginia during
the war, as the unintended effects of currency inflation and the state's tender
statute worked to corrode long-established relationships.[136] To the extent
that the gentry's power ultimately rested on its economic prowess, it had
been undermined during the war, and, worse than that, what appeared to be
bad habits had been instilled in many Virginians—not a few of them fellow
gentry. Contracts, it turned out, could be disregarded and debts discharged
at a fraction of their due; as men like Mason and Madison saw it, there had
been a dissolution of the normal bonds of society, the bonds that had kept
the lower orders in their place and extracted from them recognition that that
was indeed their place.[137] Just how traumatic the experience of wartime

inflation had been was visible in the passion with which Madison and his friends fought to rid Virginia of its effects in the 1780s. To appreciate what lay behind that campaign—with all that it implied about attitudes toward debt— it will be useful to look at what happened to some of inflation's leading victims.

Take, for example, the economic and political consequences of legal- tender paper currency for one prominent Virginia creditor, Richard Henry Lee. As Lee explained his plight to Governor Patrick Henry in May 1777, some years before the war he had decided "to break up my quarters, and rent out all my lands to a number of industrious men, who might benefit themselves, and ease me of trouble at the same time." Having carried out his plan, Lee then discovered that political developments threatened to make his major source of income disappear altogether, for once the Association's provisions forbidding exports went into effect in the fall of 1775, his tenants could not sell their crops and so lacked the means to meet their obligations to him.[138] Even in 1775, Lee told Henry, he had foreseen that it would be "a long and expensive war, that could only be supported by immense emissions of paper money, which falling in value with its excessive quantity would render my small income (but barely sufficient with the greatest economy to maintain my family in the best of times) totally insufficient."[139]

Lee's response was to change the terms of his leases. In place of the specie stipulated in the original leases, he now wanted the tenants to pay in kind— evidently, Lee expected that he would be able to find a use for their crops. The changes in his leases, he argued, embodied "two principles" of great importance: "first to put it into the power of the Tenant to pay me what was then and might become due, and second to prevent thereafter the excessive and partial injury that might be derived to me from emissions of paper money not then in existence." Privately, Lee was even more emphatic about the lack of harm to the tenants and the possibility of disaster to himself; in a set of notes on the law of contract, Lee insisted that his plan would not "be injurious to the Tenant, because commodities, Labor, and everything vend- ible, raises as the exchange does." On the contrary, he maintained, failure to revise the leases would lead to "my utter ruin, to the destruction of Jus- tice, . . . to the injury & violation of our Contract." All this was premised on Lee's conviction that "Justice plainly directs . . . [that] the common understanding of both the Contracting parties at [the] time the Contract was made" ought to govern its interpretation.[140] Lee had no difficulty establish- ing what that understanding was: The leases were intended to give him what he needed to live on, and if the legislature subsequently changed the rules of the game by introducing paper money, he would not allow that to affect his net return.[141]

Unfortunately for Lee, some of his tenants balked at accepting the changes, and following Virginia's resort to paper money backed by a legal- tender provision, word began to circulate that Lee was refusing to accept the new currency in payment of rent. Because this was contrary to the law—from his perspective, an unjust and "retrospective" law—his behavior became something of a scandal, seized on by his political enemies to discredit him.[142] Lee's position is understandable; he had a large and growing family (by 1782, there would be nine children to educate and start in life), and he had leased out his estates so as to devote his full energies to public life. Nevertheless, in Revolutionary Virginia his attitude was bound to create difficulties. Those refusing to support the state's paper currency were considered enemies of their country, and Lee was asking for special favors.[143] Moreover, Lee was, in effect, insisting that the gentry were not to suffer economically from the war, and that insistence raised the specter of internal divisions in the commonwealth, divisions that Virginia, ill-prepared to defend itself against the British threat, could not afford.[144]

Neither the rigid purity of his principles nor the radical tone of his politics could save Lee from embarrassment. In 1777, questions about his stand on paper money—questions reflecting unfavorably on his patriotism and on his fitness to represent the Old Dominion in Congress—were raised in the Virginia Assembly, and when it came time to elect delegates to Congress that spring, Lee found the legislators unwilling to renew his mandate, ostensibly because of his refusal to accept paper currency in payment of rent. This was a stunning blow, for he had served in Congress without interruption since 1774. Insisting on vindication, he returned to Virginia, appeared in person before the Assembly, and convinced it of its errors. The Assembly tendered its thanks for his services and then, when George Mason declined to serve in Congress, chose Lee to replace him.[145] But this was not the end of his troubles. In the fall of 1777, charges that Lee had violated the terms of the tender statute resurfaced, this time with the aid of a letter he had written that seemed to indicate an eagerness to circumvent the law. Now back in Congress, Lee once more took up his pen in self-defense, telling George Wythe that his "conduct" toward his tenants had been "not only innocent but laudable. For it is certainly praiseworthy," he argued, "to prevent one's family from ruin by means that are just and fair," a motive Lee did not try to square with the usual patriot rhetoric of virtue and self-sacrifice.[146] Fortunately for Lee, the mood of the Assembly had changed since the previous session, and Wythe was able to assure Lee that when his correspondence "concerning the leases was mentioned in the house [of Delegates], . . . [it was] so slighted, and treated in such manner that I had no occasion to acquaint the house with what you had written to me on that subject."[147]

Lee's enemies were relentless, however, and so, apparently, were his efforts to pry something like the normal rent out of his tenants. In the spring of 1778, new rumors circulated that Lee's insistence on a real return from his rented property was about to land him in political hot water. The Baltimore merchant George Lux, condemning Lee as "dark, subtle and designing," assured General Nathanael Greene that Lee's "existence in Congress is very short, for a Letter is at last detected from him to his Steward, in which he orders him to decline taking Continental money on the Terms prescribed by Law, a behaviour not to be forgiven in any man who pretends to call himself a Friend to American Liberty."[148] Once more, Lee survived the political challenge, though this time it was coupled with the potentially lethal charge that he was part of the congressional faction hostile to Washington as commander in chief. But Lee's escape was not complete; the Virginia legislature pointedly placed him at the bottom of the list of delegates in that fall's election, and his paranoia grew by leaps and bounds.[149]

In the end, Lee's fears of 1775 proved only too prescient. Unburdening himself to Jefferson, he told the new governor in 1779 that "I am one, who have the misfortune to [see] myself and family nearly ruined by the retrospective effect of our [tender] law." Once more, Lee rehearsed his efforts to secure an income allowing him to devote his energies to public service: "Almost the whole of my landed estate was rented out some years before the war for low cash rents, and under the faith of existing law which secur[ed] me specie for my rents." But inflation upset his plans: "The vast sums of paper money that have been issued (this being now a tender for the discharge of rents growing from old contracts) and the consequent depreciation, has well nigh effected an entire transfer of my estate to my Tenants. This year Sir, the rents of 4000 acres of fine Land will not buy me 20 barrels of Corn!" Lee urged Jefferson to support legislation that would relieve landlords like himself, but the Assembly did not act on the matter until 1781. For Lee, it was obvious that "public justice demands that the true meaning and genuine spirit of contracts should be complied with"; for other hard-pressed Virginians, the matter was not so clear.[150]

Lee's troubles, at least in their political consequences, were probably greater than those of most of his gentry contemporaries—few of whom, after all, leased out their entire estates—but a good many of them would have echoed his concern about the lack of "justice" in the workings of the tender law. Seeing one's domestic investments vanish in a hail of paper currency was, apparently, part of the price to be paid for independence, but aside from Lee—whose foresight did him no good in the end—few gentry creditors seem to have anticipated, when the decision for independence was taken in 1775 and 1776, that they would be required to contribute so much. The reaction to Lee's efforts suggests the difficulties the gentry would encounter in adjusting to the extraordinary conditions created by the war. However devoted to the cause of American liberty, many were discovering that the struggle contained unexpected and unpleasant surprises.

Washington, with the army, could only write in amazement to his family in Virginia as he watched himself founder financially. His tenants, like Lee's, evidently had their own ideas of what justice demanded, of who was to bear the sacrifices the war imposed. The general was reduced to pleading with his stepson, John Parke Custis, to redraw the leases on the family property so that he would "really and not Nominally get what was intended as a Rent."[151] And when Washington considered the fate of the £6,000 or £7,000 he had out on loan, he could barely contain himself; he told Lund Washington, his cousin and manager, that this sum was "now reduced to as many hundreds because I can get no more for a thousand at this day than an hundred would have fetched when I left Virginia."[152] He was "now receiving a Shilling in the pound in discharge of Bonds which ought to have been paid me, and would have been realized before I left Virginia, but for my indulgence to the debtors," he informed his brother-in-law Burwell Bassett in 1779.[153] By August of that year, Washington was becoming apoplectic on the subject: "I am sure that no honest Man would attempt to pay 20*l*. with one [shilling] or perhaps half a one. In a word I had rather make a present of the bonds than receive payment of them in so shameful a way." He would comply with the law, he conceded, if "Men of honor, honesty and firm attachment to the Cause" urged it, but clearly Washington had his doubts whether it was "advansive of the great cause we are imbarked in for individuals" to accept payment at 1 shilling or 6 pence in the pound, "thereby ruining themselves while others are reaping the benefit of their distress."[154]

Washington was appalled by the collapse of standards all too evident in his debtors' behavior, and his letters reflect his anger over the ways in which they used the tender law to avoid paying him what he was due. "Honor or common honesty," he thought, forbade resort to such shabby stratagems, and he told his stepson Custis that "you might as well attempt to pay men in Old News Papers and Almanacks with which I can purchase nothing as to give me paper money that has not a relative value to the Rent agreed on."[155] But Washington, like Lee, discovered that his ideas of justice were out of fashion in wartime Virginia, and he watched his debtors pay off their obligations in money that was not worth the paper it was printed on. Some of them, to be sure, "were too honest to take advantage of the tender Laws to quit scores with me," he recalled after the war, but "those who owed me, for the most part, took advantage of the depreciation and paid me off with six pence in the pound."[156]

Jefferson's experience with his debtors was much the same as Washington's; as we have seen, the lands he sold to pay his share of the Wayles debt brought him nothing. Men like Lee, Washington, and Jefferson were by no means exceptions among the gentry. In later years, the charge of having taken advantage of the tender laws would be a telling political smear, and the whole episode of paper money left an indelible impression in the minds of many gentry Virginians, Jefferson among them.[157] It was an impression of dishonesty, of injustice, of the unsettling of all the traditional values. Gentry creditors had lost too much—even if it had been the price of independence—ever to want to see a recurrence of such an "improper or wicked project," as Madison would call the "rage for paper money" in 1787.[158] Throughout the 1780s, whenever such schemes were mooted in the legislature, they took alarm, the more so because they detected behind them the powerful populist appeal of Patrick Henry.[159] Relief from these threats was cause for thanksgiving: "The resolutions of the prest. Session respecting a paper emission . . . have stamped justice and liberality on the proceedings of the Assembly," Washington exulted after the legislators had voted down a proposal to issue fiat currency.[160] Nothing frightened these members of the gentry more than the prospect of yet another round of inflation and tender laws, and they were determined to see that it did not happen again.

In the end, they got their way–or so it seemed at the time. The creation of banks of issue would raise the specter all over again, for the Constitution, in Article I, Section 10, provides that "no State shall . . . emit Bills of Credit; make any Thing but gold and silver Coin a Tender in Payment of Debts; [or] pass any . . . Law impairing the Obligation of Contracts."[161] What paper money had done to Jefferson and other members of the gentry would make the Constitution more acceptable to them; it would offer an escape from the broken faith, the violations of justice that had seemed to mark all too many of the Virginia legislature's proceedings in the years after 1775.[162] Even at the price of having to pay the British debts–for that, too, was part of the Constitutional package, given the supremacy clause in Article VI–it was a welcome escape. But in Virginia it was precisely these debt-related issues that had caused the greatest trouble for the Constitution, Madison thought. "The articles relating to Treaties–to paper money, and to contracts," he explained to Jefferson in the wake of Virginia's ratification, "created more enemies than all the errors in the System positive & negative put together."[163] Imposing "justice" on Virginia had not been easy.

In fact, much of Virginia politics in the contentious 1780s was driven by questions of debt.[164] If the issue of paper money, with all it implied for relations between debtor and creditor, provoked some of the strongest comments, there was also the continuing controversy generated by efforts to reform the state's judicial system, efforts whose goal was to strengthen professional control over the activities of the gentlemen justices who ran the Virginia trial courts. Such reforms, their advocates urged, would further the cause of "justice," since a professional judiciary, operating out of the proposed district courts, would be more inclined to see that the laws were strictly enforced, less likely to tolerate evasion of obligations and contracts.[165] Efforts to promote the Virginia economy, particularly through the Port Bill, also reflected the pervasiveness of concern about debt. Something, its sponsors argued, had to be done to improve Virginia's trading position; the solution they proposed was to foster economic independence by concentrating the import–export trade in a single seaport, thus encouraging the growth of a native merchant class that would liberate Virginians from their dependence on foreign–mainly British–capital.[166] Although the Port Bill came to grief–towns excluded from its provisions did their best to wreck the measure–it did suggest that many of the gentry had concluded that Virginians must change their traditional ways of doing things if they were ever to enjoy a debt-free existence.[167]

Throughout the period of the Revolution and the Confederation, concerned Virginians sought cures for the Commonwealth's economic ills. Just as the worthy denounced the licentious who took advantage of the tender laws, so, too, they condemned those who indulged their taste for luxury. One of the few consolations Jefferson thought he could discover in the general unpleasantness of the war was that it had forced Virginians to stop overspending–indeed, to stop spending on luxuries almost entirely. With foreign goods largely unavailable during the war, Virginians had no choice but to curb their propensity to consume, and there was hope that a permanent reformation of manners had been effected. As Jefferson put it to Alexander Donald, an old acquaintance and a tobacco merchant in Glasgow, "The maxim of buying nothing without money in our pocket to pay for it, would make of our country one of the happiest upon earth. Experience during the war proved this; as I think every man will remember that under all the privations it obliged him to submit to during that period he slept sounder, and awaked happier than he can do now."[168]

But those who thought they detected a change for the better were wrong; once the war was over and despite the state's attempts to exclude them, some of the British merchants returned, and Virginians eagerly sought the imported goods they brought with them, satisfying long-pent-up demand. Jefferson's correspondents in Virginia deplored this, Archibald Stuart asserting that "it is certain that Extravagance and dissipation has seized all Ranks of People," whereas Thomas Pleasants, Jr., noted that "every port of this Country is filled with British goods and British factors, which affords every excitement to Luxury and Extravagance." Jefferson's reflections on these and similar stories were evident in a 1787 letter to his brother-in-law Henry Skipwith: "The accounts from our country give me to believe that we are not to hope for the imitation of any thing good," he said. "All letters are filled with details of our extravagance."[169] Nevertheless, it was not to be quite like the days before 1775; merchants were now less inclined and less able to be generous in extending credit—they had been badly burned, after all, and the prewar debts remained uncollected. In any case, Virginia exports were earning less than they had before the Revolution, and there was accordingly less to spend.[170]

Moreover, the tendency of Virginians to rely on credit at stores to support their consumer purchases had been checked, at least in theory, by legislation passed during the war. This was George Mason's "Bill for Discouraging Extensive Credits, and Repealing the Act for Proving Book Debts" (1779). Setting a six-month statute of limitations on book debts (credit transactions on account, recorded by storekeepers in their shop books), the act made it impossible for merchant creditors to enforce those debts at law unless they litigated within six months of the transaction.[171] Mason's choice of a six-month limitation was, of course, intended to put an end to the old practice of running up accounts at stores during the year between the sale of one crop and the sale of the next. As he later explained his reasoning, "the extensive Credits formerly given upon open Accounts necessarily tended to ruin, and actually did ruin a great number of Familys, by involving them, unawares, in inextricable Debts." He blamed this in part on "the incautious & unguarded nature of most Men, that while they can obtain Credit, and no Demand is made for Payment, they proceed to plunge themselves deeper & deeper in the Books of their Creditors, without knowing the Amount of their Debts, or reflecting on their Ability to pay, until it is too late." Mason proposed, in effect, an early-warning system designed to alert debtors to the dangers before them at regular intervals: "Had they been called upon, at short Periods, to settle, & discharge their Accounts, or reduce them to Bonds, their Eyes wou'd have been opened in time, and their Ruin prevented," he explained.[172]

Mason also stressed the political consequences of his legislation, and here he expressed the views of a good many Virginians about the dangers to independence that debt automatically entailed: "We know from Experience, that by means of extensive Credits upon open Accounts, the Merchants, under the former Government, reduced great numbers of the People to a condition little better than Servants upon board-Wages, and . . . commanded the Produce of their Lands & Labor, upon what Terms they pleased," the master of Gunston Hall stated, sounding more than a little like Jefferson on the planters as a species of property.

But the loss of economic independence had other consequences: The merchants "had it also in their Power to influence them in Elections, and deprive them of all the Rights of free-Men."[173] Mason's expectations of the good the act would produce may or may not have been verified in practice; what seems clear is that creditors were forced by the statute to resort to the courts with increasing frequency, securing pro forma judgments on book debts that preserved the legal status of their investments while allowing the debtors more time to pay.[174]

Mason's defense of his bill suggests how emotionally charged issues of debt were in the Virginia of the Revolutionary period and the 1780s. Debt was hard to square with professions of independence; psychologically and practically, it undercut the ability of Virginians to live as the values of their corporate culture demanded. And yet, as Jefferson's case demonstrates, they could hardly escape it. The prewar economy had been built on a foundation of debt and credit, and the postwar economy was no improvement in that regard—if anything, matters were worse. The Revolution brought Virginians—male white Virginians, at any rate—the political form of the independence they esteemed; it did little or nothing to shore up the economic independence that was equally part of their ideal. Battered by the war, shaken by the failure of recovery during the Critical Period, Virginians of the gentry like Jefferson could only hope that things would improve. As we have seen, some of those Virginians, led by Madison, looked to the Constitution to bring about a restoration of virtue and justice, and Jefferson, whose doubts about the Constitution did not extend to the provisions on contracts and paper money, also hoped that better times lay ahead, confident that a stronger United States could secure trading rights for Virginians and other Americans that the impotent union under the Articles of Confederation had been unable to obtain.[175]

The political solution to Virginia's economic problems embodied in the Constitution would turn out to be something less than a panacea. Virginians who worried about their debts and how they would pay them would discover that their interests were not necessarily those of the other Americans with whom they were now more closely yoked. They would find as well that other Americans did not necessarily share the views of debt that helped fix the Virginia outlook. And as national politics took shape under the Constitution, there would grow up a distinctive Virginia posture that emphasized the dangers of debt and was hostile to banks of issue, whose paper money threatened to drive out specie and bring on inflation, just as paper money had done during the Revolution. The Virginia take on these matters would also be full of animosity toward Great Britain and sensitive to the point of hysteria on the question of the prewar obligations—in short, a stance that would draw heavily on the gentry's difficult experience with debt, particularly during the 1770s and 1780s. Jefferson would come to represent this position in national politics, and many—though not all—Virginians would fall in line behind him.

In these matters, Jefferson would reflect the Virginia experience with debt. He would, however, bring to these issues a special intensity, born of his own experiences with the problems of debt that so many other Virginians had encountered. He would add to it the fruits of his reading—as we shall see, there was a large literature on the subject of debt, and Jefferson consulted much of it—and the results of his reflections on the subject generally. The product that resulted would be peculiarly his. Yet Jefferson's lifetime of struggle against debt and of thinking about debt would be of little help. Like all too many other Virginians of his class, he would be overwhelmed by debt in the 1820s. In the end, Monticello, like the cherry orchard in Chekov's play, would have to be sold, and if it did not end up as suburban building lots, that was only because land in the Virginia Piedmont had lost its value by 1826.[176] To be a Virginian during Jefferson's lifetime was to be involved with debt, in one way or another, and in this Jefferson was Virginian to the core.

If Jefferson's financial troubles were those of his class and his state, during his years in Paris he had occasion to face not only his own creditors but others' as well, and this experience would add new dimensions to his views of debt. Even the trivial played its part in deepening his appreciation of what debt meant, and his efforts on behalf of John and Lucy Ludwell Paradise suggest why. Lucy Paradise was a Virginian—related, in the standard fashion, to half the best families in the state, and in particular to the Lees of Stratford. Her maternal aunt was the mother of the band of brothers—Richard Henry, William, Arthur, Francis Lightfoot, Philip Ludwell, and Thomas Ludwell—and her sister married William. John Paradise, her half-British, half-Greek husband, was a distinguished scholar who moved with ease in late-eighteenth-century London's literary circles. Both the Paradises were hopelessly improvident, and much of their income—it came mainly from her Virginia estates—had been sequestered during the war on the grounds that the couple, who resided in England, were British subjects.[177] Jefferson's efforts on their behalf were endless and extended well into the 1790s. He negotiated with their creditors; he arranged for them to receive an allowance; he dealt with the sometimes irascible William Lee; he did what he could to patch up their strained marriage—his sympathies were decidedly with John—and in short he devoted far more time and attention to their problems than anyone should have.[178] His involvement in their tangled affairs owed not a little to Lucy Paradise's standing in Virginia society and to the tribal instinct that overtook him when he met fellow Virginians abroad; in the end, it must have added to his own considerable worries on the score of debt, serving, in effect, as a dress rehearsal for what he would shortly be forced to do on his own account.

But the Paradises' problems were only the tip of the iceberg; far more important debts also required Jefferson's attentions. As an American diplomat in Europe—after 1784, one of three, the others being John Adams in London and William Carmichael in Madrid—Jefferson found himself dealing with the British debts on a professional level. The American failure—and it was, above all, a Virginia failure, Virginians owing the largest share of the debts—to comply with the terms of the peace treaty and permit the collection of prewar debts was the great issue in Anglo-American relations during the later 1780s.[179] As the American minister in England, Adams kept Jefferson informed of his lack of progress with the British ministry in arranging a settlement, and in March 1786 Jefferson went to England to assist Adams in what had thus far been a fruitless effort.[180] Jefferson's expertise must have been valuable to Adams, for Jefferson knew a good deal more about the practical aspects of the problem than did his colleague from Massachusetts; in addition, he was free from the inhibitions Adams must have felt as one of the American peacemakers in 1782 and 1783. It was Adams, after all, who told Benjamin Franklin, when the issue of the British debts came up during the negotiations, that "I had no Notion of cheating any Body," and who had been instrumental in satisfying the British—for whom payment of the debts was a sine qua non—on that issue.[181] Jefferson labored under none of these disadvantages, though as a member of Congress he had voted to ratify the peace treaty, including the debt article.[182] He did, however, have other and more personal inhibitions, it might be argued, that compromised his ability to deal disinterestedly with the issue—his status as a leading British debtor, his role in the drafting and enactment of the Virginia legislation sequestering the debts and providing for their discharge by payment into the state treasury, his actions as governor in administering that legislation.[183] Between them, Jefferson and Adams could hardly approach the issue free of prior commitments. But at least they could try to reach a solution.

Jefferson seems to have taken the lead in their efforts, which centered on the possibility of securing an agreement with the merchants that could then be presented to the British ministry as an equitable resolution of the debt problem. Once that question had been resolved, the American diplomats expected that they would be able to show that the United States was in full compliance with its obligations under the treaty, thus shifting the burden to the British and leading them, at least in theory, to surrender the posts they retained in the Northwest Territory and upstate New York and otherwise improve relations with the United States.[184] The problem, therefore, was to find an acceptable formula for the payment of the debts. Jefferson and Adams met on several occasions with representatives from the committee of North

American merchants—this was done with the ministry's knowledge and tacit consent—and almost managed to conclude an agreement.[185] Both sides recognized that payment in installments would be necessary. The merchants were well aware of the difficulties Virginia faced in recovering from the war; their agents in the state kept them informed of local conditions. And from long experience they knew that the planters could not be expected to pay in a lump sum, if only because there was not enough ready money in Virginia to do anything like that.[186] From the American point of view, this was heartening; the merchants did not insist on the impossible and were willing to listen to reason.

But on one critical point, the American negotiators and the merchants' representatives were unable to agree. Interest, specifically the Americans' refusal to accept the merchants' demand for interest during the eight years of the war, was the sticking point. Duncan Campbell, chief negotiator for the creditors, described the American position as "a bitter pill, and such a one as the merchants here could not swallow," but Jefferson and Adams were adamant, insisting that they could never consent.[187] It would have been extremely unpopular in America, not simply because of the substantial sum it would have added to the already heavy payments Americans would have to make. Worse, it would have been an admission, they argued, that America was at fault for the war, that its defense of constitutional claims was not legitimate, that responsibility for the Revolution rested with the Americans—who preferred to think of themselves as the victims of British tyranny—and not with the British, who in the American view were the authors of their own misfortunes.[188] The merchants refused to give way on the issue; the ministry did not encourage them to take a more accommodating position; and the negotiations ended in stalemate.[189] Jefferson and Adams were disappointed by the failure, but not greatly surprised: British unwillingness to meet the United States halfway was already an article of faith for them, particularly for Jefferson, convinced as he was that Britain "hates us, their ministers hate us, and their king more than all other men."[190]

Jefferson sent the news of their failure to John Jay, and through Jay it was made known to Congress. Jay was instructed to report on the question of the treaty and British allegations that it had been widely violated on the American side. When he did so, in the fall of 1786, his report did not make pleasant reading for Americans intent on upholding their country's honor. Congress, or what was left of it, responded in the spring of 1787 by issuing a circular to the states, urging them to comply with the treaty and, in particular, to remove any impediments to the collection of British debts.[191] The states paid little attention, and the problem was left for others to deal with. If Jay's report and Congress's circular failed to produce results, a change in the American position did come about through the adoption of the Constitution, one with considerable importance for British debtors like Jefferson and his fellow Virginians. The new federal charter, with its supremacy of treaties clause in Article VI, was generally believed to remove existing state barriers to the collection of British debts, and Jefferson himself noted that many

Virginians opposed the Constitution out of "apprehension that the new government will oblige them to pay their debts."[192]

Jefferson so understood its terms, and he further appreciated the significance of the creation of the federal courts, for which the Constitution had also made provision in Article III. These courts, it was widely expected, would be free of local "prejudices" and see to it that "justice" was done regardless of the nationality of the parties. More to the point, their jurisdiction would include cases between citizens and foreigners, as well as those arising under treaties (the treaty of 1783 included), and thus they would provide a forum in which the British creditors would be able at last to sue for recovery of the prewar debts, regardless of state laws barring them from state courts.[193] This meant, of course, that Jefferson and the rest of the Virginia debtors had lost a good deal of their bargaining power: No longer could the promise of payment despite the Virginia statutes be held out in return for favorable conditions, installments, abatements of interest, and the like.

The prospect of having to pay was at last at hand, and Jefferson could not afford to delay his visit to Virginia. By the late summer of 1788, he had learned of New York's and Virginia's ratifications, and it was apparent that the federal arrangements would go into effect the following spring. His old friend and creditor Alexander McCaul spoke for many of his peers when he wrote Jefferson of his hope that "this new constitution will be productive of good, establish an effective Government in all the states and make the debtors think seriously of paying."[194] Thus the solution to America's internal crisis came, for Jefferson as for other Virginians, in the form of a new crisis in their private affairs; however much they appreciated the necessity for the reforms the Constitution embodied, and despite their acknowledgment that the time for postponing payment had passed, they were nevertheless forced to contemplate the possibility that it might, at the same time, spell ruin for them and their families.[195]

The British debts were, then, a problem in which Jefferson's interest was more than merely professional. But there were other questions of debt that required his attention while in Paris, and of these none had greater significance than the foreign debt contracted during the American Revolution. Much of it was due to America's first and most important ally, France. In addition, there had been borrowings in Amsterdam, the great international banking center of the day.[196] In both cases, it was necessary to do whatever had to be done to preserve American credit, and that was not easily accomplished, given the weakness of American finances and the debility of Congress. Jefferson found himself in the thick of the problem, especially after John Adams's return to the United States in 1788. For the next year and a half, it was largely up to Jefferson to see that American credit in Europe did not suffer a complete collapse. The result, for Jefferson, was a lesson in depth in the ways of international high finance. He came to know intimately the bankers of the United States—in Amsterdam, the firm of Willink, Van Staphorst, and Hubbard, and in Paris, Ferdinand Grand et cie. This was a new world for Jefferson: Bankers were people Virginians had little experience of, men whose operations were mysterious and complex, difficult to penetrate, and always, therefore, more than a little suspect. "Much conversation with the bankers, brokers, and money holders gave me insight into the state of national credit there [Amsterdam] which I had never before been able satisfactorily to get," he told Washington at the time, and the lessons he learned would not be forgotten.[197]

Writing to Madison the day after his remarks to Washington, Jefferson set out the fruits of his new learning. "I am an enemy to the using our credit but under absolute necessity," he said, "yet the possessing a good credit I consider as indispensible in the present system of carrying on war. The existence of a nation, having no credit, is always precarious." Fortunately, despite the state of American finances under the Articles of Confederation, "the whole body of [the Dutch] money dealers, patriot and Stadholderian" alike, "look forward to our new government with a great degree of partiality and interest." This offered the prospect of reviving American credit in Europe, but it would be necessary to make "equal provision for the interest, adding to it a certain prospect for the principal." Thus "the first act of the new government," Jefferson concluded, "should be some operation whereby they may assume to themselves" what he was sure the United States could obtain, "the first station" in point of creditworthiness among the borrowing nations.[198] His introduction to the ways of "bankers, brokers, and money holders" was an important part of his years abroad, and by the time his European mission was finished, he had gained a firsthand acquaintance with the upper reaches of European finance that few Americans in his day could match.

Not the least of the problems Jefferson was called on to deal with in this respect was the possibility—an exceedingly dangerous one in his eyes—that France, hard-pressed for funds as the *ancien régime* staggered toward bankruptcy, might try to realize something from its American claims by selling them at a considerable discount to a consortium of bankers and speculators.[199] At the same time, well aware that the United States was not yet in a position to pay the French and fearful that an unmet call from Versailles for reimbursement would have undesirable effects on Franco-American relations, Jefferson was willing to entertain the idea that a properly managed transfer of the debt due France to suitable purchasers in Amsterdam might offer advantages to the United States. If—and at that point there was very little "if" about it—the United States could not meet its obligations, he reasoned, it was better that the burden of default fall on those who had bought with open eyes, and not on America's ally France.[200] In the end, nothing came of the scheme; the French, wisely as it turned out, decided not to sell and in due course were repaid in full by the United States.[201] But the episode did not end for Jefferson when he left Europe; Alexander Hamilton would resurrect it, insisting that Jefferson had attempted to defraud those who were planning to purchase the American debt to France. Jefferson, of course, vigorously denied the charge and was outraged by what he considered

Hamilton's misrepresentation of his own intentions.[202] Technically, Hamilton was correct; Jefferson had been willing to contemplate default–for the best of reasons–and to see it fall on others if the French could be spared. The episode suggests the growing sophistication of Jefferson's understanding of the realities of international finance, especially its political dimensions.

He was also aware of the political dimensions of the failure of the United States to pay the pensions it had promised French officers who had served with the American forces during the Revolution. These were, as he saw it, debts of honor. Not paying them was bad enough as a simple matter of ethics. Worse, many of those whose pensions were in arrears were well-placed aristocrats, men who had access to those with influence at Versailles. Their complaints could make trouble for the United States, and the sums involved were small enough that paying them would have placed no real strain on America's admittedly slender resources. Yet the Board of Treasury in New York repeatedly ignored Jefferson's pleas, and it was only toward the end of his mission that he was at last able to inform the former officers that the arrears due them would be paid.[203] In the meantime, he had to respond to their inquiries and demands, and it was not a pleasant business. Still, as Washington reminded him, the French officers were certainly in no worse a position than their American counterparts, many of whom were forced to dispose of their certificates for a fraction of their nominal value.[204] If there was a problem, it was the imbecility of American finances generally, not merely the state of American obligations in Europe.

But that was a problem Jefferson had to confront on a regular basis. European holders of American securities repeatedly sought information about their value, their negotiability, and the prospects of payment. Because the American minister in Paris seemed to be the most authoritative source, they directed their questions to Jefferson.[205] He dealt with these inquiries sympathetically, trying to assure the holders that, whatever the present state of American finances, they were sure in the end of receiving their due. He could not, of course, commit himself to anything more specific, and it is not hard to imagine that his answers were rather less than his correspondents hoped to receive.[206] If this was simply part of the public-relations side of Jefferson's duties, in line with his efforts to counter the anti-American propaganda in the British press–inspired, he was sure, by the British ministry–other requests of this nature caused him greater difficulties.[207]

During the later 1780s, American speculators attempted to support their operations by selling securities in Europe, where the market, for lack of information, was not able to judge the value of the certificates the speculators were trying to unload. On occasion, Jefferson was asked to issue what amounted to formal endorsements of the obligations these men were peddling, and his responses were always cautious in the extreme. He divided the debt into three categories: the foreign debt, the continental debt, and the debts of the individual states. He insisted that the first two categories were solid and worthwhile investments, "sacred obligations" of the Confederation and bound to be paid in full.[208] But he would not, under any circumstances, say the same of the state obligations–the category offering the greatest potential gains for the speculators and their customers. These he thought too various in kind, their underlying values too uncertain, to allow him to judge, and it is evident from his opinions that he strongly doubted that all of them were valid. When asked directly, his advice was that Europeans, who could not assess these matters firsthand, should stay away from the state certificates and, when investing in American securities, concentrate on the paper of "the confederacy," which, he told one of them, was as safe as "mortgages on land."[209] Under the circumstances, it was prudent counsel; in the late 1780s, Jefferson could hardly have known that Hamilton would valorize the state debts in 1790.

Jefferson's appreciation of the role of debt in politics was further enriched by his observation of events in France. The fall of the Bourbon monarchy, whose early stages he witnessed, was to a large degree the result of inability to manage the nation's finances, and this was certainly the view Jefferson took.[210] The budgetary deficits, the apparent impossibility of raising money from the traditional sources (including the very Dutch bankers with whom Jefferson found himself obliged to deal on behalf of the United States), the need for political reform to restore the confidence without which investors would no longer trust their funds to the French–all these were carefully reported in his official letters to Jay.[211] Jefferson became accustomed to watching fluctuations in the price of stock on the bourse for signs of rising or falling support for the government.[212] On his excursions to the booksellers and *bouquinistes*, he bought the new pamphlets on finance, passing many of them on to Madison, and he listened as the guests around his table discussed how France could be rescued from bankruptcy.[213]

In the international arena, he noted that the failure of the French-backed Patriot party in the Dutch Republic was due to France's financial collapse; unable to risk the cost of another war, the French had to step aside in 1787 and let the Prussians, behind whom stood British gold, march in and restore the Prince of Orange.[214] The result was a blow to French prestige and one to France's finances as well, for the French now found themselves cut off from the Dutch loan market, the great source of European capital and, Jefferson thought, an essential prop to any regime.[215] His own country's impotence was equally evident, if not more so, in its dealings with the Barbary pirates. True, it was cheaper to pay tribute than to fight a war, as John Adams reminded him, but Jefferson felt the humiliation keenly and looked forward to the day when America would be strong enough financially to support a navy–that "economical" means of defense; his views on this subject would later change–capable of protecting its commerce from the ravages of the piratical Algerines and their kindred.[216]

Credit was a necessity for any nation that hoped to amount to anything in the world; wars could not be fought without it, and the lessons of Europe seemed to be that wars were difficult to avoid, that the only secure maxim in international affairs was the old one–*si vis pacem, para bellum*, or, as Jefferson put it into English for Washington's benefit, "The power of making war often prevents it, and in our case would give efficacy to our desire of peace."[217] Yet it was equally evident that debt was dangerous, politically and morally as well. Jefferson, like his contemporaries, marvelled at the ability of the English to support the immense burden of their debts, but he was sure it would end in disaster.[218] In the meantime, there was the example of France, and that was obvious enough. America must see to it that it began to pay the Revolutionary debt, as quickly and as expeditiously as possible. Only then could it hope to avoid the problems that debt inevitably brought; only then would it be free to assert itself and occupy its destined position in the world.

By the time he was ready to leave France, Jefferson was fully aware of the importance of the public debt. While Jefferson was still in Europe, his thoughts had turned often enough to the question of America's debts, and he had passed on to his friends at home suggestions as to what might be done to solve the problems those debts posed.[219] Indeed, at one point he hoped to return in time to participate in the formation of a program to deal with the debts, which he was certain–correctly so–must be among the first items of business the new government took up.[220] His role in helping to salvage America's credit in Holland had given him a personal stake in any program to accomplish this, and his appreciation of the importance of a sound financial basis for the new American government, or for any other government, furnished an additional incentive for seeing to it that an adequate and lasting solution was found. And while hardly enthusiastic about the notion of debt and far from possessing any sense that it could be put to positive uses, he had gained a healthy respect for the importance of public credit, the conditions that affected it, and the ways in which it might be sustained.

Jefferson was by no means the only American to hold such views, but his European experiences had broadened his understanding of the practical realities, and there were few in the United States in 1789 who could match the extent of his acquaintance with the world of government finance, with the bankers on whose favor a nation's credit depended, and with the consequences of failure to keep that credit healthy. If the views he carried away with him when he left Europe were, on the whole, the standard wisdom of the statesmen of his time, they were, nevertheless, sound enough and constituted an adequate foundation for a safe and conservative policy of debt reduction and the preservation of credit–in short, for the kind of policy that one might reasonably expect the new federal government would adopt.

In the meantime, his efforts to come to terms with his own creditors had enhanced his determination to free himself from debt. To be sure, he was never willing to take the radical course, which alone would have brought that wish to realization, and it was perhaps more important for his future behavior that he had also come to resent deeply the pressure his creditors put on him, the diversion of resources the payments he would have to make represented, and the sorts of humiliation to which his lack of ready funds to pay them exposed him. He had worked out, in his own fashion, ways of dealing with his creditors that permitted him to retain as much latitude as possible; at the same time, he was being forced to come to terms *with* them, not merely offer terms *to* them, because the prospective opening of the federal courts to suits by British creditors removed the barrier behind which he had sheltered himself during the 1780s, whether he admitted it or not. There were senses, then, in which Jefferson must have imagined himself being backed into a corner, and he did not like it.

Nor, as we have seen, were his public concerns entirely separate from his private ones. The diplomatic impasse between Britain and America over the Virginia debts was a problem that concerned him both in his role as a debtor and in his role as an American representative in Europe, and while he and John Adams negotiated with the merchants' committee, he also met privately with his own creditors. In a wider sense, it is difficult to resist the conclusion that Jefferson's attitudes toward debt as a question of public policy were significantly affected by his attitudes toward his own debts, by that ambivalent combination of desire to do the right thing and dislike of those who might force him to do it. Indeed, as we shall see in the next chapter, there is good reason to believe that Jefferson and many of his contemporaries did not greatly differentiate between private debts and public ones; both, in the end, were dangerous and better avoided.

2

The Rights of the Living

*What a pressure on posterity, to defray the expenses of the profligate, and
wicked political schemes of the past and present days!! How horrible to be thus
manacled before it is born.*

William Branch Giles, 1824[1]

On 6 September 1789—shortly before his departure for America to settle his
debts and against the background of the French National Assembly's attempt
to dismantle the remains of feudalism and draft a declaration of rights—the
forty-six-year-old Thomas Jefferson wrote the most famous of his thousands
of letters, telling James Madison *"that the earth belongs in usufruct to the living;
that the dead have neither powers nor rights over it."*[2] Apart from the
opening of the Declaration of Independence, none of Jefferson's words are
better known than this claim on behalf of the living generation; for those
who continue to place him at the center of the American liberal tradition,
these words are the essence of the true faith.[3] Jefferson attached the greatest
importance to this idea, returning to it again and again, insisting on its
lasting relevance and urging his countrymen to take it to heart.[4] And so they
sometimes have—when they could understand what Jefferson was saying. But
that has been the problem; too often, the search for a usable past leads them
to read into the 6 September 1789 letter what they want to find. The result
has been the creation of "enduring messages" with little relation to Jefferson's
intentions in 1789—and never more than when he is credited with the notion
of a "living Constitution."[5] Yet it is worth trying to recapture Jefferson's own
sense of the principle he set out in the letter to Madison, to reestablish, if we
can, its meanings in 1789. For by stripping away accretions and recovering
the sense of 1789, we will come closer to the core of the problem I have
posed: the meaning of debt for Jefferson.

Like all complex documents, Jefferson's letter can be read in a number of
ways, and to imagine that there is one, and only one, way of understanding

his text would be a serious error. Jefferson's sense of the principle he announced in 1789 was not static; over time, he would find new applications for it, turn it to further uses. The letter's position at the core of the Jefferson canon is a tribute to its richness, to the ways it both summarizes the main tendencies in Jefferson's intellectual and emotional life through 1789 and provides a base to which he constantly returned. In this remarkable letter, long-standing preoccupations converge; in it, we have a major expression of Jefferson's views on the nature of society, on the limits of government, and, above all, on the dangers of debt. For debt is the key, and whatever else this insistence "*that the earth belongs in usufruct to the living*" means, it is first and foremost a confession of what debt meant to Thomas Jefferson.

The letter's contents are familiar, but it will be helpful to describe them in some detail. After explaining to Madison that he is writing "because a subject comes into my head which I would wish to develope a little more than is practicable in the hurry of the moment of making up general dispatches," Jefferson states his proposition—"*that the earth belongs in usufruct to the living.*" He suggests that this is a principle of the utmost importance, yet somehow it has gone unremarked. "The question Whether one generation of men has a right to bind another," he claims, "seems never to have been started either on this or our side of the water." Continuing by way of illustration, he argues that "no man can, by *natural right*, oblige the lands he occupied, or the persons who succeed him in that occupation, to the paiment of debts contracted by him." Otherwise, "he might, during his own life, eat up the usufruct of the lands for several generations to come, and then the lands would belong to the dead, and not to the living, which would be the reverse of our principle." This is as true for society as a whole as it is for the individuals who compose it: No generation has a right to burden those that come after it with a public debt. "I suppose," Jefferson goes on to say, "that the received opinion, that the public debts of one generation devolve on the next, has been suggested by our seeing habitually in private life that he who succeeds to land is required to pay the debts of his ancestor or testator: without considering that this requisition is municipal only, not moral." But, he holds, reinforcing his point that such requirements are only human contrivances, "by the law of nature, one generation is to another as one independant nation to another."[6]

Jefferson then attempts to specify the "very extensive application and consequences" of the principle. He must first define a generation, however, and this leads him into difficulties. He takes it for granted that the generation in question consists of those "of all ages above 21. years"—those, in other words, who have reached the age of majority and are thus politically competent to enter into binding agreements.[7] He admits that men are constantly dying and being born, so that the composition of society changes from one day to the next. If this Heraclitan flux seems to argue against the point he wants to make, there is a way out, and that is to find the average life span of a generation, the point at which half of those present at the time an agreement was entered into will have passed from the scene and been replaced by newcomers. Using actuarial data from tables compiled by the eighteenth-century French naturalist Comte Georges Leclerc de Buffon, Jefferson reaches the conclusion that the period of a generation is "18. years 8. months, or say 19. years as the nearest integral number."[8] That result establishes "the term beyond which neither the representatives of a nation, nor even the whole nation itself assembled, can validly extend a debt."[9] Indeed, he insists, "every constitution . . . , and every law, naturally expires at the end of 19 years," and he rejects as dangerous the argument that silence implies consent to the continuing validity of laws of any sort beyond the nineteen-year term. No, he thinks, "every practical man" must agree "that a law of limited duration is much more manageable than one which needs a repeal." The reasons are obvious: "The people cannot assemble themselves. Their representation is unequal and vicious. Various checks are opposed to every legislative proposition. Factions get possession of the public councils. Bribery corrupts them. Personal interests lead them astray from the general interests of their constituents." Only automatic expiration at the end of nineteen years will answer.[10]

Having explained his idea and described in general terms how it might operate, Jefferson then considers its immediate applications. He begins, in effect, with the French National Assembly's actions on the night of 4 August 1789, little more than a month before, and the host of technical but not unimportant questions left open by the nobility's renunciation of feudal rights.[11] As he sets them out for Madison, the problems are numerous, but his principle that the earth belongs in usufruct to the living is relevant to all of them: "It enters into the resolution of the question Whether the nation may change . . . the appropriation of lands given antiently to the church, to hospitals, colleges, orders of chivalry, and otherwise in perpetuity?" Likewise, it answers "Whether they may abolish the charges and privileges attached on lands, including the whole catalogue ecclesiastical and feudal?" And if that were not enough, "it goes to hereditary offices, authorities, and jurisdictions; . . . appellations; to perpetual monopolies in commerce, the arts with a long train of et ceteras." Most important, perhaps, "it renders the question of reimbursement" to those whose properties had been taken by the National Assembly's action "a question of generosity and not of right."[12]

Yet despite the impressive range of the principle's applications in France, for Jefferson the real issue is not what is to be done in the Old World, but what can be made of the opportunity America presents. "Turn this subject in your mind, my dear Sir, and particularly as to the power of contracting debts," he urges Madison. Now, at the outset of the American experiment in federalism, is the time to see that the principle becomes a fundamental part of American law and practice. His principle, Jefferson argues, can "furnish matter for a fine preamble to our first law for appropriating the public revenue; and it will exclude at the threshold of our new government the contagious and ruinous errors of this quarter of the globe." Indeed, he thinks, referring to the provisions of the new Constitution, "we have already given in example one effectual check to the Dog of war by transferring the power of letting him loose from the Executive to the Legislative body, from those who are to spend to those who are to pay." Even so, a "second obstacle held out by us also in the first instance" would be welcome; in matters such as these, Jefferson believes, one can never be too careful.[13] But America is especially fortunate: Because "we do not owe a shilling which may not be paid with ease, principal and interest, within the time of our own lives," no other country "can make a declaration against the validity of long-contracted debts so disinterestedly as we."[14]

In conclusion, and as though the thought had just occurred to him, Jefferson adds a final suggestion, that the principle of nineteen years' duration be applied to patents and copyrights in place of the fourteen years secured by English law. "Besides familiarising us to this term, it will be an instance the more," he notes, here interpolating another favorite theme, "of our taking reason for our guide, instead of English precedent, the habit of which fetters us with all the political heresies of a nation equally remarkable for its early excitement from some errors, and long slumbering under others."[15]

Several things stand out in this well-known text. The first—by far the most important—is Jefferson's fear of debt, whether private or public. Debt, in fact, is where Jefferson begins his letter, literally as well as conceptually. And he begins not with debt per se, but with a specific sort of debt—inherited debt, debt originally due from an ancestor or a testator, which then becomes a charge against property left at death. This is a curious way to start an argument about the rights of the living generation, and within the context of late-eighteenth-century thinking about those rights it is a highly unusual one. Others who took up the cause of the living generation at this time— Condorcet and Thomas Paine among them—made no use of the laws of inheritance when offering their versions of the rights of the living.[16] But inherited debt—as we have seen—was a matter of the greatest personal importance for Jefferson, and it is by thinking through what it means for one generation to be able to impose on another the burden of paying its debts that Jefferson arrives at his conclusion about the rights of the living generation. When all is said and done, the logic driving him in this direction can be located squarely in his own unhappy experience as a debtor.

He views debt entirely in negative terms; it is a terrible burden on the present and the future, something from which no good can ever come. Moreover, public debts are closely associated with the evils of war: Remove the ability to contract debts that run for generations, Jefferson says, and "it would bridle the spirit of war."[17] But even more striking than his well-known hostility to the very idea of a public debt is the fact that the debt provides Jefferson with the *only* specific American application for his principle, apart from the passing reference to patents and copyrights. In France, the principle's consequences would be "very extensive," but it is apparent on the face of his "whole catalogue ecclesiastical and feudal" that the abuses the principle would correct there are largely—if not entirely—unknown in the United States. What worries Jefferson, what lends conviction to his argument, is the possibility that debt may overwhelm the new Republic, just as it has already overwhelmed so much of Europe, that "the contagious and ruinous errors of this quarter of the globe" will find a second home in the New World.[18]

Next, there is the similarity between Jefferson's ideas about private debts and his views on the public debt. A common image informs both: that of the spendthrift who recklessly runs through his inherited estate, borrowing on its security to indulge himself at the heirs' expense, depriving them of their turn to enjoy the fruits of the estate in full. Nations resemble individuals in this respect; they too play the prodigal and the wastrel, destroying in a moment of folly what past generations have labored to build up and what future generations have a moral right to inherit. To underscore the importance of the parallel, Jefferson offers Madison a hypothetical illustration proving the absurdity of permitting the debts of one generation to devolve on the next. "Suppose," he suggests, "Louis XV. and his contemporary generation had said to the money-lenders of Genoa, give us money that we may eat, drink, and be merry in our day," exchanging in return a perpetual annuity to begin at the end of nineteen years. "The money is lent on these conditions, is divided among the living, eaten, drank, and squandered. Would the present generation be obliged to apply the produce of the earth and of their labour to replace their dissipations? Not at all."[19] That Jefferson saw the public debts of Europe in just this light is hardly in doubt; so many examples of riotous living by the corrupt and degenerate societies of the Old World convinced him that it was essential to prevent America from becoming another in the long train of victims.

There is, however, a certain ambivalence in Jefferson's position. Although he does not deny society's ability to make heirs—future generations— pay the debts left by their ancestors, he believes it to be a matter of convenience, not necessity. Yet he also thinks the legitimate debts that society has incurred and that can be paid within the lifetime of a generation should be paid; the American debt is a case in point.[20] Jefferson is thus far from proposing a general repudiation of debts or an agrarian law.[21] Some obligations, it seems, are binding, even if others are questions of "generosity and not of right" or, like the present French king's debts, ones of "honor, or of expediency."[22] He supplies no absolute criteria for distinguishing the different sorts of debt, except the overriding one that to be valid they must be capable of being discharged within the lifetime of the generation contracting them. But there are also debts that may be illegitimate in origin and hence morally unenforceable; as perpetual impositions on property, the feudal dues fall into this category, and so Jefferson strongly implies the absence of any obligation to compensate their owners. For Jefferson, property was not a natural right in the strict sense of the term, anterior to society, but the product of conventions that changed over time. This, as we shall see, was the view of the matter taken by leading authorities, but it did not necessarily have radical implications, and Jefferson was certainly not prepared to draw the conclusion that the only acceptable basis for property is utility.[23] Rather, it is to preserve the socially given right to property that Jefferson forbids one generation to extend its control of property unnaturally and intrude on the rights of another; his principle guarantees the equal access of all to the common heritage.

It goes without saying that Jefferson's way of thinking about debts, public and private alike, reflects the economic and emotional pressures engendered by the crisis in his own affairs during the late 1780s, and, as we have seen, some of Jefferson's letters to his creditors in those years touched on the themes discussed in the 6 September 1789 letter to Madison. Thus when he insisted that "reason" and "morality," not "authority or compulsion," would guide his conduct toward them, Jefferson came close to setting up for himself a sphere in which the dictates of the moral law would prevail over those of the municipal law. And his emphasis in the letters to his creditors on "substantial justice"– real justice, as opposed to merely formal justice–again suggests that he had his own notion of what morality demanded and that he did his best to incorporate it in his practice. Some debts, he would tell his brother-in-law Francis Eppes in 1788, were justly due, because they arose from benefits a person had had and enjoyed; but debts that were the result of the operation of law, such as those derived from securityships, lacked that status, and these there was no moral obligation to pay without contest and litigation.[24]

Set against the background of the Wayles debt–the very concern taking him back to Virginia–the 6 September 1789 letter to Madison thus becomes considerably more piquant. Jefferson's cool language about payment of ancestral debts as a mere matter of municipal law masks his resentment, but it is there, just below the surface. Although he argued for succeeding generations' unencumbered enjoyment of their property, Jefferson was condemned to pay John Wayles's debts–and pay them twice over. Unlike the French legislators, he was in no position to make this a matter of generosity; although the debts he owed were not founded in the timeless precepts of natural law, others had already made their repayment a matter of right for his creditors. To be sure, Jefferson repeatedly expressed his intention of paying those debts, but the 6 September letter shows us that he regarded them not only as economically burdensome but also as morally oppressive, examples of the way the past controlled the present, foreclosing opportunities and imposing a special kind of bondage. That such control was authorized merely by the municipal law and was thus a matter of policy with which one might well disagree only made things worse.

Another aspect of the letter also bears noticing: the idea that each generation has the right to make its own laws and constitutions. In modern readings of Jefferson's principle, this is the point most often stressed. Yet in 1789 it was not uppermost in Jefferson's mind. True, he explored it in the discussions with his Parisian friends that preceded the writing of the letter to Madison, and in later years he would return to it on more than one occasion. But in September 1789, to repeat, it was not the focus of his attentions. It is important to insist on this, for with the wisdom of hindsight and the received image of Jefferson as the apostle of American liberalism, we are likely to conclude that his primary intention in 1789 was to push forward this apparently revolutionary notion. But in fact in the letter to Madison he subordinates it to his main goal: ensuring that the infant United States remained uncontaminated by European fiscal heresies.

In suggesting that constitutional revision was not the letter's primary focus, I do not mean to deny that it was an important aspect of the general principle "*that the earth belongs in usufruct to the living*," equal in potential significance to the principle's application to debt. But it was only an aspect, not the whole or the heart of the principle itself. The principle was protean, its uses many, and what Jefferson chose to emphasize depended on context and circumstance. If modern readers are struck by the principle's political applications and therefore assume that this is the true meaning of Jefferson's claim for the living generation, that may be only a reflection of their own interests, not Jefferson's intentions in 1789. And the practice of quoting the softer–albeit more dramatically expressed–versions of the principle found in Jefferson's later letters on constitutional revision suggests that many of these modern readers prefer their Jefferson without the embarrassment of the nineteen-year limit, without too much of the language about debts.[25]

To see mandatory constitutional revision as the letter's center of gravity would also require us to adopt something like Julian Boyd's assumption that Jefferson's references to the United States are only window dressing, there to disguise his primary purpose of influencing constitutional deliberations in France. But that view–Boyd's point about France has not found support, even if his identification of the letter's central message is widely shared–would have us overlook the evidence of Jefferson's hostility to debt and ignore the ways his personal situation colored his thinking. Boyd's argument boils down to a vulgar Straussian claim that Jefferson cast a memorandum intended for use in French politics as a letter to Madison in order to avoid the appearance of interfering in French affairs; any references to America, it follows, were there to conceal his real purpose. If so, it was an extremely elaborate bit of deception, quite out of character and unlikely to achieve the desired result. Everyone who counted in Paris knew of Jefferson's relationship with Lafayette; as we shall see, it was hardly a secret that on several occasions Jefferson had provided aid and counsel to liberal members of the Estates General and National Assembly. I find it improbable that Jefferson could have hoped to conceal his responsibility for extending the right of generations; his proposition in the 6 September 1789 letter built on an earlier proposal for constitutional revision made by Lafayette in July, and few in Paris would have been fooled by the transparent disguise that Boyd has Jefferson adopting. In short, then, he had already interfered far too deeply in French politics for the deception Boyd posits to have had any effect. This is not to say, of course, that Jefferson saw no role for his principle in France–by giving Richard Gem a copy of the letter, without an injunction of secrecy, he may well have expected that it would circulate in advanced political circles Gem frequented in Paris. The principle, after all, is stated in universal terms, and Jefferson suggests several practical applications in France. Boyd's argument, then, forces us to read the letter in an unnatural way and, like a number of the interpretations in his editorial notes, is simply too contrived to be credible.[26]

Granted, Jefferson never ignored the right of future generations to make their own laws and constitutions; as the author of the Declaration of Independence, he was deeply committed to the belief that men had a right to political societies on their own terms, and the step from Lockean contractualism in 1776 to the rights of the living generation in 1789 was easily made. Yet in 1789 the United States had only just finished perfecting its Constitution, and to insist to Madison—of all people—that every generation should repeat the process was not an argument likely to win a sympathetic hearing. Jefferson knew that Madison was little more than a year removed from the hard-fought battle at the Virginia ratifying convention, and he knew as well of Madison's opposition, repeated in the pages of *The Federalist*, to his own earlier proposals for easy modes of constitutional revision.[27] Willing to disagree with Madison when the occasion demanded it—their exchange over the need for a bill of rights demonstrates that—Jefferson was also prepared to educate Madison. Thus Jefferson was probably trying to open another dialogue with his younger colleague in the 6 September letter; what "we" have been discussing in France, he hoped, would become a subject for his transatlantic conversation with Madison. While he would not conceal the principle's constitutional implications from his younger colleague, he would stress some of its consequences rather than others, and particularly the one that most concerned him in 1789—limiting debt. At the outset, then, Jefferson was eager to identify common ground with Madison—that, after all, was the route to eventual agreement—and the common ground in this case was the debt and the ways in which it could be limited. If the Constitution and the Bill of Rights—Jefferson learned in August of the amendments Congress was considering—said nothing about the power of each generation to revise the Constitution, the issue of what would be done with the American debt was still open, and thus, if only on tactical grounds, debt was Jefferson's primary and immediate focus in the letter, for the debt was something that *could* be handled in a way that conformed to his principle of generations.[28]

As it was, Madison would read the letter with his own interests and concerns in mind, reacting with Pavlovian predictability to the threat of mandatory constitutional revision inherent in Jefferson's principle.[29] Jefferson said little more about that part of the principle until the years of his retirement, and in practice he seems to have accepted a combination of constitutional custom and the amending provisions of Article V as an adequate substitute for the literal application of his principle at the federal level.[30] Thus while Jefferson explains that laws and constitutions automatically expire at the end of nineteen years, this remains simply a part of the larger principle, not the principle itself, and it is not the part he emphasizes in the 6 September 1789 letter to Madison. Another aspect of the principle, its application to debts, takes precedence, and thus it is the need to fix the term of nineteen years for the public debts of the United States on which he focuses his attention and to which he directs Madison's.

But it is not only the content of the letter that stands out; there is also the matter of its style, of the mode of argumentation Jefferson elects to use. Here, the letter to Madison brings us face-to-face with one of Jefferson's obsessions—calculation—and it is not too much to say that this was an obsession in a clinical sense.[31] We see it in his working up of Buffon's data, as he painstakingly derives the average life of a generation, then realizes his error and does it again. More to the point, it is present in his footnote calculation of the burdens of compound interest: "100£, at a compound interest of 5. per cent, makes, at the end of 19. years, an aggregate of principal and interest of £252-14, the interest of which is 12£-12s-7d which is nearly 12-5/8 per cent on the first capital of 100£."[32] Jefferson made such calculations throughout his life; his papers are full of amortization schemes and of efforts to estimate the cost of this or the profit on that. Born to collect data, Jefferson hoarded numbers with unusual intensity, responding to impulses deep within him.[33]

Those who regard Jefferson as the complete man of the Enlightenment attribute his urge to calculate to the spirit of the age, so much given to numeration. Jefferson himself once confessed to Benjamin Rush that, of all his studies, mathematics "was ever my favorite."[34] But a favorite study is favorite for a reason, and Jefferson's penchant for mathematics was more than a reflection of a prevailing cultural style: It expressed his need to control the world around him. Reduced to the regularity of numbers, unordered nature and chaotic experience (and, even more, the uncomfortable realities of daily life) could be subdued and overcome. Then Jefferson could manipulate them as he liked, demonstrating his mastery over the forces he took them to represent. This passion for mathematics finds its counterpart in Jefferson's other great passion, architecture, which in his hands was a kind of applied geometry. He is supposed to have remarked that "architecture is my delight, and putting up, and pulling down, one of my chief amusements."[35] Clearly, being able to exercise control and manipulate at will ("putting up, and pulling down") had great significance for Jefferson, and he was drawn to precisely those fields in which it was possible for him to act on these impulses without hindrance. That he chose mathematics and architecture—both disciplines that he understood as rule-bound, whether by the conventions that underlay mathematics or the Palladian principles he saw governing architecture—suggests that Jefferson sought the emotional security that comes from operating in a universe of known outcomes; because the rules were, as he understood things, universally accepted, the results he reached by following them were beyond reproach or criticism and necessarily had to be accepted by others.

As he observed to Benjamin Rush, "We have no theories there, no uncertainties remain on the mind; all is demonstration and satisfaction."[36] "Satisfaction" indeed, for problems disappeared when Jefferson could put them into tabular form. The spurious certainty of numbers enabled him to meet his critics—and his creditors—on ground he chose, with seemingly unanswerable arguments firmly rooted in the "facts" his numbers produced. If matters rarely turned out as Jefferson predicted when drawing up his schemes, failure only gave him cause to shift the blame to whatever or whomever he held responsible for his assumptions' inability to become realities.[37] The optimism so many have identified in Jefferson depended on his willingness to let calculation create its own form of reality, a reality he could control; no matter how bleak the prospects, the future seemed bearable if he could put it in numerical form. But as Freud remarked, "To order the unknown according to known categories is the task of science. Compulsive systematizing performed not for the purpose of mastering reality but in order to deny certain aspects of it, is a caricature of science."[38]

It is an irony worth mentioning that Jefferson's concern with the length of a generation was shared by Alexander Hamilton. Four months after Jefferson worked out the life span of one of his generations in September 1789, Hamilton would call on similar demographic data to support the tontine proposal included in his January 1790 *Report on Public Credit*.[39] Tontines, a form of group annuity much favored in continental eighteenth-century public finance, rewarded high life expectancy, and a good deal of the century's practical interest in demography was driven by the need to establish life tables that could be used to calculate the probabilities involved in tontines and other forms of annuities.[40] But it is perhaps appropriate that this gambling on life expectancy, for that is what the tontine amounted to, should link Hamilton to Jefferson; if the former used the data to shore up public credit in a way that would reinforce the responsibility of future generations for the debts of their ancestors, the latter used it to curtail the public debt and liberate the living generation from the very burdens Hamilton was intent on prolonging.

Finally, we come to Jefferson's preference for arguments drawn from natural law. His insistence that the nineteen-year term fix the limit beyond which debts, constitutions, and laws are no longer valid is presented as a new and more precise—far more precise—law of nature that resolves any number of practical difficulties in statecraft previously matters of debate and contention. This is an extremely important move on Jefferson's part, for it takes us to the heart of a two-sided problem that the social-contract tradition had never been able to resolve—the question of why an existing agreement can bind individual latecomers, on the one hand, and, on the other, the question of when an existing agreement ceases to bind the community as a whole. Resistance theory had always had great difficulty specifying, to any acceptable degree, exactly what acts would dissolve the contract between the sovereign and his subjects; its practical applications (for example, in 1776 by Jefferson himself) had always been ad hoc, always in the nature of laundry lists of complaints detailing a multitude of ways in which the original agreement had allegedly been violated.[41] The merit of Jefferson's nineteen-year limit is that it provides a way out of the dilemma: The regular termination he imagines is intended to make it impossible for the social contract to grow stale, for abuses to creep in. At the same time, the limit on debts also works to achieve this end: By abolishing the sovereign's right to pile up massive debts, Jefferson believes he will eliminate the conditions of corruption that give rise to breaches of the contract, thus removing the need for violent upheaval as the weapon of last resort. We may wonder whether things would work as Jefferson imagines, but his solution has the theoretical merit of resolving these issues in a way that preserves and enhances the spirit of the social-contract tradition. Given his answer, Jefferson might well suggest, as he did to Madison, that he had hit on something new.

Jefferson's emphasis on his principle as a law of nature, moreover, has important consequences for our understanding of his position within the competing political discourses open to him and other late-eighteenth-century Americans. Scholarship in recent decades has revised the image of Jefferson as the man of "French principles" who broke with the historical emphasis of the English and launched out on the uncharted waters of Enlightenment utopianism.[42] Yet for all he owed to the themes of the country party and civic humanism, Jefferson—never a consistent thinker—was open to newer currents of thought, and the letter to Madison reveals him in this light. Nothing could be more in keeping with the late eighteenth century at its most optimistic than his willingness to sweep away the dead hand of the past, to declare that the living have rights no convention, no agreement, no prior claim can displace or abridge. His principle implies that unlimited confidence in the capacity of people to decide their fate we instantly recognize as part of the traditional picture. The appeal to the teachings of natural law and the rights of men, the rejection of what custom and precedent have created in the form of the "municipal law"—all this is in accord with older views of Jefferson, even with those of scholars like Otto Vossler, who saw Jefferson undergoing a sea change in France, absorbing European radicalism and shedding the English doctrines of his youth for the liberating perspectives of the late Enlightenment.[43]

Or so it seems at first glance. Closer examination suggests that Jefferson's principle is by no means so straightforward. The irony here—one Jefferson would not have appreciated—is that in protesting against the burden that one generation wrongfully imposes on its successors, he necessarily ends by proposing a universal and perpetual entail. The earth may belong to the living, but the living enjoy only its usufruct, only its current product. That qualification is critical, for it forbids the living generation to commit waste, and thus each generation becomes a mere tenant for life, empowered only to enjoy the fruits of the estate, not to dispose of it in its entirety. Men, it appears, cannot be trusted to take the interests of the future into account. Jefferson's argument for the automatic expiration of laws and constitutions at the end of nineteen years puts a good deal of emphasis on this and does so in language reminiscent of country party themes—bribery, corruption, faction, and the like make their appearance here. It follows for Jefferson, whose belief in the power of properly drawn laws to shape society rarely faltered, that people must be forced to be virtuous by placing limits on their ability to transgress the natural law.[44] If this notion is already familiar to us from Rousseau, we can see that Jefferson has run up against a problem that would bedevil the radical reformers of his and other eras.[45] Robespierre was soon to discover how difficult it was to inaugurate, much less perpetuate, the reign of virtue; Jefferson, in the more stable setting of America, was fortunate not to have to face the problems of a genuine revolution. Spared the dilemma of working out in the public arena the contradictions inherent in his principle, he could confine his designs to paper, or to retiring the national debt.

Nevertheless, there is something odd about this, especially in an American. Jefferson's position rests on an assumption of finite resources; there is no vision here of endless expansion and limitless growth. Instead, it is as though all the world were Virginia, with its careless agriculture and its wasteful use of land—and in saying this, we are reminded that Jefferson, unlike many of his gentry contemporaries, rejected the lure of the West and cast his lot permanently in Virginia's long-settled and declining regions.[46] Yet Jefferson wants to escape the logic of his position; if history and experience suggest—as they did in his own case—that a generation is likely to misuse the resources confided to it, heaping its successors with debts that will cripple them, then he hopes to limit the damage by imposing his principle of perpetual entail, so that each generation will serve as a custodian charged with the duty of passing on intact what it receives from its predecessors. The impression such a project creates is decidedly conservative, all the more so since Jefferson sees grave dangers in the passage of time. He glimpsed one version of the future in Europe, and it appalled him. His answer is to forbid it, to husband existing resources, to avoid the challenges of change the future posed.[47]

In addition, there is the almost Burkean cast of Jefferson's letter. A year later, in 1790, Edmund Burke, envisioning society as a "partnership not only between those who are living, but between those who are living, those who are dead, and those who are to be born," would write of the limits on any one generation's right to do as it wished, of its responsibility to pass on unimpaired to the future the heritage entrusted by the past to the present.[48] The suggestion of similarity would have astonished Jefferson, but it may be that authors are not always the best readers of the texts they create.

Yet there is a positive side to Jefferson's vision, though it is only implicit in the 6 September 1789 letter and would not be fully elaborated until the years of the presidency and his retirement. If the ability to contract debts could be limited, it might be possible to escape the darker future that Jefferson had seen in Europe. Ending the tyranny of debt, Jefferson will liberate resources that would otherwise be consumed by debt service.[49] Interest payments, as his calculations in the letter show, were never far from his mind, and the rate at which interest accumulated—by the time a debt was finally discharged, interest might equal or exceed principal—was a constant worry.[50] This, as much as anything, was the problem with debt: It came at the heavy cost of interest, absorbing resources that could otherwise have been put to productive uses. Paying interest might ruin a man—or a nation—

and limiting the ability to contract debts was a way of avoiding that. Debt meant lost opportunities, but under Jefferson's principle, that danger would be reduced to manageable proportions. Once the present debt was extinguished and new debt confined to the nineteen-year term the principle allowed—Jefferson in fact hoped that the United States would be able to do without debt at all—he could imagine other ways to use the resources that debt formerly consumed. Internal improvements could be undertaken, and programs of education and enlightenment set in motion. If debt could be avoided, the possibility of transformation could be entertained; freedom from debt would mean freedom in other ways as well.[51]

A closer look at both the circumstances in which Jefferson's letter to Madison was composed and the sources scholars have suggested for the principle it announced will let us appreciate the legitimacy of Jefferson's claim to originality, an originality that came not from the discovery of the rights of the living or the rights of each generation to write its own laws and constitutions, but from his application of the generational principle of nineteen years to debt. First, we are fortunate to know a good deal about the background of Jefferson's letter to Madison. Thanks to the researches of Adrienne Koch and Julian Boyd, it is now generally accepted that the letter grew out of conversations between Jefferson and his physician in Paris, Dr. Richard Gem.[52] But Koch and Boyd may have erred in placing too exclusive an emphasis on Gem, for Gem was only the last in a long line of influences. More to the point, the ideas the two discussed were very much in the air during Jefferson's time in Paris—so much so, as we shall see, that it would be surprising if he had not taken them up at one point or another. And we can look behind the Paris experiences and trace to his early years in Virginia Jefferson's involvement with many of the elements that would later combine to form his principle. But Paris provides as good a place to begin as any; let us start there.

Jefferson's preliminary remarks in the direction of what would become his principle are well known, and they constitute some of the more rhetorically memorable passages in his correspondence during the 1780s. To Madison, he observed in 1785 that "the earth is given as a common stock for man to labour and live on." And, discussing Shays's Rebellion in 1787, he wrote to William Stephens Smith, John Adams's secretary at the American legation in London, "God forbid we should ever be 20. years without such a rebellion."[53] In themselves, these remarks may be no more than the casual asides Jefferson was accustomed to throw off in his letters, yet they suggest that his European experience was having an effect on his thinking; he was beginning to probe themes of importance to the principle of 1789. His growing appreciation of the weight of the dead hand of the past in Europe and his sense that "a little rebellion now and then" was not to be deprecated helped to prepare him for a more concerted involvement with the larger issues these comments raised.[54] That involvement came in the winter of 1788/1789, when he was caught up in the efforts of French liberals to formulate a declaration of rights.

Thus the direct course of reflection leading Jefferson to the 6 September 1789 letter may be traced to the interest of his Parisian friends, many of them members of the informal grouping known as the Américanistes, in drafting a declaration of rights and securing its adoption.[55] Conservative in his views of what the developing French Revolution could and should attempt to accomplish, Jefferson was in full sympathy with the moderates, assisting their efforts to create a new and more representative form of government in France.[56] Above all, Jefferson's American experience was an invaluable resource for reformers like Lafayette. Seeking verbal formulas that would curb the powers of the Crown and establish the French nation's rights on a firm footing, they naturally turned to Jefferson, the one man in Paris who understood how these things were done and, even more to the point, the man who had actually helped to do them. Jefferson's participation in the liberals' project—encouraging, advising, at times even serving as draftsman—is well documented, and it was no secret to contemporaries. William Pitt, the British prime minister, told his dinner companions in July 1789 that "the leading men of the popular Party" were relying on Jefferson for advice, and Jefferson eventually found it necessary to assure Louis XVI's ministers that his intentions were honorable.[57] The question of a declaration of rights, moreover, strongly interested Jefferson. Convinced that such measures were essential, he helped to popularize the 1776 Virginia bill of rights in France, and he was even now engaged in a correspondence with Madison, begun in the fall of 1787 and lasting through the summer of 1789, on the need to add a bill of rights to the new federal Constitution.[58] Jefferson's enthusiastic response when Lafayette summoned him to assist in spreading the rights of man to France was entirely in character.

Since his years in America, Lafayette had dreamed of the day when France, too, would have a constitution that protected the rights of man; in 1788 and 1789, his chance was finally at hand.[59] Early in January 1789, he gave Jefferson his initial draft of a declaration of rights. Silent on the rights of future generations and saying nothing about debts, it nonetheless provided for constitutional revision at distant but specific points in the future—"des époques éloignées mais fixes," in Lafayette's vague wording.[60] Here, in Lafayette's first proposal for constitutional revision, is the germ of what will flower in September: A fundamental question has been introduced in a setting that emphasized its importance. Jefferson passed the proposal along to Madison, commenting that "every body here is trying their hands at forming declarations of rights." In the same letter, Jefferson also included a draft by Dr. Richard Gem, calling its author "a very sensible man, a pure theorist, of the sect called the oeconomists."[61] Like Lafayette, Gem said nothing about debts or the rights of generations, nor did he mention constitutional revision.[62] Yet Jefferson's January letter to Madison is proof that the project had captured the American minister's interest.

But it was only at the beginning of June, when he took the decidedly undiplomatic step of preparing his own draft of a charter of rights, that Jefferson began to play an active role. With the crisis in Louis XVI's relations with the Estates General, it seemed likely that the king would accept limits on his power, and Jefferson thought the opportunity should not be lost.[63] He sent outlines of his ideas to Lafayette and to Jean-Paul Rabaut Saint-Étienne, the Protestant pastor and deputy for the Third Estate, both of them his guests the previous evening. In the course of their meal, they had canvassed "the difficulties which environ you," and Jefferson passed on his suggestions in the hope that they might be of use.[64] Unlike Lafayette in January, he confined himself to the immediate political impasse, proposing that the nation assume the king's debts and urging that the Estates General be given adequate powers to deal with finances. Additional provisions secured essential political liberties until a formal constitution could be adopted.[65]

Lafayette responded favorably to Jefferson's "Excellent ideas," but nothing came of this initiative.[66] Still, Lafayette continued to press for a declaration of rights, and by the end of June or beginning of July, he was ready with a second draft. Here, for the first time in Jefferson's circle, as far as we know, the rights of future generations were explicitly committed to paper, though again in connection with constitutional revision rather than with debt. The final clause of Lafayette's proposal established the nation's right to control its fundamental order: "And as the progress of knowledge, the introduction of abuses, and the right of succeeding generations [le droit des générations qui se succèdent] requires the revision of every human establishment, there should be constitutional means assuring in certain cases an extraordinary convention of representatives whose sole task it will be to examine and modify, if appropriate, the form of the government."[67] More flexible than his January proposal, Lafayette's draft allowed for response when needed rather than at fixed intervals, and in its mechanics, though not in its recital of the justifications for revision, it bore something of a resemblance to the convention options explored in American constitutional practice during the 1770s and 1780s.

Lafayette's language, invoking "le droit des générations qui se succèdent"–the right of succeeding generations–as the basis for constitutional revision was a major step forward. Neither the new American federal Constitution nor any of the state constitutions so influential in spreading the idea of a declaration of rights in France put matters in those terms, though several of the latter enshrined the right of the people to reform and change their governments.[68] Thus the 1776 Virginia declaration stated that "a majority of the community hath an indubitable, inalienable, and indefeasible right to reform, alter, or abolish it [the existing government], in such manner as shall be judged most conducive to the public weal." Pennsylvania's 1776 constitution used the same language, differing from Virginia's only by the clarifying insertion of "by that community" between "be" and "judged." Maryland's 1776 declaration of rights also addressed this issue, guaranteeing that "whenever the ends of government are perverted, and public liberty manifestly endangered, and all other means of redress are ineffectual, the people may, and of right ought, to reform the old or establish a new government"; it then denounced the doctrine of nonresistance. Less emphatically, the preamble to the 1780 Massachusetts constitution explained that "the people have a right to alter the government" whenever government failed to fulfill the ends for which it was instituted.[69] Several of the state constitutions also emphasized the importance of a Machiavellian "frequent recurrence to fundamental principles"—words found in Virginia's, copied in Pennsylvania's, and echoed in North Carolina's.[70] And a constitutional document prepared by Jefferson and included in his widely noticed *Notes on the State of Virginia* (1785), his 1783 draft Virginia constitution, also provided for amendments by way of specially chosen conventions, though without any of the language he and Lafayette would use to describe the theoretical foundations for the right of revision.[71] Similarly, Article V of the federal Constitution of 1787—in addition to the more familiar method of originating amendments in Congress—contains the option of "a convention for proposing amendments" that can be called "upon application of the legislatures of two-thirds of the several States."[72]

Moreover, four of the state constitutions, those of Pennsylvania (1776), New Hampshire (1784), Vermont (1786), and Massachusetts (1780), established procedures for constitutional revision "at distant but specific periods in the future"—every seven years in the first three, and after fifteen years in the Bay State. "In order the more effectually to adhere to the principles of the constitution and to correct those violations which by any means may be made therein, as well as to form such alterations as from experience shall be found necessary," the Massachusetts constitution provided for revision in 1795. Pennsylvania's constitution, which was widely applauded in France, established the Council of Censors, to meet in 1783 and every seven years thereafter, "whose duty it shall be to enquire whether the constitution has been preserved inviolate in every part" and to examine the conduct of public officials; the Censors were also given the "power to call a convention, to meet within two years after their sitting, if there appear any article of the constitution which appear defective." Vermont followed the Pennsylvania pattern, down to the terminology, with its own Council of Censors, whereas New Hampshire provided for a reexamination by town meetings.[73]

Lafayette's draft thus in all probability drew on clauses found in several of the American bills of rights and state constitutions—on the right of the people to alter their government, on the need for recurrence to original principles, and on constitutional revision at fixed dates—and its provisions for "une convocation extraordinaire" were doubtless influenced by Jefferson's 1783 proposal; by the Massachusetts, New Hampshire, Pennsylvania, and Vermont constitutions; and by Article V of the new federal Constitution.[74] But it was no mere copy of existing American precedents; none of the American documents spoke of the "droit des générations qui se succèdent" or invoked the "progress of knowledge"—it was rather the "introduction of abuses" that they addressed implicitly or explicitly.[75] Here, as elsewhere, we are hampered by our lack of knowledge; although we know that the two men conferred several times in early July and must have talked over the draft declaration, Lafayette and Jefferson recorded only the results of their discussions, not the discussions themselves.[76] We do not know which one of them was responsible for the striking language in Lafayette's draft or, indeed, whether it was suggested by a third party. Yet clearly Lafayette and Jefferson were working in tandem, and just as clearly there is reason to see this draft as a product of their joint efforts.

Forwarding his proposals on 9 July 1789—the day a committee of the National Assembly reported that discussion of a declaration of rights should come first in the order of constitutional business—Lafayette anxiously awaited Jefferson's response.[77] "To Morrow," he wrote, "I present my bill of rights about the middle of the sitting. Be pleased to Consider it Again, and Make Your observations."[78] Jefferson carefully reviewed the draft, suggesting changes in some provisions, but he must have been satisfied with the clause invoking the right of generations, for he let it stand as written.[79] Thus in the opening days of July 1789, shortly before events overtook theorizing, Jefferson was coming to grips with a critical element of his principle. The "droit des générations qui se succèdent" had made its way into the discussion and would soon take on a new form in Jefferson's hands. Yet the novel focus of Jefferson's 6 September 1789 letter had still to be worked out. Even in Lafayette's proposed declaration, offered to the National Assembly on 11 July—news that day that the king had dismissed Jacques Necker quickly redirected the legislators' attention to more pressing matters—there was no explicit link between each generation's right to revise the constitution and the heart of Jefferson's principle in 1789, the present generation's lack of power to burden its successors by incurring debts the latter must pay.[80] Nor should we expect such a connection: The National Assembly was attempting to repair France's shattered credit, and the introduction of such a right, even if claimed only in theory rather than exercised in practice, would have done little to restore confidence among the investing public in Paris, Amsterdam, and Geneva. In September, Jefferson would tell Madison that it was much easier to take that step when there was no difficulty in discharging the public debt within the nineteen-year limit, but in July 1789 the French did not find themselves in that position.[81]

The Lafayette–Jefferson proposal for a declaration of rights was only one of many versions in circulation, and it took the National Assembly more than six weeks to sort things out. Constitutional revision would figure in some of the proposals and be left out of others, but the "droit des générations qui se succèdent" was found only in the Lafayette–Jefferson version of 11 July.[82] Its fortunes varied during the month and a half that the National Assembly intermittently worked on the Déclaration des droits de l'homme et du citoyen, though it is probably safe to say that it never had a serious chance of being included in the final version. But it was not ignored, and it attracted supporters who continued to press for its inclusion up to the very last moment. Jefferson kept a close eye on the National Assembly as it considered the alternative declarations before it, and we can surmise that, throughout, the rights of generations were never far from his mind.

Following Lafayette's submission, the National Assembly received some twenty-seven or twenty-eight other proposals and on 19 July referred them to an eight-member constitutional committee headed by Jérôme-Marie Champion de Cicé, the archbishop of Bordeaux.[83] Hoping to bring Jefferson's talents to bear on his committee's task, Champion at this point asked the American minister to appear before the committee and "share for the benefit of France the fruits of your reason and your experience." But Jefferson declined the invitation, telling the archbishop that it would be imprudent for a known republican to offer advice.[84] One wonders what might have happened had Jefferson in fact consulted with Champion's committee rather than working behind closed doors with Lafayette and a few others. Would he have made a strong case for the right of generations, perhaps one that would have convinced the committee to adopt that part of Lafayette's 11 July proposal? It is impossible to tell, of course, and in any case the committee members, who could hardly have been unaware of Lafayette's relations with Jefferson, may have assumed that Lafayette's draft represented the American minister's views as well.

But as matters turned out, Champion's committee would have had little time in which to consider the advice Jefferson might have given. On 24 July 1789, the Assembly ordered it to report the following Monday, 27 July, which it did, with Champion introducing his fellow committee member, the conservative Jean-Joseph Mounier, who then read the committee's project.[85] This latest version of a declaration omitted a right of revision for generations—or for anyone else except under extremely limited circumstances; Mounier was profoundly opposed to the idea of constitutional change embodied in Lafayette's proposal—and debate continued until 4 August, partly in the Bureaux, the working groups into which the French National Assembly was divided, partly on the floor itself.[86] Then, at the evening session of 4 August, led by Lafayette's brother-in-law, the vicomte de Noailles, liberal members of the nobility—the sort of men with whom Jefferson had been having his constitutional conversations earlier in the year—unexpectedly intervened to quell the wave of peasant unrest by announcing their willingness to abandon feudal privileges.[87] Further debate on the French Déclaration was halted for a week while the resolutions of 4 August were turned into decrees. Although historians have discounted the practical consequences of the nobility's renunciation, the effect on Jefferson must have been electrifying.[88] For here, clearly, was an assault on the dead hand of the past, a sweeping away of the gothic rubbish he abhorred. That theme would reappear on 6 September 1789.

Having "mowed down a whole legion of abuses," as Jefferson told Jay, the acting secretary of state, the National Assembly returned to the unfinished business of a declaration of rights on 12 August.[89] It balloted for a five-man committee (its members to be chosen from those who had not previously presented a proposal for a declaration of rights) to review the existing proposals, draw up a single master version, and report back to the Assembly on the following Monday. Thus on 17 August, Mirabeau, on behalf of the

committee, presented still another project, and this one included a provision
for constitutional revision, stating, in language reminiscent of the bills of
rights of the American states, that "every political association has the inalienable right to establish, modify, or change the constitution."[90] But, like
Mounier's July proposal, Mirabeau's draft failed to meet with approval and,
after further debate, on 19 August the Assembly voted on which of three
propositions—a new version prepared by one of the working groups, the
Sixième Bureau; another offered by the Abbé Sieyès; and the last, Lafayette's
original proposal of 11 July—it would take as a basis for further discussion.
The project offered by the bureau had substantial support in the Assembly,
and unlike those presented by Lafayette, Mirabeau, and Sieyès, it made no
mention of a right of revision.[91] The bureau's draft won overwhelmingly,
receiving 620 votes to 240 for Sieyès's; with only 45 in its favor, Lafayette's
proposal was a dismal third.[92] Discussion of the bureau draft then followed
and, as often happens, those who set the agenda were able to control the
outcome—additional changes could come only by way of amendment.[93]
Thus despite last-minute efforts by Comte Mathieu de Montmorency and
others to restore the Lafayette–Jefferson language on the "droit des générations" during a debate that lasted from 20 to 26 August, the Assembly
voted on 26 August to ignore the point, and the Déclaration des droits de
l'homme et du citoyen as adopted made no provision for constitutional
revision.[94] Jefferson and his friends must have been disappointed, though he
did not say so, telling Madison simply that "their declaration of rights
is finished."[95]

Even then, the National Assembly was not quite free of the rights of
generations in one form or another. As the Assembly moved on to take up
the drafting of the constitution, speakers in the final days of August and the
opening days of September continued to raise the issue of constitutional
change.[96] Jefferson himself played a brief but important role in this phase of
the French constitutional debate, allowing his residence to be used as the site
of a conference on 26 August under Lafayette's leadership that brought
together a group including Mounier to resolve the deadlock over the proposed royal veto.[97] When discussion of this question resumed in the Assembly, speakers connected the royal prerogative to the right of constitutional
revision. Thus on 31 August the marquis de Lally-Tollendal, like Mounier a
conservative and a *monarchien*, traced the French king's traditional role in
legislation back to the days of Charlemagne, raising a basic question when he
asked, in language no doubt influenced by the debates on the "droit des
générations" in recent days and weeks, "how far a contract, sacred for so
many generations, can bind the present generation?" Lally went on to
caution that "it would be a grave mistake to act as though nothing in the
monarchy antedated the period in which we now are."[98] And if the king did
accept the constitution, would his act bind his successors? Mounier thought
it would, and so argued that it was essential for Louis XVI to sign.[99]

Then, on 4 September, two days before Jefferson sat down to write his
letter to Madison, Phillipe-Antoine Merlin de Douai reported on behalf of

the committee on feudal property rights, the Comité des droits féodaux, explaining what would be necessary to turn the August decrees into legislation. His thirty-two-page text covered many of the subjects Jefferson would list in the catalogue of questions his principle resolved, and while it is impossible to know whether Jefferson had seen Merlin's speech before he wrote his letter to Madison, there is no reason to suppose that he was unaware of its contents in a general way or unaware of the issues Merlin set before the Assembly, particularly that of compensation, a major focus of deliberations in the Comité des droits féodaux.[100] Meanwhile, the financial situation continued to deteriorate; on 27 August, Necker presented proposals for a new loan of 80 million livres, repeating the promises of 17 June and 13 July that the public creditors were under the protection of the nation's honor and loyalty and would be paid in full.[101]

But if the Déclaration was finished on 26 August, Jefferson was not. Struck down on 2 September by a migraine, one of his dreaded "periodical headaches," Jefferson called in Richard Gem for medical advice.[102] One thing must have led to another, and the two men found themselves discussing the right of generations so recently ignored by the National Assembly. Gem prepared a memorandum embodying his notion of what that right involved, and the 6 September letter to Madison (a copy of which went to Gem) was Jefferson's response. This was the moment of breakthrough, and Gem's proposition tells us why. For Gem, the earth really did belong to the living, and not merely in Jefferson's limited sense. "Individuals," Gem argued, "have the power to alienate their property or to engage it for the payment of debts. Why may not a body of men, a nation, contract debts and engage their united property for the payment of them? In this no rights of posterity seem to be violated; because the property of the present generation does not belong to them [i.e., posterity]." Gem did admit a partial objection: "The interested, ambitious and corrupt conduct of the administrators of nations" might lead them to abuse their power and misuse the proceeds of loans. "To repress" this, he thought it "expedient to declare by a law, that after a certain term of years the payment of a loan shall be void; creditors lending their money on these conditions suffer no wrong by the failure of payment."[103]

Gem's proposal–closest to Jefferson's principle in the issues with which it deals, yet not at all close in its analysis of the rights of the present generation–suggests that Jefferson was not exaggerating when he declared that the principle he was describing for Madison raised a question "never . . . started either on this or our side of the water."[104] Constitutional revision was in the air, making its way into the projects for a declaration of rights; Gem suggested as a matter of practicality a time limit on loans. But even Gem failed to understand the rights of the living as Jefferson conceived them on 6 September. Jefferson's conclusions, as we have seen, were quite different–radically so, in fact. He said that they had emerged from the "course of reflection in which we are immersed here," and something of that process is reconstructed in the preceding pages.[105] But that reconstruction suggests how novel Jefferson's version of the principle was. Set against the background of Jefferson's Paris circle, this special notion of the rights of the living takes on a distinctive and original character. And it does so, I would argue, because Jefferson is thinking of America—and himself—not merely of France, because his primary concern is not the destruction of the *ancien régime*—others were accomplishing that—but the preservation of America from the very evils bringing down the *ancien régime*.

Jefferson's insistence on priority helps us to establish what was original in his principle, but at the same time it raises further questions, if only because the body of scholarship that has grown up around his famous letter of 6 September 1789 has identified an army of contenders as intellectual progenitors of Jefferson's principle.[106] Gem and Condorcet among Jefferson's Parisian contemporaries; Locke, Montesquieu, Blackstone, Smith, Turgot, and Priestley among the writers; and, in a category all his own, Paine—each of them has been put forward at one time or another.[107] Always foolish to insist on, intellectual priority is never easily established, and in this case, as Staughton Lynd remarks before proposing his own candidates, "we are clearly dealing with an idea which was in the air among an international circle of intellectual friends and cannot, without misplaced concreteness, be attributed to any single author."[108] Yet Jefferson had long-standing interests that made him receptive to the messages he found in certain authors, and we can justifiably speak of reinforcement if not of paternity. Those interests centered on the dead hand of the past and, in particular, on feudal remnants in the law of property.

Later in life, Jefferson would recall the 1776 Virginia act to abolish entails as one of his proudest achievements.[109] That statute grew out of his reading in the 1760s, when he became convinced that feudal forms of property were incompatible with liberty. Like many of his peers in England and America, Jefferson subscribed wholeheartedly to the myth of the uncorrupted Anglo-Saxon constitution, and he praised its supposed system of allodial landholding, under which real property was held outright, not subject to feudal overlords. Embracing these notions with a fervor remarkable even in the eighteenth century—he told fellow members of the Continental Congress in 1776 that the Great Seal of the United States should bear the device of Hengist and Horsa, who led the Saxon invasion of Britain—Jefferson sought to realize them when the Revolution offered the opportunity to reform Virginia's laws.[110] "Has not every restitution of the ancient Saxon laws," he asked his colleague on the Virginia commission for the revisal of the laws, the conservative jurist Edmund Pendleton, "had happy effects?" Jefferson continued: "Is it not better now that we return at once into that happy system of our ancestors, the wisest and most perfect ever yet devised by the wit of man, as it stood before the 8th century?"[111] Entail and primogeniture, Jefferson believed, were Norman introductions, props for the "aristocracy" that stood between the people and the full enjoyment of their rights. He was convinced at the time—and later—that abolition of these pernicious practices would have only the most salutary results. Destroying primogeniture and entail, recognizing the allodial character of landhold-ing—these were essential parts of the program Jefferson worked to secure in the first flush of the Revolution, and both were intended to restore the invaluable "practice of our wise British ancestors." Thus he successfully introduced the statute abolishing entail in the first session of the newly created House of Delegates. Primogeniture, in turn, fell when the legislature adopted Jefferson's code of descent.[112] The rights of the living generation, at least with regard to real property, were now embodied in Virginia law; Jefferson had banished the dead hand of the past from his native soil.

In fact, there is little evidence that conditions in Virginia required Jefferson's reforms. Although it symbolized for him the older order he was intent on destroying, primogeniture applied only in the absence of a will and so is unlikely to have had much effect on the distribution of real property at death. In theory, Virginia entails were perpetual (in 1705, the legislature banned the practice of common recovery, the standard method of barring—ending—entails), but in fact they were easy to break, small ones by recording a deed before a country court, larger ones by legislative action.[113] Nor is there much support for Jefferson's view that entail helped maintain the dominance of "aristocracy" in Virginia politics.[114] In 1774, Jefferson had to petition the House of Burgesses for a bill to break an entail on land inherited by his wife, and while the experience may have reinforced his hostility, in all likelihood his attitudes were well established before 1774 and largely, if not entirely, ideological in origin.[115] As such, they reflected fashionable strains of eighteenth-century thought, for hostility to entail, if not to primogeniture, extended well beyond the ranks of Anglo-Saxon enthusiasts. Even Black-stone, the mainstay of legal conservatism, remarked in the second volume of his *Commentaries on the Laws of England* (1766) that "ill consequences of fettered inheritances are now generally seen and allowed" and argued for a simpler and less costly method of breaking entails based, interestingly enough, on the "usage of our American colonies."[116] Jefferson, however, was far too intent on ridding Virginia of its feudal trappings to be swayed by the realities of the case.

Although his goals were always more political than economic, Jefferson did insert a recital of practical benefits in the preamble to the act abolishing entails, stating that "the perpetuation of property in certain families by means of gifts made to them in fee-tail [entail] is contrary to good policy." (Here he was raising the specter of "aristocracy," though prudence doubtless kept him from being as explicit on this score as he would have liked.) And he went on to specify a number of more prosaic considerations: "Fair traders" were misled into extending "credit on the visible possessions of such estates"; tenants under entail had no incentive to preserve and improve their proper-ties; entails "sometimes" caused "injuries to the morals of youth by rendering them independent of, and disobedient to, their parents." Jefferson's pre-amble thus closely followed the standard contemporary criticism of entails. If these were not enough, he pointed out that "the former method of docking by special act . . . employed very much of the time of the legislature, was burthensome to the public, and also to the individuals who made applications for such acts." But despite the saving in legislative energy—the one indubitable benefit of his bill—it is safe to conclude that his primary goal in securing passage of the act was to restore to Virginians—white male Virginians—the rights enjoyed by their freedom-loving forebearers in pre-Conquest England.[117]

Neither Jefferson's letter to Pendleton on law reform nor the statute for abolishing entails relied on natural rights or natural law. Jefferson did emphasize those doctrines in his other great creation of 1776, the Declaration of Independence, and in the principle of 1789 he would rely on them exclusively, omitting any mention of the historical model furnished by the Anglo-Saxons. But the two strands of argument were not distinct for Jefferson. As he conceived them, Anglo-Saxon institutions embodied as nearly as possible the natural rights of man; any conflict between claims based on natural law and those derived from the line of historical precedents seems to have escaped him. Fortunately, given the way the two bodies of doctrine coincided—Anglo-Saxonism providing a specific instance of the more general case stemming from natural law—he had no need to bother himself with distinctions.[118] What always mattered for Jefferson was adherence to cherished convictions, not the mode of reasoning used to support them. His strategy in 1789, though different in approach from that in 1776, did not differ in intention, and we should not make too much of the apparent shift from history to natural law. Underneath, the end in view persisted. If new means could help to remove the dead hand of the past, Jefferson was happy to discover additional grounds that bolstered long-held beliefs.

As both the arguments and the language of the letter to Madison suggest, and as we would expect from a common lawyer in an age when real property was the law's great subject, even after his successes in abolishing entail and reforming the law of descent, Jefferson continued to take a strong interest in the existence of a power to direct the course of property from beyond the grave. Julian Boyd's conclusion, that "this concept of political relativism was the one great addition to Jefferson's thought that emerged from his years of residence at the center of European intellectual ferment," thus requires reconsideration.[119] His Parisian coterie may have provided a necessary stimulus, but Jefferson could draw on nearly a quarter-century of reading and reflection. He did not need exposure to "the center of European intellectual ferment"—which, in any case, Paris in the late 1780s no longer was—to learn that the living generation had rights that could not be ignored.[120]

We can see this more clearly, I think, by considering one of the sources often suggested for Jefferson's principle, Adam Smith. Entails, Smith said in *The Wealth of Nations* (1776), "are founded on the most absurd of all suppositions, the supposition that every successive generation has not an equal right to the earth, and to all that it possesses: but that the property of the present generation should be restrained and regulated according to the fancy of those who had died perhaps five hundred years ago."[121] By 1789,

Jefferson and his friend Richard Gem were undoubtedly familiar with *The Wealth of Nations*, and either or both of them could have recalled Smith's passage when they initiated their discussion of the rights of the living generation in September.[122] Had they attended Smith's lectures on jurisprudence at the University of Glasgow in 1762 and 1763, they would have heard him develop the point more fully and in a way that anticipated their own formulations a quarter-century later. "An eminent lawyer," Smith had told his students that term, "says there can be nothing more absurd than this custom of entails. . . . There is no maxim more generally acknowledged than that the earth is the property of each generation. That the former generation should restrict them in their use of it is altogether absurd; it is theirs together as well as it was their predecessors in their day."[123] And, in a further anticipation of Jefferson's language, Smith had observed to his class in 1766 that "a power to dispose of estates for ever is manifestly absurd. The earth and the fulness of it belongs to every generation, and the preceding one can have no right to bind it up from posterity. Such extension of property is quite unnatural."[124]

How are we to explain these parallels? Neither Gem nor Jefferson attended Smith's Glasgow lectures: Jefferson was safely ensconced in Williamsburg in 1762 and 1763, and by 1766 he was preparing for practice at the Virginia bar; Gem, his college years long over (he was born in 1717), spent the 1760s pursuing his medical career as physician to the British Embassy in Paris. Gem did meet Adam Smith in a professional capacity in 1766 (he was treating a pupil of Smith's), but we can dismiss the possibility that Smith showed Gem the text of his lectures, which remained unpublished until reconstructed from student notes at the end of the nineteenth century; it is equally unlikely that they discussed entails when Gem informed Smith of his pupil's condition (grave enough that Gem was unable to save him; the youth died).[125] Fortunately, there is an easy resolution to the problem: Jefferson and Smith read the same books. In his criticism of entails, Smith drew on two recently published works by Scottish jurists, Sir John Dalrymple's *Essay Towards a General History of Feudal Property in Great Britain* (1757), and the *Historical Law-Tracts* (1758) of Henry Hume, Lord Kames.[126] Jefferson's pre-Revolutionary "Commonplace Book" shows that he carefully read and excerpted both these volumes.[127] As Gilbert Chinard, the first scholar to appreciate Kames's significance for Jefferson's intellectual development, remarked more than half a century ago, "we can trace directly through the 'Commonplace Book' the sources of . . . the Law to Abolish Entails."[128]

Dalrymple, Kames, and Smith all participated in the Scottish debate of the 1750s and 1760s on the wisdom of entail. Widely noticed at the time, this controversy generated a criticism of entail stronger and more thoroughgoing than anything Jefferson could have found in the English literature of the day. The concern of Scottish jurists and intellectuals that entails were harmful and hindered Scotland's development arose from a solid foundation of fact. Following the passage of legislation authorizing their creation in 1685, entails proliferated in Scotland, in part because they offered the landowning class a way to protect its property from permanent confiscation during a period of political upheaval. Unlike the English strict settlement– but, significantly, like Virginia entails–the Scots law version of entail, the tailzie, really did entail, imposing perpetual restraints on the alienation of property. Thus it was feared that much valuable agricultural land was being tied up by entails, and tied up forever. With their interests in economic growth and what has been called "commercial society," mid-century Scottish writers had obvious reasons for attacking tailzies.[129] Their campaign, carried out on a broad front and in the strongest possible language, was grist for the young Jefferson's mill, all the more so since he could recognize in the tailzie a close relative of the Virginia entail. Had the Scots and the Virginians used the strict settlements favored in English practice, Jefferson might have been less inclined to mount his campaign against feudal survivals in the law of property; unlike entails, strict settlements were flexible and of limited duration, and while they were effective in concentrating and perpetuating family property, they did so in a way that satisfied the common-law prejudice against restraints on alienation.[130] Thus thanks to his exposure to the Scottish critique, Jefferson had already imbibed the message Smith presented to wider audiences in 1776. Jefferson did not need the salons of Paris to understand that the earth belongs to the living; he had grasped that in the quiet of his study, long before he left Virginia.

By 1789, moreover, there was a widespread American consensus against entail and primogeniture; writers in this vein shared Jefferson's belief that abolishing these remnants of feudal policy would help produce and preserve that general equality in the distribution of property the eighteenth century thought essential to the existence of republican institutions.[131] Claims of this sort were made with some frequency during the debate on the Constitution in 1787 and 1788. Noah Webster, for example, insisted: "The power of entailing estates is more dangerous to liberty and republican government, than all the constitutions that can be written on paper, or even than a standing army." It was essential to adopt "laws, irrevocable laws in every state," he urged, "destroying and barring entailments; leave real estates to revolve from hand to hand, as time and accident may direct; and no family influence can be acquired and established for a series of generations." He concluded that "the balance of wealth and power will continue where it is, in the *body of the people*." Timothy Pickering's views were similar. "The laws of most, if not all, of the states," he told a correspondent, "admit the distribution of the property of a deceased citizen among all his children, and no *entails* ought to be permitted. And when all existing entails shall be broken, & future ones forbidden, we may make ourselves easy about aristocratic ambition," sounding much like Jefferson in this regard.[132] True, Jefferson would not have agreed with Webster and Pickering that prohibiting entails virtually ensured republicanism in America–he knew that other protections were necessary–but he would not have disagreed that it was a desirable precondition.

Nor was there anything new in Jefferson's general theory of property; in this, too, he was simply following the authorities. Blackstone, like Locke before him, analyzed property and inheritance and came to similar conclusions. "The earth therefore, and all things therein, are the general property of all mankind, exclusive of other beings, from the immediate gift of the creator," Blackstone explained to his readers in 1766, repeating Locke's contention that God "*has given the Earth to the Children of Men*, given it to Mankind in Common."[133] As society becomes more complex, rights in property develop. Yet in this early state of things, property ceased the instant its owner died: "For, naturally speaking," Blackstone argued, once a proprietor dies "he ceases to have any dominion: else, if he had a right to dispose of his acquisitions one moment beyond his life, he would also have a right to direct their disposal for a million of ages after him; which would be highly absurd and inconvenient." As society grows in complexity, new needs and conditions appear, and in order to prevent "endless disturbances" and other ills, "the municipal law of the country then steps in, and declares who shall be the successor, representative, or heir of the deceased." Thus the right of inheritance is "clearly a political, establishment; since the permanent right of property, vested in the ancestor himself, was no *natural*, but merely a *civil*, right." Thus "Wills," Blackstone concluded, "and testaments, rights of inheritance and successions, are all of them creatures of the civil or municipal laws, and accordingly are in all respects regulated by them; every distinct country having different ceremonies and requisites."[134]

All this was perfectly familiar doctrine to anyone who had read the standard authorities. To be sure, there is a difference—and an important one—between Blackstone's expository account of inheritance and Jefferson's turning the same material to a more critical use. Lord Kames anticipated Jefferson in this regard, suggesting not only that "in early times property was not much distinguished from what is now called *usufruct*," but also that "the rules of succession have been established, not only from very slender circumstances, but in some measure from accident."[135] Jefferson's 6 September 1789 letter said nothing about the nature of inheritance that had not been said before. The notion that the earth belonged to the living was thus anything but novel in the late eighteenth century. In fact, its roots can be traced to the Christian Middle Ages.[136] Jefferson's 1785 observation to Madison, that "the earth is given as a common stock for man to labour and live on," repeated a theme insisted on since at least the seventeenth century.[137] Sir Robert Filmer's opponents, Locke and Algernon Sidney, used it to good effect in the polemics of the 1670s and 1680s; a century later, in the 1770s and 1780s, it provided a point of departure for the far more radical speculations on the right to property in Thomas Spence's 1775 lecture to the Newcastle Philosophical Society and the Aberdeen professor William Ogilvie's *Essay on the Right of Property in Land* (1784), and at the same time for the bland and conventional arguments of the proto-utilitarian Archdeacon William Paley's *Principles of Moral and Political Philosophy* (1785), a set text at Cambridge for decades. Thomas Paine and others would make use of it in the 1790s, again exploiting its radical potential.[138] Only as reaction to the French Revolution set in did leading Anglo-American writers come to question its implications; only then would Edmund Burke's conservative vision of generational continuity and social hierarchy find a large and appreciative audience.

The background Jefferson brought with him to Paris was constantly being reinforced. For the first time, he experienced what it meant to live in a world where feudalism had left a real mark, not merely the imaginary one that exercised him in Virginia, and we know from his letters that this slave-owning American was profoundly shaken by what he found.[139] His feelings on this score were shared by many of his French contemporaries, men whose views helped frame the debate on declarations of rights in which Jefferson participated. Demands for the abolition of feudal survivals, whether on grounds of efficiency or of natural right, were made everywhere in Europe during the waning years of the *ancien régime*. Turgot denounced these useless relics of the past in the *Encyclopédie*; his essay on perpetual endowments, attacking church property held in mortmain, attracted interest throughout the Catholic world and played a part in the assault on religious and charitable foundations that was one of the most notable developments in late-Enlightenment absolutism.[140] Insisting that "public utility" was the supreme law, Turgot deplored the persistence of a "superstitious respect" for what he called "the *founders' intentions*," especially when this meant allowing "ignorant and narrow-minded individuals" the right "to chain to their capricious desires generations not yet in being." Reforming sovereigns like Joseph in Austria and Leopold in Tuscany put Turgot's doctrines into practice, closing monasteries, banning contemplative orders, reducing the church to an arm of the increasingly utilitarian state.[141]

These views breathed a spirit Jefferson was well prepared to appreciate. Fully aware of the way European reformers were attacking the dead hand of the past, he acquired a copy of the original *Encyclopédie* in the 1780s, and while in Paris he subscribed to the *livraisons* of its successor, the *Encyclopédie méthodique*. The *Méthodique*'s volumes on finance and jurisprudence appeared during his tenure as minister, and he would have found in them ample evidence of the feudal survivals that still marked the French law of property and inheritance.[142] Jefferson himself had included a ban on mortmain that was borrowed from the British statute of 1736 in the revised code (again, as with primogeniture and entail, mortmain was a problem in Jefferson's mind, not in Virginia reality), and he had gone on to attempt the reform of Virginia's leading (and only) example of a clerical foundation, the College of William and Mary, diverting its resources from their intended religious uses to secular ends.[143] As we shall see, even after his return to the United States he remained alert to the dangers of mortmain, and he feared that the creation of powerful new corporations such as the Bank of the United States might circumvent the policy against it.[144] His dislike of the Society of the Cincinnati, which reflected in so many ways these themes of hostility to the dead hand of the past, led him to campaign against the order's hereditary principle (it was, in effect, legitimating primogeniture in a particularly dangerous way), and he equally feared that the Cincinnati, as a self-constituted perpetual body, might accumulate extensive funds and so reintroduce the evils of mortmain.[145]

Writers in Paris explored other themes in the 1780s that would recur in the letter to Madison, occasionally deploying generational arguments that anticipated Jefferson's. The prolific journalist Louis-Sébastien Mercier made telling use of such points in his prerevolutionary pamphlets and essays.[146] Mercier went so far in Jefferson's direction as to propose in a piece entitled "Génération nouvelle" (New Generation) that every generation (which he defined as thirty years) should make a new beginning and rewrite the constitution.[147] In another essay, Mercier assailed contemporary fiscal practice, condemning loans as "the worst scourge of modern states" and denouncing their devastating effects on "that unhappy race not yet in existence" as they consumed the property nature intended for those generations.[148] Mercier's comments in the latter vein were hardly original; the article on "public credit" in the *Encyclopédie méthodique* described in 1784 how "the administrators of empires . . . have not feared to charge future generations with the debts they have allowed themselves to contract." And, like Mercier, the article's author drew only gloomy conclusions: "This chain of oppression has extended itself. It must bind our descendants and weigh heavily on all peoples and all centuries."[149] Again, both Mercier's essays and that on "public credit" in the *Encyclopédie méthodique* suggest that the ideas leading to Jefferson's principle circulated widely in the years before 1789, though no one had yet combined them in quite the way that would occur to Jefferson on 6 September 1789.[150]

In Prussia, Immanuel Kant turned the argument about the rights of generations to the uses of German idealism, arguing in his famous essay of 1784, "Beantwortung der Frage: Was ist Aufklärung?" ("An Answer to the Question: 'What Is Enlightenment?' ") that the progress of enlightenment, particularly in religious matters, could not be limited by the creeds and formulas adopted in previous generations—a case Jefferson would have endorsed with enthusiasm had he been able to read Kant's words.[151] "One age [*ein Zeitalter*] cannot enter into an alliance on oath to put the next age in a position where it would be impossible for it to extend and correct its knowledge," Kant insisted. "Later generations [*die Nachkommen*]," he thought, were within their rights to dismiss these agreements as unauthorised and criminal."[152] It was a view that had much in common with Lafayette's appeal to the "progress of knowledge" as a ground for constitutional revision. Even in England, less advanced in these matters, latitudinarian Anglicans called for an end to mandatory subscription of the Thirty-Nine Articles; human, not divine, in origin, such doctrinal tests were manifestly at odds with the possibility of improving the church and, in the words of a prominent lay sympathizer, the duke of Grafton, left "our faith and worship . . . bound down, without redress by the fallible decisions of men."[153]

As for the notion that constitutions could be changed at the desire of the governed, to abolish abuses and take advantage of increases in knowledge, that was hardly new in 1789–again, it would take Burke's commanding intervention in 1790 to render the proposition suspect. In practice, Europe saw a good deal of constitutional change in the 1770s and 1780s, some of it the result of pressure by relatively broad political strata. Thus the Protestant nation in Ireland was able to secure a substantial measure of independence from Westminster during the later stages of the American Revolution, and if the Patriot movement of 1786 and 1787 in Holland failed in the face of foreign intervention, there was still hope that the Poles might be able to reform themselves in time to prevent further dismemberment of their country. In still other cases, popular movements attempted to turn back the efforts of reformers like Emperor Joseph II to do away with their ancient constitutions and the web of privileges and exemptions they embodied.[154] But it was hardly a passive decade. Above all, in France in the years before 1789 it was clear that constitutional change was under way: The debates on the composition of the Estates General, following hard on toleration for Protestants and the innovations of Archbishop Loménie de Brienne's provincial assemblies and Assembly of Notables, showed that even under the monarchy the French constitution was not immune to change, despite the Parlements' protests.[155]

On theoretical grounds, of course, the point had been established well before Jefferson's time. A century earlier Locke had argued that while a man could bind himself, he "*cannot* by any *Compact* whatsoever, bind *his Children* or Posterity.*"[156] Writing in the 1680s, Algernon Sidney, an author Jefferson revered, put the matter in classic form, asking why, "if it be lawful for us . . . to build houses, ships, and forts better than our ancestors," there should not be "the same right in matters of government, upon which all others do almost absolutely depend?" After all, Sidney continued, "If men are not obliged to live in caves and hollow trees, to eat acorns, and to go naked, why should they be forever obliged to continue under the same form of government that their ancestors happened to set up in the time of their ignorance?"[157] In the 1760s, another of Jefferson's favorites, Lord Kames, insisted that "it must also be the privilege of every society to improve its government, as well as upon manufactures, husbandry, or other art invented for their good."[158]

To be sure, not all eighteenth-century writers accepted these positions. Social-contract theory implicitly posed the question of future generations; if there was in fact an original contract, and consent was essential to legitimate it, how were those who came later to exercise their natural rights? David Hume, as we might expect, had his reservations about the original contract, and in the 1777 version of his essay on this question, he addressed the problem of future generations directly, pointing out that the argument that each generation had a right to act as it wished rested on a fundamental misunderstanding. If, he conceded, "one generation of men go off the stage at once, and another succeed," then the new generation could model government as it wished. But the fact of the matter was that the population was permanently "in flux," Hume countered, discovering a difficulty Jefferson would later try to resolve, so that there could never be the clean break the generational argument presumed. On the contrary, Hume thought, continuity was the real desideratum; to ensure stability, it was necessary to preserve established forms.[159]

Objections such as those raised by Hume were not infrequent, and the American patriot James Otis began his pamphlet *The Rights of the British Colonies Asserted and Proved* (1764) by noting the standard arguments against "the *original compact*," among them the claim that contract theory would each alot to each "generation of men . . . the same right to make original compacts as their ancestors had. If every man has such a right," Otis continued his paraphrase of the arguments against contract theory, "may there not be as many original compacts as there are men and women to be born?" Such objections, Otis observed, came from "highfliers and others in church and state who would exclude all compact between a sovereign and this people"; if answers were required, his readers would find them in "Mr. Locke's discourses on government, M. De Vattel's law of nature and nations, and their own consciences."[160] Yet for all Otis's assurances that contract theory properly understood posed no great problems for those not disposed in advance to oppose it, the very literalness with which it was presented made certain questions impossible to avoid.

In his Edinburgh University lectures, Adam Ferguson offered another reading of these issues—one Jefferson would reject, as we have seen—questioning whether it was true that "succeeding generations of men are . . . comprehended under certain legal establishments, by the deed and institution of their ancestors." On the contrary, Ferguson thought, presenting the conventional solution, every man, "as he comes of age," ratifies the contracts already made when "he mixes in society, where these conditions are already ratified by others." Thus "citizens, in every regular community, are bound, not by the institution of their ancestors on which they were not consulted, but by the consent they themselves have given" when they accepted the benefits that community provides. Accordingly, "the question, . . . whether persons of one age can bind their posterity in ages that follow," must be answered in the negative. The implications Ferguson drew from this argument allowed for change when needed: Men had the right to refuse consent to "an institution, however willingly adopted by a former age," if that institution should "prove in the sequel a mere abuse"; "injustice and wrong . . . however long continued" are of no binding force: "The oppressed, even after any indefinite period of oppression, are free to procure relief by such means as they are enable to employ for that purpose."[161] Ferguson's sensible view of the question strikes a balance that most of us, I suspect, would accept, but it leaves Jefferson's fundamental objections to tacit consent unanswered.

In the 1780s, American authors, as well, rejected Hume's position, some of them anticipating—once again—themes Jefferson would raise in 1789. Writing as "Giles Hickory" in the December 1787 issue of his *American Magazine*, Noah Webster asked: "Have we then a right to say that our posterity shall not be judges of their own circumstances? The very attempt to make *perpetual* constitutions, is the assumption of a right to control the opinions of future generations; and to legislate for those over whom we have as little authority as we have over a nation in Asia." In a later installment of his essay, Webster attacked Jefferson on this score, misreading Jefferson's comments in the *Notes on the State of Virginia* about the superiority of conventions over ordinary legislatures as proof that the Virginian was one of the utterly mistaken "advocates for *unchangeable Constitutions*."[162] The context that informs Webster's essay–the struggle over the ratification of the Constitution– helps to suggest why generational arguments began to appear spontaneously at this point. The very act of writing a constitution, especially one that was intended to replace a defective prior instrument and that did so without following the procedures for constitutional change outlined in the existing agreement, raised the issue of whether successors were bound by the decisions of their predecessors; some Antifederalists supported their charges that the 1787 Constitution was illegal by pointing out that the Articles of Confederation were specifically stated to be "perpetual" and could be altered only with the unanimous consent of the state legislatures.[163] Given those circumstances, and given the existence of the generational discourse already available in the works of authors like Locke and Sidney, it would not have been difficult for Webster–or anyone else–to make the "Giles Hickory" argument.

A year earlier, in 1786, even before the Philadelphia Convention met and the generational theme arose in the context of ratification, Thomas Paine made a similar point, in a way that prefigured some, though not all, of Jefferson's 1789 principle. Taking the side of the Bank of North America when the Pennsylvania legislature tried to revoke its charter, Paine agreed with the bank's critics on only one point: the impossibility of a perpetual charter. "As we are not to live for ever ourselves," he wrote, "and other generations are to follow us, we have neither the power nor the right to govern them, or to say how they shall govern themselves." It was, he said, "the summit of human vanity . . . to be dictating to the world to come." And he suggested thirty years as the average length of a generation, so that "any public act" could not be in force longer than that term. It would be useful as well, he thought, to have a clause "in the Constitution, that all laws and acts would cease of themselves in thirty years," for "it would prevent their becoming too numerous and voluminous, and serve to keep them in view in a compact compass."[164] Yet even Paine, in thinking along lines that later occurred to Jefferson, failed to extend his remarks to constitutions themselves and had nothing to say about debts; he was also, of course, content to take the traditional definition of a generation without stopping to ask whether a more precise figure was possible. But Paine's use of the standard argument that the legislative acts of one generation cannot bind the next is further evidence that talk about generations was becoming common in the later 1780s.[165]

These cases suggest that Jefferson did not operate in an intellectual vacuum. Apart from the crucial step of quantifying a generation and insisting that the result, his nineteen-year period, was the limit beyond which no generation had the right to bind another in matters of debt, Jefferson rarely strayed beyond well-mapped territory. Questioned on this score, no doubt he would have replied as he did when asked about the sources of the Declaration of Independence; he was not, he always insisted, creating new doctrine in 1776, but expressing the views of the best authorities and applying them to the situation at hand. The case was much the same in 1789; here, too, it was the application that was novel, not the underlying set of ideas.[166]

Thus Jefferson's Virginia preoccupations, his hostility to feudal forms of property, his work with French friends on a proposed declaration of rights, his fears for the new American republic's future, and his hope that it could escape the ruinous effects of debt—all of these impulses converged in the late summer of 1789 and moved Jefferson one step beyond his contemporaries, helping him to find the solution that had so far eluded others who shared his concern with the problem of debt. Jefferson's claim at the outset of his letter to Madison, that "the question . . . seems never to have been started on this or our side of the water," is therefore justified—justified in the sense that by giving a novel reading to an old proposition, he finds a new application for it. Linking the rights of the living generation with the public debt in order to confine the right to contract debts to a single generation, Jefferson offers something different. All the rest of his principle—the claim that the earth belongs to the living, the remarks on public debts, the analysis of property and inheritance—all of it was standard fare. Adam Smith, after all, had said twenty-five years before that "no maxim" was "more generally accepted" than that the earth belongs to the living.[167]

Rather, it was Jefferson's qualifications—the definition of a generation as nineteen years and the addition of "in usufruct"—that made the difference, moving him beyond the positions of Smith and Paine, beyond the Virginia statute abolishing entails, beyond Blackstone and Locke and the others, beyond the Parisian discussions. In Jefferson's principle, we can see the continuity between the Anglo-Saxon enthusiasms of the 1760s and the natural-rights emphasis of the 1780s, between the older and newer Jeffersons, as it were. But it is the combination, the particular mix, resting as it does on Jefferson's fear that the United States will be consumed by debt unless his principle is adopted, grounded as it is in his own sense of the burden that inherited debts imposed on him, that takes Jefferson out of the realm of the platitudes of a discourse already hackneyed. And it is his sense that he *has* found a solution, that his principle of the limited right of generations provides the answer, that makes him claim priority. Because debt is the problem Jefferson wants to address, his reading of the right of the living does describe something new, and he hastens to let Madison know of his discovery.

Ordinarily Jefferson was careful not to assert intellectual priority, and his justifiable modesty in refusing to insist on it in the case of the Declaration of

Independence has already been mentioned. But in this instance, Jefferson chose to stress that what he—or rather "we," the plural meant to include Richard Gem and probably others as well—had to say was new.[168] If Jefferson is right, and there is something original in the letter to Madison, we will find it in two places. First, there is what Jefferson himself emphasizes through his calculations—the transformation of otherwise commonplace ideas of uncertain extent and application into a law of nature, a law that, for Jefferson, has all the rigor of a scientific fact. Second, there is Jefferson's modification of the standard language of political argument. Adding the qualifying "in usufruct" to the widely accepted notion that the earth belongs to the living, and substituting "generation" for the dominant Anglo-American and French term "the people/*le peuple*," Jefferson alerts us that he is transforming familiar ideas, synthesizing and quantifying the fairly loose versions already in circulation to arrive at something new.

In any attempt to identify what is distinct in Jefferson's revision of the widely shared principle that the earth belongs to the living, his addition of the qualifying "in usufruct" is bound to strike us as significant. Unlike "generation," which comes into the picture midway in the process, "in usufruct" does not appear until the last stages in the formulation of Jefferson's doctrine. It is used expressly only in the letter to Madison; conceptually, it is not there until the early September exchange of views with Richard Gem. Yet it may be this late addition that most distinguishes Jefferson's doctrines from the other versions in circulation. Here, it seems to me, we have Jefferson the lawyer and pupil of George Wythe to thank, for in thinking of ways in which the rights of the living could be protected, Jefferson must have remembered what he learned long ago in Williamsburg. He would certainly have recalled both the traditional common-law methods of protecting estates from abuse by limiting the rights of the present occupants to ensure those of their successors, and the Roman law of property.[169] As Jefferson envisioned it in the letter to Madison, the estate any generation enjoys would be an estate for life only, an estate that must be passed on intact to the next in the line of succession.[170] Like a trusted family counsellor, Jefferson drew up a deed of settlement ensuring future generations the right to benefit from the common property, and the means he employed, the entail, was familiar doctrine to eighteenth-century Anglo-American lawyers. But "entail" is a word Jefferson could not have used—perhaps not even have imagined using—without raising eyebrows. Hence his need for a more acceptable way of putting things and, in all probability, his resort to "in usufruct," with its Roman and civil-law overtones and its relative lack of connection to the common-law practice he had earlier condemned.[171]

What will impress us in the 6 September 1789 letter to Madison, then, is Jefferson's willingness to take literally the notion of the living generation. Not content with the usual eighteenth-century measure of a generation as thirty years or so, Jefferson, always ready to calculate, went on to determine how long generations of the sort he had in mind really did last.[172] The result allowed him to be specific where others were vague, and it gave him the right to insist that he was saying something new. Claims for the living generation had been made before, but never with the precision Jefferson was able to supply; thanks to the authority of numbers, he could reduce generalities to a practicable law.

Arguably, the second of the two linguistic shifts, the adoption of "generation" as the favored term, played the key role in the gestation of Jefferson's principle. Despite the significant anticipations of Jefferson's principle I have noted, political discourse in the late-eighteenth-century United States made relatively little use of the word—it does not, for example, appear in the pages of *The Federalist*.[173] Normally one referred to "the people," and although that term obviously included the present generation, it was different in emphasis and significance. To speak of "the people" is to speak in abstractions; as Edmund S. Morgan has reminded us, "the people" is the ultimate fiction. "The people" never dies; it has the same corporate immortality and collective right of sovereignty that were attached to the king's political body in earlier theory. A "generation," however, and especially a "generation" in Jefferson's sense, is specific and identifiable. Unlike "the people," it has a precise definition and a limited duration, so that there will be a point in time after which such a "generation" no longer has rights. That limitation is critical, for it allows Jefferson to establish exactly who can exercise rights. With "the people," rights are inchoate; with a "generation," we know whom and what we are dealing with.[174] And having been able to quantify a "generation," thanks to his willingness to do the calculations required, Jefferson was able to resolve an issue that had been left open in the earlier proposals for the French Déclaration—the point in time when a generation's rights come into play. Now, at last, it would be possible to specify the "distant but fixed period" when constitutional revision was to take place; no longer would it be necessary, as in the 11 July version of the proposal, to rely on a general principle whose application would, after all, be a matter open to opinion and debate. Having a number put an end to the possibility of confusion and difference; Jefferson was able to give his principle the inflexible foundation he thought it required in order to be practicable.

It may be that the French context explains at least some of Jefferson's decision to employ the word "generation." In an atmosphere where notions of "regeneration" were on everyone's lips and where prerevolutionary pamphleteers like Louis-Sébastien Mercier occasionally made generational arguments resembling Jefferson's, it is easy to imagine how the rights of "the people"—or "the nation," the other accepted formula in 1789—might have become those of a "generation" without anyone's quite noticing, at first, the potential implications of the change.[175] But even in France, it was not yet customary in 1789 to stress the rights of generations rather than those of "the people" or "the nation."[176] Thus the early drafts of a declaration of rights in Jefferson's circle had referred to "the nation," "generation" first appearing at the end of June or beginning of July 1789.[177] Once adopted, however, the new term set in motion an argument that, for all it may have owed to standard notions of the late Enlightenment, would take on a life of its own.

Given Jefferson's difficulties with the Wayles legacy, it seems likely that what was at first a purely political "droit des générations qui se succèdent" to revise the Constitution would have led him to question his own position as a debt-ridden successor. He must, I think, have gradually come to ponder the latent meanings of the phrase "générations qui se succèdent," which, after all, described his own relationship to the Wayles legacy. On 6 September 1789, that phrase would have had a special meaning for him: It was the seventh anniversary of his wife's death in 1782.[178] And even as Jefferson was coming to his conclusions, he was being reminded of the continuing problems posed by both the French and the American public debts. He wrote to John Jay on 30 August to report Necker's latest attempt to float a loan, and on 3–4 September, despite his migraine, he engaged in a brief correspondence with the speculator James Swan on the American debt.[179] Richard Gem's early September proposition also shows that he and Jefferson were discussing the public debt, and in the circumstances it was a subject more than likely to have come up. This overlapping set of influences, then, prompting Jefferson to consider the larger implications of the traditional generational principle, set the stage for Jefferson's breakthrough.

Once he made the connection between the wording of the 11 July proposition and his own situation, Jefferson would have realized, quite suddenly, that the principle embraced far more than the right of the living generation to constitutional revision. And that the connection was *sudden* seems beyond dispute; only days before, on 28 August, in commenting on the National Assembly's completion of the Déclaration and on the American Bill of Rights, Jefferson had said nothing about the generational principle in any form; now, on 6 September, he was ready to set it out in full.[180] Drawing *bricoleur*-fashion on the other bodies of knowledge available to him, Jefferson would have recalled conventional ideas about the law of inheritance as municipal rather than natural, and about the dead hand of the past, building them into his argument. And with his penchant for calculation, at this point Jefferson would have asked himself how a generation was to be defined. Already familiar with Buffon, he would have turned to the tables, done the arithmetic, and arrived at his nineteen-year duration of a generation.[181]

If this is what happened, we can understand why Jefferson began his letter by discussing the laws of inheritance, for in linking that theme to political rights, he made what could well have struck him as an original contribution. (He was also, I suspect, using Richard Gem's proposition as an *aide-mémoire*; the order of discussion in the early pages of Jefferson's letter tracks that in Gem's brief note.) In fact, linguistic suggestions appear at several points in the letter to Madison that underscore the likelihood of Jefferson's having made a connection between the two in this fashion; he repeatedly uses the word "succeed" and its variants when describing the situation of heirs who come into property. Thus he says that "no man can, by *natural right*, oblige the lands he occupied, or the persons who succeed him in that occupation, to the paiment of debts contracted by him"; he refers to "each successive generation," "another generation or society succeeds," and "he who succeeds to lands"; and, in a political context, he speaks of "the succeeding generation."[182] The personal and the political contexts overlapped; in late August and early September—as the issue of the "droit des générations qui se succèdent" was raised once more in the French National Assembly, as Jefferson was dealing with public debts in his professional capacity, and as he would have been thinking about the return to Virginia and negotiations with his creditors—these strands must have come together, each of them reinforcing the others, with the language of successive generations—the "droit des générations qui se succèdent"—providing the link that joined them in an unusual way.

Jefferson's letter of 6 September 1789 is a remarkable statement of his conviction that debt is an evil to be avoided when at all possible and in no case to be allowed to burden the future. Written at a time when he was especially conscious of the role of debt in his own life, when his country was about to address the problem of its Revolutionary debt, and when France was in the opening stages of a revolution brought on by the inability of its governing class to deal with the debts piled up by the *ancien régime*, the letter expresses thoughts long maturing. Building on his personal experiences and on broader intellectual currents to which he had been exposed even before he left America, the letter sums up a chapter in the development of his mind.

It will, however, be necessary to examine yet another part of Jefferson's world before we can determine what is personal and what is typical in his way of looking at debt, before we can decide whether Jefferson's outlook was not merely his own but also that of his class, the Virginia gentry. In the next chapter, therefore, late-eighteenth-century Anglo-American views of the public debt and the economic and political context that informed those attitudes will be explored. With that background in place, Jefferson's reaction to Hamilton's management of American finances in the early 1790s will be easier to understand, as will the ways in which Jefferson's position on debt enabled him to emerge as Virginia's chosen voice in the new Republic. Without that context, Jefferson's views would have remained merely the idiosyncratic opinions of another Virginia gentleman. As it was, however, Jefferson would build on his obsessions and become a political force to be reckoned with.

3

Wars, Debts, and Taxes

*Wars, taxes, debts, funds, and all the consequences of our prodigious trade,
are regretted no further than as burthensome to individuals, not as parts of
that vast fabric of dependency on the crown . . . from which there is reason to
fear the worst of consequences.*

Arthur Young, 1772[1]

"Of all the enemies to public liberty," James Madison insisted in 1795, "war
is, perhaps, the most to be dreaded, because it comprises and developes the
germ of every other. War is the parent of armies; from these proceed debts
and taxes; and armies, and debts, and taxes are the known instruments for
bringing the many under the domination of the few."[2] "These truths," he
added, "are well established. They are read in every page which records the
progression from a less arbitrary to a more arbitrary government, to an
aristocracy or a monarchy."[3] Madison's trinity of evils—wars, debts, and
taxes—and the result to which they led—aristocracy or monarchy—summed
up what was perhaps the central problem of Anglo-American politics in the
eighteenth century. How to avoid the effects his contemporaries would have
agreed Madison correctly identified constituted a problem of critical importance both for the success of the republican experiment in America and for
the preservation of what remained of liberty in Europe. Unavoidably, it was
the problem to which Anglo-American politicians and publicists known to
Jefferson and the Virginians repeatedly turned their attention. For with few
exceptions, those who thought seriously about these questions shared Madison's beliefs. Occasional voices might be heard suggesting otherwise—Sir
James Steuart toward the middle of the century, and Hamilton (in some of
his moods) at its end—but on the whole there was a broad consensus in the
Anglo-American world that linked war and finance and the fate of liberty,
seeing them as necessary and inseparable elements of a common theme.

Behind this consensus lay a widespread awareness that standing armies
and modern forms of public finance were relatively new phenomena that

marked a decisive turn in history. As such, they struck many eighteenth-century observers as worthy of investigation—both for their own sake, as part of the larger project of social and historical examination undertaken by the Enlightenment and, more important, for the practical lessons they could teach. "The systems of finance are modern," Rousseau said in his *Considerations on the Government of Poland*. "I see nothing good or great emerging from them. The governments of antiquity did not even know the word 'finance.'"[4] But it was precisely this addition to the vocabulary of politics that interested men of the time, and their efforts to grasp its meaning and discover its significance for their own lives would influence the ways Jefferson, Madison, and the Virginia Republicans responded to the challenges before them in the 1790s and after.

Jefferson and his contemporaries fully accepted the eighteenth century's conventional wisdom on the public debt, its dangers, and its connections to war and taxes. Apart from his letter to Madison of 6 September 1789—the exception that proves the rule, and even then more for the solution it proposes than for the originality of its underlying analysis—rarely, if ever, will their comments on this subject strike us as new or different.[5] These were men raised on the orthodox view, and few of them abandoned it; it was an essential part of the way they understood their world. But rather than trace the orthodox view from its origins in late-seventeenth- and early-eighteenth-century England (several good accounts of those origins already exist),[6] I shall concentrate on that view as found in works late-eighteenth-century Virginians are known to have read and studied.[7] To be sure, the mid-eighteenth-century writers familiar to Jefferson and the Virginians offered little that was novel; their books echoed, even quoted, those who had written before, and the long and distinguished pedigrees these authors claimed for their ideas were part of their appeal for contemporaries. But on the whole, the Virginians spent little time reading the early-eighteenth-century originals, preferring instead the works of their own day. *Cato's Letters* might remain on their library shelves, but Hume and Blackstone and Smith, more up-to-date in their treatment, more elegant and accessible in their style, were likely to be the preferred authorities by the time of the Revolution and the early Republic.

In contrast to their predecessors, whose opinions emerged from the heat of party struggle in the opening decades of the eighteenth century, the writers Virginians admired shared a set of opinions that cut across the divisions of politics and religion. Tories like Swift had once seen the dissenters as a dangerous faction dedicated to the creation of a debt, the bank, and a standing army; by the time of the American Revolution, dissenting radicals like James Burgh, Richard Price, and Joseph Priestley would be expressing many of the fears that sixty or seventy years earlier had inspired Swift's attacks on their ancestors. If, as has been argued, Burgh, Price, Priestley, and their fellows were adapting the orthodox view to new uses and arguing against the debt not on behalf of the landed gentlemen and the country party, but in the interests of Britain's emerging petit bourgeois manufacturers and traders, the Virginians were unlikely to have noticed it.

The apparent similarity in language and subject matter, the readiness of these authors to cite with approval the views of more traditionally minded writers like Blackstone, disguised any shift, and gentry Virginians would have seen only the continuity, not the changes in emphasis and direction that may have impressed the rather differently situated groups in Britain to whom the radicals often addressed themselves and on whose behalf they spoke. But it was this very capacity of the orthodox view to win support from those who differed significantly on other questions, as well as the seeming impossibility of denying the dangers the national debt posed, that establishes it as critical for an understanding of the mid- and late-eighteenth-century Anglo-American mind; something about it, clearly, touched a vital nerve.[8]

Yet at the same time we should be careful not to see in the Virginians a simple reflection of the Augustans and the country party. If they readily accepted traditional views about the dangers of debt and the consequences of debt, they did so, it bears emphasizing, because those views continued to make sense of the late-eighteenth-century world, supplying explanations consistent both with the Virginians' experiences as planter-debtors and gentry-creditors and with the larger patterns of imperial and national politics that impinged on them. Although the Virginians may have exhibited a special sensitivity to debt in continuing to see it as a threat to independence and in insisting that spending in excess of income led straight to bankruptcy in both individuals and nations, they were far from the only Anglo-Americans in the late eighteenth century to stress the problematic character of debt or to employ a traditional language in discussing it. Again, it needs to be remembered that representatives of widely differing persuasions found common ground in attacking the debt, its causes, and its consequences. If Burke and Paine, Jefferson and John Adams could express themselves in decidedly similar terms on this issue, there must have been something about it that called forth virtually unanimous condemnation.[9] An important part of that something, I suggest, was the perception that wars did give rise to taxes and debts, and that taken together the three were the known instruments of tyranny. Radicals and conservatives alike had no trouble agreeing with this analysis, whatever their intentions in other respects.

It will be useful, then, to look at the fit between the view of debt that the Virginians, like many of their British and American contemporaries, absorbed from their reading of standard authors and the conditions that gave rise to those views, and later in this chapter I attempt to explore that relationship. That should help us to appreciate the political importance of the problem of debt in the eighteenth century and to understand the surprisingly accurate character of the analysis that contemporaries were able to develop. But I begin by looking at what a particular group of educated eighteenth-century readers—Jefferson, Madison, and the Virginia gentry—were likely to have learned about the debt as they pored over the books and essays in which it was discussed.

That ornament of the Scottish Enlightenment, William Robertson—as a historian, the Reverend Samuel Miller of New York thought, he had "perhaps . . . no superior of any age"—set out the common understanding of the origins and importance of the system of wars, debts, and taxes in his life of Charles V.[10] Robertson's brilliant and deservedly famous survey of the condition of Europe at the emperor's accession traced the rise of the modern state. As he saw it, this was above all a matter of the introduction of standing armies, a decisive innovation that appeared at the end of the fifteenth and the beginning of the sixteenth centuries. "During the obstinate struggles between France and England" in the Hundred Years' War, Robertson explained, "all the defects of the military system under the feudal government were sensibly felt." The obvious solution to those difficulties was the creation of an army as that term has since been understood, a "body of troops kept constantly on foot, and regularly trained in military subordination. . . . Such an establishment, however, was so repugnant to the genius of feudal polity, and so incompatible with the privileges and pretensions of the nobles, that during several centuries no monarch was either so bold, or so powerful, as to venture any steps toward introducing it." The break came with Charles VII of France, who "not only established that formidable body of regular troops, . . . but . . . was the first monarch of France who, by his royal edict, without the concurrence of the States-general of the kingdom, levied an extraordinary subsidy on his people." Charles "prevailed likewise with his subjects to render several taxes perpetual, which had formerly been imposed occasionally." The results of Charles's policy were striking: "He acquired such an increase of power, and extended his prerogative so far beyond its ancient limits, that, from being the most dependent Prince who had ever sat upon the throne of France, he came to possess" what Robertson called "a degree of authority which none of his predecessors had enjoyed for several ages."[11]

What Charles VII initiated was completed in the following reign: "That plan of humbling the nobility which Charles formed, his son Louis XI carried on with a bolder spirit and with greater success." Hiring foreign mercenaries, Louis could crush opposition wherever it appeared. Thanks to his father's extension of the prerogative, Louis obtained without difficulty the "great funds . . . requisite, not only to defray the expence of this additional establishment [i.e., the mercenary forces], but to supply the sums employed in the various enterprises which the restless activity of his genius prompted him to undertake." His skills extended to "the managing of great assemblies, in which the feudal policy had vested the power of granting subsidies and of imposing taxes. He first taught other Princes the fatal art of beginning their attack on public liberty, by corrupting the source from which it should flow." And when "no power remained to set bounds to his extractions, he not only continued all the taxes imposed by his father, but made immense additions to them, which amounted to a sum that appeared astonishing to his contemporaries."[12]

From France, Robertson thought, the infection spread to the rest of Europe: "The example Louis set was too inviting not to be imitated by other Princes." In England, Henry VII followed suit; Ferdinand and Isabella in Spain did likewise: "From this period, taxes went on increasing; and during the reign of Charles V such sums were levied in every state, as would have appeared prodigious at the close of the fifteenth century, and gradually prepared the way for the more exorbitant exactions of modern times." To be sure, this increase of royal power was resisted by the nobility and the representative bodies, and Robertson's account of the revolt of the Comuneros showed how difficult it was for Charles V to reduce Castile to due submission. Even in France, where the process was most advanced, the nobility, conscious of itself as a caste, and the *parlements*, with their traditional rights over legislation, continued to stand between the monarch and absolute authority. Nevertheless, "the Kings of France had thus engrossed every power which can be exerted in government; . . . the right of making laws, of levying money, of keeping an army of mercenaries in constant pay, of declaring war and of concluding peace centered in the crown." And it was the French model, in Robertson's view, toward which the rulers of other European states naturally gravitated under the pressure of the wars of the period, as they, too, discovered the advantages of standing armies and taxes imposed at the sovereign's command.[13]

Sophisticated and perceptive, Robertson's picture of what later historians would call the rise of the "new monarchies" won him high praise from contemporaries.[14] Few disagreed with his analysis of the relationship of standing armies and taxes and liberty; it was the accepted view of the age. Rousseau, who so often seems to move in directions different from those of the eighteenth-century mainstream, was in accord with Robertson on this question, and their agreement suggests how strongly an awareness of the facts Robertson presented had impressed itself on the broad eighteenth-century public. "Give money, and soon you will be in chains," Rousseau warned in the *Social Contract*. "This word 'finance' is a slave's word, unknown in the republic." In a state truly free, the citizens would form a militia and defend themselves, but in these degenerate modern days "the hustle of commerce and the arts, . . . the avid quest for profits, . . . softness and the love of ease" have induced men to abandon their civic duties and to prefer repose and private interest to the common good, relying on hired troops to do their fighting for them, all with consequences fatal to liberty.[15]

Montesquieu, equally, was convinced that the present age suffered from a dangerous condition, one he likened to an epidemic, calling it a "new distemper [that] has spread itself over Europe, infecting our princes, and inducing them to keep up an exorbitant number of troops." He explained this "contagious" condition by noting that, whenever "one prince augments his forces, the rest of course do the same, so that nothing is gained thereby but the public ruin." And, as other writers would, he drew a parallel between the state and the individual: "Were private people to be in the same situation as the three most opulent powers of this part of the globe, they would not have the necessary sustenance." Thus Europe was "poor," despite its command of "the riches and commerce of the whole world"; thus, Montesquieu thought, "soon we shall all be soldiers, and be reduced to the very same situation as the Tartars."[16]

The gloom evident in Rousseau's and Montesquieu's opinions could be found on the other side of the English Channel as well. Samuel Johnson's pamphlet *Thoughts on the Late Transactions Respecting Falkland's Islands* (1771) argued that the cycle of war and taxes and debt led nowhere. "The wars of civilized nations make very slow changes in the system of empire. The publick," the Lexicographer thought, "perceives scarcely any alteration but an increase of debt; and the few individuals who are benefitted, are not supposed to have the clearest right to their advantages." Johnson then amplified his point, which Virginia critics of Hamilton's system would repeat in 1790: "If he that shared the danger enjoyed the profit; if he that bled in battle grew rich by the victory, he might shew his gains without envy." Instead, "at the conclusion of a ten years war," what was there to show "for the death of multitudes and the expense of millions?" The survivors were reduced to "contemplating the sudden glories of paymasters and agents, whose equipages shine like meteors, and whose palaces rise like exhilations."[17]

How could this state of affairs have arisen in Britain, of all places, where free institutions continued to exist, where taxes were levied not by the king at his pleasure but only on Parliament's authorization? Here the mid-century authors found themselves grappling with the great irony of eighteenth-century British politics. The Glorious Revolution had secured the Protestant religion and defeated the absolutist designs of the Stuarts, but only at the cost of shackling other forms of tyranny on Britain, thanks to the Crown's new-found ability to command funds. For it was the discovery of ways to mobilize resources beyond the wildest dreams of Charles VII and his successors that made all the difference. The state's capacity to borrow enormous sums—the invention of public credit, in short—revolutionized politics and underwrote the cycle of wars that lasted from 1689 to 1815. It was a stunning move but, later generations would come to believe, one that threatened disaster in the long run even while supporting an imposing though temporary prosperity. Thus the unintended consequences of 1688—the series of innovations including the national debt and the Bank of England we know as the Financial Revolution—seriously compromised the liberties eighteenth-century Britons took as their birthright.

It was to these developments that William Blackstone turned his attention in 1765, in terms that met with general approval. The "natural consequences" of "our national debt and taxes," he lamented, "have . . . thrown such a weight of power in the executive scale of government, as we cannot think was intended by our patriot ancestors." The men "who gloriously struggled for the abolition of the then formidable parts of the prerogative," he concluded, "by an unaccountable want of foresight established this system in their stead."[18] As Blackstone's example suggests, the political consequences of the system produced considerable anxiety in eighteenth-century Englishmen and had done so, in fact, ever since the practice of funding debts was introduced at the end of the previous century. The tenor of his comments makes it clear that the older country party critique, embodied in the works of the Augustan satirists and in the political journalism of

Bolingbroke and the Commonwealthmen, was anything but out of date half a century later.[19] By no stretch of the imagination was Blackstone a radical, and his criticisms were cautiously phrased. He may have been the rankest of Tories at heart, as Jefferson and other Americans charged, yet on this subject his views were widely shared by many who had no use for the High Church doctrines and the Jacobite undertones that seemed to linger in his position.[20] Even in America, as we shall see, there were many—including some Virginia Republicans—who could think of no better text than Blackstone's when it came to proving the political dangers of wars, debts, and taxes.[21]

From Blackstone's perspective, the heart of the matter seemed to be that the king no longer depended on Parliament for his sustenance. At the beginning of his reign, the king received, "by long usage a truly royal addition to his hereditary revenue settled upon him for life," with the result that he needed to apply to Parliament only "upon some public necessity of the whole realm." Thus, Blackstone implied, the legislature had thrown away its best card; it was no longer in a position to control the king's policies, especially in foreign affairs, by threatening to withhold the sums he needed for the expenses of his household. The king could therefore act as he wished; when his actions led to war—as they all too often did in the eighteenth century—"the public necessity of the whole realm" left Parliament virtually without choice, and it had to come forward with supplies. Under the modern system of finance, of course, those funds would cover only a part of the cost of the campaign, and the rest would be met by borrowing, an expedient that left the nation burdened with still heavier debts and taxes. Inherent in Blackstone's reasoning was the traditional Tory condemnation of the pattern of continental involvements initiated by William III and permanently saddled on the country by the Hanoverians' German interests.[22] But, to repeat, by the 1760s such arguments had lost much of their original party character. The results of the policies pursued since 1689 were too obvious to be ignored, and Tories and opposition Whigs had no difficulty agreeing on this.[23]

Beyond the issue of the king and foreign policy, Blackstone pointed to other aspects of the new system, aspects that he, and his readers, had ample reason to distrust. In the first place, the "entire collection and management" of the enormous revenues required to service the war debt and pay for the kingdom's current expenses, "being placed in the hands of the crown, have given rise to such a multitude of officers, created by and removeable at the royal pleasure, that they have extended the influence of government to every corner of the nation." The possibilities of corruption thus opened up were endless. "All this is the natural, though perhaps the unforeseen, consequence of erecting our funds of credit, and to support them establishing our present perpetual taxes," Blackstone summed up. In addition to these dangers there was "still another newly acquired branch of power; and that is not the influence only, but the force of a disciplined army: paid indeed ultimately by the people, but immediately by the crown; raised by the crown, officered by the crown, commanded by the crown." To all intents and purposes, England had created that liberty-destroying monster, a standing army. "And there need but few words," Blackstone reminded his readers, "to demonstrate how great a trust is thereby reposed in the prince by his people. A trust, that is more than the equivalent of a thousand little troublesome prerogatives."[24]

Blackstone's warnings—and they were, it is worth emphasizing, those of a conservative and a traditionalist—were widely accepted. Radicals like James Burgh, whose *Political Disquisitions* (1774) were well received in America, found themselves citing the *Commentaries* on precisely these points. Burgh was, of course, more forthright in the way he expressed himself: "the love of *money*," he said in explaining why the forces Blackstone identified threatened English liberties, "is *our* disease, and a lousy disease (I ask the reader's pardon) it is."[25] But on the whole, radicals of Burgh's stripe could only exceed Blackstone in their rhetoric; they could hardly add to the substance of his argument. Richard Price, like Burgh a dissenter and a friend to the American cause, also found it useful to appeal to Blackstone's authority and quoted him on the dangers of imbalance in the constitution should the House of Commons become—as Price did not doubt it already had become—"subservient to the views" of the other branches of the legislature; "the men whose policy this had been," Price felt it necessary to observe, "have struck at the very heart of public liberty, and are the worst traitors this kingdom ever saw."[26] Conservatives and radicals alike, then, could agree that the constitution's condition was parlous; they had no hesitation in ascribing a major share of the responsibility to the methods of finance introduced to support the "new system of foreign politics" that had come in with the Revolution of 1688.[27]

For Englishmen in the second half of the eighteenth century, the story of how the creation and perpetuation of funding and permanent taxation upset the ideal balance of the constitution formed the major theme of their country's history in their own time. If they read, as many of them did, Tobias Smollett's immensely popular *History of England*, they were left in no doubt as to the motives and means of the corrupt gang that had accomplished this transformation in the traditional workings of the constitution, and they were equally convinced of the patriotism and virtue of those who struggled, though in vain, to stem the tide.[28] Even before Sir Robert Walpole arose to perfect the system, William III was its pioneer. "[M]aster of all the instruments and engines of corruption and violence," Smollett declared, William III had "involved these kingdoms in foreign connexions, which, in all probability, will be productive of their ruin." Indeed, in Smollett's eyes, William was the very fountainhead of evil: "In order to establish this favourite point, he scrupled not to employ all the engines of corruption, by which the morals of the nation were totally debauched." It was William who "procured a parliamentary sanction for a standing army which now seems to be interwoven in the constitution," William who "introduced the pernicious practice of borrowing upon remote funds," William who was responsible for the system that "hatched a brood of usurers, brokers, contractors, and stock-jobbers to prey upon the vitals of their country," William, in short, who "entailed upon the nation a growing debt, and a system of politics big with misery, despair, and destruction."[29]

All that remained was for someone to finish the job, and Walpole was not lacking in the requisite talents. Here was a man "well acquainted with the nature of the public funds," one who "understood the whole mystery of stockjobbing." The "connection between him and the money-corporations" followed naturally, and it "served to enhance his importance." Moreover, Walpole rightly grasped the wellsprings of human motivation; convinced "that the bulk of mankind were actuated by a sordid thirst of lucre," the minister had little difficulty achieving his ends. His "sagacity" allowed him "to convert the degeneracy of the times to his own advantage," and it was "on this, and this alone, [that] he founded the whole superstructure of his subsequent administration." Thus the Whigs, "a faction, which leaned for support on those who were enemies to the church and monarchy, on the bank, and the monied interest, raised upon usury, and maintained by corruption," secured their triumph. Yet this was to be expected, Smollett's readers were left to conclude, for the "vice, luxury, and prostitution of the age, the almost total extinction of sentiment, honour, and public spirit, had prepared the minds of men for slavery and corruption. The means were in the hands of the ministry: The public treasure was at their devotion: They multiplied places and pensions, to increase the number of their dependents."[30]

Smollett's politics were decidedly Tory–though he came from a Whigg-ish background–but it is doubtful that his partisanship lost him many readers.[31] Works like his *History*, Blackstone's *Commentaries*, and Robertson's *Charles V* were the standard fare of the educated public in the second half of the eighteenth century. They were typical of the books that introduced the provincial lawyers and gentleman planters of Virginia–and their counter-parts in the other colonies–to the history and present condition of England.[32] Carrying forward themes that first found expression in the opposition writings of the earlier part of the century, they brought the messages of the country party and the dissenting Whigs to a new audience, giving them the authority of their own considerable literary prestige. At the same time, they reflected, as we have seen, a current of thought present on the Continent as well as in England, and their interpretation found ready acceptance among the rising generation of English radicals and dissenters whose attitude in the imperial crisis made their works congenial to American audiences. To say that it was impossible to find alternative views would, of course, be incorrect–Hume's opinion that "corruption" was "inseparable from the very nature of the constitution, and necessary to the preservation of our mixed government," for example, was hardly in keeping with the dominant strain, or even with his own ideas on the national debt–but for the most part the consensus they embodied was solid and substantial.[33]

At the same time, from somewhat different but occasionally overlapping sources, the reading public began to meet with the second main branch of the orthodox view of debt and its relations to war and liberty. The rise of an interest in economics or rather, to use the more accurate term preferred by the eighteenth century, of an interest in political economy, created a body of literature that addressed itself to the economic dangers of the public debt. Those dangers were not inseparable from the political dangers, and indeed the lesson these works drew was that the economic dangers were politically created and therefore might be dealt with by political means. The political economists thus added a second dimension to the existing critique and lent it the support of their powerful reputations.[34] David Hume, above all, and Adam Smith after him established the essential lines of argument in this regard, and despite occasional voices to the contrary, for all practical purposes their opinions would be the only respectable ones until well into the twentieth century.

It was the very size of the public debt, its enormous and constantly increasing bulk, that the political economists pointed to when they wished to illustrate the dangers of the debt.[35] How, they asked themselves—and their readers asked with them—could such a burden ever be discharged?[36] In fact, there was considerable doubt that the debt ever could, or would, be paid, and it was this that gave rise to serious alarm. The nation, as a favorite metaphor suggesting the final stages of a fatal illness had it, was sinking fast beneath the weight of taxes and would soon expire. When the day of reckoning came, and it was sure to come, the results would not be pleasant. Civil war, anarchy, and chaos were confidently predicted; the people would rise up in a body against the public creditors in scenes recalling the worst of the social wars of antiquity.[37] No prudent nation, clearly, could afford to continue on a course certain to produce that result, but few contemporaries had much hope of a timely reformation.

"I must confess," Hume remarked with resignation, "that there is a strange supineness, from long custom, creeped into all ranks of men, with regard to public debts," adding that this was "not unlike what divines so vehemently complain of with regard to their religious doctrines." For everyone agreed "that the most sanguine imagination cannot hope, either that this or any future ministry will be possessed of such rigid and steady frugality, as to make a considerable progress in the payment of our debts." But even apart from the lack of willingness to address the problem, Hume doubted that there would ever be an opportunity to do so, since "the situation of foreign affairs" was unlikely "for any long time, [to] allow them leisure and tranquillity for such an undertaking." The obvious question followed: "*What then is to become of us?*" Hume's answer was somber: "Either the nation must destroy public credit," he said, "or public credit will destroy the nation." He could see no middle way, no solution less drastic than the stark alternatives he posed; it was "impossible" that both the nation and public credit could continue to "subsist, after the manner they have been hitherto managed, in this, as well as in some other countries."[38] Samuel Johnson doubted that public credit would be the winner in such a contest, and he took his usual commonsense approach to this problem: "Speaking of the national debt . . . it was an idle dream to suppose the country would ever sink under it. Let the publick creditors be ever so clamorous, the interest of millions must ever prevail over that of thousands."[39]

Hume's predictions were not unique. Thirteen years before Johnson pronounced his verdict, the title page of Malachy Postlethwayt's *Great Britain's True System* . . . (1757), bore the motto, "That an Increase of the PUBLIC DEBTS and TAXES must, in a few Years, prove the Ruin of the *Monied*, the *Trading*, and the *Landed Interests*." Postlethwayt, the most prolific writer on commerce of the mid-eighteenth century, took these matters so seriously that he went on to argue that "the ingenious Mr. *Hume* seems to entertain a more favourable Opinion of our Debts than he ought" – a conclusion he reached by misreading Hume's comments on the usefulness of public securities as a substitute for coin. Richard Price followed, urging the newly independent American states to profit from the British example; the national debt, in his view, was "a monstrous bubble – and if no very strong measures are soon taken to reduce it within the limits of safety, it must produce a dreadful convulsion. Let the United States take warning," Price admonished his transatlantic readers.[40]

Not surprisingly, given his dependence on Hume, Adam Smith's ideas differed only in minor details, and he wrote with alarm of "the enormous debts, which at present oppress and will in the long-run probably ruin, all the great nations of Europe." Smith was convinced that "the practice of funding gradually enfeebled every state which has adopted it," and adding his usual detail to the argument Hume had already laid out, Smith proceeded to pass in review for his readers the condition of the "Italian Republicks," of "Spain," of "France, [which] notwithstanding all its natural resources languishes under an oppressive load," and of "the United Provinces . . . much enfeebled by its debts." So many striking examples could lead to only one conclusion. "Is it likely," Smith ended his catalogue by asking, "that in Great Britain alone a practice, which has brought either weakness or desolation into every other country, should prove altogether innocent?"[41] His question answered itself.

Nothing, then, could be more dangerous than "mortgaging" the nation's future revenues – for that was the heart of the funding system – in order to borrow money to cover current expenses. The ancients, as Hume noted, were wiser than the moderns in this respect: Before they set off to battle, they waited until they had amassed sufficient treasure to pay for war.[42] Was it too much to expect that the moderns might be persuaded to embrace that wise policy? Lord Kames thought it was; noting that among present-day states only the Republic of Bern in Switzerland seemed to follow it, he argued that the system would never work in Britain, for "in the hands of a rapacious ministry, the greatest treasure would not be long-lived; under the management of a British ministry, it would vanish in the twinkling of an eye."[43] And there could be no doubt that the very ease with which money could be obtained under the new system of finance encouraged wars. Without funding, Smith thought, "wars would in general be more speedily concluded, and less wantonly undertaken." Thus the desire to avoid raising taxes, either out of an unwillingness to burden the people or out of fear lest they revolt, had led in the present age to the adoption of a system that succeeded only in perpetuating the vicious cycle of war, of debts to pay for war, of taxes to pay for debts, of more war, more debts, more taxes.[44]

Beneath the fears that it was impossible for funding and debts to continue without leading the nation that adopted them into disaster, there was a very simple conception of what was involved. "For why," Hume asked, "should the case be so different between the public and an individual, as to make us establish different maxims of conduct for each?"[45] Again and again, we encounter Hume's notion in eighteenth-century writing about the public debt: The state, like the private individual, could not survive if it spent more than it took in, and mortgaging the national revenues was at best a short-term expedient that only put off, but did not prevent, the inevitable consequence. Thus Montesquieu could compare the practices of modern princes to those of a young blood about to run through his inheritance: They "employ," he wrote, "what they call extraordinary means to ruin themselves—means so extraordinary, indeed, that they are hardly thought of by the most extravagant young spendthrift."[46] Hence, "like an improvident spendthrift whose pressing occasions will not allow him to wait for the regular payment of his revenue," Smith explained, "the state is in the constant practice of borrowing money of its own factors and agents, and of paying interest for the use of its own money."[47] Smith noted: "Nations, like private men, have generally begun to borrow upon what may be called personal credit, without assigning or mortgaging any particular fund for the payment of the debt; and when this resource has failed them, they have gone on to borrow upon assignments or mortgages of particular funds."[48] The road to ruin, it seemed in the eighteenth century, was remarkably uniform, whether the spendthrift in question was a nation or a private individual.

This apparent confusion of the public and the private spheres, which from the modern standpoint seems to constitute a failure of imagination and to suggest a primitive appreciation of how the economy operates, is less surprising given the perspective of the eighteenth century. Few of those who wrote on this subject could envisage the growth that makes it possible under some circumstances to borrow without fear of ruin; almost no one foresaw the transformations that would allow a nation like Britain to go on doubling and redoubling its debts without reaching the breaking point.[49] But it was not simply that men like Hume and Smith failed to understand the nature of the growth whose origins were only dimly apparent in their own day. It was, rather, a matter of the way in which the very notion of an "economy" was presented. The word itself—and this was true in French and German as well as in English—retained a strong component of its older meanings, which did little to differentiate between the public and the private spheres.[50] Thus Voltaire, following in a tradition reaching back to Aristotle, could write of "economy" that "in ordinary usage this word signifies the manner of administering one's property; it is the same for the father of a family and the superintendent of a kingdom's finances." It followed that there was no real difference between the two realms. "The economy of a state is precisely that of a large family," Voltaire insisted, and Jefferson would draw the logical conclusion when telling Madison in 1796 that "the accounts of the US. ought to be, and may be, made, as simple as those of a common farmer, and capable of being understood by common farmers."[51]

If the economy of the nation was conceived in terms equally applicable to a family, then the same rules had to apply in both cases. As long as agriculture remained the dominant form of economic activity, it was easy enough to think of debt as the wasting away of a landed estate, and the vocabulary employed to discuss the public debt—"spendthrift" nations "mortgaging" their revenues and running into national "bankruptcy"— seemed as appropriate for the state as it did for an individual.[52] The use of these terms was natural enough under the circumstances—searching for ways to describe a process new to them, early-eighteenth-century writers seized on the most obvious parallel, borrowing a familiar terminology that, in any event, suited their purposes perfectly with its implicit warnings of disaster. The king could still be seen as the national landlord and the nation's resources as his estate.[53] A landowner might "improve" his estate through good management and the adoption of new techniques, but there was a finite character to what he could achieve and an ever-present danger that the estate would be lost if debts overwhelmed it. It was, then, still too soon to speak of "the economy" in the modern sense, too soon to visualize it as endowed with a virtually endless capacity for growth.

The idea of the nation as an estate had its complement in the belief that the king should live off his own. This notion, which we now know to be in part an invention of the sixteenth and seventeenth centuries, was believed in the eighteenth to express the traditional relationship between the monarch and the nature of taxation.[54] Taxes, this view taught, were still "extraordinary" grants designed to assist the king in cases of necessity, and by definition necessity was exceptional, not the norm. The fact that kings required permanent grants of taxes to supplement their traditional revenues had something shocking about it, and it carried the implication that the king was invading spheres not properly his. As we have seen, the continental monarchs' success in destroying the barriers that separated their subjects' estates from their own was widely taken in the eighteenth century as evidence of their unlimited power, and the fear that something like this was happening in Britain, despite the apparent safeguards of the constitution, strongly affected the views of traditionalists like Blackstone. If no curb were placed on the ability of the king, supported by a corrupt Parliament, to contract debts that required ever greater amounts of taxation to service them, then what did the future hold? Under such conditions, no man could call his property truly and rightly his own, and the danger of "slavery" would no longer be merely theoretical.

Thus the vocabulary employed in contemporary discussions of the public debt—"spendthrift," "mortgage," "bankruptcy"—was more than a useful, if casual, set of metaphors; it sprang from contemporaries' underlying conceptions of the state and its relations to society. Rarely was better use made of the fundamental images at work in these notions than by Benjamin Franklin's friend Jonathan Shipley, the bishop of St. Asaph. In a speech intended for delivery in the House of Lords' debate on the Massachusetts Government bill in 1774, Shipley exploited the full range of possibilities inherent in the dominant view of the debt and its dangers, and the key passage in his text is worth quoting at length, showing as it does how these elements could be manipulated for maximum rhetorical effect. If, Shipley argued, Britain were so rash as to tax the colonies without their consent and thereby drive them into successful revolt, "Our posterity will then have reason to lament that they cannot avail themselves of those treasures of publick friendship and confidence which our fathers wisely hoarded up, and we are throwing away." Calling it "hard" and "cruel," the pro-American bishop denounced the policy that, in addition to the burden of "all our debts and taxes, and those enormous expences which are multiplying upon us every year," would "load our unhappy sons with the hatred and curses of North America." In short, he insisted, "we are treating posterity very scurvily." Soon there would be nothing left to inherit: "We have mortgaged all the lands; we have cut down all the oaks; we are now trampling down the fences, rooting up all the seedlings and samplers, and ruining the resources of another age." The consequences were all too predictable: "We shall send the next generation into the world like the wretched heir of a worthless father, without money, credit, or friends; with a stripped, incumbered, and perhaps untenanted estate."[55]

Shipley's fears for posterity and its condition were not unusual. The practice of funding, of mortgaging future revenues, was commonly understood to transfer to future generations the burdens that those who incurred them should have shouldered.[56] The present neither intended to pay nor could pay; equally, the future would be unable to pay. "The practice . . . of contracting debt will almost infallibly be abused, in every government," David Hume concluded, adding, in the now familiar comparison, that it "would scarcely be more imprudent to give a prodigal son a credit in every banker's shop in London, than to impower a statesman to draw bills, in this manner, upon posterity."[57]

Adam Ferguson, another of the Scots who thought deeply and keenly about the special character of modern society, was not sure that every resort to credit by the state was bound to be an abuse, but he was convinced that Britain's condition was serious. "States," he wrote in 1767, "have endeavoured, in some instances, by pawning their credit, instead of employing their capital, to disguise the hazards they ran." The "loans they raised" supplied "a casual resource," but the long-term costs, Ferguson thought, required careful assessment. It was true, he granted, that the system allowed "the execution of great national projects without suspending private industry," and he admitted as well that it was "plausible" and "just" that "future ages" should be responsible for "the debts contracted with a view to future emolument." Moreover, "the growing burden, too, is thus gradually laid;

and if a nation be to sink in some future age, every minister hopes it may keep afloat in his own." Yet that was precisely why the system, "with all its advantages," was "extremely dangerous"; under "a precipitant and ambitious administration," it was sure to be abused.[58]

Ferguson did not mention the British case by name, but his readers could have little doubt that his comments were meant to apply to their own country. "We are told," he transparently explained, "of a nation, who, during a certain period, rivaled the glories of the ancient world, threw off the dominion of a master armed against them with the powers of a great kingdom, broke the yoke with which they had been oppressed, and almost within the course of a century, raised, by their industry and national vigour, a new and formidable power." The results in this case were "attained by the great efforts of a spirit awakened by oppression, by a successful pursuit of national wealth, and by a rapid anticipation of future revenue." But as always there was a price to be paid, and Ferguson had no trouble identifying it: "They have sequestered the inheritance of many ages to come."[59]

The agricultural reformer and journalist Arthur Young, writing in 1772, was less certain than many of his contemporaries that the debt was insupportable from the purely economic point of view; impressed with the improvement of agriculture, the expansion of trade and manufactures, and the value of the British Empire, he quoted extensively from a pamphlet by the earl of Bath that underscored the point he wished to make. Economically, the debt might be bearable; politically, however, it was fatal. "Our ancestors," Young explained, "in recalling the constitution to its true principles . . . guarded with the utmost precaution the subjects liberty against the open power of the crown; but they could not be aware that a new monster, called *public credit*, would be born to besiege that fortress by sap, which they had laboured so indefatigably to secure against the attack by storm." Thus Young, like his contemporaries, was struck by the unintended consequences of the Glorious Revolution, and he deplored the prospect that "this hydra-headed enemy" might destroy "the mighty fabric" that the "blood and wisdom" of the patriots of an earlier day had reared.[60]

The orthodox thinkers who followed in Hume's and Smith's footsteps had little new to add, but they were eager to drive home the points that others before them had already made. Joseph Priestley, whose political and religious views gained him a reputation for heterodoxy and eventually forced him to flee Britain and seek refuge in the wilds of Pennsylvania, was as sound as anyone could be on this subject. "We shall always deceive ourselves," he declared, "when we imagine that the case of a country is, in this respect, at all different from that of an individual, or of a number of individuals, and that though debts may ruin the latter, they will not hurt the former. The only difference is, that a state cannot be compelled to pay its debts."[61] So deeply embedded was this conviction that even David Ricardo, whose penetration might have led him to reach other conclusions, endorsed it early in the following century. "That which is wise in an individual is wise also in a nation," he wrote at the end of a war that had brought the British national debt to unprecedented heights. Retrenchment and strict economy were the only cures, and Ricardo feared that another war might bring "national bankruptcy."[62]

Across the Channel, the French economist and *idéologue* Destutt de Tracy, whose works Jefferson helped to translate and have published in the United States, saw the question of debt as "a subject on which the general good sense has greatly preceded the science of the pretended adepts." As Tracy noted with some incredulity, "Men of genius believed and even wrote, not long since that the loans of a government are a cause of prosperity, and that a public debt is new wealth created in the bosom of society." But, he countered, "simple men have always known, that they impoverish themselves by spending more than their income, and that in no case is it good to be in debt."[63] Even Alexander Hamilton could sometimes be heard in this mode. Thus he wrote in the spring of 1789, in his eighth "H.G. Letter," that the policy of Congress under the Articles of Confederation had been hopelessly improvident; unable to command resources at home with which to pay the interest on the foreign debt, Congress had been forced to borrow abroad to pay that interest, "which had the pernicious effect of an accumulation of the debt, (for which all our estates must be considered as mortgaged) by the tremendous process of compound interest."[64]

Yet despite the force of the orthodox view, there were some who seemed willing—perversely willing, indeed—to espouse what Hume called "the new paradox, that public incumbrances, are, of themselves, advantageous, independent of the necessity of contracting them; and that any state, even though it were not pressed by a foreign enemy, could not possibly have embraced a wiser expedient, for promoting commerce and riches, than to create funds, and debts, and taxes, without limitation." Hume had only scorn for such reasoning, which "might naturally have passed for trials of wit among rhetoricians, like the panegyrics on folly and a fever, on BUSIRIS and NERO, had we not seen such absurd maxims patronized by great ministers, and by a whole party among us." It was impossible for the creation of debt to be, at the same time, the creation of new wealth, for at best debt merely transferred the resources of one part of society to another. And Hume found utterly implausible the argument advanced by writers like J.-F. Melon that "the public is no weaker upon account of its debts; since they are mostly due among ourselves, and bring as much property to one as they take from another."[65] In fact, those who held the debt were in the main "idle people, who live on their revenue," so that "our funds, in that view, give great encouragement to an useless and unactive life," a view endorsed by Archdeacon William Paley, who thought that taxation "takes from the industrious to give to the idle," a policy "attended with obvious evils."[66] Worse still, Hume argued, "foreigners possess a great share of our national funds," thus making "the public, in a manner, tributary to them."[67] How it could be said that the debt created wealth was a mystery, explainable only, Hume thought, by the magic that the concept of "circulation" seemed to exercise over some misguided men. But because the evidence of the debt represented nothing that was not already in existence, it could not add to circulation, and those who thought otherwise were simply blind to the facts.[68]

Hume's views, and they were those of Adam Smith and other orthodox thinkers, did encounter occasional challenges.[69] Bernard Mandeville's paradox, that private vices were often public virtues, was one of the most troubling ideas the age had to assimilate, and Hume and his followers clearly were not willing to accept it, at least where the national debt was concerned.[70] But the French publicist J.-F. Melon continued to argue that the debt had increased circulation—a notion earlier advanced by Bishop Berkeley, among others. Negotiable securities, Melon concluded, swelled the money supply and quickened the demand for goods, so producing an expansion of trade and industry; thus despite its apparent disadvantages, the debt actually increased the nation's wealth.[71] Lord Lonsdale expressed similar ideas to Hume in conversation, and the claim was sufficiently interesting that Hume thought it worth describing in a letter to Montesquieu.[72] As we have seen, Malachy Postlethwayt, who understood that government obligations could be used in this fashion, criticized Hume's approach to the benefits of a paper circulation, and in truth Hume seems never to have resolved the contradiction between his arguments in favor of circulation and his hostility to the national debt.

Other minor eighteenth-century writers also appeared as advocates of unorthodox positions, both in the middle of the century and at its close; typically, they came from the ranks of those with direct experience of the world of commerce and the stock exchange. Thus the Dutchman Isaac de Pinto, the author of a guide to the mysteries of the stock exchange, argued in the 1774 English edition of his *Traité de la circulation et du crédit* for "the great Advantages of the National Debt, to a certain Amount," though he also found value in the sinking fund idea and, warning that there could be too much of a good thing, urged a reduction in the outstanding debt. Pinto's work was, in short, an effort to refute Hume's views of the national debt and "the horrible train of evils that are supposed to attend it," according to his translator's preface, which also mocked the fear of the public debt as "a standing dish, on which an Englishman may feast his imagination, when he has no particular distress or injury to console him." Indeed, Pinto claimed that he had converted Hume (whom he met in the 1760s when Hume was serving at the British Embassy in Paris) to his view that with proper precautions the nation and public credit would not destroy each other; "I believe I have made him easy upon that point," Pinto wrote. If so, Hume's letters in the early 1770s to his London publisher, Hugh Strachan, on the dangers of the national debt, letters written in the wake of the Falkland Islands crisis, which had threatened to add still more millions to the already staggering totals of the debt, are hard to understand. Yet Pinto's case did impress Dugald Stewart, whose *Lectures on Political Economy* described the author as "the most inengious and best informed writer who has hitherto appeared as an advocate for the policy of national debt," and quoted his remarks on the change in Hume's views.[73]

But the only figure of importance to attack the orthodox position and give it a thorough examination was Sir James Steuart, whose massive treatise *An Inquiry into the Principles of Political Oeconomy* (1767) was the first sustained effort in English to describe the nature and workings of the modern economy and lay out a course of action for the statesmen responsible for guiding the nation's destinies. Prolix and poorly organized, Steuart's work was nonetheless original and thoughtful, enjoying a fair measure of public esteem until Smith's masterpiece gradually ousted it from the field.[74] Adam Smith, it is worth adding, informed a friend that he had written his own book with the express intention of providing "a clear and distinct confutation" of "every false principle"—by implication there were a good many of them—in Steuart's work and took satisfaction in his ability to do this without so much as "once mentioning" the *Inquiry*.[75] Given the distance separating their positions on the public debt, it is not difficult to see what bothered Smith in Steuart and why he was so eager to present his own quite different version of that and other matters.

Unusually for his time, and unlike Hume and Smith, Steuart distinguished the private and the public cases. "The interest of a private debtor," he wrote, "is simple and uncompounded; that of a state is so complex, that the debts they owe, when due to *citizens*, are on the whole, rather advantageous than burdensome; they produced a new branch of circulation among individuals, but take nothing from the general patrimony." Steuart further distinguished the private and the public cases by noting "essential differences" between them: The father of a family could direct it "as he sees fit," but "the *statesman* . . . is neither master to establish what oeconomy he pleases, nor, in the exercise of his sublime authority, to overturn at will the established laws of it, let him be the most despotic monarch on earth." Heretofore, Steuart suggested, "men . . . had a terror upon them in contracting debts for the public: they considered the nation as they would a private man." But as long as the debt "remains at home, it will animate every branch of circulation." Stressing again that the key was who held the debt, natives or foreigners—this was in keeping with his endorsement of mercantilist policies—Steuart insisted there was no danger to be anticipated from a well-managed debt.

"To say that a *nation* must become bankrupt to itself," he argued, "is a proposition which I think implies a contradiction." The real danger, if there was one, came from the external debt, not the domestic one; it was the balance of trade, not the public debt, that demanded attention.[76] These were propositions, it may readily be imagined, that could hardly meet with assent from those already convinced by the argument Hume had cast in its classic form, and their mercantilist tenor was utterly at odds with the arguments Smith would present in *The Wealth of Nations*.

If Steuart seems wiser, or rather more modern, than the first generation of classical economists in his appreciation of the positive role of the public debt, few contemporaries were willing to accept the lessons he tried to teach them. Nothing so paradoxical could be admitted as long as the problem of debt continued to be conceived in terms of the parallel between the finances of the individual and the finances of the state. The very suggestion that "the proper funding of the present debt, will render it a national blessing" was enough, as Alexander Hamilton discovered, to call down on oneself floods of invective, even when one qualified that principle by emphasizing, as Hamilton immediately did, his dissent from "the proposition, in the latitude in which it is sometimes laid down, that 'public debts are public benefits,' a position inviting to prodigality, and liable to dangerous abuse."[77] When Hamilton protested in his 1795 valedictory report against the all too prevalent assumption that "public Debts, . . . by facilitating the means of supporting expence, . . . encourage to enterprizes which produce it, and by furnishing in credit a substitute for revenue, [are] likely to be too freely used to avoid the odium of laying new Taxes," he protested in vain. It might indeed be true, as he thought, that such "objections to funding Systems . . . attribute to those systems effects which are to be ascribed more truly to the passions of men and perhaps to the genius of particular governments," but the weight of authority was against him.[78] Even at Columbia College, his alma mater, in the 1790s J. D. Gross, the professor of moral philosophy, could be found purveying to the students what nearly everyone seemed to admit: "Since, from the principles of nature, it cannot in any wise be made out that a public debt is a national blessing, it is a high and important duty not to anticipate the public revenue, except in cases of absolute and extreme necessity, and then to reduce it as fast as is consistent with public good."[79]

Because the debt was inseparable from the question of taxation, the political economists were also intent on investigating that question. Here they were concerned with the incidence and character of taxation, and in both cases political considerations were never far from the surface. It was universally agreed that taxation had risen to new and unprecedented heights in the course of the eighteenth century, and every increase brought with it protests from those expected to produce the additional sums. The land tax, levied on the assessed rental value of land, had been the main support of the English revenue in the late seventeenth and early eighteenth centuries, and this, as no one who has read the polemics of the period needs to be reminded, was widely denounced as an undue burden on the backbone of the nation, the landed interest.[80] But during the course of the century, the real burden on land was substantially reduced as excises and customs duties were increased and so supplied more and more of what was required to finance the wars and pay the interest on the national debt.[81] This gave rise to an extended debate on the merits of different forms of taxation. Which was the most productive with the least difficulty of administration? How far could taxes on certain items be increased without killing the goose that laid the golden eggs? Did high duties encourage smuggling (everyone agreed, in fact, that they did) and, if so, could they be lowered and still produce a net increase in yield? Did the excise, which was undoubtedly productive, justify the invasion of the rights of the subject that so obviously accompanied its collection?[82]

Certain points were axiomatic. That customs duties were easiest to collect and caused the least burden seemed clear. They fell, after all, on imported goods, which were generally products that consumers had the option of buying or not as they saw fit.[83] But other levies were considerably more controversial. Taxing the funds might be equitable, but then again it might result in higher costs of borrowing.[84] Taxing necessities was strenuously debated: Some advocated this policy because they thought it stimulated the poor to labor. Smith, however, doubted that this was the case, though he did think selective application of such taxes useful in discouraging forms of consumption not in the interest of laboring men, who would then be better able to maintain their families.[85] And, in the background, there was an awareness, muted at times, open at others, that too much taxation produced unrest and even revolt. As Smith put it, "Every new tax is immediately felt more or less by the people. It occasions always some murmur, and meets with some opposition."[86] Taxation, manifestly, called for the most diligent and careful investigation, and it did so because of the ever-larger amounts of revenue required to service the ever-increasing national debt. Without that necessity, many eighteenth-century commentators implied, the question would have been academic.[87]

In the years between the Declaration of Independence and the outbreak of the French Revolution, little was added to the orthodoxy already evident when Smith published *The Wealth of Nations*. To be sure, there was a technical development of some importance. Thanks in large part to the propaganda in its favor issuing in a steady stream from the pen of Richard Price, there was a revival of interest in the potential of the sinking fund to redeem and eventually to retire the debt.[88] The basic idea was not unknown; sinking funds had been proposed and tried in England ever since the 1720s, failing with monotonous regularity to achieve their stated purpose. For Blackstone, the sinking fund was "the last resort of the nation; on which alone depend all the hopes we can entertain of ever discharging or moderating our incumbrances"; in 1756, Francis Fauquier, Jefferson's Williamsburg patron during his tenure as governor of Virginia, called it "the favourite Child of a late Great Minister, and now deservedly become the Darling of the People." The widely shared and almost mystical belief in its efficacy encouraged reformers like Price to devise improved models.[89] Fascinated by the mathematics of compound interest—Price was fond of noting that a penny invested at simple interest in the time of Christ would have returned its lender only 7 shillings and sixpence by the middle of the eighteenth century, whereas the same penny put out at compound interest would have returned more than £1 million—this dissenting clergyman convinced himself that a sinking fund sacredly adhered to was the only feasible solution to the problem of the debt. The version he proposed would not only buy up the debt but also hold it rather than retire it, using the interest accruing to its account from the securities thus purchased to increase the amount at its disposal for the purchase of still more debt. Such a fund, Price assured his readers, would succeed where the traditional model had not, sinking the entire debt expeditiously and at far less expense than previously imagined.[90]

Initially, to be sure, Price was convinced that nothing would be done. Writing to the aging Chatham in 1773, Price had said that "all I converse with are persuaded that the national debt is one of our greatest evils, and that, if not soon put into some *fixed* course of redemption, it must terminate in all the calamities of a public bankruptcy." Yet there was, he confessed, "no probability that either mine or any other scheme for reducing it within the bounds of safety, will be ever adopted." Price was wrong about this, as it turned out, and although he had many critics—whether his proposition would work as he claimed was hotly debated—there can be no question that his ideas were influential, and Pitt's legislation in the 1780s owed more than a little to them.[91]

Yet a sinking fund was clearly second best, and there were those who confessed they could not see a way out. Sir John Sinclair, the able and tireless Scot who served as president of the Board of Agriculture, published his exhaustive three-volume *History of the Public Revenue* (1785–1803), which offered no more than cold comfort with its acknowledgment that at least the worst predictions of the debt's critics had yet to be realized. Still, it was clear to Sinclair that "the system of finance so prevalent in modern Europe, has an unavoidable tendency to public oppression; wars are perpetually arising, and the contest generally is, who can first drain the exchequer, and destroy the credit of the enemy." As with other writers in the years after the American Revolution, Sinclair concluded that an inflexible, "unalienable" sinking fund was the only hope.[92] But Thomas Paine (possibly encouraged by a subsidy from the French ministry) hardly required Sinclair's compilation to anticipate the collapse of English finance with some eagerness. "That the funding system contains within itself the seeds of its own destruction," he wrote in *Prospects on the Rubicon* (1787), "is as certain as that the human body contains within itself the seeds of death," and he continued to sound this theme throughout the 1790s.[93] As the next great contest with France approached, the British had little reason to suppose all was well.

Even the debate over the French Revolution, when it came, was not free from the traditional questions posed by debt. Paine used the occasion to praise the National Assembly's methods of handling the French debt, which, he thought, would be paid without crushing the people under heavy taxes, as was the case in England.[94] Edmund Burke, on the contrary, took the French measures to meet the problems created by their debt as evidence that behind the Revolution there stood a set of disgruntled creditors eager to destroy the existing order so that they might salvage what they could from their foolish investments.[95] Burke seemed, however, to have no doubt that this was the logical consequence of an all too patently wrong policy. "Nations," he observed in *Reflections on the Revolution in France* (1790), in words recalling Hume's earlier prophecy, "are wading deeper and deeper into an ocean of boundless debt. Public debts, which at first were a security to governments, by interesting many in the public tranquillity, are likely in their excess to become the means of their subversion." Again, like Hume before him, Burke described how public credit must destroy the nation, or the nation destroy public credit. "If," he pointed out, "governments provide for these debts by heavy impositions, they perish by becoming odious to the people. If they do not provide for them, they will be undone by the efforts of the most dangerous of all parties; I mean an extensive discontented monied interest, injured and not destroyed."[96]

Burke's attack on the French Revolution, as Sir James Mackintosh accurately noted in *Vindiciae Gallicae* (1791), was reminiscent of those that Swift and the Tories had leveled against the Whigs in the time of Queen Anne. Mackintosh himself, on the contrary, was inclined to believe that the French could discharge their debts and suggested, in any case, that the cost of freedom in France would be no greater than it had been to the English after the Glorious Revolution.[97] And, like Mackintosh, others writing to refute Burke took note of the dangers of the public debt, using language that paralleled Burke's own to suggest that not all was well in Britain. George Rous's *Thoughts on Government* (1790) deplored "the modern system of revenue" by which "the industry of the country is oppressed." It "carries," Rous said, "the seeds of its own destruction."[98]

With the outbreak of war against revolutionary France in 1793, it once again became apparent that the British national debt would go on increasing, and for the next quarter-century an endless procession of tracts and pamphlets poured from the presses, none of them, it may be said, adding much to the terms of the debate, all of them rehashing the old arguments, long familiar and well established. Pitt's resort to inconvertible paper money from 1797 on added a new interest to the question of war finance and a new urgency as well to the arguments of those who were convinced that the nation could not bear the simultaneous burden of mounting debt and rising inflation.[99] The "Friends of Peace" revived the arguments of Smith and Richard Price on the dangers of the national debt, though to little avail, while the "Friends of Liberty" at times went beyond that, demanding a cancellation of the debt and an end to taxation.[100] But the war ground on relentlessly; domestic unrest was suppressed and overt opposition crushed. There was no revolution in England, and the result, in 1815, was a nation victorious and triumphant, commanding the world's commerce, and burdened with debts that would weigh heavily on its people for a generation to come.[101]

Reflecting on the experience of England during the wars of the French Revolution and Napoleon from his safe haven in the 1840s, the historian Thomas Babbington Macaulay sought to explain why the doubters—Hume, Smith, George Grenville were mentioned by name—had been wrong. As Macaulay saw it, "there must have been some great fallacy in the notions of those who uttered and of those who believed that long succession of confident predictions, so signally falsified by a long succession of indisputable facts." Macaulay summed up the case: "Here it is sufficient to say that the prophets of evil were under a double delusion. They erroneously imagined there was an exact analogy between the case of an individual who is in debt to another individual and the case of a society which is in debt to a part of itself." This false "analogy led them into endless mistakes about the effects of the system of funding." But there was an additional reason for their mistakes: "They were under an error not less serious touching the resources of the country. They made no allowance for the effect produced by the incessant progress of every experimental science, and by the incessant efforts of every man to get on in life." Lacking that robust confidence in the future that Macaulay found so easy to adopt, these men of little faith and less foresight could see only "that the debt grew; and they forgot that other things grew as well as the debt."[102] But this was wisdom after the event; at the time, there was no reason to suppose things would necessarily turn out as well as they did—and even then Macaulay, in his confidence and his optimism, ignored the heavy price that had to be paid by those who produced Britain's wealth, a price whose burden on the farmer, the laborer, the taxpayer, and the consumer is reflected in every page of William Cobbett.[103]

But perhaps the final word should go to a man few in England had heard of. Distant from the scenes of battle and the floor of the stock exchange, Immanuel Kant was moved to reflect in 1795 on the leading problem of his age. Writing as Prussia abandoned its allies in the First Coalition (Britain first among them) and signed a separate peace with France at Basel, Kant was free to publish an argument that pointed directly to the dangers created by the Financial Revolution and embodied in the British state. From the vantage point of Königsberg, it was clear that no lasting peace could be ensured unless the funding system were abolished. "This system," he wrote in his project for a world without war, "must be prohibited by a preliminary article" of the treaty of perpetual peace; "otherwise," he feared, "national bankruptcy, inevitable in the long run, would necessarily involve other states in the resultant loss without their having deserved it."[104] In the eighteenth century, even a transcendental philosopher had no difficulty identifying the root of the evil. But it was, after all, an age in which the return of peace in 1783 could be celebrated with a thanksgiving sermon on the need to reduce the national debt.[105] Whatever else may be said, the debt was a matter of enormous concern to the eighteenth century, and it would be wrong to imagine that that concern was completely without foundation.

"Here our debt must soon produce a shocking catastrophe," Richard Price wrote in the midst of war in 1779, adding his hope that "the new world will . . . take warning and profit by the follies and corruptions and miseries of the old."[106] Jefferson and his Virginia contemporaries proved apt pupils in this regard; they paid serious attention to the considerable body of literature about public debt, much of which attributed both the political and the economic ills of modern Britain to the debt and its negative effects. There is every reason to believe that they found this literature persuasive and compelling, and its direct influence on their thought is readily identified. John Taylor of Caroline's tracts, despite their effect on John Adams's "risible

Muscles," are only the best known of the Virginia school's elaborations of these familiar themes.[107] There were plenty of others. St. George Tucker's American edition of Blackstone's *Commentaries* was full of footnotes and appendices registering the Virginia jurist's agreement with Blackstone's views on the debt, and Tucker made sure that his audience understood that Blackstone's warnings applied to the United States as well. "As geographers and navigators, in their maps and charts, do not confine themselves to countries that are beautiful," Tucker explained, "but, on the contrary, think it their duty to point out such rocky coasts as are objects of terror rather than delight . . . so, also, is it the duty of the politician to expose the concealed and insidious operations of false principles." These were, he thought, "in general, more difficult to be guarded against, than the direct invasions of open despotism." Accordingly, Tucker spent more effort annotating the first eight chapters of Blackstone's work "than might at first have appeared necessary for the use of an *American* student."[108]

Jefferson's correspondence, his addresses and his policies while president, his patronage of Destutt de Tracy's works—all these make clear how deeply and thoroughly he had accepted the truths embodied in the orthodox view of the debt. And few of the Virginia Republican pamphlets of the 1790s fail to make the obligatory mention of these themes: Wars, debt, and taxes were, as Madison said in 1795, "the known instruments of tyranny," and as such they were properly condemned by all right-thinking Virginians.[109]

Even Virginia's would-be poets added their voices to the general cry. An ode by William Munford, "The Politician in Distress. H— —n, Cidevant S— —y of the T— —y," described its subject as

> He who the fifteen states could rule,
> Teach them the skill of speculation,
> That glorious wight of his creation,
> Show them that public debt's a blessing,
> Which we are happy in possessing.

Munford went on to describe Hamilton's plot:

> He who to fix our final doom,
> The debts of states resolv'd to assume,
> And whether they said yea or nay,
> Resolv'd himself their debts to pay,
> Or what's the sae as I can shew it,
> Resolv'd to make the Union do it.[110]

St. George Tucker also tried his hand at political satire. His "To All the Great Folks in a Lump" presented a dangerous and duplicitous Hamilton, a man capable of swearing

> . . . the *nation's debt*'s a *blessing vast*
> Which far and wide its genial influence sheds,

From whence *Pactolian showers* descend so fast
On Theirs—*id est*—the Speculators' heads.

That to increase this blessing and entail
To future times its influence benign
New Loans from foreign nations cannot fail
Whilst *standing armies* clinch the *grand design*;

That *taxes* are *no burthens*—to the Rich;
That—they alone to labour *drive* the Poor;
The lazy rogues would neither plow, nor ditch
Unless *to keep the Sheriff from the door*.[111]

And an anonymous poet writing as "An American" praised Virginia's congressmen and deplored their New England colleagues, who were unworthy of their predecessors:

Oh, Massachusetts, once my boast and pride,
The nurse of Heroes and the Patriot's guide,
How hast thou fallen, all thy glory lost,
Damn'd by a speculating, stock-jobbing host.[112]

Yet why was this influence so strong? Alexander Hamilton, after all, read the same books as the Virginians, but was somehow able to reach beyond them.[113] What was it that the Virginians found in these works and in others like them that made so strong an impression? We may begin by dismissing one possibility—that the Virginians were paranoid and therefore looked to these works as support for their fantasies, fashioning out of thin air a Hamiltonian and Federalist design to enslave them when in fact there was none. The Virginians were obsessed, to be sure, but they were hardly paranoid, any more than Englishmen like Blackstone or Scots like Hume and Smith were paranoid. Admittedly, they spoke of plots and subversion and attributed to their opponents the worst of motives. But the language of conspiracy was normal in the eighteenth century, and for every monarchist the Republicans discovered, the Federalists were sure to find a Jacobin or a member of the Illuminati. Edmund Burke imagined that the French Revolution originated in a plot by monied men; Joel Barlow described the "Conspiracy of Kings" to suppress liberty.[114] Almost everyone had recourse to such figures, and we should see them as a particular style, a rhetoric that exaggerated and heightened underlying perceptions. Nor were they always lacking in foundation, for, as Richard Cobb reminds us in a brilliant discussion of the popular mind in the French Revolution, before we dismiss the revolutionaries' apparent credulity in accepting rumors of plots and conspiracies as true, we should remember that many of the plots and conspiracies in those years were in fact quite real.[115]

What, then, were the "plots" in whose existence the Virginia Republicans professed to believe? Surely they were those whose central themes Madison would insist on in 1795: the dangers to liberty inherent in the system of wars, debts, and taxes.[116] Were the Virginians wrong to imagine that such dangers existed? No, and this despite the degree to which they may have misinterpreted the intentions of Hamilton and the Federalists—and even in that they may not have been entirely wrong. For it is clear to present-day historians, as it was clear to the eighteenth-century writers whose views the Virginians shared, that strong connections existed between the rise of the modern state and the creation of standing armies, the development of government finance, and the loss of what they had in mind when they referred to "public liberty"—that is, representative institutions and limits on the powers of the monarch.[117] Charles I had indeed attempted to govern without Parliament and raise a revenue by methods that a large segment of the political nation considered unconstitutional, and after the Restoration there was a real and serious threat that absolutism on the French model might be introduced in Britain.[118]

In France, the monarchy had taken the course Robertson described in his *History of the Reign of Charles V*; representative institutions vanished or were reduced to impotence there and in most of the rest of Europe as well.[119] The tools of absolutism had been—and in the eighteenth century continued to be—armed forces over which the monarchs held undisputed control, aided, increasingly, by new information-collecting and tax-gathering bureaucracies.[120] The contests over the power of the purse, which seemed to many, including the Virginians, to be the very heart of the battle for liberty, remained a prominent theme in the political development of Europe from the middle of the fifteenth century onward, and although we may be tempted to regard them as no more than squabbles among competing elites, as in fact they often were, the outcome of those struggles in large measure determined the degree of freedom available to most individuals in the early modern and eighteenth-century West.[121]

As for the view of English history from the Glorious Revolution to their own times that the Virginians, following the lead of influential British writers, accepted, that too does not seem unreasonable on balance. The events of 1688, as Blackstone pointed out, had unintended consequences, and the achievement of political stability after 1720 came only at the price of a considerable decrease in political rights, and certainly in political participation.[122] Indeed, the view many contemporaries held of life under the Walpolean oligarchy is close to that urged by historians like the late E. P. Thompson—once again, Tory and radical seem to meet—and even Sir Robert Walpole's biographer is forced to admit that his subject's methods of governing may have had less than desirable effects.[123] Sir Lewis Namier's interpretation of the mid-eighteenth century has collapsed in recent decades, and we now understand that English politics were not entirely a matter of place rather than one of ideas or ideology.[124] But Namier's most inveterate critics would be hard pressed to suggest that jobs and corruption were not essential parts of the system, and it was at least in part that aspect of politics, together with its basis in wars, debts, and taxes, that traditionalist members of the country party and radicals and ideologues alike wished to attack and destroy.[125]

Nevertheless, that system worked remarkably well, all things considered—it made possible the careers of Lord Nelson and the younger Pitt—
and in the long run it was certainly as effective as the apparently more rational
and modern bureaucratized states on the Continent.[126] Comparison of the
weakness of Prussia bereft of Frederick the Great, or the incapacity of Austria
after the death of Joseph II, with the remarkable ability of the British system
to carry on, even with the loss of Pitt in 1806, will show that, corrupt and
inefficient though it was, riddled with anachronism and top-heavy with
patronage, eighteenth-century England had created a remarkably successful
state machine.[127] We may doubt the appropriateness of Thompson's description of the Hanoverian regime as no better than a "banana republic," but it is
difficult to deny the weight of contemporary opinion and conclude that its
victories did not come at considerable cost to those who were required to pay
for them. Now that Namier is gone, no one would argue, I think, that
Georgian England was not a deeply flawed and unsatisfactory society.[128]

But were the Virginia Republicans also reasonable in assuming, according
to the fundamental eighteenth-century precept, that like causes would always
produce similar effects, that funding in America would bring with it the evils
that funding had brought in Britain, that wars were the instruments of tyranny, that Hamilton and his friends were intent on subverting republicanism
almost from the outset?[129] These questions are, of course, impossible to answer in an ultimate sense; in the end, neither Hamilton nor his programs led
to the results the Virginians had been taught to fear—if only because Virginia
opposition successfully mobilized to ensure that they did not.[130] But every
known piece of evidence suggested that they would, and to an age trained to
find pattern and meaning in history, alert to resemblances, and deeply frightened by what it could observe elsewhere, such thoughts came naturally.[131] The
evidence that so impressed contemporaries is substantial, and it should not be
taken lightly; Virginians had reasons for reacting as they did, no matter how
strident or exaggerated their response may seem to us two centuries later.

Funding, after all, did bring speculation—though Hamilton deplored
it.[132] Employees of the Treasury Department were numerous, spread across
the land, and Federalist in their politics.[133] Under Federalist control, American foreign policy turned bellicose, and war (albeit at sea and undeclared)
became a reality, with the result that the government was forced to borrow,
at seemingly ruinous rates of interest, to finance the naval campaign against
France and, worse still, support the expansion of the army at home, an army
that could have no purpose, or so the Virginians concluded, except to crush
their liberties.[134] New taxes were imposed—land taxes, excises, stamp taxes—
and not surprisingly they provoked opposition that on occasion took the
form of active resistance.[135] Political rights did come under attack during the
closing years of the 1790s, and the relative liberality of the Sedition Act did
nothing to make it more palatable to those who understood themselves as its
intended victims.[136] None of this meant, of course, that the Federalists were
bent on turning the United States into the France of Louis XIV or even the
England of the younger Pitt, but it did seem to reasonable men that the

country was being driven in a direction a good deal less favorable to liberty. Hamilton's friends might know that he was a republican at heart; others, however, could only wonder what definition possibly justified that confidence and recall that Walpole had made his political debut in the guise of a Whig and defender of "Revolution principles."[137]

Thus the Virginia Republicans' view of Federalist behavior, if not of ultimate Federalist intentions, had much to recommend it in the context of domestic politics in the 1790s. The Federalist regime began by creating a debt not unlike Britain's, and the predictable consequences followed in due course. But the critique of the debt that Jefferson and his colleagues inherited was economic as well as political. Was it, in fact, the economic evil that Hume and Smith condemned, or the beneficial stimulus to circulation and activity that Steuart—and Hamilton—suggested? Such questions are far more difficult to resolve than the purely political ones, for we are only beginning to possess something like a satisfactory account of the impact of government borrowing and spending on the economy of eighteenth-century Britain, and we have hardly any solid information on the consequences of Hamilton's funding system for the American economy.[138] The problem is further complicated by the choice of assumptions supporting our judgment; if we agree with Smith and look to the beneficent operations of the "invisible hand," we will be inclined to doubt the usefulness of state intervention in the marketplace, especially when that intervention takes the presumably wasteful form of borrowing and spending on war; if, on the contrary, we take a more *dirigiste* position, the results may well be different.

Until recently, however, students of the economic history of Britain and America have tended to favor Smith, particularly when considering the period with which we are concerned. Government spending has been regarded, from that perspective, as an extrinsic and often disruptive factor, distorting what would otherwise be the economy's natural pattern.[139] Such intervention might impede or stimulate growth; rarely was it seen as fundamental, and, when mentioned, it was more often condemned than praised. This view, the liberal view in the classical sense of the term, is not without merit, but on the whole it seems inadequate to deal with the issues posed by state expenditure in the eighteenth century. For it should be clear that the eighteenth-century state *was* an important actor in the economic drama and that we cannot understand the Virginia Republicans' resistance to its playing a similar role in America unless we recognize, at the outset, that this was the normal, even normative, situation elsewhere.

Fortunately, recent efforts to come to terms with this problem, at least in the British case, have given us a good deal more insight into the role government played in the eighteenth century. The state, it can now be said, was an essential participant in Britain's rise to economic preeminence, and the state in this sense was, above all, the military machine financed by the national debt that enabled Britain to meet the challenge of the continental powers and, by 1815, emerge in a position of unparalleled industrial and commercial strength.[140]

One thing is undeniable. When the test came, between 1793 and 1815, Hume's prediction that public credit would ruin the nation or the nation would ruin public credit was not fulfilled in the British case.[141] The French experienced serious financial difficulties in the 1780s and witnessed the complete collapse of state finances in the 1790s; the Austrians and, to a lesser degree, the Russians achieved much the same result through runaway inflation; America was essentially bankrupt in 1814 when the government found itself unable to borrow except on ruinous terms; the war effort strained the Spanish state to the breaking point. But the British came through magnificently.[142] Hostile observers, Americans among them, were astounded; they believed, they *knew*, that what the British were doing was impossible; no nation could carry such a load of debt and long avoid collapse.[143] But precisely because Britain managed to bring off what no one imagined could be done, there is a danger that we may rule out the possibility that the debt imposed a heavy (and unnecessary?) burden on the British economy. Here, at least, the liberal view is useful in pointing to the ways in which wars, debts, and taxes may have distorted the pattern of growth and, particularly as a result of "crowding out," reduced the potential benefits of Britain's economic expansion for producers and consumers alike. And that there was a substantial burden on the British taxpayer is beyond doubt. Recent investigation has confirmed the impressions of many contemporaries that taxes in eighteenth-century Britain, on a per capita basis, were considerably higher than those in France and the other major continental states, and of course vastly higher than anything experienced in the American colonies or the new United States.[144] It may be that the returns to the taxpayers justified the impositions to which they were subjected, but that is precisely the question that needs to be answered.

What, then, were those benefits? The British government spent the money it borrowed and received by way of taxes on war; it did not waste it on the expenses of a lavish court or on pensions for royal favorites, nor did it spend it to provide social services or to create an infrastructure.[145] This was typical of *ancien régime* states generally; in the eighteenth century, had the peasantry in most countries been required to bear only the cost of the monarch's conspicuous consumption, they would have been fortunate indeed. What they and other taxpayers were called on to provide, rather, was the enormous sums of money needed to pay for the army and navy and to defray the postponed costs of past wars. As a rule, something like 50 percent of the peacetime budgets in the two leading nations, France and Britain, went to cover interest on debts accumulated in the course of the century's military campaigns, and an additional 25 to 30 percent covered current defense spending.[146] These figures help to explain why the question of the debt seemed so important to contemporaries, why it presented such apparently insoluble problems.

Spending by nations, therefore, was directed at keeping armies in the field and navies at sea. Neither came cheaply. Troops had to be fed and clothed and shod and provided with weapons; ships had to be built and provisioned and manned. All this meant that money was being spent, and being spent, moreover, in ways that might stimulate the economy. There is evidence that military expenditures had that effect, at least in Britain, though the precise dimensions cannot be quantified.[147] The vessels of the Royal Navy, after all, were among the most complex creations of the day, and the dockyards where they were built and serviced were eighteenth-century Britain's largest industrial establishments. Thousands of shipworkers took home wages; hundreds of contractors supplied goods and services.[148] Government orders for provisions, clothing, and equipment flowed out into the larger economy, often helping to take up the slack when normal export patterns were disrupted by war.[149] Undeniably, all this expenditure had important effects, perhaps even critical ones, as when, during the long wars of 1793 to 1815, the military became an important customer for the burgeoning British iron industry.[150] The state took from civil society, to be sure, but it also poured money back into it on a massive scale.

This positive side of the coin had its inevitable negative obverse: Government spending was sporadic and unpredictable. In Britain, it lasted only as long as war lasted; with the return of peace, orders ceased, retrenchment became the watchword, soldiers and sailors were discharged, and the level of state expenditure dropped dramatically. This meant, among other things, that manufacturers who had expanded their plants during the war were left with excess capacity, possibly with large inventories, and certainly with redundant hands. They coped by dismissing their laborers, shutting down their mills and forges, and dumping their goods in the first available market.[151] Thus the direct stimulus of government spending was erratically applied to the economy, and the eighteenth century witnessed the beginning of the business cycle, each wartime boom being followed by its increasingly predictable postwar depression.[152]

The impact of government spending and its relation to the business cycle were not, to be sure, the aspects of the problem that attracted the greatest attention from contemporaries. Indeed, they hardly attracted any at all, except, perhaps, from those most directly concerned, either as suppliers of labor and goods or as responsible officials at the Admiralty and the Horse Guards who knew that the on-again, off-again pattern was not, in the long run, the most economical way of maintaining an efficient defense establishment.[153] Rather, what bothered most contemporaries was the apparent drain on the nation's wealth constituted by interest payments on the debt. This, it will be recalled, was in part a function of lingering mercantilist notions that regarded the interest on the debt held by foreigners as a loss to the kingdom, and in part a function of the equally mercantilistic assumption that domestic holders of the debt were an idle lot, contributing little or nothing to the nation's economic well-being.[154] Foreigners did have substantial holdings in the British funds, and British taxes went abroad to discharge obligations due to the rentiers of Amsterdam and Geneva.[155] Whether this was a real drain is arguable; if nothing else, the avidity of foreigners for investments in the British debt must have helped to keep down the rate of interest, and surely

their investments freed domestic capital for other and possibly more productive uses. What is certain is that the British debt—and what stood behind it,
the stability of the political system that guaranteed it—was attractive enough
to continental investors that they were willing to accept a rate of return considerably below that offered, for example, by French government
securities.[156]

As for the second contention—the more interesting of the two—is it true
that the domestic fundholders were mere drones? Year in and year out, they
received their interest payments, payments that accounted for nearly half the
government's peacetime expenditures and even in wartime were not a
negligible proportion of official outlays.[157] Who were the recipients? Some of
them were the proverbial widows and orphans, and it is possible to find an
occasional defense of the debt on the grounds that it provided a safe haven
for their small capitals.[158] Others were London investors and professional
speculators—most of the debt, perhaps as much as 90 percent of that owned
domestically, was held in the London area—and there were also members of
the nobility, some of them quite large holders.[159] What use did they make of
the interest they received? Did it go to support a life of luxury and ease, or
merely one of modest rentier comfort? Was it reinvested, as occasionally
charged, in still more government debt, thus helping to perpetuate the
cycle? Was it placed in productive employments, lent out to merchants and
manufacturers seeking to enlarge their operations, or used to support the
improvement of agriculture? We do not know in detail, though some
members of the gentry and the aristocracy invested in local infrastructures
(the duke of Bridgewater's canal, for example), improved their urban real
estate, and exploited coal and other mineral deposits on their properties.[160]
Some of the interest certainly went into consumption of the luxury sort, and
probably this was true of that received by the nobility, whose capacity for
lavish spending on the building and rebuilding of country houses or at the
gaming tables knew no bounds.[161] It apparently did not find its way into the
hands of manufacturers, at least not directly, for it seems to have been the
case that much of the industrial expansion of the period was financed from
retained earnings, religiously plowed back into the enterprises from which
they came.[162] But between those two poles there is considerable room, and
we would need a great deal more information than we have about the
financing of eighteenth-century trade, for example, to be sure that the
interest from the debt had no role to play in sustaining and encouraging the
enormous growth of British commerce during the eighteenth century.[163]

There can be little doubt, however, that the debt did accomplish the
transfer of wealth of which contemporaries complained.[164] To be sure, the
English gentry was unusual in Europe in its willingness to tax itself, but it
used its political power to see that it did not bear too large a share of the cost
of the policies it directed. As the century wore on and the composition of the
British revenue shifted away from the land tax and toward taxes on consumption, whether in the form of the excise or that of customs duties, the burden
of the debt was being redistributed in ways that made it press more heavily on

the lower classes.[165] Taxes raising the price of necessities tended to decrease consumption, and even those who might have been able to pay were often willing to go without—hence such phenomena as the blocking up of windows that followed Pitt's imposition of a tax on that item in the 1790s.[166]

For those who see a prosperous British laboring class as a vast consumer market helping to fuel the nation's economic development, excises and other direct impositions on the productive population often appear as steps in the wrong direction, even apart from any consideration that decisions on expenditure are better taken by individuals than by the state.[167] There is, though, the argument that such taxes resulted in forced savings, transferring wealth from the many who tended to spend whatever small incremental gains they might have obtained from lower taxes, to those few whose incomes were large enough to permit them to save and, presumably, to invest.[168] But the evidence in this case does not seem to support that conclusion, at least as far as the interest on the debt is concerned—actual military expenditures are another matter—and it would be difficult to argue that this consequence of the state-decreed forced savings of eighteenth-century British consumers had an important effect on economic growth, let alone that they were a necessary precondition for it.[169]

There are, in addition, the questions posed by the professed objective of the spending that produced the debt—the long and dreary procession of wars from the late seventeenth century onward. Here the liberal perspective, helpful in considering issues of domestic growth, is likely to fail us, for liberalism of this sort has no place for wars, especially wars of aggression.[170] If the British originally fought, in part, to defend their liberties and protect the Protestant religion from the supposed designs of Louis XIV and his Jacobite clients—these were intangible values but hardly less important, despite our inability to quantify them, than the trade gains that would be the focus of later conflicts—the wars of the period rapidly assumed what would be their permanent character, a seemingly endless struggle for preeminence between France and Britain and their shifting casts of allies. Britain was both aggressor and victim in these wars; participation in the international state system of the eighteenth century inevitably involved even the most pacific country in bloody contests. Britain was never hesitant—except, ironically, under Walpole—to assert itself and its "rights."[171] The outcomes of the conflicts in which it engaged—the War of the League of Augsburg, the War of the Spanish Succession, the War of the Austrian Succession, the Seven Years' War, the American Revolutionary War, and the wars of the French Revolution and Napoleon—might well appear to men like Dr. Johnson hardly worth the loss and suffering they caused.

But, in fact, British taxpayers did receive something for their money—new colonies, new markets, new sources of supply for raw materials.[172] Had lenders not come forward and offered their wealth—for a suitable return, of course—had the political nation not been willing to mortgage Britain's future revenues, would the results have been more favorable? The alternatives—abstention from war or taxation at the time to cover the whole cost—

were hardly palatable, the former because it meant forgoing gains and risking losses, the latter because it would have threatened revolt by a population already taxed, or so it seemed, to the hilt.[173] In all likelihood, the national debt was thus the price Britain had to pay to become the first among nations. Distasteful as that conclusion would have been to those who feared that ruin was inevitable, it is difficult to imagine an economy so heavily dependent on the export trade performing as well as Britain's did without a substantial investment in defense and aggression.[174] Free trade and peace would be all very well in the nineteenth century, but that time had yet to come. In the eighteenth century, war was an expected and accepted part of international life, and those who imagined otherwise seemed hopelessly utopian.[175]

Ultimately, from the modern perspective, the question becomes one of sectors. Like direct military spending during wars, the interest on public securities was bound to have some effect, and the issue is whether the two streams, or either of them, flowed into those segments of the economy that were, from the standpoint of Smith and his like-thinking contemporaries, increasing the wealth of the kingdom. Indeed, we can go further and ask whether they flowed into those that were not only adding to the nation's wealth, but also transforming the very character of Britain's economic life. Or, on the contrary, did they represent a substantial diversion of the nation's resources into more traditional forms of activity, promoting, if anything, only a horizontal expansion, so that there was quantitative but not qualitative change? Setting men and women to work in foundries and cotton mills was one thing; enabling a rentier to take on an additional footman and a scullery maid or two was another and quite different one. And we may also ask whether the state, with its enormous borrowing needs, competed for capital with private borrowers in a market whose supplies of that commodity were limited, thus creating the classic "crowding out" phenomenon? Or is the very concept of a unified national capital market anachronistic in the eighteenth-century setting?[176] If, for example, government borrowing drew largely on the resources of those who would otherwise have kept their money at home in strongboxes or displayed it in the form of plate or invested it in land and country houses, there may not, after all, have been a diversion of critical resources away from the civilian economy. But what would have happened—and again we have no way of knowing—if the national debt of £127,000,000, to take the figure as it stood at the beginning of the American Revolution, had been invested over the previous eighty-five years or so in agriculture, manufacturing, and commerce? Or if the £4,612,000 in interest that debt required the taxpayers to contribute in 1774 had been left in the hands of consumers? The magnitude of the figures—a principal more than forty times the net earnings of British foreign trade in the year before Lexington and Concord, and an annual interest charge more than one and a half times that sum—suggests that contemporaries were onto something when they attacked the national debt.[177]

Hence the Virginia Republicans, with Jefferson in the lead, had valid grounds for worrying about the economic effects of a public debt, the more so because many of them believed that the American debt, on a per capita basis, was much higher than the British debt that had led Hume and Smith to their gloomy conclusions.[178] They, too, might well have wondered whether their taxes were being put to good use in paying the interest on the debt, but then they hardly needed to wonder, for they were certain the money was going straight into the pockets of speculators.[179] And, of course, they were right about that; speculators had engrossed much of the debt by the time it was funded in 1790, and many of those speculators profited enormously from operations in the public paper.[180] Thus it was easy for the Virginians to convince themselves that the debt transferred wealth from the deserving part of society to the less deserving, and they fervently echoed Hume's denunciations of fundholders as idle and unproductive members of society.[181] Moreover, as in Britain, there was the matter of foreign fundholders. By the time the Republicans took office under Jefferson's leadership in 1801, a substantial proportion of the American national debt had already been alienated abroad, and it did not help that much of it ended up in the hands of the once and future enemy.[182] To be sure, that debt was "sacred," or at least the part that had been incurred to gain independence was; the Republicans could only wonder what had been accomplished with the debt created to pay for Adams's naval war and those dangerous military preparations at home.[183] This recent addition to the debt was all the more difficult to accept because Republicans believed that there were much cheaper, better, and more humane ways of resolving international disputes than recourse to war; commercial pressure, they were certain, would bring the rest of the world to heel in short order, if consistently applied.[184]

As taxpayers, the Virginia Republicans were decidedly aware of the ways in which the Federalist debt program affected them. Large-scale consumers of imported goods, they felt the pressure of the customs duties that were the nation's primary source of revenue.[185] And their taxes, which went to pay the current expenses of the government and service the loans it continued to contract, were being used, by the late 1790s, to support a foreign policy that cut them off from their best market, France. Tobacco planters like Jefferson could only rue the opportunities they lost, thanks to the Adams administration's embargo on trade with the French, whose demand for their staple had sent prices to unprecedented levels.[186] That the Virginia Republicans thus found themselves suffering from the economic consequences of a program they were predisposed to oppose on political grounds only strengthened their hostility. And they were convinced that Federalist strength in Virginia, such as it was, rested in large part on the corps of tax gatherers and customs officials required to enforce the fiscal measures Hamilton originated and his successor Oliver Wolcott continued; in Richmond, Alexandria, Petersburg, and Norfolk, it was the federal bureaucracy—however primitive by modern standards—that seemed to offer a rallying point for the monocrats and Anglomen.[187]

Nor did appearances greatly deceive the Virginia Republicans. Other than placating South Carolina and Massachusetts—at the expense of alienating most

Virginians and a good many other Americans–it is difficult to detect any general benefit in Hamilton's solutions to the financial problems of the nation as they stood in 1790.[188] His hopes that a monetized debt, by increasing circulation, would become the foundation of a new national prosperity were doomed to disappointment; the benefits he predicted did not come to pass.[189] Prosperity, in fact, did return in the 1790s, but the "golden shower," as one newspaper called it, was the result of war abroad and America's position as the leading neutral carrier, not of Hamilton's having funded the debt.[190] Investments at home, though, the kinds of things Hamilton had envisaged, were notably unsuccessful. Few early canals or turnpikes managed to produce a decent return on the capital of those foolish enough to have invested in them; the record of manufacturing schemes was just as bad; and land speculation, the great American mania in the 1790s, all too often proved a bottomless pit.[191] The Bank of the United States, an institution the Virginia Republicans correctly associated with Hamilton's creation of the national debt, was useful, of course, but hardly indispensable. In any case, few Virginians would have agreed that its services–they went mainly to merchants, for the bank did not lend on the security of real estate and so was of little direct assistance to agriculturalists–were adequate compensation for the burden the debt had placed on them.[192]

As for Hamilton's claim that he was establishing the public credit on a firm and permanent foundation, time would reveal that accident played a greater part in his achievements than he and his friends were willing to admit. Once the French invasion of the United Provinces in 1795 closed the Amsterdam market to American loans, the government found it harder and harder to obtain the sums it required.[193] The late 1790s would show how difficult it was to locate alternative sources of capital, no matter how firmly public credit had been vindicated earlier in the decade. The 8 percent loan of 1798 left a bitter taste in many mouths; so much, it seemed, for public credit under Federalist auspices.[194] By 1796, even the Bank of the United States preferred not to lend to the government, whose calls for money seriously threatened to impede its primary tasks of supporting private credit and discounting merchants' notes.[195] And between 1812 and 1815, it would become only too obvious that public credit depended not on proper funding, not on the prompt payment of interest, not on economy in government, but on policies that met the political requirements of those with money to lend, a condition the Virginians then in power found distasteful in the extreme.[196] All of which, we may suppose, was reason enough to make Jefferson and his friends sure that they were right.

Yet even if the debt failed to perform the functions Hamilton had assigned it, it may well have had other positive effects. But if it did, we cannot be sure what they were. Economic historians have thus far failed to look closely enough at the question and provide us with the necessary information; once again, we can only speculate. The situation is different from the British case. Clearly, military spending during the Revolutionary War had energized and stimulated important parts of the domestic economy, even if its effects largely bypassed Virginia and planters like Jefferson.[197] But that spending came to an end with the close of the war between 1781 and 1783, and thereafter direct military spending had far less important a role to play in America than in the former mother country; the effects of demand by the army and navy–despite Eli Whitney and interchangeable parts–were relatively minor considerations in the American case.[198] True, even the relatively small sums spent this way could have a significant impact in a particular locality; thus the expansion of the navy during the War of 1812 helped to ease the crisis of maritime unemployment in the seaports– though privateering, which was not financed by the government, probably helped as much or more–and the frontier campaigns against the Indians in the first half of the 1790s meant windfall gains for settlers in Kentucky and the Ohio country, whose crops and services as wagoners and carters were essential to support the army's efforts in the wilderness.[199] But none of this could have had anything like the effect that military demand had on the British economy in the quarter-century or so between 1793 and Water- loo. Thus the American debt, relatively static or declining before the War of 1812 and the result of a one-time surge of government spending during the War of Independence, had some but not all the features of its British prototype and in all probability a much smaller impact on the economy over the long run.[200]

If there was an effect of major proportions in the American case, it must have come from the uses to which interest payments were put and from the ability of fundholders to employ their securities in productive ways. Here the critical data must be the extent to which the debt, originally widely distrib- uted, had been concentrated in the hands of a relative few by 1790 and the degree to which the holders sold their securities abroad, mainly to British purchasers, during the 1790s.[201] It is at this point that we come firmly up against our lack of knowledge, for we have virtually no information about the reasons that induced American speculators to dispose of their holdings, or about what became of the money they received for them. There are occasional hints, and thus we can trace the activities of the Marshalls and Robert Morris as they used their investments in the American debt to underwrite their purchase of the Fairfax lands in northern Virginia for £20,000.[202] Doubtless other land speculators followed suit.[203] Because al- most none of the dreams of those who hoped to amass fortunes through land development came true, it is unlikely that the debt was productively em- ployed when used for such purposes, though it did help to swell state treasuries (thereby reducing the level of local taxation) and facilitate settle- ment in areas that might otherwise have remained uninhabited.[204] But individual settlers could have performed many, if not all, of the same functions; those willing to purchase land from the great companies would presumably have been willing to buy the same land from the states or the federal government, and private, small-scale purchases would not have created the political problems that later resulted from the sales to the companies.[205] Land speculation, on balance, seems to have been a relatively unproductive form of investment, and the debt that was liquidated to finance it may simply have been wasted.

Some of the debt, however, must have been used by merchants to support the expansion of the carrying trade in the 1790s. As foreign demand for American maritime services rose to new heights, large numbers of ships were built, insurance companies organized, and voyages undertaken.[206] Government securities must have underwritten a part of that expansion, as merchants eager to realize their speculative gains invested the proceeds in the even more promising boom in the re-export trade. When there were fortunes to be made shipping colonial products to England and France, who would be content with a modest return of 6 percent?[207] And an important part of the remarkable prosperity of those years, Joyce Appleby reminds us, was the sale abroad of American grain. Here, too, the same factor was probably at work: Merchants liquidated their government securities to buy wheat and flour.[208] Thus the debt, concentrated in the hands of seaport speculators by 1790, could well have helped to fuel the maritime boom of the period and so create a prosperity that no one—least of all Hamilton—had foreseen when the second session of the First Congress assembled at New York in January 1790. But even here, a caveat is necessary: Would the boom have happened anyway? Surely the answer is yes. American merchants were able to join in on a large scale, thanks to their command of liquid assets in the form of the debt, but this was neither the necessary nor the sufficient cause of the boom. European grain shortages were not created by American fiscal policy, and the circumstances that made it possible for the shipowners of Boston, New York, Philadelphia, and Baltimore to reach out and seize a major share of the carrying trade had nothing to do with the visions of the treasury secretary.

We may conclude, then, that Hamilton's plans were overtaken by events, events neither he nor anyone else had foreseen. The debt may have been a secondary—very secondary—cause of American prosperity in the 1790s, but if so, it was one by chance. Without war in Europe, it is far from clear that the debt would have had the effects it did. And its alienation to British holders was probably unnecessary; orders for grain would have come to America in any case, and American shipping would have carried colonial cargoes, even if American merchants had not been able to turn their holdings of the debt into ready money or been able to use it to support their applications for credit at the banks. But because they acted as they did, American taxes went abroad, into the hands of those like the Barings, to pay interest and reimburse principal.[209] If, as a result, the American economy expanded, it was an expansion of the "horizontal" sort, an expansion in the quantitative and not the qualitative sense. The prosperity of the 1790s was of the traditional kind, familiar since colonial days, and the merchants and speculators who may have unloaded their securities so as to participate in it were simply acting in accustomed ways, following the well-worn paths of commerce they and their families before them had long known.

To the extent that they sold their securities abroad, these holders performed an important service for the still underdeveloped American economy: They brought in new capital, and they did so without increasing the country's indebtedness in an absolute sense. If–and again our lack of knowledge is crucial–that capital was put to productive uses, then the debt was indeed beneficial, just as Hamilton had claimed it would be.[210] In this, at least, the situation of the United States was different from that of Britain, where substantial proportions of the debt had been created out of domestic savings; in the United States, apart from the loans of the late 1790s and the financing of the War of 1812, the capital of the debt did not represent a current diversion of resources from other domestic employments.[211] Further, and again unlike the British case, much of the debt, as it took shape in 1790, was a pure gift to the holders, who had acquired it at bargain prices and who in no sense had performed any of the underlying services–wartime loans, supplies of goods and services to the continental army or the state troops, military service itself–to pay for which the debt had originally been issued.[212] These unearned profits–primitive accumulation in a very obvious way–were available in the hands of those who received them for investments of every kind. In an ideal sense, they should have provided the basis for significant expansion of the economy, as Hamilton had claimed they would, yet it bears repeating that we have very little evidence that this in fact happened. We do know, however, that the debt as constituted by the legislation of 1790 seemed morally dubious to a good many people and that this, in turn, helped prompt the opposition that threatened to undo Hamilton's hopes.

Finally, there is the question we have already posed in the British case, the question of the ends for which the debt was incurred. Few Americans were willing to deny that the Revolution had been worth the price; Jefferson, as we have seen, suppressed his usual abhorrence of debt when it came to this point.[213] And, apart from the Federalist malcontents in New England and Jefferson and other Old Republicans, few complained of the cost of the second war for independence between 1812 and 1815. The expense of the campaigns against the Indians on the western frontier was also approved, though not universally; the benefits from these seemed more than capable of compensating for the diversion of funds that might otherwise have gone to debt reduction.[214] And the purchase of Louisiana, the one great exception before 1812 to 1815 in the Republican policy of economizing and debt reduction, was seen in similarly positive terms by a majority of Americans.[215] On the whole, then–despite Republican objection to military spending and debt in the 1790s, despite Federalist objection to the millions of new debt for Louisiana and the far greater sums borrowed to support a needless war against Britain–it seems fair to conclude that most Americans who thought about such matters would have agreed that what was gained was worth its cost, and it would be difficult to dispute their judgment. As in Britain, debt had to be created if national goals were to be secured; the burden of paying everything out of current income would have been too great. And as for in the British case revealed, it was impossible for Americans to resist the more costly temptations that presented themselves, to pass by the opportunity to acquire more land or to submit to what were regarded as unacceptable demands from foreign powers.

In sum, national debts were a necessary part of the life of an eighteenth-century state, whether that state was traditional like Britain or professedly new and different like America. When its scale was large enough, direct military spending may have been beneficial, in the sense that it stimulated important sectors of the economy, and this seems to have been true in Britain, though probably less so in America. But we know less about the effects of the interest that had to be paid on the money borrowed for that spending. Contemporaries were disturbed by the burden that interest seemed to represent and resented the heavy taxes required to pay it. They were right to see it as a transfer of wealth from one part of society to another, but whether this forced saving did more than allow fundholders to live in ease is impossible to determine. Contemporaries were also right to associate government finance with war and standing armies; indeed, the latter were the debt's raison d'être, and without them it would not have existed. They were right as well to fear the political consequences of the system; as the victims of those consequences, they had a keen appreciation of such matters. Their sense of unease is understandable; caught up in a situation about which, apparently, little could be done, they both benefited and suffered from it, and it is probably utopian to suppose that it was possible to have one set of results without the other. If most of them were unaware of how much they owed to the willingness of those who occupied the seats of power to spend on war and to borrow to finance that spending, they had sound reasons to worry that the immediate results were not necessarily to their own advantage. Finally, the framework in which contemporaries expressed their views may, in short, have been lacking in that larger perspective capable of appreciating the Mandevillian paradox, but it was competent to identify important elements of the problems created by the system of wars, debts, and taxes. As such, it was ample enough for most purposes.

4

Errors of Political Life

I was duped . . . by the Secretary of the treasury, and made a tool for forwarding his schemes, not then sufficiently understood by me; and of all the errors of my political life, this has occasioned me the deepest regret.

Thomas Jefferson, 1792[1]

As far as the object will permit I go on the principle that a Public Debt is a Public curse and in a Rep. Govt. a greater than in any other.

James Madison, 1790[2]

If there is any part of Jefferson's engagement with debt that present-day Americans are likely to recall, it is the so-called Dinner Table Bargain of 1790. The first of the great compromises under the Constitution, this lesson in "give and take"—to borrow Jefferson's characterization of the process—retains its fascination for students of American politics: Logrolling, it seems, is as old as the Republic itself.[3] Although we still do not know precisely what happened—much remains obscure, as those who arranged the Dinner Table Bargain no doubt intended it should—in broad outline, and from the point of view of the Virginians, things are clear enough: To break the deadlock over enactment of Alexander Hamilton's financial program and, more important, to end the threat of disunion, Jefferson and Madison agreed to provide the additional votes necessary to pass the assumption of the state debts, and, on his side, Hamilton helped to arrange for the votes needed to place the permanent capital on the banks of the Potomac.[4] The Virginians were not terribly happy with the outcome, but, in the summer of 1790, they conceded that the arrangement was the best that could be made of a bad business. This grudging acceptance would not last. Jefferson discovered that he had been "duped" by Hamilton, while Madison characteristically tried to understand what had gone wrong by constructing an elaborate classification of the varying degrees of responsibility in the affair.[5] Hamilton, his two critics concluded, had put one over on them. As Virginians and therefore born connoisseurs of horseflesh, Jefferson and Madison—one cannot help thinking—might have taken the trouble to look the nag that Hamilton was selling them a little more closely in the mouth.

But it was more than simply a mistake in judgment, the loss of a round in the ongoing game of politics. For Jefferson it would become the gravest mistake of his political life, one of the few actions in a long career for which he felt compelled to offer a detailed apologia.[6] Given his principles, Jefferson was right to see the bargain in this light; it was a disaster of the first magnitude, in its own way comparable for him to the Fall of Man—with the difference that, unlike Adam, Jefferson did his best to fight his way back into the Garden of Eden. And—again unlike Adam—Jefferson had been in a position to know better. Everything he believed about debt should have kept him away from Hamilton in June 1790, and yet he ended up serving as midwife to the "brat" assumption.[7] Jefferson never overcame the sense of guilt at his part in the affair, or his anger at having been tricked into complicity; as we shall see, it would preoccupy him in the years of his retirement.[8]

Jefferson's desire to explain his mistake—to portray himself as the victim of Hamilton's superior cunning—is natural enough, though historians have been inclined to discount his insistence that he did not really understand what Hamilton had in mind.[9] But apart from the obvious aim of his exercises in apologetics, Jefferson's later reconstructions of the events of 1790 can be misleading in other ways as well. For what will strike us, in looking at those events, is the extent to which Jefferson was caught not in Hamilton's toils but in a dilemma of his own devising. In this sense, the critical point about the bargain is that it confronted Jefferson with a set of nearly impossible choices. His concern for a sound public credit, his hopes for the republican experiment then barely under way, his desire to see America strong and internationally respected—each of these was potentially in conflict with Jefferson's hatred of debt. Political configurations in 1790 made it impossible for him to have it all; some sacrifice was required, and in the end he had to choose. Agreeing to the creation of an enlarged and permanent national debt that presented serious risks to republicanism as he understood it, Jefferson chose union and the immediate restoration of public credit. No doubt this was the wisest decision he could have made—but it had its dangers, and by the spring of 1791 those dangers would become increasingly apparent.

Thus the story of the Dinner Table Bargain suggests the tensions between Jefferson's conflicting desires, illuminating the compromises he would have to make between his convictions about debt, on the one hand, and the necessities of politics in the new federal system, on the other. Jefferson would never be able to reconcile himself to the need to make choices of this sort, and with the Revolution of 1800 he would be able for a time to escape the dilemmas they posed.[10] But 1790 requires our attention for an additional reason: It marks the resumption of Jefferson's working partnership with Madison. Begun in the late 1770s around the Virginia Council table, interrupted to some extent by Jefferson's five years of residence in France and by the differences between the two men over the Constitution's lack of a bill of rights, the "great collaboration" reemerged in the spring of 1790 as the pair of Virginians discovered that Hamilton was offering a plan and a vision significantly at odds with theirs.[11]

Nor was the tangled question of funding, assumption, and the residence the only area of joint effort that spring. Jefferson and Madison would play complementary roles in a less well known but highly revealing controversy over what has been called the Arrears of Pay, a dispute growing out of frauds practiced on Revolutionary veterans in Virginia and North Carolina that pitted Hamilton against Jefferson and Madison, in the process revealing the gulf that separated the New Yorker from the Virginians.[12] Like the larger questions raised by funding and assumption, the affair of the Arrears of Pay would demonstrate the extent to which Jefferson, Madison, and a good many other prominent Virginians were not yet ready to enter Hamilton's brave new world, clinging instead to older attitudes about debt and credit that had little in common with those the treasury secretary was encouraging.

Throughout, Madison's role in these events will be of great importance, so much so that from time to time it may seem that the younger Virginian has managed to push Jefferson off the stage. There are, however, good reasons for letting Madison occupy the foreground. Jefferson was the novice in the spring of 1790; it was Madison, reversing their former roles, who was now the old hand. Jefferson had been abroad for half a decade, and in that time Madison had gradually but decisively moved to center stage. His part in the creation and adoption of the Constitution and the lead he took in the first session of Congress gave Madison a strategic position in national affairs in 1790–far more strategic, it should be added, than his senior colleague's, for Jefferson had been largely removed from national politics since 1784 and did not, in any case, expect that his new position as secretary of state would require him to resume his former involvement.[13] Hence in 1790 it was Madison who presented the Virginia point of view, and Jefferson who watched until the moment of crisis.

But precisely because Madison offered a Virginia view in 1790, and not simply his own perspective, it will be useful to examine it in some detail. Madison will introduce themes and topics with which Jefferson will feel perfectly comfortable; in this, as in his guiding Jefferson through the maze of politics in the First Congress, his service to his fellow Virginian will be invaluable. Moreover, we may safely assume that there were no secrets between the two men; what Madison knew would be known to Jefferson, and given Jefferson's comparative ignorance not only of federal politics but also of recent developments in Virginia, Madison's information becomes highly pertinent to any assessment of Jefferson's state of mind in 1790. This is not, of course, to suggest that Jefferson was merely tabula rasa on which Madison chalked his message at will; on the contrary, Jefferson had his own firmly held convictions on the subjects that occupied the attention of Congress that spring–high among them the notion that the earth belonged in usufruct to the living. But it was Madison who established the Virginia agenda in New York, and Madison who helped to set the terms of the debate to which Jefferson was a latecomer.

I have suggested that there was a degree of inevitability about Jefferson's problem in 1790, that there was nothing fortuitous about his difficulty reconciling his idea of debt with competing and sometimes contradictory convictions. There is also an inevitability about the larger conflict that generated Jefferson's dilemma, and it is easy enough to see it as the natural collapse of the jerry-built constitutional coalition of Federalists from northern commercial centers and Federalists from the plantation South.[14] Sectional and, even more, state and local interests played major roles in the drama of 1790, and with a bit of imagination it is possible to reduce the events of that spring to no more than the usual jockeying for advantage, as the Virginians insisted on holding out until Hamilton agreed to modify assumption so that its ultimate fiscal effects on the Old Dominion would be neutral.[15] But to follow the lead of such scholars as E. James Ferguson in this line of analysis would divert us from the more interesting questions the episode raises. For what it will reveal is not merely sectional or state and local interests, but significant ideological differences, differences that had a good deal to do with competing conceptions of debt and the political consequences of debt. These differences, brought out in the debates on Hamilton's program and apparent in the correspondence of prominent Virginians that spring, suggest that more was at stake than immediate questions of dollars and cents, and the traditional country party fears that Hamilton's program elicited in turn remind us that Virginians, whether at home or in New York, had their own strongly held notions about the new Republic's political economy.

Hamilton, it seems, did not realize in advance that the proposals contained in his *Report on Public Credit* would stir up a hornet's nest. But given Jefferson's and Madison's positions—and Virginia's—there was bound to be conflict. That conflict, in 1790, was sharp, but hardly as sharp as it would later become, once the Virginians had convinced themselves that they should have known better than to offer assistance to Hamilton. In 1790, their worst fears had yet to be realized. It was, rather, the fate of the new American empire that seemed to hang in the balance, and they were too committed to making it work not to compromise once the need for concessions became overwhelming. But as Jefferson was soon to discover, the season was not well calculated for advancing the rights of the living generation.

With the ratification of the Constitution and the inauguration of George Washington to signal their triumph, the nationalist reformers of the 1780s could regard the spring of 1789 as marking the moment when, at long last, they came into their own. Yet even observers disposed in advance to think well of their project must have wondered whether the Federalists would be able to use their power to translate intentions into realities. Almost everyone agreed that government under the new Constitution was an "experiment," that success could not be assumed in advance. None knew this better than the men who had worked hardest to secure the new charter and create the opportunity for a new beginning. The president, in his Inaugural Address, spoke to the issue directly; admonishing Congress in words written for him by Madison, Washington solemnly declared that "the preservation of the sacred fire of liberty, and the destiny of the Republican mode of Government, are justly considered as *deeply*, perhaps *finally*, staked on the outcome of the experiment entrusted to the hands of the American people."[16] But not even Washington could promise that all would go well; it was up to the people, or their representatives, to make the most of the chance they had been lucky enough to receive.

No doubt many of those who listened to Washington on 30 April 1789 or later read his words in their newspapers shared his sense that much was riding on the constitutional wager—for that was what Washington's language made the experiment—and the members of Congress could hardly have been unaware of what was expected of them. On the contrary, they would have been only too conscious that the public would measure the experiment's success in decidedly simple terms: Either the Constitution brought them tangible benefits, or it was a failure. After all, the people had been assured that this would happen—during the ratification campaign, the Constitution's supporters touted the new system as a panacea for every conceivable form of the nation's ills.[17]

As one of the Constitution's opponents, the Massachusetts Antifederalist who adopted the nom de guerre "John De Witt," wrote in the fall of 1787: "We are told by some people, that upon the adopting this New Government we are to become everything in a moment." As if by magic, the Constitution would make all problems disappear: "Our foreign and domestic debts will be as a feather; our ports will be crowded with the ships of all the world, soliciting our commerce and our produce; Our manufactures will increase and multiply."[18] How, incredulous Antifederalists asked, could anyone be taken in by such nonsense? "But will a new government relieve you" from debts and embarrassments, New York's Melancton Smith inquired. "The advocates for it have not yet told you how it will do it—And I venture to pronounce, that there is but one way in which it can be effected, and that is by industry and economy."[19]

Neither "De Witt" nor Smith exaggerated the tone of Federalist appeals. Hamilton had treated the matter as self-evident in *The Federalist*; appealing to widespread concern that something be done to revive trade, he insisted that "the importance of the Union, in a commercial light, is one of those points about which there is least room to entertain a difference of opinion," and he went on to paint a gratifying picture of the material advantages ratification would bring.[20] Other Federalist writers took similar positions in their contributions to the debate—with some reason, for it seems clear that a good deal of the popular support for the Constitution, particularly along the Atlantic seaboard, stemmed from the voters' willingness to swallow the Federalist argument that political change would bring about the return of prosperity.[21] As a campaign tactic, this was all very well in its way, but it carried a measure of risk.

And there was a further problem. The Federalists had not bothered to coordinate their promises—indeed, probably could not have made a consistent case throughout the nation and still have won the votes they needed. In

Virginia, the Federalists' positive promises were far less important than in other states; here, remarkably enough, most of the promises were negative. The great difficulty Virginia Federalists had to overcome was the ingrained republicanism of the commonwealth's traditional political culture, the strong appeal of opposition arguments to the gentry leaders who made up the political elite.[22] Men like Patrick Henry and George Mason were deeply attached to local values and local control, and Madison's vision of an America flourishing under the Constitution did not impress them. On the contrary, they were alarmed by the prospects of "consolidation," of heavy taxation, and of discriminatory freight rates once Congress had the power to pass navigation laws.[23] These and similar arguments made powerful impressions at the Virginia ratifying convention, and it took all the persuasive powers Madison and his allies could muster to convince the convention delegates that the Constitution was not the instrument of incipient tyranny. To do this, they had to pledge themselves—to promise that a bill of rights would be added to the Constitution, that heavy taxes would be avoided and the state left with financial resources, that Congress would not, in short, arrogate all power to itself.[24]

Madison, it is fair to say, was not optimistic about the future as the Virginia convention drew to its close in June 1788. Yes, the delegates had ratified the Constitution, but the amendments they had proposed were "many of them highly objectionable," particularly one that would have stripped Congress of the power to levy its own taxes by permitting the states to fill assigned quotas as they saw fit. Together with other amendments going to the heart of the new system, this deeply alarmed Madison.[25] He was sure that Patrick Henry would never be reconciled to the Constitution—Henry had declared that he would "wait with impatience for the favorable moment of regaining in a *constitutional way*, the lost liberties of his country"—and as long as Henry retained his powers, no one could be sure that Virginia's commitment to the Constitution would prove durable.[26] Just how strongly determined Henry and his many supporters were became apparent at the fall 1788 session of the Virginia legislature, which pointedly refused to elect Madison to a place in the United States Senate, selecting Antifederalists instead, and then went on to do its best to gerrymander him out of a seat in the House of Representatives.[27] Madison's victory in his campaign for that seat required considerable exertions on his part—and a strategic conversion to the philosophy of amendments, at least on matters like religious freedom where amendments could be conceded without damaging the essentials of the new system.[28] But not even the election of a largely Federalist Virginia delegation to the House of Representatives on 2 February 1789 could cure Madison of his sense that Antifederalism was alive and well in the Old Dominion. He continued to track Patrick Henry's activities with care, and, like other Virginia Federalists, he was well aware that, whatever the bulk of the people may have thought, the core Antifederalist leadership was still hostile, still eager for revenge, still intent on crippling revisions of the Constitution.[29]

Madison knew, therefore, that Virginia opinion bore watching. A thoroughly alienated Virginia would do the Union no good, and Madison was far too attached to the idea of Union for that to be acceptable. His strategy, then, must have been clear enough: Make sure the pledges given at the ratifying convention were kept, try not to produce further grounds for discontent, and then hope for the best, for the effects of time and the cooling of passions. Once he had taken his seat in the House, he promptly introduced amendments–though what emerged from committee and was sent to the states failed to satisfy leading Virginia Antifederalists, for whom the Bill of Rights was mere "milk and water" stuff.[30] And he kept his eye out for other sources of irritation to Virginia sentiment. But, again, all of this meant that the Federalist coalition that had secured the adoption of the Constitution was likely to run into trouble. For what would soothe Virginia might not, probably would not, go down equally well with Massachusetts or South Carolina. Madison could only hope that reason would prevail, that other states would recognize the importance of Virginia to the Union and under-stand that Virginia views and the danger of Virginia Antifederalism must be given due consideration. Had the view of politics he offered in *The Federalist*, No. 10, been correct, none of this would have mattered greatly; the myriad overlapping interests would have removed any danger of conflict and colli-sion between state and state or section and section.

Indeed, in the spring of 1789, Madison seemed to believe that this was what was happening. "In general," he told Jefferson, "the interests and ideas of the Northern & Southern States have been less averse than was predicted by the opponents or hoped by the friends of the new Government. Members from the same State, or from the same part of the Union are as often separated on questions from each other, as they are united in opposition to other States or other quarters on the Continent. This is a favorable symp-tom."[31] But Madison would discover soon enough that politics under the new Constitution contained surprises not even he had anticipated.

Nor was Madison the only Federalist to wonder how Congress was going to make good on the pledges that had been given in the heat of the battle for ratification. Whatever they and their supporters may have been willing to believe at the time, the Federalists, even with the Constitution in hand, were in no position to guarantee economic recovery and continuing prosperity. Neither the weather nor the state of the markets was under their control; the most they could hope for was restoration of confidence and relief through the normal workings of the business cycle. To be sure, a European war, with the United States now able to figure as a neutral carrier, would solve the problem in a dramatic fashion, but this prospect–which turned out to be the making of American prosperity in the 1790s–might not material-ize in time to save the Constitution.[32] In fact, there was no getting around the difficulty that the Federalists had promised too much in 1787 and 1788 and so created expectations that would be difficult to satisfy. New Jersey Federalist Jonathan Dayton feared that things had gotten out of hand: "The people," he wrote, "in their rage for the new constitution . . . think, that with a kind of *magic process* it will, at the instant of it's [*sic*]commencement rid us of all our embarrassments, & make our circumstances flourishing." But like the Antifederalists, Dayton was sure these "enthusiasts" were wrong. Only "*time* & a series of wise, prudential management and political economy will extricate us . . . from the calamities we are experiencing," he noted.[33]

As Dayton went on to observe, the great danger was that disappointing these expectations—and this was equally true of the set of expectations entertained in Virginia—"will probably furnish the first ground of discontent & give a new opening for antifederalism under more favorable auspices than theretofore to revive it's [*sic*] attacks." Dayton knew that much was at stake here. "I wish," he concluded, "that the hopes of the most sanguine may be answered but well I know that the success of an experiment like this is too apt to depend upon the impressions which it makes at it's [*sic*] outset & neither you nor I can undertake to say that this is not one of the last tryals to be afforded this or any other country, whether the people have the ability to govern themselves."[34] If Dayton, writing in October 1788, could thus anticipate Washington's inaugural sentiments in a private letter, we are entitled to suspect that a good many other Federalists were beginning to be nervous about the outcome.

But these were sober second thoughts. At the height of the struggle for ratification of the Constitution, the Federalists had not paused to think of such matters, had not confined themselves to vague assurances that a stronger Union was likely to bring better times. On the contrary, as "De Witt" pointed out, they had given remarkably concrete pledges, and in particular they had assured everyone who would listen that they would solve the problem of the Revolutionary War debt.[35] Few issues played a greater part in stimulating the movement for reform in the mid-1780s. Congress's utter inability to deal with the debt, combined with the difficulties many of the states experienced in meeting their own obligations, was a principal cause of nationalist discontent during the Critical Period. Some of the most controversial provisions of the new Constitution—high among them the broad grant of power to levy taxes and regulate commerce so alarming to Virginia Antifederalists—were intended to help Congress meet its obligations to its creditors, and it was widely expected that something would be done on that score at the first opportunity.[36] Failure now, in 1789, to act swiftly and effectively on the debt would be an open confession that the reform had failed. And that was a confession no one wanted to make, least of all Jefferson, who was running out of excuses to offer America's European creditors.[37]

Still in France, Jefferson could only urge the government at home to act; it fell to Madison, as unofficial leader of the House of Representatives, to make good on this set of Federalist promises. As the Inaugural Address he had drafted for Washington put it, "the foundations of our National Policy . . . [must] be laid in the pure and immutable principles of private morality." Madison and his friends had spent the years since 1783 trying to impose just such notions of "private morality" on recalcitrant state legislatures, and the morality they had in mind placed a high value on the payment of debts, whether public or private. We may be sure that Washington's audience knew exactly what Madison's words meant. Lest anyone miss the point, the president's speechwriter elaborated it. There was, he had the president say, "no Truth more thoroughly established, than that there exists in the oeconomy and course of nature, an indissoluble union between virtue and happiness, between the genuine maxims of an honest and magnanimous policy and the solid rewards of public prosperity and felicity." The dangers of neglecting this sound advice were emphasized as well: Divine displeasure might be incurred, since the "smiles of Heaven, can never be expected on a nation that disregards the eternal rules of order and right, which Heaven itself has ordained."[38]

Washington was not the only one to remind Congress of its duties, sacred or otherwise, on the question of the debt. Creditors at home and abroad had been put off with promises that adoption of the Constitution would work a miraculous change in the condition of American finances, that interest would be forthcoming and principal reimbursed once the new charter took effect.[39] In 1789 the creditors, not unnaturally, were expecting Congress to act, and act promptly.[40] Keenly aware of the need to demonstrate Congress's good faith, even before the inauguration Madison was urging the House, in his speech opening the debate on the revenue, that "the Union . . . ought, in its first act, to revive those principles of honor and honesty that have too long remained dormant." Clearly, "the dictates of gratitude and policy," he continued, required Congress to provide for "the numerous claims on our justice," and he warned that anything else would constitute a relapse into "the state of imbecility, that heretofore prevented a performance of [Congress's] duty" to its creditors.[41] Madison was not indulging in hyperbole. Unless the new Congress could demonstrate both its willingness and its ability to do what was right, it would show itself no more capable than its predecessor, and that, clearly, would be fatal.

Despite Madison's well-grounded pleas of urgency, the first session of Congress was largely taken up with the business of creating a government, and the creditors were left without the relief they had expected. There was, to be sure, an implied promise of things to come in the form of the first revenue statutes, though they were enacted too late to catch the spring imports and so did nothing to fill the nation's empty coffers.[42] Yet at least the preliminaries for a solution of the debt problem had been addressed. Taxes had been laid, a bureaucracy organized to collect them, and—in the long run most important of all—Alexander Hamilton had been appointed to head the new Treasury Department.[43] It was into his capable hands that the House of Representatives delivered the question of what was to be done about the debt at the close of the first session in September 1789. Convinced, as the preamble to their resolution put it, that "an adequate provision for the support of the public credit [is] a matter of high importance to the national interest and prosperity," the representatives directed Hamilton "to prepare a plan for that purpose, and to report the same to this House at its next meeting."[44]

Having left matters to Hamilton, Congress adjourned and its members scattered to their homes. Few of them could have known precisely what Hamilton would recommend for their consideration at the second session. But the secretary's views in general were no mystery, and rumors of his intentions spread rapidly among speculators and other interested parties.[45] Madison, too, seems to have had a fairly concrete sense of what was in the offing, for when Hamilton wrote to him in October, requesting his views, the Virginian replied in terms that strongly suggest familiarity with the broad outlines of Hamilton's program, at least with respect to the domestic and foreign debts.[46] While we do not know whether the two men had discussed these matters before Madison left New York at the close of the congressional session, the language of Hamilton's letter certainly implies that he had expected to go over them with Madison, and it strains credulity to imagine that the two men had never explored the issues involved in the years since their collaboration on the *Address to the States* in 1783.[47] In any case, both men had read enough of the available literature to appreciate what were the preferred solutions to questions of public credit.[48] Thus Madison would have been exhibiting less than his usual intelligence had he not had some inkling of the forms Hamilton's known preferences would take on this occasion.[49] This no doubt explains why Madison chose to treat so important a subject in a relatively brief compass; his reply to Hamilton's request for suggestions was a shorthand summary intended to remind Hamilton of the points Madison thought important, points he did not need to elaborate because he could assume that Hamilton was thoroughly familiar with them and knew that Hamilton would understand the direction Madison's own views were taking, given what he had chosen to stress.

What Madison sought to make clear in the letter was simply this: the political danger of the position he expected Hamilton to adopt. Public opinion would not countenance the sort of things Hamilton had in mind, particularly if it meant that the debt would be made permanent. "There are respectable opinions I know," Madison conceded, "in favor of prolonging if not, perpetuating it. But without entering into the general reasonings on the subject," two considerations peculiar to the United States called for the opposite course: "one, that such a policy is disrelished to a degree that will render heavier burdens for discharging the debt more acceptable than lighter ones not having that for their object—the other, that the debt, however modified must, as soon as the interest is provided for, or the permanent views of the Govt. ascertained, slide into the hands of foreigners."[50] In effect, Madison was telling Hamilton that in the United States a public debt, no matter how astutely managed, would never be considered a public blessing by the mass of the people.[51] But while he admitted that his thoughts on the subject might reflect only local notions—and he was certainly right to hint that they reflected Virginia ideas on the subject—or even mistaken ones, Madison nevertheless warned Hamilton as politely as he could against precisely the course he must have known the secretary of the treasury was intending to adopt.[52]

For all his reluctance to meet the issue head on—a reluctance, we may suppose, with roots in his realization that he and Hamilton were about to part company after a long and fruitful working partnership—Madison had made the necessary point. And he returned to the theme of public opinion repeatedly in the letter, stressing that a stamp tax was not an eligible source of revenue, given the prejudices against it, though he himself did not share them. Similarly, he urged the creation of a sinking fund; it would please many, doubtless because it would be positive evidence of a determination to extinguish the debt.[53] Hamilton, of course, was not blind to the importance of public opinion for the success of his program, but the opinion he had in mind was located elsewhere than in the Virginia Piedmont. The necessity of courting his kind of public opinion—the "monied men"—deepened Hamilton's preference for the very lines of policy Madison was sure would provoke dangerous opposition, and even as Madison was alerting him to the folly of perpetuating the national debt, Hamilton was completing his plan to do precisely that.[54]

Did Hamilton give Madison's letter much consideration? It is hard to tell, though there is certainly no evidence that it influenced his plan in any significant way. He did not write to Madison again that fall. There was little time for an extensive correspondence: Congress was due to meet early in January, and Hamilton was working against a deadline. But it is doubtful that Madison's reminders did more than alert Hamilton to the political difficulties his program would face, and Hamilton was never one to trim his sails to accommodate the prevailing breezes. What Madison had told him, after all, was hardly news, and the positions briefly noted in the Virginian's letter had no doubt been spelled out in greater detail over the past years.[55] Still, it is at least fair to conclude that Madison had given Hamilton a warning; Hamilton may have chosen to disregard it, but it had been given and he was now on notice.[56]

Indeed, had the New Yorker been paying reasonably close attention to what was going on in Congress in 1789, he would have noticed other warnings emanating from Madison, other evidence—if he needed any at that point—of his friend's attachment to orthodox positions in matters of public finance. In the spring, during the debates on the revenue—which were held a short walk from Hamilton's law office, in a legislature whose doings were of considerable interest to him, touching a subject (finance) with which Hamilton had long been identified—Madison had taken a very strong stand against a proposition that adopted the British practice of "mortgaging" specific revenues to debt service and that would have assigned the federal government's principal resource, the customs duties, in perpetuity to service the debt.[57] Madison argued that this would be contrary to "republican principles," for it would deprive the people's representatives of control over appropriations. Fully appreciating that the measure's supporters were animated by an "ardent desire to promote the general welfare, by a re-establishment of public credit; he would heartily join his labors with theirs, to effect this object, but wished to do it in a way that while they served their country, they might secure the liberties of the people, and do honor to themselves," he said in the House of Representatives on 15 May 1789.[58] In particular, Madison questioned the wisdom of tying Congress's hands, noting that changing conditions would require alterations in the law and suggesting—the theme became more familiar in future decades—that the protection offered by customs duties to certain categories of business might outlive its usefulness.[59] What would happen then if Congress tried to repeal the law? Madison imagined the worst case—a presidential veto and a majority insufficient to override, or a failure of the Senate to concur with the House. Useless revenue would then begin to pile up in the Treasury Department, and Madison pointedly referred to the possibility of executive corruption and the threats it posed: The funds, he hinted darkly, "might . . . become a convenience in the hands of some other department of the government, for the purpose of oppression."[60]

The significance of Madison's position was not lost on some of those who would back Hamilton to the hilt in 1790. Fisher Ames of Massachusetts insisted earlier in May 1789 that anything other than a permanent appropriation was "fraud on the face of it," for "nothing less than a fixed permanent system can beget confidence or give security."[61] And after the proposition had been defeated by the substantial majority of forty-one to eight, Ames confessed himself astonished at the part Madison had played, wondering what would happen when the tariff expired. Would there be enough votes to renew it? Or would local interests and Antifederalists combine to frustrate the principle of justice to creditors?[62] Outside Congress, William Bingham, who spoke for Philadelphia finance, tried to convince Madison of the error of his ways, arguing that the failure to make a perpetual assignment would decrease investor confidence and so raise interest rates. In the long run, Bingham thought, the result of this policy would be to deprive the United States of the benefits that accrued to Great Britain from placing public credit "on a permanent footing, which, in its Consequences has so increased the Capital Stock of the Country, as to furnish sufficient funds for the most extensive Operations of Industry, & Views of national Aggrandizement."[63] Ames had had a foretaste of the opposition Madison would offer in 1790, and Bingham had sketched for Madison one of those "respectable opinions in favor of prolonging the debt" that the Virginian could not accept. The lines were already drawn, well in advance of Hamilton's report to the House of Representatives.

Even as Hamilton was finishing his report in the closing days of December 1789, Jefferson was introducing Madison to the principle of the 6 September 1789 letter. When the two men met at Monticello over the Christmas holidays, Jefferson "mentioned" the letter to Madison, and we may assume that he did so in the context of what must have been a wide-ranging discussion of the current political scene. Madison may even have raised objections to some of Jefferson's points, but the older man was undeterred. Having neglected to give Madison the letter before the latter set out for New

York and the second session of Congress, Jefferson forwarded it on 9 January 1790. "After so long lying by me," he explained to Madison, "and further turning the subject in my mind, I find no occasion to alter my mind. I hazard it therefore to your consideration."[64] But before Madison had a chance to reply on 4 February 1790, matters had begun to take a turn radically at odds with Jefferson's doctrine.

Hamilton, in fact, set the new agenda even before Jefferson dispatched his argument in favor of the living generation. On 2 January 1790, the treasury secretary delivered his proposals to Washington. What the president made of them we do not know, though it is clear that he did not oppose their general thrust.[65] Like many of the report's readers, the president probably had difficulty working his way through the specific proposals, but Hamilton's statements of principle must have struck him as sound and sensible. Public credit, Hamilton urged, was essential to the nation's well-being, and Washington would have agreed with the secretary's insistence that "loans in times of public danger, especially from foreign war, are found an indispensable resource." That, Hamilton added, was all the truer in "a country which, like this, is possessed of little active wealth."[66] Given his experience during the Revolutionary War, Washington could hardly have disagreed.[67]

Moreover, Washington must have recognized that Hamilton was using the same arguments—and almost the same language—he himself had employed the previous April in his inaugural address. Justice must be upheld, Hamilton wrote in the report, and for reasons of the highest character: "While the observance of that good faith, which is the basis of public credit, is recommended by the strongest inducements of political expediency, it is enforced by considerations of still greater authority. There are arguments for it, which rest on the immutable principles of moral obligation." And he repeated the warning of the inaugural: "In proportion as the mind is disposed to contemplate, in the order of Providence, an intimate connection between public virtue and public happiness, will be its repugnancy to a violation of those principles."[68] All this would have struck Washington as both true and appropriate, and because universal applause greeted his inaugural speech the previous April, he is not likely to have imagined that Hamilton's version of it would meet with opposition, least of all from James Madison.

But there were other parts of the *Report Relative to a Provision for the Support of Public Credit* that did raise questions, particularly for Virginians, even if the president did not comment on them. Hamilton's proposal to assume the state debts was bound to be controversial, especially in its initial form, which would have penalized states like Virginia that had made substantial progress in extinguishing them.[69] Such questions were open to negotiation and might, Washington could have supposed, be settled in the normal course. Hamilton, however, had ideas that went beyond a mere settlement of the debt; for him, the debt was nothing less than an opportunity to organize the American economy as a whole. Like others with a sophisticated understanding of the British national debt, Hamilton realized that a "properly funded" debt could "be rendered a *substitute* for money," with important consequences, particularly in a country chronically short of both capital and a circulating medium.[70] The advantages were obvious, and Hamilton was careful to add that a monetized debt would aid the farmer and the landowner as well as the merchant and the mechanic.[71] Yet to use the debt in this way, as a substitute for more traditional forms of money, meant in part that the debt would have to be permanent or at least irredeemable for a considerable period, and although Hamilton avoided saying that the debt should never be paid off, the entire thrust of his plan envisaged the debt positively, as a lasting foundation for American prosperity.[72]

Moreover, to serve the purposes Hamilton had in mind, the debt had to be "an object of established confidence."[73] This had several implications, not the least of them that it ruled out any of the schemes to discriminate in favor of original holders of the debt—those who had received the debt from the government in return for loans or goods or services during the Revolution and had since parted with it at the depressed prices of the postwar years.[74] Such proposals, Hamilton explained, would violate the "*security of transfer*," thus destroying "the transferable quality of stock . . . essential to its operation as money." Unless government bonds were clearly as good as gold, they would not serve the purposes of gold, and Hamilton had no doubt that the key here was "confidence." Strengthening his case with references to the *Address to the States* issued at the end of the war in 1783, in which he and Madison had argued strongly against discrimination in favor of original holders and suggesting as well that such favoritism would be unconstitutional and violate the provisions of Article VI (which made the debts of the Confederation valid against the United States), Hamilton let Congress and the country know that discrimination was a proposition he was not prepared to entertain.[75]

There was a further consideration Hamilton found necessary to lay before his audience, one unlikely to win Virginia assent. "It cannot but merit particular attention," he announced, "that among ourselves the most enlightened friends of good government are those whose expectations are the highest." These were the men who had continued to invest in American securities, trusting that the government would redeem its pledges. To Hamilton, it was axiomatic that "those who are most commonly creditors of a nation, are, generally speaking, enlightened men."[76] This was high praise indeed for a group the Virginians in 1790 were likely to regard as unprincipled speculators, men whose claims on the common gratitude were none of the best, and the careful reader of Hamilton's *Report* would note that Hamilton seemed intent on gratifying their every wish. In private and in the past, Hamilton had placed considerable emphasis on the need to secure the support of such men, something that could be done only by conciliating their interests, and even in the *Report*, where he had to tread cautiously, it was apparent that this was the group to which his words were primarily addressed.

Such concessions to the monied part of the community—obviously, as Light-Horse Harry Lee would shortly complain, to be paid for by the landed interest—would not sit well in Virginia.[77] Nor, for that matter, would

Hamilton's maxim that "the proper funding of the present debt, will render it a national blessing," a statement Hamilton must have come to regret he had ever committed to paper.[78] For Virginians, such claims were incompatible with the understanding of debt that their experience and their reading had taught them to hold. A permanent debt? Madison had warned Hamilton in October that this idea would not be relished. Debts were burdens in Virginia, to be paid off before they drowned one in interest, not opportunities to reproduce the dubious benefits of the dangerous and corrupting English system of finance. The *Report* was, therefore, impossible to reconcile with Virginia notions on several scores; on every level, it contradicted the established Virginia way of looking at such matters, and its specific proposals—no discrimination in favor of original holders, assumption of the state debts as they now stood—were equally unpalatable.

Madison kept his initial reactions to Hamilton's *Report* to himself. Although Hamilton presented his proposals to the House on 14 January 1790, Madison had virtually nothing to say about them for another month.[79] Neither his remarks in debate nor his letters during these weeks shed much light on his views, and we have no evidence that he and Hamilton resumed the discussion initiated in their letters of the previous fall.[80] But on 4 February 1790, Madison took the time to reply to Jefferson's letter of 6 September 1789, forwarded to him on 9 January. It had, he said, reached him "a few days ago," and his answer to it indicates, not surprisingly, that it raised a number of points of particular pertinence to present considerations. "The idea which [it] evolves is a great one," Madison began, "and suggests many interesting reflections to legislators; particularly when contracting and providing for public debts." The tenor of Madison's reply to Jefferson is polite but firm; he finds his "first thoughts . . . coinciding with many of yours," but concludes that he views "the doctrine as not in *all* respects compatible with the course of human affairs," and he then proceeds "to sketch the grounds" of his own "skepticism."[81]

Systematic as ever, Madison carefully divides his answer into categories, outlining his objections to the effects of Jefferson's principle on (1) constitutions, (2) irrevocable laws, and (3) revocable laws. In the first category, Madison's remarks will come as no surprise; having recently survived the ordeal of constitution-making, he had no desire to repeat the process every nineteen years. "Would not," he asked, "a Government so often revised become too mutable to retain those prejudices in its favor which antiquity inspires, and which are perhaps a salutary aid to the most rational Government in the most enlightened age?" Yet if "antiquity," in the form of feudal oppression, was precisely what Jefferson had looked forward to abolishing, for Madison the danger was mutability—a point he had made often enough in the previous decade—and he looked as well to the practical dangers of "an actual interregnum" should government expire automatically at the end of every nineteen years.

His remarks on the third category—in effect, the bulk of ordinary legislation—also have overtones of the 1780s. He worried about what would happen to property if the positive laws supporting it automatically ceased to have effect: "The most violent struggles [would] be generated between those interested in reviving and those interested in new-modelling the former State of property," from which it followed "that the possibility of an event so hazardous to the rights of property could not fail to depreciate its value" and, as well, would "discourage the steady exertions of industry produced by permanent laws." Referring to those "motives of licentiousness already too powerful," which would draw encouragement from this state of affairs, Madison in effect read Jefferson a small lecture on the 1780s and the impulses that had led him and his fellow reformers to produce the Constitution and secure its adoption.[82]

From Madison's standpoint, Jefferson still had much to learn about the course of American politics during his absence in France. Yet, as he had noted in the beginning of his reply, the 6 September 1789 letter was directly relevant to the task before Congress, of "providing for public debts." And this was Madison's second category of legislation, that of irrevocable laws. His major point here was to insist that there were indeed burdens that might legitimately be imposed on future generations. "The *improvements* made by the dead form a charge against the living who take the benefit of them," he urged. Indeed, he would go so far as to argue that "debts may even be incurred principally for the benefit of posterity," a conception Jefferson's principle did not allow. Moving from the general to the particular, Madison characterized "the present debt of the U. States" as such a debt. In fact, he thought, that debt "far exceeds any burdens which the present generation could well apprehend for itself. The term of 19 years," he added, contradicting Jefferson's optimism on this score, "might not be sufficient for discharging the debts" in this case.[83]

If Jefferson had hoped that Madison would follow his advice and urge the adoption of his principle in the form of a "preamble" to the funding law, Madison was about to disappoint him. Not because he wished "to impeach either the utility of the principle in some particular cases; or the general importance of it in the eye of the philosophical Legislator," he explained at the end of his reply. Rather, it was because he doubted that the "spirit of philosophical legislation" was "the fashion here, either within or without Congress," that he was forced to admit that "our hemisphere must be still more enlightened before many of the sublime truths which are seen thro' the medium of Philosophy, become visible to the naked eye of the ordinary Politician." If left to him, Madison assured Jefferson, it would give him "singular pleasure to see [the principle] first announced in the proceedings of the U. States, and always kept in their view, as a salutary curb on the living generation from imposing unjust or unnecessary burdens on their successors."[84] But this was one pleasure Madison did not expect to share with his friend.

A week after writing his reply to Jefferson, Madison finally broke his silence in the House of Representatives, rising to make a major speech on Hamilton's proposals. His message was clear: He was for discrimination in favor of the original holders of the domestic debt.[85] Many of those who heard him were shocked; he was, after all, the co-author of the *Address to the States* of 1783, which had insisted on the injustice and impolitic nature of just such a measure.[86] Those who listened attentively would also have learned that Madison's larger notions about the debt differed in significant ways from Hamilton's. He took advantage of the opportunity to distance himself from what seemed to be the guiding principle of the secretary's *Report*, announcing that he had "never been a proselyte to the doctrine that public debts are public benefits. I consider them, on the contrary, as evils which ought to be removed as fast as honor and justice will permit, and shall heartily join in the means necessary for that purpose."[87] And in suggesting the criteria that ought to be employed in judging the claims under scrutiny, Madison presented a list that, again, parted company from Hamilton. For Madison, the "only principles" against which his, or Hamilton's, propositions for dealing with the debt should be measured were "1. Public justice; 2. public faith; 3. public credit; 4. public opinion."[88] As he developed these points, and particularly the first and the fourth, Madison would both repeat and enlarge themes he had raised more briefly in his letter to Hamilton the previous fall.

It was a fellow congressman from Virginia, Richard Bland Lee, representing the Northern Neck district taking in Alexandria and Mount Vernon, who provided the best explanation for Madison's decision to intervene in the question of discrimination on behalf of the original holders of the debt. Madison, Lee argued to a doubtful correspondent, had been activated by "the purest motives and a solicitude to establish the credit of the U. States on the firmest basis." As Lee recounted Madison's reasoning, "justice required that the claims Against the U. States ought to be modified in the manner proposed by him. And that such a Modification was essential to reconcile the public mind to the taxes which would necessarily be required." (Recall that Madison had discussed the question of acceptable taxes in his October letter to Hamilton.) Moreover, Lee continued, it was Madison's view that "in commencing our national existence—a sound regard to the natural dictates of Justice and gratitude would be the direct way to obtain the confidence of our own people, and that of the world." If by "so doing we should disregard maxims derived from and observed by the British nation," he added, this was hardly a valid objection to Madison's proposal, for that country, "since it contracted a national debt, never was in any situation similar to that of America and therefore would not be a proper guide on this occasion."[89]

Lee's gloss on Madison's position makes it clear that Madison was decidedly concerned with the problem of how to "reconcile the public mind" and "obtain the confidence of our own people"—with "public opinion," in short. And there is no question that Madison thought Hamilton's program would fail in precisely those respects. If nothing else, it would not be seen to do "justice," and by "justice" Madison meant something rather different from the sense in which Hamilton had used the term in his *Report*. In Madison's mind, it was the original holders forced to part with the debt at a fraction of its value who were the fitting objects of justice. They, after all, had "never really been paid" for "the value of the money, the service, or the property advanced by them." It was clear to Madison that "if any case were to happen among individuals, bearing an analogy to that of the public, a court of equity would interpose its redress."[90] It was accordingly this kind of "justice," correcting fraud and overbearing, that Madison sought to achieve, not the Hamiltonian notion of the strictest observance of contracts. And because justice must be seen to be done, not simply be done, Madison insisted on taking into account the effects on public opinion of a proposition that would leave "this exhorbitant accumulation of gain . . . made at the expence of the most meritorious part of the community" in the hands of speculators.[91] In his *Report*, Hamilton had referred to the latter as "enlightened men," and Madison now disputed that; "suffering" and "hardship" deserved more than mere verbal recognition, Madison felt, if true justice were to be done and public confidence in the moral rightness of the new government established.[92]

There were those who thought they discerned in Madison's assertion of the importance of public opinion a weakening of the Virginian's formerly stern resolve against "improper or wicked" projects.[93] Congressional supporters of Hamilton's *Report*, who found Madison's about-face on discrimination "astonishing," were sure they knew what lay behind this apparent concession to the obviously misguided views of his constituents: Madison had lost his nerve.[94] "He is so much a Virginian," Fisher Ames informed a friend, "so afraid that the mob will cry out, *crucify him*; sees Patrick Henry's shade at his bedside every night; fears so much the eastern confederacy, and perhaps thinks it unpleasant to come in as an auxiliary to support another's plan."[95] Ames may have been indulging in a little sectional pride by implicitly suggesting that Massachusetts Federalists were made of sterner stuff than the vacillating Virginian gentry, and his suggestion that Madison's amour propre had been wounded by seeing the glory go to Hamilton was probably without foundation, but he had sensed, correctly, that beneath Madison's concern for "public opinion" there lay a real anxiety about the views of Virginia and about the views of Patrick Henry and the Antifederalists in particular.

That Madison's fears were not the product of an overheated imagination was evident soon enough. His Virginia correspondents had been slow to comment on Hamilton's *Report*, but in the aftermath of his speeches on discrimination their letters began to reach New York, the contents confirming that Madison had not misread Virginia's mood.[96] Richard Bland Lee's brother and Madison's old friend and sometime partner in land speculation, Light-Horse Harry, judged the *Report* "abhorrent to political wisdom & not strictly consonant to justice," lauded the idea of discrimination, and then launched into a blistering philippic against everything the *Report* stood for. "Funding systems belong to arbitrary governments," Henry Lee pronounced, assailing "the mischief & wickedness of such policy." Lee's reading of the British "exemplum" convinced him that "a system wicked in its beginning suitable (if at all suitable) only to a nation whose situation genius

& habits direct them to commercial pursuits, & which must terminate in national bankruptcy," would be fatal to America. And he went on to explain why the adoption of such a system would harm the agricultural interest while permitting some individuals to "amass princely fortunes by stock-jobbing." The moral effects on society of encouraging such behavior would be equally deleterious, Lee insisted: "What can be denominated the habit of supporting life, subsisting family &c. by buying & selling in the funds, when contrasted with the habit of performing the same object by tilling the earth[?] Avarice, deception falsehood & constant overreaching belong to the first, while contentment, moderation, hospitality, frugality & a love to mankind result from the last." Lee spoke in the powerful clichés of the Augustan pastoral, invoking its contrast of the country and the city, ignoring his own penchant for land speculation and attributing to himself the "tilling the earth" his slaves and tenants actually performed. But he pointed to a problem that would be central for the Jeffersonians: "Ought not then the U States possessing extensive & fertile territory abominate the policy, which in addition to other evils, depretiates the morals of their citizens?" he asked.[97]

Indeed, Lee's letter was nothing if not a textbook of orthodox sentiments on the subject of debt, made more interesting by the vigor of his language and, as Madison probably did not know, by Lee's having approached Hamilton in advance of the release of the *Report* for inside information with which, presumably, he planned to shore up his none too solid finances.[98] Yet Lee's letter should not be seen as the product of a disappointed hypocrite; it is, rather, a catalogue of typical Virginia responses, responses that came naturally to members of the gentry like Lee and Jefferson and Madison. Lee's predictions of the consequences of Hamilton's program can be read as a prospectus for Virginia's position during the first three administrations—ironically so, since in time Lee would become one of the small but devoted band of Virginia Federalists.[99] In 1790, however, Lee was sure he knew where Hamilton's "wickedness" was leading: "But where the people are really free & mean to be so, where the govt. is absolutely their own property, political tricks of this kind are abominable & dangerous in their effects. If they succeed completely," he warned, "national debts will be encouraged by wanton expeditions, wars & useless expences." The results, Lee thought, could already be predicted: "This encrease of the peoples burthen, will in exact proportion encrease the operation & influence of the principle, & the one will continue to cherish the other untill the weight of oppression shall force the people to recur to first principles, or the Government shall have changed hands."[100]

Other correspondents used language less colorful than Lee's but endorsed his logic. True, it appeared at first that sentiment in Virginia's commercial centers was opposed to discrimination but, Madison dismissively told Attorney General Edmund Randolph, this was "the natural language of towns, and decides nothing."[101] Against this, Madison could weigh the approbation of George Mason and the views of such men as Walter Jones, Joseph Jones (whose "heart approved it, as I felt the force of its equitable

principles," even though he doubted its practicality), and George Lee Turberville ("I am entirely of yr. opinion").[102] Sympathy for the plight of
Revolutionary veterans was evident throughout these comments, as was
its converse, a decided distaste for the activities of the speculators who stood
to profit by the defeat of discrimination. Even Hamilton's old friend from
their days together in the army and another future Virginia Federalist,
Edward Carrington, though opposed to discrimination, conceded that
"the purchases have in many instances be[en] made under dishonorable
conduct."[103]

Like Lee, the writers of these letters were troubled by the obvious
similarity between Hamilton's plan and what they knew of the British
system of finance. Edmund Pendleton admitted that Hamilton's "plan of
finance is really too deep for my comprehension," but found it impossible to
agree "with his position that Public debt is a blessing; it may be a convenient
engine to Government, considered as having a distinct Interest from that of
the Citizens, but can never be so, where they are united, as ought to be our
case."[104] George Lee Turberville was "persuaded that the funding business
founded upon loans will never answer in America," which, unlike Britain,
was not yet "thickly populated—as commercial and as highly Cultivated."[105]
Water Jones referred Madison to the "most impartial & enlightened writers
& speakers on the Subject," who uniformly maintained "the ruinous tendency of [Britain's] national Debt & its consequences."[106] These early returns—and they would be followed by others as assumption displaced
discrimination at the center of the political stage—strongly suggest that
Madison knew precisely what he was talking about when he argued his case
for a plan that would take public opinion into account. In Virginia, that
public opinion would increasingly range itself on Madison's side.

It was, of course, assumption rather than discrimination that in the end
made all the difference. If the latter was no more than a curtain raiser, the
former was high drama, act after act of it, with enough set pieces and plot
turnings to satisfy the most rabid devotee of the cliff-hanger. In retrospect, it
is clear why assumption should have become *the* issue, especially for the
Virginians. Hamilton had managed to frame the question in such a way that
it seemed manifestly unfair to Virginians of all persuasions; no matter how
they felt about discrimination in favor of the original holders of the debt, or
even about modified forms of assumption of the debt, what Hamilton
offered was unacceptable to them.[107] Moreover, it substantially increased the
debt, and for those who were already worried about the size and permanence
of the debt, this was hardly a recommendation. But perhaps most important, by the time assumption came up for debate, Virginians had had the
opportunity to reflect on the treasury secretary's plans. Their growing
suspicions found an outlet in condemning assumption, which they would
have disliked in any case, and the two attitudes fed on each other. It was also
their last chance; the resentments that had built up ever since the *Report*'s
release would either be satisfied by the defeat of assumption or not be satisfied
at all. It only helped, of course, that the struggle over assumption went on

and on, month after month; by the time it was resolved, nearly everyone had had a chance to commit himself—against it.

It was this second phase of the struggle over the *Report*, then, that was under way when Jefferson arrived in New York toward the end of March 1790.[108] Soon thereafter, letters from Virginia denouncing assumption began reaching Madison. They—like those that followed in the months to come—had only one message. "The Idea of consolidating the debt of the States with that of the Union," George Lee Turberville informed Madison, "is a very unpopular one & for that reason ought to be laid aside."[109] Edward Carrington, too, reported its unpopularity, calling it "a subject of discontent" and wondering "whether the Constitution is yet so firmly on its legs that it cannot be shocked."[110] From Madison's own congressional district, John Dawson predicted that, if passed, assumption was likely to "draw some very spirited Resolutions from the next assembly"—which in fact turned out to be the case—"as it is thought a wanton interference of Congress and an attempt to hasten a consolidation."[111] The "ill-judged & improper measure," opined Edmund Pendleton, "fix'd a Suspicion of a Government by a Junto," adding, like Dawson, that the authority of Congress to enact an assumption "will be questioned."[112] In addition, "should the measure be at length adopted I fear it will give Disquiet to the People & perhaps produce some warm animadversions from the Legislature," Governor Beverley Randolph wrote from Richmond.[113]

Even later in the House session, as arrangements were going forward to secure the passage of a modified assumption, Virginians at home continued to urge resistance and point out the dangers of the measure in any version. "The assumption will be dislik'd here from what I can learn, under any shape it can assume," the moderate Antifederalist James Monroe insisted.[114] "I do not know any event which would cause such general discontent in this state," John Dawson warned Madison, and as late as 1 August 1790 he described the measure as "hideous in any form."[115] Governor Randolph confessed himself "sorry to find that we are still haunted by the Assumption Business. Should it be adopted in any Form I fear it will give great Disquiet in this State," he added, echoing the language he had used on an earlier occasion.[116] But perhaps the most telling comments were those invoking the name of Patrick Henry. Governor Randolph reported that Henry thought assumption "unconstitutional & will I believe oppose it upon that Ground."[117] The merchant Thomas Pleasants, Jr., a long-standing correspondent, reported that he had discovered "a prevailing Wish that Mr. H—y was in Congress," but Dawson sent word that Henry, learning of the plan for assumption, "earnestly requested the people to elect him [to the House of Delegates], which the[y] accordingly did."[118] With Henry back on the warpath, Madison and Jefferson had good cause to worry.

Yet the Antifederalists, from Henry on down, had no cause for complaint in the position adopted by the Virginia Federalists in the House of Representatives.[119] Led by Madison, the state's delegation—with the sole exception of maverick Theodorick Bland—stood firm against assumption.

Speeches by the Virginians denounced it in unmistakable terms, expounding the themes they had already begun to explore during the debate on discrimination. They warned of the effect on public opinion in Virginia. Alexander Moore assured the House that if the Virginia ratifying convention had imagined that the taxes necessary to support such a plan "would have been attempted at so early a day, I think they would have hesitated to adopt the Constitution."[120] John Page, Jefferson's friend since their days together at William and Mary, announced that assumption was obviously that "consolidation" Virginia opponents of the Constitution had predicted; it would, he said, "prove the truth of the predictions of the enemies of this Government, and wound the feelings of its friends, who so often declared that they could pledge themselves that Congress would never lay direct taxes but in cases of extreme necessity."[121]

The question of taxes was much in the Virginians' minds, and they were obviously worried about their constituents' reaction to the levies needed to support Hamilton's consolidated debt. Alexander White thought "the people would very ill brook the payment of taxes, when they saw the amount flow into the hands of a few individuals."[122] Richard Bland Lee seconded White's observation; sure that "to induce a free people to pay taxes, they must be convinced of the necessity and equity of them," he fleshed out his contention by asking rhetorically "if, on the contrary, our measures should appear irreconcilable to the popular idea of equity and right, is it probable that they would meet with that hearty support from the community, which, under our Government, is essential to a prosperous administration of it?"[123]

Nor did the House delegation lag far behind Virginia opinion when it came to denouncing the dangerous parallels between the treasury secretary's program and the British system of finance. White was alarmed by what appeared to be an intention "to fund all the debt, and to make no arrangement for the discharge thereof," nor did he understand how "perpetuating a public debt" could be "advantageous to any country." Even so, "gentlemen appear dazzled with the splendor of Great Britain, supposing that her prosperity is owing to her debts; but the reverse is the case, it was her peculiar circumstances that enable her to support her debts." And White was quite certain that things were heading for a crash: "Were he an Englishman, he would tremble for the event; sure he was, that at some future period, the nation must sink under the weight of its debt, or it must be wiped out with a sponge to the ruin of thousands." Americans, White concluded, ought to "profit from the British example, for the same consequences might follow the perpetuation of the debt in these states, though the period might be more remote."[124]

This was strong language, and Madison himself used it in his speeches on assumption, particularly in his major address of 22 April 1790, the longest to have come down to us. Here again, in addition to repeating his conviction that an unmodified assumption was essentially unfair to states like Virginia that had made good progress in discharging their debts, Madison returned once more to the theme of public opinion. As for those who claimed that failure to assume "will create a spirit of opposition to the government; in short, that it will endanger the union itself," Madison thought they were simply blind to realities: "If the refusal to assume the state debts would produce dangerous consequences to the union from the discontents that it is apprehended will grow out of the measure, much more have we to fear from an assumption." In truth, Madison thought, "if we could ascertain the opinions of our constituents, individually, I believe we should find four fifths of the citizens of the United States against assumption; I believe we should find more."[125] And he proceeded to contrast the conditions of Massachusetts and Virginia should assumption pass.

"Massachusetts will then get rid of her embarrassments; but what would be the situation of Virginia?" Virginians were indebted to one another, Madison answered his own question, "to the amount of both the public and private debts" of Massachusetts, in addition to which "the people of Virginia are indebted to foreigners to a greater amount than the whole debt of Massachusetts." Yet despite this, it was Massachusetts, not Virginia, that assumption proposed to relieve.[126] Madison ended his remarks by addressing directly the threats of disunion the controversy over assumption had produced; those in favor of the measure, he recommended, should "no longer . . . assume a pre-eminence over us in the nationality of their motives," and he hoped that they "would forebear those frequent assertions, that if the state debts are not provided for, the federal debts shall also go unprovided for; nay, that if the state debts are not assumed, the union will be endangered."[127]

Threatened, or so it seemed by the end of April 1790, with disunion if the state debts were not assumed, and with a violent revival of Antifederalism in Virginia under Patrick Henry's formidable aegis if they were, Madison found himself in a less than enviable position. Meanwhile, there would be no permanent footing for the domestic and foreign debts unless the question of assumption could be resolved to mutual satisfaction, a prospect that, as April gave way to May, appeared increasingly remote.[128] To be sure, Madison had always known that a modified assumption was a possible escape from the dilemma confronting Congress, and even at this stage there were already hints of the compromise that would eventually emerge. In early April, Richard Bland Lee was ready to assure his brother Theodorick that "the assumption of the state debts . . . will certainly operate injuriously to Virginia, unless the seat of government was so stationed as to diffuse the Wealth of the Capitol in equal measures to the extremes of the empire. In which case the poison of the measure would be very much diminished." But as matters stood, Lee thought, assumption was "very odious to the state of Virginia—from every account we receive from thence."[129] A Potomac site for the capital that would "diffuse the Wealth" as a corrective to the unfairness of assumption—Lee was not the only Virginian thinking in these terms—was an idea whose time would come, but not until the crisis had matured.[130] Something would have to overcome Madison's sense that assumption of the state debts was disastrous as a policy, and not least because it led Virginia Federalists like

Light-Horse Harry Lee to declare that "[Patrick] Henry already is considered as a prophet, his predictions are daily verifying. His declaration with respect to the division of interest which would exist under the constitution & predominate in all the doings of the govt. already has been undeniably proved."[131]

By early June, the crisis had come to a head, and the time for serious bargaining was now at hand. The states demanding assumption were implacable, the Virginians–Abigail Adams said Madison led them "like a flock of sheep"–equally reluctant to move, the more so, no doubt, because they had firmly and publicly committed themselves to a position that earned them universal applause in the Old Dominion.[132] Up until this point, Jefferson later insisted, he had scrupulously refrained from meddling in business not directly related to his duties in the State Department.[133] Nevertheless, the crisis did not catch him by surprise. Ever since his return to Virginia the previous December, Jefferson, too, had monitored both the progress of Hamilton's program and the condition of Virginia Antifederalism. Shortly after landing at Norfolk, he had observed that "Antifederalism is not yet dead in this country. The gentlemen who opposed it retain a good deal of malevolence towards the new government. Henry is it's [*sic*] avowed foe. He stands higher in public estimation than he ever did."[134] Jefferson also took time to read John Nicholas's violently anti-Henry diatribe, *The Letters of Decius*, carefully noting in the margins of his copy–a present from the author, who explained that "the Work is founded on an opinion of a *certain Statesman*, in the most essential point, similar to that of Mr. Jefferson's own"–the identities of the Virginia figures Nicholas pilloried.[135] Jefferson's worries about the persistence of Virginia Antifederalism were also evident in his 12 February 1790 reply to a welcoming address from his Albemarle County neighbors. "Let us then, my dear friends," he advised them, urging acceptance of the Constitution, "for ever bow down to the general reason of the society. We are safe with that, even in it's [*sic*] deviations, for it soon returns again to the right way."[136] And while he could assure correspondents in France like Lafayette and Richard Gem that the new Constitution faced little opposition, Jefferson knew that it had powerful enemies in Virginia.[137]

He was also following another set of developments directly affected by Hamilton's intervention, this one the fate of the American debt to France. Even before leaving Paris, Jefferson was disturbed by the possibility that financial necessity might drive the French government to sell its American debt to one of several groups of speculators eager to arrange such a transfer. Given the inability of the United States to pay, there was at least a plausible case for sale of the debt; a bird in the hand, after all, would be worth more than any number in the bush to the hard-pressed French ministry.[138] But Jefferson thought this would be a political disaster of the first magnitude for both countries and had done his best to persuade the French that the United States would act promptly, once the Constitution went into effect, to put its foreign debt on a proper–that is, paying–footing.[139] The impasse over Hamilton's program thus had serious consequences for Jefferson's hopes. By early April, disagreement about the domestic and state debts was impeding "the Act of Justice and Gratitude to the Court of France" that Jefferson was sure the United States intended to make and that alone seemed to hold out hope that a "disadvantageous Alienation" of the debt could be prevented.[140] Jefferson trusted that a copy of the unanimous resolution for funding the foreign debt would encourage the French ministry to hold onto the American debt, but as April turned into May and then May into June without passage of the necessary implementing legislation, his doubts must have grown.[141]

And there were also other problems worrying Jefferson that spring, problems that would have a bearing on his willingness to urge a compromise. Given his awareness that opposition to the Constitution was alive and flourishing in Virginia, he knew how important it was for Washington to remain in the presidency. "If," he told Lafayette, "the President can be preserved a few years till habits of authority and obedience can be established, generally, we have nothing to fear." But, he added, "I am sorry to tell you his health is less firm than it used to be."[142] Although there seemed to be no immediate danger, Jefferson was concerned by what might happen should Washington die in office–and the president's near fatal illness in May would only have increased those fears.[143] Jefferson hoped that time would heal the wounds inflicted during the struggle over the Constitution, but he also had to consider the possibility that something might interrupt the process of creating "habits of authority and obedience" before they became automatic.

Nor did Jefferson overlook the possibility that the danger might be external rather than internal. In the eighteenth-century world, war could never be ruled out, and the new United States was woefully unprepared to fight one. With an ill-equipped army of no more than a few hundred men and, as yet, neither a navy nor public credit, the country was in no position either to resist foreign aggression or to take advantage of the opportunities war might create.[144] Jefferson was sure that a neutral United States would reap a "golden harvest" from a renewal of European conflict, but even so it must have been apparent that such bounties would be more secure if the country could protect itself.[145] Just how precariously posed the nation was would become evident in mid-June 1790 when news reached New York of the likelihood of war between Britain and Spain–both colonial powers whose American possessions bounded the United States.[146] But even before the so-called Nootka Crisis added a further dimension to the complexity of high politics that summer, Jefferson knew that the United States had yet to make itself internationally respectable. A sound public credit, as he had long recognized, was an essential foundation for that respectability.

And yet, as the crisis over the debt gathered momentum, it was increasingly possible that there might not be a United States to be respectable. Until early June, Jefferson's comments on the domestic politics of funding and assumption had been relatively few and generally measured in tone. He described assumption to his son-in-law Thomas Mann Randolph, Jr., as "one of those questions which present great inconveniencies whichever way it is decided: so that it offers only a choice of evils," and to his correspondents he must have seemed far more interested in the outcome of the struggle over the location of the capital, for it was this, in early June, that he constantly mentioned in his letters.[147] Even then, it seemed more a matter of wanting to know where he should have his Parisian furniture and household goods sent than one of concern for the political implications such a decision was bound to have.[148] What Jefferson did not mention to his correspondents, though, was the impasse that had been reached in Congress; there was nothing in his letters to prepare them for the role he was now quietly about to play.

At some point in mid-June—we cannot be sure of the date, though it seems to have been on or about 20 June—Jefferson had his famous encounter with Hamilton before the president's door.[149] The treasury secretary was "in despair," Jefferson later recalled, and the two men fell into a discussion of the political crisis. Perhaps this was what Jefferson and Madison had been waiting for; only days before the encounter, Jefferson had approached Senator Robert Morris of Pennsylvania, seeking a resolution of the residence question, while Madison had let the Massachusetts delegation know that a properly modified assumption could pass if Virginia had assurances on the residence.[150] In any event, Jefferson seized his opportunity, inviting Hamilton to a dinner where Madison would be the only other guest. And then it was done: After the meal, over wine and nuts, the Virginians and the New Yorker came to some sort of terms, terms later summarized as the Dinner Table Bargain.[151] In fact, it probably took a good deal more than an afternoon's wheeling and dealing to put all the pieces together, but from the Virginia point of view what mattered was the assurance that Virginia's claims would be generously treated in the assumption of the state debts— painful though it was to agree to it on any terms—and the promise that, after ten years' temporary residence in Philadelphia, the Potomac would have the permanent location of the new capital of the United States.[152] For their part, the Virginians would have to see that sufficient votes were available to ensure passage of the blocked financial legislation, and in the end two Virginia representatives—Richard Bland Lee and Alexander White—along with two representatives and a senator from Maryland, three of the House members with districts bordering the Potomac and the fourth from Maryland's Eastern Shore, switched their votes.[153] Madison was allowed to maintain his official opposition to the bitter end, while those whose positions changed were expected to justify themselves to the voters by appealing to the benefits the Potomac site would produce in their districts.[154] The deal was done.

But the Virginians in Congress now had a good deal of explaining to do. Few of them—apart from Richard Bland Lee and, in all probability, George Washington—were entirely comfortable with the outcome.[155] It had taken considerable pressure to bring them to the bargaining table, considerable pressure to get some of them to play their assigned roles. Alexander White, Jefferson later remembered, agreed to his part "with a revulsion of the stomach almost convulsive."[156] None of them expected the Dinner Table Bargain to be popular in Virginia, and their correspondents kept assuring them that was indeed the case. Edmund Pendleton, for one, worried that so many concessions would only "fortify & Cherish an Opinion, some Gentn. appear to have entertained, that they are to dictate to the Union, against the sense of a Majority."[157] James Monroe, for another, expressed the thought that must have bothered many: What guarantee was there, when push came to shove, that the Potomac capital would ever become a reality? At the least, it was ten years away, and in the meantime who knew what nefarious tricks the Philadelphians and their supporters might manage to play?[158] The force of such reasoning and the effect it was likely to have on Virginia opinion would lead Washington, Jefferson, and Madison to spend a good deal of time over the next few years making sure that the new federal city got off the ground.[159] As for Virginia's stand on assumption, that was not going to change no matter what modifications the state's delegation secured, and the worst predictions about Virginia reactions to it, whatever its form, would be verified when the state legislature met in the fall.[160] And most of all, perhaps, Virginians with firm commitments on the question of debt had to explain how they had come to agree to the creation of a funded debt on the British model, a debt increasingly concentrated in the hands of speculators, a debt so obviously dangerous to the republican experiment. Madison had already pronounced it an "evil," and Fisher Ames reported that "he speaks of the assumption as increasing & perpetuating the *evil* of a debt. –This word *evil* is always in his mouth when he speaks of our debt."[161] But Madison was speaking for his peers at home as well as for himself. How, in that case, could he and Jefferson justify what had been done?

That some measure of justification was required seemed obvious to both men. From late June on, well before the Dinner Table Bargain had been officially recorded in the form of legislation, Jefferson, whose Virginia correspondence had hitherto touched on little other than family and business matters, began to write letters in what looks very much like the late-eighteenth-century equivalent of a public-relations campaign. He opened by addressing himself to George Mason–a powerful voice, and one to whom Madison, after the Virginia ratifying convention, could scarcely have turned for sympathetic understanding–developing what would be his standard argument, a need for compromise, "to give as well as take in a government like ours."[162] This was on 13 June 1790, and in each of several succeeding weeks the same message went out to other correspondents.[163] He wrote to his son-in-law Thomas Mann Randolph, Jr., in Albemarle and to Monroe in Fredericksburg on 20 June, to his old Albemarle acquaintance George Gilmer on 27 June, to his brother-in-law Francis Eppes of Chesterfield County on 4 July, and as the weeks passed he continued to keep them abreast of the legislation's progress as it worked its way through Congress.[164]

Throughout, he stressed the need for "some plan of compromise," without which, it seemed clear, "there will be no funding bill agreed to, our credit . . . will burst and vanish, and the states separate to take care every-one of itself." He admitted that he was not happy with the idea of even a modified assumption, but insisted that "some mutual sacrifices" were necessary "for the sake of the union, and to save us from the greatest of all calamities, the total extinction of our credit in Europe."[165] These were his words to Monroe, who needed a good deal of convincing, and he gave the same message to others. "If they separate without funding there is an end of the government," he assured his son-in-law; a total rejection of assumption, he explained to Gilmer, "will prevent their funding any part of the public debt, and will be something very like a dissolution of the government"; insisting that assumption could be modified to make it less unpalatable, he told his brother-in-law Eppes that refusing it entirely would prevent "the funding of the public debt altogether, which would be tantamount to a dissolution of the government."[166] Nothing in these letters, whose language is fairly standardized, suggests that Jefferson intended their recipients to keep the contents private; on the contrary, he must have expected his correspondents to spread the information they contained—and even more their underlying arguments in favor of the Dinner Table Bargain—among their friends and neighbors.

Madison, as befits his role in the affair, was less positive than Jefferson about what was taking place, but he, too, let his correspondents understand both the gravity of the crisis and the need for extraordinary measures to overcome it. To Monroe and Edmund Pendleton, he gave broad hints late in June that something was likely to happen, and a month later he was admitting to Monroe that "the crisis demands a spirit of accommodation to a certain extent. If the measure [i.e., the modified assumption] should be adopted, I shall wish it to be considered as an unavoidable evil, and *possibly* not the worst side of the dilemma."[167] To his father, after assumption had finally carried, Madison allowed that there had been "serious danger of a very unfavorable issue to the Session from a contrary decision," adding that it was "now incumbent on us all to make the best of what is done," the more so since, "in a pecuniary light, the assumption is no longer of much consequence to Virginia."[168] And, for distribution to his constituents in the forthcoming congressional election, he prepared a statement designed to reconcile them to the inevitable; the residence question, he said, had "been decided in a manner more favorable to Virginia than was hoped," while assumption had "been purged of some of its objections and particularly of its gross injustice to Virginia, which in a pecuniary view is now little affected one way or the other."[169] But Madison's guarded position on assumption, as expressed to the voters, revealed the problem that confronted him—and Jefferson. Modifications had "purged some" of the objectionable features, but not all.

The basic objections remained. As George Nicholas put it to Madison in May, "the funding system is dangerous. . . . A government that relies for support on it's [*sic*] creditors and not on the affections of the people cannot be durable."[170] Clearly, assumption was not likely to increase the government's store of "affections" in Virginia. From the start, Madison had realized that Hamilton's program posed precisely that danger; it would alienate the affections of Virginia, driving the Old Dominion back into the arms of Patrick Henry, undermining the republican experiment—that last chance to demonstrate the viability of free government–before it had fairly begun. Yet, by June, it had become obvious that without assumption there would be no experiment at all. Forced to choose, Jefferson and Madison weighed the alternatives and found neither of them very attractive. Assumption threatened to revive Antifederalism in Virginia; failure to assume would block the passage of any financial legislation and thus destroy both American credit in Europe and, it seemed, the Union itself. The cost of salvaging the Union and its foreign credit was high: Assumption would enlarge the funded debt–the very idea of which was anathema to right-thinking Virginians–and with it would come the political revenge of the state's Antifederalists led by Henry. Jefferson's only consolation came from his conviction that "it is not foreseen that any thing so generative of dissension can arise again, and therefore the friends of government hope that, this difficulty once surmounted in the states, every thing will work well."[171] But suppose "this difficulty"– assumption–was not in fact "surmounted" in states like Virginia? Observers on the spot were not sanguine; John Harvie, Jr., a high official in the state's land office, was calling the measure "a Bitter pill" in early August and noting that "the friends to the Government must soften it to the people as far as truth and Reason will justify."[172] Jefferson and Madison were trying to do just that, but with what success they could not be sure.

Born out of conflicting priorities, Jefferson's reluctant agreement to the passage of assumption by no means implied any surrender of his core of beliefs about debt or acceptance of the rationale behind Hamilton's program. On the contrary, shortly before the Dinner Table Bargain was arranged, he had shown himself adamantly opposed to much of the content of Hamilton's *Report* and particularly to Hamilton's insistence on "security of transfer" both as a principle of justice in itself and as an essential means of supporting public credit among those whose views really counted: the monied men of the community.[173] In his opinion on the Joint Resolutions on the Arrears of Pay, delivered to Washington on 3 June 1790, Jefferson demonstrated that he, for one, had yet to accept the logic of Hamilton's worldview.[174] The opinion, with its background, is worth considering at length, if only because it will suggest the deep differences between Jefferson's Virginia view of debt and the competing position of Hamilton and his friends, differences that the temporary compromise on assumption would only paper over, and paper over only briefly at that. Taken together with the evidence already reviewed, Jefferson's opinion will suggest how difficult it was for him to find a consistent and satisfying position in 1790; caught between irreconcilable demands, he was beginning to learn that all was not simple, direct republicanism in the new nation. As we shall see in the next chapter, the force of Jefferson's reaction to the expanding scope of Hamilton's program owes not a little to the kinds of initial compromises he had had to make in 1790.

Jefferson's opinion on the Joint Resolutions on the Arrears of Pay arose from a relatively minor incident.[175] In 1789, the first session of Congress had appropriated funds to cover some $40,000 in arrears of pay due to Revolutionary War veterans of the North Carolina and Virginia continental lines, but the Treasury Department had taken no steps to notify those entitled of the sums waiting for them.[176] This was a situation tailor-made for speculators, and thanks to his connection with a government clerk, a New York securities dealer named William J. Vredenburgh was able to obtain detailed information about the claimants and the amounts due them. He then dispatched an agent, James Reynolds, to Virginia to buy up claims.[177] Reynolds would later gain notoriety as the blackmailing husband of Hamilton's inamorata, Maria; in 1790, he was simply another of the scores of agents scouring the countryside in search of quick gains in the securities market.[178] His business techniques were simple and effective: He lied. Showing prospects what purported to be an authentic list of the sums due them, Reynolds grossly understated what they were owed. Because no provision had been made to pay the veterans' claims in Virginia, Reynolds had little difficulty convincing the former soldiers that they were better off selling out and avoiding the expense of a trip to New York, an expense that on his showing (and in fact, given the true amounts of their claims) would have been far greater than the sums they could have collected.[179] There was nothing unusual about speculators purchasing claims at a healthy discount, and while Reynolds's practices may have been sharper than most, it was hard to distinguish them from those employed by apparently more respectable men who had been taking similar advantage of the ignorance and need of veterans ever since the end of the war.[180]

What made this case different was a special and to some extent fortuitous circumstance. For once, Congress had actually appropriated money to pay the veterans in full—ordinarily, Congress and the states did no more than pay interest on outstanding obligations—and Virginians who read the newspapers were aware of this unusually generous provision.[181] Moreover, Reynolds had the bad luck to be operating in a climate increasingly hostile to speculation. Madison's stand on discrimination in favor of original holders of debt reflected this sentiment, and other Virginians like Washington's friend David Stuart found it perfectly appropriate that spring to refer to "vermin from the Northward, [who] have been posting through the Country, purchasing up, indiscrim[in]ately, all evidences of the public debt."[182] Those who dealt in securities in Virginia felt it necessary to distance themselves, one purchaser who claimed he had bought "at 2, 3, and 4 for 1" denouncing those who "purchased certificates at 8 and 10 for one"; they were, he said, *"those leeches, those usurers, who have so basely imposed on the soldiers,"* who had nothing in common with honest men and could not be sufficiently condemned.[183] Impositions had been practiced, the governor and Council of State agreed, notifying the public in 1786 that claims submitted by other than original holders had to be accompanied by an order in writing from the original holder and a certificate from a justice of the peace of the country where the original holder resided stating that the order was signed and delivered in his presence.[184] Indeed, there were even fears that some Virginians in public office might be involved in such unsavory business, and the state solicitor, Leighton Wood, found himself called on to defend clerks in his office against a charge lodged by the governor and Council of State that they were engaged in securities speculation.[185]

But the critical factor in the case seems to have been Reynolds's inability to keep quiet. He talked too much, and he talked to the wrong men. In particular, he talked to Gustavus B. Wallace of Fredericksburg, and it was Wallace–Revolutionary War officer, merchant, and staunch supporter of the Constitution–who informed his congressman, James Madison, of Reynolds's dealings with innocent and ignorant veterans. "Reynolds," Wallace reported to Madison on 25 March 1790, was "purchaseing these balances at the rate of 3/ in the pound he was in this town, shew'd me his list of Names, from the pay master books, and the ballances due to each man." At this point, Wallace had not yet grasped the full extent of Reynolds's scheme; it was simply apparent that he was buying up the claims at a fraction of their face value. Nevertheless, Wallace was outraged: "At the request of some gent. in this place I give you this information that if possible this trade may be put a Stop to and the Soldiers get the whole of their money which may be done with ease by publishing the list of Names belonging to each State in the State news paper's [*sic*] and the Sums due them."[186]

Wallace's letter reached Madison by 10 April, the date on which Madison answered him. Although Madison's reply is lost, it must have encouraged Wallace to pursue the matter, for he wrote again, this time with further–and even more alarming–details of Reynolds's dubious practice. Evidently, Reynolds continued to talk too much, for Wallace was now able to supply Madison with the name and address of the New York dealer employing Reynolds–"William J. Vriedenburg No. 40 great Dock Street"–who, so Reynolds bragged to Wallace, "got the lists from a Clerk of the Treasury." "What makes this Speculation worse," Wallace added, having discovered the secret of Reynolds's scheme, "is that he shews a Soldier a list with a smaller sum than is really due him, and gets a power of Attorney for the whole that is due him with out mentioning the sum. There are Soldiers that have £ 24 due them and some less but on his list there appears to be none over Six dollars and this he buys for 1/6 or 2/."[187]

Madison now took action. He brought the matter to the attention of those responsible for administering the congressional grant, Secretary of the Treasury Alexander Hamilton and Secretary of War Henry Knox. Urging them to protect the veterans against "so flagrant an imposition," Madison proposed that they refuse to pay any assigned claims; alternatively, he argued, Congress should put a stop to the frauds by passing appropriate legislation. But both secretaries showed considerable reluctance to alter the settled routines of their departments by scrutinizing assigned claims valid on their face, and Madison was forced to conclude that "the uncertainty and inconveniency of obtaining an interposition of Congress" made that course unsuitable. Together with Hamilton and Knox, Madison then worked out a solution that combined publicity with a legal challenge to the validity of the assignments. As Madison explained to the Virginia governor, Beverley Randolph, the federal authorities would act with the state government to right the wrongs done the veterans. Virginia would appoint an agent to gather evidence of the frauds; armed with powers of attorney from the veterans, this individual would come to New York and there bring suit "against the Officer who will be authorized to pay the Sums due (for which [suit] pecuniary aid will not be wanting) and the fraud may in this way be ascertained and redressed." The suit would call into question the validity of the assignments–that they were valid would be the defense set up by the paying officer when the agent sued to enjoin payment of claims whose assignments had been fraudulently procured–and so the question would be resolved in a manner that was both expeditious and acknowledged the position of the Treasury Department and the War Department on the need not to create unsatisfactory precedents that would complicate administrative routine and undermine investors' confidence. In the meantime, Madison hoped, "the mere institution of the suit will beget a disposition in those who have taken advantage to better their title by additional compensations to the parties injured, and . . . the appearance of such an investigation may deter from like practices in the future." Further, he urged the Virginia authorities to publish authenticated lists of the claims, thus alerting veterans to the true value of what they might otherwise be tempted to part with for a few shillings or even pennies in the pound.[188]

The measures devised by Hamilton, Knox, and Madison, and forwarded by Madison to Randolph and the Virginia Council of State, had a number of advantages. As Madison suggested, it was likely that they would put an end to the activities of James Reynolds and his ilk, and they offered a reasonable prospect of redress for those already injured. They also gave ample evidence that the administration took the matter very seriously, for there were strong suggestions in Madison's letter that the defrauded claimants would receive the government's full support in securing justice. And they were apparently acceptable to the Virginia executive, which appointed as its agent Captain Anthony Singleton (previously responsible for administering the state's sinking fund, Singleton had considerable experience in matters relating to securities) to gather information and proceed to New York. Lists were published in the Virginia newspapers and, as May began, the affair seemed well on the road to settlement.[189]

At this point, Madison could consider himself an able advocate for his constituents, taking pride in putting an unpleasant business to rest. Yet he must have regretted his inability to secure the same measure of justice for other original holders of the debt. Their case, generally put, was not so different from that of the Virginia veterans, and it would have been hard for Madison–or for Jefferson, who had arrived in New York on 21 March, four days before Gustavus Wallace wrote his letter informing Madison of the frauds–to distinguish between the two. It would certainly not have escaped their notice that in both instances Hamilton had insisted on maintaining the sanctity of contract, elevating the rights of purchasers over those of the original holders.[190] It may well have seemed to the Virginians in New York that Hamilton's willingness to permit suits in this instance was little more than window dressing, a timely concession, cosmetic in character, intended to prevent further deterioration in his relations with an important political group at a time when he needed all the support he could muster to secure the passage of his program. Nor is it entirely outside the realm of possibility that the president may have made his influence felt in this case. Years later, Madison would tell Jared Sparks that Washington had wished to see something done for his soldiers in the matter of discrimination, and if Madison's memory was accurate, Washington might well have let Hamilton and Knox know that these complaints from his old troops—many of them Virginians—deserved to be taken seriously.[191] In all, it would have been clear that this was another instance of having to extract justice—as Virginians understood it—from the Treasury Department, where that quality seemed in decidedly short supply. But to both Madison's and Jefferson's surprise, this was not the end of the matter.

Virginia's congressional delegates—whose inclination to follow Madison so impressed Abigail Adams—contained a wild card in the person of Theodorick Bland. Representing a Southside district in the heartland of Virginia Antifederalism, Bland played a curious role that spring. Flaunting his Antifederalism and engaging in pointed and no doubt embarrassing exchanges on the House floor with the rest of the delegation, he stood steadfastly behind the Treasury Department program.[192] His position on assumption was especially outrageous. Bland justified his support for Hamilton's measure on grounds that went straight to the heart of Madison's worst fears: Assumption, Bland repeatedly claimed, was exactly the kind of consolidation the Antifederalists had predicted the new Constitution would require, and by supporting it he was only drawing the logical consequences of the new system.[193] Bland had ambitions, and even as he was making a byword of himself by supporting assumption, he was casting about for ways to advance his political fortunes. He had his eye on the Virginia governorship, and it may be that he had expected to obtain it in 1788 with Patrick Henry's backing.[194] If so, one can understand his eagerness to appear as the champion of Virginia interests and something less than the tool of the Treasury Department, and the Arrears of Pay offered him the perfect opportunity. On 7 May, Bland introduced resolutions that would have required Secretary of War Knox to publish lists of claimants and the amounts due them and forbidden payment of any assigned claim except under carefully specified circumstances. The resolutions were then referred to a committee composed of Bland and one representative each from North and South Carolina.[195]

A week later, Bland's committee reported back. It offered three resolutions, two of them noncontroversial propositions to publish lists of claimants and to make arrangements for payments in the claimants' home states, and a third, and decidedly more controversial one, that would have forbidden payment except "to the original claimant, . . . or to such person or persons only as shall produce a power of Attorney, duly attested by two justices of the peace of the County in which such person or persons reside, authorizing him or them to receive a certain specified Sum."[196] The third resolution was the key; it invalidated existing assignments, which, following the procedure established in Virginia in 1786, had been attested by a single justice of the peace, not two. Securities dealers howled in protest, but Virginians were not prepared to listen.[197] In the brief House debate on the resolutions on 17 May, several members urged that the resolutions would interfere with the rights of contract and suggested that the courts provided adequate remedies for claimants alleging fraud. Madison confined his remarks to stating that the case was "extraordinary . . . , and as his colleague, Mr. White, had remarked, it could not be supposed that a poor soldier, who had but six dollars in dispute, would come all the way from Virginia to New York to commence an action against a speculator." As for the suggestion that it was improper for Congress to interfere, Madison dismissed it out of hand. "Congress had the power," he stated flatly, "and they ought to interfere in this business; for if this government has not the power to afford redress in cases like the present, it should be esteemed a government, not fit for honest men, but sharpers."[198]

None of the resolutions' opponents—and it was only the third resolution that was called into question—seem to have known of the administrative solution worked out with Hamilton and Knox, and the Virginian did nothing to enlighten the House on this score.[199] On the face of it, Madison's endorsement of Alexander White's argument about the cost of coming to New York seems less than candid; he knew, of course, that Virginia had the option of appointing an agent to act for the veterans, precisely because the authorities recognized that it would be impossible for individuals to make the trip. Because there is also nothing to suggest that the administrative arrangement had fallen apart—Hamilton would shortly cite its existence when arguing in favor of a presidential veto of the resolutions—Madison's behavior seems perplexing. Immediate political considerations must have been at work; it would have been a mistake to let Theodorick Bland reap all the credit, and, however much he disliked Bland's Antifederalism and perverse support of assumption, the issue was one on which Madison (and the rest of the Virginia delegation) could not afford to differ from their Southside colleague. Madison's support for discrimination had won considerable applause in Virginia, and he would not have wanted to risk that support, helpful as it might be in curbing Antifederalism in the Old Dominion, by opposing justice for the Virginia victims of a notorious fraud.[200]

But Madison would also have seen the resolutions as an opportunity to establish an important principle, and this was hinted at in his brief remarks. Congress did have the power to interfere, he had insisted in his effort to secure discrimination in favor of original holders; the sanctity of contract could not be allowed to mask injustice. Madison failed to convince his colleagues in the case of discrimination, but he remarked after defeat of his motion that "the prevailing sense of the people at large does not coincide with the decision, and that delay and other means might have produced a very different result."[201] Now he had a second chance, and without the complicating factor of administrative practicability.[202] That chance was too good to be missed, the principle of too much importance not to be established, and Madison seized his opportunity. If further justification were required, he could plead instructions from Virginia's governor, who wrote on 7 May 1790 in support of legislative action as the best means of dealing with the existing problem and preventing future frauds.[203] With evidence of the executive's wishes in hand–Governor Randolph's letter would have reached Madison a week after its dispatch, that is, between the date on which Madison heard Bland propose his resolutions (also 7 May) and the date of the House debate (17 May)–Madison may have felt justified in supporting the resolutions. Throughout, he had been acting on behalf of his constituents, both local and statewide, and their wishes, coinciding with his own larger goal, would have been received by him as a command. In any event, the House vote on the Bland resolutions must have been gratifying: They passed by a majority of thirty to sixteen and so in a small but significant way reversed the defeat on discrimination and established, at least in principle, that this was indeed a "government . . . fit for honest men," not "sharpers."[204]

The resolutions then went to the Senate, where they encountered considerably more opposition. Treasury forces argued strongly against the crucial third resolution and came close to securing an amendment that would have returned matters to administrative channels. As Virginia senator Richard Henry Lee asked his brother Arthur, with a fine rhetorical flourish, "are you not Astonished to be informed that the . . . Resolutions . . . should be so opposed as probably to frustrate them?" And this "altho tis certain," Lee went on to say, that "a parcel of Scoundrel Speculators went directly after the appropriation of last September & cheated the Soldiers out of 27,000 dollars for less than a penny in the pound." What was worse, "the Money is yet in the pub.[lic] Treasury–& these resolves only calculated to prevent the fraud from being carried into effect."[205] In the end, the casting vote of Vice President John Adams secured their passage–"for Once, in my Opinion," Senator William Maclay of Pennsylvania grudgingly admitted in his journal, "our [Vice-] President Voted right"–and on 2 June both houses of Congress approved the resolutions in their final version, minor changes having been imposed by the Senate.[206]

It was at this stage that Jefferson directly entered the picture. Madison in all probability had kept his friend informed of developments and shared with Jefferson the contents of the letters from Gustavus Wallace and Governor Randolph. But Jefferson's actual participation in the affair seems to have been something of a fluke. Once the resolutions had passed the Senate, Hamilton took alarm. Such brazen interference by the legislature with the rights of contract threatened to destroy investor confidence in the securities market, or so Hamilton insisted in an opinion he volunteered to Washington on 29 May.[207] Washington considered Hamilton's case for vetoing the resolutions and apparently thought it wise to obtain additional advice. For this, he turned to Jefferson. The secretary of state was hardly the logical member of the cabinet to render an opinion on the resolutions, whatever his interest in them. Under normal conditions, no doubt, it would have been Attorney General Edmund Randolph to whom Washington looked in the first instance for an authoritative view on a question of law. But pressing personal business had taken Randolph to Virginia some weeks before, and he would not return to New York until July.[208] In his absence, Jefferson was a suitable substitute. As the president knew, Jefferson had been a distinguished member of the Virginia bar before the Revolution, and Washington may also have had an inkling that he was likely to receive another point of view from his secretary of state. That point of view, of course, would be more in keeping with the Virginia outlook on such matters, and perhaps more in line, as well, with what may have been the president's desire to see justice done to his old comrades. It was, then, the accident of Randolph's absence, coupled with Hamilton's initiative in advising the president to veto the resolutions, that brought about Jefferson's direct part in the affair. But if his being asked for an opinion was the result of chance, chance had nothing to do with the advice he gave.

The position Hamilton took was straightforward, cogently argued, and pitched on the highest possible ground. "To vary the risks of parties; to supersede the contracts between them; to turn over a creditor; without his consent, from one *Debtor* to *another*; to take away a right to a *specific thing*, leaving only the chance of a remedy for retribution," Hamilton stated, "are not less positive violations of property, than a direct confiscation." It was true, he conceded, that legislative interference might be justified in "extraordinary cases . . . but it is highly important, that the nature of those cases shou'd be carefully distinguished." Hamilton was unwilling to admit that the case of the veterans fell within the special set of circumstances permitting the legislature to take such action. "Nothing therefore," he announced, "but some urgent public necessity, some impending national Calamity, something that threatens direct and general mischief to the Society, for which there is no adequate redress in the established course of things, can, it is presumed, be a sufficient cause for the employment of so extraordinary a remedy." Anything less, and "the intercourses of business become uncertain, the security of property is lessened, the confidence in Government destroyed or weakened." No interests were at stake in the present case that authorized such a departure. "Less than fifty thousand Dollars" was involved, on average no more than "twenty five Dollars per man." From Hamilton's point of view, this seemed "a very inadequate cause for a measure which breaks in upon those great principles, that constitute the foundations of property." And there was all the more reason not to upset settled and necessary rules in this case because, as Hamilton carefully outlined for Washington, there already existed an adequate legal and administrative remedy for the claimants that promised them all the relief to which they were entitled.[209]

These were the general principles that Hamilton proposed for the president's consideration, and he attempted to strengthen them by appealing to the authority of the Constitution. He could not point to any specific language in that document forbidding the course embodied in the resolutions–the Fifth Amendment, which might have helped considerably, had yet to be ratified, and it is noteworthy that Hamilton nowhere mentioned it in his opinion–but he had a superior argument, an argument from the spirit of the Constitution and the motives that led to its adoption.[210] Speaking in words that made it clear that the Constitution had been intended to provide protection for creditors, Hamilton reminded the president of what Washington surely already knew: "The Constitution of the United states interdicts the States individually from passing any Law impairing the obligation of contracts." Recalling the contests of the 1780s, Hamilton went on to make the equally obvious remark that "this, to the more enlightened part of the community was not one of the least recommendations of that Constitution. The too frequent intermeddlings of the state Legislatures, in relation to private contracts, were extensively felt and seriously lamented; and a Constitution which promised a preventative, was, by those who felt and thought in that manner, eagerly embrac'd." What Madison and his friends wanted was nothing less, Hamilton suggested, than a return to the bad old days: "Precedents of similar interference by the Legislature of the United states, cannot fail to alarm the same class of persons, and at the same time to diminish the respect of the state legislatures for the interdiction alluded to. The *example* of the national government in a matter of this kind may be expect'd to have a far more powerful influence, than the *precepts* of its Constitution."[211]

Hamilton harbored no illusions about the unpopularity of the course he was urging the president to adopt. It would win few new friends for the administration, and it had the unfortunate appearance of excessive rigor in the face of the obvious claims of humanity and sympathy. But the principle was the thing; the case did not warrant departing from it, and, Hamilton told the president, it was unlikely that his veto would be overridden by the Senate, where the margin of victory had been razor-thin in the first place.[212] Moreover, he added, those directly affected by a veto would be few in numbers, and there was something to be gained from establishing important principles at minimal cost.[213] Hamilton's deficiencies as a political observer were apparent in the last consideration, to be sure, but on the whole he had presented an able and persuasive case. The argument for a veto was carefully considered, the implications of approving the resolutions spelled out in clear and direct terms. But the opinion did not persuade Washington.

We cannot be sure that it was Jefferson's position, submitted in an opinion dated 3 June 1790, that turned the scales in favor of approval. Jefferson thought the president should sign the resolutions, of course, and that was what Washington would do, but we have no way of knowing precisely how the president made up his mind. What Jefferson did do was to provide the president with a closely reasoned set of legal arguments that may have blunted the impact of Hamilton's contention that the resolutions impaired the right of contract. Jefferson showed that, under Virginia law, only certain kinds of claims–specifically, bills of exchange, promissory notes, and bonds–could legally be assigned. "By the common law of England (adopted in Virginia)," Jefferson explained, "the conveyance of a right to a debt or other thing, whereof the party is not in possession, is not only void, but severely punishable under the names of Maintenance and champerty."[214] Hence those who had taken assignments of the veterans' claims did not, in fact, have valid contract rights, for the claims were debts not in possession and did not come under the saving exceptions of bills of exchange, bonds, and promissory notes. Jefferson was less certain about the situation in North Carolina–he confessed that he was not capable of giving an opinion on the law of that state–but he was reasonably sure the results there would be similar: "They, like Virginia, have adopted the English laws in the gross. These laws forbid in general the buying and selling of debts, and their policy in this respect is so wise, that I should presume they had not changed it, till the contrary be shewn."[215]

Jefferson's opinion was narrowly focused, confined to a technical point the secretary of the treasury had largely overlooked (Hamilton had simply stated that under "the Law of most, if not all the States, claims of this kind are in their nature assignable for valuable consideration") and that at first sight was seemingly innocuous in its import.[216] But this was a matter of strategy on Jefferson's part; he had Hamilton's opinion to work from, and he successfully located the vulnerable assumption about Virginia law.[217] What in fact stands out in Jefferson's opinion is the great care he took to deflect the real thrust of Hamilton's argument. Jefferson quickly disposed of it by appearing to concede what he took to be Hamilton's key position, insisting that he had no intention of approving "retrospective laws." "I agree," he said, "in an almost unlimited condemnation of retrospective laws," adding that the "few instances of wrong which they redress are so overweighed by the insecurity they draw over all property, and even over life itself, and by the atrocious violations of both to which they lead, that it is better to live under the evil than the remedy."[218] All that is necessary, then, is to consider whether the third resolution is such a retrospective law, and of course it is not. But in fact Jefferson avoided meeting Hamilton on the latter's chosen ground. He had nothing to say about the effects of the third resolution on opinion, and he was apparently unconcerned about the bad example being set. In truth, none of this seemed very important to Jefferson because he was unwilling, in the first place, to see anything legitimate in the buying and selling of claims or to admit that the needs of the market for certainty and security in transactions could override acts of injustice to individuals.

Thus, once again, and in the context of what may initially seem a fairly minor question, the Virginia view of debt comes up against the Hamiltonian credo. Virginians, speaking through Jefferson, stand for the older order of the common law, with its "wise policy" limiting the market economy's intrusions into the world of ordinary men. Jefferson himself, as we have seen, intensely disliked having his debts assigned by the original creditors to others who might prove less understanding or less capable of being manipulated, less restrained by long-standing ties, and we can see something of the Virginia debtor's mentality at work in the confidence with which Jefferson here asserts the moral superiority of the law in Virginia and, it seems, North Carolina.[219] Implicit, of course, is the background of events that gave rise to the resolutions: the ability and propensity of those Madison calls "sharpers"—the same men Hamilton was proudly calling "the more enlightened part of the community"—to take advantage of those without the skill or the resources to protect themselves in the sophisticated world of the marketplace.[220]

Equally revealing, and in keeping with the whole tenor of debate since Hamilton issued his *Report* in January, are the different positions on the importance of public opinion. Hamilton's plea on behalf of credit itself, so dependent on appearances, needing every support it can get from a government pledged to the inviolability of contract, even in cases where trivial sums are at stake, reflects a way of looking at the world that had yet to make itself dominant in Virginia. Jefferson insisted that no one abhorred "retrospective laws" more than he, but even this apparent concession to Hamilton reveals the gulf that separated them—and separated Virginia Federalists like Madison from their counterparts in the northern commercial centers. From the Virginia perspective, not all contracts were equal, and rights were to be determined according to principles other than those that appealed to the secretary of the treasury and his supporters. For the Virginians, in short, the law merchant, which governed the world of commerce, was still suspect; they had their own version of the economy to uphold, and Hamilton's insistence on overriding it to promote goals they could not agree to struck them as a poor portent for the future health of the Republic. "Honest men" would not and did not act like "sharpers," and it was disturbing to discover that the Constitution was already being invoked to cover the acts of the latter.

The Virginians won this battle, even if they lost the war. Washington signed the resolutions on 7 June.[221] Ironically, their author, Theodorick Bland, had died some days earlier, on 1 June.[222] He was mourned in New York by the friends of assumption, whose sole Virginia supporter he had been—thus far. Madison remarked simply that Bland had fallen "victim . . . to the influenza united with the effects & remains of a previous indisposition. His mind was not right for several days before he died."[223] Yet the passage of the resolutions that bore his name, and their signature by the president, did not put an end to the controversies they revealed. Attitudes embodied in the conflicting views over soldiers' claims would remain unaltered in the following weeks. Neither Jefferson nor Madison would see any reason to abandon the positions they expressed in the course of the controversy over the arrears; their dislike of speculation, their suspicion of the Treasury Department's motives would remain as strong as ever.

And yet, a few days after he handed the president his opinion on the resolutions, Jefferson would meet Hamilton in the street and arrange the fateful dinner. The results, as we have seen, were a grudging concession by Jefferson and Madison to the exigencies of the political crisis, but the

Virginians' eventual willingness to permit a modified assumption by no means represented any real change in their basic thinking. Madison's notions that a funded debt was an "evil," his fear that the nation was in danger of being governed for the benefit of "sharpers" rather than "honest men," were too deeply rooted to be swept away by the compromise of June 1790. So, too, was his anxiety about Virginia's reaction, his concern that the new government was acting in a way that gave far too much credence to the claims of his Antifederalist enemies.

Likewise, Jefferson's hostility to debt, his passionate belief that it was an intolerable burden, would not disappear no matter how great his relief that the nation's foreign credit had been rescued from the disaster that threatened to overwhelm it. And, like Madison, he had strong reservations about the morality of speculation and a preference for the "wise policy" of limiting it within the narrowest possible bounds. Given these attitudes, given, moreover, the alarming but not unexpected political developments in Virginia as word spread that assumption had passed, it would take very little to provoke either man. Hamilton, as always, failed to see the danger he was running, and together with those he called "the enlightened part of the community" he would shortly bring the Virginians out in force.

5

Pay as You Go

Pay as you go is the best policy; if that cannot be effected the next best is to settle and pay as soon as you can that the interest may not gradually devour the capital.

Joseph Jones, 1792[1]

The Dinner Table Bargain bore strange fruit. Virginia's consolation prize, the Potomac site for the permanent capital of the United States, proved to be worth far less than any of its advocates had imagined during the struggle over the location of the new capital. In the end, neither the economic nor the political benefits the Virginians had anticipated would materialize, and the new federal city was an embarrassment for decades after Washington helped set the cornerstone of the Capitol.[2] Nor did the Virginians' concessions put an end to intersectional strife; if the immediate crisis was resolved, unity hardly followed in its wake. In that respect, Hamilton fared no better than Jefferson or Madison. Acquiescence, as things turned out, did not mean acceptance, and Hamilton would soon discover that Madison openly and Jefferson covertly were determined to halt the progress of his program and reverse the policies he had initiated. And, by a curious sort of symmetry, what the Virginians lost in 1790 they managed to regain in part a decade later. For the hopes Hamilton had embodied in his *Report* also went unrealized. Expecting to win the powerful support of "monied men" and so make the Constitution secure, he succeeded only in creating an opposition that, with the election of 1800, would drive his party from office, burying it forever.[3] Economic benefits, as we have seen, were equally difficult to identify, at least on the scale and in the fashion Hamilton predicted them in January 1790.[4] Neither party to the Dinner Table Bargain received the gains it counted on in June 1790; both would find the results far more problematic than they originally supposed.

Yet despite Virginia fears that what had been done could still be undone, that the capital would never leave Philadelphia, the bargain endured, and one of the stranger features of politics in the 1790s, whether on the Federalist or the Republican side, was studied silence about the bargain itself.[5] After a brief flurry of squibs and articles in the New York papers in 1790, generally directed at Robert Morris, only occasionally was something said in public that hinted at what had taken place, though nothing so direct or obvious enough to raise difficult questions and force the participants to come forward with their own accounts of the events. Of course, everyone in political life knew that there had been an arrangement, even if the details—Jefferson's and Madison's roles in particular—remained obscure. Later, during Jefferson's presidency, when the Potomac location came under renewed attack by supporters of a return to Philadelphia, the federal city's defenders pointedly argued that repeal of the residence act would require repeal of the funding act; both, they said, were parts of a single whole.[6] Acknowledgment that this was indeed the case seems to have imposed itself very early on, though William Loughton Smith, the South Carolina Federalist who fought against the Potomac location in 1790, was daring enough to attack the Dinner Table Bargain, or rather to allude to it, in his pamphlet *The Politicks and Views of a Certain Party, Displayed* (1792).[7] Yet, as Madison noted in his draft of a reply, Smith's "insinuation of improper combination [of the residence] with the assumption, [was] too obscure to receive any precise answer"—a conclusion that must have allowed Madison to rest a little easier.[8] Nevertheless, he prepared a response—never published—to Smith's charges in which he carefully allotted the blame for what had happened in 1790.

There were, Madison thought, three categories into which those who had voted for the package could be divided, "if," he cautiously added, "there be any reality in the connection of the two subjects." First, there were those who had voted for it out of "disinterested respect for the aggregate good of the Union, and a belief that such a compromise was called for & justified by the state of things at the moment." These were entitled to "an indulgent tho' not an approving judgment"—a verdict just a little harsh, one would think, given Madison's role in facilitating things. Next, there were those motivated by "*Local* interest. As far as this [is] supposed to coincide with right & general interest," he concluded, "it partakes of the above motive. As far as consulted under a disregard of national considerations—it merits a high degree of censure." And last there were those with "*Interested speculations in the measure,*" and for this third category Madison had only contempt: "No indignation," he said, was "too severe" where "those who intended or used it for this purpose" were concerned.[9] But Madison must have realized that it would be dangerous to counter Smith's charges in this fashion, even anonymously; too many questions would be opened up by his first and second categories, questions he and Jefferson would not want to have to answer or have others answer for them. And so matters seem to have gone no further, at least in the press or in congressional debate.

In fact, none of the participants could have afforded to let the subject of the bargain surface, and so all of them had no choice but to remain silent. For to have introduced the issue after 1790 would have risked far too much.

Washington would never have forgiven anyone whose actions threatened to undo the agreement on the residence, and Hamilton was in no position, no matter how irritated by Republican attacks, to offend the president. That inhibition would have added to the treasury secretary's determination not to put his own program in jeopardy by revealing the part the Republican leaders had played in securing its passage in 1790, and here again he would also have risked Washington's displeasure had he done anything that reopened the issue of public credit. There were a good many things Hamilton was willing to say about Jefferson's and Madison's inconsistencies and past behavior, but the Dinner Table Bargain was the one thing he never brought up.[10] As for the Virginia duo, they too had everything to lose and nothing to gain by revealing their part in the bargain. Anything Jefferson and Madison said on the subject publicly–even to claim that they had been duped–could only expose them to charges of hypocrisy.[11] Revelations of this sort would have undermined, perhaps fatally, their leadership of the anti-Treasury forces. Old Virginia Antifederalists would have seized the opportunity their confessions created, and neither Jefferson nor Madison would have thought that cost worth the small and temporary advantage they might have gained by exposing what they had come to understand as the opening move of Hamilton's devious game. Far too much, then, depended on the silence of all the participants; only later would the story emerge, at a time when Jefferson could be reasonably sure that it would be turned to proper purposes.[12]

In any case, Jefferson and Madison had more than enough material to work with and so did not need the story of the bargain–even the story artfully recast to shed the worst possible light on Hamilton–to carry on their campaign against Treasury Department policies. That campaign would become the dominant feature of Virginia Republican politics in the 1790s, and Jefferson and Madison would use it to establish themselves at the head of a Virginia party in national politics. This in itself is perhaps the most interesting of the bargain's consequences; ironically, the very compromises to which the two men agreed helped produce the outcry in Virginia that was the making of their political fortunes. Virginia could not abide the policies adopted in 1790, or those that followed, and by rights it should have been the Virginians opposed to the new government from the start who reaped the rewards of that hostility. Patrick Henry, as we shall shortly see, immediately took this opportunity and denounced funding and assumption with his customary vehemence, reminding his audience that it was exactly what he had predicted all along–permit this new government to operate and the death warrant of liberty was as good as signed and delivered. Yet Jefferson and Madison were able to turn the situation to advantage, and it is worth considering why and how, for that will explain much of what is to follow in this chapter.

Sincerity certainly helped. Jefferson never for a moment doubted that his cause was just, even if he had suppressed his qualms about debt in the summer of 1790. The Virginia opposition to Hamiltonian finance was no

mere tactical maneuver, no bargaining chip held in reserve to extract concessions on other issues. It was *the* issue, for Hamilton's program and its
implications, ideological as well as practical, touched gentry nerves to the
quick. No one in Virginia doubted that Jefferson and Madison firmly
believed Federalist financial policy a fundamental evil or that they saw it as
setting the new Republic on the road to perdition. Their position was not a
pose, and their claim to defend the values of Virginia republicanism was
accordingly convincing. Not even Henry could dissent on this score, though
doubtless he would have insisted on the superiority of his own credentials.

Moreover, Jefferson and Madison were in the front lines, not in the rear
at Richmond, and that was an enormous advantage. Henry was never
willing to serve in Congress, though he could have been elected to the
House or Senate at any time he wished in the early 1790s. Just as he had
stayed away from the Constitutional Convention in 1787, so Henry refused
to have anything to do with the new government, and this was a fundamental mistake.[13] The other Virginia Antifederalists who went into Congress in
1789 and later years either lacked Henry's magnetism or found themselves in
the Senate, where, like Richard Henry Lee and James Monroe, they could
have little effect on public opinion, for the Senate initially operated behind
closed doors.[14] The House, on the contrary, was the forum where policy was
discussed in the open, and its debates were widely reported in the press. It
was also the branch in which money bills originated, and that, too, would
prove advantageous. Placing himself in the House, Madison had an unparalleled opportunity to take the lead, which is exactly what he did. Jefferson
was less well situated to let the public know where he stood, but it did not
take long for cabinet dissensions to become common knowledge, and by
1792 no reader of the newspapers could have been unaware that the secretary
of state stood for policies very different from those espoused by the treasury
secretary.[15] Given their positions at the center of national politics, then,
Jefferson and Madison could and did move swiftly and effectively to make
themselves the official spokesmen for the Virginia point of view.

What mattered after 1789, in short, was first New York and then, from
1790 to 1800, Philadelphia, not Richmond. However weak the Union, the
focus had shifted, and as the threats to Virginia began to come not from
within but from without, from the policies and legislation of the federal
government, it was those in national office who could most authoritatively
pose as the Old Dominion's defenders. Here it is important to remember
that the Constitution itself had helped to remove a number of the issues that
made Virginia politics unusually contentious in the 1780s. If Madison had
spent a good part of that decade struggling to defeat "improper or wicked"
projects in the House of Delegates, in the 1790s he was free of worry on that
score. The Constitution forbade the states to print paper money or to alter
the obligation of contracts, and that, combined with the gradual return of
prosperity after 1789, even in Virginia, removed whole categories of dispute
from the realm of politics.[16] Indeed, the tendency of Virginia politics after
1789 was refreshingly old-fashioned to men like Jefferson and Madison: As

before 1776, so once again there was an external enemy against which the gentry could unite in opposition on the basis of shared views. Thus the condition that had so troubled them in the 1780s—that the gentry itself could not agree on a common stand, a state of affairs contemporaries took as signifying a decline in virtue and a decay of public morality—largely disappeared after 1789.

True, there were always some Federalists in the Old Dominion— Washington was one of them—and Jefferson deplored even this slight degree of deviation from the Republican norm. As John Marshall later observed, "Those Virginians who opposed the opinions and political views of Mr. Jefferson seem to have been considered rather as rebellious subjects than legitimate enemies entitled to the rights of political war."[17] But in characteristic fashion, Jefferson explained away the Federalist presence: British merchants naturally accounted for the behavior of towns like Richmond; lack of information led others astray; and, in the later 1790s, Federalist propaganda and the artificial passions excited by the XYZ Affair were to blame.[18] On the whole, though, politically important Virginians gravitated to the Republican interest; it was their natural home, and as long as Hamilton or John Adams remained in office, most of the gentry could agree on the location of the enemy.

Hence, thanks to the harmony between their own convictions and those of their constituents, thanks to their presence where it mattered and their willingness to do battle for what Virginia thought was right, thanks above all to the inability of their old opponents among the Antifederalists to grasp the changing nature of politics after 1789, Jefferson and Madison were able to outbid Patrick Henry and his supporters and take control of Virginia politics. The similarity between Jefferson and Madison's position on Hamilton's innovations and the views of the Antifederalists on this score helped enormously; old antagonisms could thus be papered over—even if they later reappeared during Jefferson's second administration with the Quids and the movement to deny Madison the succession.[19] It goes without saying that at the outset no one had expected this turn of events, and least of all Jefferson, whose ambitions in 1789 and 1790 never for a moment included political leadership at any level. Circumstances, however, conspired to take him in a direction radically different from the one that he had anticipated when he came home on leave in 1789. Again, debt was at the bottom of things.

Jefferson returned to Virginia in the fall of 1790 to take up the threads of his affairs before returning to join the administration in its temporary new location at Philadelphia.[20] Regrettably, we have no indication of what his neighbors said to him about Hamilton's program, but doubtless he heard rumors that the Virginia legislature—just as Madison's correspondents had predicted in the spring—was about to adopt a series of resolutions on the recently enacted federal measures. By the time the Virginia House of Delegates determined their final form, Jefferson was already in Philadelphia. But both he and Madison could have guessed with considerable accuracy what the legislature was going to say: It was straight Virginia doctrine down the line, and it differed not a whit from what they had been hearing from their friends throughout the crisis of the spring and summer. They, of course, were pledged to silence, and had wanted it that way; the members of the House of Delegates, led by Patrick Henry, were not, and made their voices heard.

The Virginia delegates' resolves were pointed and straightforward. "Republican policy," they announced, "could scarcely have suggested those clauses in the aforesaid act, which limit the right of the United States, in their redemption of the public debt." (Jefferson must have been pleased to read this denunciation of permanent debts.) There was "a striking resemblance between this system and that which was introduced into England, at the revolution; a system which has perpetuated upon that nation an enormous debt, and has moreover insinuated into the hands of the executive, an unbounded influence." (The delegates evidently knew their Blackstone almost by heart.) It followed, then, that "the same causes produce the same effects!" America, the delegates implied, could look forward to corruption and the destruction of liberty, if only because "to erect, and concentrate, and perpetuate a large monied interest" in what was, after all, "an agricultural country," was bound "in the course of human events [to] produce one or the other of two evils, the prostration of agriculture at the feet of commerce, or"—worse still—"a change in the present form of the foederal government, fatal to the existence of American liberty."[21]

Hamilton was not far wrong when he denounced the resolutions as "the first symptom of a spirit which must either be killed or will kill the constitution of the United States."[22] And the Virginia legislators made it clear that their notions of the constitutional proprieties were very different from those that Hamilton was shortly to reveal in the controversy over the chartering of the first Bank of the United States. Nothing in the Constitution, they argued, authorized "Congress to assume the debts of the states!" (The delegates were liberal in their use of the exclamation point.) On the contrary, Virginia Federalists had promised them at the ratifying convention " 'that every power not granted was retained;' under this impression and upon this positive condition, declared in the instrument of ratification, the said government [i.e., the Constitution] was adopted by the people of this Commonwealth." It was their duty, the delegates concluded, to stand "as the guardians then of the rights and interests of their constituents, as sentinels placed by them over the ministers of the foederal government, to shield it from their encroachments, or at least to sound the alarm when it is threatened with invasion."[23] Wrong as policy, wrong constitutionally, both assumption and the larger program embodied in Hamilton's plan were rejected out of hand by the official voice of Virginia. For Patrick Henry, who had introduced them, passage of the resolutions must have been highly satisfying.[24]

Even Virginia Federalists in the Assembly agreed with the resolutions—except as to the constitutionally of assumption itself, a point they were unable to carry—and the line dividing Federalists from Antifederalists in this instance was highly significant. Like their friends in Congress, the Federalists were appalled by Hamilton's policy, but to call it unconstitutional was to call the Union into question, and that they were not yet prepared to do. Nevertheless, the Antifederalists understood the situation better than the Federalist minority. Hamilton did see his program as "constitutional" in the broader sense of the term. It was intended to fulfill the constitutional promise; as the secretary of the treasury conceived it, the Constitution had been adopted to secure precisely such ends. Virginia Antifederalists intuitively grasped this, taking the first opportunity to protest anything that would serve to legitimate this dangerous contention; the Federalists, like Jefferson and Madison earlier in the year, were still willing to swallow their distaste, still willing to hope that no more concessions of this sort would be extracted. They were wrong, as Hamilton would soon prove.

Governor Beverley Randolph forwarded the resolutions to Madison and the rest of the Virginia delegation in the House of Representatives on 3 January 1791.[25] By then, Hamilton's *Second Report . . . For Establishing Public Credit*, proposing the creation of a Bank of the United States, had been before Congress for nearly three weeks.[26] And it was this that marked the turning point, Dumas Malone remarked, for by the end of the struggle over the bank bill, Jefferson "was beginning to realize that if Hamiltonianism was to be combatted effectively, more aggressive tactics would have to be employed by somebody, and other weapons than constitutional arguments must be used."[27] As Jefferson and Madison pored over the *Second Report*, it became apparent that Hamilton intended to go well beyond anything they imagined they had consented to the previous summer.[28] It was further proof that the government was being run for the benefit of those "sharpers" Madison had denounced the previous spring.[29] And the broad construction Hamilton used to justify his measure was equally alarming; this was another instance of that tendency to go beyond the bounds of the document the Virginia legislators were denouncing. Jefferson had no trouble divining where such latitude would lead; if it were proper to use the general welfare clause to justify the creation of a bank, then there was no limit to what Congress might do, and the Constitution would henceforth be reduced "to a single phrase, that of instituting a Congress with power to do whatever would be for the good of the U.S. and as they would be the sole judges of the good or evil, it would be also a power to do whatever evil they pleased."[30]

In addition to the constitutional question, there were economic issues at stake, and here the Virginia mentality was fully evident in Jefferson's and Madison's criticisms of the bill authorizing the creation of a Bank of the United States. Such a bank would obviously benefit holders of the debt more than any other class of citizen, for they would have the best chance to subscribe to its stock, even though, as Madison pointed out in his draft of a veto message for the president, "it is in all cases the duty of the Government to dispense its benefits with as impartial a hand as the public interest will permit."[31] This alone would have alarmed the Virginians. That the measure would permit the proposed bank to issue notes also struck Jefferson as undesirable: "I pass over the increase of circulating medium ascribed to it as a merit," he told the president in his opinion on the bill's constitutionality, "and which, according to my ideas of paper money is clearly a demerit."[32] In any case, as Madison remarked in one of his speeches on the bank bill, Virginia had a statute "actually prohibiting the circulation of notes payable to bearer," which was exactly what the bank's notes would be. (He might have added, though he did not, that the statute had been included in his good friend Mr. Jefferson's revisal of the Virginia laws.)[33] To outsiders, and certainly to Hamilton, such objections would have seemed no more valid than the quibbles Jefferson had raised the previous June in his opinion on the Arrears of Pay, but to fail to take them seriously was to miss the seriousness with which the Virginians viewed such matters.

Nor was Hamilton likely to have caught the drift of Jefferson's opening remarks in his opinion on the bill's constitutionality. Here Jefferson pointed out to the president that the bill undertook, "among other things"–the fact that Jefferson was being selective is worthy of note, as are the features he chose to highlight–

1. to form the subscribers into a Corporation.
2. to enable them, in their corporate capacities to receive grants of land; and so far is against the laws of *Mortmain*.*
3. to make *alien* subscribers capable of holding lands, and so far is against the laws of *Alienage*.
4. to transmit these lands, on the death of a proprietor, to a certain line of successors: and so far changes the course of *Descents*.
5. to put lands out of the reach of forfeiture or escheat and so far is against the laws of *Forfeiture and Escheat*.
6. to transmit personal chattels to successors in a certain line: and so far is against the laws of *Distribution*.
7. to give them the sole and exclusive right of banking under the national authority: and so far is against the laws of *Monopoly*.

    *Though the constitution controuls the laws of Mortmain so far as to permit Congress itself to hold lands for certain purposes, yet not so far as to permit them to communicate a similar right to other corporate bodies.[34]

Of course, Hamilton would reply, these are precisely the powers that corporations have, and giving them to the proposed bank involved nothing out of the ordinary.[35]

But for Jefferson it was another matter entirely. Hamilton's bank, from Jefferson's perspective, looked like a giant engine capable of crushing the reforms of the law of property and inheritance that had been one of his principal accomplishments in Virginia. More than that, of course, it was directly counter to the principle he set forth in the 6 September 1789 letter to Madison, threatening to introduce into the United States, under the patronage of the federal government, the very abuses–mortmain, monopolies–he had insisted his principle made illegitimate. No matter to Jefferson that the bank's duration was to be only twenty years–nineteen would have been better, of course, though he did not say so in his opinion. The extent of the secretary of the treasury's failure to catch the train of Jefferson's thought, let alone Jefferson's reasons for insisting on these points, can be measured by Hamilton's comment that he did not see why the laws of descent and property were untouchable. "If these are truly the foundation laws of the several states," Hamilton remarked, "then have most of them subverted their own foundations. For there is scarcely one of them which has not, since the establishment of its particular constitution, made material alterations in some of those branches of jurisprudence especially the law of descents." One wonders whether Hamilton knew of Jefferson's role in the revisal of the Virginia laws; if he did, he obviously failed to understand Jefferson's motives. As to the duration of the charter, Madison remarked in his speech on 8 February 1791 that "twenty years . . . was to this country as a period of a century in the history of other countries—there was no calculating the events that might take place." He also suggested that the powers granted were likely to turn into perpetuities, regardless of the limits placed on them.[36]

For Jefferson, the bank bill must have been all the proof he required of the direction in which Hamilton's policies were leading the nation. Erected on the foundation Hamilton had built the previous summer (most of the proposed bank's capital would be in the form of the newly created debt), suspiciously like the Bank of England (itself an integral part of the British financial system Jefferson and other Virginians abhorred in their traditional country party way), setting aside state laws Jefferson had helped to create, and in all a dangerous precedent for activist government that might interfere in still other ways, the bank bill was the final straw. Henceforth, Jefferson would be on his guard, and his tongue was loosened. He would let his intimates know what he thought of the direction national policy had taken; he would argue with the president about the need to reverse that direction; and he would begin, in his own backstairs fashion, to lend his aid to the anti-Treasury forces within and without Congress.

Even before the president signed the bank bill, Jefferson reached out for new allies.[37] Not all Virginia Antifederalists were wedded to Patrick Henry or posed the same dangers to the Union and the Constitution, and Jefferson saw in George Mason a valuable potential recruit. In the spring of 1790, Jefferson had discreetly avoided stopping at Gunston Hall on his way to New York; now, in February 1791, he took advantage of a a letter from Mason (ostensibly reporting news from Mason's son John, a merchant in Bordeaux, it in fact asked Jefferson to patch up Mason's strained relations with Madison) to suggest that the three of them were thinking along parallel lines. "What," Jefferson asked Mason, "is said in our country of the fiscal arrangements now going on? I really fear their effect when I consider the present temper of the Southern states." But, he concluded, the bank bill and the excise (also under consideration early in 1791) would pass regardless of the arguments against them. "The only corrective of what is amiss in our present government will be the augmentation of the numbers in the lower house, so as to get a more agricultural representation, which may put that interest

above that of the stock-jobbers," he concluded.[38] And from New York at the
end of the month came a highly interesting letter from another acquaintance, Chancellor Robert R. Livingston. "I feel with you great pain in the
dissatisfaction which prevails in the Southern states," that powerful politician explained, regretting that his state's representatives and senators did not
seem to understand the seriousness of the sectional divisions their votes were
creating. Unfortunately, Livingston confessed, the general prosperity led
most New Yorkers to ignore these problems; in New York City itself, "hundreds have made fortunes by speculating in the funds and look forward to a
great encrease of them by the establishment of a bank, and have no idea of a
more perfect government than that which enriches them in six months."[39]
The New York–Virginia axis was beginning to take shape.

If the fears aroused by the bank bill led Jefferson to seek out and respond
to like-minded spirits in the spring of 1791, there were further signs that
the administration's policies were taking Jefferson back to his fundamental beliefs. In the Northwest, the newly created army was about to undertake a campaign against the Indians, and the implications of prolonged
frontier warfare disturbed Jefferson. He hoped that victory would come
quickly, telling Maryland senator Charles Carroll of Carrollton that the
next step must be to "change our tomahawk into a golden chain of friendship. The most economical as well as the most humane conduct towards
them is to bribe them into peace, and to retain them in peace by eternal
bribes." If in the 1780s he had urged war against the Barbary Pirates,
ignoring John Adams's suggestion that it was cheaper to pay tribute, Jefferson now realized the political implications of warfare and his tone changed.
The cost of the current campaign, he asserted, would have covered "presents
on the most liberal scale for 100. years."[40] This, he told James Monroe, was
the method the Spanish and the English used: "They find it the cheapest
plan, and so shall we."[41] But there was more at stake than keeping the budget
in check: What really alarmed Jefferson as he contemplated the possibility of
future expeditions to quell the Indians was the advantage the Treasury
Department's friends would derive from them. "Every rag of an Indian
depredation will serve as ground to raise troops," he predicted.[42] The linked
system of war, debt, and taxes was threatening to reproduce itself in America, and Jefferson drew the appropriate conclusions. To Monroe, he contrasted the willingness of "those who think a standing army and a public
debt necessary for the happiness of the U.S." with the same faction's unwillingness to resist the "new encroachments of Gr. Brit. on our carrying
trade . . . lest any misunderstanding with them should *affect our credit, or the
prices of our public paper*."[43]

If all this was not enough to put Jefferson's correspondents on notice, he
also let them know of the plans to create a whole new species of "paper" in the
form of "actions, or paper-shares" of "great manufacturing companies."
Jefferson was outraged. "We are ruined," he exclaimed to Monroe, "if we do
not over-rule the principles that 'the more we owe, the more prosperous we
shall be,' 'that a public debt furnishes the best means of enterprize,' 'that if

ours should once be paid off, we should incur another by all means however extravagant' &c. &c."[44] Meanwhile, as Jefferson learned from Madison in May, "the enormities produced by the spirit of speculation & fraud" continued to flourish; despite the Virginia victory in the Arrears of Pay in 1790, new schemes were afoot to take advantage of the ignorance of those with claims against the government by obtaining "administration on the effects of deceased soldiers and other claimants leaving no representatives."[45] It may have encouraged him to learn that Gouverneur Morris–by now his successor as minister to France–doubted the wisdom of Hamilton's "System of Finance" and thought that the "Bank . . . will not produce all that is expected," but otherwise the spring of 1791 was full of disturbing news.[46]

As Jefferson watched the implications of Hamilton's program turn into realities, he was reminded of the context in which he had originally conceived his principle that the earth belongs to the living–the French Revolution. Late in 1790, Edmund Burke published his *Reflections on the Revolution in France* and sparked a transatlantic controversy of considerable significance for Jefferson's political career.[47] Burke, who could hardly have known of Jefferson's 6 September 1789 letter to Madison, managed in the course of his book to raise a series of questions going straight to the heart of Jefferson's principle. If Jefferson had insisted on the rights of the living generation, Burke entered the lists as the champion of all generations, past, present, and future, insisting that "society is indeed a contract. . . . As the ends of such a partnership cannot be obtained in many generations, it becomes a partnership not only between those who are living, but between those who are living, those who are dead, and those who are to be born."[48]

The profoundly conservative implications of Burke's argument would have aroused Jefferson's hostility in any case–the author of the Declaration of Independence could hardly have accepted the argument against change–but the secretary of state must also have been struck by Burke's brilliant inversion of his own underlying metaphor. "One of the first and most leading principles on which the commonwealth and the laws are consecrated," Burke explained, going on to deploy the language of inheritance and real property we have seen Jefferson exploiting in the 6 September 1789 letter to Madison, "is lest the temporary possessors and life-renters in it, unmindful of what they have received from their ancestors or of what is due to their posterity, should act as if they were the entire masters; that they should not think it amongst their rights to cut off the entail, or commit waste on the inheritance, by destroying at their pleasure, the whole original fabric of their society; hazarding to leave those who come after them, a ruin instead of an habitation."[49] If that were to happen, "no one generation could link with the other. Men would become little better than the flies of a summer."[50] Protecting the living, as Burke saw it, required limits on their powers; Jefferson had already said that, insofar as the right to contract debts was concerned, but he had also imagined that the rights of the living to change or alter their constitutions and laws were equally valid under his principle.[51] Burke's argument, if it gained ground, would be a serious threat to principles of the highest importance for Jefferson. It was bad enough that Burke had chosen to range himself on the side of monarchy and the *ancien régime*, condemning the French Revolution, for which Jefferson had such high hopes, but to go beyond that and introduce his own version of the principle of generations was a challenge Jefferson could not ignore.

Publication of the *Reflections* unleashed a flood of replies, and some of them had the perspicacity to attack Burke on precisely those points Jefferson himself would have thought the most dangerous. Joseph Priestley's contribution to the debate, *Letters to the Right Honourable Edmund Burke, Occasioned by His Reflections* (1790), did so directly, asking in a significant footnote whether it would not "be reasonable to fix some time, beyond which it should not be deemed right to bind posterity? If our ancestors make a foolish *law*, we scruple not to repeal it; but if they make foolish *wars*, and incur foolish *debts*, we have, at present, no remedy whatever." Priestley's pamphlet would have been attractive to Jefferson on other grounds as well. He denied that a civil establishment was necessary for religion, argued in favor of closing monasteries and applying their resources to more productive ends, and looked forward to the day when surplus revenues could be put to work on projects "of great public utility, which are always wanted, and which nothing but the enormous expences of government, and of wars, chiefly occasioned by the ambitions of kings and courts, have prevented from being carried into execution"—a theme Jefferson would take up a decade and a half later in his annual messages.[52] Writing from New York, Madison brought the passage on debts to Jefferson's attention, noting "how your idea of limiting the right to bind posterity is germinating under the extravagant doctrines of Burke on that subject." And, he added, "[Thomas] Paines [*sic*] answer has not yet been recd. here. The moment it can be got [Philip] Freneau tells me it will be published in Child's paper." But Jefferson, in Philadelphia, had already seen a copy and had read it with enthusiasm.[53]

Paine's reply, *Rights of Man*, Part One (1791), was almost everything Jefferson could have wished. "Every age and generation must be free to act for itself, *in all cases*," Paine announced, "as the ages and generations which preceded it." And he went on to proclaim that "man has not property in man; neither has any generation a property in the generations that are to follow." For Paine, "it is the living, and not the dead, that are to be accommodated." Summing up his position, Paine put Jefferson's arguments into vivid language that Jefferson, with his habitual tendency toward awkward phrasing, could never have matched: "The rights of men in society, are neither devisable, nor annihilable, but are descendable only; and it is not in the power of any generation to intercept finally, and cut off the descent." Like numerous writers before him, Paine argued that a wrong does not become any less wrong with the passage of time: "If the present generation, or any other, are disposed to be slaves, it does not lessen the right of the succeeding generation to be free: wrongs cannot have a legal descent."[54] Clearly, Paine's ideas were more in keeping with American republicanism than Burke's; the time had not yet come when an old revolutionary like Richard Henry Lee could deplore the execution of Louis XVI and note that Burke had "predicted this very early, as a conclusion that wd. be come to by the ambition & avarice of the democratic faction" in France.[55]

With the American reprinting of *Rights of Man*, the fat was in the fire. Jefferson was directly implicated in the controversy that followed, for his private note endorsing Paine's pamphlet had inadvertently been used by the Philadelphia printer as a preface to the American edition.[56] Jefferson did his best to explain away his gaffe—in the note, he had made a rather rash remark about the usefulness of Paine's work in combating "the political heresies which have sprung up among us," a remark correctly understood to point in the direction of Vice President John Adams—but he was hardly in a position to disavow the work, nor did he wish to.[57] On the contrary, he thought it superb, hoped it would have the widest possible readership, and welcomed its bracing effect on the morale of American republicans, congratulating Paine on its having "been much read here, with avidity and pleasure." He told the author that, although it was "too true that we have a sect preaching up and panting after an English constitution of king, lords, and commons, and whose heads are itching for crowns, coronets, and mitres, . . . our people, my good friend, are firm and unanimous in their principles of republicanism, and there is no better proof of it than that they love what you write and read it with delight." Paine's *Rights of Man*, in short, had "served here to separate the wheat from the chaff, and to prove that tho the latter appears on the surface, it is on the surface only."[58]

Pleased though he was with *Rights of Man*, the controversy it provoked in America must have given Jefferson pause. Even if criticism stemmed only from the "chaff," it could not be entirely ignored, and in one instance, at least, it annoyed Jefferson greatly. John Quincy Adams, then a young Boston lawyer, took up Jefferson's implied challenge to his father and wrote as "Publicola" to insist that "this principle, that a whole nation has a right to do whatever it pleases, cannot in any sense whatever be admitted as true. The eternal and immutable laws of justice and of morality are paramount to all human legislation. The violation of those laws is certainly within the power, but it is not among the rights of nations."[59] The danger, according to "Publicola," was clear: "If, therefore, a majority thus constituted are bound by no law human or divine, and have no other rule but their sovereign will and pleasure to direct them, what possible security can any citizen of the nation have for the protection of his unalienable rights?"[60] Jefferson, who read "Publicola" with care, would have noticed the last phrase, so close to his own words in the Declaration, and the suggestion that dangers came from the majority—the "wheat," to borrow Jefferson's metaphor—rather than from the "chaff" of the corrupt few was utterly opposed to Jefferson's point of view in 1791, whatever he may have said about the dangers of elective despotism in the 1780s.[61] And although Jefferson devoutly believed in "the eternal and immutable laws of justice and morality," even to hint that these were in tension with the rights of the present generation was to raise a fundamental question about his principle that Jefferson neither then nor later had any wish to explore.[62] The American controversy over Burke's *Reflections* and Paine's *Rights of Man* would thus have reminded Jefferson that there were reasons to be cautious in bringing his own version of the rights of the living generation before a wider public. If Jefferson was to present his own view of the debt to an American audience, he would have to find another way of doing it, a way that would protect him from further controversy.

Jefferson did not have far to look for his means: Madison's pen was at his disposal. On 31 January 1792, the Republicans' organ, Philip Freneau's *National Gazette*, published an unsigned essay by Madison on "Universal Peace." How, Madison asked against the background of rumors of war between revolutionary France and its enemies, could wars be prevented? True, "universal and perpetual peace, it is to be feared, is in the catalogue of events, which will never exist but in the imaginations of visionary philosophers, or in the breasts of benevolent enthusiasts." Having established his credentials as a realist, Madison went on to argue that there were ways of curbing war, if not of banishing it forever. He suggested—here paraphrasing Jefferson's 6 September 1789 letter—that a "republican philosopher might have proposed as a model to lawgivers, that war should . . . only be declared by the authority of the people, whose toils and treasures are to support its burdens"—and he did not need to add that this was precisely what the American Constitution did. But more than that might be done, he thought; the philosopher might also insist that "each generation should be made to bear the burden of its own wars, instead of carrying them on, at the expence of other generations." In short, Madison was giving the Republican reading public the practical message of Jefferson's principle. Taxes to pay for those wars, he added, ought to "include a due proportion of such as by their direct operation keep the people awake, along with those, which being wrapped up in other payments, may leave them asleep, to misapplications of their money."[63]

Madison's essay also managed to refute the point that he had made to Jefferson two years before—that it was proper to burden future generations when they were to share in the benefits that loans would obtain—and did so in a typically Madisonian fashion. "To the objection," he wrote, ". . . that where the benefits of war descend to succeeding generations, the burdens ought also to descend, he [the "republican philosopher"] might have answered: that the exceptions could not be easily made; . . . that in the alternative of sacrificing exceptions to general rules, or of converting exceptions into general rules, the former is the lesser evil." And so, Madison concluded, "the only hope of UNIVERSAL AND PERPETUAL PEACE" was "in a reform of every government subjecting its will to that of the people, in a subjection of each generation to the payment of its own debts, and in a substitution of a more palpable, in place of an imperceptible mode of paying them."[64]

In a Virginia where Light-Horse Harry Lee was still fulminating against "those fashionable treasury s[c]hemes imitative of the base principles & wicked measures adopted thro necessity in corrupt monarchys and long

since reprobated (tho continued) by the wise & good in the countrys where
they exist," Madison's essay was well received.[65] Joseph Jones, his old correspondent and James Monroe's uncle, was a reader of the *National Gazette*
who found himself delighted with Madison's ideas. "Has any legislature a
right to Mortgage the property of the people forever or to say to them such
a debt wch. you owe you shall not discharge?" he asked Madison. To admit
this "wod. establish a complete legal tyranny and deprive posterity of
the means of redress or delivering themselves from the most distressing
evils." In short, for Jones—and, it is clear, for most gentry Virginians—"pay
as you go is the best policy." And when that was impossible "the next best is
to settle and pay as soon as you can that the interest may not gradually devour
the capital."[66] Jones's pointed phrases, linking Virginia attitudes toward
personal debt with the Republican position on government debt, suggest
how well prepared gentry Virginians were to receive the message of Jefferson
and Madison.

By the summer of 1791, then, with the bank bill and the storm over *Rights of
Man*, Jefferson had marked out his position. For the remainder of his years in
Washington's cabinet (he did not retire until 31 December 1793), it would
vary little. Foreign affairs occupied much of his time—there were difficult
negotiations with British minister George Hammond in 1792 over the
British debts, a subject that can only have caused Jefferson considerable
anxiety, and then came the neutrality crisis in 1793—but never for a moment
did he neglect the dangers to the Republic that Hamilton's financial system
had created. This would be a constant theme, and Madison and the other
Virginia Republicans joined him in urging it. Given the centrality of Hamilton's program to the national existence and the administration's policy on
other issues, it was inevitable that wherever Jefferson looked he saw the
malign influence of debt and speculation, always tied to the "Anglomen,"
the friends of Britain, and so pointing the way to the extinction of liberty in
America. Despite his best efforts, he was unable to persuade the president to
take his views seriously, and Madison and his other friends in Congress
seemed to make little headway against the Hamiltonian machine, their
efforts to expose the Treasury Department's duplicity and corrupting influence frustrated again and again. Understandably, Jefferson grew increasingly
shrill in his comments; too much was at stake to remain calm, and he could
only hope that somehow, sooner or later, the people would regain control.
That, of course, required political effort, and whether he wanted it or not,
Jefferson began to emerge as a party leader during his last two and a half years
in the cabinet.

Even before the controversy over Paine—and Jefferson's note of endorsement—had subsided, the secretary of state had new cause for alarm. The Bank
of the United States, he discovered, was about to drive specie out of circulation, substituting paper in its place, and costly paper at that, for the bank
would charge interest on its discounts and to that would be added the
interest the public paid on the bank's capital, composed as it was primarily of

government bonds. "Experience," he reminded James Monroe, "has proved to us that a dollar of silver disappears for every dollar of paper emitted"–that had certainly been true of Virginia during the Revolution–and he noted that the paper issued by the Bank of the United States would cost the public 13 percent per annum.[67] No one who, like Jefferson, had known Revolutionary inflation at its worst could contemplate the disappearance of specie with indifference, and it was all the more distressing that the people were scrambling to obtain their share of "the plunder" in the form of stock in the bank.[68] Madison, vacationing in New York City, witnessed the Manhattan end of the story, reporting back to Jefferson that "of all the shameful circumstances of this business, it is among the greatest to see the members of the Legislature who were most active in pushing this job, openly grasping its emoluments."[69] Jefferson coined a word for what was happening; it was "scrip-pomany," he told South Carolina's Edward Rutledge, adding that "the rage of getting rich in a day" had hobbled the country's productive forces, leaving ships idle at the docks and withdrawing funds from useful employments.[70] None of this would have happened had Hamilton's massive and largely irredeemable debt been stopped in its tracks two years before.

And there were new instances of fraud, as New York dealers once more sent their agents to the southern states to buy up government paper before the ignorant locals became aware of its true value, or so Madison reported. He could not, Madison told Jefferson, "set bounds to the daring depravity of the times. The stockjobbers will become the pretorian band of the Government–at once its tool & its tyrant; bribed by its largesses, and overawing it, by clamours & combinations." In the same letter, Madison suggested that the "abuses" stemming from the funding system "make it a problem whether the system of the old paper under a bad Government, or of the new under a good one, be chargeable with the greater substantial injustice."[71] Clearly, the Constitution was proving to be something of a mixed blessing.

Not only was debt an evil in itself, but, once again, it was leading to still other evils, and the worst of them, as Jefferson read the scene, was the undermining of the true principles of republican government. He had no doubt that it was important for American credit to be solidly established–"Our funds are near par," he boasted to Paine in the summer of 1791–but it was now apparent that Hamilton had produced a monster.[72] It was a monster with direct consequences for the economic well-being of Virginia. The system of banking and stockjobbing, Jefferson informed William Short, was causing specie to leave "the remoter parts of the union," concentrating it in Philadelphia, where, "a paper medium supplying its place, it is shipped off in exchange for luxuries." The results were disastrous. "In Virginia for instance property has fallen 25. percent in the last 12. months," Jefferson lamented.[73] And yet this was not the end of it, for the Treasury Department was proposing a further assumption of the state debts, no doubt–as Jefferson explained it to his brother-in-law Nicholas Lewis, who had managed Monticello for him during the mission to France–on the grounds that "as the doctrine is that a public debt is a public blessing, so . . . a perpetual one is a perpetual blessing" and ought to be "so large as that we can never pay it off."[74]

The evidence continued to accumulate. In 1791, Jefferson had reported to Madison that "several merchants from Richmond (Scotch, English &c.) were here [in Philadelphia] lately. I suspect it was to dabble in federal filth," and he continued to notice behavior of this sort throughout the remainder of his term at the State Department.[75] William Short, whose American investments were in Jefferson's hands, was warned of the dangers of paper and urged to transfer his fortune to the greater security of landed property.[76]

Jefferson no longer made a secret of his views. He expressed them openly in conversation, and his friends inserted them in the press, particularly in the *National Gazette*, whose editor held a sinecure in the Department of State.[77] Hamilton and his allies were alarmed, and they took appropriate steps. The political public was treated to the spectacle of open newspaper warfare between Treasury Department forces and the emerging Republican interest in the spring and summer of 1792; charges and countercharges flowed across the pages, and Hamilton made sure that no one was left in doubt about the dangers Jefferson posed. Jefferson had been the enemy of the Constitution; he had attempted to repudiate the public debt while minister to France by arranging for its transfer to shady speculators, who could then in good conscience be bilked; and he was now the chosen instrument of those who would destroy public credit.[78] And then there was the Sinking Fund, on whose board Jefferson sat ex officio, and where he conducted a minor campaign against what he saw as Hamilton's misuse of sums entrusted to the fund; the board, Jefferson thought, ought to have been buying at the lowest prices and redeeming as much of the debt as possible, especially the bonds not yet at par, the three percents and deferred sixes, which he was sure could be acquired cheaply. Instead, and it was typical, Hamilton chose to manipulate the Sinking Fund to provide an artificial support for the price of government stock.[79]

Jefferson fought back, taking his complaints to the president on 29 February 1792. In a long conversation with Washington, important enough that Jefferson carefully recorded its contents the following day, the secretary of state did his best to explain to the president the causes of the present discontents. It was not, he emphasized, a mindless opposition; above all, he argued, it had "a single source"—the policies initiated and secured by the Treasury Department. It was clear, Jefferson told Washington, "that a system had there been contrived, for deluging the states with paper-money instead of gold and silver, for withdrawing our citizens from the pursuits of commerce, manufactures, buildings, and other branches of useful industry, to occupy themselves and their capitals in a species of gambling, destructive of morality, and which had introduced it's [*sic*] poison into the government itself." For that was the core of his country party indictment: the corruption of the legislature. Jefferson told the president that "particular members of the legislature, while those laws were on the carpet, had feathered their nests with paper, had then voted for the laws, and constantly since lent all the energy of their talents, and instrumentality of their offices to the establishment and enlargement of this system." They were perverting the Constitution by "legislative construction," turning it into "a very different thing from what the people thought they had submitted to," and he cited the most recent case—the expansion of the general welfare clause apparent in Hamilton's *Report on Manufactures*.[80]

His morale no doubt strengthened by the recent bursting of the speculative bubble in the Duer Panic of March and April 1792, Jefferson now moved to secure the president's decision and so unleashed a lengthy three-sided correspondence, as Washington found himself forced to arbitrate the conflict between Jefferson and Hamilton.[81] Jefferson's letter to Washington of 23 May 1792, expanding on the themes of their conversation at the end of February, is a catalogue of his complaints and, in addition, a recital of his own innocence in the controversies of recent months. It was also intended to dissuade the president from retiring; without Washington as chief magistrate, Jefferson could only fear the worst, or at any rate something much worse than had happened thus far. Jefferson's causes for distress begin with the assumption: "A public debt, greater than we can possibly pay before other causes of adding new debt to it will occur, has been artificially created, by adding together the whole amount of the debtor and creditor sides of accounts, instead of taking only their balances, which could have been paid off in a short time."[82] Hence taxes were higher than they ought to be, and the result was public "murmurings against taxes and tax-gatherers"—in short, dangerous discontent with the federal government at a time when habits of obedience were in the early stages of formation.[83] But, Jefferson went on to suggest, what else could be expected when the burden of debt forced "resort to an *Excise* law, of odious character with the people, partial in it's [*sic*] operation, unproductive unless enforced by arbitrary and vexatious means, and committing the authority of the government, in parts where resistance is most probable, and coercion least practicable?" And now, if Hamilton's plan to assume further state obligations passed, still more debt was in the offing. Nor did Jefferson omit his outrage at the fact that specie was being driven from circulation by the Bank of the United States and was being replaced by a "paper medium" that gave those who issued it "10. or 12. percent annual profit." All of this to further the cause of speculation—"barren and useless, producing, like that on a gaming table, no accession to itself"—and at an enormous cost to "commerce and agriculture," not to speak of the deleterious effects on public morals of a system that "nourishes in our citizens habits of vice and idleness instead of industry and morality." He might have been quoting Henry Lee's 1790 letter to Madison, but he had no need to; the Virginia view of debt and Hamilton was standard enough that its leading elements could be produced by anyone.[84]

Yet this was only the half of it. Jefferson went on to insist that, quite apart from its economic and social effects, the enormous accumulation of debt had fundamentally perverted the political process. He had not the slightest doubt that the debt "furnished effectual means of corrupting such a portion of the legislature as turns the balance between the honest voters which ever way it is directed," Jefferson said, clearly thinking in country party terms. A "corrupt squadron," manipulated by the Treasury Department, aimed at nothing less than weakening the Constitution in order to "prepare the way for a change, from the present republican form of government, to that of a monarchy, of which the English constitution is to be the model." It followed, then, that of "all the mischiefs objected to the system of measures beforementioned, none is so afflicting, and fatal to every honest hope, as the corruption of the Legislature."[85]

What could be done? Even if "the republican party, who wish to preserve the government in it's [sic] present form," managed to capture the House of Representatives at the coming election (Jefferson hoped the increase in the size of the House following reapportionment after the census of 1790 would have that effect), "They will not be able to undo all which the two preceding legislatures, and especially the first have done." In other words, the debt was there, and could not be touched: "Public faith and right will oppose this." But there was something a Republican majority could accomplish: Reform the system, pursue "a liberation from the rest [of the debt] unremittingly . . . as fast as right will permit," and shut "the door . . . in future against similar commitments of the nation." Do this, of course, and "the whole monarchical and paper interest" would scream in protest, but, Jefferson assured the president, deploying a Virginian's perspective on these matters, there was no need to worry about Hamilton's concern for creating confidence among monied men—"creditors will never, of their own accord, fly off entirely from the debtors." Without a Republican majority, Jefferson could only despair of the future; when "the division of sentiment and interest happens unfortunately to be so geographical," he observed, no one could predict the result. Given that all this added fuel to the fires of "the Antifederal champions [who] are now strengthened in argument by the fulfillment of their predictions," it required little imagination to see where continued Federalist finance was likely to lead. "The confidence of the whole union is centered in you," he assured the president, once again urging him not to step down; "North and South will hang together, if they have you to hang on."[86]

As he waited for the president's response, Jefferson moved to shore up his claims in case the president asked for details. Madison was reminded to furnish a list of the individual members of Congress financially interested in the outcome of Hamilton's program, and Jefferson himself went into his library and compiled statistics on the relative weight of the national debt in various countries. It only confirmed his worst suspicions when his research revealed that the proportion of debt to annual revenue was higher in the United States (he estimated it at 20:1) than in any of the other countries for which he could find information. Even in Britain, it appeared, matters were not as bad as in the United States. "Tho the youngest nation in the world we are the most indebted nation also," he announced. To be sure, Jefferson neglected to add that the United States was the least taxed as well, but that would have gone against the grain of his argument, suggesting the need for more of those vexatious excises and other impositions he had so recently denounced to Washington.[87]

Jefferson also went on to sketch, if only for himself, an "Agenda" of what was necessary to reduce the government to its true principles, and the list leaves no doubt that he wished to destroy Hamiltonianism root and branch. The Bank of the United States was to be abolished, the Excise was to be repealed (the states were to raise the money themselves), import duties were to be lowered, the principles of the *Report on Manufactures* were to be condemned, and the debt was to lose its irredeemable quality and, moreover, be refinanced at 4 rather than the current 6 percent. To ensure that all this would happen and Hamiltonianism never return, Jefferson proposed to divide the Treasury Department, exclude "PAPER MEN" from Congress, have the government deal only in coin, not paper, and provide for more effective legislative oversight of the Treasury Department's activities.[88] Elsewhere, in an undated memorandum from this period, he showed, to his own satisfaction at any rate, that "strik[ing] off the assumption which is 3/9 of the whole debt" and refunding the balance at 4 percent instead of 6 percent would have permitted "the surplus of moderate taxes" to "have made sensible impression on the remaining capital of debt; so as to leave no hazard in pronouncing that the debt is three [times] what it needed to have been."[89] In all, it was a radical plan, and a political revolution would have been necessary to achieve it. But that was exactly what Jefferson now wanted, though he had to wait almost nine years for the day of reckoning, and even then the results, as we shall see, would not be quite as radical as he envisioned in the summer of 1792.

Jefferson was not the only one to write letters of complaint that spring; three days after his letter went off to the president, the secretary of the treasury sent his own long letter to a Virginian—Edward Carrington, supervisor of the revenue for the Virginia district and an old friend and colleague. Hamilton's letter was hot and ill-tempered, the product of a man deeply unhappy about the direction events seemed to be taking. It denounced "Mr. Madisons unfriendly intrigues" and had a good deal to say about the ways in which Madison had left him, more or less for the harlot Jefferson. As for the latter, Hamilton told Carrington, "Mr. Jefferson with very little reserve manifests his dislike of the funding system generally; calling in question the expediency of funding a debt at all. Some expressions which he dropped in my own presence (sometimes without sufficient attention to delicacy) will not permit me to doubt on this point." Admittedly, Jefferson did not advocate "directly the undoing of what has been done, but he censures the whole on principles, which if they should become general, could not but end in the subversion of the system." Nor were Jefferson and Madison the only Virginians to irk Hamilton; there was also William Branch Giles, one of the livelier young Virginia Republicans in Congress, who professed himself willing to vote "for reversing the funding system on the abstract point of the right of pledging & the futility of preserving the public faith, . . . merely to demonstrate his sense of the defect of right & the inutility of the thing."[90]

And then there was Representative John F. Mercer of Maryland—he came from the well-known Virginia family—a man with the audacity to suggest in the House on 30 March 1792 that the present generation did not have the right to bind posterity. "The God of nature has given the earth to the living," Mercer announced in yet another instance of the ways in which Jefferson's principle was beginning to germinate.[91] Hamilton was beside himself at the thought that such notions were abroad; his language at this point for once manages to surpass Jefferson's. "Upon what system of morality can so atrocious a doctrine be maintained? In me, I confess it excites *indignation & horror!*" he exclaimed after telling Carrington of Mercer's and Giles's proposals. "What are we to think of those maxims of Government by which the power of a Legislature is denied to bind the Nation by a *Contract* in an affair of *property* for twenty-four years? For this is precisely the case of the debt. . . . Questions might be multiplied without end to demonstrate the perniciousness & absurdity of such a doctrine."[92]

Hamilton complained about the *National Gazette* and Freneau's clerkship in the State Department. He denounced the Virginia leaders for their "*woman-ish attachment to France and . . . womanish resentment against Great Britain.*" Jefferson, Hamilton argued, "drank deeply of the French Philosophy, in Religion, in Science, in politics," and his vision had been clouded ever since, the more so since he returned home with "probably . . . a too partial an idea of his own powers, and with the expectation of a greater share in the direction of our councils than he has in reality enjoyed." Indeed, Hamilton added with what must have been considerable disgust, "I am not sure that he had not peculiarly marked out for himself the department of the Finances." And this creature—one can imagine Hamilton's shudder—had seduced Madison, who "had always entertained an exalted opinion of the talents, knowledge and virtues of Mr. Jefferson." Admitting that Madison's change of direction may have been prompted "by the calculation of advantage to the state of Virginia," rather than by "any peculiar opinions of Mr. Jefferson concerning the public debt," it was still "certain . . . that a very material *change* took place, & that the two Gentlemen were united in the new ideas." Hamilton could only deplore this, though there was some comfort to be had from the fact that Jefferson was "more radically wrong" than Madison. Hamilton knew that Jefferson was aiming "with ardent desire at the Presidential Chair" and so was out to destroy him, Hamilton, lest his "influence . . . with the Community" favor the cause of some other candidate once Washington retired. And so, after a concluding note assuring Carrington "on my *private faith* and *honor* as a Man" that there was not a word of truth in the rumors that he favored a monarchy, Hamilton ended by suggesting that it was rather Jefferson who was to be feared in that regard: " 'A Man of profound ambition & violent passion,' " Jefferson might well be mounting "the hobby horse of popularity" and shouting from the rooftops about "usurpation—danger to liberty &c. &c." only to " 'ride in the Whirlwind and direct the Storm.' "[93]

Washington, in the end, did decide to stand again, and both Hamilton and Jefferson would breathe more easily as a result. Jefferson's wishes were satisfied in other ways as well; the next Congress would be far more Republican than its predecessor, at least at the outset.[94] But neither man called off his troops, and the newspaper controversy continued to escalate throughout the summer of 1792. Finally, Washington was forced to intervene, and in July and August he wrote separately from Mount Vernon to each of his warring secretaries. Hamilton was the first to be called on for explanations, and in his letter Washington took Jefferson's 23 May text as his guide, suggesting that these were complaints he had heard since his arrival in Virginia. Dividing Jefferson's statements into numbered paragraphs, the president in effect asked Hamilton to reply to twenty-one charges.[95]

By mid-August, Hamilton had done so, and his "Objections and Answers respecting the Administration of the Government," as he called his paper, were the sort of finished and able production he was accustomed to turning out. (He had, of course, been going over some of the same ground in his recent newspaper essays.) As for the heart of Jefferson's complaint, the corruption of the legislature, Hamilton thought it "a strange perversion of ideas, and as novel as it is extraordinary, that men should be deemed corrupt & criminal for becoming proprietors in the funds of their Country." Hamilton would never accept that. "Can it be culpable," he asked of the attack on those who had bought stock in the Bank of the United States, "to invest property in an institution which has been established for the most important national purposes? Can that property be supposed to corrupt the holder?" To the charge that it was all tending toward monarchy, Hamilton replied that "there is no other answer than a flat denial—except this that the project from its absurdity refutes itself"; it was "one of those visionary things, that none but madmen could meditate and that no wise men will believe." And that was that. The president could do as he liked with the answers; Hamilton told Washington he would "rely on your goodness for the proper allowances."[96]

Hamilton's reply in hand, Washington then did his best to put a damper on the cabinet conflict. Both secretaries were told to stop squabbling and make peace. It did the country no good, the president insisted, and the wider party conflict that their quarrels had generated would endanger "the fairest prospect of happiness and prosperity that was ever presented to man."[97] But neither one of the two secretaries was prepared to accept the president's instructions in spirit, and Hamilton returned a vigorous defense of his conduct embodying some of the same arguments against Jefferson personally that he had already used in his May letter to Carrington. "I *know* that I have been an object of uniform opposition from Mr. Jefferson, from the first moment of his coming to the City of New York to enter upon his present office," he informed the president in the strongest possible terms. "I *know*, from the most authentic sources, that I have been the frequent subject of the most unkind whispers and insinuating from the same quarter."[98]

As for Jefferson, his letter, written from Monticello on 9 September 1792, acknowledged and defended his conduct, and then went on to answer in detail the charges in Hamilton's newspaper essays. Who had begun the conflict? he asked. Clearly Hamilton. There was only one instance in which he had ever meddled in the affairs of other departments, Jefferson confessed, and he now recognized that his conduct in that case had been a dreadful mistake: "I was duped into [it] by the Secretary of the treasury, and made a tool for forwarding his schemes, not then sufficiently understood by me; and of all the errors of my political life, this has occasioned me the deepest regret." He had always intended to explain this, he informed the president, "when, from being actors on the scene, we shall have become uninterested spectators only."[99] Washington did not need to be told what Jefferson meant; it was Jefferson's own part in arranging for assumption that he wished he could justify–that, and the lack of foresight in failing to understand where Hamilton's policies would lead.

But otherwise, Jefferson conceded nothing. Hamilton's system "flowed from principles adverse to liberty, and was calculated to undermine and demolish the republic, by creating an influence of his department over the members of the legislature." The prizes Hamilton's system created–the rise in value of the debt, the prospect of still more profits from stock in the Bank of the United States–were used as "bait" to garner votes for his projects, which would never have passed the House and the Senate had only "the disinterested majority" voted on them: "These were no longer the votes then of the representatives of the people, but of deserters from the rights and interests of the people: And it was impossible to consider their decisions, which had nothing in view but to enrich themselves, as the measures of the fair majority, which ought always to be respected."

Jefferson was outraged that Hamilton should dare to attack him, whose honor was spotless. Who was Hamilton, after all, but "a man whose history, from the moment at which history can stoop to notice him, is a tissue of machinations against the liberty of the country which has not only received and given him bread, but heaped it's [*sic*] honors on his head." If Hamilton persisted in his libels, Jefferson hinted, he would resign and justify himself to the public.[100] And, once he was back in Philadelphia and had access to his official papers, Jefferson added a postscript in the form of a detailed defense of his conduct in regard to the debt to France, rehearsing the arguments he had used in 1786 and showing that he had never intended to defraud anyone of what was justly due.[101]

There matters rested. Washington's hope that Hamilton and Jefferson would resolve their differences had been naive to begin with, and nothing came of his efforts. Each new move by the Treasury Department forces produced its countermove by Jefferson and his Republican friends; thus when Congress took up the subject of bankruptcy later that fall, Jefferson once again began compiling a list of objections not unlike those he had offered in 1790 in his opinion on the Arrears of Pay and in 1791 in his opinion on the constitutionality of the bank bill. Alarmed in particular by the fact that, unlike the British prototype statute, the bankruptcy bill as drafted made no exception for agriculturalists, Jefferson asked whether the United States was "really ripe" for a system that would allow those acting under the statute to "enter houses, break open doors, chests, &c." Worse, "the lands of the bankrupt are to be taken, sold &c. Is not this a fundamental question between the general and state legislatures?" But what could be expected from a mentality that, while departing from the British example by including agriculturalists, adhered to it by exempting "the buyers and sellers of bank stock, government paper &c.?"[102]

Yet despite the apparent stalemate in the cabinet, by the end of 1792 something *had* changed. Thanks to the newspaper controversies of the summer and fall, the public now knew a good deal about Jefferson's position on the leading political issues of the day; the secretary of state was emerging as a party leader in his own right. Madison might put his friend's ideas before the public in the anonymous fashion of the day, but Hamilton's polemics had made an issue of Jefferson's behavior, past and present, and Jefferson had been forced to defend himself. This was a notable act for a man who intensely disliked open controversy, and it was at this point that the leadership role for the opposition began to shift from Madison to Jefferson himself. Jefferson might nominally observe the president's injunctions, but the reality was different. Hamilton had to be stopped, and if it could not be done in the cabinet, Congress offered another and seemingly more promising venue. Accordingly, Jefferson worked behind the scenes to further the assault on Hamilton's handling of financial matters that culminated in the abortive Giles resolutions of early 1793, whose failure gravely disappointed him.[103] If, as Eugene R. Sheridan has noted, Jefferson did everything in his power to cover up his tracks in the Giles affair, both at the time and later, his participation could hardly have been more active. His motives were twofold. First, he hoped to be able to acquire absolute proof, proof that would convince the president, of Hamilton's illegal activities, and second, and at this stage just as important, he desperately wanted to help the fledgling French republic and was afraid that Hamilton would find a way to stop payment on the debt due France.[104]

Jefferson did, however, discover that in some instances obligations might be binding after all. Following the defeat of the Giles resolutions in the spring of 1793, as the cabinet debated what the United States should do now that America's ally France was once again at war with Great Britain, Jefferson found himself arguing that the Treaty of Alliance of 1778 was still binding, despite the change in the form of the French government and the radically different circumstances facing the United States in 1793. In contrast to Hamilton, who declared that the execution of Louis XVI in January of that year had dissolved the treaty—it had been a treaty between the king and Congress—Jefferson insisted that under the moral law "between society and society the same moral duties exist as did between the individuals composing them while in an unassociated state." It followed that "compacts then between nation and nation are obligatory between them by the same moral law which obliges individuals to observe their compacts." And while admitting that "non-performance is not immoral" when performance is "*imposs-ible*" or "*self-destructive*," he denied that nature gave man—and therefore nations—"permission to annul his obligations for a time, or for ever, whenever they are 'dangerous, useless, or disagreeable.' " That doctrine would produce the most pernicious results: "If we could free ourselves from a compact because we find ourselves injured by it," Jefferson concluded, "there would be nothing firm in the contracts of nations."[105] Hence, the United States was still bound by a treaty that, at least on paper, was intended to be perpetual.[106]

Thus fifteen years after the signing of the Treaty of Alliance with France—and only four years from the limit he had proposed for the validity of laws and constitutions—Jefferson could discuss its obligations without so much as a suggestion that there was anything wrong with perpetual treaties, any principle that barred the living from attempting to bind their successors with such agreements. Occasionally, political expediency gained the upper hand over doctrinal consistency, even for Jefferson. More important, the controversy with Hamilton over the treaty further confirms the point already made, that in the 1790s Jefferson was decidedly cautious in discussing his principle. Given the secretary of the treasury's outrage the year before when Giles protested against the funding system and Representative John Mercer suggested limitations on debts, it is improbable that Hamilton would not have made use of Jefferson's arguments against perpetual obligations at some point in the polemics of 1793, had he known of them. But neither in the cabinet nor in his newspaper essays did Hamilton so much as mention them.

On the whole, Jefferson's attitudes were fixed. The period of 1791 to 1792 was the great turning point, as Jefferson came to realize that the republicanism he prized so highly was under attack by Treasury Department forces using the debt to advance the cause of monarchy. It was then that he had come to see the need for an opposition, for a "republican interest" as he put it, that would restore the violated order. Madison explained the process for the public in still another of his *National Gazette* essays, "A Candid State of Parties," published in late September 1792, shortly after the close of Washington's correspondence with Jefferson and Hamilton. There were, Madison thought, two parties in the country, one composed of "those, who from particular interest, from natural temper, or from the habits of life, are more partial to the opulent than to the other classes of society," and the other composed of "those who believing in the doctrine that mankind are capable of governing themselves . . . are naturally offended at every public measure that does not appeal to the understanding and to the general interest of the community, or that is not strictly conformable to the principles, and conducive to the preservation of republican government." The latter, the "Republican party, as it may be termed," was naturally the political home of "the mass of people in every part of the union, in every state, and of every occupation." Unfortunately, superiority in numbers did not give it the influence it deserved; too often, apparently, the stratagems of the opposite party prevailed. Still, in the long run, the success of the Republican party was guaranteed; in the short run, however, it was best to be prepared for reverses, Madison counseled.[107] These views, which Jefferson shared, were the one ray of hope the secretary of state could find in the otherwise gloomy political picture. But Jefferson had had enough. He had fully paid the debt he owed to the public, he told Madison and others who begged him to stay on, and he was more than ready to retire.[108] Circumstances kept Jefferson in office longer than he had anticipated, but at last the president permitted his resignation to take effect at the end of 1793.[109]

Jefferson returned to Monticello knowing that he had left the Republican interest in capable hands. And he hoped that he had put politics behind him, though he continued to sound the alarm on "the shameless corruption of a portion of the Representatives to the first and second Congresses, and their implicit devotion to the treasury," if only among his Albemarle neighbors.[110] There were, of course, echoes of earlier concerns; when Vice President John Adams sent him a pamphlet on Swiss politics discussing the historical claims of the Vaudois against their Bernese overlords, Jefferson merely found it amusing. "The claims of both parties," he replied to Adams, "are on grounds which I fancy we have taught the world to set little store by. The rights of one generation will scarcely be considered hereafter as depending on the paper transactions of another."[111] Yet Jefferson could not afford to ignore national politics entirely; Madison sent a steady stream of letters from Philadelphia, and Jefferson kept his hand in by letting Madison have his comments on the latest crisis.[112]

At times it must have seemed as though 1794, 1795, and 1796 brought nothing but crisis. Jefferson worked away at the reconstruction of Monticello, the improvement of his plantations, and the reduction of his debts, but the news from Philadelphia kept intruding. First the controversy with Britain over maritime rights in 1794 and then, in 1795 and 1796, the prolonged and agonizing national debate over the Jay Treaty broke in to disturb Jefferson's retirement. These were issues Jefferson could not have ignored had he wanted to. The threat of war with Britain in 1794 led the Treasury Department's supporters to argue the case for a stronger American defense, and Jefferson hardly required Madison's reminder that "you understand . . . the old trick of turning every contingency into a resource for accumulating force in the Government."[113] Jefferson understood perfectly: "Not that the Monocrats & Papermen in Congress want war," he replied to Madison, "but they want armies & debts: and tho' we may hope that the sound part of Congress is now so augmented as to ensure a majority in cases of general interest merely, yet I have always observed that in questions of expence, where members may hope either for offices or jobs for themselves or their friends, some few will be debauched, & that is sufficient to turn the decision where a majority is at most but small."

Internal affairs intruded as well; Jefferson was horrified by the display of military force used to quell the Whiskey Rebellion, and he was even more outraged by the president's denunciations of the "self-created" Democratic Republican societies in the annual message to Congress in the fall of 1794. He had criticized the excise tax to Washington in 1792; now it produced the results he had predicted, and his fears that this "infernal" law would be the "instrument of dismembering the Union, & setting us all afloat to chuse which part of it we will adhere to" grew accordingly.[114]

In Congress, there were signs that something was being done about the debt; in the same message that angered Jefferson, the president urged the legislators to consider "a definitive plan for the redemption of the Public Debt."[115] Yet the taxes proposed by the Federalists to accomplish this—particularly the additional excises—were unpalatable to the Republicans. Madison did admit that "much as he disliked excises, he thought a perpetual debt a still greater evil."[116] Still, Madison found this all rather late in the day, and doubted that "the Treasury faction" was in earnest.[117] Once Hamilton's valedictory report as secretary of the treasury appeared in January 1795, Madison was able to tell Jefferson that its plan for reducing the debt would "require about *30 years* of uninterrupted operation. The fund is to consist of the surpluses of impost & Excise, and the temporary taxes of the last Session which are to be prolonged till 1781 [*sic*]. You will judge of the chance of our ever being out of debt, if no other means are to be used." Direct taxes would help but, Madison assumed, the public would not stand for them, and "of this dislike the partizans of the Debt take advantage not only to perpetuate it, but to make a merit of the application of inadequate means to the discharge of it."[118]

By the mid-1790s such views were to be expected in Virginia Republicanism's political discourse. Madison and his colleagues in Congress were tireless in propagating them, and Virginia authors were beginning to bring them before wider audiences. The emergence of John Taylor of Caroline as a Republican theorist was an important step in the process; although his pamphlets were prolix and tedious, they delighted Jefferson, who considered them the perfect antidotes to Federalist heresies.[119] Outside Virginia, there were those who thought they detected a strong connection between debt and Virginia politics, even if they were more inclined to suspect that the Virginians' personal debts were responsible for their opposition to Federalist policies. John Adams had no doubts on this score; the vice president knew Jefferson too well not to be sure that the £7,000 in British debts he thought Jefferson owed had an impact on his politics.[120] Virginia support for the motion to sequester British debts during the crisis of 1794 led many Federalists to conclude that the Virginia attitude toward debt was suspiciously self-serving, and so, from the mid-1790s on, the Virginians had to confront Federalist claims that they were fundamentally averse to paying debts of any kind, private or public, no matter how sacred.

It was typical when Federalist stalwart Fisher Ames—"the colossus of the monocrats and paper men," Jefferson called him—remarked after the Virginia senators urged sequestration during the crisis with Britain in 1794, "Thus, murder, at last, is out." Vice President Adams closely followed the movement to sequester the debts and was sure that Virginia unwillingness to pay debts was at the root of it all: "O! liberty. O! my country. O! debt, and O! sin? These debtors are the persons who are continually declaiming against

the corruption of Congress. Impudence! thy front is brass."[121] The irrepress-
ible William Loughton Smith made a similar claim in 1796, arguing that
Jefferson's own substantial debts to British merchants had affected his
conduct as secretary of state when negotiating with British minister George
Hammond in 1792; his *"personal* interest," Smith suggested, left Jefferson
less than eager to reach a settlement. Virginians might insist that their object was to "counteract the fatal tendency of the funding system without
endangering the public debt" and to drive from office the "faction . . . who
have adopted the false and detestable principle that a public debt is a public blessing" and "pursue the execrable systems of finance, negotiation,
and war, which have uniformly led to bankruptcy and misery," but Federalists knew better.[122] Thus the Virginians' own connection between private
and public debts would be turned against them by Federalist propaganda,
and in a way that Virginians like Jefferson, who looked on his own behavior
toward creditors as honorable to the last degree, could only regard as
insultingly wrong.

Jefferson was no longer able to permit himself the luxury of observing
these developments from afar. By 1796, Madison and others convinced him
that he would have to reenter politics, this time as a candidate for the highest
office.[123] And so, after the election of 1796, which brought John Adams to
the presidency and Jefferson to the vice presidency, he returned to the
familiar scenes of Philadelphia, there to watch the Federalists take the
Republic still further along the road that led to the extinction of liberty. Four
difficult years would be spent as vice president, years that saw the nation
engaged in an undeclared war with France, saw the national debt climb and
climb, saw taxes—and resistance to them—multiply, saw the Federalists attempt to curb the Republican opposition with repressive measures like the
Sedition Act.[124] Jefferson witnessed it all as an observer; presiding over the
Senate, and without a voice in the public councils, he could see his predictions coming true, one by one. Outside Congress, he would work to
strengthen the Republican interest and prayed for its victory by 1800, the last
chance to save the nation, or so it seemed. At times, he must have despaired
that the day would finally arrive when Hamilton and his friends would be
thrown back into richly deserved obscurity, and he was driven to desperate
measures along the way—the Kentucky Resolutions not least among them—
as he looked for means with which to combat the Federalist threat.[125]

Evil in itself, the public debt was now filling still another of the malign
roles the Republicans attributed to it. For as ever larger amounts of both the
debt itself and the debt-based shares of the Bank of the United States were
sold abroad and passed into British hands, the debt was becoming in
Jefferson's eyes an instrument, perhaps even *the* instrument, of actual British
domination of American affairs. "They are advancing fast to a monopoly of
our banks & public funds, and thereby placing our public finances under
their control," he told the Massachusetts political maverick Elbridge Gerry
early in 1797, so that in this, as in other respects, Hamilton's monster had
created the means by which American liberty would be destroyed and the

results of the Revolution undone.[126] And that was merely the state of things at the outset of Jefferson's term as vice president. The next four years would see far worse.

Throughout, Jefferson was conscious of the sacrifice he was being called on to make. And when he put it into words, it was with the metaphor that came most naturally to him, that of debtor and creditor. "There is a debt of service due from every man to his country," he instructed Edward Rutledge of South Carolina the month after learning of his election. "There is no bankrupt law in heaven, by which you may get off with shillings in the pound; with rendering to a single State what you owed to the whole confederacy. I think it was by the Roman law," he said, recalling an argument he had rejected in his 1789 letter to Madison, "that a father was denied sepulture, unless his son would pay his debts. . . . Come forward & pay your own debts."[127] High office was, then, a debt that Jefferson owed his countrymen and the principles to which he gave allegiance; at a time of crisis, no true patriot could be found wanting, and so Jefferson returned to the political battlefield he had abandoned—forever, he thought—at the end of 1793.

There was, however, the hope that heavy taxes necessary to service the mounting American debt and supply the sums being spent on the army and navy would bring the people to their senses. A land tax, Jefferson informed Virginia jurist St. George Tucker, "would awaken our constituents, and call for inspection into past proceedings," just as "the matter of finances . . . has set the people of Europe to thinking." For "war, land tax & stamp tax . . . will bring on reflection, and that, with information, is all which our countrymen need, to bring themselves and their affairs to rights," he explained as relations with France deteriorated in the spring of 1798. It was all simple and certain, he assured a nervous and rather skeptical John Taylor of Caroline: "Land tax, stamp tax, increase of public debt, &c." were bound to produce "an order of things more correspondent to the sentiments of our constituents." Jefferson was sure all would be right in the end. "A little patience," he advised Taylor, "and we shall see the reign of witches pass over, their spells dissolved, and the people recovering their true sight, restoring their government to its true principles." In the meantime, of course, "we are suffering deeply in spirit, and incurring the horrors of a war, and long oppressions of enormous public debt." By early 1799, Jefferson could congratulate himself that his predictions were coming true: "The tax gatherer has already excited discontent," he noted in reporting to Madison Republican gains in Pennsylvania and Massachusetts.[128] James Monroe and Edmund Pendleton were given similar reassurances that popular opposition to taxes would soon lead to deliverance, and by the spring of 1800 Jefferson was confident that all would shortly be right. The Federalists' "madness & extravagance" guaranteed it, he thought, for the "people through all the States are for republican forms, republican principles, simplicity, economy, religious & civil freedom." Still, Jefferson did not underestimate the seriousness of the situation, and even as he was reassuring Monroe and Pendleton, he was telling Samuel Adams that "a debt of an hundred millions growing by usurious interest, and an artificial paper phalanx overruling the agricultural mass of our country, with other &c. &c. &c., have a portentious aspect."[129]

In the end, Jefferson's confidence was rewarded. The Federalists overreached themselves, and disagreements within their ranks occasioned by the peace mission to France—dispatched by a president who shared many of Jefferson's views on the dangers of debt—helped to finish them off.[130] Now it was Jefferson's turn. The presidential election of 1800 had been nasty enough, with neither side enjoying a monopoly on scurrility. Federalists dredged up what they could about Jefferson's past; in addition to the usual stories of religious infidelity and sexual misbehavior, there were charges that he had defrauded creditors during the Revolution. Jefferson was outraged by the attacks on his character, but he accepted this as what he had to expect from the Federalists in their desperation.[131] Rather than dwell on these insults, Jefferson turned instead to consider what he hoped his administration could accomplish. In fact, he had little considering to do. In its essentials his program would be the one he had outlined for Washington in 1792. Jefferson would not touch the debt—Hamilton knew this, and it was one of the reasons he preferred Jefferson to Aaron Burr when the election went to the House of Representatives to be decided—but it would be set firmly on the road to extinction.[132] As Washington Irving later put it, exaggerating only slightly, national policy under Jefferson could be summed up in a single word: "ECONOMY, my friend, is the watchword of the nation. . . . It is a kind of national starvation; an experiment of how many comforts and necessities the body politic can be deprived of before it perishes."[133] And so Jefferson would put the nation on the strictest possible regime, relentlessly shrinking the public debt and purging the Federalist impurities that had invaded the republican system during the administrations of Washington and Adams.

Earlier, in 1795, Jefferson had explained the state of American politics as one in which the "monocrats" hoped to introduce "an English constitution" by "adopting the English forms & principles of administration, and [by] forming like them a monied interest." All of this, he added, was to be accomplished "by means of a funding system, not calculated to pay the public debt, but to render it perpetual, and to make it an engine in the hands of the executive branch of the government which, added to the great patronage it possessed in the disposal of public offices, might enable it to assume by degrees a kingly authority."[134] This, clearly, would have to go, and the sooner the better. Albert Gallatin would be Jefferson's chosen instrument; with the publication of his *A Sketch of the Finances of the United States* in 1796, the Geneva-born Pennsylvanian had established himself as the Republicans' financial expert, and he had shown himself both capable and—more to the point in 1801—far better qualified than any available Virginian to understand the mysteries of finance.[135]

Gallatin shared most, if not all, of Jefferson's ideas in these matters, and it is difficult, given the Republicans' goals, to imagine how the new president could have made a better choice. Thanks to Gallatin, who managed the details, and thanks as well to the substantial Republican majorities in both houses of Congress, little political difficulty was to be anticipated from this part—the major part—of the new administration's program. Rigorous economy in government expenditure, savings whenever possible, and the application of every spare penny to the reduction of the debt—this would be the heart of Jefferson's effort. Accomplish this, reverse the course Hamilton had set, and the danger to republicanism would be over. No debt, and no corruption; no wars, no standing armies, no navies, no hordes of internal tax collectors, and, thus, no threat that liberty would disappear. It was as simple as that—as long, that is, as customs duties continued to fill the national coffers, as long as there was no war.

"So enviable a state in prospect for our country," Jefferson later recalled, "induced me to temporize, and to bear with national wrongs which under no other prospect ought ever to have been unresented or unresisted." Jefferson's program of liberation, ironically enough, was every bit as dependent as Hamilton's on peace and good relations with Britain, though the president never acknowledged the similarity. The chance that the stream of revenue might dry up was the one factor in the equation the Republicans could not control. But for most of Jefferson's two terms in office, that danger was never very real.[136]

Yet Jefferson would also have to think of the future, and not merely of what might be done with the revenue once the public debt had disappeared, though that was a prospect that entranced him.[137] It was important, extremely important, that republican principles be firmly implanted, that the doctrines Jefferson knew so well and shared with other Virginia Republicans find their way into the hearts of the people. In 1801, after years of having to guard his words, of worrying whether private letters or chance remarks might fall into the hands of those who would make the worst of them—no idle fear, given the controversy over *Rights of Man* in 1791 or the far greater furor occasioned by the publication in 1797 of his 1796 letter to Philip Mazzei—Jefferson found himself in a position where he not only could make public statements but was expected to make them.[138] The Inaugural Address and the Annual Message became Jefferson's chosen forms of communication with the public after the election of 1800, and he used them to propagate his doctrines as widely as possible.[139] Because they constitute our best evidence of the depth of his convictions on political issues in the period of the presidency, it will be helpful to look at them in detail.

Jefferson took the opportunity of the First Inaugural to reaffirm his commitment to the republican project. "But would the honest patriot," he asked, "abandon a government which has so far kept us free and firm, on theoretic and visionary fear that this Government, the world's best hope, may by possibility want energy to preserve itself?" In effect, Jefferson was now answering the questions Washington and Madison had posed, twelve years earlier, in the original Inaugural Address; "the experiment entrusted to the hands of the American people" had indeed succeeded.[140] Pleading for an end to party strife—for the Federalists to admit that they were in error and join the victorious Republican majority, though he did not put it that bluntly—Jefferson went on to ask what was necessary to complete the list of America's "blessings" and "make us a happy and prosperous people." The answer was simplicity itself: "Still one thing more, fellow citizens—a wise and frugal government, which shall restrain men from injuring one another, which shall leave them otherwise free to regulate their own pursuits of industry and improvement, and shall not take from the mouth of labor the bread it has earned." It was "economy in the public expense, that labor may be lightly burdened; the honest payment of our debts and sacred preservation of the public faith" that would help to ensure "wise and frugal government," as would reliance on "a well-disciplined militia."[141]

Where, in this catalogue of republican verities, was Jefferson's theme of the rights of generations? No doubt readers of the Inaugural Address would discern that the administration had no plans to incur new debts, but surely it was strange that Jefferson did not strengthen his position on debt by urging Congress to pass an amendment that embodied the principle of generations. In 1798, he had gone even further than that, telling John Taylor that the Constitution needed but "a single amendment." And "that alone," he thought, would secure the "reduction of the administration of our government to the genuine principles of it's [*sic*] constitution." This would be "an additional article, taking from the federal government the power of borrowing." He admitted that paying "all proper expences within the year, would, in case of war, be hard on us." But the alternative was "ten wars instead of one. For wars would be reduced in that proportion; besides," he suggested, sounding rather like the Antifederalists of 1787 and 1788 in this regard, "the State governments would be free to lend *their credit* in borrowing quotas."[142] Yet neither in 1801 nor in any other year of his presidency did Jefferson suggest such a measure. Surely this was his opportunity. Why did he fail to seize it?

The answer, I suspect, lies in Jefferson's appreciation that such an amendment, whether in the form of a restriction of loans to nineteen years' duration or in the more drastic version of 1798—no loans at all—would have been highly controversial. He had no need for additional controversy if—and this was crucial—he could attain his ends by other means. That was what his administration would do: The debt would be set on the road to extinction, and the general maxims of republican policy, now that the Federalists had been vanquished, would then suffice to prevent future accumulations, or so he must have hoped. He had pledged himself to the "sacred preservation of the public faith"—a pledge held out to reassure Federalists that their fears the Republicans would repudiate the debt were groundless—and to have introduced his principle would have called that promise into question, as Hamilton's outrage at Representative John Mercer's speech in 1792 had demonstrated. Jefferson was far from abandoning his principle—we shall see him reviving it in his retirement—but in the presidential years prudence suggested a more cautious approach. And it was that cautious approach, insisting on the wisdom of frugality and paying off the debt, pointing to what could be accomplished once the burden was lifted, that Jefferson used again and again in his messages.

Reduction in the expenses of government, he informed Congress in December 1801, would permit the country "safely" to "dispense with all the internal taxes," and he denounced the idea of taxing simply to "accumulate treasure for wars to happen we know not when, and which might not happen but from the temptations offered by that treasure."[143] The following year, he was able to report the happy effects of this policy: "Merely by avoiding false objects of expense we are able, without a direct tax, without internal taxes, and without borrowing to make large and effectual payments toward the discharge of our public debt and the emancipation of our posterity from that moral canker." The reduction in the debt itself meant that greater resources would be available in emergencies, he noted, and of course that would further reduce the need to borrow in the event of war. The lesson, then, was clear: "preserve the faith of the nation by an exact discharge of its debts and contracts, expend the public money with the same care and economy we would practise with our own, and impose on our citizens no unnecessary burdens."[144] By the end of 1803, Jefferson was able to announce substantial reductions in the debt; since 1802, more than $8.5 million of the principal had been paid off, though it was of course true that the Louisiana Purchase added a further $13 million to the sum outstanding. Still, Jefferson thought the nation was now prosperous enough to afford that, and to keep on with the policy of paying off the old debt as well.[145] In 1804, it was much the same. "The state of our finances," Jefferson wrote, "continues to fulfil our expectations," and by the date of his message, the total principal retired amounted to $12 million.[146] Such figures, Jefferson must have felt, spoke for themselves. But he had interpolated his own comments along the way—the notion of debt as "moral canker," the reminder that the underlying principles to be observed were the same in both the private and the public spheres. These were old themes for Jefferson, and now that he was president he saw to it that they became part of his messages, knowing they would reach the widest possible audience that way.

Against this background, the opening of his second administration looked like the beginning of another four years of unparalleled prosperity and progress toward complete institutionalization of Republican financial principles. Jefferson's Second Inaugural Address accordingly moved forward to interpret the reduction of the debt in terms that would bring his favorite concepts before the public more fully. He boasted that Americans had been liberated from the vexations of internal taxation and that the existing revenue came from "the consumption of foreign articles, [and] is paid cheerfully by those who can afford to add foreign luxuries to domestic comforts." Hence it was "the pleasure and pride of an American to ask, what farmer, what mechanic, what laborer, ever sees a tax-gatherer of the United States?" And yet this revenue sufficed both to pay the current costs of government and to effect substantial reductions in the public debt. Jefferson therefore introduced his notion of what might be done once the "final redemption" of the debt had taken place. In time of peace–once the Constitution was suitably amended, of course–the funds raised by the duties on imports might be applied to "rivers, canals, roads, arts, manufactures, education, and other great objects." In time of war, he thought, there would be additional resources, now that interest on the debt no longer consumed them, so that the crisis could be met by paying "within the year all the expenses of the year, without encroaching on the rights of future generations, by burdening them with the debts of the past."[147]

Thus, in 1805, Jefferson for the first time openly referred to the rights that formed so central a part of his view of the dangers of debt. And, it is important to note, he did so in the context of an address in which he veiled his criticism of the "anti-social doctrines" of those who raised "the hue & cry . . . against philosophy & the rights of man," burying it in remarks on the need to bring the Indians into the modern world by combating "ignorance, pride, and the influence of interested and crafty individuals among them"–Jefferson's way of assailing the Federalists without, as he put it in a note to himself, engaging in "direct warfare on them."[148] But it was now possible to take up the theme of debt, even if only in this brief and undeveloped form–there was no mention of the nineteen-year limitation, let alone of the other conclusions Jefferson drew from it–because his administration had proved beyond doubt that it would pay the debt scrupulously. Hence there was no need to worry about the state of Federalist opinion, and in any case Jefferson's reelection had demonstrated–not that any demonstration was necessary by this point–that the Federalists were finished. Continuing prosperity enabled the administration to make substantial reductions in the debt, and so it was possible, and prudent as well, for Jefferson to address the question of what should be done in the future. If the First Inaugural Address had suggested how Jefferson and his colleagues would restore republicanism, the Second Inaugural Address examined the lines of policy that would preserve it for generations to come.

The messages of the second term were on the whole in the nature of progress reports. Jefferson would note the current Treasury Department surplus and its application to the remaining debt.[149] But he also took care to insert reminders of the themes he had outlined in the Second Inaugural. In 1806, he again drew Congress's attention to the question of what should be done once "the most desirable of all objects"–"the complete liberation of our revenues"–had been achieved. Internal improvements would bind the union together, he suggested; he referred to the benefits a national institution of higher learning would produce; and once more he suggested consideration of the constitutional changes necessary to accomplish such goals. The parallel passage in the Seventh Annual Message, delivered on 27 October 1807, was more muted, given the possibility that "future surpluses" might disappear if there were "a change in our public relations, now awaiting the determination of others"–a typically convoluted Jeffersonian reference to the possibility of war with Great Britain over the *Chesapeake* incident.[150]

The Eighth (and last) Annual Message, his valedictory, returned to the theme of what should be done once the debt was extinguished, after reporting that $33,580,000 "of the principal of the funded debt, being the whole which could be paid or purchased within the limits of the law and our contracts," had been discharged, with the result that $2 million formerly paid in interest was now being added "annually to the disposable surplus." If Madison in 1789 had feared that the surplus might be used for purposes of corruption and worse, Jefferson now saw it as so many lost opportunities, and the difference between those positions illustrates as well as anything can the way in which Jefferson envisioned the end of the public debt as transforming American politics.[151] Deploring the notion that such sums might "lie unproductive in the public vaults," Jefferson instead urged Congress that they should be "appropriated to the improvements of roads, canals, rivers, education, and other great foundations of prosperity and union."[152] Nor did Jefferson and his colleagues leave Congress entirely in the dark as to what might be done in this direction; Gallatin's magisterial *Report on Roads and Canals* of 6 April 1808 had already helped to direct public attention to the creation of a national system of transportation, proposing an annual appropriation of $2 million for this purpose, a sum the secretary of the treasury thought well within the country's capacity as long as peace and retrenchment prevailed.[153]

If these were Jefferson's public statements, his private views hardly differed. From the outset of the first administration, he strove to explain his policy to correspondents. In 1801, he was predicting that the entire debt could be paid off within fifteen years, even without the aid of internal taxes, though in 1802 he thought it might take eighteen.[154] And to Levi Lincoln, his first attorney general, he explained that he would "take no other revenge" on the Federalists, "than, by a steady pursuit of economy and peace, and by the establishment of republican principles in substance and in form, to sink federalism into an abyss from which there shall be no resurrection for it." Jefferson had earlier told Dr. Walter Jones that "when we reflect how difficult it is to move or inflect the great machine of society, how impossible to advance the notions of a whole people suddenly to ideal right, we see the wisdom of Solon's remark, that no more good must be attempted than the nation can bear, and that all will be chiefly to reform the waste of public money, and thus drive away the vultures who prey upon it, and improve some little on old routines."[155] There were dangers to be avoided en route, however; the Federalists' "object," he feared, was to "force us into war if possible, in order to derange our finances." But Jefferson would not permit this, and he also told the recipient of this information, James Monroe, that unlike the Federalists, who "in order to increase expense, debt, taxation, and patronage" spent lavishly on the diplomatic service, the Republicans would do no such thing, a message that Monroe, about to leave for England as a special envoy, cannot have relished.[156]

To Pierre Samuel Du Pont de Nemours, Jefferson stressed his administration's rigid financial purity: Our "great debts," he said, "will be falling due by

installments for 15. years to come, and require from us the practice of a
rigorous economy to accomplish their payment; and it is our principle to pay
to a moment whatever we have engaged, and never to engage what we
cannot, and mean not faithfully to pay."[157] The contrast between a flourishing America, rapidly reducing its debt, and the coming collapse of Britain
was a subject to which Jefferson always warmed; accepting an invitation for
the Fourth of July in 1806, he remarked on America's singular good fortune
in having "divorced [itself] from the follies and crimes of Europe, for a dollar
in the pound at least of six hundred millions sterling, and from all the ruin of
Mr. Pitt's administration."[158] But in private, if not in public, he was willing
to admit that war would derange all his plans; should the United States go to
war with Britain, he told William Short in 1807, by the second year recourse
to domestic loans would be necessary and in the years after that foreign loans
would be required.[159] That was always a danger Jefferson had to bear
in mind, and it had a decided impact on his policies at the end of the second administration; nothing must be allowed to disturb the retirement of
the debt.[160]

Yet if Jefferson was justifiably proud of his record in redeeming the
public debt (and thereby redeeming the Republic), he never ceased to regret
the mistake that had made this course essential. Early in the first administration, he told Du Pont that "the contracted English half lettered ideas of
Hamilton destroyed . . . in the bud" the chances of setting the American
republic on the right path. "We can pay off his debt in 15 years," Jefferson
continued, "but we can never get rid of his financial system. It mortifies me
to be strengthened by principles which I deem radically vicious, but this vice
is entailed on us by a just error," he added in allusion to the events of 1790.
And again, using language that would have meant a good deal more to him
than it did to the letter's recipient, he confessed that there was only so much
that could be achieved in this regard: "What is practicable must often
countroul what is pure theory, and the habits of the governed determine in a
great degree what is practicable."[161] Jefferson would do what he could, but
there was always the sense of what might have been had he and Madison fully
grasped Hamilton's intentions in 1790.

Jefferson's eight years as president saw republicanism restored and the national debt set firmly on the course of extinction. The two, in fact, were
inseparable elements of a common whole, for it was the debt—Hamilton's
debt, created in 1790 and augmented thereafter—that had been the means of
undermining republicanism and, as Jefferson and his friends understood
these things, pointing America in the direction of monarchy. Jefferson never
doubted that he had understood matters correctly or that the danger had
been narrowly averted. He knew that his party's principles had saved the
nation, and he was confident that, if left to follow their natural inclinations,
the bulk of the people were with him.

Moreover, during his terms in office, Jefferson had been able to put flesh
on the bones of what had been only a dream in 1789 when he wrote the 6

September letter to Madison. In 1809, his vision of how American society might be ordered differently seemed well on its way to realization. Without the ability to contract lengthy debts and wage costly wars at the expense of the future and to indulge in the other forms of waste that had occupied so much of eighteenth-century Anglo-America's practical politics, there would be little left for government to do except promote the good of the community. Jefferson's final messages to Congress had in fact sketched how that might be done, suggesting improvements to the common estate through the application of progressive enhancements of knowledge and science to the highest possible end. In outline, at least, it was a dazzling prospect of a world free of the burdens and corruptions national debts create, a world that would give birth to a political culture vastly different from that Jefferson had grown up with and within whose confines he had been forced to operate. Jefferson, in short, had imagined a world in which normal politics would no longer exist, in which the principle that the earth belongs in usufruct to the living generation was finally realized.

But Jefferson was realist enough to remember that the United States occupied an uncertain place in the world. Peace was integral to the success of his goals, but peace might not always be possible. And what then? Would the principles he had tried to inculcate prevail? Or would there be further accumulations of debt, further opportunities for corruption, a further struggle with those who did not share his passion for pure republicanism? Jefferson had done what he could in the nearly twenty years since his return from France to fight those battles, but it would be up to others to carry on the struggle. He could congratulate himself that so much had been achieved.

6

An Engine so Corruptive

There does not exist an engine so corruptive of the government and so demoralizing of the nation as a public debt.

Thomas Jefferson, 1821[1]

Can one generation bind another, and all others, in succession forever? I think not. The Creator made the earth for the living, not the dead.

Thomas Jefferson, 1824[2]

His retirement in 1809 brought Jefferson little of the leisure he hoped to obtain. "A correspondence afflictingly laborious"—his "epistolary corvée," he called it—kept him chained to his desk; the founding of the University of Virginia demanded every moment he could spare from other business; guests by the score had to be looked after, dined, and talked to. Monticello swarmed with his grandchildren; even in the absence of visitors, privacy was hard to achieve.[3] Jefferson found relief by escaping to his newly built Bedford County house, Poplar Forest; there, at least, he was offered some of the peace he needed, and there he was able to set down his thoughts on the questions that had interested him, free from interruption.[4] But crowded though his retirement was, it had its benefits. Debt might continue to plague him— "Instead of the unalloyed happiness of retiring unembarrassed and independent, to the enjoyment of my estate, which is ample for my limited views, I have to pass such a length of time in a thraldom of mind never before known to me," he told Kosciuszko in 1810, and that was only the beginning—yet there were compensations as well.[5] "Nature intended me for the tranquil pursuits of science, by rendering them my supreme delight," he explained two days before the end of his second term, adding with heart-felt anticipation that "never did a prisoner, released from his chains, feel such relief as I shall on shaking off the shackles of power." The image of the "Sage of Monticello" was already taking shape.[6]

Once more a private citizen—or at least one with no official responsibilities, for he would always be a public figure—Jefferson could now express himself on his favorite topics with considerably greater freedom than had been possible during his years in office. To be sure, that freedom was not unqualified; he was conscious of the limits on what he could say, and his fear of public controversy made him cautious in his choice of correspondents. Thus he would not publish his sentiments to the world during his lifetime, especially on religious and political matters, but in his quiet behind-the-scenes fashion he became something of a crusader, unveiling his ideas to a new generation that would, he hoped, see the truth of his doctrines and take them to heart.[7] Some of those he approached would find the idea that the earth belongs in usufruct to the living more than a little surprising, but Jefferson kept at it. Of all the lessons he had to teach, this was the one he was not prepared to let go by default. And there were other missions for Jefferson to pursue in the years between 1809 and 1826, other truths he wished to drive home before it was too late. High on his list was setting the historical record straight and so ensuring that future generations of Americans would not be misled by the propaganda of Federalist writers, his distant cousin Chief Justice John Marshall chief among them. Thus Jefferson would busy himself among his files—having kept so many of his papers, he was more than ready to document his case—compiling an account of his political life that would do full justice to the cause he had served. It need hardly be added that he was also out to settle old scores, or that he would return to the events of 1790, working them over until he found a satisfactory way to explain how he had made his great mistake.[8]

At the time he left office, Jefferson was convinced that he had set the public debt firmly on the road to extinction, but he also knew that the battle was not yet over. Well aware that deteriorating relations with America's major trading partner, Great Britain, could lead to a decline in revenue from the customs duties, Jefferson never doubted that the debt must be paid off, come what might. Writing to Albert Gallatin from Monticello after his departure from the capital, Jefferson insisted that this goal not be abandoned. "I consider the fortunes of our republic as depending, in eminent degree, on the extinguishment of the public debt before we engage in any war," he told Gallatin, then secretary of the treasury, who must have known this litany by heart. Failure would be fatal: "If the debt should once more be swelled to a formidable size, its entire discharge will be despaired of, and we shall be committed to the English career of debt, corruption, and rottenness, closing with revolution."[9] Jefferson prayed that America would escape this fate. "Give us peace till our revenues are liberated from debt," he pleaded, "and then, if war be necessary, it can be carried on without a new tax or loan, and during peace we may chequer our whole country with canals, roads, etc."[10] Congratulating Madison on "the triumph of our forbearing & persevering system," Jefferson predicted that it would "give us peace during your time, & by the complete extinguishment of our public debt, open upon us the noblest application of revenue that has ever been exhibited by any nation."[11] Nine months later, Gallatin would confirm the progress Jefferson hailed, showing that half of the national debt of the United States outstanding on 1 January 1801 had been redeemed by 1 January 1810.[12]

Jefferson knew, moreover, that he had left the nation in the hands of men he could depend on. "The discharge of the public debt, therefore," Gallatin was told, "is vital to the destinies of our government, and it hangs on Mr. Madison and yourself alone." Madison and Gallatin must do the job, he urged, and do it now, for "we shall never see another President and Secretary of the Treasury making all their objects subordinate to this. Were either of you to be lost to the public, that great hope is lost."[13] Yet Gallatin sensed that the time might come when he would no longer be able to remain at his Treasury Department post; he would never, he confided to Jefferson in the fall of 1809, "consent to act the part of a mere financier, to become a contriver of taxes, a dealer of loans, a seeker of resources for the purpose of supporting useless baubles, of increasing the number of idle and dissipated members of the community," and, sounding rather like Samuel Johnson some four decades earlier, he went on to denounce "contractors, pursers, and agents" and to decry the "introduction in all its ramifications [of] that system of patronage, corruption, and rottenness which you so justly execrate."[14] Gallatin's fears were warranted; it was exactly this state of affairs to which the War of 1812 would reduce the secretary of the treasury.

Although Jefferson's expectations of a diminishing public debt and a surplus to be employed on projects of public improvement would soon encounter serious obstacles, the immediate aftermath of his presidency produced some of his strongest statements of the transformations that could be achieved once the burden of debt was lifted from the nation's resources. In 1811 he was confident "that, if war be avoided, Mr. Madison will be able to complete the payment of the national debt, within his term," and he painted a glowing picture of what could be done with the "revenues once liberated by the discharge of the public debt." They could, he said, be spent on "canals, roads, schools, etc." Moreover, these improvements would be achieved at virtually no cost for the vast majority of the population; because customs duties on imported goods consumed by the wealthy would be the source of most federal revenue, America would become what no other modern society yet was, one where "the farmer will see his government supported, his children educated, and the face of his country made a paradise by the contributions of the rich alone without being called on to spare a cent from his earnings."[15] Jefferson was entranced by the vision before him. Once the law of nature in public finance was restored, progress would come without pain or controversy, harmony and brotherhood would prevail, and the true genius of republican society would at last be fully realized.

In 1812, Jefferson received a reminder of his principle from an unexpected quarter, a reminder that, with the outbreak of war, could hardly have been more timely. It came in the form of a manuscript by the French *idéologue* Destutt de Tracy, the *Traité de l'économie politique*, sent by its author to Jefferson in the hope that the former president could arrange for its translation and publication in the United States (Jefferson had already performed a similar service for Tracy's *Commentaire de Montesquieu*, a work he enthusiastically promoted).[16] As Gilbert Chinard noted in his study of Jefferson's relations with Tracy, Jefferson was bound to have been stuck by Chapter 12 of Tracy's new manuscript, with its ringing denunciation of public debts and its forthright statement of what Jefferson called, in summarizing the work's contents for a potential publisher, "the right of one generation."[17] And surely Jefferson was intrigued, perhaps even amused, by Tracy's comment that the burden on future generations was "a great question; which I am astonished to have seen no where discussed."[18] With the inevitable delays, it was not until 1817 that the *Traité* finally appeared in English as *A Treatise on Political Economy*; nevertheless, Tracy's orthodox views on public finance and strong restatement of Jefferson's principle (even if it lacked the specificity of the nineteen-year limit) may have encouraged Jefferson to enter the lists more actively on its behalf.[19]

When war did come in June 1812–Jefferson supported to the hilt Madison's decision to resort to arms against Great Britain–it was obvious that there would be new accumulations of debt, obvious that, as Jefferson had warned Gallatin, the burden of debt might grow so great that future generations would be condemned to perpetual servitude. "Having seen the people of all other nations bowed down to the earth under the wars and prodigalities of their rulers, I have cherished their opposites, peace, economy, and riddance of public debt, believing that these were the high road to public as well as private prosperity and happiness," he told South Carolina's Henry Middleton early in 1813; how, Jefferson was beginning to wonder, could the effects of this war be kept within reasonable bounds, so that the "high road" could be resumed at the earliest possible opportunity?[20] He realized that a critical moment had been reached–the more so since Gallatin was indeed "lost to the public," resigning as secretary of the treasury in April 1813.[21] With Gallatin's departure, Jefferson felt both entitled and compelled to step into the breach. And he was not without resources; if Gallatin was gone and Madison preoccupied with the day-to-day business of running the war, Jefferson had other contacts, other friends in high places who might be warned while there was still time. There was, in particular, his son-in-law John Wayles Eppes, representative from Virginia and chairman of the all-important House Ways and Means Committee.[22]

Eppes thus became the initial recipient of Jefferson's advice, tendered in three long letters dated 24 June, 11 September, and 6 November 1813.[23] In turn, Eppes showed the letters to others, and Secretary of War James Monroe, who apparently saw the first two letters while in Albemarle that fall, seems to have been impressed by them, referring favorably to the letters of 24 June and 11 September in a letter of his own to Jefferson on 1 October 1813.[24] Eppes used some of the ideas in the letters–particularly those suggesting Treasury notes as a way of avoiding the need to borrow directly–in his role as chairman of the Ways and Means Committee, for Jefferson, "preferring public benefit to all personal considerations," broke with his usual practice and permitted his son-in-law to make the letters available to others if that would help persuade Congress and the administration to alter their course before it was too late.[25] Monroe showed them in the fall of 1814 to Alexander James Dallas, the new secretary of the treasury, though that conservative financier was appalled by what he read. As we might expect, given his long-standing doubts about the rights of the living generation, Madison also rejected his friend's ideas and even went so far as to dissent from Jefferson's denunciations of paper money.[26]

Not content with reaching only a Washington audience, Jefferson also allowed his letters to be circulated among prominent Virginians whose discretion he could trust. In Richmond, the path of transmission began with Joseph Carrington Cabell, the state senator whose district included Albemarle. Soon to be Jefferson's loyal supporter in matters relating to the University of Virginia, Cabell first learned of the principle in November 1813 when Jefferson, with his new concern to propagate the idea, remarked that a bill adding a further twenty-seven years to the duration of the charter of the Rivanna Company, a local navigation improvement in which he was financially interested, violated the right of generations. Struck by Jefferson's idea, Cabell asked him for additional information; in reply, the former president sent copies of the three letters to Eppes, which Cabell returned after having shown them to a number of influential Virginians, including St. George Tucker (the federal district judge), Thomas Ritchie (editor of the powerful Richmond *Enquirer*, a journal to which Jefferson had close ties), General John Hartwell Cocke (commander of Richmond's defenses from 1814 to 1815), and Cocke's youthful aide-de-camp, Madison's future biographer William Cabell Rives.[27]

It had been nearly a quarter-century since Jefferson tried to interest Madison in his principle, and in the interim, though never abandoning it, he had worked to obtain its acceptance indirectly, above all through the debt-reduction and debt-avoidance policies of his administration. Now, in the summer and fall of 1813, there was a tremendous burst of energy, with Jefferson reaching out to new audiences, providing elaborate explanations of what he had in mind, revealing, for the first time since 1789/1790, the full extent of his principle's application to debt. It was a remarkable change of direction, and for the next thirteen years he would return again and again to the rights of the living generation. If Jefferson's confidence in his principle remained unshaken, it was nevertheless a sign of his concern for the future of the republican experiment that he now found it necessary to mount this new campaign in favor of the rights of the living; something, Jefferson began to feel, was going wrong in the years after 1812, and it did not take him long to identify what that something was or, for that matter, to offer his principle as the sovereign remedy.

Thus the three letters to Eppes, the most sustained effort Jefferson ever made to explain his principle and its implications for public finance, are full of the true gospel, warning against "the gulph yawning before us," predicting that "the overbearing clamor of merchants, speculators, and projectors, will drive us before them with our eyes open, until, as in France, under the Mississippi bubble, our citizens will be overtaken by the crush of this baseless fabric," leaving only the "satisfaction" of heaping "execrations on the heads of those functionaries, who, from ignorance, pusillanimity or corruption, have betrayed the fruits of their industry into the hands of projectors and swindlers."[28] Jefferson spared no pains in his efforts to convince Eppes. The letters were furnished with mathematical proofs and with references to Hume, Adam Smith, and other writers; in short, the full panoply of Jeffersonian argument was mobilized to support his case.[29]

If it seems more than a little familiar to us—it is, of course, 1789 all over again—it was most assuredly not familiar to his readers, and Jefferson knew he had to be convincing. Thus the first letter to his son-in-law assumes that Eppes is largely, if not entirely, ignorant of the principle; Jefferson is operating on virgin soil, even with Eppes, who as a member of Congress from 1803 to 1805 had lived in the White House.[30] This again underscores the point already made, that Jefferson had kept the specifics of his principle to himself in the years after 1790. It took the extraordinary crisis of the new war and the prospect of more debt to convince him to bring it forward in full and unabridged form, to expand on the hints he had given during the presidency. Republicans like Eppes, of course, did not require instruction in the evils of the public debt. But what they did need, as Jefferson saw it, was the more solid foundations for their beliefs that his new reading of the principle that the earth belongs to the living generation would provide; once they understood the principle in all its ramifications, he must have felt, they would also understand why the solutions he proposed were not merely a set of policy choices with which one might disagree if one chose, but moral imperatives, essential if the Republic were to be saved.

Once again, Jefferson begins by explaining the underpinnings of his theory. "What," he asks "is to hinder" the government "from creating a perpetual debt? The laws of nature, I answer. The earth belongs to the living, not to the dead. . . . Each generation has the usufruct of the earth during the period of its continuance. . . . We may consider each generation as a distinct nation, with a right, by the will of its majority, to bind themselves, but none to bind the succeeding generation." Applying the metaphor of inheritance—Eppes had studied law with Jefferson and Edmund Randolph in the early 1790s and so would have appreciated the point without difficulty—Jefferson glosses the principle and says that "the case may be likened to the ordinary one of a tenant for life, who may hypothecate the land for his debts, during the continuance of his usufruct; but at his death, the reversioner (who is also for life only) receives it exonerated from all burthen." And once again Jefferson points out how much better the world would be had the principle been widely adopted: "It is, at the same time, a salutary curb on the spirit of war and indebtment, which, since the modern theory of the perpetuation of debt, has drenched the earth with blood, and crushed its inhabitants under burthens ever accumulating."[31] It is the good old doctrine, and Jefferson preaches it tirelessly.

To strengthen his case, Jefferson gives Eppes other reasons, these new. He admits of the principle that, "like some other natural rights, this has not yet entered into any declaration of rights." Nevertheless, "it is no less a law, and ought to be acted on by honest governments." If only "this principle [had] been declared in the British bill of rights," he notes, "England would have been placed under the happy disability of waging eternal war, and of contracting her thousand millions of public debt."[32] And in his second letter to Eppes, Jefferson offers a further argument. Modern and civilized nations, he says, do not permit parents to sell their children into slavery—recall Jefferson's 1786 description of the Virginia planters as an hereditary debt-created "species of property"—and by analogy Jefferson thinks that this proves the justice of his principle: "We believe, or we act as if we believed that although an individual father cannot alienate the labor of his son, the aggregate body of fathers may alienate the labor of all their sons, of their posterity, in the aggregate, and oblige them to pay for all the enterprises, just or unjust, profitable or ruinous, into which our vices, our passions, or our personal interests may lead us." The absurdity of such a doctrine seems self-evident to Jefferson. "As he was never the property of his father, so when adult he is *sui juris*, entitled himself to the use of his own limbs and the fruits of his own exertions," he explains. "I trust," he adds, "that this proposition needs only to be looked at by an American to be seen in its true point of view."[33]

Once again, Jefferson indulges his passion for calculating. But this time his object is different; if in 1789 he had been intent on determining the life span of a generation, in 1813 his task was to set out, clearly and convincingly, the mathematics of public finance. To bolster his point that any new loan must be accompanied by a tax that will extinguish it within the lifetime of a generation, Jefferson asks "what will be . . . the annuity or tax, which will reimburse principal and interest within the given term? This problem, laborious and barely practicable to common arithmetic, is readily enough solved, Algebraically and with the aid of Logarithms," and he then proceeds to show how this can be done with the aid of a formula he had clipped from the *General Advertiser* in 1793, demonstrating for Eppes the rates of taxation that would be necessary to retire a loan within the limits set by the principle. His numbers show, he thinks, that it would be possible to redeem the debt thus far incurred "in eight or nine years," rather than the "twenty years' thraldom of debt and taxes" that our "improvident legislators . . . have exposed us to."[34]

The letters are replete with numbers. Arguing against the plan for a new national bank in the November letter, Jefferson piles number on top of number to prove how harmful the proposed Bank of the United States would be, to show that the banks already in existence were fast leading the nation to ruin, to make clear that the bank mania will end in a general crash. He describes the all-but-inevitable result: "A sum is thus swindled from our citizens, of seven times the amount of the real debt, and four times that of the fictitious one of the United States, at the close of the war" of Independence. Never, he thinks, have the prospects been so threatening. If there must be a paper circulation, it should be only between $8 million and $35 million; in fact, it was already $200 million, and the proposed national bank would issue another $90 million. The Bank of England's circulation in 1812 was only $189 million, and that sufficed for a country far more commercial and less agricultural than the United States. Jefferson's head spins at the thought of his numbers and their implications.[35]

Once again, as well, Buffon's tables are brought out to determine the life span of a generation, beyond which it is illegitimate to burden the future: "At nineteen years then from the date of a contract, the majority of the contractors are dead, and their contract with them."[36] Jefferson, of course, had used the figure of nineteen years since 1789, but it was, as he well knew, one derived from the "European tables of mortality," and in later years he questioned whether it accurately reflected the demographic experience of the United States. After all, American population had grown rapidly—by 1810, the census recorded more than 7.2 million Americans, which, if not quite doubling the 3.9 million of 1790, was still a remarkable expansion. At the same time, the population was aging, if ever so gradually (median age would rise from 16.7 years in 1820 to 19.4 years in 1860, and in all probability had been rising since 1790), and presumably that would have had its effect on the average length of a generation in Jefferson's sense.[37] Jefferson, one suspects, may not have been eager to see the term of a generation lengthen, but there is no evidence that he clearly considered the implications of a changing age structure for his doctrine. In any event, he lacked the statistical tools to track changes in the age composition of the population with the precision his principle required, for during his lifetime the census remained a fairly blunt instrument and did not supply the exact data on mortality that he had found in Buffon's tables.

In 1800, to be sure, Jefferson tried to persuade Congress to adopt a census schedule that would give a better picture of the makeup of the population; without telling the legislators that he had special reasons of his own for wanting more refined data, he explained the usefulness of "dividing life into certain epochs, to ascertain the existing numbers within each epoch, from whence may be calculated the ordinary duration of life in these States," adding that "the result will be sensibly different from what is presented by the tables of other countries." But Congress paid no attention, and the censuses of 1800, 1810, and 1820 collected little detailed information on the age distribution of the American population.[38] Thus Jefferson was left with the figure of nineteen years, though he had already realized that it was probably incorrect. Whatever its inadequacies, it still served to illustrate how the principle worked, and that was the important thing, important enough that Jefferson was willing to proceed—if that would secure the greater end—on the basis of information he had reason to question.

But even with Eppes passing his father-in-law's ideas on to his colleagues in Congress and his friends in the administration, the immediate results of Jefferson's labors were few. Jefferson told Eppes at the outset of the correspondence that he did not expect Congress to make an explicit declaration of the principle: "They wisely enough avoid deciding on abstract questions. But they may," he suggested, "be induced to keep themselves within its limits."

He then changed his mind, asking in the second of the three letters, "Ought not then the right of each successive generation to be guaranteed against the dissipations and corruptions of those preceding, by a fundamental provision in our constitution?" Even without an explicit declaration, he concluded, the principle should still govern, "there being between generation and generation, as between nation and nation, no other law than that of nature." Yet Congress did not see fit to endorse the principle either in theory or in practice; if the debts of the War of 1812 were to be redeemed within nineteen years, it would be more a matter of chance than of declared policy.[39]

What disturbed Jefferson, then, was the lack of any sign from official Washington that his views were being taken seriously. He thought the interest rates on national loans far too high. Monied Federalists showed a distressing lack of confidence in the federal government's prospects, and the administration was forced to stand hat in hand before men like John Jacob Astor and Stephen Girard to secure the funds needed to carry on the war. Even so, it took unheard-of concessions and inducements to entice these financial giants to disgorge; according to one postwar accounting, the government received only $34 million in specie for the more than $80 million in bonds it issued.[40] Jefferson was further worried that the Treasury Department was neglecting its opportunity to pay for the war cheaply and efficiently with interest-bearing notes, to be retired through taxes, concentrating instead on long-term bonds that would only bring disaster; he was, of course, remembering the lessons of "currency finance" before the Revolution, when such measures met colonial revenue needs with considerable success. In fact, Treasury notes were used extensively, particularly toward the end of the war; by 1815, almost $37 million of them had been issued, and they seemed to work remarkably well, circulating widely and experiencing relatively little depreciation. Their very success, however, must have confirmed Jefferson in his complaint: Treasury notes *were* viable, and the government should have been willing to rely on them far more heavily than it did.[41]

As his confidence that the proper course would be adopted diminished, his mood turned to despair; the war, Jefferson confessed to William Short, "has arrested the course of the most remarkable tide of prosperity any nation ever experienced, and has closed such prospects of future improvement as were never before in the view of any people." The future he had hoped to usher in was disappearing before his eyes, literally so. "Farewell all hopes of extinguishing public debt!" he wrote. "Farewell all visions of applying surpluses of revenue to the improvements of peace rather than the ravages of war."[42] He might urge Eppes that "we should keep forever in view the state of 1817"–before the war Jefferson expected that the debt would be extinguished by that date–"towards which we were advancing, and consider it as that which we must attain," but he could no longer maintain that it was a real possibility or that he would live to see his country free of debt and employing its surplus revenues on works of improvement.[43] It was that tantalizing sense of having been so close to the goal, only to see it slip away, and then for reasons that could have been avoided, that fueled Jefferson's pessimism, and who can blame him? He may have exaggerated, and he was certainly wrong–"the improvements of peace" were only postponed, not lost forever–but given his presuppositions it was the only view he could have taken.

Most of all, Jefferson was troubled by a disturbing new phenomenon, or rather by an old one in a new form: currency inflation, this time the product not of emissions by the states or the national government but the result of the proliferation of the state-chartered banks that sprang up in the wake of the demise of the Bank of the United States in 1811.[44] Jefferson had always disliked banks of issue, and now, he thought, the unfortunate results of permitting them to operate were plain for all to see. It reminded him, he said, of what he had experienced once before, during the Revolution: "We are to be ruined now by the deluge of bank paper, as we were formerly by the old Continental paper," he warned. "It is cruel," he exclaimed to Thomas Cooper, "that such revolutions in private fortunes should be at the mercy of avaricious adventurers." But the bubble would burst–of that he was certain–and what then would become of the country? "After producing the same revolutions in private fortunes as the old Continental paper did, it will die like that, adding a total incapacity to raise resources for the war." Nor was that all. "Private fortunes," he told Eppes, "in the present state of our circulation, are at the mercy of those self-created money lenders, and are prostrated by the floods of nominal money with which their avarice deluges us."[45]

It was in no small part the fact that these institutions were "self-created" (Jefferson conveniently overlooked their state-granted charters) and had arrogated to themselves decisions properly the domain of society speaking through its elected representatives that bothered Jefferson; when private groups acquired rights that rightly should have been exercised, if at all, only by government with the consent of the true majority, he reacted in alarm. "Bank paper," he argued, "must be suppressed, and the circulating medium must be restored to the nation to whom it belongs."[46] Jefferson's insistence on republican transparency–on the absence of partial or private bodies standing between the people and their servants in office–allowed no place for self-created institutions of any sort.[47] Banks of issue were thus to be feared, for they allowed a self-selected few to determine the economic fate of the nation, and that, as Jefferson rightly realized, was far too important a matter to be left in private hands. The threat of monopoly, against which Jefferson had urged Madison to guard in the Bill of Rights, was returning in a new and unanticipated form; Jefferson's fears on this score would be taken up by the Jacksonians in the next political generation, and the problematic implications of the role of banks and bankers in the American economy would become a staple of politics for the next century, to be resolved only with the New Deal and even then, as the 1980s demonstrated, less permanently than once supposed.[48]

Given Jefferson's experiences during the American Revolution, his alarm at the return of inflation is understandable; that this new episode was fueled by banks only increased it. "About the time we were funding our national debt," he recalled, "we heard much about 'a public debt being a public blessing;' that the stock representing it was a creation of active capital for the aliment of commerce, manufactures and agriculture. This paradox was well adapted to the minds of believers in dreams, and the gulls of that size entered *bona fide* into it." Times had changed, however, and for the worse. "But the art and mystery of banks is a wonderful improvement on that," he announced. "It is established on the principle that *'private* debts are a public blessing.' "[49] At least the Revolutionary inflation helped to secure independence– "if ever there was a holy war, it was that which saved our liberties and gave us independence." The inflation of the present war was different; it would only "enrich swindlers at the expense of the honest and industrious part of the nation." Jefferson could barely contain himself as he contemplated the proposal to establish a new Bank of the United States: "We are called on to add ninety millions more to the circulation. Proceeding in this career, it is infallible, that we must end where the revolutionary paper ended."[50]

Jefferson was sure that it all could have been avoided. If only the federal government had followed his advice and issued Treasury notes in small denominations to supply the want of specie, there would have been no demand for bank notes, but, he complained to Gallatin, "the treasury, for want of confidence in the country, delivered itself bound hand and foot to bold and bankrupt adventurers and pretenders to be money-holders," whose "frothy bubbles" of paper currency the people were then forced to accept. "*Aut Carthago, aut Roma delenda est,*" he declared; the choice was that simple.[51] To Eppes, Jefferson said that it recalled John Law's "Mississippi scheme," explaining for his son-in-law's benefit that "the Mississippi scheme . . . ended in France with the bankruptcy of the public treasury, the crush of thousands and thousands of private fortunes, and scenes of desolation and distress equal to those of an invading army, burning and laying waste all before it."[52] Despairing of action at the federal level, for a time he indulged the hope that Joseph Cabell, his state senator, would procure "a salutary interposition of the Legislature" in Virginia to ban out-of-state banknotes and gradually reduce the circulation of in-state ones, but this suggestion was never adopted and Jefferson was forced to conclude that there was nothing to do but wait out the storm.[53]

Describing his proposals to curtail paper emissions for John Adams, who shared his forebodings, Jefferson confessed that "it will not be done. You might as well, with the sailors, whistle to the wind, as suggest precautions against having too much money. We must scud, then before the gale, and try to hold fast, ourselves, by some plank of the wreck. God send us all a safe deliverance." Once again, he drew a sharp contrast between the paper money of the Revolution and the present situation: "Shall we build an altar to the old paper money of the revolution, which ruined individuals"–and forced him to pay the debt to Farell and Jones twice over–"but saved the republic, and burn on that all the bank charters present and future, and their notes with them?" he asked. "For these are to ruin both republic and individuals. This cannot be done," he acknowledged. "The Mania is too strong. It has seized by it's [*sic*] delusions and corruptions all the members of our governments, general, special, and individual."⁵⁴ It was, in short, a nightmare come true.

Jefferson had no difficulty identifying who was to blame in the ultimate sense: In a letter to Caesar Augustus Rodney, who had been his attorney general, he delivered a stinging indictment of Britain and the British "merchants established among us, the bonds by which our own are chained to their feet, and the banking combinations interwoven with the whole, [which] have shown the extent of their control, even during a war with her. They are the workers of all the embarrassments our finances have experienced during the war." Nor was that all. "Our government," Jefferson reflected bitterly, refused to avail itself of "this opportunity" created by the banks' suspension of specie payments "of sweeping their paper from the circulation, and substituting their own notes bottomed on specific taxes for redemption, which every one would have eagerly taken and trusted, rather than the baseless trash of bankrupt companies." That, he said, was "the British influence to which I am an enemy, and which we must subject to our government, or it will subject us to Britain."⁵⁵ British influence, ruinous inflation, a mountain of debt—for Jefferson these were the fruits of the war, and they proved to him, he told Pierre Samuel Du Pont de Nemours, "how little we understood here those sound principles of political economy first developed by the economists, since commended and dilated by Smith, Say, yourself and the luminous reviewer of Montesquieu."⁵⁶

Indeed, Jefferson became almost literally apocalyptic on the subject, insisting to Samuel Kercheval, in the famous letter of 1816, that "we must make our election between *economy and liberty*, or *profusion and servitude*." Unless the disastrous career of debt and taxation was halted, things would go on "till the bulk of the society is reduced to be mere automatons of misery, and to have no sensibilities left but for sinning and suffering. Then begins, indeed, the *bellum omnium in omnia*, which some philosophers observing to be so general in this world, have mistaken it for the natural, instead of the abusive state of man." Jefferson's sense of the lost opportunities, the tragic waste, that debt entails and the criminal mismanagement that brings it about was never more strikingly expressed. It was, he feared, the end of the republican experiment, the degradation of independent Americans to the state of misery and savagery that so frightened him in the 1780s when he observed it in Europe. And its cause was all too obvious: "The fore horse of this frightful team is public debt. Taxation follows that, and in its train wretchedness and oppression."⁵⁷

The postwar period brought no signs of improvement; intellectually and emotionally, if not financially, Jefferson was prepared for the Panic of 1819. "The paper bubble is then burst," he stoically observed to John Adams in the fall of 1819. "This is what you and I, and every reasoning man, seduced by no obliquity of mind or interest, have long foreseen."⁵⁸ Jefferson's comments on the Panic of 1819, particularly those on the banks' role in bringing it about, largely reproduce the remarks he had made during the War of 1812, with the difference that this time the ruin he had been predicting since 1813 was now a reality. As we shall see, banks and bankers had a good deal to do with the final collapse of Jefferson's fortunes during the Panic, and it is hardly surprising that paper money and inflation and the evils of banking should occupy so much of his correspondence in the postwar years.[59]

With the onset of the Missouri Crisis, Jefferson became still more pessimistic about the future of the United States. Here, too, he returned to the generational theme, seeing in the zealots on either side of the issue yet another example of a wasteful generation that destroyed what it should have handed on intact. "My only comfort and confidence is that I shall not live to see" the dissolution of the Union, he told William Short. "I envy not the present generation the glory of throwing away the fruits of their fathers' sacrifices of life and fortune, and of rendering desperate the experiment which was to decide ultimately whether man is capable of self-government." This, he said, was "treason against human hope" and would "signalize their epoch in future history."[60] It was a sorry conclusion, but in truth such conclusions came frequently in the postwar years as Jefferson watched his hopes disappear one after another.[61]

If his efforts thus far to educate his countrymen had been singularly barren of accomplishment, he kept at it, continuing to "whistle to the wind." He now had drastic remedies to offer. "The multiplication of public offices, increase of expense beyond income, growth and entailment of a public debt are indications soliciting the employment of the pruning-knife," Jefferson announced in 1821, no doubt wishing he could hack these away as he did unruly plants in the Monticello garden.[62] The sacred duty of reducing the public debt was repeatedly urged on correspondents, and for Nathaniel Macon's benefit–though this Old Republican cannot have required instruction in the subject–Jefferson explained that unless the nation was "to cease borrowing money & to pay off the national debt," the republican cause was doomed; "we are undone." Dismiss the troops and put the fleet in dry dock, he told Macon; the debt "will bring on us more ruin at home than all the enemies from abroad against whom this army and navy are to protect us." In the end, it was all simple enough: "There does not exist an engine so corruptive of the government and so demoralizing of the nation as a public debt," he insisted.[63]

Lest any of his friends miss the importance of the message he was setting before them, he reminded them of what was taking place in Great Britain, where "George the III. . . . has alienated its whole soil to creditors who could lend money to be lavished on priests, pensions, plunder, and perpetual war," where "the interest of the national debt is now equal to such a portion of the profits of all the land and labor of the island, as not to leave enough for the subsistence of those who labor."[64] The English people, he said, worked sixteen hours a day, and the earnings of fifteen of those hours went to the state in the form of taxes. No longer able to afford bread, they were condemned to subsist "on oatmeal and potatoes"; they had "no time to think, no means of calling the mismanagers to account." England "reads to us the salutary lesson," he observed, "that private fortunes are destroyed by public as well as by private extravagance." Thus, "in this example," he said, drawing the obvious moral, "let us read a lesson for ourselves, and not 'go and do likewise.' "[65]

In common with many of his American—and not a few of his British—contemporaries, Jefferson never understood how that nation managed to keep afloat despite the mountain of debt and the debilitating effects of paper money and inflation. His remarks do not differ greatly from those of the American minister to Britain in 1816, John Quincy Adams, who told his father that "whatever the result may be, the lesson may be profitable to us. If a nation can prosper in peace or war with a debt of a thousand millions sterling, it will be useful for us to make ourselves perfect masters of the mode in which such a marvellous paradox is converted into practical truth." Like his father, the younger Adams shared Jefferson's beliefs on this score, but then so did most other Americans. "If the same course of conduct which leads to inevitable and irrecoverable private ruin is the sure and only path that will conduct a nation to the pinnacle of human greatness and power," Adams continued, "let us trace it to its ultimate bounds. But if a day of reckoning for extravagance and profusion must come for nations as well as individuals, if the wisdom of the ages will ultimately vindicate its own maxims, and if prudence is not to yield forever her place as one of the cardinal virtues to prodigality"—Adams's "ifs" were purely rhetorical—"then will the catastrophe of paper credit . . . teach us at the same time the caution necessary to guard ourselves from the irreparable ruin of its explosion."[66]

No doubt Jefferson felt that the facts of the case spoke for themselves; in the aftermath of the War of 1812, the national debt stood at an astounding $127,335,000 (it had been $57,023,000 when Jefferson left office in 1809). And government expenditure had grown enormously; even with the return of peace, it was twice what it had been in the second of his administrations, averaging something like $20 million a year, with interest on the public debt accounting for about a quarter of the total.[67] Nor did it help matters that the postwar surge of nationalism led the Republican party deeper and deeper into the morass of spending, with all that implied in the way of constitutional questions and the potential for corruption. Younger Republicans like Secretary of War John C. Calhoun of South Carolina seemed to have abandoned the party's traditional inhibitions on the uses to which public money could and should be put; only the dwindling band of Old Republicans remained to testify to the true faith. "Congress," Jefferson told Albert Gallatin, then serving as minister to France, "seemed at a loss for objects whereon to squander the supposed fathomless fund of our treasury." Yet the end of what he called "this short frenzy" brought its own evils, in the form of deficits that could be met only with new loans; these, Jefferson said, threaten "to saddle us with a perpetual debt." The mania for "Consolidation," loose construction of the Constitution, lavish expenditure, abandonment of the principles that had guided his own administrations—all of this was part and parcel of the postwar political scene, and Jefferson was aghast.[68]

Time would prove that Jefferson need not have worried, or worried as much as he did. The Panic of 1819 put an end to the expansive mood of postwar nationalism; the effects of the tariff would lead many southern politicians to rethink matters; and by the mid 1820s, at least at the national level, the pendulum was swinging back in Jefferson's direction. In all but two of the twenty years from 1816 on, the federal government's budget showed an annual surplus, and debt retirement was pursued as speedily as the terms of the loans allowed (Jefferson, it goes without saying, had been horrified by the fact that limits were placed on the government's ability to redeem), with the result that, in 1836, Andrew Jackson could announce that the last of the national debt had been extinguished. Jefferson did not live to see that day, and in any case it was brief enough; deficits caused by the Panic of 1837 would force Martin Van Buren to resort to loans again, and thereafter the federal government would never be without debt.[69]

But Jefferson was unable to anticipate these developments. At the time, all he could see was that Congress refused to heed his warnings, no matter how often he repeated them to his correspondents. Still, he did not give up; he continued to press his message on his friends and likely sympathizers. If only because the "fundamental provision in our constitution" securing "the right of each successive generation . . . against the dissipations and corruptions of those preceding," of which he had briefly dreamed during the war, had not the least chance of being adopted, Jefferson's principle, as he had recognized on other occasions, would have to make its way through less formal channels.[70] Visitors to Monticello in the postwar years found themselves instructed in the doctrine; as the young Boston Brahmin George Ticknor discovered in 1815 when paying his respects to the former president shortly before sailing for Europe, Jefferson "talked very freely of the natural impossibility that one generation should bind another to pay a public debt." But Ticknor was not converted. "I considered such opinions," he remarked, "simply as curious *indicia* of an extraordinary character."[71]

Yet others were more willing to give Jefferson the attention he craved, and in the Virginia reformer Samuel Kercheval he found something like the disciple he had always wanted.[72] Contact with Kercheval brought out another side of Jefferson's principle, the theme of the right of the living generation to write its own constitution, its own laws. Although Jefferson did not abandon his insistence that the principle must be applied with respect to debt—as we have seen, his classic 1816 discussion of the principle in the letter to Kercheval put considerable stress on that aspect of the principle—in the remaining years of his life he would often return to the principle's constitutional implications. Did Jefferson realize, thanks to his experiences during the War of 1812, that there was relatively little chance, at this point, of gaining widespread acceptance for the principle in its financial aspects? We need to remember that the principle had more than one application, remember as well that Jefferson would shape his message for its recipient, and in Virginia there was a special situation bringing him into contact with Kercheval and offering a chance to put the revisionary aspect of the principle into practice. This, of course, was the movement to reform the Virginia constitution of 1776, a document Jefferson had longed wished to see replaced by something more in keeping with his own ideas of constitutional propriety.

Jefferson was otherwise occupied in Philadelphia when the Virginia legislature wrote the state's first—and thus far only—constitution in the summer of 1776, and it is not too much to say that he always believed his presence had been missed. On several occasions, he prepared drafts of a new constitution for Virginia, and his comments on the deficiencies of the existing document became common knowledge when the *Notes on the State of Virginia* appeared in 1785.[73] Efforts from various quarters over the years to convince the legislature of the need for a new constitution always failed, but with the rise in population in the western parts of the state, a movement to rewrite the Virginia constitution gradually gathered strength during the second decade of the nineteenth century. When Kercheval and others raised the banner of constitutional change, Jefferson seized his opportunity; here was a chance both to vindicate his principle and to secure the improvements he had long sought.[74]

As we should expect, then, his correspondence with Kercheval and other reformers in the postwar years breathes the spirit of liberal Jeffersonianism in what many take to be its pure and unadulterated form.[75] "Some men," Jefferson suggested—it went without saying that he was not one of them—"look at constitutions with sanctimonious reverence, and deem them like the arc of the covenant, too sacred to be touched. They ascribe to the men of the preceding age a wisdom more than human, and suppose what they did to be beyond amendment." Nineteen years, he pointed out once again—how easily Jefferson must have composed these letters—was the life of a generation, and it was "now forty years since the constitution of Virginia was formed." Two-thirds of those living in 1776 were dead; did the remaining third have the right to dictate to those who had since come into being? "This corporeal globe, and everything upon it, belong to its present corporeal inhabitants, during their generation." We must not, he insisted, "weakly believe that one generation is not as capable as another of taking care of itself, and of ordering its own affairs"; other states had already revised their constitutions, and why should Virginia not do likewise? he urged. "And lastly," he argued, "let us provide in our constitution for its revision at stated periods"—"des époques éloignées mais fixes," he might have said, so conscious is his echo of the language of Paris in 1789.[76]

There would be no revision of the Virginia constitution in Jefferson's lifetime—only in 1829/1830 would that step be taken, and then with mixed results—but Jefferson did not cease his efforts. Eight years after opening his ideas to Kercheval—through whom they were transmitted to other like-minded Virginians—Jefferson reached out to another correspondent, the veteran English reformer Major John Cartwright, to offer his valedictory statement of the principle. "Can one generation bind another? I think not," he told Cartwright. "The Creator has made the earth for the living, not the dead. Rights and powers can only belong to persons, not to things, not to mere matter, unendowed with will." No, "nothing then is unchangeable," the aging Sage of Monticello concluded with his usual self-contradictory refusal to take his principle to its ultimate point, "but the inherent and unalienable rights of man."[77]

If in the last decade of his life Jefferson had reason to despair of his country's future, fearing as he did that it was about to be swallowed up in a maelstrom of debt and corruption and paper money, his pessimism surely owed something—more than something—to his own financial collapse. While still in the White House, he was shocked to realize how much his debts had grown during his two terms in office, telling his daughter Martha Randolph in 1808 that he had "now the gloomy prospect of retiring from office loaded with serious debts, which will materially affect my tranquility of mind." Quickly adding that "not being apt to deject myself with evils before they happen, I nourish the hope of getting along," he also vowed to make economy and retrenchment the order of the day in his personal finances.[78] Granted, he was always too optimistic about what he could accomplish in that regard, nor could he change the habits of a lifetime overnight. He continued to operate his slave-run nailery and lease out the mill he had built at nearby Milton (he estimated its value at $30,000), always hoping that their profits might offset the generally negative return from his crops.[79]

But he knew that he needed to set his affairs in order, and to do this he was prepared to take steps that might surprise those who see him as self-indulgent to the end. In 1810, he sold a considerable amount of land (though it was not until 1816 that he received payment in full), and when the Library of Congress was destroyed in 1814, Jefferson was quick to recognize the opportunity this act of British vandalism presented. He disposed of a major asset, the thousands of volumes he had collected over the years, selling it to the federal government for $23,950 early in 1815.[80] We should not underestimate the sacrifice for Jefferson (or ignore the fact that he promptly set about acquiring a new library for himself, even if not on the scale of the one he sold to Congress).[81] He cherished his books, but he was willing to see them go, no doubt in part because he had come to regard them as a sort of national treasure, a collection that should one day be the public's property. He used the proceeds to reduce a number of his debts (the sum he received, large though it was, would not pay them all), debts that included $10,500 due his old friend William Short and a further $4,870 owed Thaddeus Kosciuszko; much of the remainder went to settle his outstanding accounts with merchants in Charlottesville and Richmond.[82]

Yet Jefferson's respite was brief. His crops were indifferent after the War of 1812, and he found himself relying more and more on the banks in Richmond for "accommodations." Even before leaving office, he had begun to depend on the Washington and Richmond banks for short-term loans, which he generally renewed on maturity, so that by 1806 he owed about $10,000 to banks in the District of Columbia.[83] Ironically, given his dislike of banks and his fears that the proliferation of these institutions would lead to economic disaster, he was able to benefit—if only temporarily—from the fact that Richmond now had several banks, a situation that made it possible for him to borrow from the local branch of the newly chartered Second Bank of the United States and from the Bank of Virginia and the Farmers Bank as well. But in availing himself of this facility, Jefferson was sowing the seeds of the disaster that would overtake him in 1819 and 1820. For the loans from the Bank of the United States depended in considerable part on the personal relations between Jefferson and the president of the Richmond branch, Wilson Cary Nicholas, long a stalwart of Virginia Republican politics and since 1815 the father-in-law of Jefferson's favorite grandson, Thomas Jefferson Randolph. It was Wilson Cary Nicholas, moreover, who in 1819 helped Jefferson to secure additional loans from the Farmers Bank (where the banker's brother, Philip Norbone Nicholas, was conveniently president), Wilson Cary Nicholas who provided the required endorsement for Jefferson's note at that institution.[84]

In return for favors granted and to be granted, in 1818 Nicholas asked Jefferson to serve as his endorser at the Bank of the United States in the amount of $20,000, assuring the former president that there was no danger of eventual liability. Jefferson should have known better—endorsing other people's notes was almost always guaranteed to end badly—yet he had no choice; dependent on Nicholas for favors, tied to Nicholas through bonds of kinship and respect, Jefferson could only hope that Nicholas's property was really worth the $350,000 the Richmond banker claimed. But then on 7 August 1819 Jefferson's daughter Martha wrote urgently to Poplar Forest with the alarming news that "a report has reached us that Col. Nicholas has been *protested* for a large sum. Jefferson [Martha's son and Nicholas's son-in-law] believes it and Mr. Randolph [Martha's husband] talks of sending an express to you." The report was all too true; Nicholas failed when the Panic of 1819 began to claim its victims in Virginia, and while there was initially some hope that his estate was large enough to cover the debt for which Jefferson stood responsible, it was soon evident that the assets could not begin to meet the demands of Nicholas's creditors. Reduced to dependence on the charity of his daughter, Jane, and her husband, Jeff Randolph, Nicholas died in 1820, and Jefferson was forced to confront the truth. He now owed another $20,000, and this at a time when the Richmond banks were unwilling to extend further indulgences but, on the contrary, were curtailing their notes, Jefferson's among them.[85]

What made the debt a crushing blow was not simply that it added another $20,000 to the sums Jefferson already owed; rather, it was the need to find the annual $1,200 in interest Jefferson was now obligated to pay the Bank of the United States. For it was interest that was ruining him from 1819 on, interest he could pay only by the dangerous expedient of new loans from the banks, loans that the banks were now unwilling to make. With the collapse in the price of agricultural produce and the accompanying depression in land values, particularly in the Piedmont, Jefferson had neither current income nor realizable assets—other than his slaves—with which to

meet the endless demands that seemed to come from every quarter. Even the
tenant of his mill was unable to pay the rent he counted on receiving;
nothing, apparently, was secure any longer. And there were still old debts
outstanding, old creditors from the 1790s and even earlier who pressed him
for payment. The Amsterdam bankers Van Staphorst and Hubbard, whose
loans had helped Jefferson to discharge some of his debts in the 1790s, had
never been paid in full; their American representatives, Leroy and Bayard of
New York, now came forward to require payment, and Jefferson had to
produce some $6,000 over three years beginning in 1817 to accomplish
this.[86] Still convinced that his land and slaves–at a fair valuation–more than
covered his debts, Jefferson found that the income from his property could
not cover even his basic expenses, let alone supply what he needed to meet
the interest on his outstanding obligations.

Some of his difficulty after the War of 1812, to be sure, was of his own
making, and in a way that will strike us as ironic but would have been too
painful for him to contemplate. Convinced that banks and government
stock were dangerous, he repeatedly told friends in Europe that their money
was safer when left on deposit with him. Thus he used the American funds
William Short, Thaddeus Kosciuszko, and Philip Mazzei entrusted to his
care as loans, assuring them that he would repay them when they needed the
money; in the meantime, he promised them an interest equivalent to what
they would have received from the dubious investments he warned them to
avoid. The trouble with this, apart from any ethical considerations that
modern sensibilities may discover, was that it exposed Jefferson to sudden
and unpredictable demands for large sums of money. He had been able to pay
Short and Kosciuszko, thanks to the sale of his library to Congress, but that
left Mazzei, and in Mazzei's case he was further hurt by the fact that the
sums in question had been realized from the sale of Mazzei's Virginia real
property at the height of wartime inflation. By the time Jefferson had to face
the Mazzei heirs' demands for repayment, deflation had set in, leaving him
in the difficult position of having to restore those funds in far more expensive
dollars. The sensible course of action would have been to place the proceeds
in some reasonably safe security–federal bonds, for example–but Jefferson
could never bring himself to believe that such investments were genuinely
worthwhile. He simply could not entertain the thought of putting money
into unproductive investments of this sort: Agriculture *had* to be better;
land *had* to be safer.[87]

Owing to the conjunction of his own mistakes and a severe economic
downturn that was none of his making, Jefferson began the final years of his
life with debts far more difficult to pay than any he had ever faced in all his
long years of struggle with debt. Realizing that he no longer had the capacity
to deal with his financial affairs, in 1821 he turned his estates over to his
grandson, Jeff Randolph, who took upon himself both the day-to-day
management of the remaining properties and the ultimate responsibility for
his grandfather's debts.[88] What energies he had left Jefferson must have
wished to husband for the project that now meant more than anything else–

the University of Virginia. The creation of the "academical village," the planning of the curriculum, the selection of the professors, the choice of books for the library–these were his safe haven in the remaining years of his life, and almost until the end they allowed him to escape the full gravity of his situation. They were also, of course, the pursuits he always preferred to unpleasant realities; at a time when he was no longer able to control his economic fate, he could plan a world of his own, indulge his passion for "putting up and pulling down," modeling a small universe according to his own desires. The ironies could hardly have been more obvious. But in the end, not even the university would prove a refuge from his creditors.[89]

In spite of everything, it was not until the last months of his life that Jefferson was forced to acknowledge that drastic steps were required. Through 1825, he continued to devise schemes that would pay off his debts and ensure his family a modicum of comfort once he was gone. On 1 April 1823–the date is only too appropriate, for once again, Jefferson was fooling himself about what could and could not be accomplished–he set out a plan that would have paid all his debts by 1830 without the need to sell land and still have left him 150 of his slaves. And he remained convinced that sales of land and slaves, if only their true values could be realized, would produce enough to satisfy his creditors and create a fund to support his daughter Martha and her husband, Thomas Mann Randolph, Jr., and those of their children not yet of age and established on their own.[90] For his son-in-law was now both insolvent and showing dangerous signs of mental instability, with the result that the welfare of the Randolph family devolved on Jefferson and Jeff Randolph. But by the end of 1825, it was apparent that none of Jefferson's plans would work, and no matter how Jeff Randolph struggled to make a go of things, the best he could accomplish only put off for the moment the calls that were too insistent to be ignored.[91]

Thus when Bernard Peyton, one of the Charlottesville merchants on whose indulgence Jefferson depended, sent word in December 1825 that Jefferson's debt of nearly $4,000 would have to be paid, the last act in the long melodrama of Jefferson's decline and fall began. As his daughter later remembered, the idea of a lottery as a solution to his problems came suddenly to Jefferson as he lay tossing and turning one night–here, at last, was a way out that would allow him honorably to discharge his debts, leave Monticello as a home for Martha and her family during their lifetimes, and–most important of all–realize a "fair" price for the land and slaves he proposed to sell. For it was the catastrophic decline in the price of land and slaves that had undermined Jefferson's position beyond the point of redemption; had he been able in 1825 and 1826 to realize the prices such assets brought before the Panic of 1819, he might well have been able to effect the rescue he kept trying to work out on paper. But that was precisely the problem; Jefferson had to confront a severe deflation that left him, like all debtors, in a ruinous position. A lottery, then, was the chosen vehicle of escape, but it failed. *Cohens* v. *Virginia* had recently reminded everyone, Jefferson included, that the Old Dominion banned lotteries, and the legislature initially balked at making an exception. Efforts to raise subscriptions on his behalf, once news of Jefferson's plight became general knowledge, had barely gotten under way in other parts of the country when Jefferson died on 4 July 1826, tormented by the fear that he had left his family without resources.[92]

In all, it was a sad story, and Jefferson's own reluctance to accept the realities of his situation makes it sadder still. Although Jefferson never said so, he may have recalled, toward the end, that other nations had been considerably more generous in their treatment of indebted heroes. Parliament had paid the debts of the younger Pitt after his death and was lavish in endowing the military and naval heroes of the wars of the French Revolution and Napoleon. Even the United States Congress, not known for its willingness to reward Americans, generously compensated Lafayette in 1803 and 1824. And when Jefferson wrote to congratulate Lafayette on Congress's gift of $120,000 in the latter year, telling him that "the relief from your debts will give you nights of sound sleep and the surplus I hope days of ease and comfort through the rest of your life," he can only have been comparing Lafayette's situation with his own. Jefferson's sentiments can be guessed, however, from the memorandum he drew up early in 1826, justifying his claim that an exception to the Virginia rule against lotteries should be made in his behalf. The "Thoughts on Lotteries," as this paper is called, present him in a most unusual light—he boasts for public consumption of his importance, listing his achievements in far fuller form than in the apparently modest inscription he composed for his tombstone.[93] But what the "Thoughts on Lotteries" shows us, I think, is Jefferson driven to extremes, Jefferson forced to break the reticence of a lifetime and request a favor from a public body, a body in which he had once played a leading role. It can only have been excruciating, and we can understand why he put off taking the steps that must have been all too obvious and then acted only at the last moment, only under great duress, and only in a way that still, at that late stage, allowed him to maintain the fiction of control and escape the admission that his creditors ultimately held power over him.

But even this did not work, and when news came from Richmond that the legislature was unlikely to favor his application, he wrote to his grandson, then in the capital to forward the lottery project, that it was "part of my mortification to perceive that I had so far overvalued myself as to have counted on it with too much confidence. I see, in the failure of this hope, a deadly blast of all my peace of mind, during my remaining days." Yet those days were growing short, and Jefferson knew it. "For myself," he added, "I should not regard a prostration of fortune. But I am overwhelmed at the prospect of the situation in which I may leave my family." His failure as a father, as a patriarch, as a patriot who had earned the gratitude of his fellow citizens was complete, and he gave way to a despair he had not known since his wife died in 1782. "I should not care," he said, "were life to end with the line I am writing, were it not that I may be of some avail to the family." Yet even then he was sure that it was not his fault; in his final words on the subject, he insisted that were it not for "the unfortunate fluctuations in the value of our money, and the long continued depression of farming business . . . I am confident my debts might be paid, leaving me Monticello and the Bedford estate. But where there are no bidders, property, however, great, is no resource for the payment of debts. All may go for little or nothing."[94]

Jefferson's lasting conviction that his principle was essential for the preservation of free government, whether through the consequences of limiting debt or through the liberty it gave each generation to make its own choices, was amply evident in the correspondence of his later years—more so than at any time since the early 1790s. He did his best to propagate it, but he was also worried about the reception that it and the rest of his legacy would receive at the hands of an American public whose historical understanding was at best imperfect and in practice more than a little inclined to accept what he regarded as rank Federalist propaganda.[95] "Our opponents are far ahead of us in preparations for placing their cause favorably before posterity," he lamented to Supreme Court Justice William Johnson in 1823, and that situation did not seem likely to change.[96] It was not only John Marshall's "five-volumed libel" he feared; "the life of Hamilton is in the hands of a man who, to the bitterness of the priest, adds the rancor of the fiercest federalism," Jefferson explained.[97] He then went on to note that John Adams's papers would be presented to the public by his son, John Quincy, "whose pen, you know, is pointed, and his prejudices not in our favor."[98] In recent years, though Jefferson did not say so to Johnson, the elder Adams had been a prolific publisher, rehearsing the history of his conflict with Hamilton and the High Federalists in the pages of the Boston papers, and Jefferson may well have surmised that Adams might also have a thing or two to say about his Republican opponents.[99] "Doubtless other things are in preparation, unknown to us," he warned Johnson. "We have been too careless of our future reputation," Jefferson admitted, "while our tories will omit nothing to place us in the wrong."[100] And he worried about the ways important historical material was either being suppressed, as in the case of Franklin's memoirs, which he had read in manuscript in 1790, or, like the papers of George Washington, "open to the high priests of federalism only, and garbled to say so much, and no more, as suits their views."[101]

The debates on finance during the War of 1812, moreover, had demonstrated that the issues first raised in 1790 were still alive and well. One Maryland Federalist in Congress had praised Hamilton in the highest possible terms: "He extracted order from chaos—light from darkness. He made confidence to take the place of distrust and general discontent," Alexander Contee Hanson told the House of Representatives in 1814 before going on to denounce the Madison administration for violating public faith and destroying public credit. The Republican position, to be sure, did not lack defenders, and Virginian John George Jackson, the husband of Dolley Madison's sister and a politician thought to have the president's ear, had not forgotten the events of 1790, saying of the origins of the funding system: "We all recollect the history of that nefarious peculation. The soldier's necessities, in the poverty of your government, had compelled him to sell your scrip at *2s. 6d.* in the pound. The speculator came with it into the Congressional Hall, and voted to give *himself* the full nominal value." Federalists like New York's Zebulon Shipherd could just as easily turn the tables on the Republicans, asking "where can be the policy of loading, not only the present, but unborn generations, with debt?" insisting that "a moneyed influence in a Republican Government should ever be rigidly and firmly resisted."[102] But speeches in the House of Representatives, even though they demonstrated the continuing appeal of familiar arguments, did not provide the solid account Jefferson knew was necessary.

Jefferson feared that the Republicans were falling behind in the race to capture the nation's understanding of its past. Their case, he was forced to admit, had yet to be presented in persuasive terms. "On our part we are depending on truth to make itself known, while history is taking a contrary set which may become too inveterate for correction," he warned. And what did the Republicans plan to offer by way of reply? Madison would do something, but his contribution would be limited to "particular passages of our history and these chiefly confined to the period between the dissolution of the old and commencement of the new government, which is particularly within his knowledge," Jefferson said, thinking of Madison's notes at the Philadelphia convention of 1787. For his own part, Jefferson continued, his correspondence would reveal the actions of his political life between 1790 and 1809. "My letters (all preserved)," he explained, "will furnish the daily occurrences and views from my return from Europe in 1790, till I retired finally from office." Jefferson expected that "selections from these, after my death, may come out successively as the maturity of circumstances may render their appearance seasonable." His correspondence, he knew, would "command more conviction than anything I could have written after my retirement"; with their "warmth and freshness of fact and feeling, they will carry internal evidence that what they breathe is genuine."[103]

Jefferson, who hoped Justice Johnson would write the Republican history of government under the Constitution, did not tell the justice in 1823 that he had already begun to address the problem, at least as early as 1818, when he composed the introduction to the memoranda we know as the "Anas," nor did he tell Johnson that in 1821 he had written an autobiography covering his life to the spring of 1790, when he took office as Washington's secretary of state, to the point, that is, where the "Anas" began. These works, like his collaboration between 1813 and 1815 with Louis Hue Girardin on the continuation of John Daly Burk's *History of Virginia* for the period of his governorship, were Jefferson's efforts to set the record straight before it was too late. And in these cases, Jefferson could not depend entirely on his own correspondence, for there were facts known only to him, or contained in his memoranda, that were essential to the presentation of the full story.[104]

Jefferson could only wonder what the lives and papers of Hamilton and the first Adams would contain, and clearly he feared the worst. But his distant cousin's production was already a matter of public record, and

Jefferson was more than mildly disturbed by what he found in it. He began to read John Marshall's *Life of Washington* shortly after leaving office in 1809, yet even before he opened its covers, he knew exactly the sort of infamy it would contain.[105] He tried to interest Joel Barlow in writing a suitable Republican counterblast, but Barlow, appointed minister to France by Madison in 1811, had made little progress by 1812 when death claimed him in a squalid Polish inn.[106] For Jefferson, Marshall's entire work was an abomination, and the fifth volume, which covered Washington's two administrations, was beyond contempt.[107] "Were a reader of this period to form his idea of it from this history alone," he insisted, "he would suppose the republican party (who were in truth endeavoring to keep the government within the line of the Constitution, and prevent it's [*sic*] being monarchised in practice) were a mere set of grumblers, and disorganisers." Worse, the reader would imagine that the Republicans had been only "like a British parliamentary opposition, gaping after loaves and fishes, and ready to change principles, as well as position, at any time, with their adversaries."[108] Jefferson was determined to give that reader an alternative.

There were many things in Marshall's biography of Washington to disturb him, but one passage—with its suggestions of "gaping after loaves and fishes"—must have captured Jefferson's attention. In recounting the history of the first administration, Marshall explained how it came to pass that assumption was adopted and the capital placed on the banks of the Potomac. What Marshall's account did was to state as plainly as it could be stated without actually saying so that there had been a bargain. Marshall explained that two Virginia representatives from districts on the Potomac changed their votes, thus allowing assumption to carry, and referred his readers to a note at the foot of the page. In his note, the chief justice stated: "It has ever been understood that these members were, on principle, in favour of the assumption as modified in the amendment made by the senate; but they withheld their assent from it when originally proposed in the house of representatives, in the opinion that the increase of the national debt added to the necessity of giving to the departments of the national government a more central residence." This in itself was something of a slap in the face of the Virginians who had opposed assumption, but Marshall compounded his crime by suggesting rather broadly that even those who had not voted for it would have done so under some circumstances: "It is understood," he wrote, "that a greater number would have changed had it been necessary."[109]

What, Jefferson may well have wondered, did Marshall intend his readers to make of the note, and particularly of its last sentence? Was the chief justice hinting that certain Virginia members of Congress who continued to vote against assumption even after the Dinner Table Bargain had been agreed on were ready and willing to change their votes if need be? And if this was the implication, would the well-informed understand that Madison was among them? It is impossible to know how deeply Marshall's claim affected Jefferson. It was certainly close enough to the truth to be troubling, for it raised a matter that had been largely put to sleep in the early 1790s, no doubt with the agreement of all the parties concerned.[110] Jefferson must have asked himself where and how John Marshall had obtained his information. Was there something in the Washington manuscripts that allowed Marshall to speak with authority? Had someone else, still alive when Marshall was writing the offending fifth volume, spoken to him? Had he learned it earlier, during the 1790s? All of these were possibilities, and what they would have suggested to Jefferson, I think, was that enough was known, whatever the source, that he had no choice in the matter—it had to be confronted and the misimpressions left by Marshall's account corrected.[111] We do know that Jefferson gave posterity his own version of the events of 1790, a version that did not directly contradict Marshall's but, in a sense, made it superfluous, directing attention away from the dangerous footnote if only by virtue of its color and superior quotability.[112] What makes Jefferson's version particularly interesting is that it was written especially for the "Anas," not, like the other material in that collection, simply reproduced from his contemporaneous notes.[113]

For Jefferson was still trying to explain to himself how he could have been so disastrously wrong in 1790, still trying to come to grips with the results of his willingness to mediate between Hamilton and the Virginians. Not a word that escaped from his lips or flowed from his pen since 1791 had had anything positive to say about funding, the debt, and their consequences, and in the postwar climate, with the national debt again at ruinous heights, with bank notes continuing to pour from the presses, with Jefferson more depressed by the day about republicanism's prospects, the events of 1790 were a matter he had to address. Leaving the subject untouched ran the risk that others might enter the field and say something; if that happened—and Jefferson had to allow for the possibility that it would—remaining silent would expose him to charges of hypocrisy, bad enough in any case, but even worse when he was gone and could no longer defend himself. These, then, were risks that Jefferson could not have wanted to run. And they were risks, not fantasies; as we have seen, Jefferson paid close attention to the probability that his contemporaries' papers and memoirs would be published at some point in the not very distant future. If nothing else, the activity of Hamilton's family and friends in seeking materials for a biography and in asserting Hamilton's authorship of various disputed numbers of *The Federalist* would not have allowed Jefferson the luxury of supposing that Hamilton would soon be forgotten.[114] But Hamilton was dead; he either had left some record of the events of 1790 or he had not, and nothing Jefferson could do would change that.

Others who knew something about what had happened in the summer of 1790 were still alive, however, and among them was Richard Bland Lee, one of two survivors of the five who had changed their votes.[115] Lee would just outlive Jefferson, dying in March 1827, and in the meantime, though nominally a Federalist, he was in the habit of sending his old friend James Madison reminders that he had sacrificed his political career on the altar of assumption, reminders accompanied by requests for federal employment.

"My zeal in establishing the present constitution of the U. States and my agency in fixing the seat of government at this place is well known to you," Lee told the president in 1815. A decade later, he was still at it, this time more pointedly, recalling for Madison's benefit that he "incurred considerable odium for the part I took in establishing the seat of Govemnt. on the Potowmack," and suggesting that it was not "unreasonable that I should receive some little recompense at this time"—thirty-five years later—since he wished "to bring my family to town for the purpose of education." In fact, Lee was generously treated by Madison and Monroe, who appointed him to various positions in their gift, and that would have mitigated some of his remaining rancor.[116]

Still, other members of the Lee family had not fared especially well at Jefferson's hands. There was, for example, Richard Bland Lee's brother Charles, attorney general under John Adams and one of the judges who had lost their seats when the Republicans repealed the Judiciary Act of 1800. Charles Lee had taken the Federalist side in a series of bruising cases stemming from the Republican assault on the judiciary after 1801—*Stuart* v. *Laird*, *Marbury* v. *Madison*, the Chase impeachment proceedings—and had been one of Aaron Burr's counsel.[117] Moreover, Charles and Richard Bland Lee were also Light-Horse Harry's brothers, and Jefferson's scathing remarks about Light-Horse Harry's memoirs came to the attention of the swash-buckler's son, Henry Lee, Jr. Known with good reason as "Black-Horse Harry," the younger Henry Lee had a checkered career but never wavered in his defense of his father's reputation. A delicate correspondence ensued between the former president and Light-Horse Harry's son, who was invited to Monticello for a conference in 1826 shortly before Jefferson's death.[118] The Lees had a reputation for touchiness, and there was no way of knowing what they might decide to say about a man none of them had cause to remember kindly. Hence, for this and the other reasons we have looked at, it behooved Jefferson to prepare his case in advance, and in 1818 he set himself the task of explaining what had happened, composing a suitable introduction to the "Anas" in which he would reveal—for posthumous publication, to be sure—what he had done, why he had done it, and how, in the end, responsibility was to be allocated.

Jefferson had already expressed his thoughts on these questions in the memorandum probably prepared in 1792 and, to some extent, in his correspondence with Washington that summer and fall.[119] In 1818, he reworked the material, producing what was long the standard account of the Dinner Table Bargain, modified only when twentieth-century scholars began to explore his papers and other sources in depth.[120] In comparing the versions of 1792 and 1818, what will at once be apparent is Jefferson's deftness in revising his earlier material, as he sharpens the focus, heightens the language, and suppresses any mention of Madison's role in the affair, even failing to record his presence at the celebrated dinner.

Jefferson opens the "Anas" with an attack on Marshall's *Life of Washington*, accusing the chief justice of giving way to "party feelings" and the

rankest Federalism. "Let no man believe that Gen. Washington ever intended that his papers should be used for the suicide of the cause, for which
he had lived, and for which there was never a moment in which he would not
have died," Jefferson insists, condemning Marshall's failure to make Washington's "endeavors to vindicate the rights of humanity" come alive for his
readers. But, Jefferson thinks, Marshall's "abuse of these materials is chiefly
however manifested in the history of the period immediately following the
establishment" of the Constitution, and this is what he will correct; his facts
"will shew, that the contests of the day were contests of principle between the
advocates of republican and those of kingly government."[121] After these
preliminaries, Jefferson moves on to open his narrative with the events of
1790, explaining that, on his arrival in New York, Hamilton was erecting his
"financial system," with its "two objects. 1st as a puzzle, to exclude popular
understanding & inquiry. 2dly, as a machine for the corruption of the
legislature." Hamilton's plot was only too successful. "And with grief and
shame it must be acknoledged [*sic*] that his machine was not without effect,"
Jefferson confesses, "that even in this, the birth of our government, some
members were found sordid enough to bend their duty to their interests, and
to look after personal, rather than public good."[122] Jefferson then describes
the failure of Madison's proposal for discrimination and the amazing round
of speculation that spring—"the base scramble began," he says. The moral is
obvious enough: "Men thus enriched by the dexterity of a leader, would
follow of course the chief who was leading them to fortune, and become the
zealous instruments of all his enterprises."[123]

The stage is now set for the drama of the Dinner Table Bargain: "This
game was over, and another was on the carpet at the moment of my arrival;
and to this I was most ignorantly & innocently made to hold the candle."[124]
This will be his defense: Ignorance of Hamilton's deeper intentions and
utter innocence on his own part will explain the role Jefferson played in the
assumption. His motives will be of the best; if rejection of assumption
threatened "a dissolution of our union at this incipient stage," he recalls
having told Hamilton when he encountered the secretary of the treasury "in
despair" one day "in the street," he would "deem that the most unfortunate
of all consequences, to avert which all partial and temporary evils should be
yielded." (In the 1792 memorandum, Jefferson's description of Hamilton's
condition that June morning had been considerably earthier: "His look was
sombre, haggard, and dejected beyond description. Even his dress was
uncouth and neglected.")[125]

And so, Jefferson remembers, a meeting was arranged: "I proposed to
him however to dine with me the next day, and I would invite another friend
or two, bring them into conference together," Jefferson says, explaining that
he "thought it impossible that reasonable men, consulting together coolly,
could fail, by some mutual sacrifices of opinion, to form a compromise
which was to save the union." (Thus Jefferson has it both ways; Madison is
not to be mentioned by name, but he covers himself with the language about
"another friend or two" should anyone come forward with a more accurate

list of his guests.) In due course, then, a "discussion took place" in which Jefferson "could take no part . . . but an exhortatory one, because I was a stranger to the circumstances which should govern it." (Jefferson clearly had known more at the time than he here lets on.) Agreement on assumption followed; "whatever importance had been attached to the rejection of this proposition, the preservation of the Union and of concord among the States was more important," and so "some members should change their vote." (Jefferson says not a word about the modifications that made assumption unobjectionable to Virginia from the financial point of view.) And in language that avoids the issue of who might have brought up the question ("it was observed," is his delicate way around this problem), Jefferson then notes that the permanent residence on the Potomac was agreed to in order "to sweeten" what was obviously not going to be a popular measure in the South. Putting it this way allows Jefferson to limit the damage: The "members [who] should change their votes" will be those with districts on the Potomac, Richard Bland Lee and Alexander White, though he describes White as agreeing very reluctantly—in fact, "with a revulsion of stomach almost convulsive." (In 1792, Jefferson said merely that "Mr. White had some qualms, but finally agreed.")[126]

The original version was far more direct in describing these matters, and it put Jefferson a good deal closer to the center of events. Jefferson also made it clear in the 1792 version that it was either Hamilton or Madison who brought up the question of the Potomac ("It was observed, I forget by which of them"); his 1792 language keeps the story focused on the meal as a bargaining session, whereas the more impersonal text of 1818 has the effect of distancing the reader, removing attention from Jefferson and putting the themes of corruption and trickery uppermost. In 1818, the explanation of his motives is far fuller, and it places him in the best possible light—he acts to bring "reasonable men" together "to form a compromise which was to save the union." The contrast with Hamilton could hardly be more explicit: The latter is described in the 1818 version as acting through Robert Morris to obtain the votes necessary for the Potomac residence—and, of course, for his larger goals concealed in the assumption proposal. "And so," Jefferson concludes his 1818 account, "the assumption was passed, and 20. millions of stock divided among favored states, and thrown in as a pabulum to the stock-jobbing herd. This added to the number of votaries to the treasury, and made its Chief the master of every vote in the legislature which might give to the government the direction suited to his political views."[127]

Thus Jefferson had his version, hostile to Hamilton—whose motives were spelled out in a way that did the greatest possible damage—and suitably protective of his own character. This is not even the version of 1792 he offered Washington—in which he admits that he "was duped . . . by the Secretary of the treasury and made a tool for forwarding his schemes, not then sufficiently understood by me"; it is a version in which Jefferson's role is as passive as can be.[128] Hamilton, as Jefferson tells it in 1818, planned everything in advance, knew where he was going and how to get there, and poor Thomas Jefferson merely stumbled across his path, "innocently" and "ignorantly" opening communications between the secretary of the treasury and those who were blocking his way. It helps that he has removed Madison from the picture; even the "friend or two" Jefferson said he would invite vanish from the scene after that initial mention. Without his colleague's presence, Jefferson's role can be reduced to a mere cipher, for there is nothing to remind us that he had other sources of information, that his claim of being "really a stranger to the whole subject" is less than candid. (In 1792, all the details were present, including "Mr. Madison's acquiescence in a proposition that the question should be again brought before the house . . . , that tho' he would not vote for it, nor entirely withdraw his opposition, yet he should not be strenuous, but leave it to it's [*sic*] fate.")[129] Madison's disappearance also helps to remove the onus from the future Republican interest; no one, in 1818 or later, would care much about the fact that Richard Bland Lee (who, after all, became a Federalist) and Alexander White had changed their votes (and Jefferson does his best to let White off the hook), but to have mentioned Madison would have let the cat out of the bag.

Good intentions, a desire to preserve the Union, ignorance and innocence: Jefferson creates an account in which he has none of the blame, an account in which, moreover, he does not even admit that he might have foreseen the result. Any contradiction with other views he held is ruled out. If he knew that debt was ruinous and that a national debt had political consequences hostile to republicanism, he need not try to square that with what he had done in 1790. Nor does he so much as hint that in 1790 concern to see public credit firmly established ranked high on his list of priorities—he has, in short, omitted much of what we know to have been important, constructing instead an account that explains not 1790 but what happened thereafter.

As the work of a man with a memory—and the documents that could help him refresh it—the "Anas" account is a highly interesting production. Jefferson could have given us his 1792 memorandum, but that told too much. Instead, he consciously created a new record, one that would teach the lessons he wanted the rising generation to absorb. Although it would be wrong to imply that Jefferson was fully aware of the distortions he introduced in 1818, political truth was clearly more important, at this point, than historical truth. In a sense, Jefferson was right to stress the former at the expense of the latter: Historical truth was imperfect, the story it told incomplete and, to his way of thinking, misleading. He would reveal the deeper truth, the truth apparent only in hindsight, as he had come to work it out over the course of the 1790s. The details—including Madison's presence—were there in 1792 because he wanted to create a record to use in approaching Washington and convincing the president to accept the invitation in the May and September letters to back him against Hamilton.

In 1818, however, such details were superfluous and would only confuse and distract; they would be seized on by his enemies, distorted in their polemics, and employed to deflect attention from Hamilton's antirepublican schemes. Still, it was a breathtaking maneuver, to be explained only by the utter certainty with which Jefferson in 1818 understood what had happened in the 1790s. He had, after all, no guarantee that Hamilton's papers would not provide a contrary account—but that, of course, was the point: He had to put his own version on record, endowing it with all the authority his reputation could supply, and then hope for the best. If nothing else, it would arm the faithful and persuade the wavering, and that, perhaps, was the most he could expect.[130]

Jefferson was determined that future Americans should not forget the ordeal of republicanism in the first three administrations or fail to receive the morals that story taught. His autobiographical efforts in the last decade of his life recounted in full the story of the traditional politics of debt and corruption—the account of the Dinner Table Bargain is only one of many episodes in the "Anas" to develop this theme—for this was to be history that would instruct, illustrating the dangers that republicans had to confront.[131] And in the climate of the postwar years, it was all too evident that such instruction was badly needed; with an enormous national debt, with speculation and banks—another instrument of corruption favored by Hamilton—growing at an alarming rate, Jefferson knew that the struggle was not over. But at least he could try to ensure that his role in 1790 would not be misread; though it might risk provoking further discussion of the matter, he would do his best to preempt the enemy and establish the truth.

Jefferson was seventy-five in 1818; he did not expect to live much longer, and he had done his best to prepare the materials that would vindicate him and perpetuate his message. The public, as it turned out, would have to wait another eleven years before his materials reached them, in the four volumes of his grandson's edition of the *Memoir, Correspondence, and Miscellanies, from the Papers of Thomas Jefferson*.[132] Madison was more than a little worried by the controversy their publication was sure to excite; engaged in polemics of his own over the Virginia and Kentucky Resolutions as states'-rights advocates once more claimed to know Jefferson and Madison better than they knew themselves, Jefferson's friend did not want any revelations that would damage the unionist position he was trying to defend.[133] He warned Jeff Randolph that his grandfather's remarks about Hamilton might be too strong for circulation, and he urged Randolph to be circumspect in his choice of letters, telling Lafayette that "selecting . . . the materials for the Edition" was "a very delicate task."[134] Madison was right to worry, for the *Memoir* attracted considerable attention, not all of it favorable by any measure.[135]

Still, Jefferson's account of the Dinner Table Bargain was generally accepted, if only, I suspect, because the story he told was almost too good to be true from the perspective of historians and biographers searching for colorful detail with which to enliven and personalize the otherwise dry details of early national politics.[136] Only an old clerk of Hamilton's doubted that his chief could have engaged in the horse trading that Jefferson's story seemed to hint at, and his views remained in manuscript.[137] Certainly there must have been many who, like Martin Van Buren, appreciated the story as Jefferson told it; "Hamilton," Van Buren would state in his *Inquiry into the Origins and Course of Political Parties in the United States*, "succeeded in obtaining—how much to his mortification and regret his writings show—the coöperation of Mr. Jefferson" in 1790, and that was exactly the message Jefferson wished to convey about the bargain.[138]

Jefferson may have been convinced that publication would vindicate his views to the rising generation, but critics were not impressed by his argument in favor of the rights of the living, and many readers must have agreed with Justice Joseph Story when that redoubtable figure dismissed the *Memoir* as "the most precious melange of all sorts of scandals."[139] Thus not all Americans responded favorably when given a chance to inspect Jefferson's views on the rights of the living generation. (Jeff Randolph had included several letters on this theme, including that to Madison of 6 September 1789.)[140] From New England, Theodore Dwight pronounced it one of "the strange and extravagant opinions which Mr. Jefferson had formed."[141] Despite Jefferson's efforts to appease him, Henry Lee, Jr., had neither forgotten nor forgiven what the Virginia Republicans did to his Federalist father, and he took his revenge on Jefferson's ghost. "This singular theory," he remarked of the principle, "is so exuberantly fallacious, so arborescently absurd, that it well deserves a closer examination than I can afford to bestow on it."[142] Even Madison, loyal as ever to his friend's memory, told Jefferson's granddaughter Ellen Wayles Randolph Coolidge that the principle would be difficult to reduce to practice, though he admitted that "it affords a practical lesson well according with the policy of free nations."[143]

Other Virginians also expressed their skepticism. George Tucker, Jefferson's first major biographer and his hand-picked professor of moral philosophy at the University of Virginia, was certain that it would not work in practice and was unjust to boot, though he granted that the question was academic, for the principle was "one on which no community will ever consent to act."[144] And it was not without irony that the critics seized on Madison's reply to the letter, once Tucker published it in his *Life of Thomas Jefferson* (1837); in this instance, at least, the "great collaboration" worked against Jefferson.[145] These responses to the principle would have saddened Jefferson; it was, after all, his great discovery, the deeply felt expression of his lifelong hatred of debt and what debt implied.

Jefferson found a warmer welcome in France; a two-volume abridged translation of the *Memoir* was published in Paris in 1832 under the title *Mélanges politques et philosophiques*, where it was favorably reviewed by the young Sainte-Beuve. "This period of nineteen years, at the end of which a revision and perhaps a total reorganization of society will take place, is Jefferson's favorite theme," Sainte-Beuve wrote with evident approval. And the critic explained Jefferson's notion that debts were illegitimate when entailed on one generation by the preceding one; "he opposes as strongly as he can the loans that burden a nation's future," Sainte-Beuve noted, and he further pointed out that, according to Jefferson's doctrine, once the nine-teen-year limit had expired, there was no longer any obligation "en bonne morale" to continue to pay.[146] In a France where the July Monarchy had only recently come to power, where the rising generation was conscious of itself as a generation, insisting on its right to be heard, whether in politics or in literature, Jefferson's message would have meant a great deal, far more, probably, than it did to many of Jefferson's American readers at the time. Sainte-Beuve's reception of his message would have gladdened Jefferson; deaf to irony though he was, Jefferson would have applauded his principle's return to its birthplace.[147]

In the end, then, Jefferson's career from the 1780s to the 1820s possessed a remarkable unity. Throughout, he would remain obsessed by the problem of debt—by his own debts and by the debts that threatened the future of republican America. If, as I have tried to show, it was impossible for Jefferson to separate the two, if others in Virginia shared Jefferson's sense that debt was a danger to nations as well as to individuals, perhaps we can begin to appreciate how deeply such attitudes affected the course of politics in the new nation. To be sure, Jefferson and the Virginians were not the only Americans to fear the effects of debt—John Adams's case reminds us of that—nor would every Virginian willingly subordinate all other political concerns and follow Jefferson into the Republican camp, and the state's Republicans would never adopt all his teachings. But most of the gentry did just that, and the attitudes and outlook Jefferson embodied, so firmly rooted in the gentry's collective experience, supplied the dominant themes of Virginia's position in national politics from the early 1790s through the 1820s.

Jefferson hoped that his countrymen would take to heart the lessons he preached. Republicanism would then be established on a secure and lasting foundation, at least until the inevitable progress of society, the growth of population, and the exhaustion of the public domain removed the material bases for the republican experiment in America. Jefferson's optimism was misplaced; neither Americans in general nor Virginians in particular could resist the prospects of growth and prosperity that run-ning into debt seemed to promise. Jefferson had warned against traditional eighteenth-century abuses of debt; the nineteenth century would create new forms he had not foreseen. Internal improvements, vastly expensive and requiring the full credit of the states to finance, produced mountains of state debt within little more than a decade after Jefferson's death, even in Virginia itself, which by 1861 owed some $33 million.[148] That debt would remain to haunt Virginia and Virginia politics after the Civil War, as Conservatives and Readjusters struggled over the social and economic costs that debt service imposed on an Old Dominion poorer than ever.[149] Hoping to erect barriers against the kinds of debt generated by war and military spending—the debts the eighteenth century knew—Jefferson had not imag-ined that the nineteenth century would find other ways of imposing burdens on posterity.

Still, by mid-century there was evidence that Jeffersonian lessons were spreading. After the Panic of 1837 and the collapse of many state-sponsored internal improvements, a number of states adopted constitutional bans on state borrowing.[150] And, even if it did not flourish at the federal level, there were states in which Jefferson's doctrine of periodical revision of constitutions took root.[151] Although it is impossible to know whether Jefferson's own message, that the earth belongs in usufruct to the living, influenced decisions to include such provisions in state constitutions and, even more, influenced antebellum American politicians and voters to consider such ideas in the first place, it would not be surprising to find that, here and there, readers of the Tucker biography or Jeff Randolph's edition of his grandfather's papers were captivated by the 6 September 1789 letter. And there would have been other routes of transmission as well, for claims on behalf of the living generation in a general sense could be found in the works of other writers. But what one does not see, by and large, is evidence that what Jefferson had discovered–the rights of the living generation of nineteen years–became fundamental tenets of the American political creed.

Jefferson's ideas, after all, arose in a republican–and a Virginia–context that was fading at the time of his death. Jefferson's hopes and fears had increasingly less relevance as the years passed, even to those who were proud to proclaim themselves republicans and insist that monarchy was the enemy of liberty and progress. And as that contest faded, as Virginia's role in national politics diminished, the force of Jefferson's arguments weakened.[152] On other fronts, as well, Jefferson's doctrines seemed less meaningful, given the problems that nineteenth-century American society had to confront. His commitment to the sanctity of private property was of little use in a world where private property was being identified as the root of the problem. Even in his own days, his views had hardly been radical when compared with those of the late-eighteenth- and early-nineteenth-century English pioneers of socialism, whose critiques of property and inheritance went well beyond anything Jefferson entertained.[153] American radicals in the decades following his death also found little in the Virginian's writings to inspire them; those who campaigned for land for workingmen looked to Paine, not Jefferson, for support.[154] In time, to be sure, late-nineteenth-century American critics of capitalism like Henry George would revive the Jeffersonian doctrine that the earth belongs to the living, though in an utterly literal sense Jefferson had not intended.[155] But by George's day, the original meaning of Jefferson's doctrine had already been lost, and the twentieth century would carry that process to its logical conclusion, reading Jefferson in ways the Virginian would never have recognized.

Which is not to say that there is no continuing popular tradition of opposition to the national debt that may owe something, however attenuated, to Jeffersonian inspiration. Despite the apostasy of Ronald Reagan and the modern Republican party in the 1980s, many Americans continue to accept the underlying premise that so impressed Jefferson–that nations, like individuals, cannot spend more than they take in, that a massive public debt is, somehow, a very bad thing. Visitors to Manhattan will be familiar with real-estate developer Seymour Durst's National Debt Clock on Forty-second Street, thanks to which one can sit in the restored gardens of Bryant Park behind the New York Public Library and watch the numbers spin giddily upward—Jefferson would have loved Durst's idea.[156] And then there were the television ads sponsored by W. R. Grace & Company a few presidential campaigns ago, in which a newborn infant in a crib was handed a bill for its share of the national debt—another visual presentation of the underlying thought fully in keeping with Jefferson's notions. One could also note the appeal of Ross Perot's position on the national debt to younger voters in 1992 and the emergence of groups like "Lead . . . or Leave," convinced that their rights to a secure future are jeopardized by the spendthrift habits of their elders, who have mortgaged the country's assets for generations to come.[157]

Similarly, the balanced budget amendment, whatever professionals may say about the harm that measure would cause, has attracted significant support and is likely to be with us for some time to come.[158] The historian, of course, is reminded of Hume and the other eighteenth-century critics of British policy; if a massive national debt was the apparent price of the power William Pitt the Younger and his contemporaries were unwilling to surrender, so, too, a massive debt for the victor (and bankruptcy for the defeated) has been the price of the last half-century of American foreign policy. But it would be risky to push the parallel too far, and in any case these themes have been widely discussed in recent years.[159]

As for Jefferson's notion that laws and constitutions, like debts, could last no longer than nineteen years, there, too, the record does not suggest that Jefferson's argument made as great an impact as he hoped. Constitutional theorists in the Gilded Age, influenced by Germanic notions of organic development, began to address the issue of the "living Constitution," making some of the first of many arguments that, superficially, tied Jefferson's theme of the rights of generations to the need for a Constitution capable of keeping up with changing times. Sidney George Fisher and Christopher Tiedemann, among others, adopted this approach, often in language that recalled Jefferson's, with Tiedemann claiming that "all governmental authority rests upon the commands, not of a dead generation, but of a living generation. . . . The binding authority of law, therefore, does not rest upon any edict of the people in the past; it rests upon the present will of those who possess the political power." The past is gone and has no power over the present: "No people are ruled by dead men, or by the utterances of dead men," Tiedemann concluded. Fisher had already said, in the midst of the Civil War, that there could be no "fixed, unchangeable government, for a changeable, advancing people, . . . and were it not so, it would be a sad spectacle."[160] In turn, these notions became the core of a liberal interpretation of the Constitution that came into its own in 1937; despite the resurgence of a jurisprudence of original intent, that interpretation is still very much with us.[161] But the arguments for a "living Constitution" always ignored the heart of Jefferson's principle, that only the people acting in their sovereign capacity could legitimately change the Constitution; the notion of an organically growing document, of constitutional doctrine as a product of social evolution, was utterly foreign to Jefferson's conception.

There is, to be sure, nothing unusual about such a process of change and reinterpretation or even misinterpretation; each generation reads the texts of its predecessors in light of its own needs, and the needs of late-eighteenth-century Virginia were hardly those of an America that was being transformed beyond recognition by industrial capitalism. But to say this is to return to our starting point: the original context in which Jefferson's views on debt, on the rights of the living, on the threats to republicanism took shape. For Jefferson, as for so many of his contemporaries in Virginia, debt had its own world of meaning. They knew it intimately from their experience as planter-debtors and gentry-creditors, and that experience gave them a special outlook. It heightened their attentiveness to underlying themes in the discourse of republicanism, alerting them to the dangers that debt posed to independence, whether that independence was personal or political. It made them more than usually receptive to the complaints of English opposition thought. It helped them to identify the Hamiltonian program as a threat to the republican experiment. In Jefferson's case, the impact was even more pronounced; his obsessive concern with his own debts would be combined with orthodox theories of public finance and his vision of America's future to produce a sensitivity to debt that became the hallmark of his political career in the years after 1790.

Jefferson was, it is true, subjected to countervailing pressures. He could not ignore the need for the United States to possess a strong and healthy public credit; he wished his country to figure in the world, and credit was essential if that were to be the case. But, as he discovered in 1790 and 1791, the price was more than he could accept, and therein lay his dilemma. In the end, his hatred of debt prevailed, and he would search for ways to escape the Hamiltonian nightmare to which he and Madison had mistakenly and, as it later seemed, unwittingly given their consent. That would add a special dimension to his obsessions, taking them beyond those of his fellow Virginians, increasing his sense of urgency and responsibility, even his sense of guilt. By 1809, on his retirement, he would hope that the public debt was firmly on the road to extinction and that the future of which he dreamed was well on its way to becoming a reality; by 1815, to his horror, the increase in the national debt during the War of 1812 and the proliferation of banks of issue threatened to undo what his administrations had accomplished and end any possibility of using the revenue for works of improvement. His last decade was troubled and unhappy, and so he sought, through the texts that would be included in the *Memoir*, to recall his country to the paths of republican rectitude. But the days of republicanism as Jefferson had known it were numbered. The Jacksonians might revive some of Jefferson's themes; in the long run, the world in which his doctrines had seemed appropriate responses to the problem of wars, debts, and taxes would vanish without a trace.

Thus Jefferson's attitude toward debt was at once central to his life and career and, at the same time, bound him firmly to his age and his place. Jefferson the Virginian, to borrow the title of the first volume of Dumas Malone's biography, was the essential Jefferson in many ways—in more ways, probably, than historians since Henry Adams have been willing to admit. In Jefferson's day, to be a Virginian meant to know to the full the meaning of debt. None knew it better than Thomas Jefferson.

Appendix A
Paine and Condorcet

A minor scholarly industry has grown up around the question of priority. While I address that issue in Chapter 2, two of the "sources" offered for Jefferson's principle require further comment. Did Jefferson get his idea that the earth belongs in usufruct to the living from Thomas Paine? Or did Paine borrow it from Thomas Jefferson? What of Condorcet? Did he, too, anticipate Jefferson in a way Jefferson must have been aware of? And if so, did Jefferson fail to acknowledge his sources, his inspirations? Should he have said to Madison in the 6 September 1789 letter that he took his underlying principles from the works of Paine and Condorcet or from his conversations with them? I argue in Chapter 2 that we can trust Jefferson, that he was not misleading Madison and Richard Gem when he insisted on priority.[1]

Paine's case is the more widely discussed in the literature, and Adrienne Koch was the first to raise the issue.[2] Noting the similarities between Jefferson's 6 September 1789 letter to Madison and Paine's *Rights of Man*, Part One (1791), Koch asked who was responsible for the original idea. In some ways, her question was *mal posée*: Assuming that Jefferson (or Paine) had to have been the first to discuss the rights of generations, she naturally concluded that one of them derived his ideas from the other. Her review of the evidence in 1950 led her to conclude that it had been Jefferson who inspired Paine, not vice versa.[3] Although Koch's argument was, as we shall see, convincing on its own terms, not everyone was satisfied, and Alfred O. Aldridge and David Freeman Hawke have insisted that Jefferson must have been inspired by Paine, pointing to Paine's use of a generational argument in his *Dissertations on Government* (1786) as evidence that the Anglo-American pamphleteer had given the idea to the Virginia statesman.[4] The flaw at the outset in the argument is the assumption of novelty; as I suggest in Chapter 2, the generational argument was too widely discussed in the late eighteenth century to allow us to conclude that it originated with either Paine or Jefferson.

Koch, who did not notice Paine's use of the argument in 1786, was able to demonstrate to her satisfaction that the documentary evidence offered no support for the conclusion that it was Paine who had priority and therefore influenced Jefferson. Yet she also concluded that Paine's generational arguments could only have come from Jefferson and so went back through the evidence to construct a plausible case for Jefferson as Paine's inspiration. Conversations in Paris between these Americans in 1788, she believed, turned to the issues underlying the principle of generations, and she pointed to the Jefferson–Paine correspondence, with its discussion of natural and civil rights, as evidence that fundamental questions of this sort had arisen in those conversations. Given her conclusion that Jefferson was the first to commit the idea to paper, it followed easily enough, with only a slight gap in the evidentiary chain, that Paine must have seen Richard Gem's copy of the 6 September 1789 letter when he returned to Paris shortly after Jefferson left for America. Remembering Jefferson's letter, Paine then incorporated its ideas in *Rights of Man*, Part One, the following year.[5]

But either man could have reached his formulation independently of the other, and I would argue that is exactly what happened. Jefferson had a copy of Paine's *Dissertations on Government* in his library—when and how acquired is not clear—and for proponents of Paine's priority, its presence is the smoking gun.[6] Yet even if Jefferson read Paine's pamphlet before 6 September 1789—let us assume for the sake of argument that he did—why give it greater priority than the other works Jefferson read that also contained a generational argument in one form or another? And, of course, why credit the argument to Paine in the first place? The argument that Paine got it from Jefferson or Jefferson got it from Paine also fails to confront the absence of acknowledgment on either side. Jefferson never credits Paine; Paine never credits Jefferson. And neither of them says a word about the rights of generations in their letters to each other.[7] They may have discussed those rights—this is one of those things that will remain a mystery in the absence of further documentation—though it seems unlikely, for the letters growing out of their conversations of 1788 never mention them, and it was, moreover, only in late June and early July 1789 that the issue of constitutional revision was tied to the theme of the rights of the living generation in Jefferson's Parisian circle. But if they did discuss the rights of generations, neither man ever alluded to it in published writings or in letters to each other, nor did they do so in their letters to other correspondents. When Madison told Jefferson in 1791 that Joseph Priestley's reply to Edmund Burke showed how "your"—Jefferson's—idea was "germinating," Jefferson did nothing to correct any error this statement contained.[8] I find it improbable that Jefferson was so invested with the idea of priority that he consciously refused to acknowledge Paine's role, even to his trusted friends.

Paine did not need Jefferson to remind him of the rights of generations. He used the argument in its standard eighteenth-century form in 1786, and there is no reason to suppose that it would have disappeared from his intellectual arsenal in the years between 1786 and the publication of *Rights of Man*, Part One, in 1791. Here, it seems to me, the Jefferson–Paine correspondence between 1788 and 1791 has something to say. Significantly, I think, Jefferson's letter to Paine of 11 July 1789 is silent on this issue, even though 11 July was the very day Lafayette offered his proposed Déclaration, containing the "droit des générations qui se succèdent," and even though Jefferson went into great detail on other matters in that letter.[9] Nor did Jefferson send Paine a copy of the 6 September 1789 letter or otherwise describe its contents in his further correspondence with Paine. Unless we assume that Jefferson was somehow unwilling to let Paine know that he had appropriated Paine's idea, we are forced to conclude that Jefferson did not see the idea as linked to Paine in any significant way and so did not think it worth discussing in their correspondence.

If we want an explanation for Paine's stirring assertion of the rights of the living in *Rights of Man*, Part One, there is a much easier and certainly more direct answer than that offered by Paine's alleged–and unprovable– appropriation. We need look no further than the man and the book Paine attacked in *Rights of Man*–Edmund Burke and his *Reflections on the Revolution in France* (1790). For it was Burke who challenged Paine and produced the latter's response, Burke's assertion of the rights of the past over the present and the future that provoked Paine's counterattack on behalf of the living. Burke's claims moved Paine to an appropriate reply without any need for intellectual midwifery on Jefferson's part. If nothing else, the interest that arguments for and against the living generation provoked in other participants in the Burke–Paine exchange suggests that no one reading either *Reflections* or *Rights of Man* could ignore the issue.[10] Paine, then, did not require a hypothetical and in any case undocumented prompting by Jefferson.

But there is a final and even more conclusive reason for supposing that Jefferson and Paine arrived at their formulations independently: Their formulations exhibit major differences. Paine's is far closer to the stock run of eighteenth-century ideas on the subject than is Jefferson's. It shows no signs of having been influenced by the novel twists that Jefferson would incorporate in his version. There is nothing about the nineteen years' duration, only the standard suggestion that each generation, undefined, has a right to make its own choices. Nor is there the insistence, the insistence that follows from Jefferson's limitation, that *all* laws and constitutions automatically cease to be valid at the end of nineteen years. On the contrary, Paine simply argues that laws and constitutions can be changed at the behest of the current generation whenever the living want to change them. And although Paine has much to say about debt, it always remains within the framework of the eighteenth century's standard approach to the subject—there is nothing here to suggest that Paine has adopted Jefferson's notion of the nineteen-year limit, nothing to suggest that he had altered his 1786 view that a generation lasted thirty years. If Paine did see a copy of Jefferson's letter sometime after 6 September 1789—and that is, of course, a possibility that cannot be ruled out, given that Paine returned to Paris in November 1789 and might well have encountered Richard Gem or someone else with access to the copy Jefferson left with Gem—he must not have been overly impressed with it, for the things that make Jefferson's doctrine Jefferson's are the things Paine leaves out.[11]

We can dispose of the Jefferson–Paine problem in what I am convinced is an acceptable fashion, but it will not be so easy to dispose of the Jefferson-–Condorcet problem.[12] For one thing, the documentation here is far more scanty and the need for assumptions correspondingly greater. The basic difficulty is the remarkable resemblance between aspects of Jefferson's formulation and Condorcet's, particularly that in Condorcet's 6 September 1789 letter to Comte Mathieu de Montmorency. What is immediately obvious to any reader of Condorcet's letter is the way in which he manipulates the numbers—exactly as Jefferson does, and to the same end as far as constitutions are concerned.[13] Condorcet was a gifted mathematician, an expert of international standing in a realm in which Jefferson was only an amateur, and, more important, he had a long-standing interest in what might be called "social mathematics," the application of mathematics to the solution of social and political problems, particularly those involving group decision-making procedures such as voting.[14] It should not surprise us that he is able to work out for Montmorency what the life of a generation is and, accordingly, when the right of revision will come into play. Thus there is something of a tie—both Jefferson and Condorcet set down their ideas on the same day (assuming that the 6 September 1789 date of the published letter to Montmorency is accurate). Again, as so often in this business, we are always able to posit parallel lines of action—working with the same general assumptions, both Jefferson and Condorcet could, of course, have arrived independently at the same conclusions.

But these were not rival scientists working in widely distant laboratories; they were prominent men, known to each other, living in the same city, with similar interests and a number of mutual friends and acquaintances.[15] The possibility cannot be excluded that there was some contact between the two, either directly or through an intermediary (Richard Gem?) in the period around 6 September 1789.

Unfortunately, their biographies shed no light on this—though we do know that, on 17 September 1789, Condorcet was present at a farewell dinner Jefferson gave and the question of constitutional revision could well have been canvassed during their meal.[16] But 17 September was a week and a half after Jefferson first set down his principle and more than a week after he completed work on it with the 9 September note of correction to Gem. It was also a week and a half after Condorcet dated his 6 September letter to

Mathieu de Montmorency, and thus will not give us the link we require, however suggestive it is about the possibility the two *could* have been in contact at the end of August and the beginning of September.[17] It would be unwise to go further without additional evidence.

What can be said, however, is that Jefferson was not the only person in Paris to think out the implications of Lafayette's July proposition about the "droit des générations qui se succèdent" at the end of the summer of 1789; Condorcet was reaching similar conclusions on some points. But not on all points, and this is important to emphasize. For while Condorcet was decidedly interested in constitutional revision in 1789 and would remain so until his suicide in 1794, his writings on the subject show no interest in applying the principle to limit debts.[18] If Condorcet borrowed from Jefferson, then, he did so selectively. It might, therefore, be easier to assume that the current of influence flowed in the other direction–that Jefferson picked up the idea of the correct mathematical demonstration of the life of a generation from Condorcet. This is possible, for the letter to Mathieu de Montmorency of 6 September 1789 was probably published soon after its date–and perhaps Jefferson learned of its contents even before its appearance in print. But Sowerby does not record a copy, and it is difficult to imagine that Jefferson would have let a copy of the *Lettres à Montmorency* out of his sight once he had acquired it.[19] Again, as with Paine, there is no sign of a discussion of the rights of the living generation in the Jefferson–Condorcet correspondence after September 1789. That correspondence–and there was relatively little of it–was largely confined to another interest the two men shared: reform of the system of weights and measures.[20] Thus we are left in this case with speculation and supposition. Clearly, there is a good deal more reason to suppose a connection in this case than there is in the Jefferson- -Paine case, but the current state of the evidence does not allow us to determine what the nature of that connection was–if, indeed, there was any connection.

We may conclude, then, that Jefferson and Paine in all probability arrived at independent conclusions, drawing on some of the same readily available eighteenth-century materials. As for Jefferson and Condorcet, we are confronted with tantalizing possibilities that prove impossible to resolve. But perhaps the more important point to be made, in each case, is the way in which the connections and parallels, such as they are, confirm the original character of Jefferson's composition. Both Paine and Condorcet speak of generations, and Condorcet's twenty-year definition is close enough to Jefferson's. But neither Paine nor Condorcet uses the crucial qualifier "in usufruct," and neither of them advances the principle with the single-minded literalness that characterizes Jefferson's position. Nor does either of them start from or refer to debt as the foundation. These differences are enough to suggest that Jefferson worked by himself for the most part, arriving at a set of conclusions that, however derivative, took on a form distinctly his own.

Appendix B
Selected Virginia Libraries

What follows is a sampling of the contents of the libraries of eighteenth-century Virginians, and, in two cases, of proposed libraries whose catalogues are either known or thought to have been drawn up by Virginians. The sample is not exhaustive, nor is it meant to be. But it will suggest that some prominent Virginians—Washington, Jefferson, Madison, and Patrick Henry among them—were acquainted with the eighteenth-century works discussed in the text. Except for the fact that Hume's *Essays* does not seem to have been a staple in the collections, there are no surprises here. Montesquieu and Blackstone are found more often than any other works, and this is in keeping with what we should expect, given their prominence and the utility of their books. Looking over the results—summarized in the table that follows—will suggest that gentry Virginians were, broadly speaking, familiar with major mid-eighteenth-century works of history and political economy and, moreover, that they thought it important—for whatever reason—to have such works in their personal collections.

Selected Eighteenth-Century Works in Virginia Libraries

Works	*Libraries*								
	a	*b*	*c*	*d*	*e*	*f*	*g*	*h*	*i*
Swift		X			X				
Montesquieu	X	X	X			X	X	X	
Hume			X						
Kames	X	X							
Smollett		X			X	X			
Steuart	X		X	X			X		X
Robertson		X	X		X		X	X	
Blackstone		X	X	X		X	X	X	X
Burgh	O		X					X	
Price	O	O	X						
Smith	O	O	X		X		X	X	
Sinclair	O	O	O				X	X	
Burke	O	O	O				X		
Paine	O	O	O		X			X	

Note: *X* indicates the presence of a work in a library; *O* indicates that the inventory of a library was taken before the work in question was published. Libraries (identified by letter) and works (identified by author's last name) are described in the key.

a Thomas Jefferson, pre-1770 collection (so-called first library). Reconstructed in H. Trevor Colbourn, *The Lamp of Experience: Whig History and the Intellectual Origins of the American Revolution* (Chapel Hill, N.C., 1965), 217.

b Robert Carter of Nomini, library as catalogued in 1774 by Philip Vickers Fithian. The catalogue is printed in Hunter Dickinson Farish, ed., *Journal and Letters of Philip Vickers Fithian: A Plantation Tutor of the Old Dominion, 1773–1774* (Charlottesville, Va., 1957), 221–29.

c James Madison, 1783 book list of a proposed library for Congress, in *PJM*, 6:65–115.

d John Breckinridge, library of 1791, as ordered from his bookseller. See Wheeldon & Butterworth to Donald & Burton, 17 Feb. 1791; Donald & Burton to Robert Rives, 17 Feb. 1791, Breckinridge Family Papers, vol. 7, LC.

e George Washington, library as inventoried in 1800, after his death. The inventory is printed in Eugene E. Prussing, *The Estate of George Washington, Deceased* (Boston, 1927), 418–33.

f Patrick Henry, library as inventoried in 1802, after his death. The inventory is printed in Robert Douthat Meade, *Patrick Henry: Practical Revolutionary* (Philadelphia, 1969), 455–59.

g The original collection of the Library of Congress, 1800. The catalogue is printed in *The First Booklist of the Library of Congress: A Facsimile* (Washington, D.C., 1981). As Dana J. Prat notes in the Foreword to the *Booklist*, although there is no record of how the joint committee charged with setting up the Library of Congress made its book selections, "it is reasonable to assume that the advice of the great bibliophile Thomas Jefferson was sought." (Jefferson was, of course, serving as vice president in 1800.)

h Thomas Jefferson, collection of 1770 to 1815 (so-called second library). Catalogued in *Sowerby*.

i Works cited in St. George Tucker's annotated edition of *Blackstone's Commentaries: With Notes of Reference, to the Constitution and Laws, of the Federal Government of the United States; and of the Commonwealth of Virginia* . . . , 5 vols. (Philadelphia, 1803).

Blackstone, Sir William. *Commentaries on the Laws of England*, 4 vols. (1765–1769).

Burgh, James. *Political Disquisitions* (1774).

Burke, Edmund. *Reflections on the Revolution in France* (1790).

Hume, David. *Essays* (1741; many later editions).

Lord Kames [Henry Hume]. *Historical Law-Tracts* (1758).

Montesquieu, Charles de Secondat, baron de. *The Spirit of the Laws* (1748); English trans. Thomas Nugent (1756). Both English and French editions of this work were present in

Virginia collections; thus Patrick Henry, as one might expect, had the translation (f), while Jefferson had the original (a, h).

Paine, Thomas. *Rights of Man*, Part One (1791).

Price, Richard. *Additional Observations on the Nature of Civil Liberty* (1776).

Robertson, William. *History of the Reign of Charles V* (1769).

Sinclair, Sir John. *History of the Public Revenue*, 2 vols. (1785, 1789).

Smith, Adam. *The Wealth of Nations* (1776).

Smollett, Tobias. *History of England* (1757).

Steuart, Sir James. *Principles of Political Oeconomy* (1767).[1]

Swift, Jonathan. *Works*. Numerous eighteenth-century editions existed, and it has not been possible to identify specifically those in Virginia collections.

Notes

Abbreviations

The following short citation forms are used in the notes.

AHR   *American Historical Review*

Boyd   Julian P. Boyd et al., eds., *The Papers of Thomas Jefferson*, 25 vols. to date (Princeton, N.J., 1950–)

Cappon   Lester G. Cappon, ed., *The Adams–Jefferson Letters: The Complete Correspondence between Thomas Jefferson and Abigail and John Adams*, 2 vols. (Chapel Hill, N.C., 1959)

DHFFC   Linda Grant De Pauw, ed., *The Documentary History of the First Federal Congress of the United States of America, March 4, 1789–March 3, 1791*, 11 vols. to date (Baltimore and London, 1972–)

DHRC   Merrill Jensen et al., eds., *The Documentary History of the Ratification of the Constitution*, 10 vols. to date (Madison, Wis., 1976–)

Family Letters   Edwin Morris Betts and James Adam Bear, Jr., eds., *The Family Letters of Thomas Jefferson* (Columbia, Mo., 1966)

Farm Book   Edwin Morris Betts, ed., *Thomas Jefferson's Farm Book, with Commentary and Relevant Extracts from Other Writings* (Princeton, N.J., 1953)

Ford   Paul Leicester Ford, ed., *The Works of Thomas Jefferson*, 12 vols. (New York and London, 1904–1905) ("Federal Edition")

JAH   *Journal of American History*

L&B	Andrew A. Lipscomb and Albert Ellery Bergh, eds., *The Writings of Thomas Jefferson*, 20 vols. (Washington, D.C., 1903–1904) ("Memorial Edition")
LC	Library of Congress, Washington, D.C.
LofA	Thomas Jefferson, *Writings*, ed. Merrill D. Peterson (New York, 1984) (Library of America edition)
Malone	Dumas Malone, *Jefferson and His Time*, 6 vols. (Boston, 1948–1981)
MHS	Massachusetts Historical Society, Boston
PAH	Harold C. Syrett, ed., *The Papers of Alexander Hamilton*, 27 vols. (New York, 1961–1987)
PJM	William T. Hutchinson et al., eds., *The Papers of James Madison*, 17 vols. (Chicago and Charlottesville, Va., 1962–1991)
Sowerby	E. Millicent Sowerby, comp., *Catalogue of the Library of Thomas Jefferson*, 5 vols. (Washington, D.C., 1952–1959)
TJ	Thomas Jefferson
UVa	University of Virginia Library, Charlottesville
VMHB	*Virginia Magazine of History and Biography*
WMQ	*William and Mary Quarterly*, 3rd ser.

Introduction

1. Steven Harold Hochman, "Thomas Jefferson: A Personal Financial Biography" (Ph.D. diss., University of Virginia, 1987), offers the best view to date of Jefferson's private finances in dollars and cents terms. Hochman does not, however, connect the private and the public Jefferson, and is probably overly cautious in drawing conclusions about the significance of debt as a theme in Jefferson's life. Others have also been struck by the ways in which debt provides a key to much about Jefferson; see, for example, Fawn M. Brodie, *Thomas Jefferson: An Intimate History* (New York, 1974), 456, and Edmund S. Morgan, *American Slavery, American Freedom: The Ordeal of Colonial Virginia* (New York, 1975), 383. Dumas Malone, Jefferson's principal biographer, whose six-volume life is the source to which all students of the third president repair when in doubt—and to which most of us go when beginning our projects—had relatively little to say about the deeper meaning of debt for Jefferson. But in the last volume, he puts things in words that I think must command assent, speaking of Jefferson's "obsession regarding debt" (*Malone*, 6:138). As will be apparent, I see that observation as the starting point.

2. Andrew Burstein, the author of an important forthcoming study of Jefferson as a letter writer, has cautioned me in conversation against taking Jefferson's tactic too seriously. Jefferson, Burstein says, is writing with tongue in cheek. Burstein is right; Jefferson clearly draws up the account with an implied chuckle. But that is precisely the point: Debt is so much a presence in Jefferson's life that it even colors his attempts at wit. For the letter itself, see TJ to Ellen Wayles Randolph, 21 May 1805, *Family Letters*, 271:

MISS ELEANOR W. RANDOLPH TO TH: JEFFERSON   DR.

1805. May 21. To a letter which ought to be written once every 3.

weeks, while I am here, to wit from Jan. 1. 1805. to this day 15. weeks   5

CR.

Feb. 23.   By one single letter of this day's date 1
Balance due for E. W. Randolph to Th: J Letters   4
                                                                        ——
                                                                          5

For other examples of the language of debtor and creditor in the correspondence between Jefferson and his grandchildren, see TJ to Ellen Wayles Randolph, 4 Mar. 1805; E. W. Randolph to TJ, 30 Jan., 17 Feb. 1807; TJ to E. W. Randolph, 1 Mar. 1807; E. W. Randolph to TJ, 6 Mar. 1807; TJ to E. W. Randolph, 8 Dec. 1807; 23 Feb. 1809; TJ to Cornelia Jefferson Randolph, 3 Apr. 1808, ibid., 268, 294, 296 (bis), 298, 316, 329, 339.

3. For the phrase, see TJ to Charles Thompson, 9 Jan. 1816, in Dickson W. Adams, ed., *Jefferson's Extracts from the Gospels: "The Philosophy of Jesus" and "The Life and Morals of Jesus"* (Princeton, N.J., 1983), 356.

4. The literature on Jefferson has long since become all but unmanageable. Peter S. Onuf provides a guide to recent work in "The Scholars' Jefferson," *WMQ* 50 (1993): 671–99; earlier studies are surveyed in Merrill D. Peterson, *The Jefferson Image in the American Mind* (New York, 1960), and, with respect to Jefferson and slavery, in Scott A. French and Edward L. Ayers, "The Strange Career of Thomas Jefferson: Race and Slavery in American Memory, 1943–1993," in Peter S. Onuf, ed., *Jeffersonian Legacies* (Charlottesville, Va., 1993), 418–56. The standard bibliographies are those by Eugene L. Huddleston, *Thomas Jefferson: A Reference Guide* (Boston, 1982), and Frank Shuffleton, *Thomas Jefferson: A Comprehensive, Annotated Bibliography of Writings About Him, 1826–1980* (New York, 1983) and *Thomas Jefferson, 1981–1990: An Annotated Bibliography* (New York, 1992). For a sense of the breadth of the literature, see the essays in Merrill D. Peterson, ed., *Thomas Jefferson: A Reference Biography* (New York, 1986); those in Onuf, ed., *Jeffersonian Legacies*, suggest the current direction of scholarship on many of the topics of most interest to historians.

5. Lance Banning, *The Jeffersonian Persuasion: Evolution of a Party Ideology* (Ithaca, N.Y., 1978); John G. Murrin, "The Great Inversion, or Court versus Country: A Comparison of the Revolution Settlements in England (1688–1721) and America (1776–1816)," in J. G. A. Pocock, ed., *Three British Revolutions: 1641, 1688, 1776* (Princeton, N.J., 1980), 368–453, esp. 405–28; Gordon S. Wood, *The Radicalism of the American Revolution* (New York, 1992), 367–68, and "The Trials and Tribulations of Thomas Jefferson," in Onuf, ed., *Jeffersonian Legacies*, 412–15.

6. The literature on republicanism and liberalism in the new nation is enormous. Most students of these interpretations would begin with two important review essays by Robert E. Shalhope: "Toward a Republican Synthesis: The Emergence of an Understanding of Republicanism in American Historiography," *WMQ* 29 (1972):49–80, and "Republicanism in Early American Historiography," *WMQ* 39 (1982): 334–56, and then proceed to sample the following works. On the liberal side, one would look first to Joyce O. Appleby's pioneering *Capitalism and a New Social Order: The Republican Vision of the 1790s* (New York, 1984) and her collected essays, *Liberalism and Republicanism in the Historical Imagination* (Cambridge, Mass., 1992). Isaac Kramnick, *Republicanism and Bourgeois Radicalism: Political Ideology in Late Eighteenth-Century England and America* (Ithaca, N.Y., 1990), provides further support for the liberal interpretation. Paul Rahe, *Republics Ancient and Modern: Classical Republicanism and the American Revolution* (Chapel Hill, N.C., 1992), attempts to demonstrate the utter incompatibility of classical republicanism and

eighteenth-century America. Thomas L. Pangle, *The Spirit of Modern Republicanism: The Moral Vision of the American Founders and the Philosophy of Locke* (Chicago, 1988), offers a reading of the Founding that emphasizes its liberal character. The republican interpretation can be followed in J. G. A. Pocock, *The Machiavellian Moment: Florentine Political Thought and the Atlantic Republican Tradition* (Princeton, N.J., 1975), and *Virtue, Commerce, and History: Essays on Political Thought and History, Chiefly in the Eighteenth Century* (Cambridge, 1985); Banning, *Jeffersonian Persuasion*; Drew R. McCoy, *The Elusive Republic: Political Economy in Jeffersonian America* (Chapel Hill, N.C., 1980), and *The Last of the Fathers: James Madison and the Republican Legacy* (Cambridge, 1989); Bernard Bailyn, *The Ideological Origins of the American Revolution* (Cambridge, Mass., 1967); Milton M. Klein et al., eds., *The Republican Synthesis Revisited: Essays in Honor of George Athan Billias* (Worcester, Mass., 1992); and "Republicanism in the History and Historiography of the United States" [special issue], *American Quarterly* 27 (1985): 461–598. Daniel T. Rogers, "Republicanism: The Career of a Concept," *JAH* 79 (1992): 11–38, is a wry account of this paradigm's fortunes. See Appleby's comments in "A Different Kind of Independence: The Postwar Restructuring of the Historical Study of Early America," *WMQ* 50 (1993): 260–65.

7. As J. G. A. Pocock notes in "Conservative Government and Democratic Revolutions: American and French Cases in British Perspective," *Government and Opposition* 24 (1989): 99, "Jefferson was not immune from this double vision, . . . his ideals were rooted in a past as well as a future, and . . . he viewed the movement of history with one auspicious and one drooping eye." For arguments that republicanism was only one of several competing discourses in the founding era, see James T. Kloppenberg, "The Virtues of Liberalism: Christianity, Republicanism, and Ethics in Early American Political Discourse," *JAH* 74 (1987): 9–33; Isaac Kramnick, "The 'Great National Discussion': The Discourse of Politics in 1787," in *Republicanism and Bourgeois Radicalism*, 260–88; and Michael Lienesch, *New Order of the Ages: Time, the Constitution, and the Making of Modern American Political Thought* (Princeton, N.J., 1988). Both Lance Banning and Joyce O. Appleby have contributed to this shift; see Banning's "Quid Transit: Paradigms and Process in the Transformation of Republican Ideas," *Reviews in American History* 17 (1989): 199–204, and "Jeffersonian Ideology Revisited: Liberal and Classical Ideas in the New American Republic," and Appleby's reply, "Republicanism in Old and New Contexts," *WMQ* 43 (1986): 3–19, 20–34. Peter S. Onuf reviews the field in: "Reflections on the Founding: Constitutional Historiography in Bicentennial Perspective," *WMQ* 46 (1989): 341–75, and "Scholars' Jefferson," esp. 675–84. John Ashworth, "The Jeffersonians: Classical Republicans or Liberal Capitalists?" *Journal of American Studies* 18 (1984): 425–35, is worth consulting. But as Peter Onuf and Nicholas Onuf have noted, "The current debate has no clear winner. Even its structure has broken down, as participants and positions proliferate. This impasse suggests two possibilities about the founders' debate. It is possible that the debate was inconclusive and that current scholarship fairly reflects this discursive confusion. It is also possible that today's scholars misconstrue the terms of earlier debate because of unexamined propensities in their own discourse" (*Federal Union, Modern World: The Law of Nations in an Age of Revolutions, 1776–1814* [Madison, Wis., 1993], 20). As confirmation of the emerging consensus that Jefferson was neither all republican nor all liberal, consider the following comments by Ruth H. Bloch and Norman K. Risjord. As Bloch sees it, "even some of the articulate ideological spokesmen—such as Thomas Jefferson—were, to our minds, often frustratingly contradictory, perfectly capable of entertaining

seemingly opposite sets of convictions at the same time" ("Religion, Literary Sentimentalism, and Popular Revolutionary Ideology," in Ronald Hoffman and Peter J. Albert, eds., *Religion in a Revolutionary Age* [Charlottesville, Va., 1994], 310). According to Risjord, "Jefferson was not a man of keen introspection; he was fully capable of embracing competing 'persuasions' that seem to us today incompatible" (*Thomas Jefferson* [Madison, Wis., 1994], xii).

8. See, for example, Joyce O. Appleby's comment that "the light touch of the past on Jefferson's thinking can be accounted for in part by the looming presence of the future" ("The Radical *Double-Entendre* in the Right to Self-Government," in Margaret Jacob and James Jacob, eds., *The Origins of Anglo-American Radicalism* [London, 1984], 281).

9. Isaac Kramnick, "Republican Revisionism Revisited," *AHR* 87 (1982): 629–64, now amplified in *Republicanism and Bourgeois Radicalism*, 163–99. For Kramnick's reliance on Appleby to support the American side of his argument, see 171n.19, 179n.35. For a different reading of the evidence, see J. G. A. Pocock, "Radical Criticisms of the Whig Order in the Age between Revolutions," in Jacob and Jacob, eds., *Origins of Anglo-American Radicalism*, 32–57,

10. See, for example, Richard J. Twomey, "Jacobins and Jeffersonians: Anglo-American Radical Ideology, 1790–1810," in Jacob and Jacob, eds., *Origins of Anglo-American Radicalism*, 284–99, and Michael Drury, "Thomas Paine's Apostles: Radical Emigrés and the Triumph of Jeffersonian Republicanism," *WMQ* 44 (1987): 661–88, on radical immigrant Jeffersonians who quite literally came from the milieux Kramnick investigated. Appleby's arguments often seem to fit the Democratic Republicans of the seaports better than they fit Jefferson himself, which is not particularly surprising, given the capaciousness of the Democratic Republican tent and the nature of coalition politics. On the latter point, see Ashworth, "Jeffersonians," 427.

11. On the links between party and denomination in Massachusetts, see James M. Banner, *To the Hartford Convention: The Federalists and the Origins of Party Politics in Massachusetts, 1789–1815* (New York, 1970), 197–215, and Paul Goodman, *The Democratic-Republicans of Massachusetts: Politics in a Young Republic* (Cambridge, Mass., 1964), 86–96.

12. On Federalist science at Yale, see Chandos Michael Brown, *Benjamin Silliman: A Life in the Young Republic* (Princeton, N.J., 1989); for American science in this period generally, see John C. Greene, *American Science in the Age of Jefferson* (Ames, Iowa, 1984), and, of course, Daniel J. Boorstin, *The Lost World of Thomas Jefferson* (New York, 1948). Linda Kerber's *Federalists in Dissent: Imagery and Ideology in Jeffersonian America* (Ithaca, N.Y., 1970) should not be read to suggest that Federalists were implacably opposed to science, though the politicization of culture in the period may have led them to attack some of its Republican practitioners.

13. On late-eighteenth-century Americans' sense of American exceptionalism, see Jack P. Greene, *The Intellectual Construction of America: Exceptionalism and Identity from 1492 to 1800* (Chapel Hill, N.C., 1993), 163–99, which can be seen as amplifying the arguments implicit in his *Pursuits of Happiness: The Social Development of Early Modern British Colonies and the Formation of American Culture* (Chapel Hill, N.C., 1988). Bailyn, *Ideological Origins of the American Revolution*, and Wood, *Radicalism of the American Revolution*, also offer compelling evidence of late-eighteenth-century Americans' belief that they *were*, in fact, different.

14. On the ward system, see TJ to Joseph C. Cabell, 2 Feb. 1816, *LofA*, 1379–81; TJ to John Taylor, 28 May 1816; TJ to Samuel Kercheval, 12 July 1816, *Ford*, 11:529–30, 12:8–10. For his sense that the ancients had little to teach the moderns,

see his dismissal of Aristotle's *Politics* in TJ to Isaac H. Tiffany, 6 Aug. 1816, *L&B*, 15:65–66.

15. McCoy, *Last of the Fathers*, is particularly helpful in depicting Madison's cautiously optimistic pessimism.

16. On Jefferson's educational programs, see Harold Hellenbrand, *The Unfinished Revolution: Education and Politics in the Thought of Thomas Jefferson* (Newark, Del., 1990), and Lorraine Smith Pangle and Thomas L. Pangle, *The Learning of Liberty: The Educational Ideas of the American Founders* (Lawrence, Kans., 1993).

17. Frances Trollope, *Domestic Manners of the Americans* (1832), ed. Donald Smalley (New York, 1949). Wood's depiction of Jefferson's increasing irrelevance, by the time of his death, to the emerging pattern of American life seems irrefutable; see *Radicalism of the American Revolution* and "Trials and Tribulations of Thomas Jefferson."

18. Joyce Appleby, "Jefferson and His Complex Legacy," in Onuf, ed., *Jeffersonian Legacies*, 14–15.

19. And even then in general only for a very select group. I have found no evidence, for example, that Jefferson ever discussed his principle of the living generation with his treasury secretary and close collaborator, Albert Gallatin. Gallatin was sound enough on the question of not burdening the future that Jefferson may not have felt it necessary to specify things. On Jefferson's failure to offer a practical program of internal improvements that might have put some flesh on the bones of his vision, see John Lauritz Larson, "Jefferson's Union and the Problem of Internal Improvements," in Onuf, ed., *Jeffersonian Legacies*, 340–69,

20. TJ to Martha Randolph, 5 Jan. 1808, *Family Letters*, 319.

21. Thus Hochman speaks of the "almost incredible, yet characteristic, optimism of Jefferson when it came to evaluating his financial situation" ("Personal Financial Biography," 55; see also 288–89).

22. I discuss the final collapse of Jefferson's fortunes in Chapter 6. For the special significance of spending on the mill, see Hochman, "Personal Financial Biography," 231–32.

23. On these efforts to clear his debts, see Chapter 6.

24. TJ to Thomas Jefferson Randolph, 8 Feb. 1826, *Family Letters*, 469. The context makes it clear that by "family" Jefferson meant only his white family. Note as well the characteristic conditional; Jefferson was still hoping at this point that something might come of the lottery effort.

25. For Jefferson's 1823 plan to clear his debts by 1830 through the sale of 80 of his slaves, see *Malone*, 6:448–49. For a striking instance of Jefferson's awareness that he stood to profit from an increase in the number of his slaves, a conclusion on his part that makes sense only in the context of slave sales, see also TJ to Joel Yancey, 17 Jan. 1819, *Farm Book*, 43.

Chapter 1

1. TJ to Nicholas Lewis, 19 Dec. 1786, *Boyd*, 11:640.

2. TJ to John Jay, 19 Nov. 1788, ibid., 14:215, and cf. TJ to James Madison, 18 Nov. 1788, ibid., 189; TJ, Account Book, 10 Oct. 1788. Scattered in a number of repositories, Jefferson's account books will be published in James A. Bear, Jr., and Lucia C. Stanton, eds., *Jefferson's Memorandum Books: Accounts, with Legal Records and Miscellany, 1767–1826* (forthcoming in Series Two of *The Papers of Thomas Jefferson*). Accordingly, I shall simply cite them by year; readers who wish to follow up can do so

by consulting Bear and Stanton under the appropriate date. My thanks to Stanton for allowing me to check my readings of the manuscripts against the editors' text.

3. Jay did not write back until 9 Mar. 1789, and Jefferson did not receive the letter until 28 July 1789. Jay to TJ, 9 Mar. 1789, *Boyd*, 14:628, 629n. Acknowledging receipt of Jefferson's request, Jay noted the absence of a working representation in the old Congress since the previous October and the fact that the new federal Congress had not yet organized itself, promising to pass the letter on to Washington when he arrived in New York. Ibid., 628–29.

4. TJ to George Washington, 4 Nov. [Dec.] 1788; TJ to Madison, 18 Nov. 1788; TJ to Francis Eppes, 15 Dec. 1788; TJ to Lewis, 16 Dec. 1788, ibid., 331–32, 189, 357, 362.

5. TJ to Madison, 11 May 1789, ibid., 15:121; see TJ to Madison, 15 Mar., 18 June, 22 July 1789, ibid., 14:662; 15:195, 301.

6. Jay to TJ, 19 June 1789, ibid., 14:202–3. He received Jay's letter on 23 Aug. 1789, ibid., 203n.

7. List of Baggage Shipped by Jefferson from France [ca. 1 Sept. 1789], ibid., 375–77, 377n; for the details of his departure, see *Malone*, 2:235.

8. TJ to Eppes, 15 Dec. 1788; TJ to Madison, 28 Aug. 1789, *Boyd*, 14:357; 15:368–69.

9. See Chapter 2.

10. Madison to TJ, 27 May 1789, *PJM*, 12:185. Jefferson received this letter on 6 Aug. 1789, *Boyd*, 15:154n, and for the reply, see TJ to Madison, 28 Aug. 1789, ibid., 369. As Jefferson later remembered, Gouverneur Morris also told him of a possible offer from Washington. TJ to Morris, 7 Nov. 1792, ibid., 24:594–95. On the broader significance of his desire to retire to private life, see Jan Lewis, " 'The Blessings of Domestic Society': Thomas Jefferson's Family and the Transformation of American Politics," in Peter S. Onuf, ed., *Jeffersonian Legacies* (Charlottesville, Va., 1993), 109–46.

11. TJ to Madison, 18 Nov. 1788; TJ to Washington, 4 Nov. [Dec.] 1788; TJ to Madison, 28 Aug. 1789, *Boyd*, 14:189, 332; 15:368.

12. His letters stress the importance of escorting his daughters (TJ to Madison, 18 Nov. 1788; TJ to Washington, 4 Nov. [Dec.] 1788, ibid., 14:189, 332), but it seems clear that the timing of his trip was dictated by the need to attend to his debts; another year or so in France would not have been fatal for his daughters.

13. Steven Harold Hochman, "Thomas Jefferson: A Personal Financial Biography" (Ph.D. diss., University of Virginia, 1987), is now standard on Jefferson's financial history, confirming what readers had derived from *Malone*, esp. 1:435–46; 3:529–30; 6:505–12. Boyd's editorial note, "The Debt to Farell & Jones and the Slave Ship *The Prince of Wales*," *Boyd*, 15:643–49, together with the documents that follow, is an important contribution.

14. For Jefferson's assets, see Jackson Turner Main, "The One Hundred," *WMQ* 11 (1954): 354–84, esp. 377; Francis Eppes and Henry Skipwith, like Jefferson sons-in-law of John Wayles, are on this list of the hundred wealthiest Virginians, as is Thomas Mann Randolph, soon to be the father-in-law of Jefferson's daughter Martha. Ibid., 374, 380, 381. Main's sources provided no information on the claims against these estates; as we shall see, John Wayles's sons-in-law did not hold their properties free and clear, and the same was true of Randolph. For some of Randolph's debts, see Charles F. Hobson, "The Recovery of British Debts in the Federal Circuit Court of Virginia, 1790 to 1797," *VMHB* 91 (1984): 198n.61, and editorial note, "*Scott* v. *Jones's Administrator*," in Herbert A. Johnson et al., eds., *The Papers of John Marshall*,

7 vols. to date (Chapel Hill, N.C., 1974–), 5:389–91. One of many cases involving Farell and Jones and Jefferson's extended family, *Scott* v. *Jones's Administrator* is also of interest in that it arose from Randolph's standing surety, all too often a road to ruin in Virginia.

15. TJ to Farell & Jones, 9 July 1773, *Boyd*, 15:657–61, provides details of the estate's debts and assets and the executors' plans. For the estate's gross value, see ibid., 659, where Jefferson also notes debts to Cary & Co. of London (£1,000), to Mr. Flood of Virginia (£600 [Va. currency]), and to Thomas Waller, a London book-seller, all of which the executors intended to defer and pay from the produce of the plantations. In 1990s dollars, the inheritance would be worth something on the order of $2.25 million. For the conversion factors used here, see John J. McCusker, *How Much Is That in Real Money? A Historical Price Index for Use as a Deflator of Money Values in the Economy of the United States* (Worcester, Mass., 1992), 333. But as McCusker cautions (308–9, 312–313, 315), it is extremely difficult to make accurate comparisons over long periods of time, all the more so given dramatic changes in the standard of living and what there is for money to buy. One way of thinking about the value of the Wayles inheritance is to consider that it would have purchased something like 800 adult slaves at prices then prevailing in Virginia, for which see "Sales of Slaves Imported in *The Prince of Wales*" [Sept.–Dec. 1772], *Boyd*, 15:654–55. A decade or so later, "fewer than one hundred persons [in Virginia] had a hundred slaves"; the largest holding, that of Charles Carter, numbered 783 slaves, and many of them, of course, were not yet adults. Jackson Turner Main, "The Distribution of Property in Post-Revolutionary Virginia," *Mississippi Valley Historical Review* 41 (1954): 249, 249n.22.

16. For the amount of indebtedness recognized by the executors, see Boyd, "Debt to Farell & Jones," *Boyd*, 15:646–47; for the "Guineaman" and the problems it created, see ibid., 647–48, and Farell & Jones to Richard Randolph (Wayles's partner in the consignment), 10 Dec. 1773; William Jones to R. Randolph, 31 May 1783; William Jones to TJ, 11 June 1788, ibid., 665, 673; 13:251; and editorial note, "*Wayles's Executors* v. *Randolph et al.*," in Johnson, ed., *Papers of John Marshall*, 5:117–20. None of the pre-Revolutionary correspondence between the executors and Farell and Jones deals with liability for the slave shipment, probably because Randolph was still alive and recognized as having primary responsibility. It was only after the war, when the Wayles heirs realized that Randolph could not pay and was, moreover, in poor health that they seem to have become worried that the onus would fall on them. On Farell and Jones as the most important tobacco firm in Bristol at this time, see Kenneth Morgan, *Bristol and the Atlantic Trade in the Eighteenth Century* (Cambridge, 1993), 160–61.

17. Will of John Wayles, 5 Mar. 1773, *Tyler's Quarterly Historical and Genealogical Magazine* 6 (1924): 269–70; Wayles's directions in the codicil are quoted in TJ to Farell & Jones, 9 July 1773, *Boyd*, 15:658.

18. TJ to Farell & Jones, 9 July 1773, *Boyd* 15:658.

19. George Mason to Washington, 21 Dec. 1773, in Robert A. Rutland, ed., *The Papers of George Mason, 1725–1792*, 3 vols. (Chapel Hill, N.C., 1970), 1:185; Martha Randolph to TJ, 16 Jan. 1808, *Family Letters*, 322.

20. See the executors' advertisements in the *Virginia Gazette*, 15 July and 9 Sept. 1773, *Boyd*, 1:100, 103. Distribution of the estate seems to have taken place on 14 Jan. 1774. See "Roll of the Slaves of John Wayles which were allotted to T.J. in right of his wife on a division of the estate Jan. 14, 1774," facsimile in *Farm Book*, 7. See TJ, Account Book, 14 Jan. 1774, for his payment of £710 to Henry Skipwith for 226 acres

of the Elkhill estate, part of a series of transactions in which the heirs swapped assets and arranged the division of the Wayles estate in a way that suited them all. Jefferson had assured Farell and Jones six months earlier that the estate (apart from land being sold immediately for the Bristol firm's benefit) would be kept together until the debt was paid. TJ to Farell & Jones, 9 July 1773, *Boyd*, 15:658.

21. Jacob M. Price, "Credit in the Slave Trade and Plantation Economies," in Barbara L. Solow, ed., *Slavery and the Rise of the Atlantic System* (Cambridge, 1991), 309 (italics in original), quoting the statute of 5 George II, c.7. Ordinary creditors could reach Virginia real estate, with some difficulty, by a writ of *elegit*; it allowed them to receive "a portion of the rents and profits from the land until the debt was satisfied" (Peter J. Coleman, *Debtors and Creditors in America: Insolvency, Imprisonment for Debt, and Bankruptcy, 1607–1900* [Madison, Wis., 1974], 192).

22. On the plea of *plene administravit*, see Johnson, ed., *Papers of John Marshall*, 5:40n.6.

23. For an introduction to executors' liability, see editorial note, "*Payne v. Walden's Executor*," in ibid., 34–35. Under Virginia law, debts were to be paid from the testator's personal estate (including slaves if necessary). Ibid., 46. For further details, including the *devastavit*, see Henry St. George Tucker, *Commentaries on the Laws of Virginia. . .* , 2 vols. (Winchester, Va., 1831), 1:425–26, 436–39.

24. TJ to Madison, 6 Sept. 1789, *Boyd*, 15:393, 395; for a full discussion of this important text, see Chapter 2.

25. TJ to W. Jones, 5 Jan. 1787, recounts the sales and Evans's refusal, as does TJ to John Dobson, 1 Jan. 1792, *Boyd*, 11:15–16; 23:4.

26. For the payment, see *Malone*, 1:443. For his role in drafting the statute, see *Boyd*, 2:168–71, with the text proposed by Jefferson; the adopted version, which differs only in details, is in William Waller Hening, comp., *The Statutes at Large. . .* , 13 vols. (Richmond, Va., 1809–1823), 9:377–80. For further evidence of his role in creating the legislation, see also TJ, "Draft of a Resolution Concerning Money Due British Subjects" [ca. 13 Jan. 1778], *Boyd*, 2:171–72. As governor between 1779 and 1781, Jefferson signed the certificates of discharge received by those who paid into the treasury. Ibid., 6:645, and accompanying plate 12. His own description of the payments can be found in ibid., 10:46. Emory G. Evans, "Private Indebtedness and the Revolution in Virginia, 1776 to 1796," *WMQ* 28 (1971): 349–74 (on Jefferson, see 355), and Hobson, "Recovery of British Debts," discuss the British debts during and after the war.

27. For the text of Article IV of the Treaty of Paris (1783), see Charles I. Bevans, comp., *Treaties and Other International Agreements of the United States of America, 1776–1949*, 13 vols. (Washington, D.C., 1968–1976), 12:11. But as Edmund Pendleton reminded Madison in 1790, it was not clear what this meant; did it, he asked, repeal every impediment to the collection of debts or was it only a promise by each side to remove those impediments added during the war? Pendleton to Madison, 21 July 1790, *PJM*, 17:548.

28. TJ to W. Jones, 5 Jan. 1787, *Boyd*, 11:16.

29. Jefferson understood that the debtors would receive credit for only the real, not the nominal, value of the payments and would owe the balance to the creditor. TJ, "Observations on Démeunier's Manuscript," 22 June 1786, ibid., 46. For Francis Eppes, this helped to make "the Peace rather a curse than a blessing" (Eppes to TJ, 16 Sept. 1784, ibid., 15:616). The issue of payments into the treasury was ultimately taken to the Supreme Court, whose decision in *Ware v. Hylton*, 3 Dall. 199 (1796), put an end to any hope the debtors may have had of benefiting from their actions.

Note that Eppes, Daniel L. Hylton's surety on the bond to Farell and Jones at issue in *Ware*, was Hylton's co-defendant in that case, yet another of the British debt suits in which Wayles heirs figured. Jefferson may have played a role in *Ware*. Between July 1795 and April 1797, he and John Marshall, counsel for the *Ware* defendants, exchanged letters now lost. For the missing letters, their existence reconstructed on the basis of entries in Jefferson's Summary Journal of Letters, see Johnson, ed., *Papers of John Marshall*, 2:317, 318, 321, 322, 323; 3:46, 47, 69. Given the letters' dates, Jefferson may have been helping Eppes in the appeal stage of *Ware* v. *Hylton* by instructing Marshall on the conduct of the case, a suspicion deepened by TJ to Eppes, 28 Aug. 1794, Jefferson Papers, UVa. Another possibility is that the correspondence arose in connection with *Wayles's Executors* v. *Randolph et al.* –Marshall represented Randolph's executors–for which see note 16. Whether and to what extent Jefferson's and Marshall's legal dealings in the 1790s colored their later relations remains unexplored.

30. The inheritance of Martha Wayles Skelton Jefferson more than doubled Jefferson's estate. *Malone*, 1:445. He now faced the prospect that nothing of that increase would remain. Francis Eppes also feared that he would have little to leave his son, John Wayles Eppes, and begged Jefferson, with whom the young man was studying law, "for gods sake indevour to impress on his mind the necessity of qualifying himself for some profession which will enable him to git his bread for shou'd this business [Farell and Jones's claim for the slave shipment] go against us it will not be in my power to do much for him" (Eppes to TJ, 27 Apr. 1791, *Boyd*, 20:313).

31. As Jefferson hinted in his negotiations with some of his creditors. See TJ to Alexander McCaul, 4 Jan. 1787; TJ to W. Jones, 5 Jan. 1787, *Boyd*, 11:11, 14.

32. In May 1784, Jones notified Richard Randolph that he was sending Richard Hanson with full powers to settle his affairs in Virginia. Hanson called on Eppes in the summer of 1784, and Eppes reported the visit to Jefferson. W. Jones to R. Randolph, 31 May 1784; Eppes to TJ, 16 Sept. 1784, ibid., 15:673, 616. For further evidence of Hanson's efforts, see Eppes to TJ, 23 Oct. 1786, ibid., 10:483. William Jones had much at stake in Virginia; the £80,000 due him in the Old Dominion was exceeded only by the claims of three large Glasgow firms. Morgan, *Bristol and the Atlantic Trade*, 164 and n.37.

33. On Jefferson's losses, see *Farm Book*, 503–6. He was, of course, careful to point this out to his major creditor. TJ to W. Jones, 5 Jan. 1787, *Boyd*, 11:16. For Virginia's condition in the immediate postwar period, see text at notes 127–35 and 158–75, and Norman K. Risjord, *Chesapeake Politics, 1781–1800* (New York, 1978), 96–103, 109–16.

34. On paying the local debts first, see TJ to Lewis, 19 Dec. 1786, 29 July 1787, 11 July 1788, *Boyd*, 10:614; 11:640; 13:341.

35. For the appointment and his decision to accept, see *Malone*, 1:419–20; for his later complaint that Congress had failed to provide an outfit and a salary that would allow him to live in the style of other diplomats in Paris, see TJ to James Monroe, 11 Nov. 1784, *Boyd*, 7:512–13. For recognition that something had to be done to make his lands more profitable, see TJ to Lewis, 29 July, 17 Sept. 1787, 11 July 1788, ibid., 11:640; 12:135; 13:339–43.

36. Wakelin Welch to TJ, 31 May 1783, *Boyd*, 6:272–73. Welch was also sending reminders to other Virginia debtors. Welch to Washington, 31 May 1783, Washington Papers, LC. For Washington's irate reply, see Washington to Welch, 30 Oct. 1783, in John C. Fitzpatrick, ed., *The Writings of George Washington. . .* , 39 vols. (Washington, D.C., 1933–1944), 27:211–13.

37. TJ to Welch, 24 July 1784; Welch to TJ, 17 Sept., 10 Dec. 1784; TJ to Welch, 5 Jan. 1785, *Boyd*, 7:384, 423, 568, 587.

38. TJ to Eppes, 22 Apr. 1786, ibid., 9:396, 397n; TJ, Account Book, 1 Apr., 25 Apr. 1786.

39. TJ, Account Book, 20 Jan. 1797. See TJ to Benjamin Waller, 21 Dec. 1793, Jefferson Papers, UVa; TJ to Eppes, 1 Aug. 1796, Jefferson Papers, LC; John Wickham to TJ, 8 Dec. 1796; TJ to Wickham, 20 Jan. 1797, Jefferson Papers, MHS.

40. Hochman, "Personal Financial Biography," 261–62; TJ, Account Book, 13 July 1810.

41. TJ, Account Book, Mar. 1823, Statement of Debts. *Malone*, 6:511, does not list the debt as outstanding on 4 July 1826, but I have seen no evidence of its having been paid between 1823 and the date of Jefferson's death, and the probability that it would not have been is high.

42. For Peter Jefferson's estate, see *Malone*, 1:435–37, and for his debts, see TJ to James Lyle, 16 Oct., 3 Nov. 1790, *Boyd*, 17:599–600, 674–75. For his mother's debt—as of 1771, it had been only £95—see Henderson, McCaul & Co., Account with Thomas Jefferson, 14 May 1808, Jefferson Papers, UVa. For his own debts to the firm, see the discussion later in the chapter.

43. TJ to McCaul, 19 Apr. 1786; Alexander Donald to TJ, 6 Sept. 1792 ("your Old Friend Mr. Alexr. McCaul whom you will remember in Richmond many years before the Revolution"), *Boyd*, 9:388; 24:343.

44. See text at notes 179–90.

45. TJ to McCaul, 19 Apr. 1786, 4 Jan. 1787, *Boyd*, 9:388–90; 11:11.

46. McCaul to TJ, 14 Aug. 1788, ibid., 13:513.

47. TJ to McCaul, 4 Jan. 1787, ibid., 11:11–12.

48. McCaul to TJ, 2 Feb. 1787; TJ to McCaul, 19 Feb. 1787, ibid. 11:109n, 167–68.

49. TJ to McCaul, 12 July 1788; McCaul to TJ, 14 Aug. 1788, 25 June 1789; TJ to McCaul, 3 Aug. 1789; Robert and Hugh Ingram to TJ, 10 Aug. 1789, ibid., 13:349, 512; 15:212, 213, 328, 339.

50. TJ, Account Book, 4 Mar. 1790.

51. He began promptly, sending Lyle £325 the day before he left Richmond for New York and his post as secretary of state. Ibid., 7 Mar., 8 Mar. 1790; TJ to Lyle, 7 Mar. 1790, *Boyd*, 16:212. For further developments, see TJ to Lyle, 11 May 1791, 15 Apr. 1793, ibid., 20:388–89; 25:550–51; Lyle to TJ, 25 Oct. 1796; Lyle, Thomas Jefferson in Account with Henderson, McCaul & Co., 1 June 1800, Jefferson Papers, UVa.

52. Ibid.

53. TJ, Account Book, 24 June 1811, 7 Nov. 1808.

54. Ibid., 16 June 1821.

55. Of the bonds Jefferson gave Lyle on 16 June 1821, three (Nos. 1, 2, and 3) survive, and their endorsements provide information on the payments. Jefferson Papers, UVa.

56. Jones died in the early 1790s—his brother-in-law Farell had died during the war—and he may have been eager to wind up the affairs of his firm and so pressed Jefferson more than McCaul. Jones's date of death is not known, but it occurred between May 1791, when suit was brought in his name against Wayles's executors and Daniel Hylton, Richard Randolph's executor, to recover on the 1772 shipment of slaves, and 23 May 1793, when it was revived in the name of John Tyndale Ware, his executor. Barbara Jeanne Bennett, "Settling the Revolutionary Debt Question: *Ware v. Hylton* and *Jones v. Walker*, 1791–1796" (M.A. thesis, Columbia University, 1966),

40, 64. Jones referred to Farell's death in a letter to R. Randolph, 31 May 1783, *Boyd*, 15:672.

57. For Jones's efforts, see note 32.

58. TJ to Eppes, 22 Apr. 1786; TJ to Henry Skipwith, 6 May 1786; TJ to W. Jones, 5 Jan. 1787; TJ to Lewis, 29 July 1787; TJ to Eppes, 30 July 1787; W. Jones to TJ, 11 June 1788; TJ to W. Jones, 9 July 1788; TJ to Eppes, 10 July, 15 Dec. 1788, *Boyd*, 9:395–96, 465; 11:14–16, 639; 13:251–52, 324–26, 327–29; 14:357–58.

59. Jefferson outlined the plan in a 5 Jan. 1787 letter to Jones; see TJ to Eppes, 10 July 1788. For Jones's refusal, see W. Jones to TJ, 11 June 1788; TJ to W. Jones, 9 July 1788, 17 May 1789, ibid., 11:16–17; 13:327–28, 251, 325; 15:131–32.

60. TJ to Lewis, 29 July 1787, ibid., 11:640.

61. Ibid., 639–40.

62. TJ to Lewis, 17 Sept. 1787; TJ to Eppes, 30 July 1787, ibid., 12:135; 11:653–54.

63. TJ to W. Jones, 5 Jan. 1787, and, for a comparable statement to another creditor, TJ to McCaul, 4 Jan. 1787, ibid., 11:16, 11.

64. In July 1788, Jefferson believed he would be able to negotiate with Jones from his base in Paris, but this was before he learned of the failure of his Virginia property to produce a return. TJ to Eppes, 10 July 1788, and for his change of plans, TJ to Eppes, 15 Dec. 1788; TJ to Lewis, 16 Dec. 1788, ibid., 13:327; 14:357, 362.

65. TJ to McCaul, 12 July 1788, reporting bad news from his manager (apparently a missing letter from Lewis to TJ, 15 Apr. 1788, mentioned as received "last night" in TJ to Lewis, 11 July 1788), and see TJ to W. Jones, 9 July 1788, ibid., 13:349, 339, 324–25.

66. Boyd, "Debt to Farell & Jones," and Memorandum of Agreement between Richard Hanson and Executors of John Wayles, 7 Feb. 1790, ibid., 15:643–49, 674–76.

67. For land sales, see TJ to William Ronald, 20 Sept. 1790, Agreement of Sale, 5–13 Oct. 1790; TJ to Eppes, 14 Mar. 1791; TJ to Lewis, 4 Apr. 1791; TJ to Hanson, 5 Apr. 1791; TJ to Thomas Mann Randolph, Jr., 15 May 1791, 8 Jan. 1792; TJ to Hanson, 20 Jan. 1793, ibid., 17:512–13, 569–71; 19:554; 20:102–4, 153–54, 415–16; 25:69–70. For sales of slaves, see TJ to Eppes, 11 Mar. 1792, describing the proceeds as "short"; TJ to T. M. Randolph, Jr., 12 Oct. 1792, ibid., 23:253; 24:473. For further borrowing, see TJ to Van Staphorst & Hubbard, 26 Feb. 1796; Van Staphorst & Hubbard to Harrison & Sterrett, 21 May 1796; Van Staphorst & Hubbard to TJ, 21 May 1796, Jefferson Papers, LC. For delays in payment, see TJ to John Dobson, 4 July 1791; TJ to T. M. Randolph, Jr., 17 July 1791; TJ to Eppes, 7 Aug. 1791; TJ to J. Dobson, 4 Dec. 1791; TJ to Richard Dobson, 15 Apr. 1793, *Boyd*, 20:597–98, 641; 22:10, 374–75; 25:549–50; TJ to Hanson, 18 Oct. 1793, Jefferson Papers, UVa. Even then, it was not until 1807 that the firm Farell and Jones was satisfied in full with a final payment of £108.15.0 (Virginia currency). TJ, Account Book, 7 Mar. 1807.

68. Monroe to TJ, 20 May 1790, *Boyd*, 16:432, reporting that Hanson is about to bring suit. For the case itself, see Boyd, "Debt to Farell & Jones," ibid., 15:643–49. For Marshall's view that Wayles was liable on the slave shipment, see Andrew Ronald and John Marshall, Opinion, 1 Apr. 1791, in Johnson, ed., *Papers of John Marshall*, 2:89–90. Marshall recorded a fee of £7 for his work. Ibid., 413. Jefferson refused to accept the opinion, insisting that the executors mount a strong defense. For the heirs' alarm at the opinion, see Skipwith to TJ, 7 Apr. 1791; Eppes to TJ, 27 Apr. 1791; and, for Jefferson's reassurances, TJ to Skipwith, 6 May 1791; TJ to Eppes, 15 May 1791, *Boyd*, 20:166–67, 313, 373–76, 412.

69. TJ to Peter Carr (his nephew), 8 May 1791; TJ to Martha Jefferson Randolph, 26 Apr. 1790, *Boyd*, 20:379; 16:387.

70. TJ to Eppes, 7 Aug. 1791; TJ to Daniel L. Hylton, 17 Mar. 1792; Hylton to TJ, 25 Mar. 1792, ibid., 22:10; 23:290, 333.

71. Hobson, "Recovery of British Debts," takes the story to 1797; further developments can be followed in Johnson, ed., *Papers of John Marshall*, 5 (Marshall's law practice), 6, 7 (Marshall's Supreme Court years, 1801–1813), and in forthcoming volumes of the series.

72. TJ to Thaddeus Kosciuszko, 26 Feb. 1810, *L&B*, 12:370.

73. TJ, "Answers to Démeunier's Additional Queries" [ca. Jan.–Feb. 1786], *Boyd*, 10:27. Démeunier used this and other information from Jefferson in his *Encyclopédie méthodique* article on the United States. In his translation, which did not catch the flavor of the original, it read, "Les dettes étoient devenues héréditaires de père en fils, depuis plusieurs générations, ensorte que les planteurs sembloient appartenir à quelques maisons de commerce de Londres" (*Encyclopédie méthodique: Économie politique et diplomatique* . . . , 4 vols. [Paris, 1784–1788], 2:392).

74. On Jefferson and slavery, see John Chester Miller, *The Wolf by the Ears: Thomas Jefferson and Slavery* (New York and London, 1977), and Lucia C. Stanton, " 'Those Who Labor for My Happiness': Thomas Jefferson and His Slaves," in Onuf, ed., *Jeffersonian Legacies*, 147–180. Paul Finkelman presents the prosecution's case in "Jefferson and Slavery: 'Treason Against the Hopes of the World,' " in ibid., 181–221. For contemporary use of the term "species of property" to refer to slaves, see, for example, Washington to David Stuart, 15 June 1790, in Fitzpatrick, ed., *Writings of George Washington*, 31:52.

75. TJ to Madison, 6 Sept. 1789, *Boyd*, 15:393, 395.

76. See, for example, Bernard Bailyn, *The Ideological Origins of the American Revolution* (Cambridge, Mass., 1967), 232–34.

77. For the Revolutionary era, see Sylvia R. Frey, *Water from the Rock: Black Resistance in a Revolutionary Age* (Princeton, N.J., 1991), and the essays in Ira Berlin and Ronald Hoffman, eds., *Slavery and Freedom in the Age of the American Revolution* (Charlottesville, Va., 1983). For what came next, see Douglas R. Egerton, *Gabriel's Rebellion: The Virginia Slave Conspiracies of 1800 and 1802* (Chapel Hill, N.C., 1993), and Eugene D. Genovese, *From Rebellion to Revolution: Afro-American Slave Revolts in the Making of the Modern World* (Baton Rouge, La., 1979).

78. TJ to McCaul, 4 Jan. 1787; TJ to W. Jones, 1 June 1789, *Boyd*, 11:10; 15:161.

79. TJ to Eppes, 10 July 1788, ibid., 13:328.

80. TJ to Lyle, 11 Mar., 29 July 1792; Lyle to TJ, 11 Aug. 1792, ibid., 23:255; 24:265–66, quotation on 286. For good examples of what Jefferson was reduced to during and after the War of 1812, see *Farm Book*, 301–4. For a stimulating reading of the vocabulary of debt-induced "mortification" in the letters of Jefferson's contemporaries, see Toby L. Ditz, "Shipwrecked; or Masculinity Imperiled: Mercantile Representations of Failure and the Gendered Self in Eighteenth-Century Philadelphia," *JAH* 81 (1994): 51–80, esp. 70–72.

81. TJ to W. Jones, 5 Jan. 1787; TJ to Carr, 8 May 1791; TJ to J. Dobson, 1 Jan. 1792, *Boyd*, 11:15–16; 20:379; 23:4.

82. See, for example, TJ to Lyle, 11 Mar., 29 July 1792; Lyle to TJ, 11 Aug. 1792, ibid., 23:255; 24:265–66, and *Farm Book*, 301–4.

83. TJ to J. Dobson, 1 Jan. 1792; TJ to Lewis, 19 July 1787, *Boyd*, 23:4; 11:640.

84. For his expenditure on Monticello in the 1790s, see *Malone*, 3:232–35, 240–42. Susan R. Stein, *The Worlds of Thomas Jefferson at Monticello* (New York,

1993), which represents the catalogue of the exhibit honoring Jefferson's 250th birthday, provides as good a sense as we are likely to get of the results of his passionate desire to furnish Monticello in the best contemporary taste. *Sowerby* records Jefferson's efforts to create a library second to none. While in Europe, Jefferson spent lavishly to acquire household goods and books. See TJ, Account Book, Apr. 1786, which shows him spending hundreds of pounds on trinkets while in London meeting his creditors Welch and Jones. Examples of his chronic inability to stop consuming could easily be multiplied. Nevertheless, as I suggest in the Introduction, it is not realistic to blame his final debacle on his lifelong habit of buying only the best. For some sense of what a real spender could lay out in France, see Jean-Jacques Fiechter's account of Gouverneur Morris's purchases while American minister in Paris in the early 1790s, in *Un Diplomate américain sous la Terreur: Les années européennes de Gouverneur Morris, 1789–1798* (Paris, 1983), 327–38. Morris's acquisitions make Jefferson's look modest indeed.

85. I discuss these matters in Chapter 6.

86. TJ to Hanson, 5 Apr. 1791; TJ to Lyle, 11 May 1791; Hanson to TJ, 30 Apr. 1791; Lyle to TJ, 20 May 1791, *Boyd*, 20:153–54, 388–89, 326, 389. For Hanson's transfer of the bonds to Dobson, see TJ to J. Dobson, 4 July 1791, ibid., 597. The agreement between Hanson and the Wayles executors provided that bonds received by the executors when they sold land and slaves could be turned over to Hanson for collection, but only when the proceeds were actually in would they be credited to the executors' accounts. Memorandum of Agreement between Richard Hanson and Executors of John Wayles [7 Feb. 1790], ibid., 15:676. It was just this sort of hiatus that drove Jefferson to distraction.

87. Cf. TJ to J. Dobson, 1 Jan. 1792, ibid., 23:4.

88. For Madison, see Irving Brant, *James Madison: Commander in Chief, 1812–1836* (Indianapolis, 1961), 446–49, 510–11, 514, 523–24; for Monroe, see Harry Ammon, *James Monroe: The Quest for National Unity* (New York, 1971), 546–48, 553–60, 569–70, and Gerard W. Gawalt, "James Monroe, Presidential Planter," *VMHB* 101 (1993): 251–72. Lucius Wilmerding, Jr., *James Monroe: Public Claimant* (New Brunswick, N.J., 1960), adds details and is more critical than Ammon and Gawalt of Monroe's efforts to retrieve his fortunes through favorable settlement of his claims against the United States. As Wilmerding shows, grants to Monroe from Congress barely prevented his ruin.

89. On Randolph–his problems resulted in part from his inability to account for his official expenditures as secretary of state–see John J. Reardon, *Edmund Randolph: A Biography* (New York, 1974), 349, 354–59; on Lee, see Charles Royster, *Light-Horse Harry Lee and the Legacy of the American Revolution* (New York, 1981), 170–85, 231–33, 240–47; Boyd, editorial note, "Locating the Federal District," *Boyd*, 19:9–20, 25–26; and, for effects on his family, see Douglas Southall Freeman, *Robert E. Lee: A Biography* (New York, 1934), 1:1–2, 6–17, 31–33. William H. Gaines covers "Colonel Tom" and his troubles in *Thomas Mann Randolph: Jefferson's Son-in-Law* (Baton Rouge, La., 1966), 101–9, 131–32, 142, 148–49, 155–62, 186–87.

90. For the Bizarre scandal, a deep wound to the pride of the Randolphs (and their Jefferson connections, since Jefferson's daughter Martha was the sister-in-law of several principals), see editorial note, "*Commonwealth* v. *Randolph*," in Johnson, ed., *Papers of John Marshall*, 2:161–68, and Robert Bloom's fictional account, *A Generation of Leaves* (New York, 1991). For Wythe, see Julian P. Boyd, "The Murder of George Wythe," and W. Edwin Hemphill, "Examinations of George Wythe Sweeny for Forgery and Murder: A Documentary Essay," *WMQ* 12 (1955): 513–42, 543–74.

Boynton Merrill, Jr., *Jefferson's Nephews: A Frontier Tragedy*, 2d ed. (Lexington, Ky., 1987), tells the story of Isham and Lilburne Lewis and is the best study of downward mobility among the lesser gentry. For Meriwether Lewis, another member of the Jefferson–Lewis clan, see Howard I. Kushner, "The Suicide of Meriwether Lewis: A Psychoanalytic Inquiry," *WMQ* 38 (1981): 464–81.

91. See Robert Dawidoff, *The Education of John Randolph* (New York, 1979), and, for the will, Frank F. Mathias, "John Randolph's Freedmen: The Thwarting of a Will," *Journal of Southern History* 39 (1973): 263–72.

92. On the Tuckers, see Robert C. McLean, *George Tucker: Moral Philosopher and Man of Letters* (Chapel Hill, N.C., 1961), and Robert J. Brugger, *Beverley Tucker: Heart over Head in the Old South* (Baltimore, 1978), the latter, like Dawidoff's *Education of John Randolph*, exploring the pessimism and nostalgia of the younger generation of Virginia intellectuals after the War of 1812. For modern studies of Taylor, see Lance Banning, *The Jeffersonian Persuasion: Evolution of a Party Ideology* (Ithaca, N.Y., 1978), 192–201, 226–27, and Robert E. Shalhope, *John Taylor of Caroline: Pastoral Republican* (Columbia, S.C., 1980). For Wirt, see his *Letters of the British Spy* (Richmond, Va., 1803), and note the argument of William R. Taylor, identifying this orphaned son of an innkeeper who became the leader of the Supreme Court bar, attorney general, and candidate for president in 1832 as one of the early nineteenth century's "new men" filling the places opened up by the decay of the gentry. Taylor, *Cavalier and Yankee: The Old South and American National Character* (New York, 1961), 67–94. For additional reflections, see Robert P. Sutton, "Nostalgia, Pessimism, and Malaise: The Doomed Aristocrat in Late-Jeffersonian Virginia," *VMHB* 76 (1968): 41–55.

93. George Tucker, *The Valley of the Shenandoah: Or, Memoirs of the Graysons* (1824), ed. Donald R. Noble, Jr., 2 vols. in 1 (Chapel Hill, N.C., 1970). For Tucker's place in the canon of Virginia novels, see Richard Beale Davis, "The Virginia Novel Before *Swallow Barn*," in *Literature and Society in Early Virginia, 1608–1840* (Baton Rouge, La., 1973), 233–56. On the novel itself, see McLean, *George Tucker*, 75–89. The final straw in Jefferson's collapse, for which see Chapter 6, came from endorsing a friend's note. Tucker was Jefferson's first important biographer; his *Life of Thomas Jefferson* (Philadelphia, 1837) was solid but not uncritical. On the *Life*, see Merrill D. Peterson, *The Jefferson Image in the American Mind* (New York, 1960), 122–27.

94. By the 1820s, John Randolph of Roanoke, related to Tucker through his stepfather, St. George Tucker, also repented the Jacobinical excesses of his youth. Dawidoff, *Education of John Randolph*, 198–238.

95. In 1820, Virginia had 1,075,069 inhabitants; New York (1,372,812) surpassed it, and Pennsylvania (1,049,458) almost did. By 1860, to take matters to the logical point, Virginia was fifth (1,596,318), behind New York (3,880,735), Pennsylvania (2,906,215), Ohio (2,339,511), and Illinois (1,711,951). U.S. Bureau of the Census, *Historical Statistics of the United States: Colonial Times to 1957*, vol. 13, Series A 123–180, *Population, for States: 1790–1950* (Washington, D.C., 1960).

96. On the population exodus, see Avery O. Craven, *Soil Exhaustion as a Factor in the Agricultural History of Virginia and Maryland, 1606–1860* (Urbana, Ill., 1925), 119–25, though note that Craven's long-accepted account of soil exhaustion is challenged by Jack Temple Kirby, "Virginia's Environmental History: A Prospectus," *VMHB* 99 (1991): 464–67. Richard Beale Davis describes the export of talent in "The Jeffersonian Virginia Expatriate in the Building of the Nation," in *Literature and Society in Early Virginia*, 306–24. On the ways early-nineteenth-century Virginians "looked to more fertile lands" in the West and South "for a new

beginning," see Jan Lewis's discussion in *The Pursuit of Happiness: Family and Values in Jefferson's Virginia* (Cambridge, 1983), 142–47. For contemporary comment, see Joseph G. Baldwin, *The Flush Times of Alabama and Mississippi* (1853), ed. William A. Owens (New York, 1957), 52–76.

97. Allan Kulikoff, "Uprooted Peoples: Black Migrants in the Age of the American Revolution, 1790–1820," in Berlin and Hoffman, eds., *Slavery and Freedom*, 143–71, and Richard Sutch, "The Breeding of Slaves for Sale and the Westward Expansion of Slavery," in Stanley L. Engerman and Eugene D. Genovese, eds., *Race and Slavery in the Western Hemisphere: Quantitative Studies* (Princeton, N.J., 1975), 173–210); for Jefferson's slaves, see *Malone*, 6:488–89, 511–12, and Stanton, " 'Those Who Labor for My Happiness,' " tracing the fate of Jefferson's slaves through the life of Monticello's blacksmith, Joe Fossett.

98. For statistical confirmation, see Tadahisa Kuroda, "The County Court System in Virginia from the Revolution to the Civil War" (Ph.D. diss., Columbia University, 1970), 20, 47–48; Kuroda finds a decline of 25 percent between 1780 and 1820 to 1830 in holdings of slaves, land, and horses by justices of the peace. Given their traditional importance in their communities and the criteria for their selection, Kuroda's data say a good deal about Virginia's ruling class. But the decline may be less than he suggests: A. G. Roeber, *Faithful Magistrates and Republican Lawyers: Creators of Virginia Legal Culture, 1680–1810* (Chapel Hill, N.C., 1981), 201–30, shows that the post-Revolutionary District Courts reduced the importance of the County Courts, where justices of the peace sat; if so, local notables may have been less willing to serve and their places taken by the less affluent.

99. For positive views of Virginia's condition, see Kathleen Bruce, *Virginia Iron Manufacture in the Slave Era* (New York, 1930), vii–viii, 81–87, and "Virginian Agricultural Decline to 1860: A Fallacy," *Agricultural History* 6 (1932): 3–13; Lewis Cecil Gray, *History of Agriculture in the Southern United States to 1860*, 2 vols. (Washington, D.C., 1933), 2:881–82, 915–17, 919–21; Carter Goodrich, "The Virginia System of Mixed Enterprise: A Study of State Planning of Internal Improvements," *Political Science Quarterly* 64 (1949): 355–87; and Robert McColley, *Slavery and Jeffersonian Virginia*, 2d ed. (Urbana, Ill., 1973), 24–30, 225–26. Still, it is hard to avoid the conclusion reached by Lorena S. Walsh: "The Chesapeake economy," she says, "had entered a long-term decline by 1820" ("Slave Life, Slave Society, and Tobacco Production in the Tidewater Chesapeake, 1620–1820," in Ira Berlin and Philip D. Morgan, eds., *Cultivation and Culture: Labor and the Shaping of Slave Life in the Americas* [Charlottesville, Va., 1993], 198). But Virginia was more than the older agricultural sections of the Tidewater and the Piedmont, and for assessments of economic life in other regions, see David R. Goldfield, *Urban Growth in the Age of Sectionalism: Virginia, 1847–1861* (Baton Rouge, La., 1977), though see 1–28, presenting a picture of Virginia in decay before his period; Frederick F. Siegel, *The Roots of Southern Distinctiveness: Tobacco and Society in Danville, Virginia, 1780–1865* (Chapel Hill, N.C., 1987); and John E. Stealey III, *The Antebellum Kanawha Salt Business and Western Markets* (Lexington, Ky., 1993). We know all too little about early-nineteenth-century Virginia; any opinion on its overall prosperity or poverty is at best provisional. Van Beck Hall makes this clear in "A Fond Farewell to Henry Adams: Ideas on Relating Political History to Social Change During the Early National Period," in James Kirby Martin, ed., *The Human Dimensions of Nation Making: Essays on Colonial and Revolutionary America* (Madison, Wis., 1976), 328–61.

100. Lewis's study of domestic relations among the gentry, *Pursuit of Happiness*, shows that many gentry families escaped these fates. Randolph is quoted in Elizabeth

Langhorne et al., *A Virginia Family and Its Plantation Houses* (Charlottesville, Va., 1987), 110. For Jefferson's grandchildren, see George Green Shackelford, ed., *Collected Papers to Commemorate Fifty Years of the Monticello Association of the Descendants of Thomas Jefferson* (Princeton, N.J., 1965), 67–153, 167–78. Not all of them did as well as Jeff Randolph and his brother, George Wythe; still, as Shackelford remarks, "the second and third generations of the Monticello family acquitted themselves with distinction," producing (the list includes those who married Jefferson and Randolph daughters) "one Governor of Virginia, one U.S. Senator, two members of the U.S. House of Representatives, five members of the Virginia General Assembly, one cabinet member, one general, one presidential secretary, one diplomat, one Territorial Secretary, one financier, two frontiersmen, and one Rector of the University of Virginia and one member of its Board of Visitors" (vii). For Jeff Randolph's standing as the wealthiest man in Albemarle in the 1840s and 1850s, see ibid., 84. Shackelford notes that some of that wealth came from the unpaid "labor of maiden sisters and daughters" who in addition to "supervising the household, . . . conducted a fashionable girls' school" at Edgehill for decades (85, 86). For fuller accounts of the brothers, see Joseph C. Vance, "Thomas Jefferson Randolph" (Ph.D. diss., University of Virginia, 1956), and George Green Shackelford, *George Wythe Randolph and the Confederate Elite* (Athens, Ga., 1988).

101. For contemporary comment, see Sutton, "Nostalgia, Pessimism, and Malaise."

102. On the depressed conditions of agriculture in Virginia and the South from 1815 to 1819 on, see Charles S. Sydnor, *The Development of Southern Sectionalism, 1819–1848* (Baton Rouge, La., 1948), 104–19, 249–52; Paul W. Gates, *The Farmer's Age: Agriculture, 1815–1860* (New York, 1960), 3–4, 100–107; and Joseph C. Robert, *The Tobacco Kingdom: Plantation, Market, and Factory in Virginia and North Carolina, 1800–1860* (Durham, N.C., 1938), 135–40. Joyce Appleby makes the point in "Commercial Farming and the 'Agrarian Myth' in the Early Republic," *JAH* 68 (1982): 840, that it was not the ending of the Napoleonic Wars per se but increased European output after 1815 that cut foreign demand for American grain, ending the wheat-based era of prosperity (ca. 1790–ca. 1820) that enriched so many American— and some Virginia—farmers. For responses to the Panic of 1819 in Virginia, see Murray N. Rothbard, *The Panic of 1819: Reactions and Policies* (New York, 1962), 35–38, 66–67, 137–40. But planters could make money if they devoted their energies to it rather than entering politics and trying to do two things at once and if, unlike the former presidents, they did not entertain on a lavish scale. McColley, *Slavery and Jeffersonian Virginia*, 22–23, 28. William Wirt expressed the views of many when he wrote in 1830 that "they have been pressing me here to become a politician, but I think of Monticello and Oak Hill, and I shake my head" (John P. Kennedy, *Memoirs of the Life of William Wirt*, 2 vols. [Philadelphia, 1856], 2:266).

103. This figure includes fifteen years (1775–1790) of simple interest at 5 percent, but does not include any debts to British creditors that Virginians incurred between 1783 and 1790. Jacob M. Price, *Capital and Credit in British Overseas Trade: The View from the Chesapeake, 1700–1776* (Cambridge, Mass., 1980), 6–10, Table I. Richard B. Sheridan, "The British Debt Crisis of 1772 and the American Colonies," *Journal of Economic History* 20 (1960): 181, notes that a group of thirty-seven Glasgow firms "had upwards of 31,000 debts owing from 112 stores in Virginia," and a full examination of all accounts due to other merchants would add thousands more to that figure. For the number of families in Virginia (excluding Kentucky) counted by the census of 1790, see Edward Carrington to Alexander Hamilton, 4 Oct. 1791, *PAH*, 9:278. On the activities that produced these debts, see T. M. Devine, *The*

Tobacco Lords: A Study of the Tobacco Merchants of Glasgow and Their Trading Activities, c. 1740–90 (Edinburgh, 1975); Alan L. Karras, *Sojourners in the Sun: Scottish Migrants in Jamaica and the Chesapeake, 1740–1800* (Ithaca, N.Y., 1992); and Price, *Capital and Credit*. Some economic historians have attempted to dismiss the British debts as figments of the Virginia imagination. James F. Shepherd, Jr., and Gary M. Walton, *Shipping, Maritime Trade, and the Economic Development of Colonial North America* (Cambridge, 1972), 130–32, 165–66, conclude that the debts did not exist, a claim repeated in Walton and Shepherd, *The Economic Rise of Early America* (Cambridge, 1979), 98, 105–8. This would be astounding if it were true, but it is not. The authors assume that British exports to the colonies should be valued at British wholesale prices plus a 7.5 percent profit for the importing merchant in America. Shepherd and Walton, *Shipping, Maritime Trade*, 135. But as Price and others more familiar than Shepherd and Walton with the mechanics of the tobacco trade show, markups of up to 80 percent were not unusual at the retail stores operated by Scottish tobacco merchants in Virginia, and the profits those markups generated were intended for repatriation to Great Britain. Price, *Capital and Credit*, 149–51. Debts at these stores–classified by Shepherd and Walton as merely internal and so irrelevant to their argument–were actually debts due merchants in Britain. There is no mystery about the debts; they did exist. What is more mysterious is Shepherd and Walton's failure to see this.

104. Evans, "Private Indebtedness and the Revolution in Virginia"; Hobson, "Recovery of British Debts."

105. See Madison's remarks on internal debts during the 1790 House debates, quoted in Chapter 4, and text at note 126.

106. T. H. Breen, *Tobacco Culture: The Mentality of the Great Tidewater Planters on the Eve of Revolution* (Princeton, N.J., 1985), is a stimulating introduction to the economic practices and psychology of the gentry and lesser Virginians; it should be read in conjunction with Jack P. Greene, review of *Tobacco Culture*, by T. H. Breen, *VMHB* 94 (1986): 477–80. For Jefferson's use of bonds, see text at notes 25, 86.

107. For Washington's loans of £6,000 or £7,000 when he left to join the army in 1775, see Washington to Lund Washington, 18 Dec. 1778, in Fitzpatrick, ed., *Writings of George Washington*, 13:424. For Mason's loans, see his Will, 20 Mar. 1773, in Rutland, ed., *Papers of George Mason*, 1:147. Aubrey C. Land explains the origins of this practice in "Economic Behavior in a Planting Society: The Eighteenth-Century Chesapeake," *Journal of Southern History* 33 (1967): 469–85.

108. Breen, *Tobacco Culture*, 84–123.

109. In *The Economy of British America, 1607–1789* (Chapel Hill, N.C., 1985), 124–43, John J. McCusker and Russell R. Menard review and synthesize the literature on late–colonial Virginia's economy.

110. Oliver Ellsworth, speech at the Connecticut ratifying convention, 7 Jan. 1788, *DHRC*, 15:277.

111. Breen, *Tobacco Culture*, 84–123.

112. For Carter and other late-colonial planters, see ibid, 69–82. For Jefferson, see TJ to Henry Remsen, 17 May 1799, *Farm Book*, 271: "My tobaccos have always been considered here in Philadelphia, London & Glasgow as of the very first quality, & . . . I have always been able to command for them from half a dollar to a dollar a hundred more than the market price of the best James River. In Philadelphia I . . . have always had a dollar more than any body else." For his continuing belief in the high quality of his tobacco and his confusion when the market no longer seemed to recognize it, see George Jefferson to TJ, 25 June 1806; TJ to James Maury, 16 June 1815; TJ to Patrick Gibson, 23 Apr. 1820, ibid., 292, 303, 305.

113. Breen, *Tobacco Culture*, 147–50, describes Washington's experiences in this regard during the 1760s.

114. Joseph Jones to Madison, 6 Apr. 1792, *PJM*, 14:280; TJ to Mary Eppes, 7 Jan. 1798; TJ to M. Randolph, 5 Jan. 1808, *Family Letters*, 152, 320.

115. On the theme of independence, see Jack P. Greene's contributions: *Landon Carter: An Inquiry into the Personal Values and Social Imperatives of the Eighteenth-Century Virginia Gentry* (Charlottesville, Va., 1967); "Society, Ideology, and Politics: An Analysis of the Political Culture of Mid-Eighteenth-Century Virginia," in Richard M. Jellison, ed., *Society, Freedom, and Conscience: The American Revolution in Virginia, Massachusetts, and New York* (New York, 1976), 14–76; " '*Virtus et Libertas*': Political Culture, Social Change, and the Origins of the American Revolution in Virginia, 1763–1776," in Jeffrey J. Crow and Larry E. Tise, eds., *The Southern Experience in the American Revolution* (Chapel Hill, N.C., 1978), 55–108; and "Character, Persona, and Authority: A Study of Alternative Styles of Political Leadership in Revolutionary Virginia," in W. Robert Higgins, ed., *The Revolutionary War in the South: Power, Conflict, and Leadership: Essays in Honor of John Richard Alden* (Durham, N.C., 1979), 3–42. Lewis adds valuable information about the persistent appeal of this ideal in *Pursuit of Happiness*, 106–20. In "The Concept of Virtue in Late Colonial British America," in *Imperatives, Behaviors, and Identities: Essays in Early American Cultural History* (Charlottesville, Va., 1992), 208–35, Greene explores the links between independence and civic virtue, suggesting that we cannot assume that the latter had the same meaning for colonial Americans that it had for the eighteenth-century Englishmen described by J. G. A. Pocock; "free British colonial Americans," he writes, "seem to have put less emphasis on the material than on the moral foundations of virtue" (220). Greene may be right, but the point is that they placed "less emphasis," not none at all.

116. For Washington's problems meeting his creditors' demands, see, for example, Washington to Richard Conway, 4 Mar., 1789; Conway to Washington, 6 Mar. 1789; Washington to James Mercer, 18 Mar. 1789, in W. W. Abbot, ed., *The Papers of George Washington: Presidential Series* (Charlottesville, Va., 1987), 1:361–62, 368, 405–6. The letters discuss his having to borrow £500 to finance his trip to New York for the inauguration and to pay for other pressing needs; he is appalled by the "very *hard* conditions" of the loan.

117. Essential in exploring this theme is Breen's discussion of the "etiquette of debt" in *Tobacco Culture*, 93–106.

118. On the Virginia law of debtor and creditor, see Coleman, *Debtors and Creditors in America*, 191–206.

119. For the British background, see Neil McKendrick et al., *The Birth of a Consumer Society: The Commercialization of Eighteenth-Century England* (Bloomington, Ind., 1982); on its American and Virginia aspects, see T. H. Breen, "An Empire of Goods: The Anglicization of Colonial America, 1690–1776," *Journal of British Studies* 25 (1986): 467–99, and " 'Baubles of Britain': The American and Consumer Revolutions of the Eighteenth Century," *Past and Present* 119 (1988): 73–104. An illuminating Virginia comment by Jefferson's father-in-law is John Hemphill, "John Wayles Rates His Neighbors," *VMHB* 66 (1958): 302–6. For an introduction to the problem of consumption during Jefferson's lifetime, see Carole Shammas, *The Pre-Industrial Consumer in England and America* (Oxford, 1990). Julian Hoppit, "Attitudes to Credit in Britain," *Historical Journal* 33 (1990): 305–22, is a survey with comparative implications. Richard L. Bushman's study of how Americans learned to be "genteel," *The Refinement of America: Persons, Houses, Cities*

(New York, 1992), offers insights into the tensions engendered by the need to be at once a producer and a consumer. Gordon S. Wood, *The Radicalism of the American Revolution* (New York, 1992), describes the broader framework within which these changes occurred. Michael Zuckerman speculates on these matters in "A Different Thermidor: The Revolution Beyond the Revolution," in James A. Henretta et al., eds., *The Transformation of Early American History: Society, Authority, and Ideology* (New York, 1991), 170–93, esp. 174–79. Daniel Horowitz, *The Morality of Spending: Attitudes Toward the Consumer Society in America, 1875–1940* (Baltimore, 1985), xxiv–xxviii, cautions that most Americans remained outside the consumer society until the late nineteenth century.

120. John Sekora, *Luxury: The Concept in Western Thought, Eden to Smollett* (Baltimore, 1977); M. M. Goldsmith, "Liberty, Luxury and the Pursuit of Happiness," in Anthony Pagden, ed., *The Languages of Political Theory in Early-Modern Europe* (Cambridge, 1987), 225–52. Instructive on matters of gentry style is Rhys Isaac, *The Transformation of Virginia, 1740–1790* (Chapel Hill, N.C., 1982), 32–42, 70–79, 118–20.

121. For a classic example of the desire to keep up, see the discussion of Washington's early purchases through his London agents in Douglas Southall Freeman, *George Washington: A Biography* (New York, 1951), 3:27–28, 78–80, 91, 110–13, 114–16. On gambling and horse races, see T. H. Breen, "Horses and Gentlemen: The Cultural Significance of Gambling Among the Gentry of Virginia," *WMQ* 34 (1977): 239–57.

122. The Virginia role in the tobacco sector of the Atlantic economy is explored in Jacob M. Price, *France and the Chesapeake: A History of the French Tobacco Monopoly, 1674–1791, and of Its Relationship to the British and American Tobacco Trades*, 2 vols. (Ann Arbor, Mich., 1973). For the implications of Price's magisterial work, see Elizabeth Fox-Genovese, "Merchant Capital and State Power: Jacob Price on the Tobacco Trade and Its Political Consequences," in Elizabeth Fox-Genovese and Eugene D. Genovese, *Fruits of Merchant Capital: Slavery and Bourgeois Property in the Rise and Expansion of Capitalism* (New York, 1983), 76–89.

123. For the argument that wheat offered planters an escape from a stagnating tobacco trade and the prospect of debt and yet more debt, see, for example, Appleby, "Commercial Farming and the 'Agrarian Myth,' " and Peter V. Bergstrom, *Markets and Merchants: Economic Diversification in Colonial Virginia, 1700–1775* (New York, 1985), 149–52, which notes that tobacco's share of the value of Virginia exports dropped from 76.6 percent in 1773 to 60.8 percent in 1773, but also cautioning that on the eve of the Revolution, Virginia was not "an integrated, or even a balanced economy" (151). See also Breen, *Tobacco Culture*, 180–82, 204–10, and "The Culture of Agriculture: The Symbolic World of the Tidewater Planter," in David D. Hall et al., eds., *Saints and Revolutionaries: Essays on Early American History* (New York, 1984), 275–84, and, by implication, Paul G. E. Clemens, *The Atlantic Economy and Colonial Maryland's Eastern Shore: From Tobacco to Grain* (Ithaca, N.Y., 1980). Anyone who looks at Jefferson's correspondence will doubt that wheat offered a solution in the long run; by the 1790s, when he began to raise it, wheat was no longer a panacea. See Jefferson's letters on his troubles raising and marketing wheat in *Farm Book*, 203–25. Merrill notes of Albemarle agriculture in the 1790s that "in the eight years from 1792 to 1800, there were only two years in which crops were harvested and sold without the occurrence of some calamity" (*Jefferson's Nephews*, 46). Greene is skeptical that wheat had the ability to transform the lives of pre-Revolutionary planters; see his review of Breen, *Tobacco Culture*. Walsh is persuasive on the limitation of wheat as a

solution to the region's problems in "Slave Life, Slave Society, and Tobacco Production," 194–96, 198. Tobacco production, measured by exports (thus not taking account of domestic consumption, which would have risen as population grew), was stagnant in the years between 1788 and 1826; not until 1826 to 1830 did average annual exports exceed those for 1788 to 1792. See Roberts, *Tobacco Kingdom*, 130–31. Jefferson's concern with the southward progress of the Hessian fly can be followed in *Farm Book*.

124. See, generally, McCusker and Menard, *Economy of British America*, 117–43.

125. "Never were such hard times seen as we have here now," Jefferson told Joel Yancy in 1820, and to James Leitch, for once abandoning optimism, he admitted that "I have been led on by the flattering expectations that a good crop the next year, and the next year, and so on would enable me to do you justice; but finding the expectation delusive and that the next year, like tomorrow, never comes," he would sell lands pay his debts (TJ to Yancy, 22 Apr. 1820; TJ to Leitch, 8 June 1819, Jefferson Papers, MHS).

126. For earlier efforts to describe the relationships between the British debts and the gentry's decision for independence, see Emory Evans, "Planter Indebtedness and the Coming of the Revolution in Virginia," *WMQ* 19 (1962): 511–33, and Gordon S. Wood, "Rhetoric and Reality in the American Revolution," *WMQ* 23 (1966): 3–32. For a more recent discussion, see Breen, *Tobacco Culture*, 160–203.

127. Gordon C. Bjork, *Stagnation and Growth in the American Economy, 1784–1792* (New York, 1985), 20–27, 129–33, 158–59, presents a more favorable picture of the tobacco economy in the postwar period, arguing that "the years up to 1790 were a time of real prosperity for the tobacco planters of the Upper South" (159). Bjork's case is less than convincing, given what we know of the politics of the period. For a recent study of Charles County, Maryland (across the Potomac from Mt. Vernon), that reaches conclusions similar to mine about the Revolution as a negative turning point in the Chesapeake economy, see Jean B. Lee, *The Price of Nationhood: The American Revolution in Charles County* (New York, 1994), 7–10, 223–62.

128. Price, *France and the Chesapeake*, 2:728–87.

129. The return of the British merchants has yet to find its student, but for a brief account, see Devine, *Tobacco Lords*, 161–67. Manuscript collections in the Library of Congress offer rich possibilities; see John R. Sellers et al., comps., *Manuscript Sources in the Library of Congress for Research on the American Revolution* (Washington, D.C., 1975), entries 47, 54, 248, 303, 316, 344, 355, 1003. Thus James Ritchie & Co., Glasgow, "Instructions," to James Anderson et al., 31 Mar. 1784, Dunlop Family Papers, Box 6-Business Papers, sets out in twenty-two paragraphs the strategy of this important firm, which had decided to reopen its Virginia stores "to facilitate the payment of our old debts by having it in our power to supply our old Debtors with necessaries . . . but on no account and for no prospect of profit will we give Credit for longer time than betwixt Crop and Crop as more particularly aftermentioned" (Para. 1).

130. George Mason was alarmed by the rumors of opposition to this section of the treaty that reached him early in 1783; see Mason to Arthur Lee, 25 Mar. 1783; Mason to William Cabell, 6 May 1783; Mason to Patrick Henry, 7 May 1783; Mason to Henry Tazewell, 6 May 1783; Mason to Arthur Campbell, 7 May 1783, in Rutland, ed., *Papers of George Mason*, 2:765–66, 768–69, 700–72, 774–75, 776–77. As the recipients' names and the letters' dates suggest, Mason was mobilizing gentry opinion to block legislative interference with the treaty's execution. He was unsuccessful.

131. On the debts as a nonmotive, or rather one that needs careful handling, see Evans, "Planter Indebtedness"; Wood, "Rhetoric and Reality in the American Revolution"; and Breen, *Tobacco Culture*, 160–203. Contrary arguments can be found in, for example, Marc Egnal, "The Economic Development of the Thirteen Continental Colonies, 1720 to 1775," *WMQ* 32 (1975): 191–222, and Marc Egnal and Joseph A. Ernst, "An Economic Interpretation of the American Revolution," *WMQ* 29 (1972): 3–32. More recently, in *A Mighty Empire: The Origins of the American Revolution* (Ithaca, N.Y., 1988), Egnal has preferred a land-speculation explanation. For the court-closing episode at the start of the Revolution, see George M. Curtis III, "The Role of the Courts in the Making of the Revolution in Virginia," in Martin, ed., *Human Dimensions of Nation Making*, 121–46, esp. 138–39. On the debts as an issue in postwar Virginia, where there is no denying their reality, see Risjord, *Chesapeake Politics*, 96–103, 109–16. The latest discussion of the Revolution's economic causes, Larry Sawers, "The Navigation Acts Revisited," *Journal of Economic History* 65 (1992): 262–84, emphasizes the substantial burden placed on the planters by tobacco's status as one of the enumerated products and is confident that this helps explain the coming of the Revolution. That there was some burden is certain– Sawers's figures may be right–but establishing that planters were dissatisfied does not prove that they were therefore driven to revolt. The ideological explanation, properly used, remains persuasive; what colonial elites like the Virginia gentry saw from 1765 on was a carefully orchestrated imperial assault on their privileges, and in 1775 they went to war to preserve them from further erosion.

132. For his losses, see TJ, affidavit, 27 Jan. 1783, and TJ to W. Jones, 5 Jan. 1787; TJ to William Gordon, 16 July 1788, *Farm Book*, 504–6. For background, see Elizabeth Cometti, "Depredations in Virginia During the Revolution," in Darrett B. Rutman, ed., *The Old Dominion: Essays for Thomas P. Abernethy* (Charlottesville, Va., 1964), 135–51.

133. On the merchants' "inability" to prevent the war, see John A. Sainsbury, *Disaffected Patriots: London Supporters of Revolutionary America, 1769–1782* (Kingston, Ont., 1987), 55–97; for a typical postwar view, see TJ to McCaul, 19 Apr. 1786, *Boyd*, 9:390.

134. Adams's claim is in his diary for 3 Nov. 1782, in L. H. Butterfield, ed., *The Diary and Autobiography of John Adams* (Cambridge, Mass., 1962), 3:43. For an outraged Virginia response, see Meriwether Smith's twenty-eight-page pamphlet, *Observations on the Fourth and Fifth Articles of the Preliminaries for a Peace with Great Britain . . .* (Richmond, Va., 1783), esp. 6–8, 21–22, 24–28.

135. For Virginia divisions over compliance with the treaty, see Risjord, *Chesapeake Politics*, 109–16, 201–3.

136. A problem throughout Revolutionary America, the effects of inflation were widely felt. In Virginia, they seem to have been uniformly adverse; unlike the nascent entrepreneurs of the northern and middle states, few of the gentry responded to the war as an economic *opportunity*. See Gordon S. Wood, "Interests and Disinterestedness in the Making of the Constitution," and Janet Riesman, "Money Credit and Federalist Political Economy," in Richard Beeman et al., eds., *Beyond Confederation: Origins of the Constitution and American National Identity* (Chapel Hill, N.C., 1987), 69–109, 128–61. For the failure of the gentry to show the entrepreneurial spirit evident in the Philadelphia merchant community, see Thomas M. Doerflinger, *A Vigorous Spirit of Enterprise: Merchants and Economic Development in Revolutionary Philadelphia* (Chapel Hill, N.C., 1986), 356–64.

137. The best contemporary expressions of this view are in George Mason's letters cited in note 130. "Frequent Interference with private Property & Contracts,

retrospective Laws destructive of all public Faith, as well as Confidence between Man & Man, and flagrant Violations of the Constitution must disgust the best & wisest Part of the Community, occasion a general Depravity of Manners, bring the Legislature into Contempt, and finally produce Anarchy & public Convulsion," Mason told Cabell on 6 May 1783 (his language to other correspondents was similar), in Rutland, ed., *Papers of George Mason*, 2:768. If this sounds like Virginia's version of Colonel Blimp, it was nonetheless the authentic voice of high-gentry statesmanship.

138. Richard Henry Lee to Henry, 26 May 1777, in Paul H. Smith, ed., *Letters of Delegates to Congress, 1774–1789*, 21 vols. to date (Washington, D.C., 1976–), 7:122–23. Lee also rented out his slaves to the tenants; see the list of amounts due for slave hire in Richard Parker to R. H. Lee, 7 Mar. 1776, in Paul P. Hoffman, ed., *Lee Family Papers, 1742–1795* (Charlottesville, Va., 1966), microfilm, reel 2, no. 0555. For another gentry patriot who foresaw inflation even at the beginning of the war, see Mason to Washington, 14 Oct. 1775, in Rutland, ed., *Papers of George Mason*, 1:256. Ronald Hoffman discusses the problem as experienced on the other side of the Potomac in *A Spirit of Dissension: Economics, Politics, and the Revolution in Maryland* (Baltimore, 1973), chap. 9. Like Lee and Mason, Charles Carroll of Carrollton anticipated the economic disruption that the war would bring; unlike the two Virginians, the Marylander had no illusions about his family's ability to preserve its fortune intact, telling his father that they would be lucky if a third of their land and slaves remained at the end of the war. Ibid., 213.

139. R. H. Lee to Henry, 26 May 1777, in Smith, ed., *Letters of Delegates*, 7:122–23

140. Ibid., 122–23; R. H. Lee, "Notes on the Law of Contract," ca. 10 Jan. 1776, in Hoffman, ed., *Lee Family Papers*, reel 2, no. 0539.

141. In "Notes on the Law of Contract," Lee characterized such legislative interference as "ex post facto" laws.

142. For the tenants' reluctance, see Parker to R. H. Lee, 7 Mar. 1776, in Hoffman, ed., *Lee Family Papers*, reel 2, no. 0555, reporting negotiations on Lee's behalf. Lee to TJ, 3 May 1779, Boyd, 2:263, has the "retrospective" characterization. Lee insisted the issue was a pretext: "Would any but bad Men, hardly pressed for argument against an innocent Character, have misrepresented, and miscalled this absolutely faultless and justifiable conduct?" he asked the governor. R. H. Lee to Henry, 26 May 1777, in Smith, ed., *Letters of Delegates*, 7:122–23.

143. For Lee's difficulty in balancing responsibility to family with his desire to participate in public life, see Pauline Maier, "A Virginian as Revolutionary: Richard Henry Lee," in *The Old Revolutionaries: Political Lives in the Age of Samuel Adams* (New York, 1980), 164–200. On the failure to support the currency as evidence of lack of Whig virtue, see TJ to R. H. Lee, 17 June 1779, *Boyd*, 2:298, which deplores "the cursed arts of our secret enemies," who "combining with other causes, should effect by depreciating our money, what the open arms of a powerful enemy could not".

144. On tensions in Revolutionary Virginia, see Warren M. Billings et al., *Colonial Virginia: A History* (White Plains, N.Y., 1986), 346–49; Allan Kulikoff, *Tobacco and Slaves: The Development of Southern Cultures in the Chesapeake, 1680–1800* (Chapel Hill, N.C., 1986), 300–13; and Herbert Sloan and Peter Onuf, "Politics, Culture, and the Revolution in Virginia: A Review of Recent Work," *VMHB* 91 (1983): 367–79. Richard R. Beeman, "The Political Response to Social Conflict in the Southern Backcountry: A Comparative View of Virginia and the Carolinas," in Ronald Hoffman et al., eds., *An Uncivil War: The Southern Backcountry during the*

American Revolution (Charlottesville, Va., 1985), 213–39, argues that Virginians were better able to contain these tensions than were their neighbors to the south. Lee was not, however, a Virginia version of Robert Morris, pressing for freedom of contract and preaching the gospel of an unregulated market. Supporting price controls, at least as a temporary expedient, he regularly denounced speculation in language typical of those Maier calls the "old revolutionaries." For Lee on price regulation, see Benjamin Rush, "Notes of Debates," 14 Feb. 1777; R. H. Lee to Henry, 15 Apr. 1777; Lee to Samuel Adams, 23 Nov. 1777, in Smith, ed., *Letters of Delegates*, 6:274–75, 538, 8:311. For Maier's characterization, see "Virginian as Revolutionary."

145. On this aspect of the campaign against Lee, see Boyd's note to TJ, "Bill for Regulating the Appointment of Delegates to the Continental Congress" [12 May 1777], *Boyd*, 2:16–18; Mason to R. H. Lee, 4 Mar. 1777, in Rutland, ed., *Papers of George Mason*, 1:333–34; and R. H. Lee to Henry, 26 May 1777; R. H. Lee to John Page, 26 May 1777, in Smith, ed., *Letters of Delegates*, 7:121–25. For comment on Lee's successful defense, see James Lovell to William Whipple, 7 July 1777; William Duer to Robert R. Livingston, 9 July 1777; and Samuel Adams to R. H. Lee, 22 July 1777, ibid., 315, 327, 345.

146. R. H. Lee to Wythe, 19 Oct. 1777, in Smith, ed., *Letters of Delegates*, 8:146–47.

147. Wythe to R. H. Lee, 6 Nov. 1777, in Hoffman, ed., *Lee Family Papers*, reel 3, no. 0587.

148. Lux to Greene, 28 Apr. 1778, in Richard K. Showman, ed., *The Papers of General Nathanael Greene* (Chapel Hill, N.C., 1980), 2:366.

149. Henry to R. H. Lee, 7 Apr., 18 June 1778, in H. R. McIlwaine, ed., *Official Letters of the Governors of the State of Virginia* (Richmond, Va., 1926), 1:261, 291.

150. R. H. Lee to TJ, 3 May 1779, *Boyd*, 2:263; for the statute, see Hening, comp., *Statutes at Large*, 10:471–74; see petitions from citizens of Loudoun County, 8 June 1776, and from citizens of Prince William County, 2 Nov. 1776, requesting relief from high money rents, in Randolph W. Church, comp., *Virginia Legislative Petitions: Bibliography, Calendar, and Abstracts from Original Sources, 6 May 1776–21 June 1782* (Richmond, Va., 1984), 70-P, 189-P, the latter signed by some of Lee's tenants; for evidence that Lee's views were not universally popular at the time of his letter to Jefferson, see petitions from citizens of Frederick and Berkeley counties, 2 June 1779, protesting refusals to accept paper money in payment of bills, bonds, and mortgages, ibid., 973-P, 973 A–P through 973 E–P.

151. Washington to John Parke Custis, 28 Sept. 1777, in Fitzpatrick, ed., *Writings of George Washington*, 9:282.

152. Washington to Lund Washington, 18 Dec. 1778, ibid., 13:424.

153. Washington to Burwell Bassett, 22 Apr. 1779, ibid., 14:432.

154. Washington to L. Washington, 17 Aug. 1779, ibid., 16:125.

155. Washington to L. Washington, 17 Aug. 1779; Washington to Custis, 20 Jan. 1780, ibid., 124–25, 413–14.

156. Washington to Fielding Lewis, 27 Feb. 1784, ibid., 27:345–46. For further comments in this line, see Washington to John Augustine Washington, 26 Nov. 1778; Washington to L. Washington, 18 Dec. 1778; Washington to Benjamin Harrison, 18 [-30] Dec. 1778; Washington to Custis, 24 Aug. 1779, ibid., 13:325, 424–25, 467; 16:166–67.

157. For its use against Washington, apparently by George Mason, see L. Washington to Washington, 6 Mar. 1789, in Abbot, ed., *Papers of George Washington: Pres. Ser.*, 1:369; for use against Jefferson in the campaign of 1800, see TJ to Uriah

McGregory, 13 Aug. 1800, Jefferson Papers, LC; for its use in the aftermath of the ratification controversy in Virginia, see [John Nicholas], *Decius's Letters on the Opposition to the New Constitution in Virginia, 1789* (Richmond, Va., 1789), 15, 20–21, 42–43, 91–92 (accusing Patrick Henry), and 71 (accusing Henry's brother-in-law, Colonel John Syme).

158. James Madison, *Federalist*, no. 10, 22 Nov. 1787, in *The Federalist*, ed. Jacob E. Cooke (Middletown, Conn., 1961), 65.

159. For gentry reactions to the explosive combination of paper money and Patrick Henry, see Edmund Randolph to Madison, 11 Apr. 1787; Madison to Edmund Pendleton, 22 Apr. 1787; Madison to TJ, 23 Apr., 6 June 1787; James McClurg to Madison, 5 Aug. 1787; John Dawson to Madison, 25 Sept. 1787, *PJM*, 9:373, 369, 401; 10:30, 135, 173.

160. Washington to Henry Knox, 21 Dec. 1786, in Fitzpatrick, ed., *Writings of George Washington*, 29:122.

161. On banks of issue and Jefferson's fear of an inflation that would rival–indeed, surpass–that of the Revolutionary years, see Chapter 6.

162. Mason to Cabell, 6 May 1783, quoted in note 137, reminds us that not every Virginian opposed to paper money was willing to sacrifice personal liberty for the protections of the Constitution. R. H. Lee was, of course, another.

163. Madison to TJ, 17 Oct. 1788, *PJM*, 11:297. Madison was right about this; see index to *DHRC*, 8–10, s.v. "Bankruptcy," "Contracts, obligation of," "Debt," "Installments," "Paper Money," "Tender Laws," and "Treaties."

164. For an overview, see Risjord, *Chesapeake Politics*, 82, 114–16, 135–38, 151–56, 175–79, 182–84. See also Myra L. Rich, "The Experimental Years: Virginia, 1781–1789" (Ph.D. diss., Yale University, 1966). Rich's article "Speculations on the Significance of Debt: Virginia, 1781–1789," *VMHB* 76 (1968): 301–17, does not begin to do justice to her important thesis.

165. Roeber, *Faithful Magistrates*, 171–202.

166. Drew R. McCoy, "The Virginia Port Bill of 1784," *VMHB* 83 (1975): 288–303. John E. Crowley sets this in wider perspective in *The Privileges of Independence: Neomercantilism and the American Revolution* (Baltimore, 1993), chap. 4, "The Recolonization of Anglo-American Trade," and chap. 5, "The Madisonian Definition of National Economic Interests."

167. For comments along these lines, see, for example, Washington to Harrison, 10 Oct. 1784; Washington to James Warren, 7 Oct. 1785, in Fitzpatrick, ed., *Writings of George Washington*, 27:473–74; 28:290–91; TJ to Washington, 15 Mar. 1784; TJ to G. K. Van Hogendorp, 13 Oct. 1785; TJ to John Jay, 23 Aug. 1785, *Boyd*, 7:26; 8:426–27, 633.

168. TJ to Donald, 28 July 1787, and see also TJ to Skipwith, 28 July 1787; TJ to James Currie, 4 Aug. 1787, *Boyd*, 11:633, 636, 682.

169. Archibald Stuart to TJ, 17 Oct. 1785; Thomas Pleasants, Jr., to TJ, 24 Oct. 1785; TJ to Skipwith, 28 July 1787, ibid., 8:645, 667; 11:636, and see also Currie to TJ, 2 May 1787, ibid., 328–29. For the controversy surrounding the return of the British merchants, see, for example, E. Randolph to Madison, 9 May, 15 May 1783; Pendleton to Madison, 17 May 1783, noting that the failure to open the ports to British ships was "a great mortification of some Gentlemen, who seem to long for the Flesh pots of Egypt, particularly some cheese and Porter in a vessel from Ireland"; J. Jones to Madison, 25 May 1783, *PJM*, 7:33–34, 45, 51, 76.

170. On the decline of Virginia tobacco exports in the 1780s, see Price, *France and the Chesapeake*, 2:729. The impact of that decline, however, varied; some of the newer

producing regions, such as the Southside, were less affected than the Tidewater or parts of the Piedmont. On the rise of tobacco culture in the Southside, see Richard R. Beeman, *The Evolution of the Southern Backcountry: A Case Study of Lunenburg County, Virginia, 1746–1823* (Philadelphia, 1984); Siegel, *Roots of Southern Distinctiveness*, carries the story of the new tobacco regions into the nineteenth century.

171. Hening, comp., *Statutes at Large*, 10:133–34; for Mason's authorship, see Rutland, ed., *Papers of George Mason*, 2:539n.

172. Mason, Fairfax County Petition Protesting Repeal of the Act to Prevent Extensive Credits [18 June 1783], in Rutland, ed., *Papers of George Mason*, 786.

173. Ibid., 786–87.

174. Or so one might conclude from Freeman H. Hart, *The Valley of Virginia in the American Revolution, 1763–1789* (Chapel Hill, N.C., 1942), 124–25. Hart shows that for 1,871 cases tried in Berkeley County in 1784, there were 457 executions of judgments, which suggests that most of the suits were brought simply to comply with the terms of the act; once a judgment had been recorded, the debt was secured, and the creditor could then allow the debtor to take his time paying up.

175. For what Jefferson did dislike about the Constitution, see his letters to John Adams, 13 Nov. 1787; to Madison, 20 Dec. 1787, *Boyd*, 12:350–51, 439–42. For a strong statement of his view that the Constitution would help secure American commerce, see TJ to Washington, 4 Nov. [Dec.] 1788, ibid., 14:328.

176. On the decline of Piedmont land values, see Craven, *Soil Exhaustion*, 123–24, and Charles Henry Ambler, *Sectionalism in Virginia from 1776 to 1861* (Chicago, 1910), 110–13. Monticello was sold by Jefferson's executor for a mere $7,000 in 1831; for the 1826 lottery, the mansion house and adjacent lands were valued at $71,000. Frederick D. Nichols and James A. Bear, Jr., *Monticello: A Guidebook* (Monticello, Va., 1982), 69; *Malone*, 7:511.

177. For the Paradises and Jefferson, see Archibald Bolling Shepperson, *John Paradise and Lucy Ludwell of London and Williamsburg* (Richmond, Va., 1942), 195–244, 308–397, 410–16, 418–24, printing most, though not all, of the letters. For additional material, consult *Boyd* with the help of vol. 21, the index. See Shepperson, *Paradise*, 451–56 (on Lucy Ludwell Paradise's relatives); 80–138 (on John Paradise); 146–48 (on financial problems).

178. Does this suggest that Jefferson was less than fully occupied with his diplomatic duties? If so, it would confirm what we sense from his extended tours of France, northern Italy, and the Rhineland.

179. For Anglo-American relations after the peace treaty, see Charles R. Ritcheson, *Aftermath of Revolution: British Policy Toward the United States, 1783–1795* (Dallas, 1969), 3–144, esp. 63–87 on the debt issue.

180. Adams urged Jefferson to come to London to join him in negotiating a commercial treaty with Portugal. Adams to TJ, 21 Feb. 1786, *Cappon*, 1:123. Once there, Jefferson was drawn into the ongoing effort to adjust Anglo-American differences. For the status of that effort, see Adams to TJ, 19 Jan. 1786, ibid., 117.

181. Adams, Diary, 3 Nov. 1782, in Butterfield, ed., *Diary and Autobiography of John Adams*, 3:43. For the debts as an issue in the peace negotiations, see Richard B. Morris, *The Peacemakers: The Great Powers and American Independence* (New York, 1965), 350–52, 361, 366–67.

182. For his role in the treaty's ratification, which was dramatic enough, see TJ, Autobiography, 1821, *LofA*, 50–54.

183. For his role as legislator, see note 26. The statute was in force during his term as governor (1779–1781).

184. Ritcheson, *Aftermath of Revolution*, 84–86, offers a different reading of the negotiations, suggesting that Jefferson's role was minor at best. But against this it may be urged that Jefferson's interest in the question of the debts was on any grounds greater than Adams's, that his references to it are more frequent than Adams's, and that, while it may have been no more than a coincidence, it was Jefferson, not Adams, who wrote the dispatch to Jay describing the meetings. TJ to Jay, 23 Apr. 1786, *Boyd*, 9:403–5. Jefferson's private meetings with his creditors gave him an opportunity Adams lacked to test the merchants' sentiment. Note, as well, that Jefferson continued to employ the line of reasoning espoused in 1786 after he became secretary of state; it formed the core of his argument to British minister George Hammond in 1792, for which see TJ to Hammond, 29 May 1792, ibid., 23:551–601, esp. 568–80.

185. TJ to Jay, 23 Apr. 1786, ibid., 9:403–4; see also TJ to Madison, 25 Apr. 1786; TJ to Monroe, 10 May 1786, ibid., 433–34, 500–501.

186. James Ritchie & Co., "Instructions," to Anderson, 31 Mar. 1784, Dunlop Family Papers, LC.

187. Campbell is quoted in TJ to Jay, 23 Apr. 1786, *Boyd*, 9:404. The statement is reported in similar terms in TJ to Eppes, 22 Apr. 1786; TJ to Madison, 25 Apr. 1786, ibid., 396, 434.

188. At the standard rate of 5 percent simple interest, the claim for the war years would have added a hefty 40 percent to the debts outstanding in 1775. For the rejection on political grounds, see TJ to McCaul, 19 Apr. 1786, ibid., 389. I have assumed that Jefferson's arguments to Campbell were those he made to McCaul; it is unlikely that he would have made a different case in a letter likely to have been shown to other creditors in Glasgow.

189. As Jefferson put it to Jay, after receiving the American proposition, Campbell "took leave, and we never since heard from him or any other person on the subject" (23 Apr. 1786, ibid., 405). Shortly thereafter, Jefferson returned to France. TJ to Lord Carmarthen, [ca. 26 Apr. 1786], ibid., 436.

190. TJ to John Page, 4 May 1786, and see TJ to R. H. Lee, 22 Apr. 1786, ibid., 446, 397–99. For additional evidence of Jefferson's conviction that the British and, above all, the king hated him, see Charles R. Ritcheson, "The Fragile Memory: Thomas Jefferson at the Court of George III," *Eighteenth-Century Life* 6 (1981): 1–16.

191. TJ to Jay, 23 Apr. 1786, *Boyd* 9:403–5; for Jay's 13 Oct. 1786 report and Congress's recommendations to the states the following April, see Worthington Chauncey Ford, ed., *Journals of the Continental Congress*, 34 vols. (Washington, D.C., 1904–1937), 21:781–84; 32:177–84.

192. TJ to Lewis Littlepage, 8 May 1789, *Boyd*, 15:106.

193. See Alexander Hamilton's discussion in *Federalist*, Nos. 80–83, in Cooke, ed. *The Federalist*, 534–74. The Constitution, Article VI, Section 2, made "all treaties made . . . under the authority of the United States . . . the supreme law of the land," while Article III, Section 2, granted jurisdiction in "all cases, in law and equity, arising under this Constitution, the laws of the United States, and treaties made, or which shall be made, under their authority" and further granted jurisdiction "in all cases . . . between a State, or the citizens thereof, and foreign States, citizens or subjects." For the provisions of the Judiciary Act of 1789 embodying these grants, see *DHFFC*, 5:1154, 1158.

194. McCaul to TJ, 14 Aug. 1788 (with news of Virginia's ratification), *Boyd*, 13:513.

195. See, for example, E. Randolph to Madison, 12 Sept. 1788, 27 Mar., 19 May 1789, *PJM*, 11:252; 12:32, 168.

196. On the Dutch debt, see James C. Riley, "Foreign Credit and Fiscal Stability: Dutch Investment in the United States, 1781–1794," *JAH* 65 (1978): 654–78; on the French debt, see E. James Ferguson, *The Power of the Purse: A History of American Public Finance, 1776–1790* (Chapel Hill, N.C., 1961), 40–42, 44–46, 55–56, 126–30, 234–38.

197. TJ to Washington, 2 May 1788, *Boyd*, 13:126–28, quotation on 127. This aspect of Jefferson's mission is summarized in *Malone*, 2:146–47, 188–91.

198. TJ to Madison, 3 May 1788, *Boyd*, 13:129–30. For evidence that Jefferson's views were having an effect on his American correspondents–"The last loan in Holland and that alone, saved the U.S. from Bankruptcy in Europe; and that loan was obtained from a belief that the Constitution then depending wd. be certainly speedily, quietly, and finally established, & by that means put America into a permanent capacity to discharge with honor & punctuality all her engagements"–see Madison to George Lee Turberville, 2 Nov. 1788, *PJM*, 11:332.

199. TJ to Jay, 26 Sept., 12 Nov. 1786, *Boyd*, 10:406, 519–23, provides details of the proposals and Jefferson's cautiously favorable reaction, which he would later modify. For a guide to the episode, see Boyd, editorial note, "Proposals for Funding the Foreign Debt," ibid., 190–94; as might be expected, it casts Jefferson in the best possible light.

200. TJ to Jay, 26 Sept. 1787, ibid., 10:406.

201. The decision was not taken until late in 1789. William Short to TJ, 19 Nov. 1789, ibid., 15:550. Even then, the speculators continued to promote schemes for transfer of the debt. TJ, "Opinion on Fiscal Policy," 26 Aug. 1790, ibid., 17:425–27. See Short's correspondence on the subject with Jefferson, ibid., 16–19, and Hamilton, *PAH*, 6–12.

202. *Malone*, 2:470–71, describes the episode, defending Jefferson against Hamilton's charges. The best that can be said about this is that Hamilton should have left it alone, while Jefferson's defense was necessarily less than candid. In 1792, with public credit reestablished, the expedients of the 1780s were better left unmentioned; what then passed for wisdom was no longer politically possible in 1792, and Jefferson's response was shaped by the exigencies of politics then current.

203. See, for example, La Rouërie to TJ, 25 Sept. 1786; TJ to La Rouërie, 16 Sept. 1788; La Rouërie to TJ, 19 Sept., 26 Dec. 1788; and Sauvage to TJ, 25 Oct. 1788; TJ to Sauvage, 24 Nov. 1788, *Boyd*, 10:401; 12:614–15, 617–19; 14:390, 37, 284–85. Jefferson's concern can be followed in Commissioners of Treasury to TJ, 16 Feb. 1787; TJ to Commissioners, 17 June 1787, 16 May 1788; TJ to Jay, 5 Sept. 1788; TJ to Willink, Van Staphorst, & Hubbard, 9 Apr., 3 Aug. 1789, ibid., 11:160–61, 474–75; 13:168, 569; 15:40–41, 331–32.

204. Washington to TJ, 31 Aug. 1788, ibid., 13:556. An old hand at speculating in soldiers' certificates, Washington must have had a keen appreciation of the plight of his former officers and men. For his purchases of certificates after the Seven Years' War, see Bernhard Knollenberg, *George Washington: The Virginia Period, 1732–1775* (Durham, N.C., 1964), 91–100, 135–37.

205. See Brissot de Warville to TJ, 3 Jan. 1787, *Boyd*, 11:6–9.

206. For Jefferson's reply to one such inquiry, see Jacob Gerrit Dirks to TJ, 2 July 1788; TJ to Dirks, 2 July 1788, ibid., 13:302, 303.

207. *Malone*, 2:92–93, notes this aspect of the mission.

208. For Jefferson's general account of the American debt, intended to receive wide circulation through its appearance in the new *Encyclopédie méthodique*, see his "Answers to Démeunier's First Queries," 24 Jan. 1786, and "Answers to the Additional Queries" [ca. Jan.–Feb. 1786], *Boyd*, 10:12–17, 23–27.

209. TJ to James Swan, 4 Aug. [Sept.] 1789, ibid., 15:382–83.

210. "The pecuniary distresses of France," he recalled in 1821, referring to the Assembly of the Notables, "produced this year [1786] a measure of which there has been no example for near two centuries, and the consequences of which, good and evil, are not yet calculable" (TJ, Autobiography, 1821, *LofA*, 62).

211. See TJ to Jay, 20 Aug., 13 Sept. 1788, 11 Jan., 9 May, 27 Aug., 30 Aug., 19 Sept., 30 Sept., 1789, *Boyd*, 13:529–30, 564; 14:431–32; 15:111–12, 358, 373, 457, 501.

212. TJ to Jay, 11 Jan., 19 Sept. 1789, ibid., 14:432; 15:458.

213. For his collection of pamphlets on French finances, see *Sowerby*, 3:53, 57–60. For those shipped to Madison, see Madison, Memorandum of Books, [ca. Aug. 1790], *PJM*, 13:286–89. For some of his conversations, see Chapter 2 and TJ to Madison, 11 May 1789, enclosing "Abstract of Mr. G[ouverneur] Morris's plan of American finances," *Boyd*, 15:123–24.

214. TJ to Jay, 3 Nov. 1787, and cf. TJ to John Brown Cutting, 3 Nov. 1788, *Boyd*, 12:309–10; 14:47. For the Patriot movement in Holland and its failure–the bankers Willink, Van Staphorst & Hubbard had strong ties to the Patriots–see Simon Schama, *Patriots and Liberators: Revolution in the Netherlands, 1780–1813* (New York, 1977).

215. TJ to Jay, 3 Nov. 1787 (private), *Boyd*, 12:315.

216. On the Barbary pirates, see *Malone*, 2:27–32, and the editorial note in *Boyd*, 10:560–66, which uses the opportunity to boost Jefferson's reputation at the expense of John Jay. For some of Jefferson's comments on the need for a navy (linked, because of the cost, to the need for a reform of the Articles of Confederation to allow the national government to tax), see TJ to Monroe, 11 Aug. 1786 (arguing that a navy "can never endanger our liberties, nor occasion bloodshed; a land force would do both"), ibid., 225, and TJ to Adams, 11 July 1786, *Cappon*, 1:142–44. By 1792, his views had changed; he now thought it preferable to purchase peace with the Algerines. TJ, "Considerations on Policy toward Algiers," enclosed in TJ to GW, 1 Apr. 1792, *Boyd*, 23:362.

217. TJ to Washington, 4 Nov. [Dec.] 1788, *Boyd*, 14:328.

218. See Chapter 6.

219. See Boyd, "Proposals for Funding the Foreign Debt," *Boyd*, 14:190–97, and the accompanying documents, ibid., 197–209. For Jefferson's concern in this regard, see TJ to Washington, 2 May, 4 Nov. [Dec.] 1788; TJ to Madison, 3 May, 18 Nov. 1788, 11 May 1789, ibid., 13:126–28; 14:328; 13:128–29; 14:189; 15:122–24.

220. TJ to Madison, 18 Nov. 1788, ibid., 14:189.

Chapter 2

1. William Branch Giles, "Political Schemers–Hard Times. II: Public Credit–Funding Scheme" (1824), in *Political Miscellanies* (Richmond, Va., 1829), 15. The essay first appeared in the Richmond *Enquirer*, Republican orthodoxy's voice in the Old Dominion.

2. TJ to James Madison, 6 Sept. 1789, *Boyd*, 15:392–97, quotation on 392. According to Blackstone's successor at Oxford, "usufruct" meant the "right to make all the use and profit of a thing that can be made without injuring the substance of the thing itself. . . . This estate regularly lasted for life" (Sir Robert Chambers, *A Course of Lectures on the English Law, Delivered at the University of Oxford, 1767–1773*, ed. Thomas M. Curley, 2 vols. [Madison, Wis., 1986], 2:85). The *Encyclopédie*

defined "usufruit" as "le droit de jouir indéfiniment d'une chose appartenante à autrui, sans en diminuer la subsistance" (*Encyclopédie, ou dictionnaire raisonné des sciences, des arts et des métiers*, 39 vols. [Lausanne, 1781–1782], 36:370). Jefferson owned a copy of this edition of the *Encyclopédie. Sowerby*, 5, no. 4890. Dr. Johnson defined "usufruct" as "temporary use; enjoyment of the profits, without power to alienate" (Samuel Johnson, *A Dictionary of the English Language*. . . , 4th ed., 2 vols. [London, 1774], 2, s.v. "usufruct").

Useful commentaries on the letter include Boyd, editorial note, "The Earth Belongs to the Living," *Boyd*, 15:384–91; Franz Bühler, *Verfassungsrevision und Generationenproblem: Studie zur Verfassungsrevisionstheorie Thomas Jeffersons* (Freiburg, 1949); Adrienne Koch, *Jefferson and Madison: The Great Collaboration* (New York, 1950), 62–96; Staughton Lynd, *Intellectual Origins of American Radicalism* (New York, 1968), 77–86; Merrill D. Peterson, "Thomas Jefferson's 'Sovereignty of the Living Generation,' " *Virginia Quarterly Review* 52 (1976): 437–44; *Jefferson and Madison and the Making of Constitutions* (Charlottesville, Va., 1987), esp. 11–13; and "Thomas Jefferson, the Founders, and Constitutional Change," in J. Jackson Barlow et al., eds., *The American Founding: Essays on the Formation of the Constitution* (Westport, Conn., 1988), 275–93; and Garry Wills, *Inventing America: Jefferson's Declaration of Independence* (Garden City, N.Y., 1978), 132–48. The following are also of interest: Hannah Arendt, *On Revolution* (New York, 1963), esp. chap. 6; Daniel J. Boorstin, *The Lost World of Thomas Jefferson* (New York, 1948), 204–13; Harold Hellenbrand, *The Unfinished Revolution: Education and Politics in the Thought of Thomas Jefferson* (Newark, Del., 1990), 121–25; Stephen Holmes, "Precommitment and the Paradox of Democracy," in Jon Elster and Rune Slagstad, eds., *Constitutionalism and Democracy* (Cambridge, 1988), 195–240; Stanley N. Katz, "Thomas Jefferson and the Right to Property in Revolutionary America," *Journal of Law and Economics* 14 (1976): 467–88, and "Republicanism and the Law of Inheritance in the American Revolutionary Era," *Michigan Law Review* 76 (1977): 1–29; Richard K. Matthews, *The Radical Politics of Thomas Jefferson: A Revisionist View* (Lawrence, Kans., 1984), 19–29; and Charles A. Miller, *Jefferson and Nature: An Interpretation* (Baltimore, 1988), chap. 5, esp. 161–64. Most recently, Gregory S. Alexander, in "Time and Property in American Republican Legal Culture," *New York University Law Review* 66 (1991): 273–352, has read the principle, in part, as implying the right of each generation "to re-create the configuration of property rights, allowing the republican polity to limit the alienation of land to whatever extent was needed to create the necessary conditions for republican politics" (300–301).

3. As Joyce Appleby notes, "Few enthusiasts for reform in America fail to mention Jefferson's belief that the world belongs to the living and that laws should, therefore, be subjected to generational plebiscites" ("Historians, Community, and the Pursuit of Jefferson: Comment on Professor Tomlins," *Studies in American Political Development* 4 [1990]:40).

4. See Chapters 5 and 6.

5. On the New Deal's discovery of Jefferson as the patron of the "living Constitution," see Merrill D. Peterson, *The Jefferson Image in the American Mind* (New York, 1960), 356. That doctrine, he reminds us, was never Jefferson's but rather John Marshall's in *McCulloch* v. *Maryland*, 4 Wheat. 316 (1819). See Peterson, "Thomas Jefferson, the Founders, and Constitutional Change," 284. Michael Kammen's conclusion in " 'A Vehicle for Life': Continuity and Change in Americans' Perception of Their Constitution," in *Sovereignty and Liberty: Constitutional Discourse in American Culture* (Madison, Wis., 1988), 145, that Jefferson "*shared* with Chief

Justice John Marshall, a political foe whose ideas and tactics he detested, a strong belief in the necessity of a living Constitution–a belief they both acted upon when they occupied positions of power and responsibility," seems wrong, no matter what Jefferson did in acquiring Louisiana or enforcing the Embargo. For Jefferson's views on what Marshall was doing to the Constitution, see David N. Mayer, *The Constitutional Thought of Thomas Jefferson* (Charlottesville, Va., 1994), 268–94.

6. TJ to Madison, 6 Sept. 1789, *Boyd*, 15:392–93, 395. In summarizing the letter's contents, I have rearranged its order slightly, the better to follow Jefferson's logic.

7. Ibid., 396, 394. See TJ to John Wayles Eppes, 24 June 1813, *Ford*, 11:298–99, which explains this more directly: "I turn, for instance, to Buffon's tables, of twenty-three thousand nine hundred and ninety-four deaths, and the ages at which they happened, and I find that of the numbers of all ages living at one moment, half will be dead in twenty-four years and eight months. But (leaving out minors, who have not the power of self-government) of the adults (of twenty-one years of age) living at one moment, a majority of whom act for the society, one half will be dead in eighteen years and eight months."

8. TJ to Madison, 6 Sept. 1789, *Boyd*, 15:394. He may have been responding to David Hume's point in "Of the Original Contract" (1741), in Eugene F. Miller, ed., *Essays, Moral, Political, and Literary* (Indianapolis, 1985), 476, that because the population was always "in flux," there was never a distinct succeeding generation with the right to wipe the slate clean and devise its own system of rule. Jefferson avoids Hume's problem by creating an artificial generation. Note that he apparently assumes the population was static in size; on this, see Chapter 6 and text at notes 37, 38.

9. TJ to Madison, 6 Sept. 1789, *Boyd*, 15:394. After finishing the letter on 6 September, Jefferson realized he had erred in his initial assumptions about how to calculate the life of a generation; the text quoted here reflects his corrections. See TJ to Richard Gem [9 Sept. 1789], ibid., 398–99. For the possibility that a pamphlet by Condorcet may have alerted him to his error, see Appendix A.

10. TJ to Madison, 6 Sept. 1789, *Boyd*, 15:396. These comments echo ones in Querry XVII of TJ, *Notes on the State of Virginia* (1785), ed. William Peden (Chapel Hill, N.C., 1954): "Our rulers will become corrupt, our people careless." Jefferson's refusal to let silence imply consent reflects a recurring theme in the social contract literature: After the original contract is formed, how do latecomers ratify it? For eighteenth-century discussion of this issue, see text at notes 159–62. Modern treatments include Holmes, "Precommitment and the Paradox of Democracy," and Sanford Levinson, *Constitutional Faith* (Princeton, N.J., 1988). The latter, though only briefly mentioning Jefferson, has much to say about the larger issues the principle raises. For theoretical discussions that do not invoke Jefferson, see Peter Laslett and James S. Fishkin, eds., *Justice Between Age Groups and Generations* (New Haven, Conn., 1992).

11. For the decrees abolishing feudalism in France, see John Hall Stewart, ed., *A Documentary Survey of the French Revolution* (New York, 1951), 107–10. Unlike some modern historians, certain that feudalism did not exist in late-eighteenth-century France, Jefferson had no doubts on that score. What he had in mind were practices surviving from earlier times, especially those limiting the right to dispose of property–primogeniture, entail, mortmain. He thought they bolstered the illegitimate political power of "aristocrats" by concentrating property in their hands. For contemporary French views, see J.Q.C. Mackrell, *The Attack on "Feudalism" in*

Eighteenth-Century France (London, 1973); Ernst Hinrichs, "Die Ablösung von Eigentumsrechten: Zur Diskussion über die droits féodaux in Frankreich am Ende des Ancien Régime und in der Revolution," in Rudolf Vierhaus, ed., *Eigentum und Verfassung: Zur Eigentumsdiskussions im ausgehenden 18. Jahrhundert* (Göttingen, 1972), 112–78; and Gerd van den Heuvel, "Féodalité, Féodal," in Rolf Reichardt and Eberhard Schmidt, eds., *Handbuch politisch-sozialer Grundbegriffe in Frankreich, 1680–1820* (Munich, 1988), 10:7–54. Gustave Flaubert may have been right to define "feudalism" in his dictionary of "received ideas" as "*Féodalité*–N'en avoir acune idée précise, mais tonner contre" (*Dictionnaire des idées reçues*, ed. Lea Caminiti [Naples, 1966], 273).

12. TJ to Madison, 6 Sept. 1789, *Boyd*, 15:396. Several of his illustrative cases appear to be taken from the National Assembly's decrees; compare the text of the decrees in Stewart, ed., *Documentary Survey*, 107–10. Note the many applications to church property. Having helped disestablish the Anglican church in Virginia and seen his efforts triumph in the 1785 Statute for Religious Freedom, Jefferson hoped that the French would go and do likewise. But the Statute left church property in limbo; disputes over the glebe lands continued into the nineteenth century. Jefferson may thus have seen his principle as applying to these unresolved cases. For the background, see Thomas E. Buckley, S.J., *Church and State in Revolutionary Virginia, 1776–1787* (Charlottesville, Va., 1977); on the glebes, see Buckley, "Evangelicals Triumphant: The Baptists' Assault on the Virginia Glebes, 1786–1801," *WMQ* 45 (1988): 33–69, and *Terrett* v. *Taylor*, 9 Cranch 43 (1815), a decision that must have appalled Jefferson, erecting as it did–four years before *Dartmouth College* v. *Woodward*, 4 Wheat. 518 (1819)–a class of "private" corporations that legislation could not reach.

13. TJ to Madison, 6 Sept. 1789, *Boyd*, 15:397. Jefferson is invoking Shakespeare; see *Julius Caesar*, act 3, sc.1, line 270.

14. TJ to Madison, 6 Sept. 1789, *Boyd*, 15:396.

15. Ibid. Boyd took this passage as evidence that Jefferson had not written "an authentic letter to Madison," but "a thesis stated for a pressing need, being intended to provide an instrument of justification for the constitutional reforms then under discussion" in France ("Earth Belongs to the Living," ibid., 390). The principle's American applications, including this one, were so trivial, Boyd thought, that Jefferson could not seriously have intended it to apply to American cases. But Jefferson was interested in patents and copyrights and had recently suggested adding to the Bill of Rights protection against such "monopolies" by limiting their duration, though without specifying what that duration should be. TJ to Madison, 28 Aug. 1789, ibid., 368. The surprise in the 6 September 1789 letter is his willingness to *lengthen* the term of protection. For his lasting opposition to intellectual monopolies, see TJ to Oliver Evans, 2 May 1807, *L&B*, 11:200–202; TJ to Isaac McPherson, 13 Aug. 1813, *LofA*, 1291–92. In the Evans letter, Jefferson says the English period of protection is too short because America is too "sparsely populated" for inventions to become well known within its term, but he does not offer the nineteen-year period–or any other–as an alternative.

16. For Paine, see *Dissertations on Government, the Affairs of the Bank, and Paper Money* (1786), in Michael Foot and Isaac Kramnick, eds., *The Thomas Paine Reader* (Harmondsworth, 1987), 186–88, and *Rights of Man*, Part One (1791), ed. Henry Collins (Harmondsworth, 1969), 40–45, 66; for Condorcet, see *Déclaration des droits* (1789), *Lettres à M. le comte de Montmorency* (1789), and *Sur la nécessité de faire ratifier la Constitution par les citoyens . . .* (1789), in A. Condorcet O'Connor and M.F.

Arago, eds., *Oeuvres* (Paris, 1847), 9:210–11, 367–68, 371–72, 389–90, 415–16. For further detail, see Appendix A.

17. TJ to Madison, 6 Sept. 1789, *Boyd*, 15:395.

18. Ibid., 396. For one exception, the glebes, see note 12. Another was the College of William and Mary, which Jefferson did his best to reform, though with little success. For this, see TJ, reform bill, *Boyd*, 2:535–43, and *Notes on the State of Virginia*, 150–51; Hellenbrand, *Unfinished Revolution*, 85–94.

19. TJ to Madison, 6 Sept. 1789, *Boyd*, 15:395.

20. Ibid., 397; for his different position on the French debt, see also 395.

21. Gordon S. Wood describes the fears aroused during the 1780s in the United States by the specter of agrarian laws in *The Creation of the American Republic, 1776–1787* (Chapel Hill, N.C., 1969), 404–13.

22. TJ to Madison, 6 Sept. 1789, *Boyd*, 15:396, 395.

23. On the nature of property for Jefferson, see David M. Post, "Jeffersonian Revisions of Locke: Education, Property-Rights, and Liberty," *Journal of the History of Ideas* 47 (1986): 147–57, and Mayer, *Constitutional Thought of Thomas Jefferson*, 77–80. On the limitations of Jefferson's thinking about property, see Katz, "Jefferson and the Right to Property," 469, though note that Katz thinks Jefferson held that property was a natural right. Elsewhere in his essay, arguing that Jefferson believed that the earth literally belonged to the living, Katz links the letter to Madison with Jefferson's never-adopted 1776 plan to give each propertyless adult white male in Virginia fifty acres of public land (the amount necessary to vote). If there is a connection, Jefferson himself did not make it; he soon dropped the 1776 proposal, though not the effort to make property in land more widely available, for which see John E. Selby, *The Revolution in Virginia, 1775–1783* (Williamsburg, Va., 1988), 153–55, 229–32. Acquisition of the trans-Appalachian West in 1783 and Louisiana in 1803 created a vast national domain, reducing Jefferson's fears that yeomen would not be able to acquire property. See Drew R. McCoy, *The Elusive Republic: Political Economy in Jeffersonian America* (Chapel Hill, N.C., 1980), esp. chap. 8, "The Jeffersonians in Power: Extending the Sphere."

24. For these strategies, see Chapter 1.

25. Levinson, *Constitutional Faith*, 9 is one example; Arendt, *On Revolution*, 234–35, is another. Fascinated by the American Founding, Arendt nevertheless deemed the principle "too fantastic (especially if one considers the then prevailing tables of morality, according to which there was a 'new majority' every nineteen years) to be taken seriously"; calling it a "somewhat awkward attempt" to secure each generation's right to express its views on the fundamentals of the political order, she explained that Jefferson "was carried away by such impracticabilities" because he understood, "however dimly, that the Revolution, while it had given freedom to the people, had failed to provide a space where this freedom could be exercised." Unlike communitarians and republican revivalists among present-day constitutional lawyers and political theorists, who ignore Jefferson's arguments and endorse Madison's warnings against frequent change—for example, Bruce Ackerman, *We the People: Foundations* (Cambridge, Mass., 1991)—Arendt saw Jefferson's larger goal. Another case in point is Joyce Appleby, who uses the version of the principle found in the 1816 letter to Samuel Kercheval (for which see Chapter 6) in, for example, "Comment to Leonard Levy," in John Allphin Moore, Jr., and John E. Murphy, eds., *A Grand Experiment: The Constitution at 200: Essays from the Douglass Adair Symposia* (Wilmington, Del., 1987), 14. John R. Vile notes the frequency of references to the 1816 letter by would-be reformers of the federal Constitution in

Rewriting the United States Constitution: An Examination of Proposals from Reconstruction to the Present (New York, 1991), 156.

26. Boyd's argument is set out in "Earth Belongs to the Living," *Boyd*, 15:384–91, note 15. For the copy of the letter given to Gem, see ibid., 398–99.

27. Edward Carrington sent *The Federalist* to Jefferson as it appeared in book form. Carrington to TJ, 14 May, 10 Aug. 1788, *Boyd*, 13:157, 495. For Jefferson's enthusiastic reaction, see TJ to Madison, 18 Nov. 1788, ibid., 14:188.

28. For Madison's transmittal of the amendments in their early form, see Madison to TJ, 13 June, 30 June 1789, *PJM*, 12:217–18, 272. Jefferson received the first of these letters on 15 August, and the second on 27 August. *Boyd*, 15:181n, 229n. As Boyd notes, we do not know which contained the information. But see TJ to Madison, 28 Aug. 1789 ("I must now say a word on the declarations of rights you have been so good as to send me"), suggesting that it arrived on 27 August. Ibid., 367. The 28 August letter proposes several additions to the Bill of Rights, but says nothing about constitutional revision.

29. For Madison's reactions, see Chapter 4 and text at notes 81–84. Drew R. McCoy explores this aspect of Madison's conservatism in *The Last of the Fathers: James Madison and the Republican Legacy* (Cambridge, 1989), 45–61. For the Founders' ambiguity as to whether the union *would* be perpetual–a different question from that implied by Jefferson's principle–see Kenneth M. Stampp, "The Concept of a Perpetual Union," *JAH* 65 (1978):5–33. On the mid-nineteenth-century implications of the sense that the founding was over, see George Forgie, *Patricide in the House Divided: A Psychological Interpretation of Lincoln and His Age* (New York, 1979); it can be read as evidence that the country would have been better off had Jefferson's idea received more support at the federal level. For a strong argument that the Founders understood constitutions by their nature to be permanent, see Philip A. Hamburger, "The Constitution's Accommodation of Social Change," *Michigan Law Review* 88 (1989): 239–327, which concludes that the Founders "did not want the Constitution to change in adaptation to the economic, political, cultural or moral development of American society" (325).

30. The ease with which ten of the first twelve proposed amendments were adopted (1791), followed by Amendments 11 (1798) and 12 (1804), may have convinced him that the clause sufficed. I know of no statement by Jefferson that the federal Constitution violated his principle (the Virginia constitution was another matter; see Chapter 6). For his willingness to accept constitutional custom in place of formal amendments, see his comments on the two-term precedent established by Washington. TJ to John Taylor, 6 Jan. 1805, *Ford*, 10:124–25. He did, however, continue to think that a formal amendment to that effect was desirable. See TJ to Robert J. Garnett, 14 Feb. 1824, ibid., 12:341–42.

31. On the obsessive personality, see Otto Fenichel, *The Psychoanalytic Theory of Neurosis* (New York, 1945), 269–310, esp. 284–86. That his obsession involved money–the subject of so many of Jefferson's calculations–raises further issues. For guidance in this area, see Ernst Borneman, ed., *The Psychoanalysis of Money*, trans. Michael Shaw (New York, 1976).

32. TJ to Madison, 6 Sept. 1789, *Boyd*, 15:395 n.*; the calculation shows how Jefferson arrived at the annual interest on the hypothetical Genoese loans.

33. For a revealing case, see TJ, "Notes on the Payment of the National Debt" [ca. 28 Mar. 1793], in which Jefferson uses a formula printed in Benjamin Franklin Bache's *General Advertiser* to calculate how long it would take to extinguish the American national debt under certain conditions; for earlier efforts, see Boyd,

editorial note, "Proposals for Funding the Foreign Debt, and Jefferson's Plan" [Oct. 1788], computing that the French debt could be paid by 1803, the Dutch by 1805. *Boyd*, 25:465–66; 14:202–4, 206–8. Other examples can be found throughout the text and notes. On Jefferson as calculator, see Patricia Cline Cohen, *A Calculating People: The Spread of Numeracy in Early America* (Chicago, 1982), 86, 112–14, and, more critically, Wills, *Inventing America*, 111–24, 132–48.

34. TJ to Benjamin Rush, 17 Aug. 1811, *Ford*, 11:212.

35. D. L. Rayner, *Life of Thomas Jefferson* (Boston, 1834), 524, quoted in Susan R. Stein, *The Worlds of Thomas Jefferson at Monticello* (New York, 1993), 13.

36. TJ to Rush, 17 Aug. 1811, *Ford*, 11:212.

37. For examples of this behavior, especially in regard to his creditors, see Chapter 1.

38. Sigmund Freud, *The Problem of Anxiety* (1935), quoted in Fenichel, *Psychoanalytic Theory of Neurosis*, 286.

39. Hamilton, *Report on Public Credit*, 9 Jan. 1790, *PAH*, 6:95, 128. Along with a good many other fancy devices in Hamilton's original proposal, the tontine did not survive in the enacted version, for which see *DHFFC*, 5:713–21.

40. David R. Weir, "Tontines, Public Finance, and Revolution in France and England, 1688–1789," *Journal of Economic History* 69 (1989): 95–124; Robert M. Jennings et al., "Alexander Hamilton's Tontine Proposal," *WMQ* 45 (1988): 107–15; a more exhaustive treatment is Robert M. Jennings and Andrew P. Trout, *The Tontine: From the Reign of Louis XIV to the French Revolutionary Era* (Philadelphia, 1982).

41. Bentham's principle of utility offered a way out of the difficulties of contract theory—which, of course, he proposed to abandon altogether. See Jeremy Bentham, *A Fragment on Government* (1776), ed. J.H. Burns and H.L.A. Hart (Cambridge, 1988), 53–59. This method of cutting the Gordian knot was one Jefferson would never adopt.

42. For newer views situating Jefferson in a republican context, see Introduction. The older views I have in mind can be found in, for example, Vernon Louis Parrington, *Main Currents in American Thought*, vol. 1, *The Colonial Mind, 1620–1800* (New York, 1927), bk. 3, pt. 2, situating Jefferson and Paine as part of the "French Group" of "political thinkers," and in the works of Henry Steele Commager: *Jefferson, Nationalism, and the Enlightenment* (New York, 1975) and *The Empire of Reason: How Europe Imagined and America Realized the Enlightenment* (Garden City, N.Y., 1977).

43. Otto Vossler, *Die Amerikanischen Revolutionsideale in ihrem Verhältnis zu den Europäischen, untersucht an Thomas Jefferson, Historische Zeitschrift*, Supplement 17 (1930): esp. 116–30 (with discussion of the letter to Madison), 187 (after Jefferson's return to America, "unter seiner Führung, lernt Amerika, seinen Freiheitskampf mit europäischen Augen zu sehen und nimmt die Ideale von 1789 als eigene auf"). On this contribution to the study of Jefferson, see R. R. Palmer, "A Neglected Work: Otto Vossler on Jefferson and the Revolutionary Era," *WMQ* 12 (1955): 462–71.

44. On Jefferson's goals as law reformer, see Ralph Lerner, "Jefferson's Pulse of Republican Reformation," in *The Thinking Revolutionary: Principle and Practice in the New Republic* (Ithaca, N.Y., 1987), 60–90; for qualifications, see Bernard Bailyn, "Political Experience and Radical Ideas in Eighteenth-Century America" (1962), in *Faces of Revolution: Personalities and Themes in the Struggle for American Independence* (New York, 1990), 191–92, and John V. Orth, "After the Revolution: 'Reform' of the Law of Inheritance," *Law and History Review* 10 (1992): 33–44.

45. Cf. Jean-Jacques Rousseau, *Du contrat social* (1762), in Bernard Gagnebin and Marcel Raymond, eds., *Oeuvres complètes*, (Paris, 1954), 3:364: "quiconque refusera d'obéir à la volonté générale y sera contraint par tout le corps: ce qui ne signifie autre chose sinon qu'on le forcera d'être libre." On the tensions in Rousseau's ideas and the ways they played out after 1789, see Carol Blum, *Rousseau and the Republic of Virtue: The Language of Politics in the French Revolution* (Ithaca, N.Y., 1986).

46. For Virginia's agricultural decline, see Chapter 1. On Jefferson's refusal to buy western lands and activities as a gentleman farmer and agricultural reformer, see *Malone*, 1:435–45; 3:194–206; 6:36–54. His views on Virginia agriculture can be followed in the extracts from his correspondence in *Farm Book*.

47. McCoy describes Jefferson's fears for the future in *Elusive Republic*, 13–15, 126–27, 185–88, 192–96, 236–39, 248–52.

48. Edmund Burke, *Reflections on the Revolution in France* (1790), in *The Writings and Speeches of Edmund Burke*, vol. 8, *The French Revolution, 1790–1794*, ed. L. G. Mitchell (Oxford, 1989), 147. Like Jefferson, Burke exploited the property-law metaphor inherent in the idea of generational rights, later remarking that "with regard to futurity, we are to treat it like a ward. We are not so to attempt an improvement of his fortune, as to put the capital of his estate to any hazard" (*An Appeal from the New to the Old Whigs* [1791], in *Further Reflections on the Revolution in France*, ed. Daniel E. Ritchie [Indianapolis, 1992], 91). In this pamphlet, Burke replied to Paine's generational claims made earlier that year in *Rights of Man*. For the context, see Carl B. Cone, *Burke and the Nature of Politics*, vol. 2, *The Age of the French Revolution* (Lexington, Ky., 1964), 355, 359–64, and for development of the generational argument in the early 1790s, see Chapter 5.

49. John Lauritz Larson, "Jefferson's Union and the Problem of Internal Improvements," in Peter S. Onuf, ed., *Jeffersonian Legacies* (Charlottesville, Va., 1993), 340–69, describes the problems Jefferson encountered in attempting to realize this vision.

50. See TJ to George Hammond, 29 May 1792, *Boyd*, 23:589–95, esp. 591–this is his official reply to British minister Hammond's letter on American infractions of the peace treaty–for his view that interest on debts is not "sacred" and "not part of the debt," and courts will take circumstances into account before awarding it. Jefferson is appealing to traditional (and negative) views of interest as usury at this point; there is no reason to suppose that his personal views on this differed from his official ones.

51. For the role this concept plays in situating Jefferson historiographically, see Introduction.

52. Koch, *Jefferson and Madison*, 77–78, 84–88; Boyd, "Earth Belongs to the Living," *Boyd*, 15:384–87.

53. TJ to Madison, 28 Oct. 1785, *Boyd*, 8:682; TJ to William Stephens Smith, 13 Nov. 1787, ibid., 12:356.

54. TJ to Abigail Adams, 22 Feb. 1787, *Cappon*, 1:173.

55. For the *Américanistes*, see Joyce Appleby, "The Jefferson–Adams Rupture and the First French Translation of John Adam's *Defence*," *AHR* 73 (1968): 1087–88, and "America as a Model for the Radical French Reformers of 1789," *WMQ* 28 (1971): 273–75.

56. For Jefferson on the developing revolution, see R. R. Palmer, "Dubious Democrat: Thomas Jefferson in Bourbon France," *Political Science Quarterly* 72 (1957): 388–404. The best narrative of his activity in circles connected to Lafayette is Louis Gottschalk and Margaret Maddox, *Lafayette in the French Revolution: Through the October Days* (Chicago, 1969). Older accounts of value include Gilbert Chinard,

La Déclaration des droits de l'homme et du citoyen d'après ses origines américaines (Washington, D.C., 1945), and Henry E. Bourne, "American Constitutional Precedents in the French National Assembly," *AHR* 8 (1908): 466–86. For the Déclaration's drafting, see Marcel Gauchet, *La Révolution des droits de l'homme* (Paris, 1989); Stéphane Rials, *La Déclaration des droits de l'homme* (Paris, 1989), introduction; and Sigmar-Jürgen Samwer, *Die französische Erklärung der Menschen- und Bürgerrechte von 1789/91* (Hamburg, 1970), esp. chap. 2, "Die Debatten in der Reichsstände- und Nationalversammlung." Gauchet's comparisons between the French and the American foundings need to be taken with caution. Like other revisionists, he accepts at face value the idea that pragmatism made the American Founding more successful than the 1789 French effort. "On the Latent Illiberalism of the French Revolution," *AHR* 95 (1990): 1452–70, Isser Woloch's wide-ranging review of revisionism's principal monument—François Furet and Mona Ozouf, eds., *A Critical Dictionary of the French Revolution*, trans. Arthur Goldhammer (Cambridge, Mass., 1989)—gives special attention to Gauchet's essay on the Rights of Man. Woloch notes that Gauchet and other authors in the collection "obliquely invoke" American pluralism without taking account of the collapse of the Constitution in 1861 and the eighty years of post-Reconstruction failure ("a reign of terror," Woloch properly calls it) to make rights a reality for African Americans. Ibid., 1460. See also Claude Mazauric, "Autour du bicentenaire," in *Jacobinisme et Révolution: Autour du bicentenaire de Quatre-vingt-neuf* (Paris, 1984), 20.

57. For Pitt's gossip, see Matthew Montagu to Mrs. Elizabeth Montagu, 13 July 1789, in Reginald Blunt, ed., *Mrs. Montagu, "Queen of the Blues": Her Letters and Friendships from 1762 to 1800*, 2 vols. (Boston, 1924), 2:237; for Jefferson's assurances, see *Malone*, 2:229–31. Jefferson's own recollections of his activity can be found in his Autobiography, 1821, *LofA*, 94–97.

58. See TJ to Madison, 20 Dec. 1787, 31 July, 18 Nov. 1788, 15 Mar., 28 Aug. 1789, *Boyd*, 12:439–42; 13:442–43; 14:188–89, 659–61; 15:367–68; TJ to George Washington, 2 May 1788, ibid., 13:128. *Malone*, 2:92–111, covers Jefferson's activities as a publicist while in France.

59. Lafayette would later remark that the age of the American Revolution was "l'ère des déclarations des droits" (*Mémoires, correspondance et manuscrits du Général Lafayette* [Paris, 1837], 2:303).

60. Lafayette, draft [ca. Jan. 1790], *Boyd*, 14:439. Lafayette's proposal thus apparently antedates a similar one published by Condorcet in February providing for special revisionary "Conventions" that would meet at "des époques déterminées" (*Déclaration des droits* [1789], in Rials, *Déclaration*, 550).

61. TJ to Madison, 12 Jan. 1789, *Boyd*, 14:436–37; in a letter to Richard Price, 8 Jan. 1789, ibid., 423, he described the course he thought the Estates General would take, saying, "Perhaps they may make a declaration of rights. It will be attempted at least."

62. Lafayette, draft [ca. Jan. 1790], ibid., 439. For another early 1789 contribution by Gem, a proposal for "Loix fondamentales d'une société politique," see ibid., 15:232n.

63. Gottschalk and Maddox, *Lafayette*, 55–59.

64. TJ to Lafayette; TJ to Rabaut St. Étienne, both 3 June 1789, *Boyd*, 15:165–66, 166–67, quotation on 166. This seems to have been Jefferson's first meeting with Rabaut, but Rabaut and Lafayette had been acquainted since 1785, when Lafayette took up the cause of the French Protestants. Louis Gottschalk, *Lafayette Between the American and the French Revolutions (1783–1789)* (Chicago, 1950), describes their relations.

65. TJ, "Draft of a Charter of Rights" [3 June 1789], *Boyd*, 15:167–68.

66. Lafayette to TJ, [3 June 1789], ibid., 166, and see Gottschalk and Maddox, *Lafayette*, 57–58.

67. Gottschalk and Maddox, *Lafayette*, 80–98; Lafayette, "Draft of a Declaration of Rights," *Boyd*, 15:230–31, quotation on 231 (my translation). The original reads as follows: "Et comme le progrès des lumieres l'introduction des abus et le droit des générations qui se succèdent nécéssitent la révision de tout etablissement humain, il droit être indiqué des moyens constitutionels qui assurent dans certains cas une convocation extraordinaire des représentants dont le seul objet soit d'examiner et modifier, s'il le faut, la forme du gouvernement." For the problems in dating this document, see *Boyd*, 15:231n, and Gottschalk and Maddox, *Lafayette*, 82n.42.

68. For an overview of the revisionary clauses in the state constitutions, see Willi Paul Adams, *The First American Constitutions: Republican Ideology and the Making of the State Constitutions in the Revolutionary Era*, trans. Rita Kimber and Robert Kimber (Chapel Hill, N.C., 1980), 139–41. On the novelty of the state constitutions' provisions for "orderly constitutional change," see Peterson, "Jefferson, the Founders, and Constitutional Change."

69. Francis Newton Thorpe, comp., *The Federal and State Constitutions . . . ,* 7 vols. (Washington, D.C., 1909), 7:3831 (Va.); 5:3083 (Pa.); 3:1687 (Md.); 3:1889 (Mass.). For the French texts of these provisions available to Lafayette and others in 1789, see Rials, *Déclaration*, 496, 499, 504, 512. Durand Echeverria describes both the Rochefoucauld collection of state constitutions used by Rials and other versions available at the time in France in "French Publications of the Declaration of Independence and the American Constitutions, 1776–1783," *Papers of the Bibliographical Society of America* 47 (1953): 313–38.

70. Thorpe, comp., *Federal and State Constitutions*, 7:3814 (Va.); 5:3083 (Pa.); 5:2788 (N.C.); for the French translations, see Rials, *Déclaration*, 497, 501, 511. The French were reminded of the principle by a pamphlet, *Aux Bataves sur le Stathoudérat* (1788), that quoted—without attribution—the language of the Virginia bill of rights. Ibid., 520–21.

71. TJ, "Draft of a Constitution for Virginia" [May–June 1783], *Boyd*, 6:304; a special convention to consider amendments could be called whenever two of the three branches of government (each by a two-thirds majority) requested one. In addition to including the draft constitution as an appendix to the *Notes*, Jefferson criticized the Virginia constitution on the grounds that, as the product of the legislature, it could be repealed or altered by any subsequent legislature and so lacked what he took to be the hallmark of constitutionality; only a convention specially elected for the purpose, he said, could create a genuine constitution. See TJ, *Notes on the State of Virginia*, 121–25 (criticism), 221 (appendix).

72. On the thus far unused convention route under Article 5, see Russell L. Caplan, *Constitutional Brinksmanship: Amending the Constitution by National Convention* (New York, 1988).

73. Thorpe, comp., *Federal and State Constitutions*, 3:1911; 4:2470; 5:3091–92; 6:3760–61. Pennsylvania's 1776 constitution was the state constitution best known to the French. The most radical of the state constitutions, some of its features (unicameralism and the revisionary mechanism of the Council of Censors) influenced French constitution-making in the 1790s. See Horst Dippel, "De la constitution de la Pennsylvanie de 1776 à la constitution jacobine de 1793," *Francia* 16 (1989): 61–73. Note that, when the opportunity came in 1795, no revisions were made in the Massachusetts constitution. Oscar Handlin and Mary Flug Handlin, *Commonwealth: A Study of the Role of Government in the American Economy: Massachusetts,*

1774–1861 (Cambridge, Mass., 1947), 56. Why Massachusetts chose fifteen years, rather than the others' seven, is not clear.

74. On French interest in the federal constitution of 1787, see Durand Echeverria, *Mirage in the West: A History of the French Image of American Society to 1815* (Princeton, N.J., 1957), 162–64.

75. The issue of American influence on the Déclaration des droits de l'homme et du citoyen has been debated for a century. See Rials, *Déclaration*, 355–73. Georges Lefebvre's verdict, in *The Coming of the French Revolution* (1939), trans. R.R. Palmer (Princeton, N.J., 1947), 214–15, still stands: "The influence of America is beyond question," but the United States and France, and England before them, "were alike tributaries to a great stream of ideas" common to the culture of the West as a whole.

76. Lafayette to TJ, 6 July 1789; TJ to Lafayette, 6 July 1789; Lafayette to TJ, 9 July 1789, *Boyd*, 15:249, 250, 255.

77. Antoine de Baecque, ed., *L'An 1 des droits de l'homme* (Paris, 1988), 63–64.

78. Lafayette to TJ, 9 July 1789, *Boyd*, 15:255.

79. Or so his silence allows us to infer. For the changes he did make, see ibid., 231n, 233n.

80. For Necker's dismissal and the events it unleashed, taking Lafayette away from the National Assembly and leaving defense of his proposal to others, see Gottschalk and Maddox, *Lafayette*, Chaps. 6–9. Lafayette himself did not expect the Assembly to take immediate action, telling an unnamed correspondent on 11 July 1789 that "aujourd'hui . . . je présenterai mon projet de déclaration des droits qui sera envoyé dans les bureaux. Il n'y aura acune délibération prise, et je pense qu'on attendra, pour débattre les différens plans, qu'on ait travaillé sur la constitution" (*Mémoires*, 2:313).

81. TJ to Madison, 6 Sept. 1789, *Boyd*, 15:397. But he also thought the French should apply the limit to "future debts" (395).

82. Of the forty-eight proposals for declarations of rights offered in the National Assembly and out of doors and reprinted in Rials, *Déclaration*, nineteen provide for constitutional revision. Only two–Lafayette's late June–early July draft and his formal motion of 11 July 1789–ascribe the right of revision to generations. Ibid., 568, 591. For the other plans with a right of revision, see ibid., 529 (Lafayette), 550 (Condorcet), 563 (Brissot), 606 (Sieyès), 612 (Target), 612 (Mounier), 621 (Sieyès), 626 (anon.), 632 (anon.), 636 (Thouret), 640 (Thouret), 645 (Custine), 661 (Duport), 725 (Pison), 725 (Pétion), 731 (Boislandry), 748 (Mirabeau).

83. On the progress of the Déclaration after 11 July, see Gauchet, *Révolution des droits*, 61–64. For the 19 July action, see de Baecque, ed., *L'An 1*, 70.

84. J.-M. Champion de Cicé to TJ, 20 July 1789; TJ to Champion, 22 July 1789, *Boyd*, 15:291, 298 (my translation).

85. De Baecque, ed., *L'An 1*, 83–88.

86. See ibid., 86–88, for Mounier's draft (the first paragraph declared that once the king had accepted the constitution, it could be changed only by following the methods the constitution itself would set out), and ibid., 88–125, for the debates, which produced a decision on 4 August that the *Déclaration* should stand at the head of the constitution. On 12 August 1789, Mounier (sounding like Madison in *The Federalist*, No. 49) published a fifty-four-page pamphlet in which he admitted constitutions could never be eternal but insisted there were "les plus grands dangers dans le système de ceux qui voudroient annoncer des époques fixes, & des convocations extraordinaires pour corriger la Constitution; c'est comme si l'on vouloit, à des temps marqués, rompre tous les ressorts du Gouvernement, &

livrer la France à toutes les fureurs de la discorde" (*Considérations sur les Gouvernements, et principalement sur celui qui convient à la France* [Paris, 1789], 33, quotation on 50).

87. Patrick Kessel, *La Nuit de 4 août* (Paris, 1969), has a minute-by-minute account of the events of the famous night.

88. See, for example, P. M. Jones, *The Peasantry in the French Revolution* (Cambridge, 1988), 81–85.

89. TJ to John Jay, 5 Aug. 1789, *Boyd*, 15:334.

90. De Baecque, ed., *L'An 1*, 125–26, quotation on 128 (my translation).

91. Sieyès, draft, late July 1789: "Un peuple a toujours le droit de revoir & de réformer sa constitution. Il est même bon de déterminer des époques fixes, où cette révision aura lieu, quelle qu'en soit la nécessité" (Rials, *Déclaration*, 621). For Lafayette's 11 July motion, see text at note 67. For the Sixième Bureau, see Philip Dawson, "Le 6ᵉ bureau de l'Assemblée Nationale et son projet de Déclaration des Droits de l'Homme, juillet 1789," *Annales historiques de la Révolution française* 50 (1978): 161–79; additional background is in Georges Lefebvre, "Les Bureaux de l'Assemblée Nationale en 1789," *Annales historiques de la Révolution française* 22 (1950): 134–40.

92. For the resumed debates, see de Baecque, ed., *L'An 1*, 125–48, and, for the final vote, 149.

93. For the final debate, see ibid., 149–95.

94. The last day of discussion was 26 August 1789. The National Assembly was slated to consider omitted articles on 27 August, but when the president proposed taking up the order of the day, he was met with a successful motion to limit the Déclaration to the articles already adopted and proceed at once to work on the constitution. There would, in fact, be a revisionary clause in the constitution, adopted on 3 September 1791 and ratified by Louis XVI ten days later. The nation's right to amend the document was declared "imprescriptible," but exercising this right was difficult–it required uniform resolutions by three consecutive legislatures and adoption of the proposed changes by a fourth, which would be augmented by doubling the number of members sent by each département. Influenced by Condorcet, the Girondin constitution of 24 June 1793 provided a more liberal standard, recalling the failed 1789 proposal: Article 28 of its Declaration of Rights stated that "un peuple a toujours le droit de revoir, de réformer et de changer sa Constitution. Une génération ne peut assujettir à ses lois les générations futures." Revisionary provisions in later constitutions became ever more complex and then disappeared entirely, understandably so given the need for stability in the aftermath of Thermidor. For the 1791 and 1793 constitutions, see Jacques Godechot, ed., *Les Constitutions de la France depuis 1789* (Paris, 1979), 66–67, 82–83, and, for later provisions, index, s.v. "Révision des constitutions." For Condorcet's role in framing the 1793 document, see Elisabeth Badinter and Robert Badinter, *Condorcet (1743–1794): Un intellectuel en politique* (Paris, 1988), 533–44, and Keith Michael Baker, *Condorcet: From Natural Philosophy to Social Mathematics* (Chicago, 1975), 320–29. Franck Alengry pays special attention to Condorcet's insistence on a generationally based right of revision in *Condorcet: Guide de la Révolution française, théoricien du droit constitutionnel, et precurseur de la science sociale* (Paris, 1904), 589–606. On the search for order after Thermidor, see Bronislaw Baczko, *Comment sortir de la Terreur: Thermidor et la Révolution* (Paris, 1989), which explicitly contrasts (343 and n. 1) the cumbersome revisionary machinery of the 1795 constitution with Condorcet's generational principle.

95. TJ to Madison, 28 Aug. 1789, and cf. TJ to Jay, 27 Aug. 1789, *Boyd*, 15:364, 358. Jefferson may have muted his disappointment to avoid giving the impression of playing an active role; this would be consistent with his discretion in 1789 letters to American correspondents. In contrast, on 30 August 1789, Condorcet protested the omission in a letter to Mathieu de Montmorency. Condorcet, *Lettres à Montmorency*, in O'Connor and Arago, eds., *Oeuvres*, 9:367–68, 371–72. His second letter to Montmorency, interestingly dated 6 September 1789, returns to this theme. Ibid., 389–90.

96. On developments after 26 August, see Keith Michael Baker, "Fixing the French Constitution," in *Inventing the French Revolution: Essays on French Political Culture in the Eighteenth Century* (Cambridge, 1990), 271–305.

97. TJ, Autobiography, 1821, *LofA*, 95–96. His memory of the episode was not exact; for details, see Gottschalk and Maddox, *Lafayette*, 227–29

98. *Rapport de M. le comte Lally-Tollendal* (31 Aug. 1789), in *Procès Verbal de l'Assemblée Nationale* 5 (27 Aug–18 Sept. 1789), 4:4–5 (my translation). The Procès Verbal lacks continuous pagination; organized chronologically, its reports can be found under the appropriate date.

99. *Rapport de M. Mounier* (31 Aug. 1789), in ibid., 2.

100. *Rapport fait au comité des droits féodaux . . . par M. Merlin* (4 Sept. 1789), in ibid., esp. 24–28.

101. *Mémoire envoyée à l'Assemblée Nationale par M. Necker, Directeur-Général des Finances* (27 Aug. 1789), in ibid., 9: The National Assembly, Necker says, "a mis les Créanciers de l'État sous la sauve-grade de l'honneur et de la loyauté françoise." Necker's language may have influenced Jefferson's description of the king's debts as ones "of honor."

102. Boyd, "Earth Belongs to the Living," *Boyd*, 15:384n.1; TJ to John Trumbull, 9 Sept. 1789, ibid., 407.

103. Gem, Proposition [ca. 1–6 Sept. 1789], ibid., 391–92. For the dating, see Boyd, "Earth Belongs to the Living," ibid., 391–92.

104. TJ to Madison, 6 Sept. 1789, ibid., 392.

105. Ibid.

106. For the major literature on the principle, see note 2.

107. Merrill D. Peterson, *Thomas Jefferson and the New Nation: A Biography* (New York, 1970), 383, suggests Locke and Smith; Lynd, *Intellectual Origins*, 78–81, urges Locke, Blackstone, Turgot, Condorcet, and Priestley; Boyd focuses on Gem in "Earth Belongs to the Living," *Boyd*, 15:384–91, and refers readers to Koch; Koch, *Jefferson and Madison*, 65, 76, 78, mentions Locke and Montesquieu; Bühler, *Verfassungsrevision*, 31–33, cites Condorcet and is followed by Wills, *Inventing America*, 132, both seeing Jefferson's mathematical emphasis as in keeping with the spirit of Condorcet; Alfred O. Aldridge, *Thomas Paine's American Ideology* (Newark, Del., 1984), 265, and see also 237–39, insists that Jefferson took his idea from Paine, while David Freeman Hawke, *Paine* (New York, 1974), 178, faults Jefferson for not acknowledging Paine. On Paine and Condorcet, see Appendix A.

108. Lynd, *Intellectual Origins*, 79.

109. TJ, "Services to My Country" [ca. 1800], *Ford*, 9:164, and for similar statements, see Autobiography, 1821, *LofA*, 32–33, and "Thoughts on Lotteries," Feb. 1826, *Ford*, 12:447. The Supreme Court seems to agree with Jefferson's view of his achievements; in *Hawaii Housing Authority* v. *Midkiff*, 426 U.S. 229, 241–42 (1984), Justice O'Connor noted early state efforts "to reduce the perceived social and economic evils of a landed oligopoly traceable to their monarchs."

110. Jefferson had, of course, made strong claims for allodial landholding on the Saxon model in *A Summary View of the Rights of British America* (1774), *Boyd*, 1:121–22, 132–33. On his Anglo-Saxonism, see H. Trevor Colbourn, *The Lamp of Experience: Whig History and the Intellectual Origins of the American Revolution* (Chapel Hill, N.C., 1965), 168–71, and Peterson, *Jefferson and the New Nation*, 56–61, 180–82, 183–84. For these themes in eighteenth-century Britain, see Christopher Hill, "The Norman Yoke" (1954), in *Puritanism and Revolution: Studies in the Interpretation of the English Revolution* (New York, 1964), 50–122; S.L. Kliger, *The Goths in England* . . . (Cambridge, Mass., 1952), passim; J.G.A. Pocock, *The Ancient Constitution and the Feudal Law: A Study of English Historical Thought in the Seventeenth Century*, 2d ed. (Cambridge, 1987), 243–45; and R.J. Smith, *The Gothic Bequest: Medieval Institutions in British Thought, 1688–1864* (Cambridge, 1987), esp. chap. 4. For an English enthusiast who became Jefferson's correspondent, see John W. Osborne, *John Cartwright* (Cambridge, 1972). On the Great Seal, see John Adams to Abigail Adams, 14 July 1776, in L.H. Butterfield, ed., *Adams Family Correspondence* (Cambridge, Mass., 1963), 2:96–97. Adams's preference was strictly classical– the Choice of Hercules. Ibid.

111. TJ to Edmund Pendleton, 13 Aug. 1776, *Boyd*, 1:492. The letter was written from Philadelphia the day before Adams noted Jefferson's design for the Great Seal.

112. For the reforms, see *Malone*, 1:247–57. The statute of descent–included in the revisal of Virginia law that Jefferson helped to prepare–was not adopted until 1785 and took effect only on 1 January 1787. TJ, "A Bill directing the Course of Descents," *Boyd*, 2:391–93 (text), 393n (enactment). The fact that Jefferson did not wait for the revisal to press ahead with the abolition of entail is worthy of note.

113. C. Ray Keim, "Primogeniture and Entail in Colonial Virginia," *WMQ* 25 (1968): 545–86; Robert E. Brown and B. Katharine Brown, *Virginia, 1705–1786: Democracy or Aristocracy?* (East Lansing, Mich., 1964), 80–95; Orth, "After the Revolution." The legislative route involved some difficulty: Acts breaking entails had to go to Westminster for confirmation, with the usual delays and costs. But independence removed that objection. Jefferson clearly had more in mind than making life easy for the great landowners of Virginia. For inheritance practice in his own county, Albemarle, see Daniel Blake Smith, *Inside the Great House: Planter Family Life in Eighteenth-Century Chesapeake Society* (Ithaca, N.Y., 1980), chap. 6, "Providing for the Living: Inheritance and the Family." Using data for the period 1750 to 1799, Smith shows that fathers tended "to provide for all sons as equally as possible" in their wills; daughters typically received marriage portions and shares of the personal rather than the real estate. Ibid., 246–47.

114. For his views, see, for example, TJ to J. Adams, 28 Oct. 1813, *Cappon*, 2:389; TJ, "Services to My Country," *Ford*, 9:164; Autobiography, 1821, *LofA*, 32–33; and "Thoughts on Lotteries," *Ford*, 12:447.

115. For his reaction to the Wayles entail, see *Malone*, 1:253, 442, and Peterson, *Jefferson and the New Nation*, 113.

116. William Blackstone, *Commentaries on the Laws of England* (1766) (Chicago, 1979), 2:358–61, quotations on 360, 361. Was Blackstone thinking of the Virginia practice?

117. The preamble to the statute, adopted on 1 November 1776, is in *Boyd*, 1:560. It horrified Landon Carter; for some of his comments (he took exception to the point about youths), see Carter, undated diary entry 1776, in Jack P. Greene, ed., *The Diary of Colonel Landon Carter of Sabine Hall, 1752–1778*, 2 vols. (Charlottesville, Va., 1965), 2:1068–69, and Carter to Washington, 31 Oct. 1776 (denouncing Jefferson by name), quoted in

Malone, 1:255. In the 1770s and 1780s, Jefferson was preoccupied with the issue of disobedient youth; in *Notes on the State of Virginia*, 162, he argued that slavery added to the problem by early accustoming members of the master class to dominate others, thus making them less willing to accept restraints on their own behavior. For the political and cultural implications of establishing order in a context that made paternal authority suspect, see Jay Fliegelman, *Prodigals and Pilgrims: The American Revolution Against Patriarchal Authority, 1750–1800* (Cambridge, 1982), and Melvin Yazawa, *From Colonies to Commonwealth: Familial Ideology and the Beginnings of the American Republic* (Baltimore, 1985). For parallels between Jefferson's criticism of entail and those of contemporaries, see Blackstone, *Commentaries*, 2:116; Adam Smith, *An Inquiry into the Nature and Causes of the Wealth of Nations* (1776), ed. R.H. Campbell and A.S. Skinner, 2 vols. (Oxford, 1976), 1:382, 384–85; and Lord Kames, [Henry Hume], "Property," in *Historical Law-Tracts* (1758), 4th ed. (Edinburgh, 1817), 152–56.

118. Cf. Isaac Kramnick on Jefferson's contemporaries among the English reformers: "To re-establish the Saxon constitution, then, was seen as recapturing inalienable rights of free men" ("Republican Revisionism Revisited," *AHR* 87 [1982]: 649). As James Tully notes in "Placing the 'Two Treatises,' " in Nicholas Phillipson and Quentin Skinner, eds., *Political Discourse in Early Modern Britain* (Cambridge, 1993), 256–57, "natural law and ancient constitutional arguments were used interchangeably by writers such as James Tyrell and Algernon Sidney," and he points to the ease with which Jefferson functioned in exactly the same way (271).

119. Boyd, "Earth Belongs to the Living," *Boyd*, 15:384.

120. By the time Jefferson arrived in Paris on 6 August 1784, the last great figures of the French Enlightenment were dead: Voltaire and Rousseau in 1778, Turgot in 1781, d'Alembert in 1783, Diderot on 31 July 1784. The "center of European intellectual ferment" in the 1780s would not have been Paris, where the ferment was political, but Königsberg or Weimar. "By the mid-1780s, Kant, in distant Königsberg, was the only indisputable literary and intellectual giant left in Europe; those who came closest to him were fellow Germans like Herder, Goethe, and Schiller" (William Doyle, *The Old European Order, 1660–1800*, 2d ed. [Oxford, 1992], 215). Nor is there much evidence to support Boyd's picture of Jefferson as an active participant in Parisian intellectual circles—though in 1788 and 1789, as we have seen, he played an important role in political ones.

121. For suggestions of Smith's paternity, see Peterson, *Jefferson and the New Nation*, 383. For the quoted language, see Smith, *Wealth of Nations*, 1:384.

122. When did Jefferson first read *The Wealth of Nations*? The copy in his "second" library was the 1784 London edition (*Sowerby*, 3, no. 3546), but we do not know when he acquired it, nor does its presence rule out earlier acquaintance. It would have been hard to come by in America before the peace of 1783–though Robert Morris had a copy in 1781, when he lent it to Edmund Randolph. Morris, Diary, 27 Dec. 1781, in E. James Ferguson, ed., *The Papers of Robert Morris, 1781–1784* (Pittsburgh, 1977), 3:447. In 1790, Jefferson recommended it to his son-in-law: "In political economy I think Smith's wealth of nations the best book extant" (TJ to Thomas Mann Randolph, Jr., 30 May 1790, *Boyd*, 16:449). This letter is his first known mention of Smith.

123. Adam Smith, *Lectures on Jurisprudence*, ed. R.L. Meek et al. (Oxford, 1978), 69–70. For similar points in the lectures of Smith's successor at Glasgow, see Thomas Reid, *Practical Ethics: Being Lectures and Papers on Natural Religion, Self-Government, Natural Jurisprudence, and the Law of Nations*, ed. Knud Haakonssen (Princeton, N.J., 1990), 150–53, 207, 213–14, 333 n.46, 334.

124. Smith, *Lectures on Jurisprudence*, 468.

125. For Gem's biography, see Boyd, "Earth Belongs to the Living," *Boyd*, 15:384–87. For the Gem–Smith encounter, see Adam Smith to Lady Frances Scott, 15 Oct., 19 Oct. 1766, in Ernest Campbell Mossner and Ian Simpson Ross, eds., *The Correspondence of Adam Smith*, rev. ed. (Oxford, 1987), 119–21; for the history of Smith's students' notes, see "Introduction," in Smith, *Lectures on Jurisprudence*, 5–13. A further possible connection is by way of Smith's pupil and friend Dugald Stewart, who spent the summer of 1789 in Paris and was often in Jefferson's company. *Malone*, 2:215, 266; TJ to J. Adams, 14 Mar. 1820, *Cappon*, 2:561. For Stewart's career as Smith's successor at the head of the Scottish school of political economy, see Biancamaria Fontana, *Rethinking the Politics of Commercial Society: The Edinburgh Review, 1802–1832* (Cambridge, 1985). But did Jefferson take up with Stewart the threads of his conversations with Lafayette and Gem? We do not know.

126. Smith, *Lectures on Jurisprudence*, 69 nn. 66–67, 70 (information supplied by the editors). Both works were in Smith's library. Ibid., 592, 593. But if Kames actively opposed entail, Dalrymple was only descriptive, providing a straightforward account of the development of feudal institutions in England and Scotland. Insofar as he addressed the policy implications of entails in the *Essay*, it was to note that they were not as bad as critics claimed. John Dalrymple, *An Essay Towards a General History of Feudal Property in Great Britain*, 3rd ed. (London, 1758), 192–95. Like Smith, Jefferson read Dalrymple by extracting information and putting it in an already established "anti-feudal" framework. It is not clear whether he knew Dalrymple's *Considerations upon the Policy of Entails*, 2d ed. (Edinburgh, 1765), in which Dalrymple expands themes briefly touched on in the *Essay* into 115 pages, showing that ending entails would lower the price of land in Scotland and so ruin the economy. Its argument would not have persuaded Jefferson.

127. *The Commonplace Book of Thomas Jefferson: A Repertory of His Ideas on Government*, ed. Gilbert Chinard (Baltimore, 1926), 93–135, esp. 107–10 (Kames), 145–49 (Dalrymple). On the dating of the *Commonplace Book* extracts, see Douglas L. Wilson, "Thomas Jefferson's Early Notebooks," *WMQ* 42 (1985): 433–52, esp. 446. Jefferson's first library (destroyed in the 1770 Shadwell fire) included Kames's *Historical Law-Tracts* and Dalrymple's *Essay*; he acquired new copies of both by 1783. Colbourn, *Lamp of Experience*, 217–18. For additional information, see *Sowerby*, 2, No. 2005 (Dalrymple), No. 2008 (Kames).

128. Gilbert Chinard, *Thomas Jefferson, the Apostle of Americanism* (Boston, 1929), 30.

129. On Scottish entails, see David Burgess, *Perpetuities in Scots Law* (Edinburgh, 1979); R.H. Campbell, "Continuity and Change: The Perpetuation of the Landed Interest," in T. M. Devine, ed., *Conflict and Stability in Scottish Society, 1700–1850* (Edinburgh, 1990), 122–35; David Lieberman, *The Province of Legislation Determined: Legal Theory in Eighteenth-Century Britain* (Cambridge, 1989), 156–58; Nicholas T. Phillipson, "Lawyers, Landowners, and the Civic Leadership of Post-Union Scotland: An Essay on the Social Role of the Faculty of Advocates 1661–1830 in 18th-Century Scottish Society," *Juridical Review*, n.s., 21 (1976): 97–126; Ian Simpson Ross, *Lord Kames and the Scotland of His Day* (Oxford, 1972), 210–12, 225–26, 343, 364; and A.W.B. Simpson, "Entails and Perpetuities," *Juridical Review*, n.s., 24 (1979): 1–20. The subject was treated in fiction; John Galt's *The Entail; Or, The Lairds of Grippy* (1822), ed. Ian A. Gordon (Oxford, 1970), is the story of a Glasgow merchant whose efforts to set up a landed dynasty end in disaster.

130. For the distinction between entail and strict settlement; see Simpson, "Entails and Perpetuities." For the strict settlement itself, see A. W. B. Simpson, *An Introduction*

to the History of the Land Law (Oxford, 1961), 218–24. J.P. Cooper offers a broader perspective in "Patterns of Inheritance and Settlement by Great Landowners from the Fifteenth to the Eighteenth Centuries," in Jack Goody et al., eds., *Family and Inheritance: Rural Society in Western Europe, 1200–1800* (Cambridge, 1976), 192–327; John Cannon reviews the debate on the strict settlement's economic effects in *Aristocratic Century: The Peerage of Eighteenth-Century England* (Cambridge, 1984), 132–37.

131. On revolutionary changes in the law of inheritance in the direction of greater equality, see, for example, Katz, "Republicanism and the Law of Inheritance"; Orth, "After the Revolution"; Carole Shammas et al., *Inheritance in America from Colonial Times to the Present* (New Brunswick, N.J., 1987), 63–79; and Gordon S. Wood, *The Radicalism of the American Revolution* (New York, 1992), 182–83. As several of these studies note, the claims made at the time for these changes seem out of all proportion to the results. In "The American Revolutionaries, the Political Economy of Aristocracy, and the American Concept of the Distribution of Wealth, 1765–1900," *AHR* 98 (1993): 1090, 1093–95, James L. Huston argues, correctly, that hostility to entail was fundamental to republican values in the new nation; Jack P. Greene notes contemporaries' emphasis on the free circulation of property as a barrier to aristocracy in America in *The Intellectual Construction of America: Exceptionalism and Identity from 1492 to 1800* (Chapel Hill, N.C., 1993), 179.

132. "A Citizen of America" [Noah Webster], *An Examination into the Leading Principles of the Federal Constitution* . . . (1787), in Bernard Bailyn, ed., *The Debate on the Constitution*, 2 vols. (New York, 1993), 1:158–59, 157–58. Writing as "America" in the New York *Daily Advertiser* on 31 December 1787, Webster again argued that true republican liberty and entails were incompatible. *DHRC*, 15:195–96. For the view that equal division of property promoted republicanism, see also Oliver Ellsworth writing as "Landholder," 6, and "The Republican: To the People," *Connecticut Courant* (Hartford), 10 Dec. 1787, 7 Jan. 1788, ibid., 14:402; 3:529. For Pickering, see his letter to Charles Tillinghast, 24 Dec. 1787, ibid., 14:194.

133. Blackstone, *Commentaries*, 2:3; John Locke, *Second Treatise*, in *Two Treatises of Government*, ed. Peter Laslett (Cambridge, 1988), 286, where Locke invokes Psalm 115:16. His views on property are explored in James Tully, *A Discourse on Property: John Locke and His Adversaries* (Cambridge, 1980).

134. Blackstone, *Commentaries*, 2:3, 10, 11, 12. Blackstone's view remained standard in American law; see *Magoun* v. *Illinois Trust & Savings Bank*, 170 U.S. 283, 287–88 (1898), and *Knowlton* v. *Moore*, 178 U.S. 41, 55–58 (1900), and the discussion of those cases in Robert Stanley, *Dimensions of Law in the Service of Order: Origins of the Federal Income Tax, 1861–1913* (New York, 1993). Jefferson would later comment that "it is agreed by those who have seriously considered the subject, that no individual has, of natural right, a separate property in an acre of land, for instance. By an universal law, indeed, whatever, whether fixed or moveable, belongs to all men equally and in common, is the property for the moment of him who occupies it; but when he relinquishes the occupation, the property goes with it. Stable ownership is the gift of social law, and is given late in the progress of society" (TJ to McPherson, 13 Aug. 1813, *LofA*, 1291).

135. Lord Kames, [Henry Hume], *Essays upon Several Subjects Concerning British Antiquities* . . . , 3d ed. (Edinburgh, 1763), 130 n.*, 144; for a similar statement, see Kames, "Property," in *Historical Law-Tracts*, 126.

136. Janet Coleman, "Property and Poverty," in J. H. Burns, ed., *The Cambridge History of Medieval Political Thought, c. 350–c. 1450* (Cambridge, 1988), 617–25, 643–46.

137. TJ to Madison, 28 Oct. 1785, *Boyd*, 8:682. Note that in this letter, Jefferson also endorsed "the descent of property of every kind . . . to all the children, or to all the brothers and sisters, or other relations in equal degree" as a way of avoiding too great a concentration of property in the hands of a few.

138. See Thomas A. Horne, *Property Rights and Poverty: Political Argument in Britain, 1605–1834* (Chapel Hill, N.C., 1990), for a survey of this theme in seventeenth- and eighteenth-century Britain; I have drawn on it extensively. On Sidney, see Alan Craig Houston, *Algernon Sidney and the Republican Heritage in England and America* (Princeton, N.J., 1991), 105–7. Spence and Ogilvie are reprinted in M. Beer, ed., *The Pioneers of Land Reform: Thomas Spence, William Ogilvie, Thomas Paine* (New York, 1920). For Paley and Cambridge, see John Gascoigne, *Cambridge in the Age of the Enlightenment: Science, Religion, and Politics from the Restoration to the French Revolution* (Cambridge, 1989), 241–44.

139. Perhaps the best examples of this are TJ to Madison, 28 Oct. 1785; TJ to George Wythe, 13 Aug. 1786; TJ to George Washington, 14 Nov. 1786, *Boyd*, 8:681–82; 10:244–45, 532–33. For his reaction to Europe generally, see *Malone*, 2:18–19, 112–30.

140. Turgot, "Fondations," *Encyclopédie*, 14:892–97. Owen Chadwick chronicles the travails of the eighteenth-century church at the hands of reformers in Austria, Italy, and Spain in *The Popes and European Revolution* (Oxford, 1981), 246–52, 391–94; the best study in English of the secularization of Church property in a single country is Richard Herr, *Rural Change and Royal Finances in Spain at the End of the Old Regime* (Berkeley, 1989); and for a skeptical look at *Josephinismus*, see P. G. M. Dickson, "Joseph II's Reshaping of the Austrian Church," *Historical Journal* 36 (1993): 89–114, esp. 110–12, contrasting Joseph's reforms with those of the French Revolution and finding the former less thorough-going than the latter, even between 1789 and 1791.

141. Turgot, "Fondations," *Encyclopédie*, 14:897 (my translations). Jefferson owned the *Encyclopédie* and was probably familiar with this essay, one of its most celebrated articles. *Sowerby*, 5, No. 4890.

142. See, for example, "Féodal," in *Encyclopédie méthodique: Finances* (Paris, 1784), 2:110–17. For Jefferson's acquisition of the two encyclopedias, see *Sowerby*, 5, No. 4889 (*Méthodique*), No. 4890 (*Encyclopédie*). Robert Darnton mentions Jefferson's key role in the diffusion of the *Méthodique* in the United States in *The Business of Enlightenment: A Publishing History of the Encyclopédie, 1775–1800* (Cambridge, Mass., 1979), 318–19. For prerevolutionary criticism of French inheritance law, see Gary Kates, *The Cercle Social, the Girondins, and the French Revolution* (Princeton, N.J., 1985), 112, 114–15. For changes under the Revolution and Napoleon, see James F. Traer, *Marriage and the Family in Eighteenth-Century France* (Ithaca, N.Y., 1980), esp. Chaps. 5, 6, and Lynn Hunt, *The Family Romance of the French Revolution* (Berkeley, 1992), 40–41, 65–66, 161–63; a more detailed account is André Dejace, *Les Règles de la dévolution successorale sous la Révolution, 1789–1794* (Brussels, 1957). The complex and often contradictory French initiatives in these matters are in contrast to the relative simplicity of Jefferson's scheme, for which see *Boyd*, 2:391–93.

143. When the legislature, at Madison's prompting, took up the revised code in 1785, it considered but did not adopt Jefferson's ban on mortmain. *Boyd*, 2:414 (text of bill), 414n (inaction). Jefferson was probably aware that in 1743 the Virginia General Court had held that the British Mortmain Act of 1736 did not apply in Virginia, and his bill would have filled that gap. Howard S. Miller, *The Legal Foundations of American Philanthropy, 1776–1844* (Madison, Wis., 1961), 7. On the

British statute, heavily influenced by Whig anticlerical sentiments Jefferson shared, see Gareth Jones, *History of the Law of Charity, 1532–1827* (Cambridge, 1969), 109–19, and for its effects on particular institutions, see W. R. Ward, *Georgian Oxford: University Politics in the Eighteenth Century* (Oxford, 1958), 157–60, and G.F.A. Best, *Temporal Pillars: Queen Anne's Bounty, the Ecclesiastical Commissioners, and the Church of England* (Cambridge, 1964), 104–10. Jefferson's opposition to mortmain seems to have struck a responsive chord in Virginia, where since 1851 the state constitution has prohibited the incorporation of religious bodies. See A.E. Dick Howard, *Commentaries on the Constitution of Virginia*, 2 vols. (Charlottesville, Va., 1974), 1:545–47. Howard believes this is unconstitutional under the Fourteenth Amendment. For Jefferson's plans for William and Mary, see his reform bill, *Boyd*, 2:535–43; TJ, *Notes on the State of Virginia*, 150–51; and Hellenbrand, *Unfinished Revolution*, 85–94.

144. For his opposition to the Bank of the United States because its charter would violate the policy against mortmain, see Chapter 5, text at note 34. Pauline Maier, "The Revolutionary Origins of the American Corporation," *WMQ* 50 (1993): 69–71, shows that his fears were widely shared; for contemporary legal opinion, see James Kent, *Commentaries on American Law* (New York, 1827), 2:227–32. In later years, Madison condemned "Perpetual monopolies" in the form of "Corporations" and "Ecclesiastical Endowments" ("Madison's 'Detached Memoranda,' " ed. Elizabeth Fleet, *WMQ* 3 [1946]: 552, 554, 556–58).

145. TJ to Washington, 16 Apr. 1784; TJ, "Answers to Démeunier's Queries," 22 June 1786, *Boyd*, 7:105–8; 10:48–52; TJ to Madison, 28 Dec. 1794; *PJM*, 15:427. *Malone*, 2:107–8, 155–56, summarizes Jefferson's efforts against the Cincinnati.

146. On Mercier's popularity, see Robert Darnton, "The Forbidden Books of Prerevolutionary France," in Colin Lucas, ed., *Rewriting the French Revolution: The Andrew Browning Lectures, 1989* (Oxford, 1991), 14–15, 17, 24. Jefferson apparently did not meet Mercier while in Paris. For their known correspondence, see Mercier to TJ, 30 Aug. 1802; TJ to Mercier, 6 Feb. 1803, Jefferson Papers, LC; in this purely formal exchange, Mercier wrote in his capacity as a member of the Institut. Norman Hampson discusses Mercier's politics, unfortunately shedding no light on the problem at hand, in *Will and Circumstance: Montesquieu, Rousseau, and the French Revolution* (London, 1983), 65–83. Other studies of Mercier have even less to say about his political journalism in the 1780s.

147. Mercier, "Génération nouvelle," in *Tableau des empires, ou notions sur les gouvernements*, 4 vols. (Amsterdam, 1788), 3:63: "& par l'experience des siècles, que quatre-vingt-dix ans composent trois ages d'homme, nous devons en conclure, que tous les trente ans il devroit y avoir une assemblée générale pour établir une refonte dans les grandes sociétés." Jefferson apparently did not own the *Tableau des empires*, though he or others in his Paris circle could easily have seen it. For works by Mercier that Jefferson did own (predictably, they include the *Tableau de Paris* and the famous utopian novel *Mémoires de l'an 2440*), see *Sowerby*, 1, No. 173; 2:1351, No. 1352; 4, No. 3890, No. 4593.

148. Mercier, "Emprunts d'un Souverain," in *Tableau des empires*, 6:109 ("scourge"), 105: "Les emprunts, après avoir donné la fièvre des combats à la génération présente, alienent encore la bonheur de la posterité. Ils vont consummer la ruine de cette malheureuse race qui n'est pas encore née. . . . [N]ous leur ['nos neveux'] transmettons un héritage grevé de la manière la plus cruelle. Ce poids de dettes & de misère va donc retomber sur cette race qui n'existe pas encore, & anéantir les biens que la Nature lui avoit preparés." Both this essay and "Génération nouvelle" were reprinted without significant changes in Mercier's *Fragmens de politique et d'histoire*, 3

vols. (Paris, 1792), 3:30–37 ("Génération nouvelle"), 120–26 ("Emprunts"). The essays reprinted in *Fragmens* also appeared in English translation: *Fragments of Politics & History*, 2 vols. (London, 1795), 2:47–51 ("The Loans of a Sovereign"), 197–203 ("The New Generation").

149. "Crédit," in *Encyclopédie méthodique: Finances*, 1:435–36 (my translation). For other eighteenth-century discussion of the debt as a burden on future generations, see Chapter 3.

150. For Condorcet, who came close to doing this, see Appendix A.

151. For Jefferson's inability to read German, see TJ to Dr. Benjamin Smith Barton, 10 Oct. 1810, quoted in *Sowerby*, 1, No. 443. Having received from its author, J.S. Vater, a copy of *Untersuchungen über Amerika's Bevölkerung* (Halle, 1810), Jefferson told Barton that "not understanding a word of German, the book is lost on me." For an instance of the confusion this caused, see TJ to J. Adams, 24 Jan. 1814, *Cappon*, 2:421. We are so used to thinking of Jefferson as a linguistic polymath that we may forget that he did not read the language of the major developments in European intellectual life after 1780. In this, as in other ways, he remained firmly fixed in the mid-eighteenth century, largely unaware of the intellectual changes transforming Europe and setting the stage for the century to come.

152. Immanuel Kant, "Beantwortung der Frage: Was ist Aufklärung?" (1784), in *Ausgewählte kleine Schriften* (Hamburg, 1965), 5–6, translation in "An Answer to the Question: What Is Enlightenment?" in Kant, *Political Writings*, ed. Hans Reiss, trans. H. B. Nesbit (Cambridge, 1991), 57. On the significance of Kant's project for free discussion and publicity, see Jürgen Habermas, *Strukturwandel der Öffentlichkeit* (Darmstadt, 1962), 127–43.

153. On the subscription controversy, see Gascoigne, *Cambridge*, 130–34, 190–202, quotation on 192.

154. R. R. Palmer, *The Age of the Democratic Revolution: A Political History of Europe and America, 1760–1800*, 2 vols. (Princeton, N.J., 1959–1964), is the classic overview of political change in the second half of the century; in *The End of the Old Regime in Europe*, trans. R. Burr Litchfield, 3 vols. (Princeton, N.J., 1989–1991), Franco Venturi draws on Italian literary and journalistic sources to provide an extended commentary on these events and, at the same time, illustrates the breadth of interests of the literate public then in formation.

155. On constitutional changes before the meeting of the Estates General, see Jean Egret, *The French Prerevolution, 1787–1788*, trans. Wesley D. Camp (Chicago, 1971); Jeffrey Merrick describes the significance of religious toleration in *The Desacralization of the French Monarchy in the Eighteenth Century* (Baton Rouge, La., 1990), 135–64. For his expectation that constitutional change would come relatively easily, see TJ to Washington, 4 Dec. 1788; TJ to Richard Price, 8 Jan. 1789, *Boyd*, 14:329–30, 420–23.

156. Locke, *Second Treatise*, in *Two Treatises*, ed. Laslett, 346.

157. Algernon Sidney, *Discourses Concerning Government*, ed. Thomas G. West (Indianapolis, 1990), 357–58. For the rejection of the Filmerian argument, see Houston, *Sidney*, 140–45.

158. Kames, *Essays Concerning British Antiquities*, 197.

159. Hume, "Of the Original Contract," 476, 643 (addition in 1777 edition). Hume died on 25 August 1776; this passage, which did not appear in earlier editions, including the preceding one of 1770, may have been prompted by the American Revolution, though the Declaration probably came too late to influence Hume. He may also have been responding to Rousseau's *Contrat social* (1762). Note that there

was a well-established conservative tradition in eighteenth-century Germany hostile to social-contract notions and fully prepared to receive Burke's doctrines in 1790. See Klaus Epstein, *The Genesis of German Conservatism* (Princeton, N.J., 1966), and Jonathan B. Knudsen, *Justus Möser and the German Enlightenment* (Cambridge, 1986).

160. James Otis, *The Rights of the British Colonies Asserted and Proved* (1764), in Bernard Bailyn, ed., *Pamphlets of the American Revolution, 1750–1776* (Cambridge, Mass., 1965), 1:420–21. Modern readers may find it ironic that his list of objections to contract theory included the following: "Are not women born as free as men? Would it not be infamous to assert that the ladies are all slaves by nature?" (420). Otis was the elder brother of Mercy Otis Warren, who may have taken these lines more literally than he intended.

161. Adam Ferguson, *Principles of Moral and Political Science; Being Chiefly a Retrospect of Lectures Delivered in the College of Edinburgh*, 2 vols. (Edinburgh, 1792), 2:233–35. The date of publication makes it surprising that he was willing to put this (by then) somewhat daring set of ideas before a wider audience; already, Dugald Stewart was being forced to tone down his teaching and remove favorable references to France from his work. On this, see Emma Rothschild, "Adam Smith and Conservative Economics," *Economic History Review*, 2nd ser., 45 (1992): 74–96.

162. [Noah Webster], "Giles Hickory," 1, 3, in Bailyn, ed., *Debate on the Constitution*, 1:671; 2:307. See Wood's discussion of the essays ("an extraordinary series of articles"), *Creation of the American Republic*, 376–82, quotation on 376. In November 1790, Webster sent Jefferson his *Collection of Essays and Fugitive Pieces* . . . (Boston, 1790), which reprinted "Giles Hickory." His cover letter drew the secretary of state's attention to the passages on perpetual constitutions. This led to a brief exchange in which Jefferson tried to explain himself to Webster, but Webster persisted in thinking he had caught Jefferson in a solecism. In fact, Webster's views were closer to Jefferson's than the New Englander realized; his conclusion that all rights other than those that "*rest wholly on the moral law*" may "vary with circumstances" is one Jefferson would have endorsed. Webster to TJ, 14 Oct. 1790; TJ to Webster, 4 Dec. 1790; Webster to TJ, 12 Dec. 1790, *Boyd*, 17:598–99; 18:132–33, 153–54, quotation on 154, and see Boyd's note, ibid., 133–34. For Jefferson's copy of this work, see *Sowerby*, 5, No. 4928.

163. For the argument that the Philadelphia Convention was "in direct violation" of the Articles, in which the states "had solemnly engaged that the confederation now subsisting should be inviolably preserved by each of them, and the union thereby formed, should be perpetual, unless the same should be altered by mutual consent," see "The Address and Reasons of Dissent of the Minority of the Convention of the State of Pennsylvania to their Constituents," 18 Dec. 1787, *DHRC*, 15:34. For the minority's textual basis, see Section XIII of the Articles of Confederation, ibid., 1:93; the claim is correct.

164. Paine, *Dissertations on Government*, 186. He also thought that peace treaties should have limited duration; it would reflect reality, and periodic renegotiation would correct injustices and inconveniences. Ibid., 187.

165. Jefferson may have been familiar with Paine's work on the bank. For his copy, see *Sowerby*, 3, No. 3035. For the question of priority, see Appendix A.

166. TJ to Henry Lee, Jr., 8 May 1825, *Ford*, 12:409.

167. Smith, *Lectures on Jurisprudence*, 69–70.

168. TJ to Madison, 6 Sept. 1789, *Boyd*, 15:392. In a comment also applicable to the present case, Otto Vossler remarks of Jefferson's role in the creation of Lafayette's

11 July 1789 proposal that he was not so modest ("so bescheiden war er gewiss nicht") that he would not have claimed credit if it was due ("Studien zur Erklärung der Menschenrechte," *Historische Zeitschrift* 142 [1930]: 544). Vossler probably underestimates Jefferson's part in the 11 July proposal.

169. Neither Paine nor Condorcet—for whose versions of the rights of generations see Paine, *Dissertations on Government* and *Rights of Man*, and Condorcet, *Déclaration des droits, Lettres à M. le comte de Montmorency*, and *Sur la necessité de faire ratifier la Constitution*—was trained in the common law; neither would have conceived the matter in these terms, which came naturally to Jefferson.

170. In later versions of the letter, Jefferson continued to employ the language of property law that I suggest he had in mind. As he put it to John Wayles Eppes on 24 June 1813, "The case may be likened to the ordinary one of a tenant for life, who may hypothecate the land for his debts, during the continuance of his usufruct; but at his death, the reversioner (who is also for life only) receives it exonerated from all burthen" (*Ford*, 11:298).

171. On usufruct as a doctrine of Roman and civil law, see Chambers, *Course of Lectures on the English Law*. For the impact of Roman law notions on Jefferson and his Virginia contemporaries, especially George Wythe, see W. Hamilton Bryson, "The Use of Roman Law in Virginia Courts," *American Journal of Legal History* 28 (1984): 135–46. Bryson notes that Jefferson's statute of descents "was clearly based on Roman law ideas and was so considered by later jurists" (139). Jefferson's mastery of Roman and civil law concepts is evident in his 1810 memoir on the Batture, for which see *L&B*, 18:1–132. How he came to deploy his learning in this fashion is explained in *Malone*, 6:55–73, and George Dargo, *Jefferson's Louisiana: Politics and the Clash of Legal Traditions* (Cambridge, Mass., 1975), 74–101.

172. For his struggles to get the numbers right, see TJ to Gem, 9 Sept. 1789, *Boyd*, 15:398–99. The conventional figure of thirty years was used in 1786 by Paine, *Dissertations on Government*, 186, and in 1788 by Mercier, "Génération nouvelle," in *Tableau des empires*, 3:63; "Génération," in *Encyclopédie*, suggested "trente-trois ans ou environ" (15:890).

173. Searching *The Federalist* with WordCruncher shows that it used "people" 527 times, and "generation" never. On the respective frequency with which "people" and *peuple* appear in *The Federalist* and works by members of the Société de 1789, see Mark Olsen, "Translating a Revolution: American Political Vocabulary in the Discourse of the *Société de 1789*," in William Roosen, ed., *Proceedings of the Annual Meeting of the Western Society for French History* (Flagstaff, Ariz., 1988), 15:154–67, esp. 157–60. For the growing significance of "generation" after the Restoration, see Chapter 6, text at nn. 147, 148.

174. Edmund S. Morgan, *Inventing the People: The Rise of Popular Sovereignty in England and America* (New York, 1988), 82–83, 153–54, 267. On the immortality of the king's political body, see Ernst Kantorowicz, *The King's Two Bodies: A Study in Mediaeval Political Theology* (Princeton, N.J., 1957).

175. Mona Ozouf, "Regeneration," in Furet and Ozouf, eds., *Critical Dictionary*, 781–91.

176. Olson, "Translating a Revolution"; Rolf Reichardt, "Revolutionäre Mentalitäten und Netze politischer Grundbegriffe in Frankreich, 1789–1795," in Reinhart Koselleck and Reichardt, eds., *Die Französische Revolution als Bruch des gesellschaftlichen Bewusstseins* (Munich, 1988), 185–215. *Génération* is not on this list of the Revolution's key words.

177. For Lafayette's drafts, see *Boyd*, 14:439; 15:231.

178. On Martha Wayles Skelton Jefferson's death and its impact on Jefferson, see *Malone*, 1:393–98. Fawn Brodie, *Thomas Jefferson: An Intimate History* (New York, 1974), 245, suggests that Jefferson may also have recalled that he had met his wife nineteen years before and hence that the nineteen-year term for a generation may have had more than simply scientific importance. Any conclusions must remain matters of speculation, but it will not be pressing things too far to suggest that Jefferson was deeply involved on many levels in the contents of the 6 September letter.

179. TJ to Jay, 30 Aug. 1789; James Swan to TJ, 3 Sept. 1789; TJ to Swan, 4 Aug. [Sept.] 1789, *Boyd*, 15:373–74, 381–82, 382–83. The 30 August letter to Jay discusses Necker's proposals of 27 August, for which see text at note 101.

180. For the comments, see TJ to Madison, 28 Aug. 1790, ibid., 364, 367–68.

181. On the work from which Jefferson took the data, Buffon's *Histoire naturelle* . . . —it ultimately reached seventy-one duodecimo volumes and took over half a century (1752–1805) to appear—see *Sowerby*, 1, No. 1024, and *Boyd*, 15:398n.

182. TJ to Madison, 6 Sept. 1789, *Boyd*, 15:393, 394, 395, 396.

Chapter 3

1. [Arthur Young], *Political Essays* . . . (London, 1772), 54.

2. [James Madison], *Political Observations*, 20 Apr. 1795, *PJM*, 15:518. For similar warnings, see Madison's anonymous essay "Political Reflections," *Aurora General Advertiser* (Philadelphia), 23 Feb. 1799, ibid., 17:240–42, David Hume, it will be recalled, had given a rather different explanation of how the many govern the few in "Of the First Principles of Government" (1741), in Eugene F. Miller, ed., *Essays, Moral, Political, and Literary* (Indianapolis, 1985), 32–36.

3. [Madison], *Political Observations*, *PJM*, 15:518.

4. Jean-Jacques Rousseau, *Considérations sur le gouvernement de Pologne*, in Bernard Gagnebin and Marcel Raymond, eds., *Oeuvres complètes* ([Paris], 1964), 3:1005 (my translation). Cf. his *Projet de constitution pour la Corse* of 1769: "Ce mot de finance s'étoit pas plus connu des anciens que ceux de taille et de capitation" (929).

5. Jefferson's 6 September 1789 letter to Madison is discussed at length in Chapter 2.

6. In "Virtue and Commerce in the Eighteenth Century," *Journal of Interdisciplinary History* 3 (1972): 119–34; *The Machiavellian Moment: Florentine Political Thought and the Atlantic Republican Tradition* (Princeton, N.J., 1975), 401–505; and "*The Machiavellian Moment* Revisited: A Study in History and Ideology," *Journal of Modern History* 53 (1981): 49–72, J. G. A. Pocock provides the starting point for any study of the impact of the public debt on the eighteenth-century Anglo-American mind. For a succinct but powerful statement of his position, see his "The Political Limits to Premodern Economics," in John Dunn, ed., *The Economic Limits to Modern Politics* (Cambridge, 1992), 121–41, esp. 131–33. Also essential are Isaac Kramnick, *Bolingbroke and His Circle: The Politics of Nostalgia in the Age of Walpole* (Cambridge, Mass., 1968), 39–38, and, for the less often studied middle decades of the century, Edwin G. Burrows, "Albert Gallatin and the Political Economy of Republicanism, 1761–1800," 2 vols. (Ph.D. diss., Columbia University, 1974), 2:378–85. For the development of the debt itself, as opposed to ideas about it, see P. G. M. Dickson's classic *The Financial Revolution in England, 1688–1756* (London, 1967); John Brewer, *The Sinews of Power: War, Money and the English State, 1688–1783* (New York, 1989), supplements Dickson and carries the story forward to the end of the American Revolution. For an important collection of essays that further deepens our

understanding of the eighteenth-century British military-fiscal state, see Lawrence Stone, ed., *An Imperial State at War: Britain from 1689 to 1815* (London, 1994); the essays in this collection by E. A. Wrigley, "Society and the Economy in the Eighteenth Century," 72–95; Joanna Innes, "The Domestic Face of the Military-Fiscal State," 96–127; and Daniel A. Baugh, "Maritime Strength and Atlantic Commerce," 185–223, are particularly useful. For the wider context, of which the English experience is a special case, see Charles P. Kindleberger, *A Financial History of Western Europe* (London, 1984), 158–76, and Geoffrey Parker, "The Emergence of Modern Finance in Europe, 1500–1700," in Carlo M. Cipolla, ed., *The Fontana Economic History of Europe*, vol. 2, *The Sixteenth and Seventeenth Centuries* (Glasgow, 1974), 527–94.

7. For the presence in Virginia libraries—Washington's, Jefferson's, Madison's, and Patrick Henry's among them—of the major works discussed in the text, see Appendix B.

8. For the argument that the dominant civic humanist mode of political thought, with its fear of debt and standing armies, managed to encompass almost—though not quite—everyone in the eighteenth century, see Pocock, "Virtue and Commerce," 122, 133, and *Machiavellian Moment*, 506–9. The argument for a cacaphony, or at least a multiplicity, of voices can be found in, for example, Isaac Kramnick's essays in *Republicanism and Bourgeois Radicalism: Political Ideology in Late Eighteenth-Century England and America* (Ithaca, N.Y., 1990), esp. 260–88. For my discussion of this problem, see Introduction.

9. For a summary of Adams's attitudes in this regard, see Manning J. Dauer, *The Adams Federalists* (Baltimore, 1968), 64–66.

10. Samuel Miller, *A Brief Retrospect of the Eighteenth Century* . . ., 2 vols. (New York, 1803), 2:136. There is a Virginia connection: According to Patrick Henry's first biographer, Robertson was Patrick Henry's father's uncle. William Wirt, *Sketches of the Life and Character of Patrick Henry*, 3rd ed. (Philadelphia, 1818), 19. For his popularity in the colonies, see H. Trevor Colbourn, *The Lamp of Experience: Whig History and the Intellectual Origins of the American Revolution* (Chapel Hill, N.C., 1965), index, s.v. "Robertson, William." Richard B. Sher, *Church and University in the Scottish Enlightenment: The Moderate Literati of Edinburgh* (Princeton, N.J., 1985), places Robertson in his Scottish setting; for a more critical view of Robertson as a historian, see D. A. Brading on *History of America* (1771) in *The First America: The Spanish Monarchy, Creole Patriots, and the Liberal State, 1492–1867* (Cambridge, 1991), 432–41.

11. William Robertson, *The History of the Reign of Charles the Fifth* . . . (1769), 3 vols. (Philadelphia, 1774), 1:73, 76.

12. Ibid., 78–79.

13. Ibid., 80, 80–82, 93; 2:102–25; 1:136–38, 135, 71, 74, 93.

14. Madison repeated this analysis in *The Federalist*, No. 41, and while he did not attribute it to the Scottish historian, Robertson may have been his source. "The fifteenth century," Madison wrote, "was the unhappy epoch of military establishments in time of peace. They were introduced by Charles VII. of France. All Europe has followed, or been forced into the example" (*The Federalist*, ed. Jacob E. Cooke [Middletown, Conn., 1961], 270–71). For another possible Virginia borrowing, see John Page, *An Address to the Freeholders of Gloucester County* . . . (Richmond, Va., 1799), 26: "*What has been* (as the English proverb says) *may be again*, and it is certain that the parliaments, or the *cortes* of Spain, which once exercised a constitutional right of determining in what manner taxes should be levied and to what amount, and

so stood as barriers against the attacks of royal authority on the rights of the people, became corrupt, sacrificed their own rights, and left their Kings uncontrolled."

15. Jean-Jacques Rousseau, *Du contrat social* (1762), in Gagnebin and Raymond, eds., *Oeuvres complètes* 3:429. Rousseau was repeating an argument widely diffused since its appearance in Niccolo Machiavelli's *Discorsi* (ca. 1515–1520), for which see Quentin Skinner, *The Foundations of Modern Political Thought*, 2 vols. (Cambridge, 1978), 1:130–31, 173–76, 226–27, 308–12, 349–51, and Pocock, *Machiavellian Moment*, 289–95.

16. Charles de Secondat, baron de Montesquieu, *The Spirit of the Laws* (1748), trans. Thomas Nugent, 2 vols. in 1 (New York, 1949), 1:217. The eighteenth-century Nugent translation was widely read, and I have thus used it rather than the French original; on English-language copies of Montesquieu in America, see Colbourn, *Lamp of Experience*, 200, 204, 209, 211, 216, 217, 221. Jefferson excerpted the quoted passage in his commonplace book. *The Commonplace Book of Thomas Jefferson: A Repertory of His Ideas on Government*, ed. Gilbert Chinard (Baltimore, 1926), 277.

17. Samuel Johnson, *Thoughts on the Late Transactions Respecting Falkland's Islands* (1771), in *The Yale Edition of the Works of Samuel Johnson*, vol. 10, *Political Writings*, ed. Donald J. Greene (New Haven, Conn., 1977), 371. Johnson was writing to justify the North ministry's refusal to go to war with Spain over the Falklands.

18. William Blackstone, *Commentaries on the Laws of England* (1765) (Chicago, 1979), 1:324.

19. For the country party view, see Kramnick, *Bolingbroke and His Circle*.

20. Julius S. Waterman discusses Blackstone's Tory side and American hostility to him on that ground in "Thomas Jefferson and Blackstone's Commentaries" (1933), in David H. Flaherty, ed., *Essays in the History of Early American Law* (Chapel Hill, N.C., 1969), 451–88.

21. See text at note 108, and the Virginia Assembly's 1790 resolutions condemning assumption in Chapter 5, text at note 21.

22. Blackstone, *Commentaries*, 1:323, 315–16, 323.

23. By the 1750s, moreover, English politics was breaking out of its early Hanoverian stranglehold, and Tories were no longer automatically proscribed. If the results of this shift produced less than Tories and opposition Whigs hoped, it suggests again how generally respectable their ideas were, provided they no longer threatened the dynasty. For a recent narrative of political change in mid-century Britain, see Paul Langford, *A Polite and Commercial People: England, 1727–1783* (Oxford, 1989), chap. 5, "Patriotism Unmasked, 1742–1757," and chap. 8, "Patriotism Restored, 1757–1770."

24. Blackstone, *Commentaries*, 1:324, 324–35, 325.

25. James Burgh, *Political Disquisitions; or, An Enquiry into Public Errors, Defects, and Abuses* (1774), 3 vols. (Philadelphia, 1775), 1:271, quotation on 267. Burgh's major discussion of the public debt (267–78, and see 400–404, 485–86, for further treatment) comes in Book 5, "Of Parliamentary Corruption." On Burgh, see Oscar Handlin and Mary Handlin, "James Burgh and American Revolutionary Theory," Massachusetts Historical Society, *Proceedings* 73 (1962): 38–57; Carla H. Hay, "The Making of a Radical: The Case of James Burgh," *Journal of British Studies* 18 (1979): 90–117; and Isaac Kramnick, "James Burgh and 'Opposition' Ideology in England and America," in *Republicanism and Bourgeois Radicalism*, 220–59.

26. Richard Price, *Additional Observations on the Nature and Value of Civil Liberty . . .* (1777), in *Two Tracts on Civil Liberty, the War with America, and the Debts and Finances of the Kingdom . . .* (London, 1778), 45–46, 45. On Price, see the life by

Carl B. Cone, *Torchbearer of Freedom* (Lexington, Ky., 1952), and Isaac Kramnick, "Republican Revisionism Revisited," in *Republicanism and Bourgeois Radicalism*, 176–79.

27. Blackstone, *Commentaries*, 1:315.

28. Tobias Smollett, *The History of England from the Revolution to the End of the American War . . .*, 6 vols. (Philadelphia, 1796). First published in 1759, this work filled the need for a readable sequel to Hume's *History*, and the edition I cite contains both Smollett's text and a continuation to 1783 by other hands. Ibid., 1:iv–v. For other histories of contemporary Britain popular in eighteenth-century America (Burgh's *Disquisitions* among them), see Colbourn, *Lamp of Experience*, 40–56; on Smollett as a historian, see Donald J. Greene, "Smollett the Historian: A Reappraisal," in G. S. Rousseau and P.-G. Bouce, eds., *Tobias Smollett: Bicentennial Essays Presented to Lewis M. Knapp* (New York, 1971), 25–56.

29. Smollett, *History of England*, 1:16, 331.

30. Ibid., 2:137, 16, 136. On the importance for Smollett's understanding of history of luxury and the corruption of virtue it produced, see John Sekora, *Luxury: The Concept in Western Thought, Eden to Smollett* (Baltimore, 1977), 136–54.

31. Lewis Mansfield Knapp, *Tobias Smollett: Doctor of Men and Manners* (Princeton, N.J., 1949), 186–94; Sekora, *Luxury*, 138–40.

32. For evidence of their popularity in the colonies, see Colbourn, *Lamp of Experience*, app. 2, "History of Eighteenth-Century American Libraries," 199–232; Jack P. Greene, *The Intellectual Heritage of the Constitutional Era: The Delegates' Library* (Philadelphia, 1986); David Lundberg and Henry F. May, "The Enlightened Reader in America," *American Quarterly* 28 (1976): 262–93; Donald S. Lutz, "The Relative Influence of European Writers on Late Eighteenth-Century American Political Thought," *American Political Science Review* 78 (1984): 189–97; and Robert A. Rutland, *"Well Acquainted with Books": The Founding Framers of 1787* (Washington, D.C., 1987).

33. David Hume, "Of the Independence of Parliament" (1741), in Miller, ed., *Essays*, 45. Hume's comment did not endear him to American republicans, and his *History* was often seen as a defense of such views on a broad scale. For a striking instance, see TJ to John Adams, 25 Nov. 1816; Adams to TJ, 16 Dec. 1816, *Cappon*, 2:498–99, 502–3. Douglas L. Wilson describes Jefferson's lifelong battle against the *History* in "Jefferson vs. Hume," *WMQ* 46 (1989): 49–70. However, Hume's dislike of the national debt was in keeping with republican opinion; for this, see text at notes 38–45.

34. The Augustan critics raised this earlier, but foresaw only the ruin of the landed classes (who bore much of the weight of taxation at a time of low agricultural prices), not, like the mid-century critics for whom Britain consisted of much more than the agricultural interest, the ruin of the nation as a whole. On the Augustans, see Kramnick, *Bolingbroke*, 42–44, 51–52, 70–71, 170, and Pocock, *Machiavellian Moment*, 441–61. Jonathan Swift is rich in such predictions: "If," he wrote in 1710, "the war [of the Spanish Succession] continues some Years longer, a landed Man will be little better than a Farmer at rack Rent, to the Army, and to the publick Funds" ("Examiner," No. 13, 2 Nov. 1710, in Herbert Davis, ed., *The Prose Works of Jonathan Swift*, 14 vols. (Oxford, 1939–1968), 3:5). For trenchant comments on the origins, purposes, and effects of funding systems, see also the most famous of Swift's political pamphlets, *The Conduct of the Allies . . .* (1711), in ibid., 4:5–7, 10, 18–19, 54–56.

35. In round numbers, the debt (in millions) stood at £3.1 in 1691, £14.1 in 1701, £22.4 in 1711, £54.9 in 1721, £51.7 in 1731, £48.8 in 1741, £78.1 in 1751, £114.2 in

1761, £128.9 in 1771, £190.4 in 1781, £243.2 in 1791, £456.1 in 1801, £609.6 in 1811, and £838.3 in 1821. B. R. Mitchell, *Abstract of British Historical Statistics* (Cambridge, 1962), 401–2.

36. As a practical matter, the only appreciable reductions (in percentage terms) until after 1815 came during Walpole's ministry, when it fell from £54.9 million in 1721 to £46.9 million in 1739–an £8 million decrease in eighteen years of peace and economizing. Despite his fame as a reformer and his determination to reduce the debt, between 1784 and 1792 the younger Pitt managed to effect a decrease of no more than £1.3 million. Previous peacetime ministries, in 1748 to 1756 and 1763 to 1775, did better, with reductions of £5.9 million and £6.9 million, respectively. Ibid. Regardless of the ministry and the politicians' professions, progress in eliminating the debt was glacial by any standard.

37. Adam Smith, *An Inquiry into the Nature and Causes of the Wealth of Nations* (1776), ed. R. H. Campbell and A. S. Skinner, 2 vols. (Oxford, 1976), 2:912, 928, 929–32; David Hume, "Of Public Credit" (1754), in Miller, ed., *Essays*, 364–65. For Smith's and Hume's presence in Virginia libraries, see Appendix B.

38. Hume, "Of Public Credit," 360–61. See Duncan Forbes, *Hume's Philosophical Politics* (Cambridge, 1975), for Hume's views on political questions and, on the debt in particular, Istvan Hont, "The Rhapsody of Public Debt: David Hume and Voluntary State Bankruptcy," in Nicholas Phillipson and Quentin Skinner, eds., *Political Discourse in Early Modern Britain* (Cambridge, 1993), 321–48.

39. James Boswell, *Life of Johnson* (1791), ed. George Birkbeck Hill, rev. L. F. Powell, 6 vols. (Oxford, 1934–1950), 2:127. Johnson's sympathies were obviously not with the creditors.

40. Malachy Postlethwayt, *Great Britain's True System* . . . (London, 1757), title page, 213–17, quotation on 213; Richard Price, *Observations on the Importance of the American Revolution* . . . (1785), in Bernard Peach, ed., *Richard Price and the Ethical Foundations of the American Revolution: Selections from His Pamphlets* . . . (Durham, N.C., 1979), 186. Earlier, Price had expressed this view in a private letter to Arthur Lee, Jan. 1779, ibid., 313.

41. Smith, *Wealth of Nations*, 2:911, 928.

42. Hume, "Of Public Credit," 349–50; Smith, *Wealth of Nations*, 2:907–9.

43. Lord Kames [Henry Home], *Six Sketches of the History of Man* . . . (1774) (Philadelphia, 1776), 96. According to Sir Francis d'Ivernois, *On the Downfall of Switzerland* (n.p., 1798), 12, the French seized £600,000 from the Bernese treasury when they overran Switzerland. Kames was wrong to claim that Bern was the only *state* to have amassed a treasure; as Smith pointed out, it was the only *republic* to have done so, for both Frederick the Great and his father, Frederick William, were able to accumulate "considerable treasure" (*Wealth of Nations*, 2:909). On Prussian finance, see Walther Hubatsch, *Frederick the Great of Prussia: Absolutism and Administration*, trans. Patrick Donan (London, 1975), 137–40, 147, stressing the importance of subsidies Prussia received from foreign powers, including England, in aiding Frederick to attain his goal–a strong treasury and no debt. For John Adams's unfavorable comments on the Prussian system of "thesaurization," see Zoltan Haraszti, *John Adams and the Prophets of Progress* (Cambridge, Mass., 1952), 263–64 and illustration opposite 257. Jefferson and Madsion also had their doubts about the wisdom of piling up treasure simply to support war; see Chapter 4, text at note 60, and Chapter 5, text at note 152.

44. Smith, *Wealth of Nations*, 2:926, 919–20, 921, 926. And see Blackstone, *Commentaries*, 1:315.

45. Hume, "Of Public Credit," 351.

46. Montesquieu, *Spirit of the Laws*, 1:218.

47. Smith, *Wealth of Nations*, 2:912. The practice Smith mentions was typical of early modern and eighteenth-century public finance. In Britain, as elsewhere, those handling public funds, whether tax collectors or disbursing agents, were permitted to regard balances in their hands as their property, accounting for them only at intervals. This allowed temporary investments, often in the public debt, and it was thought great fortunes could be gained this way. During the Seven Years' War, the paymaster-general of the forces, Henry Fox, Lord Holland, notoriously used his position to considerable advantage in this regard. See John M. Norris, *Shelburne and Reform* (London, 1963), 199–239, and J. E. D. Binney, *British Public Finance and Administration, 1774–92* (Oxford, 1958), 189–219, and, for Fox, Lucy S. Sutherland and J. Binney, "Henry Fox as Paymaster-General of the Forces" (1955), in Rosalind Mitchison, ed., *Essays in Eighteenth-Century History from the English Historical Review* (London, 1966), 231–59. For France, see J. F. Bosher, "French Administration and Public Finance in their European Setting," in *The New Cambridge Modern History*, vol. 8, *The American and the French Revolution, 1763–93*, ed. A. Goodwin (Cambridge, 1965), 565–91, esp. 580–84, and, for detail, Bosher, *French Finances 1770–1795: From Business to Bureaucracy* (Cambridge, 1970).

48. Smith, *Wealth of Nations*, 2:911.

49. See text at note 102, and J. R. McCulloch, *A Treatise on the Principles and Practical Influence on Taxation and the Funding System* (1863), ed. D. P. O'Brien (Edinburgh, 1975), 413, holding that Hume and Smith *were* right but failed to give sufficient attention to the possibility of countervailing factors such as the growth of industry.

50. For an introduction to the changing meanings of "economy" in the major European languages and its historical roots in the notion of the household, see Günter Bien, "Haus," and H. Rabe, "Ökonomie," in Joachim Ritter, ed., *Historisches Wörterbuch der Philosophie*, 8 vols. (Basel, 1971–1992), 3:cols. 1007–17; 7:cols. 1049–153. For more detailed discussions, see Otto Brunner, "Das 'ganze Haus' und die alteuropäische 'Ökonomik,' " in *Neue Wege der Verfassungs- und Sozialgeschichte*, 2d ed. (Göttingen, 1968), 103–27; Karl Polanyi, "Aristotle Discovers the Economy" (1957), in *Primitive, Archaic and Modern Economies*, ed. George Dalton (Garden City, N.Y., 1968), 78–115; and Keith Tribe, *Land, Labour, and Economic Discourse* (London, 1978). The locus classicus is Aristotle; see *The Politics*, ed. Stephen Everson (Cambridge, 1988), 4–20.

51. Voltaire, "Économie," in *Questions sur l'Encyclopédie* (1771), in *Oeuvres complètes de Voltaire* (Paris, 1878), 18:453, 458. Rousseau, however, disagreed in the *Discours sur l'économie politique* (1755), in Gagnebin and Raymond, eds., *Oeuvres complètes*, 3:241–44. The *Discours* was originally published in the *Encyclopédie*, and Voltaire was responding to Rousseau's article in his *Questions*.

52. Examples of eighteenth-century use of such terminology will be found throughout this and later chapters.

53. On the notion of the king as landlord, see Herbert H. Rowen, *The King's State: Proprietary Dynasticism in Early Modern France* (New Brunswick, N.J., 1980).

54. The emergence of modern concepts of sovereignty, cutting through traditional limits on the right to tax, is discussed in F. H. Hinsley, *Sovereignty*, 2d ed. (Cambridge, 1986), 45–157. G. L. Harriss, "Medieval Doctrines in the Debates on Supply," in Kevin Sharpe, ed., *Faction and Parliament: Essays on Early Stuart History* (Oxford and New York, 1978), 73–104, shows the difficulty early-seventeenth-

century English parliaments had in creating an acceptable rationale for taxation in a period when rising revenue needs made it harder to rely on old ones.

55. [Jonathan Shipley], *A Speech Intended to Have Been Spoken by the Bishop of St. Asaph* . . . (1774), in Paul H. Smith, comp., *English Defenders of American Freedoms, 1774–1778: Six Pamphlets Attacking British Policy* (Washington, D.C., 1972), 40. For his relations with Franklin, see Carl Van Doren, *Benjamin Franklin* (New York, 1938), 413–17, 481–82, 717. In 1785, still friendly to America and Americans, he officiated at the London wedding of John Adams's daughter Abigail to William Stephens Smith. Page Smith, *John Adams*, 2 vols. (Garden City, N.Y., 1962), 2:675.

56. For examples, see this chapter and Chapter 2.

57. Hume, "Of Public Credit," 352.

58. Adam Ferguson, *An Essay on the History of Civil Society* (1767) (New Brunswick, N.J., 1980), 234, quotation from pt. 5, sec. 5, "Of National Waste."

59. Ibid.

60. [Young], *Political Essays*, 52–53, 55.

61. Joseph Priestley, *Lectures on History, and General Policy* . . . (1788), 2 vols. (Philadelphia, 1803), 2:420.

62. David Ricardo, *On the Principles of Political Economy and Taxation* (1817), in Pierro Sraffa, ed., *The Works and Correspondence of David Ricardo*, 11 vols. (Cambridge, 1951–1973), 1:248–49.

63. Antoine Louis Claude, comte Destutt de Tracy, *A Treatise on Political Economy* . . . (Washington, D.C., 1817), 235–36. On Jefferson's role in the publication of this work, see Chapter 6, text at notes 16–19. Discussions of Tracy include Emmet Kennedy, *A Philosophe in the Age of Revolution: Destutt de Tracy and the Origins of "Ideology"* (Philadelphia, 1978), and Cheryl B. Welch, *Liberty and Utility: The French Idéologues and the Transformation of Liberalism* (New York, 1984). On Jefferson's relations with Tracy, see Joyce Appleby, "What Is Still American in the Political Philosophy of Thomas Jefferson?," *WMQ* 39 (1982): 287–309; her use of Tracy to prove that Jefferson had abandoned republicanism is not convincing.

64. [Alexander Hamilton], H.G. Letter 8, 2 Mar. 1789, *PAH*, 5:280.

65. Hume, "Of Public Credit," 352, 356, 636n.d–637. For Smith's treatment of this point, see *Wealth of Nations*, 2:924–25, where Smith, too, denies the debt creates new capital. J.-F. Melon's argument in *Essai politique sur le commerce* (1734) is noted in Hume, "Of Public Credit," 636n.d; Melon held that "les dettes d'un Etat sont les dettes de la main droite à la main gauche, dont le corps ne se trouvera point affaibli, s'il a la quantité d'aliments nécessaire, et s'il sait les distribuer" (*Essai*, in Eugène Daire, ed., *Economistes financiers du XVIIIe siècle* . . . [Paris, 1851], 749). For Smith's comments on Melon, see *Wealth of Nations*, 2:924–25, 926–27, where he remarks that "in the payment of the interest of the publick debt, it has been said, it is the right hand which pays the left. . . . This apology is founded altogether in the sophistry of the mercantile system."

66. Hume, "Of Public Credit," 355; William Paley, *The Principles of Moral and Political Philosophy*, 7th ed. (1785), 2 vols. (Philadelphia, 1789), 1:475.

67. Hume, "Of Public Credit," 355. Interestingly, Smith does not follow Hume in considering either this aspect of the debt or its concentration in the hands of the idle. Rather, he thinks that the majority of public creditors in England are wealthy merchants who see the debt as a sound investment and otherwise would not have purchased it. Smith could not have endorsed Hume's complaints without invoking the mercantilist policies he wished to discredit. This is the only important respect in which his analysis of the debt differs from Hume's. Smith, *Wealth of Nations*, 2:918.

68. Hume, "Of Public Credit," 636n.d–637. His position here is in contrast to his praise for paper currency, which increases circulation, in "Of Money" (1741) and "Of the Balance of Trade" (1741), in Miller, ed., *Essays*, 284–85, 318–21. On this, see Albert O. Hirschman, *The Passions and the Interests: Political Arguments for Capitalism Before Its Triumph* (Princeton, N.J., 1977), 75–76. Jefferson's references to Hume are generally unfavorable, but for evidence that he was acquainted with the economic essays, and in particular with "Of Money," which he thought "well explained" the price mechanism, see TJ to John Wayles Eppes, 6 Nov. 1813, *Ford*, 11:319.

69. Hume's doctrine would remain standard well into the nineteenth century, fully accepted by the classical school. D. P. O'Brien, *The Classical Economists* (Oxford, 1975), 259–65, has a useful summary.

70. On Mandeville's paradox and reactions to it, see M. M. Goldsmith, *Private Vices, Public Benefits: Bernard Mandeville's Social and Political Thought* (Cambridge, 1985).

71. For Melon, see *Essai*, 749, and for Smith's comments on this proposition, see *Wealth of Nations*, 2:924–25; for Berkeley, see "The Querist" (1735–1737), No. 233, in A. A. Luce and T. E. Jessop, eds., *The Works of George Berkeley, Bishop of Cloyne* (London, 1953), 6:124.

72. Hume to Montesquieu, 10 Apr. 1749, in J. Y. T. Grieg, ed., *The Letters of David Hume*, 2 vols. (Oxford, 1932), 1:137, where Hume endorses "l'enumeration que vous faites des inconvenients des dettes publiques" but suggests Lonsdale's ideas as a possible exception.

73. Pinto's arguments are discussed in Charles Wilson, *Anglo-Dutch Commerce and Finance in the Eighteenth Century*, 2d ed. (Cambridge, 1966), 71, 75–78, and Robert James Parks, *European Origins of the Economic Ideas of Alexander Hamilton* (New York, 1977), 80–85. For the quotations, see Isaac de Pinto, *An Essay on Circulation and Credit . . .*, trans. S. Baggs (London, 1774), v (translator), 1, 104. For Hume's doubts, see his letters to Strachan, 21 Jan.; 11 Mar., 25 Mar.; 25 June; 19 Aug. 1771, in Grieg, ed., *Letters*, 2:234, 237, 242, 245, 248. Hume did not alter the text of "Of Public Credit" to reflect the views Pinto attributed to him. Dugald Stewart's remarks are in his *Lectures on Political Economy, Now First Published*, in Sir William Hamilton, ed., *The Collected Works of Dugald Stewart, Esq., . . .*, (Edinburgh, 1855), 9:218, 220. For a later example of positive evaluation of the debt, see P[atrick] Colquhoun, *A Treatise on the Wealth, Power, and Resources, of the British Empire . . .*, 2d ed. (London, 1815), 283.

74. On Steuart and his work, see S. R. Sen, *The Economics of Sir James Steuart* (Cambridge, Mass., 1957), and Andrew Skinner's Introduction to his edition of Steuart's *Inquiry into the Principles of Political Oeconomy*, 2 vols. (Edinburgh, 1966). While it is usually held that *The Wealth of Nations* immediately destroyed the reputation of Steuart's work, it has been suggested that only around 1790 did Smith clearly overtake Steuart in public estimation. Salim Rashid, "Adam Smith's Rise to Fame: A Reexamination of the Evidence," *Eighteenth Century: Theory and Interpretation* (1982), 23:64–85, and Richard F. Teichgraeber III, " 'Less Abused Than I Had Reason to Expect': The Reception of *The Wealth of Nations* in Britain, 1776–90," *Historical Journal* 30 (1987): 337–66. For Steuart's popularity in Virginia, see Appendix B.

Although it is difficult to assess Steuart's influence in Virginia—his ideas on the public debt did not find an audience there—the work was still being used in the 1790s as a reference tool. The questions raised by the federal carriage tax of 1794—was it an excise as its proponents insisted or, as many Virginians claimed, a direct tax and thus one constitutionally apportionable according to population?–led advocates on both sides to consult Smith and Steuart for definitions of the different forms of taxation. A test case was brought, and the defendants' counsel, John Taylor of Caroline, based his argument on Steuart's definition of direct taxes, under which it appeared that the levy on carriages fell into that category. The United States, in opposition, urged that Smith's discussion proved that the tax was an excise. For this episode, which ended in the Virginians' defeat in *Hylton* v. *United States*, 3 Dall. 172 (1796), see Julius Goebel, Jr., and Joseph H. Smith, eds., *The Law Practice of Alexander Hamilton: Documents and Commentary* (New York, 1980), 4:297–340, esp. 323–36. Taylor's use of Steuart was a tactical move and should not be seen as evidence that he was deeply impressed with Steuart's insights. Robert E. Shalhope, *John Taylor of Caroline: Pastoral Republican* (Columbia, S.C., 1980), 103, is in error on this point (note Shalhope's reference, which may explain his mistake, to "Sir James Steuart and his pupil, Adam Smith" [ibid.]).

75. Smith to William Pulteney, 3 Sept. 1772, in Ernest Campbell Mossner and Ian Simpson Ross, eds., *The Correspondence of Adam Smith*, rev. ed. (Oxford, 1987), 164.

76. Sir James Steuart, *An Inquiry into the Principles of Political Oeconomy* . . , 2 vols. (London, 1767), 2:625; 1:16–17; 2:357, 444, 445, 463.

77. Alexander Hamilton, *Report on Public Credit*, 9 Jan. 1790, *PAH*, 6:106. Hamilton earlier argued that "a national debt if it is not excessive will be to us a national blessing; it will be powerfull cement of our union" (Hamilton to Robert Morris, 30 Apr. 1781, ibid., 2:635), and that in fact remained his position in the *Report*. But see also his remarks on the debt in H. G. Letter 8, 2 Mar. 1789, ibid., 5:280.

78. Alexander Hamilton, *Report on a Plan for the Further Support of Public Credit*, 16 Jan. 1795, ibid., 18:109.

79. Johan. Daniel Gros, *Natural Principles of Rectitude, for the Conduct of Man* . . . (New York, 1795), 380. The first American textbook of moral philosophy to appear during the early national period, the work set a pattern for those that followed "into the middle of the nineteenth century" (Wilson Smith, *Professors and Public Ethics: Studies of Northern Moral Philosophers Before the Civil War* [Ithaca, N.Y., 1956], 81). For Gros's life and thought, see 81–94.

80. On the land tax, see W. R. Ward, *The English Land Tax in the Eighteenth Century* (London, 1953), esp. 15, 19, 70–74. For figures on the composition, by source, of the British revenue in the eighteenth century, see Mitchell, *Abstract of British Historical Statistics*, "Public Finance 1. Net Receipts of the Public Income . . . 1688–1801," 386–88.

81. Ibid; Brewer, *Sinews of Power*, 202–6, 212–17. For an example proving the soundness of his general case, see R. A. C. Parker, *Coke of Norfolk: A Financial and Agricultural Study, 1707–1842* (Oxford, 1975), 2–3, 127–28.

82. David Hume, "Of Taxes" (1752), in Miller, ed., *Essays*, 345; Blackstone, *Commentaries*, 1:298–315; Steuart, *Principles of Political Oeconomy*, 2:485–591; Smith, *Wealth of Nations*, 2:825–906; Josiah Tucker, *A Treatise Concerning Civil Government* (1781), in Robert Livingston Schuyler, ed., *Josiah Tucker: A Selection from His Economic and Political Writings* (New York, 1931), 443–50.

83. Hume, "Of Taxes," 345; Blackstone, *Commentaries*, 1:306; Smith, *Wealth of Nations*, 2:883–86.

84. Smith was sure that "a tax upon the interest of money would not raise the rate of interest" (*Wealth of Nations*, 848); Hume thought the principal difficulty in taxing

the funds was political ("Of Public Credit," 358–59); and for the argument against taxing them, see Hamilton, *Report on a Plan for the Further Support of Public Credit*, 16 Jan. 1795, *PAH*, 18:115–22, esp. 120–21.

85. Smith, *Wealth of Nations*, 1:85–92, 95–104; 2:869–78; Hume, "Of Taxes," 343.

86. Smith, *Wealth of Nations*, 2:920–21.

87. For example, Blackstone, *Commentaries*, 1:315.

88. On Price and the sinking fund, see Carl B. Cone, "Richard Price and Pitt's Sinking Fund of 1786," *Economic History Review*, 2d ser., 4 (1951): 243–51, which should be supplemented by John Ehrman, *The Younger Pitt: The Years of Acclaim* (New York, 1969), 260–67.

89. Blackstone, *Commentaries*, 1:318–19; Francis Fauquier, *An Essay on Ways and Means for Raising Money for the Support of the Present War, Without Increasing the Public Debts . . .* (London, 1756), 12. See also Smith, *Wealth of Nations*, 2:915–16, 920–24, and Price, *Two Tracts on Civil Liberty . . .* (1778), and *Observations on the Importance of the American Revolution* (1785), in D. O. Thomas, ed., *Political Writings* (Cambridge, 1991), 98, 121. For Jefferson's relations with Fauquier, see *Malone*, 1:53, 73–74, 78.

90. For Price's example of compound interest, see *Observations on the American Revolution*, 121. His initial proposals for the sinking fund are in *An Appeal to the Public on the Subject of the National Debt* (1774), in John R. McCulloch, ed., *A Collection of Scarce and Valuable Tracts . . . on the National Debt and the Sinking Fund* (London, 1857), 301–58, esp. 340–43. Price thought the population was shrinking; hence the need to tackle the debt, for soon there would be fewer taxpayers to discharge it. Ibid., 343–46. Cone describes the mechanics of Price's fund in "Price and Pitt's Sinking Fund," 244–45.

91. Price to Lord Chatham, 11 Mar. 1773, in D. O. Thomas and W. Bernard Peach, eds., *The Correspondence of Richard Price* (Durham, N.C., 1983), 1:57–58. Price's assumptions became critical with the great increase in the debt after 1793. Ricardo and others in the next generation of classical economists devoted much attention to them. For Ricardo's views, see his contribution to the 1820 edition of the *Encyclopaedia Britannica*, "Funding System," in Sraffa, ed., *Works and Correspondence of Ricardo*, 4:143–200, esp. 149, where Ricardo acknowledges his reliance on Robert Hamilton's *Inquiry Concerning . . . the National Debt of Great Britain and Ireland*, 3d ed. [1818], in McCulloch, ed., *Collection of Scarce and Valuable Tracts*, 421–688. For Hamilton on Price, see ibid., 555–72, describing Price's views as "completely delusive" (567).

92. Sir John Sinclair, *The History of the Public Revenue of the British Empire . . .*, 3 vols., 3rd ed. (London, 1803), 1:4, 475, 513. (First published in 1785, vol. 1 was reprinted in 1803 with "little variation from the original publication" [viii].) Sinclair presented a copy of Vol. 2 to Jefferson. *Sowerby*, 3, No. 2939. For evidence of the work's popularity in Virginia, see Appendix B.

93. Paine's prediction is in *Prospects on the Rubicon . . .* (1787), in Moncure Daniel Conway, ed., *The Writings of Thomas Paine*, 4 vols. (New York, 1894–1895), 2:216. David Freeman Hawke, *Paine* (New York, 1974), 178, suggests that Paine may have been paid by the French to write it. For Paine's comments in the 1790s, see, for example, *The Decline and Fall of the English System of Finance* (1796), in Conway, ed., *Writings of Thomas Paine*, 3:, esp. 287, 290–91, 300, 307, 310.

94. Thomas Paine, *Rights of Man*, Part One (1791), ed. Henry Collins (Harmondsworth, 1969), 133–38.

95. Edmund Burke, *Reflections on the Revolution in France* . . . (1790), in *The Writings and Speeches of Edmund Burke*, vol. 8, *The French Revolution, 1790–1794*, ed. L. G. Mitchell (Oxford, 1989), 158–60, 167–74, 203–4. For a discussion of Burke's fear of "monied men," see J. G. A. Pocock, "The Political Economy of Burke's Analysis of the French Revolution," *Historical Journal* 25 (1982): 331–49. Emma Rothschild, however, cautions against seeing Burke in the tradition of Smith *et al.*, suggesting that much of Burke's *Reflections* "consists of an attack on Smith's friends, on his language, and on his beliefs" ("Adam Smith and Conservative Economics," *Economic History Review*, 2d ser., 45 [1992]: 76). If Rothschild is correct, this is another example of the way the debt built bridges between otherwise dissimilar temperaments.

96. Burke, *Reflections*, 203–4, and see also 158–60.

97. Sir James Mackintosh, *Vindiciae Gallicae: Defence of the French Revolution* (1791) (Philadelphia, 1792), 75–78, 85 (debt); 69–70 (Burke).

98. George Rous, *Thoughts on Government: Occasioned by Mr. Burke's Reflections* . . . , 2d ed. (London, 1790), 45–46.

99. On wartime debates over inflation and the debt, see Norman J. Silberling, "Ricardo and the Bullion Report" (1924), in Frederick C. Lane, ed., *Enterprise and Secular Change: Readings in Economic History* (Homewood, Ill., 1953), 360–90.

100. J. E. Cookson, *The Friends of Peace: Anti-War Liberalism in England, 1793–1815* (Cambridge, 1982), 55–63; Albert Goodwin, *The Friends of Liberty: The English Democratic Movement in the Age of the French Revolution* (Cambridge, Mass., 1979), 481–82.

101. E. P. Thompson, *The Making of the English Working Class* (New York, 1964), is the classic account of protest and its containment in this period; on the results of the wars of the French Revolution and Napoleon, in terms of debts and taxes, see J. H. Clapham, *An Economic History of Modern Britain: The Early Railway Age, 1820–1850* (Cambridge, 1959), 311–12, 317–30. The continuing emphasis on the national debt as the source of evil in radical circles in post-1815 Britain is explored in Noel W. Thompson, *The People's Science: The Popular Political Economy of Exploitation and Crisis, 1816–34* (Cambridge, 1984).

102. Lord Macaulay, *History of England* (1848) (London, 1906), 3:515.

103. William Cobbett, *Rural Rides* (1830), ed. George Woodcock (Harmondsworth, 1967), passim.

104. Immanuel Kant, *Zum ewigen Frieden: Ein philosophischer Entwurf* (1795), trans. as "Perpetual Peace: A Philosophical Sketch," in Hans Reiss, ed., H. B. Nisbet, trans., *Political Writings*, 2d ed. (Cambridge, 1991), 95; the work should be read in light of Prussia's abandonment of the British-led First Coalition and its separate peace with France at Basel in 1795. In 1798, borrowing from Hume's "Of Public Credit," Kant returned to the theme of inevitable bankruptcy in *Der Streit der Facultäten*, trans. as "The Contest of the Faculties," in ibid., 189–190, 281n.22. For Kant's dislike of British policy (he had earlier admired the American rebels), see Karl Vorländer, *Immanuel Kant: Der Mann und das Werk*, 2 vols. (Leipzig, 1924), 2:213, 216–18.

105. The clergyman was Pitt's secretary and future biographer, George Pretyman, soon to be appointed bishop of Lincoln, and his sermon was delivered to the House of Commons at St. Margaret's, Westminster, in July 1784. Ehrman, *Younger Pitt*, 13–14, 469, 469n.

106. Price to Lee, Jan. 1779, in Peach, ed., *Price and the Ethical Foundations of the American Revolution*, 313.

107. John Adams to TJ, 15 Sept. 1813, *Cappon*, 2:376. John Taylor's principal works include *Definitions of Parties; or, the Political Effects of the Paper System* (Philadelphia, 1794); *An Enquiry into the Principles and Tendency of Certain Public Measures* (Philadelphia, 1794); *An Inquiry into the Principles and Policy of the Government of the United States* (Fredericksburg, Va., 1814); *Construction Construed and Constitutions Vindicated* (Richmond, Va., 1820); *Tyranny Unmasked* (Washington, D.C., 1823); and *New Views of the Constitution* (Washington, D.C., 1824). Their titles suggest the direction of his thought. Even in his agricultural essays, *Arator: Being a Series of Agricultural Essays, Practical and Political . . .*, 6th ed. (Petersburg, Va., 1818), he found room in the first twelve numbers to discuss "The Political State of Agriculture," with heavy emphasis on the evils of debt and funding.

108. St. George Tucker, ed., *Blackstone's Commentaries: With Notes of Reference to the Constitution and Laws of the Federal Government of the United States and of the Commonwealth of Virginia*, 5 vols. (Philadelphia, 1803), 2:337n.56. For Tucker's endorsement of Blackstone's warnings on the dangers of the debt, see ibid., 1:246–47; 2:328n.49, n*, 329n.50, n*, 337nn.54, 55 (the last six references cover Blackstone, *Commentaries*, 1:316–26).

109. In addition to Taylor's pamphlets of the 1790s, *Definitions of Parties* and *Enquiry into the Principles and Tendency of Certain Public Measures*, and Madison's *Political Observations*, 20 Apr. 1795, *PJM*, 15, see John Page, *An Address to the Citizens of the District of York . . .* (Philadelphia, 1797), 11, 25–26, 31–32, and *An Address to the Freeholders of Gloucester County . . .* (Richmond, Va., 1799), 3, 5, 26; Edmund Pendleton, "Address to the Citizens of Caroline," [Nov. 1798], *An Address of the Honorable Edmund Pendleton, of Virginia, to the American Citizens* (Boston, 1799), and "The Danger Not Over," 5 Oct. 1801, in David John Mays, ed., *The Letters and Papers of Edmund Pendleton, 1734–1803*, 2 vols. (Charlottesville, Va., 1967), 2:652–53, 660, 665–66, 698; and [John Thompson], *The Letters of Curtius, Addressed to General Marshall* (Richmond, Va., 1798), 16, 31–32.

110. William Munford, *Poems, and Compositions in Prose on Several Occasions*, 2d ed. (Richmond, Va., 1798), 152.

111. [St. George Tucker], *The Probationary Odes of Jonathan Pindar . . .* (Philadelphia, 1796), 16. For other examples, see "To Atlas" and "To Midas," 18–19, 25–26.

112. "An American," *Virginia Gazette, & Richmond & Manchester Advertiser*, 27 Feb. 1794.

113. Alexander Hamilton's early pamphlets were standard Whig productions, able to pass muster anywhere in the colonies, even Virginia. See *A Full Vindication of the Measures of Congress . . .* (New York, 1774); *The Farmer Refuted . . .* (New York, 1775); "Remarks on the Quebec Bill, Part One," 15 June 1775, and "Remarks on the Quebec Bill, Part Two," 22 June 1775, *PAH*, 1:45–78, 81–165 (esp. 144–46), 165–69, 169–76. For a review of Hamilton's likely acquaintance with orthodox writers, as reflected in the 1790 *Report on Public Credit*, see the editors' Introductory Note, ibid., 6:51–56. The issue of "influences" on Hamilton's views is not settled. Forrest McDonald claimed a special place for Jacques Necker in *Alexander Hamilton: A Biography* (New York, 1979), 84–85, 134–35, 160–61, 188, 196, 234, 264, 382n.24, 398n.33, 408nn.13–409, later providing a more nuanced evaluation in *Novus Ordo Seclorum: The Intellectual Origins of the Constitution* (Lawrence, Kans., 1985), 135–42. For other efforts, see Donald F. Swanson, *The Origins of Hamilton's Fiscal Policies* (Gainesville, Fla., 1963), and Parks, *European Origins of the Economic Ideas of Hamilton*. My candidate for a major and not fully acknowledged influence is

Steuart, both for his positive view of the debt and for his emphasis on the role of the statesman. On Steuart, see text at notes 74–76. E. A. J. Johnson states that "Hamilton's basic doctrines were much more closely related to those of Malachy Postlethwayt and Sir James Steuart than they were to the atomistic theory of Adam Smith" (*The Foundations of American Economic Freedom: Government and Enterprise in the Age of Washington* [Minneapolis, 1973], 123). McDonald says that on reading the whole of Steuart's *Principles* in 1984, "Hamilton's debt to Steuart became obvious to me" (*Novus Ordo Seclorum*, 136n.66).

114. Bernard Bailyn, *The Ideological Origins of the American Revolution* (Cambridge, Mass., 1967), 144–59; John R. Howe, Jr., "Republican Thought and the Political Violence of the 1790s," *American Quarterly* 19 (1967): 147–65; Marshall Smelser, "The Jacobin Frenzy: The Menace of Monarchy, Plutocracy, and Anglophobia, 1789–1798," *Review of Politics* 21 (1959): 239–58; "The Jacobin Phrenzy: Federalism and the Menace of Liberty, Equality, and Fraternity," *Review of Politics* 13 (1951): 457–82; and "The Federalist Period as an Age of Passion," *American Quarterly* 10 (1958): 391–419. For a more extended treatment, see Richard Buel, Jr., *Securing the Revolution: Ideology in American Politics, 1789–1815* (Ithaca, N.Y., 1972). As Richard Hofstadter and David Brion Davis remind us, this mood was not peculiar to the eighteenth century. Hofstadter, "The Paranoid Style in American Politics," in *The Paranoid Style in American Politics, and Other Essays* (New York, 1965), 3–5, 38–40; Davis, *The Slave Power Conspiracy and the Paranoid Style* (Baton Rouge, La., 1969), 3–31. Gordon S. Wood adds a new dimension to our understanding of this problem in "Conspiracy and the Paranoid Style: Causality and Deceit in the Eighteenth Century," *WMQ* 39 (1982): 401–41.

115. "Le révolutionnaire est *crédule*," Richard Cobb insists. "Une telle crédulité n'était pourtant sans fondement. Ces complots, auxquels on croyait tant, ils ont bel et bien existé" ("Quelques aspects de la mentalité révolutionnaire (avril 1793–thermidor an II)," in *Terreur et subsistances, 1793–1795* [Paris, 1965], 11, 16).

116. [Madison], *Political Observations*, 20 Apr. 1795, *PJM*, 15.

117. The literature on state-building in the early modern period and the eighteenth century is enormous; I shall not try to cite it all. Among the better works are Perry Anderson, *Lineages of the Absolutist State* (London, 1974), esp. 15–42, 397–432; Gabriel Ardant, "Financial Policy and Economic Infrastructure of Modern States and Nations," in Charles Tilly, ed., *The Formation of National States in Western Europe* (Princeton, N.J., 1975), 161–242; Trevor Aston, ed., *Crisis in Europe, 1500–1660* (Garden City, N.Y., 1967); Roger Bigelow Merriman, *Six Contemporaneous Revolutions* (Oxford, 1938); Brian M. Downing, *The Military Revolution and Political Change: Origins of Democracy and Autocracy in Early Modern Europe* (Princeton, N.J., 1992); Robert Forster and Jack P. Greene, eds., *Preconditions of Revolution in Early Modern Europe* (Baltimore, 1970); Jack A. Goldstone, *Revolution and Rebellion in the Early Modern World* (Berkeley, 1991); H. G. Koenigsberger, *Estates and Revolutions: Essays in Early Modern European History* (Ithaca, N.Y., 1971), 1–93, 125–43, 176–210, 224–77; Michael Mann, *The Sources of Social Power*, vol. 2, *The Rise of Classes and Nation State, 1760–1914* (Cambridge, 1993); Joseph A. Schumpeter, "The Crisis of the Tax State" (1918), in *The Economics and Sociology of Capitalism*, ed. Richard Swedberg (Princeton, N.J., 1991), 99–140; Theda Skocpol, *States and Social Revolutions: A Comparative Analysis* . . . (Cambridge, 1979); and Perez Zagorin, *Rebels and Rulers, 1500–1660*, 2 vols. (Cambridge, 1982), esp. 1:87–139; 2:1–8. From differing perspectives, these works pay close attention to the role of war and taxation in shaping the early modern and eighteenth-century state and to the political causes and

consequences of the financial crises these states encountered in their quests for survival and supremacy. In that sense, they continue the discussion begun in the eighteenth century. In "Negotiated Authorities: The Problem of Governance in the Extended Polities of the Early Modern Atlantic World," in *Negotiated Authorities: Essays in Colonial Political and Constitutional History* (Charlottesville, Va., 1994), 1–24, Jack P. Greene has argued the case for the limited power of the early modern states and their continuing reliance on negotiated solutions; early absolutism, in short, was anything but absolute. Granting Greene's point, it remains the case that contemporaries were more impressed by the degree to which liberty had been lost than by the extent of its survival.

The "military revolution"–the quantitative and qualitative change in the size and scale of warfare in the early modern period–has attracted several students whose works deepen and refine the story told in the studies just listed. See, for example, Michael Roberts, *The Military Revolution* (Belfast, 1956); Geoffrey Parker, "The 'Military Revolution,' 1560–1660–A Myth?," *Journal of Modern History* 48 (1976): 195–214; and William H. McNeill, *The Pursuit of Power* (Chicago, 1982).

118. Conrad Russell, *The Crisis of Parliaments: English History, 1509–1660* (Oxford, 1971), describes the impact of the "military revolution" on sixteenth-century England, Tudor responses, and continuing problems under the early Stuarts; J. P. Kenyon, *Stuart England*, 2d ed. (Harmondsworth, 1985), covers the seventeenth century as a whole; and, for the dangers of absolutism under the Restoration, see J. R. Jones, *Country and Court: England, 1658–1714* (Cambridge, Mass., 1978). Stephen Saunders Webb argues in *The Governors-General: The English Army and the Definition of the Empire, 1569–1681* (Chapel Hill, N.C., 1979) that the military element (and hence, potentially, the absolutist element) was the dominant one in the creation and administration of the British Empire until the middle of the eighteenth century. For a summary of his arguments, see 436–59, and, for his view that this situation lasted until the Seven Years' War, see 461–66. Webb's work has not won universal assent– see, for example, J. M. Sosin, *English America and the Restoration Monarchy of Charles II: Transatlantic Politics, Commerce, and Kinship* (Lincoln, Neb., 1980), 302–12, 323n.15, and the exchange between Richard R. Johnson and Webb in *WMQ* 43 (1986): 408–59–but it seems convincing to me, suggesting moreover that early Americans were familiar with the experience, and not merely the ideas, of the seventeenth-century constitutional struggle.

119. In France, it would take the reign of Louis XIV to complete the process, on which see Anderson, *Lineages*, 98–106. For the decline of representative institutions elsewhere in Europe, see F. L. Carsten, *The Origins of Prussia* (Oxford, 1954), 184–201 (Brandenburg), 216–18 (Prussia), 243–51 (Cleves and Mark), and for other German states, *Princes and Parliaments in Germany from the Fifteenth to the Eighteenth Century* (Oxford, 1959). On southern Europe, see H. G. Koenigsberger, *The Habsburgs and Europe, 1516–1660* (Ithaca, N.Y., 1971), 33–37 (Castile), 47–55, 100–104 (Sicily, Naples, and Milan), 109–10 (Savoy), 276–83 (Florence), 279–85 (general considerations). On the later developments in central Europe, see R. J. W. Evans, "Maria Theresa and Hungary" and "Joseph II and Nationality in the Habsburg Lands," in H. M. Scott, ed., *Enlightened Absolutism: Reform and Reformers in Later Eighteenth-Century Europe* (Ann Arbor, Mich., 1990), 189–207, and 209–19, and H. M. Scott, "Reform in the Habsburg Monarchy, 1740–90," in ibid., 145–87. Michael Roberts tracks the fate of the Swedish Riksdag in *The Age of Liberty: Sweden, 1719–1772* (Cambridge, 1986); for Denmark, see H. Arnold Barton, *Scandinavia in the Revolutionary Era, 1760–1815* (Minneapolis, 1986). R. R. Palmer describes the

remains of the representative system at mid-eighteenth century, stressing survivals, in *The Age of the Democratic Revolution: A Political History of Europe and America, 1760–1800*, vol. 1, *The Challenge* (Princeton, N.J., 1959), 27–52. For another survey, based on contemporary observations by Italian writers, see Franco Venturi, *The End of the Old Regime in Europe*, trans. R. Burr Litchfield, 3 vols. (Princeton, N.J., 1989–1991). Studies of smaller German principalities offer a sense of how those survivals worked; see Charles W. Ingrao, *The Hessian Mercenary State: Ideas, Institutions, and Reform under Frederick II, 1760–1785* (Cambridge, 1987), and James Allen Vann, *The Making of a State: Württemberg, 1593–1793* (Ithaca, N.Y., 1984).

120. On eighteenth-century European militarism, see Walter L. Dorn, *Competition for Empire, 1740–1763* (New York, 1940), 3–16. Americans in 1776 had only to look to the presence of the Hessians to appreciate the point, which Jefferson underscored in the Declaration. One of the stranger features of Michel Foucault's investigation of the invigilating absolutist and modern states was his relative neglect of the larger context within which the new bureaucracies took shape; Foucault's clinics and prisons appear in a world that, it seems, has nothing to do with international conflict.

121. Revisionist writing on early Stuart politics tends in this direction, and the struggle between Crown and Parliament no longer has the special character it had before historians abandoned nineteenth-century pieties. Still, as J. H. Hexter, among others, stresses, there *were* important issues at stake; see, for example, his Introduction to Hexter, ed., *Parliament and Liberty: From the Reign of Elizabeth to the English Civil War* (Stanford, Calif., 1992), 1–19.

122. Blackstone, *Commentaries*, 1:324. J. H. Plumb, *The Growth of Political Stability in England, 1765–1725* (London, 1967), is the standard account, and see also W. A. Speck, *Stability and Strife, England, 1714–1760* (Cambridge, Mass., 1979), 1–30, 143–66.

123. For Thompson and his school, see E. P. Thompson, *Whigs and Hunters: The Origin of the Black Act* (New York, 1975), esp. 190–218; "The Peculiarities of the English" (1966), in *The Poverty of Theory and Other Essays* (New York, 1978), 258–61; and his revised essays in *Customs in Common* (New York, 1991), esp. "The Patricians and the Plebs," 16–96; Douglas Hay et al., eds., *Albion's Fatal Tree: Crime and Society in Eighteenth-Century England* (New York, 1975); and Peter Linebaugh, *The London Hanged: Crime and Civil Society in the Eighteenth Century* (Cambridge, 1992). Thompson was criticized by some on the left for overlooking the enormous achievements under the Hanoverians. See Perry Anderson, *Arguments within English Marxism* (London, 1980), 87–99, who notes the parallel between Thompson's position and that of the early-eighteenth-century Tory humanists. Bernard Bailyn accepts the contemporary critique of Walpole; according to him, "the opposition literature of early eighteenth-century politics" in England should be seen "not as neurotic fantasies but as realistic responses to the recent history and existing conditions of public life in England" (*The Origins of American Politics* [New York, 1968], 53). Richard L. Bushman, *King and People in Provincial Massachusetts* (Chapel Hill, N.C., 1985), shows that these attitudes were not confined to Britain. For comments by Walpole's biographer, Sir John Plumb, see his *Sir Robert Walpole*, vol. 2, *The King's Minister* (Boston, 1961), 326–28, 330–33, and *Origins of Political Stability*, 187–88, suggestive on the long-term effects.

124. What Namier's interpretation meant can be measured by a comment in Richard Pares, *King George III and the Politicians* (Oxford, 1953), 5: "When this controversy [i.e., the direction of foreign policy] slept—as it often did—there was nothing to think about, in the middle of the eighteenth century, but the control and

composition of the executive government itself. Indeed, when there is nothing to do but to govern, no other subject is worth thinking about." On Namierism, see Jack P. Greene, "The Plunge of Lemmings: A Consideration of Recent Writings on British Politics and the American Revolution," *South Atlantic Quarterly* 67 (1968): 140–75. The title of John Brewer's *Party Ideology and Popular Politics at the Accession of George III* (Cambridge, 1976) confirms that Namier's reign was over. Paul Langford, *Public Life and the Propertied Englishman, 1689–1798* (Oxford, 1991), suggests an even more drastic re-reading of eighteenth-century politics, while Linda Colley, *Britons: Forging the Nation, 1707–1837* (New Haven, Conn., 1992), goes beyond the London crowd to show how widening circles of the population—including women—were incorporated through a triumphalist British nationalism. For a different effort to restore the role of ideas and ideology, see J. C. D. Clark, *English Society, 1688–1832: Ideology, Social Structure, and Political Practice During the Ancien Regime* (Cambridge, 1985), and *Revolution and Rebellion: State and Society in England in the Seventeenth and Eighteenth Centuries* (Cambridge, 1986).

125. See, for example, Lewis Namier, " 'So Come and Join the Dance . . .': An Eighteenth-Century Political Transaction with a Dismal Conclusion" (1928), in *In the Margin of History* (London, 1939), 171–76, and, on a slightly broader scale, L. P. Curtis, *Chichester Towers* (New Haven, Conn., 1966). For evidence that post-1750 radicals continued to object to such "corruption," see Kramnick, "Republican Revisionism Revisited," 165–66, 194–96.

126. Nelson, one of many younger sons of a country clergyman who was himself the younger son of a younger son, owed the beginnings of his career to his mother's family, the Sucklings, related to the Walpoles and ensconced in various offices in the navy. Carola Oman, *Nelson* (Garden City, N.Y., 1946), 1–26. Pitt, another younger son, was blessed with a famous father but no fortune. Nevertheless, he entered Parliament at twenty-one (he sat for Appleby, a borough controlled by the notorious Sir James Lowther), becoming prime minister at twenty-four. Ehrman, *Younger Pitt*, 19–20, 25, 49, 127.

127. As James J. Sheehan remarks, "Defeated in 1793–4, neutral from 1795 to 1806, defeated again in 1806–7, the Hohenzollern were no more successful in their efforts to withstand the revolution than the Habsburgs or the Wittelsbachs; and for them, military failure was also attended by political disruption, territorial rearrangement, and fiscal catastrophe" (*German History, 1770–1866* [Oxford, 1989], 291).

128. For Thompson's comment, see *Whigs and Hunters*, 197–98, and cf. his "Eighteenth-Century English Society: Class Struggle Without Class?" *Social History* 3 (1978): 139–40, and "Peculiarities of the English," 258–60.

129. On eighteenth-century habits of mind, see Arthur O. Lovejoy, *Reflections on Human Nature* (Baltimore, 1961), and, for their role in shaping late-eighteenth-century American politics, two essays by Douglass G. Adair: "That Politics May Be Reduced to a Science: David Hume, James Madison, and the Tenth Federalist," *Huntington Library Quarterly* 20 (1957): 343–60, and "Experience Must Be Our Only Guide: History, Democratic Theory, and the United States Constitution," in Ray A. Billington, ed., *The Reinterpretation of Early American History: Essays in Honor of John Edwin Pomfret* (San Marino, Calif., 1966), 129–48. Lance Banning describes reactions to Hamilton's program in *The Jeffersonian Persuasion: Evolution of a Party Ideology* (Ithaca, N.Y., 1978), 127–60; my own treatment will be found in the next chapter.

130. John G. Murrin, "The Great Inversion, or Court versus Country: A Comparison of the Revolution Settlements in England (1688–1721) and America

(1766–1816)," in J. G. A. Pocock, ed., *Three British Revolutions: 1641, 1688, 1776* (Princeton, N.J., 1980), 368–453.

131. For alternative readings of the Republicans, see Introduction.

132. "I observe that certain characters continue to sport with the Market & with the distresses of their fellow Citizens," Hamilton wrote during the 1792 Duer Panic, adding that it was time for "a line of separation between honest Men & knaves; between respectable stockholders and dealers in the funds, and mere unprincipled Gamblers," and concluding that "Contempt and Neglect must attend those who manifest that they have no principle but to get money" (Hamilton to Philip Livingston, 2 Apr. 1792, *PAH*, 11:218–19). His distinction between "respectable stockholders and dealers" and "unprincipled Gamblers" should be compared with Madison's 1790 distinction between "honest men and sharpers," for which see Chapter 4, text at note 198.

133. For the personnel policies of the Treasury Department and the political effects at the local level, see Carl E. Prince, *The Federalists and the Origins of the U.S. Civil Service* (New York, 1977), 1–182, passim. For summaries of Prince's findings, see Tables 1, 3, 4.

134. For the Quasi-War, see Alexander DeConde, *The Quasi-War: The Politics and Diplomacy of the Undeclared War with France, 1797–1801* (New York, 1966); Manning J. Dauer, *The Adams Federalists* (Baltimore, 1968), 172–97, 212–32; and Stephen G. Kurtz, *The Presidency of John Adams: The Collapse of Federalism, 1795–1800* (Philadelphia, 1957), 284–373. The expansion of the army at home and the reactions it provoked are treated in detail in Richard H. Kohn, *Eagle and Sword: The Federalists and the Creation of the Military Establishment in America, 1783–1802* (New York, 1975), 193–273, 280–86, 299–302. In *The Age of Federalism* (New York, 1993), 529–743, Stanley Elkins and Eric McKitrick have taken a new look at the Quasi-War and the politics of the Adams administration that casts serious doubt on the viability of Adams's "third way"; their conclusions do not, however, affect the point made here, that the Republican reaction to the war, additional debt, taxes, and repression was both entirely predictable and, given the Republican worldview, entirely understandable.

135. For the taxes and resistance to them, see Kurtz, *Presidency of Adams*, 305–6, 336–39, 357–66, 371, and Davis Rich Dewey, *Financial History of the United States*, 2d ed. (New York, 1903), 109–10, 111–12.

136. See, generally, James Morton Smith, *Freedom's Fetters: The Alien and Sedition Laws and American Civil Liberties* (Ithaca, N.Y., 1956), which, like John C. Miller, *Crisis in Freedom: The Alien and Sedition Acts* (Boston, 1952), is something of a tract for its times. A more measured view is Leonard W. Levy, *Emergence of a Free Press* (New York, 1985) and "Liberty and the First Amendment: 1790–1800" *AHR* 68 (1962): 22–37. Jeffrey A. Smith's refutation of Levy, *Printers and Press Freedom: The Ideology of Early American Journalism* (New York, 1988), does not convince. The best-known of the Virginia responses is covered in Adrienne Koch and Harry Ammon, "The Virginia and Kentucky Resolutions: An Episode in Jefferson's and Madison's Defense of Civil Liberties," *WMQ* 5 (1948): 145–76.

137. Gerald Stourzh establishes Hamilton's republican bona fides in *Alexander Hamilton and the Idea of Republican Government* (Stanford, Calif., 1970).

138. In 1982, in *Pursuit of Power*, 210–11, McNeill offered a critique of the literature on the eighteenth-century British economy with respect to this point. Since then, Patrick K. O'Brien and others have improved our understanding, at least for the period of the wars of the French Revolution and Napoleon (1793–1815).

O'Brien's "Political Preconditions for the Industrial Revolution," in Patrick K. O'Brien and Roland Quinault, eds., *The Industrial Revolution and British Society* (Cambridge, 1993), 124–55, is now the starting point for consideration of these issues. For a similar account, see O'Brien's "Central Government and the Economy, 1688–1815," in Roderick Floud and Donald McCloskey, eds., *The Economic History of Britain Since 1700*, vol. 1, *1700–1860*, 2d ed. (Cambridge, 1994), 205–41; significantly, the first edition of Floud and McCloskey's collection (1981) contained no such extended treatment of this issue. For the difficulty of dealing with the American case, compare the positions in the following authorities: Stuart Bruchey, *The Roots of American Economic Growth, 1607–1861: An Essay in Social Causation* (New York, 1965), 112, argues that the transfer of income from taxpayers to securities holders must have had beneficial results; E. James Ferguson, "Political Economy, Public Liberty, and the Formation of the Constitution," *WMQ* 40 (1983): 410, contends that "the consequent redistribution of national wealth generated capital for business," qualifying this by adding: "How much of it was actually applied to that purpose is uncertain"; Curtis P. Nettels, *The Emergence of a National Economy, 1775–1815* (New York, 1962), 94–98, 109–29, esp. 121–26, suggests a stimulus to foreign trade (125–26); Douglass C. North, *The Economic Growth of the United States, 1790–1860* (Englewood Cliffs, N.J., 1961), 17–58, ignores the matter entirely, and in *Growth and Welfare in the American Past: A New Economic History* (Englewood Cliffs, N.J., 1966), 56–57, devotes two sentences to suggesting that Hamilton's plans helped to create a "better capital market" and then drops the subject.

139. For American examples, see note 138. As for Britain, Phyllis Deane, doyenne of historians of the Industrial Revolution, devoted the chapter "The Role of Government" in *The First Industrial Revolution*, 2d ed. (Cambridge, 1979), 219–37, to the rise of laissez-faire and the gradual emergence during the first half of the nineteenth century of more effective government, capable of intervening in ways beneficial rather than harmful. In reviewing the effects of the wars of 1793 to 1815 on the British economy, Deane simply noted that while gross government expenditure amounted to one-quarter of national expenditure, it was not "a serious break on British industrial progress" ("War and Industrialization," in J. M. Winter, ed., *War and Economic Development: Essays in Memory of David Joslin* [Cambridge, 1975], 94, 100).

140. See O'Brien, "Political Preconditions for the Industrial Revolution," and, for an earlier argument in this line, A. H. John, "War and the English Economy, 1700–1763," *Economic History Review*, 2d ser., 7 (1955): 329–44. McNeill makes this point in *Pursuit of Power*, 206–15, emphasizing 1793 to 1815. Comparison of the first and second editions of Peter Mathias, *The First Industrial Nation: An Economic History of Britain, 1700–1914* (New York, 1969; London, 1983) suggests that by the 1980s economic historians were beginning to give this issue its due. The first edition stresses the instability created by state intervention in the eighteenth-century economy (48); the second shows a far keener interest in war's impact on the economy (esp. 40–45).

141. For Hume's prediction, see text at note 38.

142. On France, see Jacques Godechot, *Les Institutions de la France sous la Révolution et l'Empire*, 2d ed. (Paris, 1963), 160–87, 389–98, and, for Bonaparte's cautious financial policy in the wake of revolutionary inflation and debt repudiation, Louis Bergeron, *France under Napoleon*, trans. R. R. Palmer (Princeton, N.J., 1981), 37–51. Some of the emperor's comments on these matters—decidedly similar to Jefferson's—are in J. Christopher Herold, ed. and trans., *The Mind of Napoleon: A Selection from His Written and Spoken Words* (New York, 1955), 93–94. For a revisionist view of the French

situation, see Eugene Nelson White, "Was There a Solution to the Ancien Régime's Financial Dilemma?" *Journal of Economic History* 49 (1989): 545–68, arguing against the idea of "inevitable decline" and suggesting that "the return of the venal financial aristocracy" in the early 1780s sealed France's doom. For Austria, see C. A. Macartney, *The Habsburg Empire, 1790–1918* (New York, 1969), 179–80, 183, 195–98, and, on Russia, Hugh Seton-Watson, *The Russian Empire, 1801–1917* (Oxford, 1967), 157. American financial difficulties in the War of 1812 are discussed in Chapter 6. For Spanish problems, see Jacques S. Barbier and Herbert S. Klein, "Revolutionary Wars and Public Finances: The Madrid Treasury, 1784–1807," *Journal of Economic History* 41 (1981): 324–36. For Britain's conduct of the war's financial side and avoidance of bankruptcy–though not of considerable inflation–see Michael D. Brodo and Eugene N. White, "A Tale of Two Currencies: British and French Finance During the Napoleonic Wars," *Journal of Economic History* 51 (1991): 303–16.

143. For expressions of such views in the 1790s, see Chapter 5.

144. Peter Mathias and Patrick O'Brien, "Taxation in Britain and France, 1715–1810: A Comparison of the Social and Economic Incidence of Taxes Collected for the Central Governments," *Journal of European Economic History* 5 (1976): 601–50, esp. 604–9. Palmer, *Age of the Democratic Revolution*, 1:155, has per capita tax data for various European nations and American states showing that in 1785 only the Dutch paid more than the British; Donal R. Wier, "Tontines, Public Finance, and Revolution in France and England, 1688–1789," *Journal of Economic History* 69 (1989): 95–124, Table 1, suggests that the ratio of taxes to GNP was 6.8 percent in France and 12.4 percent in Britain (between 1792 and 1794, it was 2.0 percent in the United States). On the negative effects of taxation on the Dutch economy, see Charles Wilson, "Taxation and the Decline of Empires, an Unfashionable Theme" (1963), in *Economic History and the Historian: Collected Essays* (New York, 1969), 114–27.

145. Mitchell shows this clearly in *Abstract of British Historical Statistics*, "Public Finance 2. Net Public Expenditure–Great Britain 1688–1801," 389–91. Compare the column headed "Total Net Expenditure" with those headed "Civil Government-Civil List," which includes spending on the court, and "Civil Government-Total."

146. For Britain, see ibid.; for France, see Michel Vovelle, *La Chute de la monarchie, 1787–1792* (Paris, 1972), 92–93, with data from 1786 showing that debt service took 51 percent and military spending 26 percent of state outlays. See also Wier, "Tontines, Public Finance, and Revolution," Table 1. The situation was similar in Naples, according to the British minister; debt service took 60 percent and military spending 20 percent of the revenue in 1764. Brian Fothergill, *Sir William Hamilton: Envoy Extraordinary* (New York, 1969), 42–43. In Prussia, with no permanent debt to service, military spending took 80 percent of the budget in 1740 (a war year), but only about 50 percent in 1786 (a peace year). Rudolf Braun, "Taxation, Sociopolitical Structure, and State-Building: Great Britain and Brandenburg-Prussia," in Tilly, ed., *Formation of National States*, 294. Russia's situation resembled Prussia's, with military expenses falling from some 80 percent of government outlay at mid-century to about 50 percent in the 1780s. Isabel de Madariaga, *Russia in the Age of Catherine the Great* (New Haven, Conn., 1981), 487. In the new United States, military charges and interest on the debt dominated the budget in the 1790s, tending to run at about 75 to 80 percent of total government spending. U.S. Bureau of the Census, *Historical Statistics of the United States: Colonial Times to 1957*, Series Y 350–356, *Expenditures of the Federal Government: 1789–1957* (Washington, D.C., 1960), 719. All these figures reflect only central government expenditures; local and provincial or state expenditures would alter the picture somewhat.

147. O'Brien, "Political Preconditions for the Industrial Revolution," 146; McNeill, *Pursuit of Power*, 206–15; John, "War and the British Economy."

148. On the dockyards, see Robert Greenhalgh Albion, *Forests and Sea Power: The Timber Problem of the Royal Navy, 1652–1862* (Cambridge, Mass., 1926), 68–71, and Mathias, *First Industrial Nation* (1969), 121. Linebaugh's treatment of workers' perquisites in *London Hanged*, 371–401, shows that more than money wages was involved.

149. On the magnitude of such orders, see Norman Baker, *Government and Contractors: The British Treasury and War Supplies, 1775–1783* (London, 1971), esp. 64–90, and, for the shipping–much of it private–required to transport supplies to America, see David Syrett, *Shipping and the American War, 1775–83: A Study of British Transport Organization* (London, 1970). T. S. Willan, *An Eighteenth-Century Shopkeeper: Abraham Dent of Kirkby Stephen* (Manchester, 1970), 60–11, shows the effects of war on a small hosier in the Pennines, the decline in colonial orders after 1774 being offset by increased military demand.

150. McNeill, *Pursuit of Power*, 212.

151. Mathias, *First Industrial Nation* (1969), 44–48. At the end of the Seven Years' War, for example, the army was reduced from 120,000 to 30,000 men. J. Steven Watson, *The Reign of George III, 1760–1815* (Oxford, 1960), 103.

152. For this, see Charles P. Kindleberger, *Manias, Panics, and Crashes: A History of Financial Crises* (New York, 1978), 120–24. Note, however, the argument of James C. Riley, in *The Seven Years War and the Old Regime in France: The Economic and Financial Toll* (Princeton, N.J., 1986), that, at least in France, merchants anticipated the destablizing effects of war, with the result that the apparent peaks and valleys of charted economic activity represent rational responses rather than a war-induced distortion of what would otherwise be an unbroken upward trend. Riley's discussion of this and related issues (104–31) is the most sophisticated attempt so far to measure the economic impact of eighteenth-century war on a major European economy. It remains to be seen whether his conclusions apply to the British case.

153. For Admiralty complaints of starvation at the hands of an economy-minded (-blinded?) ministry, see Watson, *Reign of George III*, 103–4. The desire to keep the army at adequate strength played a role in the decision to station permanent forces in North America after 1763. John Shy, *Toward Lexington: The Role of the British Army in the Coming of the American Revolution* (Princeton, N.J., 1965), 68–83.

154. On this, see text at note 66.

155. The extent of Dutch holdings in the British funds is a matter of debate. See Wilson, *Anglo-Dutch Commerce*, 78, and, for discussion of his controversy with Alice Clare Carter over this, see his "Author's Foreword." Carter's views are in her collected essays, *Getting, Spending and Investing in Early Modern Times: Essays on Dutch, English and Huguenot Economic History* (Assen, 1975); for her conclusion that Dutch investment in British public securities was greatly overestimated by students like Wilson, see, for example, "The Dutch and the English Public Debt in 1777," 20–41. For the Dutch as bankers to the European states in the eighteenth century, see James C. Riley, *International Government Finance and the Amsterdam Capital Market, 1740–1815* (Cambridge, 1980). For Genevan investments, see Herbert Lüthy, *La Banque protestante en France de la révocation de l'édit de Nantes à la Révolution* (Paris, 1961), 2:57–58. The Republic of Bern (see note 43) held some £357,311 in the British funds in 1750. Dickson, *Financial Revolution*, 292–93.

156. Wilson, *Anglo-Dutch Commerce*, 75–78; Riley, *International Government Finance*, 111.

157. Mitchell, *Abstract of British Historical Statistics*, "Public Fiance 2," 389–91.

158. Dickson supplies data on the distribution of ownership at mid-century in *Financial Revolution*, 284–300; for women—many of them no doubt widows—see 298. Dickson's tables include Bank, South Sea, and East India stock, as well as "purely" governmental loans.

159. On the concentration of ownership in the London area, see ibid., 301–2, and, for the two largest individual holdings that Dickson's mid-century survey turned up—the Marlborough estate, with £85,000 or so, and Lord Godolphin, with about £70,000—see 296. On the rather different distribution of East India shares, see H. V. Bowen, "Investment and Empire in the Later Eighteenth Century: East India Stockholding, 1756–1791," *Economic History Review*, 2d ser., 42 (1989): 186–206. Although ownership was concentrated in London and the home counties and in fairly large blocks, aristocratic holdings were scarce (194–95, 199).

160. J. V. Beckett suggests the range of aristocratic economic activity in *The Aristocracy in England, 1660–1914* (Oxford, 1986), pt. 3, "The Aristocracy and the Economy."

161. For a survey going beyond the bounds of our period, see ibid., 287–343. See also J. H. Plumb, "The Noble Houses of Eighteenth-Century England," in *Men and Centuries* (Boston, 1963), 67–79 (on building), and H. J. Habakkuk, "England," in Albert Goodwin, ed., *The European Nobility in the Eighteenth Century: Studies of the Nobilities of the Major European States in the Pre-Reform Era* (London, 1953), 7–8, 10 (on gambling). The great example of how unlimited spending at the gaming tables could be is Charles James Fox, who ran through £100,000 before coming of age. See George Otto Trevelyan, *The Early History of Charles James Fox* (New York, n.d.), 418–26. For the origins of the fortune that made his gambling possible, see note 47. John Cannon provides an overview of the sources of aristocratic wealth that supported these habits in *Aristocratic Century: The Peerage of Eighteenth-Century England* (Cambridge, 1984), chap. 5, "The Sinews of Power: Economic,"

162. François Crouzet, "Editor's Introduction," in Crouzet, ed., *Capital Formation in the Industrial Revolution* (London, 1972), 1–69, esp. 29–64, summarizes the literature on this.

163. The critical role of credit in the expansion of an important branch of Britain's foreign commerce, that with the tobacco colonies, is emphasized in Jacob M. Price, *Capital and Credit in British Overseas Trade: The View from the Chesapeake, 1700–1776* (Cambridge, Mass., 1980), esp. 63–95, for bank credit. In Price's opinion, this was not the most important source (95), but arguably interest deposited in banks helped support short-term business credit. Price has since taken a more positive position on the ability of the debt to provide underpinning for business credit, noting that "in some respects state debt in those countries where state credit was strongest could sustain and help expand semiofficial and private credit," as in the case of the Bank of England, whose holdings of government debt gave it credibility. He adds that government securities held privately "could also be used as the basis for credit" ("Transaction Costs: A Note on Merchant Credit and the Organization of Private Trade," in James D. Tracy, ed., *The Political Economy of Merchant Empires* [Cambridge, 1991], 294–95).

164. Mathias, *First Industrial Nation* (1969), 39–42, argues that the regressive tax structure had two effects: (1) it fell on demand, since mass consumption items were taxed, and therefore did not have adverse consequences for capital accumulation; and (2) it shifted income back to those with a higher propensity to save. In view of the fact that capital for expansion seems to have come from retained earnings (Crouzet,

"Editor's Introduction,"), it is not clear that the first argument would be true of such important and highly taxed industries as brewing. While he is right to urge that there was a shift, it does not follow that those who profited had a higher propensity to save. J. V. Beckett and Michael Edward Turner explore these issues further in "Taxation and Economic Growth in Eighteenth-Century England," *Economic History Review* 43 (1990): 377–403.

165. Mathias and O'Brien, "Taxation in Britain and France," 614–15, 621.

166. M. Dorothy George, *London Life in the 18th Century* (London, 1925), 77.

167. See, for example, Samuel Hollander, *The Economics of Adam Smith* (Toronto, 1973), 138–39, 253–58, which suggests that Smith was of two minds about this.

168. Mathias, *First Industrial Nation* (1969), 39–52.

169. This is not the same as saying that capital accumulation itself was unnecessary; clearly it was. But to the extent that it took place, it seems to have been more efficiently managed by individual entrepreneurs and investors.

170. Note O'Brien's reference to "that entirely unbalanced preoccupation of liberal thought since the time of Adam Smith with the costs of taxes and loans" ("Political Preconditions for the Industrial Revolution," 137).

171. Josiah Tucker, ever the iconoclast, makes the point about Walpole in *The Case of Going to War* (1763), in Schuyler, ed., *Josiah Tucker: A Selection*, 293n*.

172. The argument that war was a necessary part of British economic development in this sense can be found in, for example, E. J. Hobsbawm, *The Making of Modern English Society*, vol. 2, *Industry and Empire, 1750 to the Present Day* (New York, 1968), 33–38, and, more recently and on the basis of considerably more evidence, in O'Brien, "Political Preconditions for the Industrial Revolution," 124–29, 135–44, 151. Similarly, P. J. Cain and A. G. Hopkins make a strong case for the importance of the state (and hence the debt) in the laying the foundations of empire and prosperity in *British Imperialism: Innovation and Expansion, 1688–1914* (London, 1993), esp. chap. 2, "Prospective: Aristocracy, Finance and Empire, 1688–1850." In contrast, Deane, *First Industrial Revolution*, devotes a chapter to the expansion of foreign trade ("The Commercial Revolution," 53–71) and only in passing mentions (57) the effects of British naval supremacy after 1793.

173. For the contemporary perception that the national debt had been instituted in part because higher taxes were politically impossible, see Blackstone, *Commentaries*, 1:315–16, and Smith, *Wealth of Nations*, 1:920–21.

174. On the importance of the export sector in pacing British growth, see, for example, Deane, *First Industrial Revolution*, 69–71; Mathias, *First Industrial Nation* (1969), 103–6; and P. K. O'Brien and S. L. Engerman, "Exports and the Growth of the British Economy from the Glorious Revolution to the Peace of Amiens," in Barbara L. Solow, ed., *Slavery and the Rise of the Atlantic System* (Cambridge, 1991), 177–209.

175. Eighteenth-century peace plans are discussed in F. H. Hinsley, *Power and the Pursuit of Peace: Theory and Practice in the History of Relations Between States* (Cambridge, 1963), 33–80. For American efforts after 1789–not always successful–to realize some of that utopian vision, see Doron S. Ben-Atar, *The Origins of Jeffersonian Commercial Policy and Diplomacy* (Manchester, 1993); Merrill D. Peterson, "Thomas Jefferson and Commercial Policy, 1783–1793," *WMQ* 22 (1965): 584–610; Burton Spivak, *Jefferson's English Crisis: Commerce, Embargo, and the Republican Revolution* (Charlottesville, Va., 1979); Robert W. Tucker and David C. Hendrickson, *Empire of Liberty: The Statecraft of Thomas Jefferson* (New York, 1990); and Peter Onuf and Nicholas Onuf, *Federal Union, Modern World: The Law of Nations in an Age of Revolutions, 1776–1814* (Madison, Wis., 1993).

176. Cf. Crouzet, "Editor's Introduction," 48–53. Deane suggests that "there was a good deal of capital invested in the Funds, in land, and in game preserves and country-houses in the second half of the eighteenth century, that was yielding a very low return indeed, in either money or in goods and services, compared with what it could be made to yield in canals and turnpike trusts" (*First Industrial Revolution*, 84). The problem was thus not the lack of capital but the unproductive use much of it was put to.

177. Mitchell, *Abstract of British Historical Statistics*, "Public Finance 5. Nominal Amount of the Unredeemed Capital of the Public Debt . . .," 401 (total debt, 1774), "Public Finance 2," 390 (total debt charges, 1774), "Overseas Trade I, Official Values of Overseas Trade" . . . Great Britain 1772–1803," 281 (domestic imports and re-exports, less imports, 1774).

178. TJ to James Madison, 4, 21 June 1792, *Boyd*, 24:26, 106.

179. The classic statement is Jefferson's in the "Anas," 1818, *LofA*, 666–67.

180. For speculators' holdings, see Whitney K. Bates, "Northern Speculators and Southern State Debts: 1790," *WMQ* 19 (1962): 30–48, and E. James Ferguson, *The Power of the Purse: A History of American Public Finance, 1776–1790* (Chapel Hill, N.C., 1961), 251–86, 327–30.

181. Cf. John Taylor, *An Inquiry into the Principles and Policy of the Government of the United States* (1814), ed. Loren Baritz (Indianapolis, 1969), 223–28, 237–38.

182. For an overview, see Mira Wilkins, *The History of Foreign Investment in the United States to 1914* (Cambridge, Mass., 1989), 31–41. By 1795, foreigners held $20,288,637 of the American debt; by 1801, the figure was $33,041,135. Ralph W. Hidy, *The House of Baring in American Trade and Finance: English Merchant Bankers at Work, 1763–1861* (Cambridge, Mass., 1949), 34. The latter amount was some 40 percent of the $83,038,000 federal debt then outstanding. Bureau of the Census, *Historical Statistics*, Series Y 368–379, *Public Debt of the Federal Government: 1791–1957*, 721. Foreign ownership also accounted for 13,000 of the 25,000 shares of the Bank of the United States in 1798; by 1809, two years before the Bank's charter expired, it would be 18,000. Hidy, *House of Baring*, 34. For data on who in England bought American stock, see Charles R. Ritcheson, *Aftermath of Revolution: British Policy toward the United States, 1783–1795* (Dallas, 1969), 205–9. For a Belgian patrician family's investments in American securities during this period, see Margaret Law Callcott, ed., *Mistress of Riversdale: The Plantation Letters of Rosalie Stier Calvert, 1795–1821* (Baltimore, 1991). There was a small reverse flow; by 1810, Americans held £438,455 in the British funds. Larry Neal, *The Rise of Financial Capitalism: International Capital Markets in the Age of Reason* (Cambridge, 1990), 209.

183. For the sacredness of the debt, see TJ to Madison, 6 Sept. 1789, *Boyd*, 15:397. For some of his comments on the illegitimate uses to which the loans raised during the Quasi-War were put, see his letters to Virginia correspondents early in 1799: to James Monroe, 23 Jan. 1799; to Edmund Pendleton, 29 Jan. 1799, *Ford*, 9:9–10, 28; to Nicholas Lewis, 30 Jan. 1799, *L&B*, 10:89–91; to Madison, 30 Jan. 1799, *PJM*, 17:223; to Monroe, 11 Feb. 1799; to Archibald Stuart, 13 Feb. 1799, *Ford*, 9:36–37, 41–42; and see also to Samuel Adams, 26 Feb. 1800, ibid., 114.

184. On Republican alternatives to war, less successful in the long run than their proponents hoped, see Ben-Atar, *Origins of Jeffersonian Commercial Policy*; Peterson, "Thomas Jefferson and Commercial Policy"; Spivak, *Jefferson's English Crisis*; and Tucker and Hendrickson, *Empire of Liberty*. In *Federal Union, Modern World*, Onuf and Onuf set Republican policy preferences in the broader context of the shift from the traditional law of nations to the then emerging concept of international law.

185. Changing patterns of trade make it impossible to determine the extent of Virginia's consumption of imports after 1790 and hence to establish the burden that import duties posed. Before the Revolution, goods were imported directly from Britain; but after the Revolution, the decline of the tobacco trade and the rise of Philadelphia and Baltimore as wholesaling centers led many Virginians to turn to those cities for imports. This was true of Washington and Jefferson, and no doubt of many less prominent consumers as well. Thus while available statistics show Virginia lagging behind Pennsylvania and Maryland in the volume of imports after 1790, it is probably the case that the Virginians paid (through price markups) a good deal more in the way of import duties than official figures suggest. Hence the data on the burden of federal taxes in Virginia in the 1790s in H. James Henderson, "Taxation and Political Culture: Massachusetts and Virginia, 1760–1800," *WMQ* 47 (1990): 112, Table 6, probably require upward revision. For the shift from direct imports to importing via Philadelphia, see, for example, Washington's letters to his agent in Philadelphia, "Selections from the Correspondence of Colonel Clement Biddle," *Pennsylvania Magazine of History and Biography* 42 (1918): 310–43; 43 (1919): 53–76, 143–62, 193–207; and Jedidiah Morse, *The American Universal Geography . . .*, 2 vols. (Boston, 1802), 1:534. I conjecture that this was also the case with the rising port of Baltimore, on which see Garry Lawson Browne, *Baltimore in the New Nation, 1789–1861* (Chapel Hill, N.C., 1980).

186. TJ to Thomas Mann Randolph, Jr., 2 Feb. 1800, *L&B*, 10:152–53, and, for more detail, see TJ to Randolph, 13 Jan., 4 Mar. 1800, Jefferson Papers, LC; and TJ to Henry Remsen, 4 Mar. 1800, *Farm Book*, 273–74.

187. Prince supplies details of the Federalist organization in Virginia, such as it was in *Federalists and the Origins of the Civil Service*, 105–17, 145–46.

188. For a concise statement of the case in Hamilton's favor, see Bruchey, *Roots of American Economic Growth*, 108–16. As will be clear from what follows, it seems to me that the problem with this and similar interpretations is that they tend to take Hamilton's wish for the deed, much as Hamilton himself would in his valedictory report. On the latter, see note 189.

189. Hamilton, *Report on Public Credit*, 9 Jan. 1790, *PAH*, 6:67, 70–71, contains his claims for the advantages of a "properly funded" debt that "answers most of the purposes of money" (70). On retiring, he was confident that these predictions had been realized; see his *Report on a Plan for the Further Support of Public Credit*, 16 Jan. 1795, ibid., 18:127: "If the individual Capital of this Country has become more adequate to its exigencies than formerly, 'tis because individuals have found new resources in the public *Credit*, in the funds to which *that* has given value and activity." For his view that a monetized debt could support the expansion of American manufacturing and commerce, see the *Report on the Subject of Manufactures*, 5 Dec. 1791, and the *Second Report on the Further Provision Necessary for Establishing Public Credit*, 13 Dec. 1790, ibid., 10:277–83; 8:320–21.

190. For the quoted language, see Elkins and McKitrick, *Age of Federalism*, 441. The carrying trade as the source of American prosperity in the 1790s is persuasively urged in North, *Economic Growth of the United States*, 24–58, and see also Donald R. Adams, Jr., "American Neutrality and Prosperity, 1793–1808: A Reconsideration," *Journal of Economic History* 40 (1980): 713–37, esp. the conclusions on the geographic and social limitations of that prosperity (734–35).

191. On the generally dismal performance of these enterprises, see Joseph Stancliffe Davis, "Eighteenth-Century Business Corporations in the United States," in *Essays in the Earlier History of American Corporations* (Cambridge, Mass., 1917),

2:173–85, 279–83. For land speculation, see Nettels, *Emergence of a National Economy*, 149–54.

192. For the bank's policies, see its 1791 Ordinance and By-Laws, in John Thom Holdsworth, "The First Bank of the United States," in Holdsworth and Davis R. Dewey, *The First and Second Banks of the United States* (Washington, D.C., 1910), 133–35.

193. Shortly after the French invaded the United Provinces, Hamilton was warned by the United States' bankers in Amsterdam that this would be the case. Willink, Van Staphorst, and Hubbard to Hamilton, 5 Jan. 1795, *PAH*, 18:23, where the bankers note that this was in some ways simply the coup de grâce for the Dutch money market, already weakened by the Dutch East India Company and French state bankruptcies. For the difficulties these new conditions presented to Hamilton's successor, Oliver Wolcott, see, for example, Wolcott to Hamilton, 21 Dec. 1798, ibid., 22:382–83, and Dewey, *Financial History of the United States*, 111–13, 117. James C. Riley notes the extreme dependence of American finances on the Amsterdam money market in the early 1790s in "Foreign Credit and Fiscal Stability: Dutch Investment in the United States, 1781–1794," *JAH* 65 (1978): 654–78.

194. John Adams was one of those appalled by the loan's expense. Dauer, *Adams Federalists*, 241–42. For Jefferson's reactions, see the letters cited in note 183.

195. Holdsworth, *First Bank*, 45–47.

196. For the collapse of American credit during the War of 1812, see Chapter 6.

197. Gordon S. Wood, "Interests and Disinterestedness in the Making of the Constitution," in Richard Beeman et al., eds., *Beyond Confederation: Origins of the Constitution and American National Identity* (Chapel Hill, N.C., 1987), 77–79; the activities of the military supply system are studied in E. Wayne Carp, *To Starve the Army at Pleasure: Continental Army Administration and American Political Culture, 1775–1783* (Chapel Hill, N.C., 1984), and Ena Risch, *Supplying Washington's Army* (Washington, D.C., 1981). For an account of activity in a single state, see Richard Buel, Jr., *Dear Liberty: Connecticut's Mobilization for the Revolutionary War* (Middletown, Conn., 1980). For the less flourishing condition of Revolutionary Virginia, see John E. Selby, *The Revolution in Virginia, 1775–1783* (Williamsburg, Va., 1988), chap. 9, "The Economy in War," esp. 167–68, 182–83. Thomas M. Doerflinger, *A Vigorous Spirit of Enterprise: Merchants and Economic Development in Revolutionary Philadelphia* (Chapel Hill, N.C., 1986), 356–64, speculates on the failure of Virginia planters (in contrast to his Philadelphia merchants) to develop a business culture that would have taken advantage of the state's resources and led the Old Dominion to a more productive economy.

198. Bureau of the Census, *Historical Statistics*, Series Y 350–356, *Expenditures of the Federal Government: 1789–1957*, 719, shows that between 1789 and 1810 spending on the army and navy amounted to $57,808,000, while interest payments on the public debt amounted to $68,848,000.

199. The number of seamen in the navy rose from 1,425 in 1808 to 7,500 in 1814. Ibid., Series Y 736–775, *Military Personnel on Active Duty: 1789–1957*, 737. For suggestions as to the importance of military spending for the frontier economy, see Elkins and McKitrick, *Age of Federalism*, 468, and for the possibilities for peculation en route, see Boyd, editorial note, "Threat of Disunion in the West," *Boyd*, 19:442–469.

200. I deliberately bracket the argument that the way in which Hamilton managed the debt–by insisting that it not be repudiated or unfavorably modified and that present holders be paid more or less in full–helped to secure the dominance of

market relations and provided essential backing for the newer kinds of contract rights underpinning capitalist notions of property. In the first place, as early- and mid-nineteenth-century experience with state and local debt demonstrates, the values Hamilton contended for took decades to establish, and the story of American public finance below the federal level is often one of repudiation and readjustment; in the second, as students of nineteenth-century American law have shown, the transition from a traditional moral economy to full-blown capitalism was only just beginning in 1790. Hamilton may have provided a model, but it was only a model, and neither he nor John Marshall could impose it fully. For Hamilton and the security of property rights, see Stuart Burchey, *Enterprise: The Dynamic Economy of a Free People* (Cambridge, Mass., 1990), 127–28, 129; B. U. Ratchford, *American State Debts* (Durham, N.C., 1941), discusses state debt repudiation and readjustment; on municipal bond repudiation, see Charles Fairman, *Reconstruction and Reunion, 1864–88, Part One* (New York, 1971), 918–1116; and Morton J. Horwitz, *The Transformation of American Law, 1780–1860* (Cambridge, Mass., 1977), treats changes in antebellum American law favoring capitalist development.

201. On the concentration of the debt in a relatively small number of hands, see Bates, "Northern Speculators and Southern State Debts," and Ferguson, *Power of the Purse*, 251–86, 327–30.

202. Albert J. Beveridge, *The Life of John Marshall*, 4 vols. (Boston, 1916–1919), 2:202–5, 210–11; John Marshall, Receipts, 10 Feb. 1792, 30 Sept., 3 Oct. 1793; Articles of Agreement, 1 Feb. 1793; Robert Morris to Marshall, 30 Dec. 1796, 23 Jan. 1797, in Herbert A. Johnson et al., eds., *The Papers of John Marshall*, 7 vols. to date (Chapel Hill, N.C., 1974–   ), 2:109, 215, 153; 3:60–61, 63.

203. For the dangers of land speculation in the 1790s, see the survey in Nettels, *Emergence of a National Economy*, 149–54.

204. Ibid., 149, 153–54.

205. On the political problems, notably present in New York, see Pieter J. Van Winter, *American Finances and Dutch Investment, 1780–1805: With an Epilogue to 1840*, trans. James C. Riley, 2 vols. (New York, 1977), 2:734–41, an account sympathetic to the investors.

206. North, *Economic Growth of the United States*, 24–32, 38–45, 47–51.

207. For the profits to be made in an expanding area of American commerce, the India trade, see Kenneth Wiggins Porter, *The Jacksons and the Lees: Two Generations of Massachusetts Merchants, 1765–1844*, 2 vols. (Cambridge, Mass., 1937), 1:71–73, which concludes that before 1815, barring "some unforeseen calamity, the East India trade seemed to be capable of producing, at the least, normal interest of 6% per annum on the investment and occasionally as much as 40% and 60%" (73).

208. "You will perceive by the newspapers," Jefferson wrote from Philadelphia to the American minister in Paris, Gouverneur Morris, on 12 Mar. 1793, "a remarkable fall in the price of our public paper. This is owing chiefly to the extraordinary demand for the produce of our country, and a temporary scarcity of cash to purchase it. The merchants holding public paper are obliged to part with it any price, to raise money" (*Boyd*, 25:369).

209. On the Barings' role as agents, first for the Bank of the United States and then for the federal government itself, see Hidy, *House of Baring*, 30, 32–35.

210. For these claims, see note 189.

211. The Louisiana Purchase was financed by giving bonds to the French, who sold them, promptly and at a discount, to British investors, thus increasing foreign holdings of the American debt. Hidy, *House of Baring*, 33–34.

212. Ferguson, *Power of the Purse*, 256–58, notes the low prices prevailing up to the end of 1789–never more than 50 and more commonly around 20 cents on the dollar.

213. TJ to Madison, 6 Sept. 1789, *Boyd*, 15:397, and see also Chapters 1 and 2.

214. Despite their dislike of military expense, many southern Republicans warmly supported the western campaigns of the early 1790s. On their endorsement of the Indian war in 1792, see Gerard Clarfield, "Protecting the Frontiers: Defense Policy and the Tariff Question in the First Washington Administration," *WMQ* 32 (1975): 444–48, 450–51.

215. On reaction to the acquisition of Louisiana, see *Malone*, 4:297, 302–3, 325, 338–39, 345, contrasting Federalist and Republican attitudes.

Chapter 4

1. TJ to George Washington, 9 Sept. 1792, *Boyd*, 24:352.

2. James Madison to Henry Lee, 13 Apr. 1790, *PJM*, 13:148.

3. For Jefferson's characterization, see TJ to George Mason, 13 June 1790, *Boyd*, 16:493. Although it entered his vocabulary late in his life, Jefferson was delighted to discover the word "logrolling," eagerly explaining its uses and derivation to his correspondents. TJ to Albert Gallatin, 16 June 1817; TJ to William Branch Giles, 26 Dec. 1825, *L&B*, 15:134–35; 16:148. As Joyce Appleby reminds us in *Without Resolution: The Jeffersonian Tension in American Nationalism* (Oxford, 1992), 11–12, Jefferson was always an enthusiast for neologisms.

4. For modern accounts of the Dinner Table Bargain and its context, suggesting that matters were more complex than Jefferson's recollection would indicate–probably more complex than he knew–see Jacob E. Cooke, "The Compromise of 1790," *WMQ* 27 (1970): 523–45; Kenneth R. Bowling, "Dinner at Jefferson's: A Note on Jacob E. Cooke's 'The Compromise of 1790,' " and Cooke's rebuttal, *WMQ* 28 (1971): 629–48; Boyd, editorial notes, "Opinions on the Constitutionality of the Residence Bill," "Fixing the Seat of Government on the Potomac," and "Locating the Federal District," *Boyd*, 17: 163–83, 452–60; 19:3–58; editorial note, "From Josiah Parker," *PJM*, 13:243–46; Norman K. Risjord, *Chesapeake Politics, 1781–1800* (New York, 1978), 363–93, and "The Compromise of 1790: New Evidence on the Dinner Table Bargain," *WMQ* 33 (1976): 309–14; and Kenneth R. Bowling, *The Creation of Washington, D.C.: The Idea and Location of the American Capital* (Fairfax, Va., 1991), 161–207.

5. See TJ to Washington, 9 Sept. 1792, *Boyd*, 24:352, and Madison, "Notes on William Loughton Smith's *Politicks and Views*" [ca. 4 Nov. 1792], *PJM*, 14:396–400, esp. 398–99, discussed in Chapter 5.

6. For Jefferson's efforts to explain himself, see TJ to Washington, 9 Sept. 1792, *Boyd*, 24:352, and, for his 1818 effort, posthumously published as the introduction to the "Anas," Chapter 6.

7. For references in this vein to the Dinner Table Bargain, see Donald H. Stewart, *The Opposition Press of the Federalist Period* (Albany, N.Y., 1969), 49–50. Norman K. Risjord cites "the sly maneuvers, unholy alliances, and public half-truths that accompanied the compromise of 1790–in which the Virginians won not only the capital but a financial windfall through assumption," asking whether "Jefferson and Madison [could] seriously contend that the Federalists were the architects of corruption and national decay?" (review of *The Jeffersonian Persuasion*, by Lance Banning, *WMQ* 35 [1978]: 746). Risjord wants to question Banning's ideological analysis, but the

point is that ideology made Jefferson intensely aware that he had sinned, and grievously so.

8. See Chapter 6.

9. See, for example, E. James Ferguson, *The Power of the Purse: A History of American Public Finance, 1776–1790* (Chapel Hill, N.C., 1961), 320. Jefferson's principal biographer notes that his comments on assumption in 1790 were less categorical about his lack of understanding of Hamilton's intentions than they later became. *Malone*, 2:300–301.

10. On his inability to admit that there might be a range of legitimate choices in a given situation, see John Lauritz Larson, "Jefferson's Union and the Problem of Internal Improvements," in Peter S. Onuf, ed., *Jeffersonian Legacies* (Charlottesville, Va., 1993), 353–56.

11. The phrase is borrowed from Adrienne Koch's classic account, *Jefferson and Madison: The Great Collaboration* (New York, 1950).

12. Boyd presented a version of the incident that differs in significant ways from mine; see his editorial note, "Cabinet Opinions on the Resolutions Concerning Arrearages in Soldiers' Pay," and "Appendix: The First Conflict in the Cabinet," *Boyd*, 16:455–62; 18:611–88. Those familiar with Boyd's self-appointed role as prosecutor of Alexander Hamilton at the bar of history will recall that most of the "Appendix" is given over to proving that Hamilton faked his correspondence in the Reynolds affair in order to cover up his countenancing of wrongdoing at the Treasury Department; Boyd's exercise in innuendo and speculation has convinced no one. His eagerness to present further grounds on which to convict Hamilton of general heinousness led him into errors of fact and interpretation. For example, in *Number 7: Alexander Hamilton's Secret Attempts to Control American Foreign Policy* (Princeton, N.J., 1964), an expanded version of an editorial note in *Boyd*, 17, he demonstrated, if only to himself, that Hamilton was a traitor. I point these out in the notes at appropriate places in my account of the Arrears incident.

13. Or so he would later insist, claiming that "when I embarked in the government, it was with a determination to intermeddle not at all with the legislature, and as little as possible with my co-departments" (TJ to Washington, 9 Sept. 1792, *Boyd*, 25:352).

14. The conflict between Hamilton and Madison in 1790 can be taken to symbolize this.

15. The best case along these lines is in Ferguson, *Power of the Purse*, 309–20, 323–25; for a more colorful version, see Forrest McDonald, *Alexander Hamilton: A Biography* (New York, 1979), 163–88.

16. George Washington, First Inaugural Address, 30 Apr. 1789, in W. W. Abbot, ed., *The Papers of George Washington: Presidential Series* (Charlottesville, Va., 1987), 2:175.

17. For an overview of the Federalists' argument, see David F. Epstein, "The Case for Ratification: Federalist Constitutional Thought," in Leonard W. Levy and Dennis J. Mahoney, eds., *The Framing and Ratification of the Constitution* (New York, 1987), 283–98.

18. "John De Witt," "To the Free Citizens of the Commonwealth of Massachusetts," No. 1, 22 Oct. 1787, in Cecelia M. Kenyon, ed., *The Antifederalists* (Indianapolis, 1966), 95.

19. "A Plebian" [Melancthon Smith], *Address to the People of the State of New York* (1788), in Paul Leicester Ford, ed., *Pamphlets on the Constitution of the United States . . .* (Brooklyn, N.Y., 1888), 106–7.

20. "Publius" [Hamilton], *Federalist*, No. 11, 24 Nov. 1787, in *The Federalist*, ed. Jacob E. Cooke (Middletown, Conn., 1961), 65.

21. See, for example, "A Jerseyman to the Citizens of New Jersey," *Trenton Mercury*, 6 Nov. 1787; "Philanthrope: To the People," *American Mercury*, 19 Nov. 1787; James Campbell, *Oration Delivered in Philadelphia* (1787); "A True American," *Massachusetts Centinel*, 29 Sept. 1787; Petition of New Castle County Inhabitants, 24 Oct. 1787, DHRC, 1:147–50, 469; 2:164, 267; 3:55–56. On the success of these appeals, see Van Beck Hall, *Politics Without Parties: Massachusetts, 1780–1791* (Pittsburgh, 1972), 273–93, and Alfred F. Young, *The Democratic Republicans of New York: The Origins, 1763–1797* (Chapel Hill, N.C., 1967), 83–105.

22. For a survey of the literature on the Virginia gentry's political ethos, see Herbert Sloan and Peter Onuf, "Politics, Culture, and the Revolution in Virginia: A Review of Recent Work," *VMHB* 91 (1983): 267–74, 279–82. T. H. Breen, *Tobacco Culture: The Mentality of the Great Tidewater Planters on the Eve of Revolution* (Princeton, N.J., 1985), is an important subsequent addition.

23. On the Virginia convention, see Lance Banning, "Virginia: Sectionalism and the Common Good," in Michael Allen Gillespie and Michael Lienesch, eds., *Ratifying the Constitution* (Lawrence, Kans., 1989), 261–99; John Kukla, "A Spectrum of Sentiments: Virginia's Federalists, Antifederalists, and 'Federalists Who Are for Amendments,' 1787–1788," *VMHB* 96 (1988): 277–96; Norman K. Risjord, "Virginians and the Constitution: A Multivariant Analysis," *WMQ* 31 (1974): 613–32; and J. Thomas Wren, "The Ideology of Court and Country in the Virginia Ratifying Convention of 1788," *VMHB* 93 (1985): 398–408. The documents are in *DHRC*, 8–10.

24. For the Virginia amendments, see Helen E. Veit et al., eds., *Creating the Bill of Rights: The Documentary Record of the First Federal Congress* (Baltimore, 1991), 17–21. Virginians were not alone in proposing amendments, particularly on the taxing power. For similar proposals from Pennsylvania, New York, and North Carolina, see Thomas P. Slaughter, "The Tax Man Cometh: Ideological Opposition to Internal Taxes, 1760–1790," *WMQ* 41 (1984): 585. H. James Henderson, "Taxation and Political Culture: Massachusetts and Virginia, 1760–1800," *WMQ* 47 (1990): 90–114, esp. 109–14, explains why federal taxation appeared to hit Virginia especially hard; Antifederalists were not mistaken. Roger H. Brown, *Redeeming the Republic: Federalists, Taxation, and the Origins of the Constitution* (Baltimore, 1993), reviews the links connecting the nationalist drive to strengthen central government in the 1780s by providing dependable and independent sources of revenue, the conservative desire to impose economic discipline on the population, and the program that resulted in 1789 and 1790.

25. Madison to Hamilton, 27 June 1788 (quotation); Madison to Washington, 27 June 1788; to TJ, 24 July 1788; Madison to Tench Coxe, 30 July 1788; Madison to Edmund Randolph, 22 Aug. 1788; Madison to TJ, 23 Aug., 21 Sept. 1788, *PJM*, 11:181, 182–83, 196–97, 210, 237, 238–39, 257–58.

26. Madison to Hamilton, 27 June 1788, ibid., 182. For additional commentary on Henry's opposition after the convention, see Madison to TJ, 24 July 1788 ("But altho' the leaders, particularly H—y & M–s–n, will give no countenance to popular violences it is not to be inferred that they are reconciled to the event, or will give it a positive support"); Madison to E. Randolph, 2 Nov. 1788 (Henry's "enmity was levelled, as he did not scruple to insinuate agst the *whole System*; and the destruction of the whole System, I take to be still the secret wish of his heart, and the real object of his pursuit"), ibid., 196–97, 329.

27. On Antifederalist efforts to take revenge on Madison in the fall of 1788, see the surviving correspondence and legislative material in Gordon DenBoer, ed., *The Documentary History of the First Federal Elections, 1788–1790* (Madison, Wis., 1984), 2:280–82 (Senate elections), 283–97 (gerrymandering), and 257–73 (commentary in correspondence). For a narrative, see Risjord, *Chesapeake Politics*, 322–26.

28. For Madison's contest with Monroe, see DenBoer, ed., *Documentary History of First Elections*, 2:317–49, and see Madison to George Thompson, 29 Jan. 1789, ibid., 341–44, for his refusal to compromise on direct taxes, a position in decided contrast to his willingness to permit amendments on other scores, particularly liberty of conscience, on which see Madison to George Eve, 2 Jan. 1789, ibid., 330–31.

29. For the date of the Virginia elections, see ibid., 256. Steven R. Boyd argues that "the first federal elections in Virginia demonstrated, even as they fostered its further development, the high degree of acceptance of the Constitution among the state's voters" (*The Politics of Opposition: Antifederalists and the Acceptance of the Constitution* [Millwood, N.Y., 1979], 158). Emphasizing voter willingness to elect Federalists, Boyd ignores (as Madison never did) the extent to which Antifederalist leaders remained unrepentant. Since the chief of the party was the most charismatic politician Virginia ever knew, Federalists like Madison did not make Boyd's mistake of assuming the struggle was over. For Antifederalism's continuing appeal, see Richard E. Ellis, "The Persistence of Antifederalism After 1789," in Richard Beeman et al., eds., *Beyond Confederation: Origins of the Constitution and American National Identity* (Chapel Hill, N.C., 1987), 295–314, and, for a detailed study of the Virginia case, see Richard R. Beeman, *The Old Dominion and the New Nation, 1788–1801* (Lexington, Ky., 1972).

30. For the official Virginia Antifederalist reaction, see Richard Henry Lee and William Grayson to the speaker of the House of Delegates, 28 Sept. 1789, in Veit, ed., *Creating the Bill of Rights*, 299–300 (Lee and Grayson were Virginia's senators, both moderate Antifederalists). Madison's reaction to the letter was to tell the president that it was "well calculated to keep alive the disaffection to the Government, and is accordingly applied to that use by the violent partizans," blaming it on Lee and expressing surprise that Grayson had signed. Madison to Washington, 5 Dec. 1789, *PJM*, 12:458.

31. Madison to TJ, 9 May 1789, *PJM*, 12:142. Lance Banning has suggested that Madison's record in Congress in the 1780s shows him "urging mutual concessions and almost instinctively inclined to associate Virginia's interests with the long-term needs of the country as a whole" ("The Hamiltonian Madison: A Reconsideration," *VMHB* 92 [1984]: 17). Banning's sense of Madison's position in the 1780s is further developed in "James Madison and the Nationalists, 1780–1783," *WMQ* 40 (1983): 227–55, and "The Practicable Sphere of a Republic: James Madison, the Constitutional Convention, and the Emrgence of Revolutionary Federalism," in Beeman et al., eds., *Beyond Confederation*, 162–87. Drew McCoy's essay in the same collection, "James Madison and Visions of American Nationality in the Confederation Period: A Regional Perspective," ibid., 226–58, suggests additional reasons for Madison's optimism at the outset of the federal experiment. But his problem from 1789 on is that it becomes increasingly less easy to square Virginia's interests with those the Federalists from commercial centers and the North insist are national, hence less easy to obtain concessions.

32. TJ to Washington, 4 Dec. 1788; TJ to Alexander Donald, 8 Apr. 1790, *Boyd*, 14:328; 16:325.

33. Jonathan Dayton to John Cleves Symmes, 22 Oct. 1788, in Beverley W. Bond, Jr., ed., *The Correspondence of John Cleves Symmes, Founder of the Miami Purchase* (New York, 1926), 206.

34. Ibid., 206–7.

35. This is not to argue that the purpose of the Constitution was to enrich securities holders; in that sense, Beard was wrong. Nevertheless, as Ferguson remarks, "It seems indisputable that as a group the [public] creditors supported the Constitution. . . . Constitutional reform had always involved public finance. The decision to establish a national government entailed federal taxation and the payment of the debt, irrespective of the designs of creditors, who assisted the process, reaped its benefits, but did not create it" (*Power of the Purse*, 340–41). See also Brown, *Redeeming the Republic*.

36. Ferguson, *Power of the Purse*, 289–92; Madison, speech on Import Duties, 15 May 1789, *PJM*, 12:163–65.

37. TJ to Madison, 18 Nov. 1788, *Boyd*, 14:189, and, for the question generally, see Boyd, editorial note, "Proposals for Funding the Foreign Debt," ibid., 190–97.

38. Washington, Inaugural Address, 30 Apr. 1789, in Abbott, ed., *Washington Papers: Pres. Ser.*, 2:175. On Madison as draftsman, see editorial note, "First Inaugural Address," ibid., 152–54, and editorial note, "Address of the President to Congress," *PJM*, 12:120–21. The Madison editors are more certain than the Washington editors about Madison's role in creating the address.

39. The Nationalists of the 1780s and their understanding of how this would be done are discussed in E. James Ferguson, "Political Economy, Public Liberty, and the Formation of the Constitution," *WMQ* 40 (1983): 401–7.

40. Even so, the first formal memorial on the debt was not presented to Congress until late August. Memorial of the Public Creditors of Pennsylvania, 28 Aug. 1789, *DHFFC*, 5:738–42. Clearly, the creditors were alarmed that Congress was about to rise without having addressed the debt.

41. Madison, speech on Import and Tonnage Duties, 8 Apr. 1789, *PJM*, 12:65.

42. As Edmund Pendleton pointed out to Madison on 9 June 1789, ibid., 17:535. His first day in office saw Hamilton appealing to the Philadelphia Bank of North America for a $50,000 loan to meet the government's immediate needs. Hamilton to Thomas Willing, 13 Sept. 1789, *PAH*, 5:370–71.

43. For the appointment, see *DHFFC*, 2:38–39; on the work of the Treasury Department, see Leonard D. White, *The Federalists: A Study in Administrative History* (New York, 1948), 117–27, and Carl E. Prince, *The Federalists and the Origins of the U.S. Civil Service* (New York, 1977), 21–182.

44. House of Representatives, Resolution, 21 Sept. 1789, *DHFFC*, 3:220.

45. Ferguson discusses his ties to speculators in New York, concluding that "Hamilton was scrupulous, but he could not keep from imparting information to such companions" (*Power of the Purse*, 270–71). See also Joseph Stancliffe Davis, "William Duer, Entrepreneur, 1747–99," in *Essays in the Earlier History of American Corporations* (Cambridge, Mass., 1917), 1:188–192. The French minister, comte de Moustier, referred to Hamilton's "rapports avec des speculateurs et agioteurs hardis et bien reconnus" (conversation with Comte de Moustier, 13 Sept. 1789, *PAH*, 5:367). In the hands of Boyd, such comments would become the foundation for the indictment in "Appendix," *Boyd*, 18:611–88. Ferguson's judgment is preferable; unwise in the company he kept, Hamilton was not personally corrupt.

46. Hamilton to Madison, 12 Oct. 1789, *PAH*, 5:439; Madison to Hamilton, 19 Nov. 1789, *PJM*, 12:449–51.

47. For the *Address to the States* of 26 April 1783, an important but ineffectual statement of Congress's policy on its debt, urging among other points a policy of nondiscrimination against transferees, see ibid., 6:488–94.

48. On this literature, see Chapter 3. The sources of Hamilton's ideas in the *Report on Public Credit* are discussed in editorial note, *PAH*, 6:51–65, and for further detail, see the treatments cited in Chapter 3, note 113.

49. Later, Madison would state that his reply had not been fully considered, explaining that, "in a hasty answer to a letter from the Secretary of the Treasury which followed him after the adjournment, he did not suggest the idea of discrimination as one of the ingredients in a funding system"; this, and his own earlier opposition to such a measure, might have given Hamilton the wrong impression. But the "idea of discrimination" was already present, and it "grew rapidly on him on his return to Congress as the subject unfolded itself; and the outrageous speculations on the floating paper pressed on the attention. Such was the spirit which was stimulated by the prospect of converting the depreciated paper into par value, that it seized members of Congress who did not shrink from the practice of purchasing thro' Brokers the certificates at little price, and contributing by these at the same moment to transmute them into the value of the precious metals" (James Madison, "Autobiography" [ca. 1832–1836], ed. Douglass Adair, *WMQ* 2 [1945]: 204–5).

50. Madison to Hamilton, 19 Nov. 1789, *PJM*, 12:451.

51. On this maxim, which struck most eighteenth-century Englishmen and Americans as the height of paradox, see Chapter 3, text note 77 and note 77.

52. Madison to Hamilton, 19 Nov. 1789, *PJM*, 12:451.

53. Ibid., 449–50 (taxes), 450 (sinking fund).

54. On Hamilton and "monied men," see Lance Banning, *The Jeffersonian Persuasion: Evolution of a Party Ideology* (Ithaca, N.Y., 1978), 135–40.

55. Again, this would have been in conversation; the surviving correspondence does not suggest it.

56. Although not, of course, on discrimination (for which see Madison's recollections quoted in note 49). But though it mattered a great deal to Madison, discrimination was not the heart of the opposition to Hamilton's programs, and Madison's statement that debt itself was "disrelished" captures the real point at issue.

57. Madison, speech on Import Duties, 15 May 1789, *PJM*, 12:163–65.

58. Ibid., 163–64.

59. Ibid., 164. For the southern tradition in this regard, see Joseph J. Persky, *The Burden of Dependency: Colonial Themes in Southern Economic Thought* (Baltimore, 1992).

60. *PJM*, 12:164–65. Other Virginia representatives also spoke against the measure—Richard Bland Lee, Alexander White, Theodorick Bland, John Page. *DHFFC*, 10:680, 685, 690–91, 692.

61. Fisher Ames, speech on Import Duties, 15 May 1789, *DHFFC*, 10:689.

62. Ames to George Richards Minot, 16 May 1789, in W. B. Allen, ed., *Works of Fisher Ames*, 2 vols. (Indianapolis, 1983), 1:624–26.

63. William Bingham to Madison, 17 June 1789, *PJM*, 12:230–31.

64. TJ to Madison, 9 Jan. 1790, *Boyd*, 16:92.

65. Washington recorded receipt of the *Report* in his diary; see entry for 2 Jan. 1790, in Donald Jackson and Dorothy Twohig, eds., *The Diaries of George Washington* (Charlottesville, Va., 1979), 6:1.

66. Alexander Hamilton, *Report Relative to a Provision for the Support of Public Credit*, 9 Jan. 1790, *PAH*, 6:67. A 20 January 1790 entry in the president's household

expense account noted the purchase of Adam Smith's *Wealth of Nations*; perhaps the president wanted help with the technicalities. See Stephen Decatur, Jr., *Private Affairs of George Washington, from the Records and Accounts of Tobias Lear, Esquire, His Secretary* (Boston, 1933), 113.

67. In 1792, the president defended the funding system to Jefferson on the grounds that "he had seen our affairs desperate and our credit lost, and . . . this was in a sudden and extraordinary degree raised to the highest pitch" by Hamilton's measures. TJ, memorandum, 1 Oct. 1792, *Boyd*, 24:435.

68. Hamilton, *Report*, *PAH*, 6:69.

69. Hamilton, *Report*, ibid., 78–83, has the proposal. For the implications, see Ferguson, *Power of the Purse*, 306–11.

70. Hamilton, *Report*, *PAH*, 6:70–71.

71. Ibid., 71, 72.

72. He conceded that "the advantages, described as likely to result from funding the public debt, would [not] be instantaneous" (ibid., 72). And the plan he set forth limited the extent to which the government could redeem the debt. Ibid., 90, 92, 93, 94. As enacted, the limited redemption feature meant it would take twenty-four years to retire the debt (thirty-four in the case of the deferred 6 percents). Donald F. Swanson and Andrew P. Trout, "Alexander Hamilton's Hidden Sinking Fund," *WMQ* 49 (1992): 112. As Swanson and Trout note elsewhere, "Hamilton did agree with Necker that nominal redemptions of the principal were advisable—if only for the sake of appearances" ("Alexander Hamilton, 'the celebrated Mr. Necker,' and Public Credit," *WMQ* 47 [1990]: 428), and see also the same authors' "Alexander Hamilton's Report on the Public Credit (1790) in a European Perspective," *Journal of European Economic History* 19 (1990): 627, and "Alexander Hamilton, Conversion, and Debt Reduction," *Explorations in Economic History* 29 (1992): 419–20.

73. Hamilton, *Report*, *PAH*, 6:70.

74. Ibid., 73–78; Hamilton began his discussion by explaining that he "has too much deference for the opinions of every part of the community, not to have observed one, which has, more than once, made its appearance in the public prints, and which is occasionally to be met with in conversation. It involves this question, whether a discrimination ought not to be made between original holders . . . and present possessors" (73). In the fall, Madison had written him that "the modification of the public debt is a subject on which I ought perhaps to be silent, having not enough revolved it to form any precise ideas. . . . The domestic debt is well known to be viewed in different lights by different classes of people." But he said nothing specifically in favor of discrimination. Madison to Hamilton, 19 Nov. 1789, *PJM*, 12:450. For Madison's later explanation of his silence, see ibid., 451.

75. Hamilton, *Report*, *PAH*, 6:76, 77–78.

76. Ibid., 70, 68.

77. H. Lee to Madison, 4 Mar. 1790, *PJM*, 13:89–90.

78. Hamilton, *Report*, *PAH*, 6:106, adding at once that he was "so far from acceding to the position, in the latitude in which it is sometimes laid down, that 'public debts are public benefits,' a position inviting to prodigality, and liable to dangerous abuse,—that he ardently wishes to see it incorporated, as a fundamental maxim, in the system of public credit of the United States, that the creation of debt should always be accompanied with the means of extinguishment." This was not sufficient to satisfy his critics. What he had in mind, presumably, was the permanent assignment of revenues to the debt—a measure Madison had successfully argued against the previous spring. See text at notes 56–62.

79. Madison did not arrive in New York until six days after Hamilton's presentation to the House. See Madison to James Madison, Sr., 21 Jan. 1790, *PJM*, 13:1, and, for action in the House, *DHFFC*, 3:263.

80. For the brief and unilluminating comments he did make to his correspondents, see Madison to Madison, Sr., 21 Jan.; Madison to TJ, 24 Jan.; Madison to Edward Carrington, 2 Feb.; Madison to TJ, [ca. 11 Feb. 1790], *PJM*, 13:1–2, 4, 14, 31. Again, if his later recollection is right, it was now that the enormity of speculation and the inequity of the outcomes Hamilton proposed began to make a serious impression on him. See his "Autobiography," quoted in note 49.

81. Madison to TJ, 4 Feb. 1790, *PJM*, 13:18–19.

82. Ibid., 19, 20.

83. Ibid., 19, 20.

84. Ibid., 21. Shortly after this comment on Congress's lack of enthusiasm for "philosophical legislation," Madison reported to Jefferson the failure of his own effort in that direction, an occupational schedule for the census, intended to obtain "a kind of information extremely requisite to the Legislator, and much wanted for the science of Political Economy." The Senate rejected it "as a waste of trouble and supplying materials for idle people to make a book," he added. "Judge by this little experiment of the reception likely to be given to so great an idea as that explained in your letter of September" (Madison to TJ, 14 Feb. 1790, ibid., 41). For evidence that Madison would not always be so skeptical, see Chapter 5, text at notes 63, 64; for his later return to his original position, see Chapter 6, text at note 144.

85. Madison, speech on Discrimination, 11 Feb. 1790, *PJM*, 13:34–38. For a discussion of the ways Madison's position in the controversy reflected his understanding of Hume's analysis of interests in politics, see Robert J. Morgan, "Madison's Analysis of the Sources of Political Authority," *American Political Science Review* 75 (1981): 613–25.

86. For Madison's efforts to reconcile his positions in 1783 and 1790, see his speech on Discrimination, 18 Feb. 1790, *PJM*, 13:50, acknowledging that "he had been repeatedly reminded of the address of Congress in 1783, which rejected a discrimination between original and purchasing holders" and condemning the "enormous and flagrant" "injustice" that had taken place between that date and the present, as veterans were forced to dispose of their holdings at a fraction of their value. Note his rejection of the charge that his proposal was an "ex post facto" law, disputing Hamilton's interpretation of the Constitution on this point, and his insistence that it would help, not hurt, public credit: "It was in vain to say that government ought never to revise measures once decided. Great caution on this head ought, no doubt, to be observed: but there were situations in which, without some legislative interposition, the first principles of justice, and the very ends of civil society, would be frustrated" (52).

87. Madison, speech on Discrimination, 11 Feb. 1790, ibid., 38, and, for similar statements as the debate developed, see his remarks on 1 Mar., 10 Mar., 12 Mar., and 22 Apr. 1790, ibid., 75, 99–100, 101, 102, 167.

88. Madison, speech on Discrimination, 11 Feb. 1790, ibid, 35.

89. R. B. Lee to ——, 23 Feb. 1790, R. B. Lee Papers, LC; Madison to Hamilton, 19 Nov. 1789, *PJM*, 12:449–50.

90. Madison, speech on Discrimination, 11 Feb. 1790, *PJM*, 13:36, 38.

91. Madison, reply to Egbert Benson, 18 Feb. 1790, ibid., 57.

92. "Gentlemen say [discrimination] will work injustice; but are we not as much bound to repair the injustice done by the United States?" Madison asked on 19

February 1790. Admitting that his proposal would involve "some difficulty" in administration, he concluded that "it is enough for me that it is not insuperable; and I trust, with the assistance which the cause of equity and justice will ever obtain from the members of the national legislature," that it will be overcome. Ibid., 58–59. On 22 February, the proposal was defeated in the Committee of the Whole. *DHFFC*, 5:724.

93. "Publius" [Madison], *Federalist*, No. 10, 22 Nov. 1787, in Cooke, ed., *The Federalist*, 65.

94. Theodore Sedgwick to — Van Schaack, 13 Feb. 1790, Sedgwick Papers III, box 1, MHS.

95. Ames to William Tudor, 8 Mar. 1790, in Allen, ed., *Works of Fisher Ames*, 1:729. Ames had already commented on Madison's sensitivity to Virginia opinion; see Ames to Minot, 3 May, 14 May, 29 May ("he is afraid, even to timidity, of his state"), 2 July ("the people of Virginia [whose murmurs, if louder than a whisper, make Mr. Madison's heart quake]"), 9 July ("The spectre of Patrick Henry haunts their dreams"), 23 July 1789, ibid., 569, 582–83, 638, 680, 687, 694.

96. The first surviving letter to comment on the *Report* is from Edward Carrington, 5 Feb. 1790 ("I have seen the Sketch of the plan for supporting the public Credit . . . but will not at present hazard an opinion upon it"), *PJM*, 13:27. Not until 26 February 1790 did one of Madison's Virginia correspondents, John Dawson, send a detailed reaction. Ibid., 63. Lack of comment reflects the slowness with which news circulated in 1790; it does not reflect lack of interest.

97. H. Lee to Madison, 4 Mar. 1790, ibid., 87–91. For the cultural context informing Lee's stereotypes, see Raymond Williams, *The Country and the City* (New York, 1973).

98. H. Lee to Hamilton, 16 Nov. 1789; Hamilton to H. Lee, 1 Dec. 1789, *PAH*, 5:517; 6:1. On Lee's checkered career, see Charles Royster, *Light-Horse Harry Lee and the Legacy of the American Revolution* (New York, 1981).

99. On Lee and the Virginia Federalists, see Norman K. Risjord, "The Virginia Federalists," *Journal of Southern History* 33 (1967): 486–517, and Norman K. Risjord and Gordon DenBoer, "The Evolution of Political Parties in Virginia, 1782–1800," *JAH* 60 (1974): 961–984.

100. H. Lee to Madison, 4 Mar. 1790, *PJM*, 13:88.

101. E. Randolph to Madison, 6 Mar., 10 Mar. 1790; Madison to E. Randolph, 21 Mar. 1790, ibid., 92, 96, 110.

102. See letters to Madison from Walter Jones, 25 Mar. 1790; Joseph Jones, 26 Mar. 1790; E. Randolph, 6 Mar. 1790 (reporting Laurence Washington's information that "Colo. Geo. Mason was strenuously in favor of your motion"); George Lee Turberville, 7 Apr. 1790, ibid., 119, 123, 92, 144.

103. Edward Carrington to Madison, 27 Mar. 1790, ibid., 125. On his future Federalism, see Prince, *Federalists and the Civil Service*, 106.

104. E. Pendleton to Madison, 2 Apr. 1790, *PJM*, 17:545.

105. Turberville to Madison, 7 Apr. 1790, ibid., 13:143.

106. W. Jones to Madison, 25 Mar. 1790, ibid., 119.

107. For reactions to the assumption of the state debts among Madison's correspondents, see the text. Madison made the point in debate on 24 February 1790: "The citizens of a state will be burthened, in proportion as their state has made exertions to discharge its obligations; for instance–if one state had paid the whole of her debt and another paid none, if you assume the unpaid without the paid, the state which has already paid off what it owed will be burthened to pay the debts of the

other" (ibid., 63). He would go on to speak of the "great injustice" Hamilton's plan would do and of the "great inequality" it would create (1 Mar. 1790) and of the "disproportioned burthen" it would place upon a "particular part of the community" (22 Apr. 1790) (72, 74, 165).

108. Jefferson arrived in New York on 21 March 1790. Madison to E. Randolph, 21 Mar. 1790, ibid., 110.

109. Turberville to Madison, 7 Apr. 1790, ibid., 114.

110. Carrington to Madison, 7 Apr. 1790, and see also Carrington to Madison, 27 Mar. 1790 (assumption as proposed "is truly iniquitous" to states that have already paid off much of their debt, and "Virga. [Virginia] would be a great sufferer"), ibid., 142, 127.

111. Dawson to Madison, 13 Apr. 1790, ibid., 154.

112. E. Pendleton to Madison, 21 Apr. 1790, ibid., 154.

113. B. Randolph to Madison, 26 May 1790, ibid., 230.

114. James Monroe to Madison, 2 July 1790, ibid., 261.

115. Dawson to Madison, 4 July, 1 Aug. 1790, ibid., 262, 291.

116. B. Randolph to Madison, 12 July 1790, ibid., 277.

117. Ibid.

118. Thomas Pleasants to Madison, 10 July 1790; Dawson to Madison, 5 June 1790, ibid., 271, 239.

119. For reports of the popularity that Madison's positions were winning him in Virginia, see E. Randolph to Madison, 20 May 1790 ("Some of the strongest antifoederalists here are high in their eulogiums on all of you, who have opposed" assumption), ibid., 224, and Peter Carr to TJ, 30 Apr. 1790, *Boyd*, 16:393. William Short, Jefferson's secretary, now chargé d'affaires in Paris, could not believe the news that reached him of Madison's plea for discrimination; having invested heavily in securities, he would see "the half of my fortune" disappear if it passed. "It is with anxious expectation that I await the result of this proposition, which I should have thought wild, and ill designed if it had not come from Madison, but even his name cannot prevent my concieving it highly unjust and impolitic, if not impracticable," he said. Short to TJ, 9 May 1790, ibid., 419. A Virginian, Short was surely one of the few gentry to see it this way. For Madison's comments on Bland's position, see Madison to E. Randolph, 14 Mar. 1790 ("the whole Delegation is agst. the measure except *Bland*!!"), and Madison to Pendleton, 4 Apr. 1790, *PJM*, 13:106, 138.

120. Alexander Moore, 25 Feb. 1790, *Annals of the Congress of the United States, 1789–1824*, 42 vols. (Washington, D.C., 1834–1856), 2:1348.

121. John Page, 31 Mar. 1790, and see his similar remarks of 25 Feb. 1790, ibid., 1499, 1354.

122. Alexander White, 25 Feb. 1790, ibid., 1345.

123. R. B. Lee, 18 Feb. 1790, ibid., 1271–72.

124. White, 25 Feb. 1790, ibid., 1343. Cf. Hume's claims cited in Chapter 3, text at note 38.

125. Madison, speech on Assumption of the State Debts, 22 Apr. 1790, *PJM*, 13:163–74, quotations at 166.

126. Ibid., 171. Madison's reference is to the British debts, which the Virginians were now obliged to pay, thanks to the Constitution's supremacy clause.

127. Ibid., 173.

128. For a general view of the stalemate on the debt in April and May, see Ferguson, *Power of the Purse*, 317–19.

129. R. B. Lee to Theodorick Lee, 9 Apr. 1790, R. B. Lee Papers, LC.

130. For literature on the residence question, see note 4.

131. H. Lee to Madison, 3 Apr. 1790, *PJM*, 13:136–37. Lee had previously written to Madison that he wished Patrick Henry were part of the Virginia delegation in the House, a thought that must have horrified Madison. H. Lee to Madison, 13 Mar. 1790, ibid., 103.

132. Abigail Adams to Cotton Tufts, 30 May 1790, Adams Papers microfilm, reel 373. All references to the Adams Papers are to the microfilm edition published by the Massachusetts Historical Society, Boston, which owns the originals.

133. TJ to Washington, 9 Sept. 1792, *Boyd*, 24:352. Out of commission most of May, felled by one of his "periodical headaches," Jefferson stayed home and worked on his *Report on Weights and Measures*—another of those exercises in calculation that so entranced him, in this case one that would allow him quite literally to impose his views on the world, or so he hoped. For the migraine, see TJ to Mary Jefferson, 23 May 1790; TJ to Thomas Mann Randolph, Jr., 23 May 1790; TJ to Short, 27 May 1790, ibid., 16:435, 436, 443. See George Gilmer to TJ, 21 May 1790, ibid., 433, with news that he had dined with Justices John Blair and James Wilson, then on circuit in Charlottesville, learning from them of Jefferson's migraine. For the *Report*, see Boyd, editorial note, "Report on Weights and Measures," ibid., 602–17.

134. TJ to Short, 14 Dec. 1789, ibid., 26.

135. John Nicholas, Jr., to TJ, 3 Feb. 1790, ibid., 139; for Nicholas's pamphlet see Chapter 1.

136. TJ, Response to Albemarle Address, 12 Feb. 1790; for the background, see Boyd, editorial note, "The Holy Cause of Freedom: Address of Welcome by the Citizens of Albemarle and Jefferson's Response," *Boyd*, 16:179, 167–77.

137. TJ to Lafayette, 2 Apr. 1790; TJ to Richard Gem, 4 Apr. 1790, ibid., 293, 297. Such letters were in the nature of press releases and should be evaluated accordingly.

138. For the background, see TJ to Washington, 2 May 1788 ("I am anxious about every thing which may affect our credit"); TJ to Madison, 3 May 1788 ("The existence of a nation, having no credit, is always precarious"); and TJ to John Jay, 4 May 1788, ibid., 13:126–28 (quotation at 127), 129–31 (quotation at 129), 133–34. After Jefferson's departure for America, Short continued to keep the government informed of developments. See Short to TJ, 19 Nov. 1789, ibid., 15:7–8; Short to Hamilton, 30 Nov. 1789, *PAH*, 5:570–74; Short to TJ, 25 Dec. 1789, *Boyd*, 16:43.

139. Boyd, editorial note, "Proposals for Funding the Foreign Debt," *Boyd*, 14:190–97, details Jefferson's efforts to shore up American credit in Europe, particularly after the departure of John Adams, who had managed the Amsterdam end of the business since the early 1780s. For this aspect of Jefferson's mission, see Chapter 1.

140. TJ to Short, 6 Apr. 1790, *Boyd*, 16:316.

141. Jefferson enclosed the resolution with the letter cited in the previous note; for the resolution's text, see *DHFFC*, 3:347–48.

142. TJ to Lafayette, 2 Apr. 1790, *Boyd*, 16:293.

143. For Washington's severe illness in May, see Douglas Southall Freeman, *George Washington*, vol. 6, *Patriot and President* (New York, 1954), 259–61, and, for Jefferson's response, see his letters to Martha Randolph, 16 May 1790 ("yesterday . . . he was thought by the physicians to be dying" but is now recovering); to M. Jefferson, 23 May 1790; to T. M. Randolph, Jr., 23 May 1790; to Short, 27 May 1790 ("A successful effort of nature however relieved him and us. You cannot conceive the public alarm on this occasion."), *Boyd*, 16:429, 435, 436, 444. One result of Washington's illness—a case of pneumonia—is a 10 May–24 June 1790 gap in his diary,

robbing us of the light it might have shed on the Dinner Table Bargain. See Jackson and Twohig, eds., *Diaries of George Washington*, 6:77.

144. On the army in 1790–it would shortly and disastrously go into battle against the Indians in Ohio–see Richard H. Kohn, *Eagle and Sword: The Federalists and the Creation of the Military Establishment in America, 1783–1802* (New York, 1975), 91–107.

145. TJ to Donald, 8 Apr. 1790, *Boyd*, 16:325.

146. Word of the Nootka Crisis reached Jefferson in late June. TJ to Monroe, 20 June 1790, ibid., 538. For a partisan view of what happened next, see Boyd, *Number 7*; for Jefferson's initial policy response, see TJ to Washington, 12 July 1790, enclosure, *Boyd*, 17:109: "Consider our abilities to take part in a war. Our operations would be by land only. How many men should we need to employ?–Their cost? Our resources of taxation and credit equal to this. Weigh the evil of this new accumulation of debt Against the loss of markets, and eternal expence and danger from so overgrown a neighbor." Had Jefferson not been reasonably sure, by the middle of July, that the Dinner Table Bargain was signed, sealed, and all but delivered, it is doubtful he could have contemplated war so cavalierly, though to be sure he does not forget to mention the "evil" of "new accumulation of debt," debt that would depend on the existence of a viable public credit.

147. TJ to T. M. Randolph, Jr., 18 Apr. 1790 (quotation); TJ to Short, 27 May 1790; TJ to M. Randolph, 6 June 1790; TJ to Short, 6 June 1790; and, most notably, letters to the following correspondents all written on 13 June 1790: Peter Carr, Donald, Elizabeth Wayles Eppes, Francis Hopkinson, William Hunter, Jr., and Nicholas Lewis, ibid., 16:351, 444–45, 474, 475, 488–92. Virginia Antifederalists in Congress, however, saw only the evils of funding and assumption and had nothing to say about disunion. See R. H. Lee to Patrick Henry, 10 June 1790, in James Curtis Ballagh, ed., *The Letters of Richard Henry Lee* (New York, 1914), 2:524.

148. Jefferson was quite concerned on this score. See TJ to Short, 6 Apr., enclosure, 1 July 1790, *Boyd*, 16:321–24, 589–90.

149. The authorities agree that the encounter took place in the middle weeks of June, but the precise date cannot be fixed. The best guess seems to be 20 June 1790. See the accounts cited in note 4.

150. Bowling unravels these complicated maneuvers in *Creation of Washington, D.C.*, 182–83.

151. For Jefferson's characterization of Hamilton, see his 1792 memorandum, The Assumption, *Boyd*, 17:205. Jefferson did not refer to the outcome of the meeting as a bargain. With ever so slightly a guilty conscience, he insisted, with respect to the residence, that the "Pennsylvania and Virginia delegations have conducted themselves honorably and unexceptionably. . . . Without descending to talk about bargains they have seen that their true interests lay in not listening to insidious propositions made to divide and defeat them" (TJ to Monroe, 20 June 1790, ibid., 16:538).

152. Late-eighteenth- and early-nineteenth-century Americans normally dined in the afternoon, and one assumes this was the case with Jefferson and his guests in June 1790. See Barbara G. Carson, *Ambitious Appetites: Dining, Behavior, and Patterns of Consumption in Federal Washington* (Washington, D.C., 1990), 75–76, 78–79.

153. For these maneuvers, see TJ, The Assumption, *Boyd*, 17:207; Jefferson discusses only the Virginia votes that changed. On the Maryland votes, see Bowling, *Creation of Washington, D.C.*, 185–86.

154. TJ, The Assumption, *Boyd*, 17:206–207: "It ended in Mr. Madison's acquiescence in a proposition that the question should again be brought before the house by way of amendment from the Senate, that tho' he would not vote for it, nor entirely withdraw his opposition, yet he should not be strenuous, but leave it to it's [*sic*] fate."

155. See R. B. Lee to T. Lee, 26 June 1790, R. B. Lee Papers, LC, reporting that "this week will decide the fate of the potowmack forever. If we are successful the place to be selected will be left to the discretion of the President[.] Georgetown as is probable should be the fortunate spot . . . the Bill will be framed as to admit Alexandria if it shoud be deemed proper into the ten miles square." As Alexandria's congressman, Lee was elated at the prospect of capturing the capital. As for the president's reaction, that must be inferred from Washington's belief in the future of the Potomac valley, but we will do no violence to historical truth by taking it for granted.

156. This was how Jefferson put it in 1818, in the "Anas," for which see Chapter 6; in 1792, he had said only that "White had some qualms, but finally agreed" (TJ, The Assumption, *Boyd*, 17:207).

157. E. Pendleton to Madison, 21 July 1790, *PJM*, 17:547.

158. Monroe to Madison, 26 July 1790, ibid., 13:283–84.

159. For a review of this activity, see Boyd, "Fixing the Seat of Government on the Potomac," "Locating the Federal District," and "Fixing the Seat of Government," *Boyd*, 17:452–60; 19:3–58; 20:3–72. For Jefferson's correspondence relating to the federal district during his tenure as secretary of state, see also Saul K. Padover, ed., *Thomas Jefferson and the National Capital* (Washington, D.C., 1946). A good secondary account is Bowling, *Creation of Washington, D.C.*, 208–34.

160. See Chapter 6.

161. Ames to John Lowell, 2 May 1790, in Allen, ed., *Works of Fisher Ames*, 1:733. Ames heard Madison correctly; for references to the debt as an "evil" in his speeches before the date of Ames's letter, see those of 1 Mar. and 22 Apr. 1790, *PJM*, 13:74, 75, 167.

162. TJ to Mason, 13 June 1790, *Boyd*, 16:493.

163. The timing of these letters clearly depended on the schedule of the southern mail, and Jefferson did not necessarily write them on the days of their dates. He may, instead, have dated them as of the day of dispatch.

164. TJ to T. M. Randolph, Jr., 20 June 1790; TJ to Monroe, 20 June 1790; TJ to Gilmer, 27 June 1790; TJ to Francis Eppes, 4 July 1790; TJ to Lewis, 4 July 1790; TJ to Edward Rutledge, 4 July 1790; TJ to Monroe, 11 July 1790; TJ to T. M. Randolph, Jr., 11 July 1790; TJ to Eppes, 25 July 1790; TJ to Gilmer, 25 July 1790; TJ to John Harvie, 25 July 1790; TJ to T. M. Randolph, Jr., 25 July, 14 Aug. 1790, *Boyd*, 16:540–41, 536–38, 574–75, 598, 599, 601; 17:25, 26, 266–67, 269–70, 270–71, 276, 390–91.

165. TJ to Monroe, 20 June 1790, ibid., 16:537.

166. TJ to T. M. Randolph, Jr., 20 June 1790; TJ to Gilmer, 27 June 1790; TJ to Eppes, 4 July 1790, ibid., 540, 575, 598.

167. Madison to Monroe, 17 June, 24 July 1790; Madison to Pendleton, 22 June 1790, *PJM*, 13:246–47, 282–83, 252–53.

168. Madison to Madison, Sr., 31 July 1790, ibid., 285.

169. Madison to Madison, Sr., 14 Aug. 1790, enclosure, ibid., 293.

170. George Nicholas to Madison, 3 May 1790, ibid., 187.

171. TJ to T. M. Randolph, Jr., 14 Aug. 1790, *Boyd*, 17:390–91.

172. Harvie to TJ, 3 Aug. 1790, ibid., 296.

173. For Hamilton's position, see *Report*, *PAH*, 6:76.

174. TJ to Washington, 3 June 1790, *Boyd*, 16:468–70.

175. Boyd's editorial note, "Cabinet Opinions," and "Appendix," ibid., 455–62; 18:611–29, were long the only sustained efforts to discuss this incident. As I have suggested in note 12, Boyd's version of the story is to be taken with a grain of salt.

176. For the Act of 29 September 1789, see *DHFFC*, 4:49. And for outstanding warrants the appropriation would cover, see *Report of the Secretary of the Treasury*, 25 Sep. 1789, ibid., 100–102.

177. Boyd discusses Vredenburgh and his activities in "Appendix," *Boyd*, 18: 618–23. For the basic contemporary references to Vredenburgh and Reynolds, see Gustavus B. Wallace to Madison, 25 Mar., 20 Apr. 1790, *PJM*, 13:122, 152. For reasons one can only guess at, Boyd cites Wallace's 20 April 1790 letter to Madison as "Gustavus B. Wallace to TJ, 20 Apr. 1790" and then goes on to cite "Adam Stephen to TJ, 25 Apr. 1790; Carrington to TJ, 27 Mar. 1790" ("Cabinet Opinions," *Boyd*, 16:456n.5). There are no such letters to Jefferson, and the reader of volume 16 of *Boyd*, covering 30 November 1789 to 4 July 1790, will search for them in vain. Like the 20 April 1790 Wallace letter, the Carrington and Stephen letters can be found in their proper places in *PJM*, 13:124–27, 176–77. Boyd silently corrects his mistake with regard to the Wallace letter in "Appendix," *Boyd*, 18:623n.44, properly citing it as "Wallace to Madison, 20 Apr. 1790." Because the letters in question are used in the "Cabinet Opinions" editorial note to establish a minor point, rumors that Hamilton had been killed in a duel, Boyd's carelessness does not directly weaken his argument, but it does underscore the need for caution in dealing with his more argumentative editorial notes.

178. For Jefferson's discovery of Reynold's second career, see TJ, "Notes on the Reynolds Affair," 17 Dec. 1792, ibid., 24:751, and see editorial note on the affair in *PAH*, 21:121–44, a more reliable treatment of than that in Boyd, "Appendix," *Boyd*, 18:629–88.

179. Wallace to Madison, 25 Mar., 20 Apr. 1790, *PJM*, 13:122, 152.

180. On speculation in the Revolutionary debt, see Ferguson, *Power of the Purse*, 251–86; Whitney K. Bates, "Northern Speculators and Southern State Debts: 1790," *WMQ* 19 (1962): 30–48; and Davis, "William Duer," 179–94. Bates shows that New Yorkers were active in acquiring Virginia debt, a point of relevance to Virginia attitudes on both assumption and speculators as a class; Davis allows us to penetrate the workings of an influential group of speculators with contacts in the Treasury Department.

181. For publication of information on Congress's grant in the *Gazette of the United States*, see Boyd, "Cabinet Opinions," *Boyd*, 16:455n.1.

182. David Stuart to R. B. Lee, 23 May 1790, R. B. Lee Papers, LC. In late January, Madison was reporting to Jefferson that, shortly before Hamilton's *Report* was issued, speculators sent agents into the countryside "to take advantage of the ignorance of the holders" (Madison to TJ, 24 Jan. 1790, *PJM*, 13:4).

183. "To the Freeholders of Virginia," *Virginia Independent Chronicle* (Richmond), 10 Oct. 1787. The anonymous author described himself as "a foreigner."

184. John Pendleton, Auditor's Office, 14 Mar. 1786, *Virginia Gazette, and Weekly Advertiser* (Richmond), 30 Mar. 1786.

185. Leighton Wood to B. Randolph, 6 Feb. 1790, in William P. Palmer et al., eds., *Calendar of Virginia State Papers* (Richmond, Va., 1885), 5:109.

186. Wallace to Madison, 25 Mar. 1790, *PJM*, 13:122. For Wallace's background, see Boyd, "Appendix," *Boyd*, 18:614n.16.

187. Wallace to Madison, 20 Apr. 1790, *PJM*, 13:152.

188. Madison to B. Randolph, 27 Apr. 1790, ibid., 178. Boyd, in both his accounts of the Arrears, ignores this critical letter. Without it, he can make Hamilton's record seem far worse than it was. Boyd may not have known of the letter's existence; the manuscript is at the Historical Society of Pennsylvania, rather than in the Madison papers at the Library of Congress, on which Boyd seems to have relied. Volume 13 of *PJM*, which prints the letter, did not come out until 1981, long after Boyd's essays were published ("Cabinet Opinions" in 1961 and "Appendix" in 1971). One wonders what difference access to the letter to Randolph would have made to Boyd's analysis; if Hamilton cooperated from the start, the case for a cover-up begins to collapse.

189. On Singleton's appointment, see Sandra Gioia Treadway, ed., *Journals of the Council of the State of Virginia*, vol. 13, *November 1788–29 November 1791* (Richmond, Va., 1982), 182, and Dawson to Madison, 14 May 1790, *PJM*, 13:215. On his activities as agent of the sinking fund, see Singleton to B. Randolph, 8 Feb. 1790, in Palmer et al., eds., *Calendar of Virginia State Papers*, 5:113.

190. For Hamilton's opposition to discrimination, see *Report, PAH*, 6:73–78.

191. In a memorandum summarizing their 1827 conversations, the historian Jared Sparks recorded Madison's memory that "the Mind of Washington was strongly exercised by Hamilton's funding system. He had given strong pledges to the army, that justice would be done them, and when the plan was proposed for paying the whole amount of the bills to the present holders, and thus deprive of their just claims the soldiers, who had been obliged to take the bills at par, when they were no more than 2s. 6d. on the pound, and had thus sacrificed 17s. 6d. on the £, he could not easily be reconciled to it" (Herbert B. Adams, *The Life and Writings of Jared Sparks . . .*, 2 vols. [Boston, 1893], 1:565–66). This statement of Washington's position is plausible, but one wishes there were positive confirmation for it in 1790, when Madison presumably heard Washington make the remarks later summarized for Sparks. At the time, the president did tell David Stuart that "Mr. Madison, on the question of discrimination, was actuated, I am convinced, by the purest motives, and most heart-felt conviction; but the subject was delicate, and perhaps had better never been stirred" (Washington to Stuart, 28 Mar. 1790, in John C. Fitzpatrick, ed., *The Writings of George Washington . . .* (Washington, D.C., 1939), 31:30.

192. Boyd either ignores the problem of Bland or finesses it by describing him as "a Virginia representative respected for his character if not for his intellectual prowess" ("Cabinet Opinions," *Boyd*, 16:456). For Madison's comments on Bland, hardly suggesting "respect," see Madison to E. Randolph, 14 Mar. 1790; Madison to E. Pendleton, 4 Apr. 1790, *PJM*, 13:106, 138. Nor did Madison say anything positive about Bland during the first session of the First Congress in 1789. See Madison to TJ, 29 Mar. 1789, ibid., 12:37, predicting that Bland would be "very inveterate" in opposition. For Bland's election as an Antifederalist and for the character of his district, see DenBoer, ed., *Documentary History of First Elections*, 2:267–68, 359, 364, 366, 382–83 (Carrington to Madison, 19 Dec. 1788, reporting that he had not run for Congress because Bland was unbeatable), 384, 386, 404, 405.

193. For Bland's speeches of 18 February 1790 (opposing discrimination), 9 March 1790 (assumption), 19 March 1790 (objecting to motion to inquire into Robert Morris's official conduct; Madison supported it), 30 March 1790 (assumption), and 31 March 1790 (assumption), see *Annals of Congress*, 2:1287, 1417–18, 1465, 1481–84, 1499–1500, 1515–17. Why, Bland asked on 9 March 1790, were gentlemen "so squeamish at this time of day on the subject of direct taxes?" He for

one had always thought "that the adoption of the Constitution would necessarily absorb all the efficient revenue of the United States" (1418, 1417). See also Bland to St. George Tucker, 6 Mar. 1790, Tucker–Coleman Papers, Box 16, Swemm Library, College of William and Mary, Williamsburg, Va.: "a Politician of no great depth—may easily see what is like to be the Issue of the Fiscal arrangements of the Present System–Absorption of revenue will Certainly follow Assumption of debt–so that our state governments will have little else to do than to eat drink and be merry–all this I think I foresaw would be the case."

194. For his efforts in 1790, see Bland to Tucker, 6 Mar. 1790, Tucker–Coleman Papers (reporting the illness of Virginia's senator William Grayson and announcing his willingness to replace Grayson), and Dawson to Madison, 13 Apr. 1790 (noting that the voters in Bland's district were not likely to reelect him, thanks to his stand on assumption, a consideration that might well have prompted Bland to seek other office, especially if election to it could be engineered by someone like Patrick Henry), *PJM*, 13:149. Bland had been mentioned for the governorship in 1788. DenBoer, ed., *Documentary History of First Elections*, 2: 261, 264.

195. For the legislative history of Bland's resolutions, see the calendar in *DHFFC*, 6:2064–65; for the text, see 2068.

196. Ibid., 2068–69.

197. For the dealers' protests, see Boyd, "Appendix," *Boyd*, 18:620–23.

198. For the debate, see *Annals of Congress*, 2:1582, and Madison, speech on Pay Arrearages to Virginia and North Carolina Veterans, 17 May 1790, *PJM*, 13:221.

199. Madison to B. Randolph, 27 Apr. 1790, *PJM*, 13:178.

200. This is what might be called the Fisher Ames interpretation of Madison's position; unfortunately, Ames was too busy fighting for assumption to describe Madison's stand on the arrears, and so we lack his usual comments. Note that here I differ from the account in Boyd, "Appendix," *Boyd*, 18:616, which claims that, while Bland introduced the resolutions, "there can be no doubt that the directing hand was his"–that is, Madison's.

201. Madison to E. Randolph, 14 Mar 1790, *PJM*, 13:106.

202. On the question of practicality, see Madison to Madison, Sr., 27 Feb. 1790, ibid., 66.

203. B. Randolph to Madison, 7 May 1790, ibid., 189–90. This is another piece of the picture Boyd ignores or fails to investigate; Randolph's letter is cited in neither of his essays on the arrears.

204. Madison, speech on Pay Arrearages to Virginia and North Carolina Veterans, 17 May 1790, ibid., 221.

205. For the text as amended by the Senate, see *DHFFC*, 6:2069–70; for calendar of the legislative history, see also 2064–65. For Lee's comments, see R. H. Lee to A. Lee, 19 May 1790, Ballagh, ed. *Letters of R. H. Lee*, 2:517.

206. For the Pennsylvania senator's diary entries on the arrears issue, see *DHFFC*, 9:272–74, quotation on 274.

207. Hamilton to Washington, 28 May 1790, enclosed in Hamilton to Washington, 29 May 1790, *PAH*, 6:433–39, 447–48.

208. On Randolph's absence, see E. Randolph to Madison, 15 Mar., 20 May 1790, *PJM*, 13: 107–8, 224; for his return, see John J. Reardon, *Edmund Randolph: A Biography* (New York, 1974), 425n.18.

209. Hamilton to Washington, 28 May 1790, *PAH*, 6:435–38. Boyd, "Cabinet Opinions," *Boyd*, 16:459, ignores Hamilton's quite justified insistence that an adequate arrangement for dealing with the problem was already in place.

210. Hamilton to Washington, 28 May 1790, *PAH*, 6:436–37.

211. Ibid.

212. Ibid., 438–39.

213. Ibid.

214. TJ to Washington, 3 June 1790, *Boyd*, 16:468–70. Boyd's analysis of Washington's decision to sign the resolutions is wide of the mark. "It can scarcely be supposed that he was persuaded to approve the resolutions solely by Jefferson's technical argument and by a general disinclination to use the veto power," Boyd writes. "For the case presented to him by the secretary of state amounted almost to a challenge to ask for further proof of the alleged frauds" ("Cabinet Opinions," ibid., 460). But because Boyd's intention is to convict Hamilton for concealing fraud at the Treasury Department, it goes without saying that any excuse to mention its existence will be seized on.

215. TJ to Washington, 3 June 1790, ibid., 470.

216. Hamilton to Washington, 28 May 1790, *PAH*, 6:433. For discussions of what kinds of paper could and could not be assigned at the time, see editorial note, "Bills and Notes," in Julius Goebel, Jr., ed., *The Law Practice of Alexander Hamilton: Documents and Commentary* (New York, 1969), 2:211–22 (on mercantile practice familiar to Hamilton and the changing state of the law in New York); editorial note, "*Harwood* v. *Lewis*, 1792–1794," in Charles F. Hobson, ed., *The Papers of John Marshall*, vol. 5, *Selected Law Cases, 1784–1800* (Chapel Hill, N.C., 1987), 201–5 (on assignments and in particular the 1705 Virginia statue governing this and mentioned in Jefferson's opinion); and Morton J. Horwitz, *The Transformation of American Law, 1780–1860* (Cambridge, Mass., 1977), 213–26 (on the broader implications of the shift from the common law's policy forbidding the assignment of choses in action). Note, however, that the changes described by Horowitz came more slowly in some regions than in others. In this regard, see F. Thornton Miller, *Judges and Juries versus the Law: Virginia's Provincial Legal Perspective, 1783–1828* (Charlottesville, Va., 1994), esp. 34–46, and Tony A. Freyer, *Producers versus Capitalists: Constitutional Conflict in Antebellum America* (Charlottesville, Va., 1994), which looks closely at New Jersey, Pennsylvania, Maryland, and Delaware. For parallel British developments—important doctrinally in giving American jurists materials from which to fashion new law for an emerging capitalism and because they suggest the American case is part of a larger pattern—see P. S. Atiyah, *The Rise and Fall of Freedom of Contract* (Oxford, 1979), 135–38, 484–85. His comments on the willingness of reactionary early-nineteenth-century Tory judges and politicians to support freedom of contract and laissez-faire (506–12) help to call into question—like Jefferson's position in the arrears controversy—some of Joyce Appleby's claims for Jefferson as the harbinger of a liberal capitalism, as discussed in the Introduction. Jefferson's legal conservatism requires treatment of its own, not possible here; his image as a law reformer is in real need of modification.

217. As Boyd notes, "There is no written request from Washington for an opinion . . . in the case of . . . TJ" ("Cabinet Opinions," *Boyd*, 16:459n.10). Clearly, however, Washington let Jefferson see Hamilton's opinion.

218. TJ to Washington, 3 June 1790, ibid., 468.

219. Ibid., 470; for Jefferson's dislike of assignments, see Chapter 1, text at notes 83, 86.

220. Madison, speech on Pay Arrearages to Virginia and North Carolina Veterans, 17 May 1790, *PJM*, 12:220. For Hamilton and the "enlightened men," see text at notes 78, 79.

221. *DHFFC*, 6:2065.

222. Ibid., 3:441.

223. Madison to Monroe, 1 June 1790, *PJM*, 13:234. Richard Henry Lee, however, was grief-stricken at the death of "our much valued friend Colo. Bland" (R. H. Lee to [Thomas Lee Shippen], 1 June 1790, in Ballagh, ed., *Letters of R. H. Lee*, 2:520).

Chapter 5

1. Joseph Jones to James Madison, 6 Apr. 1792, *PJM*, 15:280.

2. James Sterling Young, *The Washington Community: 1800–1828* (New York, 1966); Stanley Elkins and Eric McKitrick, *The Age of Federalism* (New York, 1993), 163–93.

3. The literature on the first party system and the rise of the Democratic Republicans is extensive and varied in approach. Modern study of the question begins with Charles A. Beard's *Economic Origins of Jeffersonian Democracy* (New York, 1915), a far better work than his more celebrated *An Economic Interpretation of the Constitution of the United States* (New York, 1913) and one that can still be read with profit. After Beard, pride of place goes to Joseph Charles, *The Origins of the American Party System: Three Essays* (1956) (New York, 1961), and to the studies of Noble E. Cunningham, Jr., *The Jeffersonian Republicans: The Formation of Party Organization, 1789–1801* (Chapel Hill, N.C., 1957) and *The Jeffersonian Republicans in Power: Party Operations, 1801–1809* (Chapel Hill, N.C., 1963). Also in this vein is William Nisbet Chambers, *Political Parties in a New Nation: The American Experience, 1776–1809* (New York, 1963). More recently, two trends have dominated the subject: the republican and liberal approaches (discussed in the Introduction) and quantitative studies. The latter include Mary P. Ryan, "Party Formation in the United States Congress, 1789 to 1796: A Quantitative Analysis," *WMQ* 28 (1971): 523–42; H. James Henderson, "Quantitative Approaches to Party Formation in the First United States Congress" [with a reply by Mary P. Ryan], *WMQ* 30 (1973): 307–24; and Rudolph M. Bell, *Party and Faction in American Politics: The House of Representatives, 1789–1801* (Westport, Conn., 1973). Of special importance are Richard Hofstadter, *The Idea of a Party System: The Rise of Legitimate Opposition in the United States, 1780–1840* (Berkeley, 1969), and Richard Buel, Jr., *Securing the Revolution: Ideology in American Politics, 1789–1815* (Ithaca, N.Y., 1972). John F. Hoadley, *Origins of American Political Parties, 1789–1803* (Lexington, Ky., 1986), uses "spatial analysis" to confirm what we already knew. The new master narrative of these events is Elkins and McKitrick, *Age of Federalism*. Michael Lienesch, *New Order of the Ages: Time, the Constitution, and the Making of Modern American Political Thought* (Princeton, N.J., 1988), and James Roger Sharp, *American Politics in the Early Republic: The New Nation in Crisis* (New Haven, Conn., 1993), supply briefer accounts, the former exploring how the Founders explained things to themselves, the latter emphasizing polarization and political passions.

4. For economic conditions in the 1790s and Hamilton's plans, see Chapter 3.

5. On the fears that headquartering the Bank of the United States in Philadelphia might keep the capital there permanently, see Kenneth R. Bowling, *The Creation of Washington, D.C.: The Idea and Location of the American Capital* (Fairfax, Va., 1991), 215–19, and Benjamin B. Klubes, "The First Federal Congress and the First National Bank: A Study in Constitutional Interpretation," *Journal of the Early Republic* 10 (1990): 19–41.

6. Attacks on the residence deal as a "bargain" are described in Bowling, *Creation of Washington, D.C.*, 198–203, and Boyd, editorial note, "Opinions on the Constitutionality of the Residence Bill," *Boyd*, 17:180–81, and see xxxiv–xxxvii, for a description of several 1790 cartoons on the subject, reproduced following 426. Bowling describes later removal efforts and the replies they elicited in *Creation of Washington, D.C.*, 241–43.

7. For Smith's position in 1790, see *Boyd*, 17:173, 176–83.

8. William Loughton Smith, *The Politicks and Views of a Certain Party, Displayed* (n.p., 1792), hints at the Dinner Table Bargain (9) and calls the residence "the offspring of a political cohabitation (for it cannot be called a marriage) between Pennsylvania and Virginia. . . . [I]t was begotten in darkness and its Nurses were afraid of its being exposed to the light" (13). For Madison's draft reply (not published), see Notes on William Loughton Smith's *Politicks and Views*, [ca. 4 Nov. 1792], *PJM*, 14:396–400, quotation on 398.

9. *PJM* 14:398–99.

10. For a summary of his charges against the two Virginians, see, for example, Alexander Hamilton to Edward Carrington, 26 May 1792, *PAH*, 11:426–45, and for Hamilton's 1792 newspaper campaign against Jefferson, see text at note 78. Hamilton's willingness to support Jefferson over Burr in the election of 1800 was due in part to confidence that Jefferson could be trusted on the debt, confidence that must have owed something to the fact that the Dinner Table Bargain had never come up in the polemics of the 1790s. For his letters insisting that Jefferson was sound on the debt, see Hamilton to Gouverneur Morris, 24 Dec. 1800; Hamilton to James Ross, 29 Dec. 1800; Hamilton to Oliver Wolcott, Jr., [7 Dec. 1800], Hamilton to James McHenry, 4 Jan. 1801; Hamilton to John Ruttedge, Jr., 4 Jan. 1801, *PAH* 25:272–73, 281, 288, 292–93, 298.

11. Jefferson did, however, privately admit to the president that he had been duped by the secretary of the treasury. TJ to George Washington, 9 Sept. 1792, *Boyd*, 24:352. Washington, of course, would not have been an entire stranger to the events Jefferson discussed.

12. For Jefferson's efforts to control the damage that details of the Dinner Table Bargain were likely to cause, see Chapter 6.

13. For Henry's refusal to accept a federal office or attend the convention, see Richard R. Beeman, *Patrick Henry: A Biography* (New York, 1974), 140–42, 165–92.

14. The Republicans urged opening Senate debates to the public, but the fact that they were closed in the early 1790s left Madison without competition for the attention of Virginia readers. On the closed-door policy, see Madison to Horatio Gates, 23 Feb. 1794, *PJM*, 15:264, and for long-standing Virginia complaints on this score, see ibid., 265n.2.

15. Thus Jefferson's important earlier disagreements with Hamilton—whether over the arrears of pay in 1790 or the chartering of the Bank of the United States in 1791—were unknown to the public, though the political elites of New York and Philadelphia were obviously better informed on these matters.

16. See Chapter 1.

17. Quoted in Charles Royster, *Light-Horse Harry Lee and the Legacy of the American Revolution* (New York, 1981), 226.

18. For Jefferson's explanations of the appeal of Federalism, see, for example, Notes on Professor Ebeling's Letter of July 30, 1795, *Ford*, 8:209–10, and for the effects of the XYZ Affair—a considerable, albeit temporary, setback for the Republican cause—see TJ to John Taylor, 1 June 1798; TJ to Elbridge Gerry, 26 Jan. 1799,

ibid., 430–31; 9:16–17, 20–23. For modern secondary accounts of the party struggle in Virginia, see Richard R. Beeman, *The Old Dominion and the New Nation, 1788–1801* (Lexington, Ky., 1972); James H. Broussard, *The Southern Federalists, 1800–1816* (Baton Rouge, La., 1978); Norman K. Risjord, *Chesapeake Politics, 1781–1800* (New York, 1978); and Lisle A. Rose, *Prologue to Democracy: The Federalists in the South, 1789–1800* (Lexington, Ky., 1968), among the book-length treatments; article-length studies include Harry Ammon, "The Formation of the Republican Party in Virginia, 1789–1796," *Journal of Southern History* 19 (1953): 283–310, and "The Jeffersonian Republicans in Virginia: An Interpretation," *VMHB* 71 (1963): 153–67; Norman K. Risjord, "The Virginia Federalists," *Journal of Southern History* 33 (1967): 486–517; and Norman K. Risjord and Gordon DenBoer, "The Evolution of Political Parties in Virginia, 1782–1800," *JAH* 60 (1974):961–84.

19. On political problems in Jefferson's second administration, see *Malone*, 5. David Nicholas Mayer, ed., "Of Principles and Men: The Correspondence of John Taylor of Caroline with Wilson Cary Nicholas," *VMHB* 96 (1988): 345–88, esp. 358–61, provides illustrations of the alarm Madison excited in some Virginia Republican quarters.

20. Jefferson left New York for Monticello on 1 September 1790 (he and Madison traveled together as far as Montpelier, stopping en route to visit Mount Vernon and perform some important business connected with the creation of the new federal city). Jefferson (once more traveling with Madison) was back in the capital, now relocated to Philadelphia, by 27 November 1790. *Malone*, 2:319–20; Madison to Madison, Sr., 28 Nov. 1790, *PJM*, 13:308.

21. For the text of the resolutions, see William Waller Hening, comp., *The Statutes at Large. . .* , 13 vols. (Richmond, Va., 1809–1823), 13:234–35.

22. Hamilton to John Jay, 13 Nov. 1790, *PAH*, 7:149. Jay's reply suggested that he did not appreciate how serious things were: "The assumption will do its own work," he counselled Hamilton, "–it will justify itself and not want advocates" (Jay to Hamilton, 28 Nov. 1790, ibid., 167). From Amsterdam, William Short reported that while news of the resolutions had reached the banking community there, he had been assured they would not affect the loans the United States was negotiating. Short to Hamilton, 30 Dec. 1790, ibid., 393–94.

23. Virginia resolutions, in Hening, comp., *Statutes at Large*, 13:234–35.

24. For the history of the resolutions and Henry's role, see Beeman, *Old Dominion and New Nation*, 78–82.

25. Governor Beverley Randolph to Madison et al., 3 Jan. 1791, *PJM*, 13: 345–46.

26. For the *Second Report on the Further Provision Necessary for Establishing Public Credit*, 13 Dec. 1790, see *PAH*, 7:305–42.

27. *Malone*, 3:350.

28. For a convenient summary, see ibid., 337–50. Madison's views can be found in his 2 February, 8 February 1791 speeches and his 21 February 1791 draft veto message for Washington, *PJM*, 13:373–81, 383–87, 395. The main source for Jefferson's views is his Opinion on the Constitutionality of the Bill for Establishing a National Bank, 15 Feb. 1791, *Boyd*, 19:275–80.

29. For Madison's denunciation of "sharpers," see Chapter 4; for 1791 variants on that formula, see text at note 71.

30. TJ, Opinion, 15 Feb. 1791, *Boyd*, 19:277.

31. Madison, Draft Veto, 21 Feb. 1791, *PJM*, 13:395. The bill creating the Bank of the United States required subscribers to the initial stock offering to make three-

fourths of their payment in 6 percent United States bonds (the bonds that Hamilton's 1790 plan created). This gave those already holding federal securities an advantage in buying into the bank, promising further gains on top of the substantial profits from the effects of funding and assumption. For the act creating the Bank, see *DHFFC*, 4:164–70; for subscriptions, see 164–65.

32. TJ, Opinion, 15 Feb. 1791, *Boyd*, 19:278.

33. Madison, Speech on the Bank, 2 Feb. 1791, *PJM*, 13:375. For the statute, see Hening, comp., *Statutes at Large*, 12:166–67, and for inclusion of the statute in his revisal of the laws, see *Boyd*, 2:435 (Boyd notes that it was apparently drafted not by Jefferson, but by George Wythe).

34. TJ, Opinion, 15 Feb. 1791, *Boyd*, 19:275–76.

35. Hamilton, Opinion on the Constitutionality of an Act to Establish a Bank, [23 Feb. 1791], *PAH*, 8:107–10.

36. Ibid., 108. On Jefferson and reform of the law of property, see Chapter 2. For the charter's duration, see the statute, *DHFFC*, 4:165. For Madison's comments, see *PJM*, 13:387, 383–84.

37. The bill was signed on 2 March 1791. *DHFFC*, 4:212.

38. For Jefferson's avoidance of Mason in 1790, see his note of explanation to Mason, 13 June 1790, *Boyd*, 16:493; for the 1791 approach, see TJ to Mason, 4 Feb. 1791, ibid., 19:241–42. For evidence of the flourishing state of the resumed relationship, see TJ, Notes of a Conversation with George Mason, 30 Sept. 1792, and TJ to Madison, 1 Oct. 1792, ibid., 24:428–29, 432. For the excise bill, see *DHFFC*, 4:551–82. On 3 March 1791, Washington signed the bill, which was introduced in December 1790 and cleared all legislative hurdles by 26 February 1791. Ibid., 572, 581–82.

39. Robert R. Livingston to TJ, 20 Feb. 1791, *Boyd*, 19:296; Livingston was replying to yet another feeler Jefferson had put out, for which see TJ to R. R. Livingston, 4 Feb. 1791, ibid., 241.

40. TJ to Charles Carroll, 15 Apr. 1791, ibid., 20:214–15. On Jefferson's fear that war would involve the nation in still more accumulation of dangerous debts, in addition to the discussion in this chapter and in Chapter 6, see Reginald C. Stuart, *The Half-way Pacifist: Thomas Jefferson's View of War* (Toronto, 1978), 13–14, 31, 35–36, 47, 53, 57, 61–62; Stuart's *War and American Thought: From the Revolution to the Monroe Doctrine* (Kent, Ohio, 1982) also helps to set Jefferson's beliefs in the larger context of early national America's attitudes toward the nature, effects, and purposes of war. Lawrence Delbert Cress, *Citizens in Arms: The Army and Militia in American Society to the War of 1812* (Chapel Hill, N.C., 1982), goes well beyond Stuart's explorations and is essential to any consideration of Jefferson's alternatives to war and debts; for seventeenth- and eighteenth-century English debates on these issues, see, for example, Lois G. Schwoerer, *"No Standing Armies": The Antiarmy Ideology in Seventeenth-Century England* (Baltimore, 1974); J. R. Western, *The English Militia in the Eighteenth Century: The Story of a Political Issue, 1660–1802* (London, 1965); and J. E. Cookson, *The Friends of Peace: Anti-War Liberalism in England, 1793–1815* (Cambridge, 1982). Theodore J. Crackel, *Mr. Jefferson's Army: Political and Social Reform of the Military Establishment, 1801–1809* (New York, 1987), suggests a Jefferson less hostile to the military than most scholars have recognized. Robert W. Tucker and David C. Hendrickson, *Empire of Liberty: The Statecraft of Thomas Jefferson* (New York, 1990), offer a critical overview of the aims of Jefferson's foreign policy and the means he used to achieve his goals. For the period at issue, see Merrill D. Peterson, "Thomas Jefferson and Commercial Policy, 1783–1793," *WMQ* 22 (1965): 584–610, and

Doron S. Ben-Atar, *The Origins of Jeffersonian Commercial Policy and Diplomacy* (New York, 1993).

41. TJ to James Monroe, 17 Apr. 1791, *Boyd*, 20:235.

42. Ibid., 236. Other Southerners responded more with enthusiasm. See Gerard Clarfield, "Protecting the Frontiers: Defense Policy and the Tariff Question in the First Washington Administration," *WMQ* 32 (1975): 444–48, 450–51.

43. TJ to Monroe, 17 Apr. 1791, *Boyd*, 20:236. John R. Nelson, *Liberty and Property: Political Economy and Policymaking in the New Nation, 1789–1812* (Baltimore, 1987), 52–63, follows the Republicans in seeing Hamilton's policy as permanently shackling the United States to Great Britain. Nelson is correct to insist that Hamilton's financial arrangement required a steady stream of revenue from the customs duties and hence good relations with the former mother country, but one can wonder what positive benefits "economic independence" would have conferred on the United States at this point.

44. TJ to Monroe, 17 Apr. 1791, *Boyd*, 20:236.

45. Madison to TJ, 1 May 1791, *PJM*, 14:15–16.

46. Morris to TJ, 26 Feb. 1791, *Boyd*, 19:343–44.

47. For an introduction to this controversy, see Boyd, editorial note, "*Rights of Man*: The 'Contest of Burke and Paine . . . in America,' " *ibid.*, 20:268–90; on the English side of the controversy excited by Burke's publication, see R. R. Fennessy, *Burke, Paine, and the Rights of Man* . . . (The Hague, 1963), for a guide to the flood of pamphlets and books responding to Burke and Paine–several of them reprinted and widely read in America.

48. Edmund Burke, *Reflections on the Revolution in France* (1790), in *The Writings and Speeches of Edmund Burke*, Vol. 8, *The French Revolution, 1790-1794*, ed. L. G. Mitchell (Oxford, 1989), 146–47. *Sowerby*, 5, index, s.v. "Burke, Edmund," lists no copy of the work in the library that Jefferson sold to Congress in 1815, but it is highly unlikely that he did not see a copy in 1791 or 1792.

49. Burke, *Reflections*, 145. For Jefferson's variations on these themes, see Chapter 2.

50. Burke, *Reflections*, 145. Burke's reference to flies echoes David Hume's use of the word to make a similar point, in "Of the Original Contract" (1741), in Eugene F. Miller, ed., *Essays, Moral, Political, and Literary* (Indianapolis, 1985), 476.

51. See Chapter 2.

52. Joseph Priestley, *Letters to the Right Honourable Edmund Burke, Occasioned by His Reflections* . . . (1790), 3d ed. (New York, 1791), 56n* (debts), 38–41 (religious establishments), 50–53 (closing monasteries), 69–70 (liberating revenues). There is no evidence that Priestley had seen a copy of Jefferson's 6 September 1789 letter to Madison, and his "posterity" lacks the concreteness of Jefferson's nineteen-year generation. For Jefferson's use of arguments similar to Priestley's in his annual messages, see text at notes 150–52. For his copy of this work, see *Sowerby*, 3, No. 2544.

53. Madison to TJ, 1 May 1791, *PJM*, 14:15. Jefferson–as his letter to Jonathan B. Smith, 26 Apr. 1791, *Boyd*, 20:290, reveals–had already seen an imported copy, but Madison, writing from New York, was unaware of this.

54. Thomas Paine, *Rights of Man*, Part One (1791), ed. Henry Collins (Harmondsworth, 1969), 63, 64, 67.

55. Richard Henry Lee to Thomas Lee Shippen, 15 Apr. 1793, in James Curtis Ballagh, ed., *The Letters of Richard Henry Lee* (New York, 1914), 2:556.

56. For the private note, see TJ to J. Smith, 26 Apr. 1791, *Boyd*, 20:290. For Jefferson's immediate comments on the ensuing controversy, see his letters to George

Washington, 8 May 1791; to Madison, 9 May 1791; to Thomas Mann Randolph, Jr., 3 July 1791; to Monroe, 10 July 1791; to John Adams, 17 July, 30 Aug. 1791; to Thomas Paine, 29 July 1791, ibid., 291–92, 293–94, 295–96, 297–98, 302–3, 310–11, 308–9.

57. TJ to J. Smith, 26 Apr. 1791, ibid., 290, has Jefferson's remark about heresies. For the vice president's own understanding that the remarks were directed at him, see J. Adams to TJ, 29 July 1791, ibid., 305–6.

58. TJ to Paine, 29 July 1791, 19 June 1792, ibid., 308, 312. For *Rights of Man*'s popularity among anglophone publics on both sides of the Atlantic, see Eric Foner, *Tom Paine and Revolutionary America* (New York, 1976), 219; David Freeman Hawke, *Paine* (New York, 1974), 223–25, 240, 254, 267; and E. P. Thompson, *The Making of the English Working Class* (New York, 1964), 90–96. Paine's directness of style and unrivaled gift for memorable phrases made his work far more accessible than Burke's elaborate and often hysterical production. On style and language in the Burke–Paine controversy, see Olivia Smith, *The Politics of Language, 1791–1819* (Oxford, 1984), 34–67; for an explanation of Burke's unexpectedly hostile reaction to the Revolution, see Isaac Kramnick, *The Rage of Edmund Burke: Portrait of an Ambivalent Conservative* (New York, 1977).

59. For the impact of "Publicola" on Jefferson, see Boyd, *"Rights of Man," Boyd*, 20:280–86. For the quotation, see [John Quincy Adams], "Letters of Publicola," 8 June–27 July 1791, in Worthington Chauncey Ford, ed., *Writings of John Quincy Adams* (New York, 1913), 1:70.

60. [Adams], "Letters of Publicola," 71.

61. For Jefferson's concern with elective despotism—his primary reference was to the Virginia legislature—see *Notes on the State of Virginia* (1785), ed. William Peden (Chapel Hill, N.C., 1954), 120.

62. As Jefferson famously put it in his letter to Major John Cartwright, 5 June 1824, *L&B*, 16:48: "Nothing then is unchangeable but the inherent and unalienable rights of man."

63. James Madison, "Universal Peace," *National Gazette*, 31 Jan. 1792, *PJM*, 14:207–8.

64. Ibid., 208. Madison would later change his mind, once again returning to his original posture of skepticism. See Chapter 6, text at note 144.

65. Henry Lee to Madison, 8 Jan. 1792, *PJM*, 14:183. For similar comments from Virginia correspondents in late 1791 and early 1792, see letters to Madison from H. Lee, 24 Aug. 1791, 17 Jan., 6 Feb. 1792; from Francis Corbin, 25 Oct. 1791; from Walter Jones, 10 Feb. 1792; from J. Jones, 2 Mar. 1792, ibid., 73–74, 189, 219, 85, 229, 243–44.

66. J. Jones to Madison, 6 Apr. 1792, ibid., 280; on Jones as a subscriber to Freneau's paper, see Madison to J. Jones, Aug. 1791, and J. Jones to Madison, 2 Mar. 1792, ibid., 71–72, 259, 260n.1. I have conjectured that his comments were provoked by Madison's essay; if not, they still suggest that the piece was fully in line with Virginia opinion.

67. TJ to Monroe, 10 July 1791, *Boyd*, 20:297–98; cf. TJ to Madison, 10 July 1791, ibid., 616.

68. "Plunder" was Madison's term in his 13 July 1791 letter to TJ, *PJM*, 14:47.

69. Madison to TJ, 10 July 1791, ibid., 43.

70. TJ to Edward Rutledge, 25 Aug. 1791, *Boyd*, 22:74.

71. Madison to TJ, 8 Aug. 1791, *PJM*, 14:69.

72. TJ to Paine, 29 July 1791, *Boyd*, 20:309.

73. TJ to Short, 18 Mar. 1792, ibid., 23:319.

74. TJ to Nicholas Lewis, 12 Apr. 1792, ibid., 408.

75. TJ to Madison, 24 July 1791, ibid., 20:667; for Jefferson's comments on speculation, see especially his memorandum of 23 March 1793, listing members of Congress known by him or John Beckley to be "paper-men"; his memorandum of 7 April 1793 on William Duer; and his memoranda of 7 May and 12 May 1793 on Hamilton's abuse of the sinking fund, ibid., 25:432–33, 517, 673; Franklin B. Sawvel, ed., *The Complete Anas of Thomas Jefferson* (New York, 1903), 120–22; and TJ to Monroe, 5 May 1793, *Boyd*, 25:661.

76. See, for example, TJ to Short, 16 Mar. 1791, 18 Mar. 1792, *Boyd*, 19:579; 23:319. On Jefferson as agent for Short's considerable American investments, see George Green Shackelford, *Jefferson's Adoptive Son: The Life of William Short, 1759–1849* (Lexington, Ky., 1993), 135–39.

77. On the *National Gazette*'s role as the instrument of Republican propaganda, see Boyd, editorial note, "Jefferson, Freneau, and the Founding of the *National Gazette*," *Boyd*, 20:718–53, with citations to the secondary literature. Madison's contributions to the paper, an important series of essays in 1791 and 1792, are discussed in editorial note, "Madison's *National Gazette* Essays, 19 November 1791–20 December 1792," *PJM*, 14:110–12, with emphasis on the surviving notes and drafts for the essays. For a previously unidentified contribution to the series, see also ibid., 17:559–60, and on the preparatory work for the essays, see Colleen A. Sheehan, "The Politics of Public Opinion: James Madison's 'Notes on Government,' " *WMQ* 49 (1992): 609–27.

78. For the charges raised by Hamilton, see *Malone*, 2:457–77. Hamilton's essays—especially the T.L. series of 25 July, 28 July, 11 Aug. 1792; the An American series of 4 Aug., 11 Aug., 18 Aug. 1792; the Civis series of 5 Sept., 11 Sept. 1792; the Amicus article of 11 Sept. 1792; the Fact series of 11 Sept., 17 Oct. 1792; and, above all, the Catullus series of 15 Sept., 19 Sept., 29 Sept., 17 Oct., 24 Nov., 22 Dec. 1792–can be found under their respective dates in *PAH*, 12–13; the editors' notes help readers make their way through the maze of Republican replies and countercharges.

79. *Malone*, 3:24–25. For one such protest by Jefferson, see, for example, Meeting of the Commissioners of the Sinking Fund [4 Apr. 1792], *PAH*, 11:224, 224nn.2–25; his 7 May 1793 memorandum on the sinking fund, *Boyd*, 25:673, records another instance in which Jefferson clearly felt he was being manipulated. Henry Remsen to TJ, 23 Apr. 1792, ibid., 23:451, complains of the Treasury Department's buying at fixed prices during the Duer Panic rather than taking advantage of the market to reduce the debt. For his sketch of a statute that would force the fund to reduce the debt, see TJ, A Bill to Redeem the Public Debt, [3 Dec. 1792], ibid., 24:692.

80. TJ, Memoranda of Conversations with the President, 1 Mar. 1792, *Boyd*, 23:186–87; for additional evidence from this period of his fears that the Constitution was being stretched beyond its proper limits by Hamiltonian loose construction, see TJ, Notes on Constitutionality of Bounties to Encourage Manufacturing, [Feb. 1792], and Comments on Hamilton's Notes on Report of Instructions for the Commissioners to Spain, [1–5 Mar. 1792], ibid., 172–73, 181–82.

81. For his comments on the Duer Panic, see TJ to T. M. Randolph, Jr., 16 Mar., 19 Apr. 1792; TJ to Short, 18 Mar., 24 Apr. 1792 (describing the losses as worse than those of the South Sea and Mississippi bubbles); TJ to David Humphreys, 9 Apr. 1792; TJ to Henry Remsen, 14 Apr. 1792; TJ to C. W. F. Dumas, 3 June 1792, ibid.,

287, 436, 319, 459, 387, 425–26; 24:20–21. For his conclusion that "treasury influence was tottering" in Congress even before Duer collapsed, see TJ, Memorandum on References by Congress to Heads of Departments. [10 Mar. 1792], ibid., 247. On the Panic itself, see Joseph Stancliffe Davis, "William Duer, Entrepreneur, 1747–99," in *Essays in the Earlier History of American Corporations* (Cambridge, Mass., 1917), 1:278–315; Robert F. Jones, "William Duer and the Business of Government in the Era of the American Revolution," *WMQ* 32 (1975): 411–13; and Cathy Matson, "Public Vices, Private Benefit: William Duer and His Circle, 1776–1792," in William Pencak and Conrad Edick Wright, eds., *New York and the Rise of American Capitalism: Economic Development and the Social and Political History of an American State, 1780–1870* (New York, 1989), 105–7.

82. TJ to Washington, 23 May 1792, *Boyd*, 23:535–40, quotation on 536. On the treatment of state debts in the 1790 legislation, see E. James Ferguson, *The Power of the Purse: A History of American Public Finance, 1776–1790* (Chapel Hill, N.C., 1961), 321–24; as Ferguson shows, Virginia was a decided beneficiary of the generous approach Congress eventually adopted.

83. TJ to Washington, 23 May 1792, *Boyd*, 23:536. On Virginia fears that high taxes would be resented and resisted, undermining the new government before it could properly establish itself, see Chapter 4.

84. TJ to Washington, 23 May 1792, *Boyd*, 23:536, 537. For Lee's comments, see Chapter 4. And see TJ to J. P. P. Derieux, 6 Jan. 1792 ("Agriculture, commerce, and every thing *useful* must be neglected, when the *useless* employment of money is so much more lucrative"), ibid., 23:27. On the excise on distilled liquor and the problems it caused through 1792, see Thomas P. Slaughter, *The Whiskey Rebellion: Frontier Epilogue to the American Revolution* (New York, 1986), 93–105, 109–24.

85. TJ to Washington, 23 May 1792, *Boyd*, 23:537.

86. Ibid., 537–39.

87. TJ to Madison, 4 June, 21 June 1792, ibid., 24:26, 106. On relative levels of taxation, see Chapter 3 note 144.

88. TJ, Note of Agenda to Reduce the Government to True Principles, [ca. 11 July 1792], *Boyd*, 24:215. For Jefferson's view of the *Report on Manufactures*, see TJ, Notes on the Constitutionality of Bounties to Encourage Manufacturing, [Feb. 1792], and Memorandum of Conversations with Washington, 1 Mar. 1792, ibid., 23:172–73, 187. He embodied the proposal to divide the Treasury in his Resolutions on the Secretary of the Treasury, [pre-27 Feb. 1793], ibid., 25:293, intended for use by William Branch Giles in the early 1793 Republican campaign to expose Hamilton, though Giles did not, in fact, make that part of the resolutions he offered the House, for which see ibid., 294–96.

89. TJ, Note on the National Debt [1792–93?], ibid., 24:810. Earlier in 1792, Alexander Donald had twice written from London to suggest that the United States take advantage of favorable market conditions in Europe and refinance the debt at 4 or 4.5 percent, 6 percent being far higher than was necessary. Donald to TJ, 3 Jan., 15 Feb. 1792, ibid., 23:9, 118.

90. Hamilton to Carrington, 26 May 1792, *PAH*, 11:426–45, 434 (intrigues), 427–29, 432–36 (charges against Madison), 429 (Jefferson), 436–37 (Giles).

91. Ibid., 436; see Mercer's speech, 30 Mar. 1792—two months after the publication of Madison's essay on "Universal Peace" discussed above, text at nn. 63–64—in *Annals of the Congress of the United States, 1789–1824*, 42 vols. (Washington, D.C., 1834–1856), 3:504. For Mercer's Virginia connections, see *DAB*.

92. Hamilton to Carrington, 26 May 1792, *PAH*, 11:437.

93. Ibid., 439–40, 441, 443. Hamilton may have been right about Jefferson's desire to have a say in the finances; for evidence that Jefferson had hoped to play a role in American finances at one point in the late 1780s, see Chapter 1, text at note 220. Hamilton's language echoes Joseph Addison, *The Campaign: A Poem, to His Grace the Duke of Marlborough* (London, 1710), 11.

94. For Jefferson's hopes for the Third Congress, see his letter to T. M. Randolph, Jr., 16 Nov. 1792, *Boyd*, 24:623; for the debuts of the Third Congress, which heartened the Republicans, and the subsequent collapse of their expectations, see editorial note, "Madison in the Third Congress, 2 December 1793–3 March 1795," *PJM*, 15:145–58.

95. Washington to Hamilton, 29 July 1792, *PAH*, 12:129–34.

96. Hamilton to Washington, 18 Aug. 1792, ibid., 229–58, quotations on 229, 249–50, 251. The newspaper essays are listed in note 78.

97. Washington to Hamilton, 26 Aug. 1792, *PAH*, 12:276–77; Washington to TJ, 23 Aug. 1792, *Boyd*, 24:315–18.

98. Hamilton to Washington, 9 Sept. 1792, *PAH*, 12:347–50, quotation on 348.

99. TJ to Washington, 9 Sept. 1792, *Boyd*, 24:351–59, quotation on 352.

100. Ibid., 353, 358–59.

101. TJ, Observations on the French Debt, [ca. 17 Oct. 1792], enclosed in TJ to Washington, 17 Oct. 1792, ibid., 496–97. For the events giving rise to Jefferson's 1786 correspondence, see Chapter 1, text at notes 199–202.

102. TJ, Thoughts on the Bankruptcy Bill, [ca. 10 Dec. 1792], enclosed in TJ to Madison, [ca. 10 Dec. 1792], *Boyd*, 24:722. Jefferson repeated much of this analysis in his letters of 19 Dec. 1792 to John F. Mercer and 21 Dec. 1792 to T. M. Randolph, Jr., ibid., 757–58, 775. The bill did not pass, but a measure introduced in 1797 was eventually adopted in 1800; the debates on that measure, which lasted from 1797 to 1800, produced a similar outpouring of Republican objections. See Charles Warren, *Bankruptcy in United States History* (Cambridge, Mass., 1935), 10–22, and Drew R. McCoy, *The Elusive Republic: Political Economy in Jeffersonian America* (Chapel Hill, N.C., 1980), 178–84.

103. On the Giles Resolutions, see Eugene R. Sheridan, "Thomas Jefferson and the Giles Resolution," *WMQ* 49 (1992): 589–608, and Boyd, editorial note, "Jefferson and the Giles Resolutions," *Boyd*, 25:280–92. Together, these essays replace earlier accounts and confirm what many suspected, that Jefferson was intimately involved in preparing the censure resolutions that Giles pressed the House to adopt. Also lost was a constitutional amendment offered by the Virginians that would have forced members of the House and Senate to declare their "property in public and Bank Stock of every kind" and would have forbidden them to "purchase or deal in any such paper, or any public lands, or any other public property whatever" during their terms in Congress. On this, see Madison, Notes on Proposed Constitutional Amendments [ca. 3 Mar. 1792], *PJM*, 14:470, 470n.1.

104. On the issue of the debt to France and Jefferson's covering his tracks, see Sheridan, "Jefferson and the Giles Resolutions," 598–99, 607.

105. See Jefferson's 28 April 1793 opinion, *Boyd*, 25:608–18, quotations on 609, 616. Jefferson's position foreshadows the compact theory he later developed in the Kentucky Resolutions.

106. See Article XI of the Treaty of Alliance of 1778, providing that the treaty's territorial guarantees would run "from the present time and forever against all other powers." Charles I. Bevans, comp., *Treaties and Other International Agreements of the United States of America, 1776–1949*, 13 vols. (Washington, D.C., 1968–1976), 7:779.

107. Madison, "A Candid State of the Parties," *National Gazette*, 22 Sept. 1792, *PJM*, 14:371–72.

108. On Jefferson's decision to retire in 1793, see *Malone*, 3:9–10, 123–24, 132–33, 161; for his insistence that he had "fully & faithfully paid" his "debt of service" to the public, see TJ to Madison, 9 June 1793, *PJM*, 15:26.

109. For the official letter of resignation, see TJ to Washington, 31 Dec. 1793, *L&B*, 9:278–79.

110. TJ to Edmund Randolph, 3 Feb. 1794, ibid., 280.

111. J. Adams to TJ, 4 Apr. 1794, enclosing a copy of *Lettres de Jean Jacques Cart à Bernard Demuralt, trésorier du pays de Vaud, sur le droit public de ce pays* . . . (Paris, 1793), and TJ to J. Adams, 25 Apr. 1794, *Cappon*, 1:253, 254. For Jefferson's copy of the work, see *Sowerby*, 3, No. 2681. Cart's book is more important than Jefferson realized, if only because a German translation of it was Hegel's first publication. H. S. Harris, *Hegel's Development: Toward the Sunlight, 1770–1801* (Oxford, 1972), 158, 418–21.

112. Thus during the spring 1794 session of Congress, Madison wrote to Jefferson on 2 Mar., 9 Mar., 12 Mar., 14 Mar., 24 Mar., 26 Mar., 31 Mar., 14 Apr., 28 Apr., 11 May, 25 May, and 1 June describing the crisis in relations with Britain and the shifting course of congressional opinion and action. *PJM*, 15:269–71, 274–75, 278–79, 284, 288, 294–95, 299, 306–7, 315–16, 327–28, 337–38, 340–41. Jefferson's replies were far fewer, of course; see TJ to Madison, 3 Apr., 15 May 1794, ibid., 301–2, 332–33.

113. Madison to TJ, 14 Mar. 1794, ibid., 284.

114. TJ to Madison, 3 Apr., 28 Dec. 1794, ibid., 301–2, 427.

115. On this, see editorial note on Hamilton's *Report on a Plan for Further Support of Public Credit*, 16 Jan. 1795, *PAH*, 18:46–56. "My own opinion was, that from the commencement of this government to the time I ceased to attend to the subject, we had been increasing our debt about a million of D. annually," Jefferson told Madison in 1796, urging him to have Albert Gallatin "reduce this chaos to order" (TJ to Madison, 6 Mar. 1796, *PJM*, 16:250). At the end of the 1796 legislative session, Jefferson could tell Monroe that his worst suspicions had been confirmed by Gallatin's speeches (TJ to Monroe, 12 June 1796, *Ford*, 8:244), and the publication in November of Gallatin's extended examination of this question, *A Sketch of the Finances of the United States* (1796), Henry Adams, ed., in *The Writings of Albert Gallatin*, 3 vols. (Philadelphia, 1879), 3:143–68, settled the doubts–could there really have been any?–Republicans had on this score, then and for all time.

116. Madison, Speech on Excise, 16 Jan. 1795, *PJM*, 15:447.

117. Madison to TJ, 26 Jan. 1795, ibid., 455.

118. For the *Report* itself, see *PAH*, 18:56–148; for the comment, see Madison to TJ, 15 Feb. 1795, *PJM*, 15:474–75. For Republican proposals on how to pay off the national debt, see John Taylor Memorandum, 11 May 1794, ibid., 329–30.

119. For Jefferson's delight with Taylor, see TJ to Madison, 1 Sept., 8 Sept. 1793; Madison to Taylor, 20 Sept. 1793, *PJM* 15:89, 104, 121 (on Taylor's *Enquiry into the Principles* [1793]); TJ to Madison, 15 May 1794, ibid., 333 (on Taylor's *A Definition of Parties* [1794]). For Taylor's record as a Republican publicist, see Chapter 3, note 107.

120. J. Adams to Abigail Adams, 3 Jan. [1794], Adams Papers, MHS, microfilm, reel 377.

121. Fisher Ames to Thomas Dwight, 6 May 1794, in W. B. Allen, ed., *Works of Fisher Ames*, 2 vols. (Indianapolis, 1983), 2:1042; TJ to T. M. Randolph, Jr., 16 Nov. 1792, *Boyd*, 24:623; J. Adams to A. Adams, 1 Apr., 5 Apr., 7 Apr., 10 May 1794, in

Charles Francis Adams, ed., *Letters of John Adams, Addressed to His Wife*, 2 vols. (Boston, 1841), 2:148, 152, 153, quotation on 159. Adams is improving on the language of Joseph Addison in Act 4 of *Cato: A Tragedy* (1713), in Ricardo Quintana, ed., *Eighteenth-Century Plays* (New York, 1952), 48. Linda K. Kerber notes that such charges remained an active part of the Federalist repertory after the defeat of 1800 in *Federalists in Dissent: Imagery and Ideology in Jeffersonian America* (Ithaca, N.Y., 1970), 25, 30, 61–62.

122. [William Loughton Smith], *The Pretensions of Thomas Jefferson to the Presidency Examined; . . . Part the Second* (Philadelphia, 1796), 6–8; [John Thompson], *The Letters of Curtius, Addressed to General Marshall* (Richmond, Va., 1798), 31, 32. For similar Virginia comments, see, for example, [John Taylor], *A Definition of Parties* (Philadelphia, 1794), 3–4; [James Madison], *Political Observations* (1795), *PJM*, 15:511; John Page, *An Address to the Citizens of the District of York . . .* (Philadelphia, 1799), 11, 25–32, and *An Address to the Freeholders of Gloucester County . . .* (Richmond, Va., 1799), 3, 4–5, 26–27; and circular letters to their constituents from Virginia congressmen Samuel J. Cabell, 12 July 1797, 28 Mar. 1800, and Anthony New, 17 June 1797, in Noble E. Cunningham, Jr., ed., *Circular Letters of Congressmen to Their Constituents, 1789–1829*, 3 vols. (Chapel Hill, N.C., 1978), 1:70, 178–79, 93.

123. For Jefferson's decision to contest the presidency in 1796, see *Malone*, 3:273–76.

124. The travails of the Adams administration are recounted in Stephen G. Kurtz, *The Presidency of John Adams: The Collapse of Federalism, 1795–1800* (Philadelphia, 1957); the new reading of the evidence by Elkins and McKitrick in *Age of Federalism* suggests that Kurtz's pro-Adams interpretation is a good deal less solid than historians have supposed. Jefferson's reactions can be followed in *Malone*, 3:295–339, 359–483.

125. On the Virginia and Kentucky Resolutions and Jefferson's part in their creation, see Adrienne Koch and Harry Ammon, "The Virginia and Kentucky Resolutions: An Episode in Jefferson's and Madison's Defense of Civil Liberties," *WMQ* 5 (1948): 145–76, and Adrienne Koch, *Jefferson and Madison: The Great Collaboration* (New York, 1950), 178–211, and, for the episode of the Alien and Sedition Acts more generally, see James Morton Smith, *Freedom's Fetters: The Alien and Sedition Laws and American Civil Liberties* (Ithaca, N.Y., 1956); John C. Miller, *Crisis in Freedom: The Alien and Sedition Acts* (Boston, 1952); Leonard W. Levy, *Emergence of a Free Press* (New York, 1985), and "Liberty and the First Amendment: 1790–1800," *AHR* 68 (1962): 22–37; Jeffrey A. Smith, *Printers and Press Freedom: The Ideology of Early American Journalism* (New York, 1988); and Adrienne Koch and Harry Ammon, "The Virginia and Kentucky Resolutions: An Episode in Jefferson's and Madison's Defense of Civil Liberties," *WMQ* 5 (1948): 145–76. Note that the Seventh Kentucky Resolution protested against Federalist loose construction of the necessary and proper clause and implicitly promised repeal of the charter of the Bank of the United States. TJ, draft of Kentucky Resolutions, fair copy; [Nov. 1798], *Ford*, 8:468–69.

126. TJ to Elbridge Gerry, 13 May 1797, *Ford*, 8:285. Later, Madison made similar charges in the essay "Foreign Influence," *Aurora General Advertiser* (Philadelphia), 23 Jan. 1799, *PJM*, 17:218–19. The two Virginians were correct about substantial British ownership of American securities; for details, see Chapter 3, note 182. The conclusions they drew are open to question.

127. TJ to Edward Rutledge, 27 Dec. 1796, *Ford*, 8:258.

128. TJ to St. George Tucker, 28 Aug. 1797; TJ to James Lewis, Jr., 9 May 1798; TJ to Taylor, 1 June 1798, ibid., 419, 9:337, 416, 431, 432–33; TJ to Madison, 3 Jan. 1799, *PJM*, 17:193. For Taylor's mood–he did not find Jefferson's reassurances convincing–see Robert E. Shalhope, *John Taylor of Caroline: Pastoral Republican* (Columbia, S.C., 1980), 98–101.

129. TJ to Monroe, 23 Jan. 1799; TJ to Edmund Pendleton, 29 Jan. 1799; TJ to Edward Livingston, 30 Apr. 1800; TJ to Samuel Adams, 26 Feb. 1800, *Ford*, 9:11, 27–28, 132, 115.

130. For Adams's comments on the dangers of national debts–he was particularly alert to the role of war in helping to create them–see, for example, J. Adams to Benjamin Rush, 25 Dec. 1811, in John A. Schutz and Douglass Adair, eds., *The Spur of Fame: Dialogues of John Adams and Benjamin Rush, 1805–1813* (San Marino, Calif., 1966), 201 (Jefferson "disapproved of the eight per cent loan [of 1798], and with good reason. For I hated it as much as any man, and the army, too, which occasioned it"), and J. Adams to A. Adams, 5 May 1794, Adams Papers, MHS, microfilm, reel 377 ("I lament the introduction of Taxes and expences which will accumulate a perpetual Debt, and lead to future Revolutions"). For a general discussion of Adams's ideas of government finance, see Manning J. Dauer, *The Adams Federalists* (Baltimore, 1968), 64–66.

131. For the charges raised by the Federalists in 1800, see, generally, *Malone*, 3:479–83. Jefferson learned of the charge of financial impropriety when Uriah McGregory of Derby, Conn., wrote to him of the rumors being spread by the Reverend Cotton Mather Smith. McGregory to TJ, 19 July 1800, and see TJ to McGregory, 13 Aug. 1800, Jefferson Papers, LC.

132. Hamilton to Morris, 24 Dec. 1800; Hamilton to Ross, 29 Dec. 1800; Hamilton to Wolcott, [Dec. 1800]; Hamilton to McHenry, 4 Jan. 1801; Hamilton to Rutledge, 4 Jan. 1801, *PAH*, 25:272–73, 281, 288, 292–93, 295.

133. Washington Irving, *Salmagundi* . . . , "improved edition," 2 vols. (New York, 1814), 1:101.

134. TJ, Notes on Ebeling's Letter, *Ford*, 8:208.

135. Gallatin, *Sketch of the Finances*, 143–68. Gallatin's post-1800 career lacks a good full-length study; in the meantime, see Raymond Walters, Jr., *Albert Gallatin: Jeffersonian Financier and Diplomat* (New York, 1957), and, on the technical aspects, Alexander Balinky, *Albert Gallatin: Fiscal Theories and Policies* (New Brunswick, N.J., 1958). Noble E. Cunningham, Jr., *The Process of Government under Jefferson* (Princeton, N.J., 1978), shows how effectively Gallatin worked with the president, other cabinet members, as well as Congress, to achieve Jefferson's goals.

136. For the quotation, see TJ to John Wayles Eppes, 11 Sept. 1813, *Ford*, 11:307. On the problems that Jefferson's policies encountered when such dangers *were* real, as they became in the last two years of the second term, see Burton Spivak, *Jefferson's English Crisis: Commerce, Embargo, and the Republican Revolution* (Charlottesville, Va., 1979), and for an appraisal of the deficiencies of Jefferson's foreign policy generally, see Tucker and Hendrickson, *Empire of Liberty*.

137. For a critical reading of Jefferson's hopes, see John Lauritz Larson, "Jefferson's Union and the Problem of Internal Improvements," in Peter S. Onuf, ed., *Jeffersonian Legacies* (Charlottesville, Va., 1993), 340–69.

138. For the controversy over *Rights of Man*, see text at notes 56–62. The letter to Philip Mazzei, 24 Apr. 1796, is in *Ford*, 8:235–41; for the controversy it occasioned, see *Malone*, 3:267–68, 302–7. For concern during the Quasi-War that his letters were being opened and read, see, for example, TJ to Taylor, 26 Nov. 1798, *Ford*, 8:480.

139. On the role of the Annual Message, the chief vehicle through which Jefferson communicated to the nation, see Cunningham, *Process of Government*, 84–86. Jefferson's preference for written communications with Congress–his predecessors delivered their messages in person–should not obscure the fact that he intended the Annual Message to receive the widest possible circulation; the message was a constitutional duty, and he could make use of it without appearing to engage in party propaganda.

140. TJ, First Inaugural Address, 4 Mar. 1801, *LofA*, 493; for Washington's question, see his First Inaugural Address, 30 Apr. 1789, in W. W. Abbot, ed., *The Papers of George Washington: Presidential Series* (Charlottesville, Va., 1987), 2:175.

141. TJ, First Inaugural Address, 4 Mar. 1801, *LofA*, 494.

142. TJ to Taylor, 26 Nov. 1798, *Ford*, 8:481.

143. TJ, First Annual Message, 8 Dec. 1801, ibid., 9:333–34.

144. TJ, Second Annual Message, 15 Dec. 1802, ibid., 412, 415. Note that Jefferson's remarks did not differ greatly from George Washington's in the latter's Farewell Address of 1796, in which Washington had urged "vigorous exertions in time of Peace to discharge the Debts which unavoidable wars may have occasioned, not ungenerously throwing upon posterity the burthen which we ourselves ought to bear" (Farewell Address, 19 Sept. 1796, in John C. Fitzpatrick, ed., *The Writings of George Washington . . .* , 39 vols. [Washington, D.C., 1933–1944), 35:320.

145. TJ, Third Annual Message, 17 Oct. 1803, *Ford*, 10:39–40.

146. TJ, Fourth Annual Message, 8 Nov. 1804, ibid., 116.

147. TJ, Second Inaugural Address, 4 Mar. 1805, ibid., 130.

148. TJ, undated Notes of a Draft of a Second Inaugural Address; Second Inaugural Address, ibid., 127, 132.

149. On the development of what came to be called in the cabinet "the financial paragraph," see Cunningham, *Process of Government*, 78–79. For the paragraphs themselves, see TJ, Fifth Annual Message, 3 Dec. 1805; Sixth Annual Message, 2 Dec. 1806; Seventh Annual Message, 27 Oct. 1807, *Ford*, 10:195–96, 316, 524–25.

150. TJ, Sixth Annual Message, 2 Dec. 1806; Seventh Annual Message, 27 Oct. 1807, *Ford*, 10:317–18, 526.

151. For Madison's fears, see Chapter 4, text at note 60.

152. TJ, Eighth Annual Message, 8 Nov. 1808, *Ford*, 11:71.

153. The critical portions of the *Report* are in E. James Ferguson, ed., *Selected Writings of Albert Gallatin* (Indianapolis, 1967), 229–40.

154. TJ to John Dickinson, 19 Dec. 1801; TJ to Thaddeus Kosciusko, 2 Apr. 1802, *L&B*, 10:302, 310.

155. TJ to Levi Lincoln, 25 Oct. 1802, *Ford*, 9:401; TJ to W. Jones, 31 Mar. 1801, *L&B*, 10:256.

156. TJ to Monroe, 13 Jan. 1803, *Ford*, 9:418, 420.

157. TJ to Pierre Samuel Du Pont de Nemours, 1 Feb. 1803, ibid., 438.

158. TJ to Thomas Digges, 1 July 1806, *L&B*, 11:113.

159. TJ to Short, 15 Nov. 1807, ibid., 393.

160. For Jefferson's comments in retirement on the need to keep the course he had set, see Chapter 6.

161. TJ to Du Pont, 18 Jan. 1802, in Gilbert Chinard, ed., *The Correspondence of Jefferson and Du Pont de Nemours . . .* (Baltimore, 1931), 37.

Chapter 6

1. TJ to Nathaniel Macon, 19 Aug. 1821, *Ford*, 12:207.
2. TJ to Major John Cartwright, 5 June 1824, *L&B*, 16:48.
3. TJ to Charles Thompson, 9 Jan. 1816, in Dickinson W. Adams, ed., *Jefferson's Extracts from the Gospels: "The Philosophy of Jesus" and "The Life and Morals of Jesus"* (Princeton, N.J., 1983), 365. In 1818, Jefferson said he was "no longer equal to the labors of the writing table" and declined to enter a correspondence with John Stevens, adding, in yet another allusion to his generational principle, that "there is moreover a natural term when age should know itself, withdraw from observation, and leave to the new generation the management of its own concerns" (TJ to John Stevens, 23 Nov. 1818, "Correspondence of Thomas Jefferson," *Glimpses of the Past* 3 [1936]: 122). Using Jefferson's carefully maintained register of correspondence, John Catanzariti provides a sense of what the "epistolary corvée" after 1809 actually amounted to—about 400 letters a year received and about 300 a year written. Catanzariti, "Thomas Jefferson, Correspondent," Massachusetts Historical Society, *Proceedings* 102 (1990): 16.
4. For Jefferson in retirement, see *Malone*, 6; for the escapes to Poplar Forest, see ibid., 14–15, 153–68, 285–93. While at Poplar Forest in September 1813, Jefferson wrote one of the trio of letters to Eppes on the rights of the living generation. Merrill D. Peterson, ed., *Visitors to Monticello* (Charlottesville, Va., 1989), 45–110, collects the accounts of those who visited him in retirement.
5. TJ to Thaddeus Kosciuszko, 26 Feb. 1810, *L&B*, 12:370; on the debts, see *Malone*, 6:34–43, 301–15, 448–51, 453–54, 473–82, 495–96, 505–12, and Steven Harold Hochman, "Thomas Jefferson: A Personal Financial Biography" (Ph.D. diss., University of Virginia, 1987), 249–89.
6. TJ to Pierre Samuel Du Pont de Nemours, 2 Mar. 1809, in Gilbert Chinard, ed., *The Correspondence of Jefferson and Du Pont de Nemours . . .* (Baltimore, 1931), 144. The best picture of Jefferson as the "Sage of Monticello" is in the Adams–Jefferson correspondence, *Cappon*, 2:283–614; for John Adams's own reference to Jefferson as Monticello's "Sage," see J. Adams to TJ, 20 Dec. 1814, ibid., 441.
7. See, for example, TJ to Joseph Cabell, 17 Jan. 1814, *L&B*, 14:68, requesting his discretion in showing others Jefferson's letters condemning banks ("I am too desirous of tranquility to bring such a nest of hornets on me as the fraternity of banking companies"). But Jefferson agreed to let Cabell print a letter to his nephew Peter Carr on the establishment of what would become the University of Virginia "if it will promote the interests of science" (TJ to Cabell, 2 Feb. 1816, ibid., 419). Even old correspondents could prove unfaithful; for his embarrassment when George Logan released to the press part of a letter condemning Napoleon, see TJ to Logan, 19 May, 20 June 1816, *Ford*, 11:525–27, 527n.1. For concern lest his religious views become public—Jefferson knew they would alarm the orthodox—see TJ to Levi Lincoln, 26 Apr. 1803; TJ to Charles Clay, 29 Jan. 1815; TJ to Francis Adrian Van der Kemp, 25 Apr. 1816; TJ to William Short, 13 Apr. 1820; TJ to Timothy Pickering, 27 Feb. 1821; TJ to Benjamin Waterhouse, 19 July 1822; TJ to James Smith, 8 Dec. 1822; TJ to John Davis, 18 Jan. 1824; TJ to George Thacher, 26 Jan. 1824, in Adams, ed., *Jefferson's Extracts from the Gospels*, 337–38, 363, 368–69, 391, 403, 406–7, 409, 414, 415.
8. On Jefferson's promotion of a Republican history, see *Malone*, 6:200–212, and see 213–30 on his efforts to have the history of Virginia, including his governorship, correctly written. Merrill D. Peterson, *The Jefferson Image in the American Mind* (New

York, 1960), tells us how posterity came to see Jefferson; we know less about his own efforts to shape that image. For his instruments in setting the record straight on his governorship, see Edith Philips, *Louis Hue Girardin and Nicholas Gouin Dufief and Their Relations with Thomas Jefferson* (Baltimore, 1926), and Joseph I. Shulim, *John Daly Burk: Irish Revolutionist and American Patriot*, American Philosophical Society, *Transactions*, n.s., 54 (1964), pt. 6. For materials he prepared toward this end, see TJ, Notes and Documents Relating to the British Invasions in 1781, *Boyd*, 4:256–78.

9. TJ to Albert Gallatin, 11 Oct. 1809, *Ford*, 9:124–25.

10. TJ to Thomas Leiper, 23 May 1808, *L&B*, 12:65–66.

11. TJ to James Madison, 27 Apr. 1809, in Robert A. Rutland et al., eds., *The Papers of James Madison: Presidential Series*, 2 vols. to date (Charlottesville, Va., 1984–), 1:139.

12. Albert Gallatin, Statement of the Public Debt from January 1, 1791 to January 1, 1810, in E. James Ferguson, ed., *Selected Writings of Albert Gallatin* (Indianapolis, 1967), 208–9; as Gallatin noted, the debt was also increased during Jefferson's tenure, and $11 million of the $53 million due in 1810 represented the cost of Louisiana.

13. TJ to Gallatin, 11 Oct. 1809, *Ford*, 11:125.

14. Gallatin to TJ, 8 Nov. 1809, in Henry Adams, ed., *The Writings of Albert Gallatin*, 3 vols. (Philadelphia, 1879), 1:465–66. For Dr. Johnson, see Chapter 3, text at note 17.

15. TJ to Du Pont, 15 Apr. 1811, in Chinard, ed., *Jefferson and Du Pont*, 163–64. The remarks on the rich as the sole objects of taxation echo the claim in the 1805 Second Inaugural that ordinary Americans never saw a federal tax collector. For this, see Chapter 5, text at note 144.

16. *Malone*, 6:208–12; Gilbert Chinard, ed., *Jefferson et les idéologues . . .* (Baltimore, 1925), 31–96. Jefferson does not seem to have been affected by Tracy's remark in the *Commentary on Montesquieu* that declarations of rights were signs of political immaturity. Tracy made the point while nevertheless praising Lafayette's 11 July 1789 proposal, for which see Chapter 2, text at note 67; Tracy's daughter had married Lafayette's son, and perhaps the favorable mention was no more than politeness on Tracy's part. For Tracy's position, see Jeremy Jennings, "The *Déclaration des Droits de l'Homme et du Citoyen* and Its Critics in France: Reaction and *Idéologie*," *Historical Journal* 35 (1992): 857.

17. Chinard, ed., *Jefferson et les idéologues*, 102–4; the quotation is in TJ to William Duane, 22 Jan. 1813, ibid., 106.

18. For comments on the generational theme, see Antoine Louis Claude, Comte Destutt de Tracy, *A Treatise on Political Economy . . .* (Washington, D.C., 1817), 238–40, 246–47, quotation on 238. Jefferson seems never to have explored this question with Tracy, though in a letter to Tracy of 26 December 1820 he did say that "it is incumbent on every generation to pay it's [*sic*] own debts" (Chinard, ed., *Jefferson et les idéologues*, 203). Tracy, of course, was aware of the generational principle in its political form (note 16), but apparently did not see the connection between generational limits on debts and generational limits on constitutions.

19. On the delays, see TJ to Tracy, 3 Aug. 1819, in Chinard, ed., *Jefferson et les idéologues*, 159–61, and *Malone*, 6:305–6.

20. TJ to Middleton, 8 Jan. 1813, *L&B*, 13:202.

21. On Gallatin's resignation–he was driven to it, but it is clear he would have found life at the Treasury Department difficult in the war's remaining years–see J. C. A. Stagg, *Mr. Madison's War: Politics, Diplomacy, and Warfare in the Early American Republic, 1783–1830* (Princeton, N.J., 1983), 301.

22. For an overview of this episode, see *Malone*, 6: chap. 10, "The Political Economy of a Country Gentleman."

23. For conditions in 1813 prompting Jefferson to write to Eppes, see Stagg, *Madison's War*, 292–348. On 10 June 1813, Eppes introduced emergency loan legislation authorizing the government to borrow $7.5 million. *Annals of the Congress of the United States, 1789–1824*, 42 vols. (Washington, D.C., 1834–1856), Extra Session, 1813, 148. Jefferson's first letter, dated two weeks later, was no doubt prompted by that news. Redeemable at the government's option after twelve years, the loan was not accompanied by a tax to extinguish it. Rafael A. Bayley, *The National Loans of the United States, from July 4, 1776, to June 30, 1880* (Washington, D.C., 1881), 51, 126. Eppes needs a biography, but in the meantime see *DAB* and George Green Shackelford, "Maria Jefferson and John Wayles Eppes," in Shackelford, ed., *Collected Papers to Commemorate Fifty Years of the Monticello Association of the Descendants of Thomas Jefferson* (Princeton, N.J., 1965), 154–66. For the letters, 24 June, 11 Sept., 6 Nov. 1813, see *Ford*, 11:297–306, 306–15, 315–32. The 24 June letter lays out the principle and its applications in the present crisis, the 11 September letter discusses what kinds of loans will satisfy the principle, and the 6 November letter, reacting to the news of plans for a new national bank, condemns banks of issue and paper currency and advocates Jefferson's favorite scheme of treasury notes.

24. *Malone*, 6:140; James Monroe to TJ, 1 Oct. 1813, in Stanislaus Murray Hamilton, ed., *The Writings of James Monroe* . . . (New York, 1901), 5:273–74.

25. TJ to Eppes, 24 Sept. 1814, *Ford*, 11:314.

26. Stagg, *Madison's War*, 438–39. For Madison's reaction, see TJ to James Madison; 24 Sept. 1814, *L&B*, 14:195–96; Madison to TJ, 10 Oct. 1814 (dissent on paper money), in Gaillard Hunt, ed., *The Writings of James Madison* . . . , 9 vols. (New York, 1900–1910), 8:313–16; TJ to Madison, 15 Oct. 1814, *Ford*, 11:432–36; Madison to TJ, 23 Oct. 1814, in Hunt, ed., *Writings of James Madison*, 8:314n.2. Madison had evidently abandoned the views expressed in his essay "Universal Peace" (1792), for which see Chapter 5, text at notes 63, 64. For Dallas, see Raymond Walters, Jr., *Alexander James Dallas: Lawyer–Politician–Financier, 1759–1817* (Philadelphia, 1943), 190–91.

27. TJ to Cabell, 7 Nov. 1813; Cabell to TJ, 29 Nov. 1813; TJ to Cabell, 17 Jan. 1814; Cabell to TJ, 6 Mar. 1814, in Nathaniel Francis Cabell, ed., *Early History of the University of Virginia, as Contained in the Letters of Thomas Jefferson and Joseph C. Cabell* (Richmond, Va., 1856), 9, 24; *L&B*, 14:67–68. On Cabell, see Carol Minor Tanner, "Joseph C. Cabell, 1778–1856" (Ph.D. diss., University of Virginia, 1948); for the careers of those he showed the letters, see *DAB*. Rives has finally received the attention he deserves. See Drew R. McCoy's depiction of this last of the Madisonians in *The Last of the Fathers: James Madison and the Republican Legacy* (Cambridge, 1989). For Jefferson and the *Enquirer*, see *Malone*, 6:esp. 115, 325, 357–59, 375, 431.

28. TJ to Eppes, 24 June, 6 Nov. 1813, *Ford*, 11:305, 330n.1.

29. For references to Smith (Jefferson quotes him extensively on banks and paper money and cites by book, chapter, and page), see TJ to Eppes, 11 Sept., 6 Nov. 1813, ibid., 314, 319–24, 314; he also cites Buffon's tables (299), Hume (319), Thomas Cooper's *Political Arithmetic* (Philadelphia, 1798) (321), and Richard Price on annuities (314). For mathematical exercises, see ibid., 311–13.

30. On Eppes at the White House, see *Malone*, 4:368.

31. TJ to Eppes, 24 June 1813, *Ford*, 11:298, 300. For Eppes's law studies, see Shackelford, "Maria Jefferson and John Wayles Eppes."

32. TJ to Eppes, 24 June 1813, *Ford*, 11:300.

33. TJ to Eppes, 13 Sept. 1813, ibid., 309, 308–9. For the 1786 remark, see Chapter 1, text at notes 73–77.

34. TJ to Eppes, 13 Sept. 1813, *Ford*, 11:311–14, quotations on 311, 314; for the formula, see TJ, Notes on the Payment of the Public Debt, [ca. 28 Mar. 1793], *Boyd*, 25: 464–65. See also TJ to Madison, 15 Oct. 1814, *Ford*, 11:432–36.

35. TJ to Eppes, 6 Nov. 1813, *Ford*, 11:326–29, quotation on 329; circulation figures are on 323, 327.

36. TJ to Eppes, 24 June 1813, ibid., 299.

37. The length of a Jeffersonian generation today would be forty-eight years. M. L. Burstein, *Understanding Thomas Jefferson: Studies in Economics, Law and Philosophy* (New York, 1993), 206, citing F. Gunter, "Thomas Jefferson on the Repudiation of Public Debt" (unpublished paper, 1990), 12–14.

38. For Jefferson's efforts in 1800, see Memorial of the American Philosophical Society, 10 Jan. 1800, in U.S. Congress, *House Report*, 41st Cong., 2d sess., no. 3, 18 Jan. 1879, 35. For census schedules from 1790 to 1820, see Carroll D. Wright, *The History and Growth of the United States Census* (Washington, D.C., 1900), 18, 20–21, 26, 132–33. Without that more refined data, Jefferson had to fall back on Buffon's tables on more than one occasion. In 1792, he used them to estimate the profits that could be made from the labor of a male slave aged twenty-five; he used them again in 1805 when working on the proposal for a naval militia. Prime examples of his penchant for calculation are TJ, Notes on Arthur Young's Letter to George Washington, 18 June 1792, *Boyd*, 24:95; TJ to Gallatin, 3 Nov. 1805, *Ford*, 10:209–11.

39. TJ to Eppes, 24 June, 11 Sept. 1813, *Ford*, 11:301, 310. No such amendment as Jefferson proposed was introduced, let alone debated seriously. See Herman V. Ames, "The Proposed Amendments to the Constitution of the United States During the First Century of Its History," American Historical Association, *Annual Report for the Year 1896* (Washington, D.C., 1897), 306–421, "A Calendar of Amendments Proposed to the Constitution of the United States. . . ."

40. On the cost of the loans, see Davis Rich Dewey, *Financial History of the United States*, 2d ed. (New York, 1903), 134. On Girard, see Donald R. Adams, Jr., *Finance and Enterprise in Early America: A Study of Stephen Girard's Bank, 1812–1831* ([Philadelphia], 1978), 26–27, 30–44.

41. There is no adequate financial history of the War of 1812, but for an overview suggesting why Jefferson was worried, see Dewey, *Financial History of the United States*, 128–42. For details of the loans, see Bayley, *National Loans of the United States*. On the legislative history of interest-bearing notes, see Donald H. Kagan, "Monetary Aspects of the Treasury Notes of the War of 1812," *Journal of Economic History* 44 (1984): 68–88; a numismatist, Kagan ignores Jefferson's role in stimulating Eppes to press for larger issues of the notes. Jefferson's preference for interest-bearing notes to be retired through taxation reflects both colonial methods of currency finance and the practice in some states, including Virginia, during the 1780s of retiring war debt through taxes payable in certificates. E. James Ferguson, *The Power of the Purse: A History of American Public Finance, 1776–1790* (Chapel Hill, N.C., 1961), 3–24. For political aspects of wartime fiances, see Stagg, *Madison's War*, esp. 88–91, 141–43, 150–52, 279–80, 291–99, 375–80, 437–53. Henry Adams's account of these matters still has value; see his *History of the United States of America During the Second Administration of James Madison*, 3 vols. (New York, 1890), 1:387–90; 2:212–15, 239–62. For Jefferson's complaints, in addition to the three letters to Eppes, see TJ to Thomas Cooper, 10 Sept. 1814 (treasury notes); TJ to Madison, 24 Sept. 1814 (Treasury notes), *L&B*, 14:188–89, 195–96; TJ to Madison, 15 Oct. 1814 (Treasury

notes, loans), *Ford*, 11:432–36; TJ to Monroe, 16 Oct. 1814 (Treasury notes), *L&B*, 14:207–8; TJ to William Harris Crawford, 11 Feb. 1815 (Treasury notes), *Ford*, 11:452; TJ to Caesar A. Rodney, 16 Mar. 1815 (Treasury notes); TJ to Gallatin, 16 Oct. 1815 (Treasury notes, loans), *L&B*, 14:286–87, 356–58.

42. TJ to Short, 28 Nov. 1814, *L&B*, 14:214.

43. TJ to Eppes, 11 Sept. 1813, *Ford*, 11:308.

44. On bank proliferation, see Bray Hammond, *Banks and Politics in America: From the Revolution to the Civil War* (Princeton, N.J., 1957), 144–96, 227–50; for Virginia, see George T. Starnes, *Sixty Years of Branch Banking in Virginia* (New York, 1931), 27–56.

45. TJ to Cooper, 16 Jan. 1814, *L&B*, 14:61; TJ to Eppes, 24 June 1813, *Ford*, 11:305.

46. TJ to Eppes, 11 Sept. 1813, *Ford*, 11:311.

47. For additional evidence of his dislike of "self-created" societies, see his comments on Jedidiah Morse's association to support Indian missions, which he feared would enable the clergy (the bulk of its members) to supplant the authority of the people's representatives. It was a dangerous precedent, he told Morse. Commenting on the proposal to Madison and Monroe, he was even more explicit, seeing in Morse's suggestion the blueprint for associations that would allow zealots to impose their policy choices on the nation regardless of the will of the majority. TJ to Jedidiah Morse, 6 Mar. 1822; TJ to Madison, 25 Feb. 1822; TJ to Monroe, 19 Mar. 1822, *Ford*, 12:222–26, 227–28, 228.

48. For an introduction, see Hammond, *Banks and Politics*.

49. TJ to Cabell, 17 Jan. 1814, *L&B*, 14:69.

50. TJ to Eppes, 6 Nov. 1813, *Ford*, 11:330, 328.

51. TJ to Gallatin, 16 Oct. 1815, *L&B*, 14:357, 356.

52. TJ to Eppes, 6 Nov. 1813, *Ford*, 11:324. At other times, he used the story of the South Sea Bubble to the same effect, often referring to these early-eighteenth-century episodes in tandem. See, for example, TJ to Henry Remsen, 14 Apr. 1792; TJ to Short, 24 Apr. 1792; *Boyd*, 23:425, 459 – both comment on the Duer Panic–TJ to Charles Yancey, 6 Jan. 1816, *Ford*, 11:494. References to the South Sea Bubble would be in keeping with standard Republican and country party rhetoric, on which see Lance Banning, *The Jeffersonian Persuasion: Evolution of a Party Ideology* (Ithaca, N.Y., 1978), 67–69; Jefferson's use of the Mississippi Bubble may reflect Adam Smith's treatment of paper money, which Jefferson cites to Eppes at this point in the 6 November 1813 letter.

53. TJ to Cabell, 17 Sept., 23 Sept. 1814, in Cabell, ed., *Early History of the University of Virginia*, 24–27, 27–30. For his efforts to procure legislative action, see TJ to Rives, 28 Nov. 1819, *Ford*, 12:149–50 (reviving his wartime plan for gradual reduction of the paper circulation). For the legislature's actions, see Murray N. Rothbard, *The Panic of 1819: Reactions and Policies* (New York, 1962), 35–38, 137–40.

54. TJ to J. Adams, 24 Jan. 1814, *Cappon*, 2:424–25.

55. TJ to Rodney, 16 Mar. 1815, *L&B*, 14:286, 286–87.

56. TJ to Monroe, 1 Jan. 1815, *Ford*, 11:443; TJ to Du Pont, 28 Feb. 1815, in Chinard, ed., *Jefferson and Du Pont*, 211. The "luminous reviewer of Montesquieu" was Destutt de Tracy, as Joyce Appleby reminds us in "What Is Still American in the Political Philosophy of Thomas Jefferson?" *WMQ* 39 (1982): 287–91, 297–301.

57. TJ to Samuel Kercheval, 12 July 1816, *Ford*, 12:10–11.

58. TJ to J. Adams, 7 Nov. 1819, *Cappon*, 2:546.

59. For Jefferson's financial collapse, see Hochman, "Personal Financial Biography," 273–74, 275, 276, 278.

60. TJ to Short, 13 Apr. 1820, in Adams, ed., *Jefferson's Extracts from the Gospels*, 393–94.

61. Cf. Gordon S. Wood, "The Trials and Tribulations of Thomas Jefferson," in Peter S. Onuf, ed., *Jeffersonian Legacies* (Charlottesville, Va., 1993), 413–14.

62. TJ to Spencer Roane, 9 Mar. 1821, *Ford*, 12:201.

63. TJ to Macon, 19 Aug. 1821, ibid., 207. On Macon, see J. Adams to Benjamin Rush, 22 June 1806, in John A. Schutz and Douglass Adair, eds., *The Spur of Fame: Dialogues of John Adams and Benjamin Rush, 1805–1813* (San Marino, Calif., 1966), 55: "I must give to Mr. Macon . . . the praise of system and consistency. [His] fundamental principle is that the moment you raise a public force, you give up your liberties; and therefore there must be neither an army, navy, fortifications, a select militia, or even a revenue because if any of those exist, they must be entrusted to the executive authority, establish a system of patronage, and overthrow the Constitution." Macon was willing to suppress his hatred of the debt during the War of 1812, because, as he put it, he hated British impressment of American seamen more. Macon, 3 Mar. 1814, in *Annals of Congress*, 13th Cong., 2d sess., 1782.

64. TJ to Samuel Kercheval, 5 Sept. 1816, *Ford*, 12:15–16; TJ to J. Adams, 14 Oct. 1816, *Cappon*, 2:492. For similar comments, see TJ to Eppes, 11 Sept. 1813, *Ford*, 11:310; TJ to J. Adams, 25 Nov. 1816, *Cappon*, 2:496–97.

65. TJ to Kercheval, 12 July, 5 Sept. 1816, *Ford*, 12:10–11, 15.

66. J. Q. Adams to Abigail Adams, 5 Jan. 1816, in Worthington Chauncey Ford ed., *The Writings of John Quincy Adams* (New York, 1915), 5:462–63.

67. U.S. Bureau of the Census, *Historical Statistics of the United States: Colonial Times to 1957*, Series Y 350–356, *Expenditures of the Federal Government: 1789–1957* (Washington, D.C., 1960), 719; ibid., Series Y 368–379, 721.

68. *Malone*, 6:328–61, 426–43, describes Jefferson's reactions to national politics in the years after the war; for the quotation, see TJ to Gallatin, 26 Dec. 1820, *Ford*, 12:186. On government finances between 1819 and 1821—there were loans of $3 million in 1820 and $5 million in 1821—see Dewey, *Financial History of the United States*, 166–67. John Lauritz Larson comments on his hostility to energetic government in "Jefferson's Union and the Problem of Internal Improvements," in Onuf, ed., *Jeffersonian Legacies*, 364. Jefferson's final intervention in politics, the December 1825 "Solemn Declaration and Protest of the Commonwealth of Virginia on the principles of the Constitution of the US. of America & on the violations of them," enclosed in TJ to Madison, 24 Dec. 1825, *Ford*, 12:418–21, saw him offering a solution to congressional usurpations: Until an amendment authorized Congress to spend on internal improvements, unconstitutional acts of Congress would be made constitutional by having the Virginia legislature adopt them as state statutes.

69. On the eventual extinction of the debt, see Robert V. Remini, *Andrew Jackson and the Course of American Democracy, 1833–1845* (New York, 1984), 218–19, 222–26, 280, 412–13, 476, suggesting the continuity of republicanism in this regard. Jacksonianism could be quite Jeffersonian, as Marvin Meyers's remarks on a debt limitation proposal at the New York constitutional convention of 1846 suggest: "Here is the chart of the Jacksonian conscience, indignant at what it has seen, half-ashamed at what it has condoned, and fiercely resolved to extirpate for ever one whole order of public evil" (*The Jacksonian Persuasion: Politics and Belief* [Stanford, Calif., 1957], 205). For additional evidence of the way Jacksonians perpetuated this part of Jefferson's legacy, see L. Ray Gunn, "The Crisis of Distributive Politics: The Debate

over State Debts and Development Policy in New York, 1837–1842," in William Pencak and Conrad Edick Wright, eds., *New York and the Rise of American Capitalism: Economic Development and the Social and Political History of an American State, 1780–1870* (New York, 1989), 168–201, esp. 181.

70. TJ to Eppes, 11 Sept. 1813, *Ford*, 11:310.

71. George Ticknor to E. Ticknor, 1 Feb. 1815, in *Life, Letters, and Journals of George Ticknor*, 2 vols. (London, 1876), 1:37–38. For the favorable impression this young New Englander made, see TJ to John Vaughan, 5 Feb. 1815, *L&B*, 14:239; TJ to J. Adams, 10 June 1815, *Cappon*, 2:443.

72. Jefferson and Kercheval corresponded before 1816, the date of the famous letter, on educational and other topics. See Kercheval to TJ, 28 Sept., 12 Dec. 1809; TJ to Kercheval, 15 Jan., 19 Jan. 1810, Jefferson Papers, LC.

73. On the Virginia constitution of 1776 and the movement for reform, see, for an overview, Fletcher M. Green, *Constitutional Development in the South Atlantic States, 1776–1860: A Study in the Extension of Democracy* (Chapel Hill, N.C., 1930), 101–4, 139–41, 173–76, 210–24, 287–96, and, for a narrative, Robert P. Sutton, *Revolution to Secession: Constitution Making in the Old Dominion* (Charlottesville, Va., 1989), 21–102. William W. Freehling, *The Road to Disunion* (New York, 1990), 166–77, is brief but suggestive. Also helpful in understanding Jefferson's 1816 exchange with Kercheval are J. R. Pole, *Political Representation in England and the Origins of the American Republic* (New York, 1966), 281–338, and Dickson D. Bruce, Jr., *The Rhetoric of Conservatism: The Virginia Convention of 1829–30 and the Conservative Tradition in the South* (San Marino, Calif., 1982), 1–29. Peterson, *Jefferson Image*, 40, notes the impact of the 1816 correspondence with Kercheval on the reformers who pressed the cause of constitutional change. See Willi Paul Adams, *The First American Constitutions: Republican Ideology and the Making of the State Constitutions in the Revolutionary Era*, trans. Rita Kimber and Robert Kimber (Chapel Hill, N.C., 1980), for a comparison of the Virginia document with those of other states. On Jefferson's role in the creation of that document, see Boyd, editorial note, "The Virginia Constitution," *Boyd*, 1:329–37; Robert A. Rutland, editorial note, "Virginia Constitution of 1776," in Rutland, ed., *The Papers of George Mason, 1725–1792*, 3 vols. (Chapel Hill, N.C., 1970), 1:295–99, and see also 302–4, and Brent Tarter and Robert L. Scribner, eds., *Revolutionary Virginia: The Road to Independence* (Charlottesville, Va., 1983), 7, pt.2:594–98, 603–6, 636–39, 641–44, 649–54, 656–58. For Jefferson's published comments, see *Notes on the State of Virginia* (1785), ed. William Peden (Chapel Hill, N.C., 1954), 117–29.

74. For Jefferson's 1783 effort to draft a new constitution for Virginia, see Boyd, editorial note, "Jefferson's Proposed Revision of the Virginia Constitution," *Boyd*, 6:278–84, and for the text itself, ibid., 294–305; for Madison's observations on the draft, see also ibid., 308–16. Edmund Randolph tried unsuccessfully to obtain a new constitution in 1789; for details, see Richard R. Beeman, *The Old Dominion and the New Nation, 1788–1801* (Lexington, Ky., 1972), 49, 51–55, and Joseph Jones to Madison, 2 Nov. 1789; John Dawson to Madison, 17 Dec. 1789, *PJM*, 12:441, 461. Randolph sent his plan to Madison and Jefferson. E. Randolph to Madison, 23 Mar. 1790, ibid., 13:116.

75. See, for example, Joyce Appleby, "Republicanism in Old and New Contexts," *WMQ* 43 (1986): 22, and Chapter 2. For the letters, see TJ to Kercheval, 12 July, 5 Sept. 1816, *Ford*, 12: 3–15, 15–17.

76. TJ to Kercheval, 12 July 1816, *Ford*, 12:11–13. On the Parisian origins of "revision at periodic intervals," see Chapter 2. For the two states (New Hampshire

and Vermont) providing for periodic revision at this point, see Francis Newton Thorpe, comp., *The Federal and State Constitutions* . . . , 7 vols. (Washington, D.C., 1909), 5:2470, 2489–90; 6:3748–49, 3760–61, 3762–78. What Jefferson seems to have in mind, however, is that fact that a number of states had already adopted new constitutions to replace their Revolutionary ones–Delaware (1792), Georgia (1789, 1798), Kentucky (1799), New Hampshire (1784, 1792), Pennsylvania (1790), South Carolina (1778, 1790), and Vermont (1786, 1793). Ibid., 1:568–81; 2:785–90, 791–802; 3:1277–92; 4:2435–70, 2471–90; 5:3092–103; 6:3248–57, 3258–65, 3749–61, 3762–78.

77. TJ to Thomas Earle, 24 Sept. 1824, TJ to Cartwright, 5 June 1824, *L&B*, 15:470, 16:48.

78. TJ to Martha Randolph, 5 Jan. 1808, 27 Feb. 1809, *Family Letters*, 319 (quotations), 320, 386. On Jefferson's finances during the presidency, see Hochman, "Personal Financial Biography," 216–48.

79. On the mill and the nailery as a source of income (and in the case of the mill, of considerable expense as well), see Hochman, "Personal Financial Biography," 221–22, 229–30, 231–40, 255–56, 280. As Hochman notes of Jefferson's investment in the mill, "the venture proved to be a disaster of mammoth proportions. If he had not gone ahead with the project during his vice-presidency and presidency, he could have left office free of debt and might actually have had the tranquil retirement for which he yearned" (231–32). For additional material on the tangled history of the milling operations, see Boynton Merrill, Jr., *Jefferson's Nephews: A Frontier Tragedy* (Princeton, N.J., 1976), 55–70.

80. Hochman, "Personal Financial Biography," 256–57, 268.

81. On the sale of Jefferson's library to Congress, see *Malone*, 6:167–84, and on the creation of a final collection, ibid., 185–99.

82. Hochman, "Personal Financial Biography," 269–70.

83. Ibid., 245.

84. Ibid., 273–74, 275. On Jefferson's relationship with Nicholas, see *Malone*, 6:161, and the other sources cited.

85. Hochman, "Personal Financial Biography," 274, 276, 278; *Malone*, 6:303–4, 305, 309–11, 314–15. Jefferson was not the only sufferer by Nicholas's fall; see Kathryn R. Malone, "The Fate of Revolutionary Republicanism in Early National Virginia," *Journal of the Early Republic* 7 (1987): 45–46. See also Ludwell H. Johnson III, "Sharper Than a Serpent's Tooth: Thomas Jefferson and His Alma Mater," *VMHB* 99 (1991): 145–62, and Victor Dennis Golladay, "The Nicholas Family of Virginia, 1722–1820" (Ph.D. diss., University of Virginia, 1973), 150–62, both critical of Jefferson and his heirs. For the quotation, see M. Randolph to TJ, 7 Aug. 1819, *Family Letters*, 430.

86. On troubles with the mill, see *Malone*, 7:315, 449, and Hochman, "Personal Financial Biography," 280; on the debt to Van Staphorst and Hubbard, see Account Book, 24 May, 25 May 1817, and TJ to Leroy and Bayard, 25 May 1817, Jefferson Papers, LC. In 1819, the firm agreed to allow Jefferson to postpone the last installment if interest were paid. At the time of his death, Jefferson still owed $1,120 on this obligation. *Malone*, 6:308, 511.

87. On Jefferson's dealings with Mazzei and his heirs, see Howard R. Marraro, "Jefferson Letters Concerning the Settlement of Mazzei's Virginia Estate," *Mississippi Valley Historical Review* 30 (1943):235–42, "Unpublished Mazzei Letters to Jefferson," *WMQ* 2 (1944):374–96, and "The Settlement of Philip Mazzei's Virginia Estate: Unpublished Correspondence," *VMHB* 63 (1955):306–31. The heirs would

not be paid in full until 1841. *Malone,* 6:510. For his argument that banks were unsafe and government securities illiquid, see TJ to Giovanni Carmignani, 18 July 1817, in Marraro, "Settlement of Mazzei's Virginia Estate," 313.

88. On Thomas Jefferson Randolph's assumption of the management of his grandfather's affairs, see Hochman, "Personal Financial Biography," 278, 286.

89. There is no modern full-length study of the creation of the University of Virginia; in the meantime, see *Malone,* 6:233–82, 365–425, 463–69, 482–88. For the quotation, see Chapter 2, text at note 35.

90. For details of his plan, see *Malone,* 6:448; the plan, dated 1 April 1823, is in the Jefferson Papers, UVa. The concerns it addressed were genuine, and Jefferson had expressed them often enough in earlier years; see TJ to M. Randolph, 5 Jan., 6 Feb. 1808, 27 Feb. 1809, *Family Letters,* 320, 327, 386.

91. For the fall of Thomas Mann Randolph, Jr., and Jeff Randolph's desperate efforts to keep things afloat, see William H. Gaines, Jr., *Thomas Mann Randolph, Jefferson's Son-in-Law* (Baton Rouge, La., 1966), 101–9, 131–32, 142, 148–49, 155–62, 186–87; Hochman, "Personal Financial Biography," 280–81; and *Malone,* 6:453–56, 460.

92. On the lottery and its failure, see *Malone,* 6:473–82, 488, 495–96. For *Cohens* v. *Virginia,* 6 Wheat. 264 (1821), see G. Edward White, *The Marshall Court and Cultural Change, 1815–35* (New York, 1988), 504–24; for Jefferson's hostile reaction to Marshall's decision, see *Malone,* 6:357–58, and David N. Mayer, *The Constitutional Thought of Thomas Jefferson* (Charlottesville, Va., 1994), 277–92.

93. On the donations, see Gilbert Chinard, ed., *The Letters of Lafayette and Jefferson* (Baltimore, 1929), 187–94, 359–60, and for the quotation, TJ to Lafayette, 16 Jan. 1825, ibid., 428. For Parliament's payment of £40,000 of Pitt's debts after his death, see *DNB;* for its generosity to Nelson's heirs and to Wellington, see Carola Oman, *Nelson* (Garden City, N.Y., 1946), 662, and Elizabeth Longford, *Wellington: Pillar of State* (New York, 1972), 19, 45.

94. TJ to Thomas Jefferson Randolph, 8 Feb. 1826, *Family Letters,* 469–70. For his prostration on the death of Martha Wayles Skelton Jefferson on 6 September 1782, see *Malone,* 1:393–98.

95. This concern would remain with Jefferson until the end; "Take care of me when dead," he begged Madison in the letter that closed their nearly half-century of correspondence. TJ to Madison, 17 Feb. 1826, *Ford,* 12:459.

96. TJ to William Johnson, 12 June 1823, *L&B,* 15:439. Jefferson was attempting to get Johnson to take up his pen in the cause; see Donald G. Morgan, *Justice William Johnson: The First Dissenter . . .* (Columbia, S.C., 1954), chap. 9, "Report to Monticello."

97. TJ to Johnson, 4 Mar. 1823, *Ford,* 12:278. Hamilton's biographer was the Reverend Dr. John Mitchell Mason (1770–1829), who attended the dying statesman in 1804 and was the author of a violent anti-Jefferson polemic, *The Voice of Warning to Christians, on the Ensuing Election of a President . . .* (New York, 1800). Mason was the family's choice as biographer, and he did his best to begin the work. See Jacob Van Vechten, *Memoirs of John M. Mason, D.D. . .* (New York, 1856), 311–12, 325–26; for additional material on the family's and Mason's efforts to gather data for the planned life, see Robert Troup to Mason, 22 Mar. 1810, in Nathan Schachner, ed., "Alexander Hamilton Viewed by His Friends: The Narratives of Robert Troup and Hercules Mulligan," *WMQ* 4 (1947): 203–25. In 1810, Mason contacted Madison, asking for access to Madison's notes of debates at the Constitutional Convention. See William Lewis to Madison, 30 Dec. 1809; Madison to John Mitchell Mason, 12 Jan.

1810; Mason to Madison, 29 Jan. 1810; Madison to Mason, 5 Feb. 1810; Madison to TJ, 17 July 1810; TJ to Madison, 26 July 1810; Eppes to Madison, 1 Nov. 1810, in Rutland, ed., *Papers of James Madison: Presidential Series*, 2: 151–53, 174, 210–11, 219–20, 418–19, 440, 610. By 1819, Mason's "impaired health had rendered it necessary for him to relinquish what he had regarded as a very responsible undertaking–the Life of General Hamilton" (Van Vechten, *Memoirs of Mason*, 497). For the family's efforts to enlist a new biographer, see John Jay to Rufus King, 8 Oct. 1818, in Henry P. Johnston, ed., *The Correspondence and Public Papers of John Jay* (New York, 1890), 4:420. Jefferson seems to have been unaware of this change of plans.

98. TJ to Johnson, 4 Mar. 1823, *Ford*, 12:278. Jefferson, who had a long memory for this sort thing, was no doubt recalling the younger Adams's *Publicola* (1791), for which see Chapter 5. In 1825, he remarked that "J. Q. Adams, the son, was more explicit than the father" in his "monarchism," citing "his answer to Paine's *rights of man*" as proof. TJ to Short, 8 Jan. 1825, *Ford*, 12:395. Nor was he wrong on the main point; for John Quincy Adams's reaction to Jefferson's posthumous works, see text at note 140.

99. For Adams's publications in retirement, see Joseph J. Ellis, *Passionate Sage: The Character and Legacy of John Adams* (New York, 1993), 75–80.

100. TJ to Johnson, 4 Mar. 1823, *Ford*, 12:278, 277–78.

101. For his fears for Franklin's manuscript, see TJ, Autobiography, 1821, *LofA*, 99–101, and Boyd's editorial note on Jefferson's efforts to get William Temple Franklin to publish his grandfather's memoirs, *Boyd*, 18:87–97; in fact, although Jefferson did not know it at the time he was writing his Autobiography, Franklin's *Autobiography* had been published in full in 1818. See J.A. Leo Lemay and P.M. Zall, eds., *Benjamin Franklin's Autobiography: An Authoritative Text, Backgrounds, Criticism* (New York, 1986), 361. For comments on the Washington papers, see TJ to Johnson, 12 June 1823, *L&B*, 15:442.

102. *Annals of Congress*, 13th Cong., 2nd sess., 14 Feb. 1814 (Hanson), 1378–79; 17 Feb. 1814 (Jackson), 1496; 18 Feb. 1814 (Shipherd), 1506, 1526.

103. TJ to Johnson, 4 Mar. 1823, *Ford*, 12:278–79.

104. On Jefferson's role in writing Virginia history, see TJ to Du Pont, 2 Mar. 1809, in Chinard, ed., *Jefferson and Du Pont*, 144; *Cappon*, 2:283–614; J. Adams to TJ, 20 Dec. 1814, ibid., 441. For the "Anas," see Charles T. Cullen, editorial note, "The 'Anas,' " *Boyd*, 22:33–38. The Autobiography has yet to find its student.

105. See TJ to Joel Barlow, 3 May 1802, *Ford*, 9:372, 9 July 1806, Jefferson Papers, LC, 8 Oct. 1809, *Ford*, 40:121–22.

106. For what remains of Barlow's history and an account of its genesis, see Christine M. Lizanich, " 'The March of this Government': Joel Barlow's Unwritten History of the United States," *WMQ* 33 (1976): 315–30.

107. An abomination, but one that obsessed him; Jefferson began to take notes on volume 5 in 1809, and in 1815, having sold his library to Congress and his set of Marshall with it, he purchased another. *Malone*, 5:356–59; for the notes, see *Ford*, 11:122n., 123n.

108. TJ, "Anas," 1818, *LofA*, 663.

109. John Marshall, *The Life of George Washington* . . . , 5 vols. (Philadelphia, 1804–1807), 5:233–71, much of this being paraphrase or verbatim transcription of the recorded debates. For the footnote, see ibid., 260n*.

110. See Chapter 5.

111. The surviving Marshall papers, in Herbert A. Johnson et al., eds., *The Papers of John Marshall*, 7 vols. to date (Chapel Hill, N.C., 1974–   ), shed no light on this,

but of course some Virginians at the time *had* known fairly well what was taking place.

112. In *A Political and Civil History of the United States of America, from the Year 1763 to . . . 1797 . . .* , 2 vols. (New Haven, Conn., 1828), 2:345, Timothy Pitkin, without citing his source, appears to have taken up the suggestion in Marshall's footnote, writing that "it has been supposed, and probably with truth, that this decision [the Potomac location] had some influence on the settlement of the question, concerning the assumption of the state debts." Pitkin's book was published before Jefferson's account appeared in 1829, but later nineteenth-century works seem to make no use of Marshall's footnote, and the twentieth-century commentary on the Dinner Table Bargain—for which see Chapter 5—also ignores it, no doubt because historians, properly, have preferred Jefferson's firsthand testimony and accepted the *Life*'s reputation as a dull compilation from secondary sources. Marshall left his remarks unaltered in the abridgment published several years after Jefferson's version was released in 1829. John Marshall, *The Life of George Washington . . .* , 2 vols. (Philadelphia, 1836), 2:191n*.

113. The account of the bargain is in Jefferson's introductory remarks of 4 February 1818; Jefferson describes his collection as consisting of "memorandums on loose scraps of paper, taken out of my pocket in the moment, and laid by to be copied fair at leisure, which however they hardly ever were" ("Anas," *LofA*, 668–69, 661). His description gives the memoranda the same qualities of immediacy and "warmth" he told Johnson would add to his letters' credibility (see text at note 103); they were what Jefferson as a lawyer would have seen as in the nature of spontaneous declarations, hence to be given great evidentiary weight. All of this makes more interesting his decision to recast his memorandum on the Dinner Table Bargain. On that memorandum, see Boyd, editorial note, "Opinions on the Constitutionality of the Residence Bill"; Boyd's source note to the memorandum, convincingly assigning it a 1792 date; and the text of the memorandum itself, *Boyd*, 17:170–71, 207–8, 205–7.

114. For the dispute over *The Federalist*, see Douglass Adair, "The Authorship of the Disputed Federalist Papers" (1944), in *Fame and the Founding Fathers: Essays by Douglass Adair*, ed. H. Trevor Colbourn (New York, 1974), 27–74, esp. 32–35.

115. The other four were Charles Carroll of Carrollton, who lived until 1832; Daniel Carroll, who died in 1796; George Gale, who died in 1815; and Alexander White, who died in 1804. Madison also approached a fifth congressman, Michael Jenifer Stone of Maryland, who refused to change his vote (he died in 1812). Kenneth R. Bowling, *The Creation of Washington, D.C.: The Idea and Location of the American Capital* (Fairfax, Va., 1991), 186. For death dates, see *Biographical Directory of the United States Congress, 1774–1989* (Washington, D.C., 1989).

116. For Lee's dates and career, see *DAB* and Wesley Frank Craven's sketch in Richard A. Harrison, ed., *Princetonians, 1776–1783: A Biographical Dictionary* (Princeton, N.J., 1981), 266–69. In 1816, Madison made Lee one of the commissioners for adjudicating claims for property lost or destroyed in the District of Columbia during the War of 1812; in 1819, Monroe appointed him to the bench of the District Orphan's Court, a position he held until his death. Ibid., 268. His financial difficulties in later years are described in Paul C. Nagel, *The Lees of Virginia: Seven Generations of an American Family* (New York, 1990), 185–87. For Lee's letters to Madison, see Lee to Madison, 31 Jan. 1815, 15 Apr. 1825, Richard Bland Lee Papers, LC.

117. On Charles Lee, see Wesley Frank Craven's sketch in Richard A. Harrison, ed., *Princetonians, 1769–1775: A Biographical Dictionary* (Princeton, N.J., 1980), 493–98.

118. For Jefferson's correspondence with Henry Lee, Jr., see Henry S. Randall, *The Life of Thomas Jefferson*, 3 vols. (New York, 1857), 3:appendix 32, 662–64. On this episode, see Charles Royster, *Light-Horse Harry Lee and the Legacy of the American Revolution* (New York, 1981), chap. 6, "Mr. Jefferson"; Peterson, ed., *Visitors to Monticello*, 108–110; and for the younger Lee's life and times, Nagel, *Lees of Virginia*, 203–30.

119. For the memorandum, see *Boyd*, 17:170–71, 207–8, 205–7, and for the letter to the president, see TJ to George Washington, 9 Sept. 1792, ibid., 24:352–53.

120. For the historiography of the Dinner Table Bargain, see Chapter 5.

121. TJ, "Anas," 1818, *LofA*, 662–63.

122. Ibid., 666.

123. Ibid., 667.

124. Ibid.

125. Ibid., 668; *Boyd*, 17:205.

126. *LofA*, 668–69; *Boyd*, 17:207.

127. *Boyd*, 17:207; *LofA*, 669.

128. TJ to Washington, 9 Sept. 1792, *Boyd*, 24:352.

129. *Boyd*, 17:206–7; *LofA*, 668.

130. One result of Jefferson's effort to preempt the discussion of the bargain is that we lack an account by Madison. In autobiographical notes written late in life, he passed over the incident in silence; see James Madison, "Autobiography" [ca. 1832–1836], ed. Douglass Adair, *WMQ* 2 (1945): 204–5. Even his major nineteenth-century biographer, William Cabell Rives, apparently did not know that Madison was present at the June 1790 dinner. William C. Rives, *History of the Life and Times of James Madison* (Boston, 1868), 3:113–15.

131. See, for example, Jefferson's notes on members of Congress financially interested in the outcome of legislation, the information from John Beckley, 23 Mar. 1793, the notes of a conversation with Washington, 6 Aug. 1793, and the notes on whether Fisher Ames was a speculator, 11 Mar. 1800, *Boyd*, 25: 432–33; "Anas," *LofA*, 684–88; Franklin B. Sawvel, ed., *The Complete Anas of Thomas Jefferson* (New York, 1903), 202–3.

132. Thomas Jefferson Randolph, ed., *Memoir, Correspondence, and Miscellanies, from the Papers of Thomas Jefferson* (Charlottesville, Va., 1829). The second edition was published in Boston in 1830. On the publication of the *Memoir*, see Peterson, *Jefferson Image*, 29–36. In addition to these editions, there were others, which I have not seen, published in New York and in London, both in 1830.

133. For some of Madison's problems, see McCoy, *Last of the Fathers*, 115–18, 123–51.

134. Madison to T. J. Randolph, 28 Feb. 1829, Madison Papers, LC; Madison to Lafayette, 20 Feb. 1828, in Hunt, ed., *Writings of James Madison*, 9:306.

135. For reactions to the *Memoir*, see Peterson, *Jefferson Image*, 32–36.

136. For adoption of the "Anas" account of the Dinner Table Bargain, always uncritically, see, for example, George Tucker, *The Life of Thomas Jefferson* . . . , 2 vols. (Philadelphia, 1837), 1:329–31; Richard Hildreth, *The History of the United States of America* . . . *1788–1821* (1851) (New York, 1875), 3:122–12; Randall, *Life of Thomas Jefferson*, 1:608–10; and Rives, *Life and Times of James Madison*, 3:113–15. Not until Edward Channing's *History of the United States* (New York, 1917), 4:77–79, which made use of the diary of Senator William Maclay, do we find a real effort to go beyond the "Anas." In contrast, the Hamilton family preferred silence on the Dinner Table Bargain, concentrating its efforts on the more important task of redeeming its

progenitor from Jefferson's charges of corruption and monarchism. See John C. Hamilton, *History of the Republic of the United States of America, As Traced in the Writings of Alexander Hamilton* . . . (New York, 1859), 4:137n* (the barest of allusions to a bargain, with quotations from Madison's correspondence to suggest the impetus came from the Virginians), and James A. Hamilton, *Reminiscences of James A. Hamilton; or, Men and Events* . . . (New York, 1869), 16–19, 21–22, 35–38.

137. See "Memoirs of the life of General Alexander Hamilton By Mr. Meyer Clerk in the General's Office," Hamilton Papers, LC.

138. Martin Van Buren, *Inquiry into the Origin and Course of Political Parties in the United States* (New York, 1867), 216, and see also 175. Van Buren's discussion of the public debt, which he sees as Hamilton's means to corrupt Congress, is another instance of the way Jacksonians preserved some of Jefferson's teachings. Ibid., 142–54, 162–63, 170–232.

139. Joseph Story to Samuel P. P. Fay, 15 Feb. 1830, in William W. Story, *The Life and Letters of Joseph Story*, 2 vols. (Boston, 1851), 2:33. For John Quincy Adams's acrid verdict, see his diary entries for the period 11 January to 3 February 1831, in Charles Francis Adams, ed., *Memoirs of John Quincy Adams* . . . (Philadelphia, 1876), 8:270–310. Unfortunately, Adams does not seem to have read much beyond the Autobiography and the correspondence through May 1785; if he did read the 6 September 1789 letter, he does not mention it. But on 23 January 1831, he discussed with Story Jefferson's 5 June 1824 letter to Major Cartwright. Although that letter is an important reaffirmation of the generational principle, Adams says only that he and Story agreed in dismissing as historically unfounded the part of the letter in which Jefferson attempted to show that Christianity was not part of the common law. Ibid., 291, and for the letter to Cartwright, see text at note 77.

140. On the rights of the living generation, Jeff Randolph included Jefferson's letter to Madison, 6 Sep. 1789; the note of correction to Gem; and the letters to Eppes, 24 June, 6 Nov. 1813; to Kercheval, 12 July, 5 Sept. 1816; to Cartwright, 5 June 1824, in Randolph, ed., *Memoir*, 4:27–31, 32, 196–201, 207–22, 285–92, 295–96, 393–99.

141. Theodore Dwight, *The Character of Thomas Jefferson, as Exhibited in His Own Writings* (Boston, 1839), 82. Dwight quotes the text in full (82–89), as well as the note of correction to Gem (89–90), the letter to Eppes of 24 June 1813 (90–92), and the letter to Cartwright of 5 June 1824 (92–93); sets out his own objections in detail (93–96); and supports them by quoting from Madison's reply of 4 Feb. 1790 (96–101), taken from Tucker's 1837 biography, which quotes the Madison letter in full (Tucker, *Life of Jefferson*, 1:292–96). Dwight's book is 371 pages long, and the 18 pages he spends on the letter to Madison and associated texts (about 5 percent of the work) suggest that Dwight was genuinely struck by the—to him—absurd principle.

142. Henry Lee, [Jr.], *Observations on the Writings of Thomas Jefferson, with Particular Reference to the Attack They Contain on the Memory of the Late Gen. Henry Lee* . . . (New York, 1832), 77–78, quotation on 78 (Lee understands Jefferson to mean that the longer one avoids paying a debt, the less valid it becomes). The *Observations* were reprinted seven years later, edited by Charles Carter Lee, who added a note referring the reader to Madison's 4 February 1790 reply as printed in Tucker's *Life of Jefferson* and suggesting that comparison with Burke's *Reflections* would be instructive—the first time, as far as I can discover, that Jefferson's and Burke's views of the rights of generations were directly compared. Henry Lee, Jr., *Observations*, ed. C.C. Lee (Philadelphia, 1839), 79n*.

143. Madison to Ellen Wayles Randolph Coolidge, 3 Apr. 1830, Madison Papers, LC.

144. Tucker, *Life of Jefferson*, 1:291–98, quotation on 297. Given Tucker's position on the national debt, his reaction is no surprise; see "A Citizen of Virginia" [George Tucker], "On National Debt" (1815), in [Tucker], *Essays on Various Subjects of Taste, Morals, and National Policy* (Washington, D.C., 1822), 127–56. For Tucker's comments on the 1813 Eppes correspondence, see *Life of Jefferson*, 2:370–75, again critical of Jefferson's economics. As Joseph Dorfman noted, "Jefferson's ideas, those of the legendary Jefferson more than the actual one, were still anathema to [Tucker], but he managed to surround his objections with Jefferson's rhetoric" (*The Economic Mind in American Civilization, 1606–1865* [New York, 1946], 2:881). On Tucker's appointment, see Robert Colin McLean, *George Tucker: Moral Philosopher and Man of Letters* (Chapel Hill, N.C., 1961), 24–28.

145. Tucker, *Life of Jefferson*, 1:292–96, prints Madison's reply in full. Both Dwight, *Character of Thomas Jefferson*, and Lee, *Observations* (1839), used the reply to refute Jefferson.

146. Charles Augustin Sainte-Beuve, review of Thomas Jefferson, *Mélanges politiques et philosophiques extraits des Mémoires et de la correspondance de Thomas Jefferson* . . . , ed. L.-P. Conseil (Paris, 1833), in *Le National* (Paris), 25 Feb. 1833, in Sainte-Beuve, *Oeuvres*, ed. Maxim Leroy ([Paris], 1956), 1:485.

147. On Sainte-Beuve's audience, see Alan B. Spitzer, *The French Generation of 1820* (Princeton, N.J., 1987).

148. On internal improvements and the Virginia state debt, see Carter Goodrich, "The Virginia System of Mixed Enterprise: A Study of State Planning of Internal Improvements," *Political Science Quarterly* 64 (1949): 355–87, and Richard L. Morton, "The Virginia State Debt and Internal Improvements, 1820–38," *Journal of Political Economy* 25 (1917): 339–73. Even before Jefferson's death, not every Virginia Republican was hostile to banks and other state-sponsored enterprises. On the creation of the Bank of Virginia in 1803–1804, see Malone, "Fate of Revolutionary Republicanism," 27–51, esp. 34–43.

149. See B. U. Ratchford, *American State Debts* (Durham, N.C., 1941), 197–229, and James Tice Moore, *Two Paths to the New South: The Virginia Debt Controversy, 1870–1883* (Lexington, Ky., 1974). These discussions do not reveal whether the Readjusters made use of "the earth belongs to the living" in their efforts to scale down the state debt.

150. These are described in A. James Heins, *Constitutional Restrictions Against State Debt* (Madison, Wis., 1963), 3–9; for Virginia's experience with debt limitation, see A. E. Dick Howard, *Commentaries on the Constitution of Virginia*, 2 vols. (Charlottesville, Va., 1972), 2:1095–1113.

151. See, generally, Walter Farleigh Dodd, *The Revision and Amendment of State Constitutions* (Baltimore, 1910). Kermit Hall's forthcoming study of nineteenth-century state constitutions promises to enlarge our understanding of this process. Note that at the time Jefferson wrote his 1816 letters on constitutional revision, both New Hampshire and Vermont did provide for periodic revision, or rather for discussion of whether it was needed, in the former by town meetings, in the latter by the Council of Censors. In both states, the reexaminations took place at seven-year intervals. Thorpe, comp., *Federal and State Constitutions*, 5:2470, 2489–90 (New Hampshire), 6:3748–49, 3760–61, 3762–78 (Vermont). It is not clear that Jefferson was aware of this practice.

152. Corruption hardly disappeared; it was a major theme for Calhoun, who upheld the purity of Republican doctrine in this respect. See William W. Freehling, "Spoilsmen and Interests in the Thought and Career of John C. Calhoun," *JAH* 52

(1965): 25–42, and J. William Harris, "Last of the Classical Republicans: An Interpretation of John C. Calhoun," *Civil War History* 30 (1984): 255–67.

153. For radical critiques by Jefferson's British contemporaries, see William Stafford, *Socialism, Radicalism, and Nostalgia: Social Criticism in Britain, 1775–1830* (Cambridge, 1987).

154. Or so one concludes from Helene S. Zahler, *Eastern Workingmen and National Land Policy, 1829–1862* (New York, 1941); it is, of course, possible that a reexamination of the sources would turn up Jeffersonian influences that Zahler and other students missed. An exception can be found in the New York anti-rent wars; one tenant agitator, the immigrant Irish radical Thomas Ainge Devyr, appealed to Jefferson's ideas in his case against the patroons, arguing in a 4 July 1842 speech that "the immortal author of the Declaration of Independence has left us his opinion that the present generation is entitled only to the usufruct of the earth, and that they are bound to leave it free for the use of the generation that is to succeed them. Those who please to invert the laws of Nature and adopt the doctrine of the thickheaded Dutch Company are, of course, at full liberty to do so—but for my part I cling to the law which is stamped upon creation—and I have more respect for the least sentence that ever fell from the pen of Thomas Jefferson than for all the dirty greasy tobacco-dyed parchments that ever chronicled the wisdom of the big-breeched sages of Old Amsterdam' " (*Our Natural Rights; A Pamphlet for the People* [Williamsburg, N.Y., 1842], as quoted in Henry Christman, *Tin Horns and Calico: A Decisive Episode in the Emergence of Democracy* [New York, 1945], 56). For additional suggestions that Jefferson's principle resonated in advanced political circles in New York, see Meyers, *Jacksonian Persuasion*, 205, and Gunn, "Crisis of Distributive Politics." And in an editorial in the *Working Man's Advocate*, 7 Sept. 1844, George Henry Evans, prominent in the land reform movement and one of Devyr's associates, quoted with approval an editorial from another reform paper, the *Phalanx*, that referred to the right of each generation to the usufruct of the earth, adding that "Jefferson, also, in some part of his writings, (not now at hand,) asserts the right in almost the same terms as the *Phalanx*" (John R. Commons et al., eds., *A Documentary History of American Industrial Society* [Cleveland, 1910], 8:355). For similar possible echos of Jefferson's doctrine, see ibid., 328, 340.

155. John L. Thomas notes the impact of George's reading of Jefferson in *Alternative America: Henry George, Edward Bellamy, Henry Demarest Lloyd, and the Adversary Tradition* (Cambridge, Mass., 1983), 118–19.

156. On the national debt clock, see James Barron, " 'Does Anybody Here Know What Time It Is?' " *New York Times*, 30 Jan. 1994, sec. 4, 2.

157. On Perot, "Lead . . . or Leave," and similar expressions of fears for the future, see Felicity Barringer, " 'Lead . . . or Leave' Asks: Who's Spending Our Inheritance?" *New York Times*, 14 Mar. 1993, sec. 4, 3, and Andrew Cohen, "Me and My *Zeitgeist*," *The Nation*, 19 July 1993, 96–100. In *13th Gen* (New York, 1993), Neil Howe and Bill Strauss, though less overtly political than Perot or the "twentysomethings" behind "Lead . . . or Leave," express similar views on the prospects facing the next generation. Peter G. Peterson's *Facing Up: How to Rescue the Economy from Crushing Debt and Restore the American Dream* (New York, 1993) is the grown-ups' version of these arguments; in addition to invoking Jefferson's principle from time to time, the author, a prominent investment banker who leads the "Concord Coalition," offers a plan that would bring the budget into balance by the year 2000 and stop the onward spiral of debt and federal spending. These works follow on a spate of popular books in the late 1980s that raised the alarm at the deficits of the

Reagan years and wondered when and how the bill would be paid. see, for example, Alfred L. Malabre, Jr., *Beyond Our Means: How America's Long Years of Debt, Deficits, and Reckless Borrowing Now Threaten to Overwhelm Us* (New York, 1987); Lawrence Malkin, *The National Debt: How America Crashed into a Black Hole and How We Can Crawl Out* (New York, 1987); and Benjamin M. Friedman, *Day of Reckoning: The Consequences of American Economic Policy* (New York, 1988). The most recent contribution to this debate I have seen is John H. Makin and Norman J. Ornstein, *Debt and Taxes* (New York, 1994), a work sponsored by the American Enterprise Institute. Robert Heilbroner and Peter Bernstein, *The Debt and the Deficit: False Alarms/Real Possibilities* (New York, 1989), takes a more nuanced view, but on the whole it met with no favor from either politicians or the public. And in *Balanced Budgets and American Politics* (Ithaca, N.Y., 1988), James D. Savage supplies an overview to educate the reading public on the long history of American attitudes toward deficits and national debt; like other efforts to insert a measure of rationality into the debate, it seems to have fallen on deaf ears.

158. On the balanced budget amendment, see Savage, *Balanced Budgets*, and, for the Article V convention method advocated by some as a way of achieving it, see Russell L. Caplan, *Constitutional Brinksmanship: Amending the Constitution by National Convention* (New York, 1988), esp. 78–79, 84–85.

159. Paul M. Kennedy's best-selling *The Rise and Fall of the Great Powers: Economic Change and Military Conflict from 1500 to 1800* (New York, 1987) is the most significant example of this literature, not only because of what it says but more importantly, perhaps, because of the way it has been received.

160. Quoted in Paul W. Kahn, *Legitimacy and History: Self-Government in American Constitutional Theory* (New Haven, Conn., 1992), 78; for this strain generally, see ibid., 71–72, 77–78. For the quotation from Sidney George Fisher's *The Trial of the Constitution* (1862), see ibid., 71.

161. For the current debates, see Jack N. Rakove, ed., *Interpreting the Constitution: The Debate over Original Intent* (Boston, 1990).

Appendix A

1. See Chapter 2.

2. For the literature on "influences," see Adrienne Koch, *Jefferson and Madison: The Great Collaboration* (New York, 1950), 82–88; Alfred O. Aldridge, *Thomas Paine's American Ideology* (Newark, Del., 1984), 265, 237–39; and David Freeman Hawke, *Paine* (New York, 1974), 178.

3. Koch, *Jefferson and Madison*, 82–88.

4. Aldridge, *Thomas Paine's American Ideology*, 132, and see also 237–39; Hawke, *Paine*, 178.

5. Koch, *Jefferson and Madison*, 82–88, and note her description of this conclusion as a "hypothesis" (88).

6. For Jefferson's copy, see *Sowerby*, 3, No. 3035.

7. For their letters in the relevant period, see Thomas Paine to TJ, 3 May, 10 May 1789; TJ to Paine, 19 May 1789; Paine to TJ, 17 June, 18 June, 11 July 1789; TJ to Paine, 13 July 1789; Paine to TJ, 13 July 1789; TJ to Paine, 17 July, 23 July, 13 Sept. 1789; Paine to TJ, 15 Sept., 18 Sept. 1789; TJ to Paine, 14 Oct. 1789; Paine to TJ, 28 Sept. 1790; TJ to Paine, 29 July 1791; Paine to TJ, 13 Feb. 1792; TJ to Paine, 19 June 1792, *Boyd*, 15:137n, 136–37, 193–94, 197–99, 266–69, 273, 274–75, 279, 302, 424, 429–30, 449, 522; 17:533–34; 20:308–9; 22:115; 20:312. As Boyd noted,

after the letter to Paine of 19 June 1792, Jefferson let a decade pass before again writing to Paine, leaving, in the meantime, all of Paine's letters to him (Boyd identified eight of them between 1792 and 1801) unanswered. Ibid., 312–13n.

8. James Madison to TJ, 1 May 1791, *PJM*, 14:15.

9. TJ to Paine, 11 July 1789, *Boyd*, 15:266–69; for Lafayette's proposal, see Chapter 2, text at note 67. Jefferson's silence in the 11 July letter underscores two things: First, the main point, that he did not associate the generational principle with Paine and so did not mention it; second, the principle had yet to assume the importance for Jefferson himself that it later came to have with the breakthrough in the 6 September letter to Madison. Paine, of course, would have seen Lafayette's proposal in the newspapers, and in *Rights of Man*, Part One, ed. Henry Collins (Harmondsworth, 1969), 45, he says that as he writes, "some proposals for a declaration of rights by the Marquis de Lafayette . . . to the National Assembly, on the 11th of July 1789" happen to be "accidentally before me." Paine, therefore, was aware of Lafayette's proposal by 1791, and by that time he may also have been aware of Jefferson's role in its creation. But he says nothing about this in *Rights of Man* or in his correspondence.

10. See, for example, Joseph Priestley, *Letters to the Right Honourable Edmund Burke, Occasioned by His Reflections* . . . (London, 1790), who responded to precisely this point in Burke's argument.

11. For Paine's return to Paris, see Hawke, *Paine*, 200.

12. For claims that Condorcet influenced Jefferson, see Lynd, *Intellectual Origins*, 78–81; Bühler, *Verfassungsrevision*, 31–33; and Wills, *Inventing America*, 132. For these and other discussions of influences, see Chapter 2, note 2.

13. See Condorcet, *Lettres à M. le comte de Montmorency* (1789), in *Oeuvres*, ed. A. Condorcet O'Connor and M. F. Arago (Paris, 1847), 9:389–90.

14. See Keith Michael Baker, *Condorcet: From Natural Philosophy to Social Mathematics* (Chicago, 1975), and Éric Brian, *La Mesure de l'etat: Administrateurs et géomètres au XVIII siècle* (Paris, 1994), 147–205, 256–92, which describes the sources and nature of Condorcet's interest in demography.

15. Hard information about Condorcet's relations with Jefferson is difficult to come by. They knew each other, had interests in common, and occasionally corresponded. But there seems to have been no close friendship, despite the impression created by Condorcet's will in 1794, which left his daughter to Jefferson's—and others'—protection. On Jefferson's relations with Condorcet, see *Malone*, 2:15, 109–10, 194. In *Condorcet*, Baker never mentions Jefferson; Elisabeth Badinter and Robert Badinter, *Condorcet (1743–1794): Un intellectuel en politique* (Paris, 1988), mentions Jefferson six times—always briefly—in a text of 621 pages. For the conclusion that "on ne sait pas grand chose sur les influences mutuelles de Condorcet, Jefferson et Gem entre 1785 et 1789," see Arnold B. Urken, "Condorcet-Jefferson: Un chaînon manquant dans la théorie du choix social?" in Pierre Crépel and Christian Gilain, eds., *Condorcet: Mathématicien, économiste, philosophe, homme politique* (Paris, 1989), 114.

16. The other guests were Lafayette, the duc de La Rochefoucauld, and Gouverneur Morris. Gouverneur Morris, *A Diary of the French Revolution*, ed. Beatrix Cary Davenport, 2 vols. (Boston, 1939), 1:220–21. Morris's account does not record any discussion of the rights of the living, but it does note that Condorcet was already there when he, Morris, arrived—Lafayette and La Rochefoucauld arrived after Morris.

17. For the possibility that Jefferson may also have dined with Condorcet on 14 September 1789, see Condorcet to TJ, [12 Sept. 1789]; TJ to John Churchman, 18 Sept. 1792 (forwarding material received from Condorcet), *Boyd*, 15:419, 439.

18. For Condorcet's continuing interest, see Chapter 2, note 94.

19. Jefferson did have three copies of Condorcet's early 1789 *Déclaration des droits*. *Sowerby*, 3, Nos. 2442, 2522, 2568. Note that these were the edition containing both the French original and a translation into English by Dr. Richard Gem, who may well have been a critical link between Condorcet's circle and Jefferson's.

20. See TJ to William Short, 26 July 1790 (with a copy of the Report on Weights and Measures for Condorcet); Condorcet to TJ, [ca. 3 May 1791] (with a copy of the Académie des sciences' report on the unit of measure); TJ to Condorcet, 30 Aug. 1791 (critical of the metric unit). Condorcet's final letter to Jefferson, 21 Dec. 1792, introduced Citizen Genet and criticized Lafayette's political conduct. *Boyd*, 17:281; 20:353; 22:98–99; 24:760–62.

Appendix B

1. Contemporary reviews of Steuart's book prompted such prominent Virginians as colony treasurer Robert Carter Nicholas (who called it "much celebrated"), president of the council William Nelson, and George Wythe to order copies from their agent in England. Nicholas to John Norton, 20 May 1768; Nelson to Norton, 20 May 1768; Wythe to Norton, 15 Aug. 1769, in Frances Norton Mason, ed., *John Norton and Sons: Merchants of London and Virginia*, 2d ed. (Newton Abbot, 1968), 52, 105, 52.

Index